Third Edition

CRIME CONTROL IN AMERICA

WHAT WORKS?

John L. Worrall

The University of Texas at Dallas

PEARSON

Boston   Columbus   Indianapolis   New York   San Francisco   Upper Saddle River
Amsterdam   Cape Town   Dubai   London   Madrid   Milan   Munich   Paris   Montréal   Toronto
Delhi   Mexico City   São Paulo   Sydney   Hong Kong   Seoul   Singapore   Taipei   Tokyo

Editorial Director: Vernon R. Anthony
Executive Editor: Gary Bauer
Program Manager: Megan Moffo
Editorial Assistant: Kevin Cecil
Director of Marketing: David Gesell
Senior Marketing Manager: Mary Salzman
Senior Marketing Coordinator: Alicia Wozniak
Marketing Assistant: Les Roberts
Team Lead for Project Management: JoEllen Gohr
Project Manager: Steve Robb and Susan Hannahs
Creative Director: Jayne Conte
Cover Designer: Bruce Kenselaar
Cover Images: (top to bottom): © Tupungato/Shutterstock, © Rob Byron/Shutterstock, © Volodymyr Kyrylyuk/Shutterstock
Full Service Project Management: Nitin Agarwal, iEnergizer Aptara Limited/Falls Church
Composition: iEnergizer Aptara Limited/Falls Church
Text Printer/Bindery: RR Donnelley
Cover Printer: RR Donnelley
Text Font: Minion Pro Regular

Credits and acknowledgments borrowed from other sources and reproduced, with permission, in this textbook appear on the appropriate page within the text.

Library of Congress Cataloging-in-Publication Data

Worrall, John L.
    Crime control in America: what works? /
John L. Worrall, University of Texas at Dallas.—Third edition.
        pages cm
    ISBN-13: 978-0-13-349548-5
    ISBN-10: 0-13-349548-5
    1. Criminal justice, Administration of—United States.   2. Criminology—United States.
3. Crime—Government policy—United States.   4. Crime prevention—United States.
5. Law enforcement—United States.
I. Title.
    HV9950.W67 2015
    364.973—dc23
                                                                    2013041313

ISBN 13: 978-0-13-349548-5
ISBN 10:   0-13-349548-5

To Jordyn, for keeping me grounded and reminding me what's important in life.

CONTENTS

FOREWORD

AMERICA HAS LIVED THROUGH A GENERATION OF CRIME PREVENTION

Crime rates in the United States began to rise in the 1960s, and people started to be concerned toward the end of that decade. By the 1970s, perhaps partly as a result of President Richard M. Nixon's "War on Crime," a general public sentiment developed that crime was a grave threat to our democracy and that "something needed to be done."

Since then, a great deal has been done. For one thing, the criminal justice system has grown inexorably for almost 40 years. In 1971, there were about 200,000 prisoners and about 1 million people under authority of the corrections system. The penal system has grown every year since that year, and today there are over 2 million people behind bars and another 6 million under community supervision. This is somewhere in the range of a 600 percent growth in penal control, a dynamic that has not been seen in any other nation ever in history. This enormous growth of the penal system has been nearly matched by an equivalent increase in law enforcement and the courts.

This growth represents a major shift in public expenditures and government priorities. For most of the 1980s and 1990s, when many types of government jobs were in decline or stagnant, criminal justice was a reliable growth industry. Jobs as corrections officers, police officers, and correctional personnel, were plentiful. To match (or feed) this steady increase in employment opportunities, higher education invented a new field of study: criminal justice. In the mid-1960s, there were but a handful of criminal justice academic departments located in the nation's universities and colleges, and most of what was taught in the field of crime and justice amounted to little more than a course here and there on criminology or the criminal justice system. By the end of the century, there were several hundred colleges and community colleges offering majors in criminal justice, perhaps a hundred MA-level programs, and more than three dozen doctoral programs. People who wanted to prepare for a career that was a seller's market could do well to enter the field of criminal justice.

As government geared up in the generation of crime control, so did the private sector. Crime prevention became an industry. There was also growth in the area of private security equivalent to that taking place in the public sector, and today the private security profession is far larger than the public police force. On the technology side, the last third of the 20th century saw the invention of privately owned security as a new idea. From burglary prevention systems in houses to auto theft devices, from neighborhood watch programs in hard-hit locations to perimeter security systems in vulnerable buildings, a great profit-making potential lay in finding ways to sell to private interests (individuals and companies) their privately owned and often personal crime prevention capacity. This trend has not abated, and now there are satellite systems of car-theft prevention, entry-proof key systems, and the like—all designed to help people feel more confident that their vulnerability to crime is being reduced.

The coalition of the private and public crime prevention apparatus has been a natural consequence of growth in both spheres. Private prisons, faith-based treatment programs, and auxiliary police services are but a few of the more prominent examples.

The dominance of the generation of crime control is so complete that, today, we do not even notice its effects. We are entirely used to showing personal identification when entering buildings, going through metal detectors when leaving public space and entering private space, and allowing ourselves to be searched as a price of going into certain vulnerable places, such as airports. It may surprise some of us to remember that *none* of these infringements in passage existed 40 years ago. We are the generation of crime prevention.

WHAT HAS THAT CRIME PREVENTION WROUGHT?

For the first third of that time, crime continued to rise, sometimes precipitously. Crime hit a peak in the early 1980s then and fell for a few consecutive years until the middle of the decade. Few people noticed, and when crime again began to rise, it was as though the short respite in ever-increasing crime rates had never happened. Crime again peaked in the early 1990s and then began a period of steady decline that has lasted nearly 20 years.

The actual experience of crime has not been easily translated into public perception of crime. Even though crime rates are down nationally, most places approaching the (dare we say) halcyon levels of the mid-1970s, people are not likely to think so. Until recently, when terrorism intruded into the picture, crime remained one of the top two or three concerns people expressed in almost all the public surveys tapping the American sentiment. Maybe even partly as a consequence of the way crime dominates public thought, it dominates entertainment as never before; on nightly television, prime time is a panoply of murder and mayhem.

One of the products of a generation of crime prevention is the solidification of a set of expectations we have for the state. We expect that the state is too lenient with criminals, and we expect, equally, that the state will try to figure out how to get tougher. We expect that the costs of crime prevention will be high, and we expect these costs to increase, drawing ever more from other budgets, such as those for education or health. We expect to see a crime story lead the six o'clock news.

So, for the generation of crime prevention, this has been a story of ever-increasing resources devoted to the prevention of crime, an explosion of innovation (by the public and private sector alike) in dealing with crime, and an oddly generalized sense that it is for naught—that no matter what we are doing, crime is getting worse. The irony, of course, is that for all the attention given to the former, we are wrong in our sense about the latter. For the crime prevention generation—for whatever reason—crime is being prevented now more than ever before.

HAS THE GENERATION OF CRIME PREVENTION PRODUCED TODAY'S DROP IN CRIME?

It seems reasonable to think that the excessive interest in preventing crime has been why there is a currently dropping rate of crime. As is true for almost all ideas about crime and justice, this one is both partly right and partly wrong.

It is right in that the great and consuming interest in crime that has dominated our popular culture has spawned a vast array of ways to deal with crime. From private business to public action, crime prevention is a high priority and a main motivation.

It is illogical in the extreme to think that a generation that could be thought of as the crime prevention generation could have lived with this obsessive attention to crime and yet have had no impact on it.

On the other hand, crime rates go up and down in relation to so many forces that have nothing to do with the honed nature of our crime prevention apparatus. The size of the at-risk age group of poor males, the economy, whether we are at war, drug markets, immigration, and popular culture all seem to have something to do with crime and to have little capacity to be directly affected by narrow crime prevention strategies. Surely any account of crime rates in the face of the crime prevention generation has to take these forces into account as well.

THE TASK AT HAND

If we are to make sense of this great puzzle, we must begin with a careful assessment of the tools of crime prevention that we have designed, developed, and perfected since we, as a generation, turned our attention to this problem 35 years ago or so. Some say this is emblematic of a new era in crime and justice—the Era of Evidence—a time when we carefully craft our responses to crime in ways we know will reduce the threat of crime. This is not a simple task. It requires three kinds of care.

First, we must classify the various strategies of crime prevention into some logical categories so that we can make sense of them. There are, we know, so many strategies of crime prevention that we cannot even begin to think about them without an organizing framework.

Second, we must carefully sift the evidence about them. This is a dispassionate responsibility, in which we review literally hundreds of studies of different methodologies offering different results and try to find the best way to make sense of their complexities—find their themes and consistencies—so that we can draw some wisdom from them.

Third, we must put into order the strengths and weaknesses of the exercise so that something can be gained from it. We have to suggest lessons in some order of magnitude: "This kind of strategy will count for more than that" and so on. Only by taking a position on what strategies matter more than others can we truly be helpful.

John Worrall has done this for us. In the book you are holding in your hands, you have a rare gem. It is thorough and exacting in its coverage, and it is a reliable review of the evidence. It is profound in its organizational and presentation logic. It is that best of things in a book: authoritative.

Enjoy this book.

Todd R. Clear

PREFACE

The purpose of this book is to identify what works and what does not work to control crime in the United States. This is a difficult task—Herculean, as one reviewer of the first edition put it—but still a necessary one. A few books (cited several times throughout the chapters to come) have attempted to do what this book does, but most of them have not been very accessible to nonexperts, particularly undergraduate students in the fields of criminal justice, criminology, and policy studies. The first reason I decided to write this book was therefore to reach a wider audience, especially people with little background in the area, while keeping the content to a reasonable length.

Other crime control books do not cover enough of what is done to control crime in America. That is, the amount of material on crime control that has made its way into textbooks and into the crime policy literature in general has been relatively modest. This book will make it abundantly clear that a great deal is done in the United States in response to crime, much of which has yet to be researched or laid out in the pages of a textbook—until now. I believe that the field needs a more comprehensive look at crime control in America, which was my second reason for writing this book. I'm sure you will agree, after having read the book, that the range of alternatives for dealing with crime is quite extensive.

Some competitive texts tend to take a strong ideological stance, almost to the point at which a balanced review of the literature is not presented. My third reason for writing this book, then, was to present a comprehensive view of crime control in America while maintaining a neutral ideological stance. To be sure, even the driest of introductory textbooks cannot be totally objective. Every book reflects a perspective; this one reflects mine. But whether you agree or disagree with my perspective, you will come to realize that it is not a predictable one. I lean in no particular ideological direction, I am not registered with any specific political party, and I have no specific agenda to further by writing this book.

I have been teaching crime control courses at the university level for more than 15 years. They are the courses I most look forward to teaching. The subject of crime control tends to liven up discussions in many a course, much more than other topics. (When was the last time undergraduates expressed excitement over chi-square tests or theoretical integration?) Even the most reserved students tend to chime in when opinions are voiced as to the best method of targeting crime in America. Three-strikes laws, the death penalty, and other approaches have brought some of my classes to the brink of an all-out brawl. I hope that this book leads to much (constructive) discourse in other university classes, as well.

PRESENTATION

There is no easy way to organize the study of crime control in the United States. Some authors have organized it according to ideological perspectives. Others have presented it in something of a linear fashion, in the order in which the criminal process plays out (starting with police, then going on to courts, sentencing, corrections, and so forth). I part with past approaches and present crime control from its point of origination. That is, most of the chapters in this book discuss crime control in terms of who does it and/ or where it comes from. But I also follow something of a linear progression by beginning with police and then moving on to prosecution, courts, sentencing, and corrections before getting into less traditional topics.

Importantly, much is done to control crime that is informal in nature, which does not rely on involvement by the criminal justice system or other forms of government intervention. For example, when a person purchases a firearm to protect himself or herself, that person is engaging in informal crime control. Likewise, a person who installs a home security system is engaging in informal crime control. Approaches such as these have been largely overlooked in previous books on crime control, so a significant effort has been made to include them here. Indeed, three chapters discuss the effectiveness (and ineffectiveness) of what I call "approaches beyond the criminal justice system."

CRIME CONTROL APPROACHES

As will become clear in Chapter 1, the title of this book was chosen quite deliberately. In fact, the book's title is the first point at which my perspective comes out. I have chosen the term crime "control," not because I don't believe in crime prevention, but because most of what is done to deal with crime is not proactive. Additionally, I have avoided the term crime control "policy" and elected instead to discuss "approaches" to the crime problem. Doing so, makes it possible to discuss not just formal crime control policies, but also some of the less formal methods governmental entities and private parties take to make America a safer place. For those who prefer "prevention" in lieu of "control. " Even so, I think you will come to agree that most approaches to the crime problem that have been taken in the United States amount to control rather than prevention.

UNIQUE CONTENT

Another one of my motivations for writing this book was to include topics and approaches that always seem to come up in my classes but have rarely been included in the text I assigned for the course (for example, I have yet to find a book in our field that discusses the effect of civil asset forfeiture on the drug problem). Yet another impetus for this project was a desire on my part to educate readers about many of the lesser-known and underexplored methods of crime control in America. When I share these with my students, many of whom are outgoing seniors who have already received the bulk of their criminal justice education, they often express surprise, if not total shock.

By way of overview, some of the relatively unique content (in comparison to competitive texts) consists of sections or chapters on residency requirements for cops, college degrees for cops, police–corrections partnerships, multijurisdictional drug task forces, Compstat, citizen patrol, citizen police academies, no-drop prosecution policies, federal–state law enforcement partnerships, community prosecution, deferred sentencing and prosecution, fines, fees, forfeiture, sentence enhancements, chemical castration of sex offenders, civil commitment, anti-gang injunctions, job training, shaming, problem-solving courts, self-protective behaviors, and several others.

DOES IT WORK?

As Chapter 1 will discuss at great length, it is nearly impossible to claim that a particular form of crime control is effective or ineffective. Additional research, new analytic techniques, and the like can cast doubt on what has been considered gospel truth. At the other extreme, a slew of studies confirming a single finding would tend to suggest an effective approach, but time passes and things change, which makes scientific knowledge very tenuous and uncertain, especially in the crime control context. Yet in an effort to avoid beating the "we-just-don't-know-for-sure" horse to a bloody pulp, I have decided to include "Does It Work?" sections in all but the first and last chapters. In these sections, I attempt to summarize the state of the literature as it currently stands.

REVISIONS FOR THE THIRD EDITION

Several changes have been made to this, the third edition. Aside from updating the book with the latest research, the following key changes have been made:

- Learning objectives have been added at the beginning of every chapter.
- Key term definitions are provided in the margins.
- The first and second edition's dedicated juvenile justice chapter has been removed and the content has been integrated throughout the book to improve flow and organization.
- "Does It Work?" sections have been updated, consistently formatted, and set off from the rest of the narrative for quick reference.
- Various recent approaches to the crime problem have been added (e.g., fusion centers, juvenile waivers).

CHAPTER OVERVIEW

The book is divided into five sections. The first section lays a foundation for assessing the evidence. Chapter 1 discusses what is meant by crime, crime control, and effectiveness. It also discusses many of the issues associated with research in the social sciences. For example, Chapter 1 points out how difficult experimental research is in our field, and it highlights the tentative nature of scientific knowledge. Chapter 2 continues in this vein by introducing various crime control perspectives that readers should be familiar with. Chapter 2 also presents the goals of crime control, including deterrence, retribution, incapacitation, and rehabilitation—each of which informs, to varying degrees, the approaches discussed throughout the book.

     The second section consists of the law enforcement approach to the crime problem. Because most research on the law enforcement approach has been concerned with police, three chapters are devoted to the effectiveness of police approaches. Chapter 3 discusses traditional policing (e.g., hiring more cops), then Chapters 4 and 5 discuss more imaginative approaches, including directed patrol and community policing. Chapter 6 discusses the effectiveness of prosecutorial approaches to the crime problem. This is another unique feature of this book; it does not appear that anyone has attempted to publish a summary of prosecutorial approaches to the crime problem with attention to their effectiveness.

Section Three consists of courts, corrections, and legislative approaches to the crime problem. Chapter 7 discusses crime control through legislation, including legislative bans, gun control, sex offender laws, and laws aimed at control of white-collar crime and terrorism. Chapter 8 covers crime control in the courts and beyond. It looks at the effectiveness of approaches ranging from pretrial incapacitation, diversion, shaming to restorative justice, anti-gang injunctions, and problem-solving courts.

Chapter 9 focuses on sentencing policy, including the effectiveness of fines, forfeiture, civil commitment, mandatory sentencing, sentence enhancements, capital punishment, castration, and several other sentencing strategies. Chapter 10 focuses on probation, parole, and intermediate sanctions. Examples of the latter include intensive supervision probation, home confinement, electronic monitoring, boot camps, shock probation, halfway houses, and day reporting centers. Finally, Chapter 11 examines the effectiveness of rehabilitation, treatment, and job training.

Section Four moves the book's focus away from the criminal justice system to approaches taken by individuals, families, schools, and communities. Chapter 12 begins with individual-level crime control, including buying a gun to protect oneself, risk avoidance, and risk management behaviors. It then discusses the effectiveness of household and family-based crime control. Chapter 13 covers both community and school-based crime control. Examples of the former include financial assistance to communities, resident mobilization programs, and youth mentoring. School-based approaches include targeting the school environment, such as through efforts to build administrative capacity, and interventions aimed at students, such as Drug Abuse Resistance Education, Gang Resistance Education, and behavior modification. Continuing with the focus on crime control beyond the criminal justice system, Chapter 14 looks at efforts to reduce criminal opportunities through environmental manipulation. In that chapter, we cover efforts to discourage crime by altering the physical appearance of places.

Section Five consists of a single chapter, one that summarizes previous chapters and then presents and critically reflects on several explanations that have been offered for the crime decline that took place throughout the 1990s. Explanations are organized into liberal, conservative, and miscellaneous categories. The message that this section presents is that there were (and continue to be) many different forces at work that help to explain national trends in crime.

APPENDIX

I assume that not everyone who picks up this book is intimately familiar with the criminal justice system in America. Accordingly, the Appendix presents an ultra-brief introduction to the criminal justice system. It discusses sources of crime statistics, the actors involved in the justice system (in terms of executive, legislative, and judicial functions), the criminal process (pretrial, adjudication, and beyond conviction), and sanctions. It is not intended to replace an introductory text, but I feel that it gets much important information across.

INSTRUCTOR SUPPLEMENTS

MyTest and *TestBank* represent new standards in testing material. Whether you use a basic test bank document or generate questions electronically through MyTest, every question is linked to the text's learning objective, page number, and level of difficulty.

This allows for quick reference in the text and an easy way to check the difficulty level and variety of your questions. MyTest can be accessed at www.PearsonMyTest.com.

PowerPoint Presentations   Our presentations offer clear, straightforward outlines and notes to use for class lectures or study materials. Photos, illustrations, charts, and tables from the book are included in the presentations when applicable.

Other supplements are:

- Instructor's Manual with Test Bank
- Test Item File for ingestion into an LMS, including Blackboard and WebCT.

To access supplementary materials online, instructors need to request an instructor access code. Go to **www.pearsonhighered.com/irc**, where you can register for an instructor access code. Within 48 hours after registering, you will receive a confirming email, including an instructor access code. Once you have received your code, go to the site and log on for full instructions on downloading the materials you wish to use.

ALTERNATE VERSIONS

eBooks   This text is also available in multiple eBook formats including Adobe Reader and CourseSmart. *CourseSmart* is an exciting new choice for students looking to save money. As an alternative to purchasing the printed textbook, students can purchase an electronic version of the same content. With a *CourseSmart* eTextbook, students can search the text, make notes online, print out reading assignments that incorporate lecture notes, and bookmark important passages for later review. For more information, or to purchase access to the *CourseSmart* eTextbook, visit **www.coursesmart.com**.

ACKNOWLEDGMENTS

The author wishes to thank researchers everywhere for their efforts to inform crime control policy. This book is a literature review, and it would not have been possible but for their efforts. Thanks also go to Gary Bauer, Megan Moffo, and Steve Robb at Pearson, plus Nitin Agarwal at Aptara, Inc., for their help in producing this edition. Also, the reviewers who provided valuable feedback on this edition deserve thanks. They are: Tim Goddard, Florida International University; Krystal E. Noga-Styron, Central Washington University; and Cody Stoddard, Central Washington University. Finally, I must once again thank my family, especially my wife, Sabrina, for putting up with me on yet another book project; the compulsion to write is difficult to shake.

ABOUT THE AUTHOR

 **John L. Worrall** is Professor and Criminology Program Head at The University of Texas at Dallas. He has published articles and book chapters on a wide range of topics ranging from legal issues in policing to crime measurement. He is also the author of several other books, including *Criminal Procedure: From First Contact to Appeal* (5th ed., Pearson, forthcoming), coauthor, with Larry Siegel, of *Introduction to Criminal Justice* (15th ed., Cengage, forthcoming) and *Essentials of Criminal Justice* (9th ed., Cengage, 2015), and co-editor of *The Changing Role of the American Prosecutor* (SUNY, 2009). He currently serves as editor of the journal *Police Quarterly*, as well.

Identifying and Evaluating Crime Control

LEARNING OBJECTIVES

- Distinguish between crime control and prevention.
- Discuss the dimensions of the crime problem in America.
- Explain various "approaches" to the crime problem.
- Summarize the importance of definitions in the crime control debate.
- Discuss what crime control evaluations are problematic.
- Define displacement and diffusion.
- Explain why scientific knowledge is tentative.
- Explain how resources and political ideologies guide crime control priorities.
- Summarize the concept of evidence-based justice.

The United States of America has a crime problem. In response to it, we spend billions of dollars annually on everything from prison construction, police salaries, and courthouse operations to home security systems, gated communities, and self-defense courses. We cannot turn on the evening news without being witnesses to the violence and mayhem that result from criminal activity. We flock to movie theaters to watch crime-fighter movies. We elect politicians who promise to get tough with criminals and lock them up and throw away the key. We long for safe neighborhoods, free from violence and victimization.

Whether we like it or not, all Americans are influenced by the crime problem. Some of us make a living because of the crime problem. This book wouldn't have been written but for the presence of crime! Others of us have been victims of crime, ranging from violent assaults to petty theft. Even a person who has not been a direct victim of crime pays for the costs of crime. Car insurance premiums, for example, are determined partly by the incidence of fraudulent claims. The locks on our doors probably wouldn't be in place but for the threat of burglary.

It is often said that people who make their living because of the presence of crime enjoy a secure future in the United States. People ranging from the powerful Chief Justice of the U.S. Supreme Court all the way down to the police motor pool mechanic enjoy at least a part of their livelihood because of criminals. There are, quite literally, millions of Americans who make their living from some dimension of the crime problem. It would seem that we cannot live without it, but to say that we are content to let the problem thrive is obviously not true. We do a great deal in response to this nation's crime problem—hence the reason for this book. It is about methods of dealing with the crime problem.

CRIME CONTROL AND PREVENTION

This book is about crime control. At a glance, the term *control* connotes a reactive approach to the crime problem. It suggests that crime is inevitable and that all we can hope for is that it does not get worse. Some people prefer the term *prevention* because it carries connotations of a proactive approach that seeks to stop crime before it can occur. But many forms of crime *prevention* are also methods of crime *control*. For example, three-strikes legislation is intended to both prevent and control crime. It is preventive in the sense that the threat of a long prison term might deter would-be offenders. It is also reactive because there would be no such thing as "three-strikers" if there were no serious crimes.

The term *prevention* may therefore be hyperbole; police officers responding to 911 calls are not preventing crime, and prisons certainly are not built so that we don't have to use them. Accordingly, this book uses the term *control* loosely to refer to both reactive and preventive methods of dealing with crime.

THE CRIME PROBLEM IN AMERICA

Although there is clearly a crime problem in the United States, people's definitions of the problem vary considerably across time and space. For one thing, there are many types of crimes. One person might be concerned with the prospect of being murdered, while another might perceive a more direct threat of being the victim of car theft. The incidence of crime can also factor into someone's definition of the problem. One burglary might be too much to bear for one community, while another community might be more tolerant of such activity.

Crime also varies from one place to another. South Central Los Angeles is clearly different from, for instance, Beverly Hills. Washington, D.C., is clearly different from Minot, North Dakota. Each city, county, or state has a crime problem that is its own. Also, we all know that the crime problem fluctuates with time. The manner in which it fluctuates, however, is difficult to understand. During the "dot-com" heyday of the late 1990s, crime rates were at historic lows. Many were convinced that crime and the health of the economy were positively correlated. But the economy took a significant downturn starting around 2008 and crime also declined. According to the Federal Bureau of Investigation (FBI), for example, the "2011 estimated violent crime total was 15.4 percent below the 2007 level and 15.5 percent below the 2002 level."[1]

Next, the cost (or the lack thereof) of crime often factors into people's perceptions of whether crime is a problem. Some people say, "If it doesn't affect me, why should I be concerned about it?" Others feel that if one extra dollar of their hard-earned money is lost, something needs to be done to address the root causes of crime. Finally, some people confuse the crime problem with fear of crime. In many ways, fear of crime is worse than the crime problem itself. The following sections consider each of these issues in more detail.

Types of Crime

It is easy to talk about crime in the abstract, but crime is a multifaceted concept. It is "multifaceted" because there are many varieties of crime. Just look at your state's penal code, and this fact will become clear. Crime is a "concept" because it is something that needs to be defined. In other words, most types of crimes are considered criminal acts because they are defined as such by appropriate authorities. Certain crimes are almost universally considered wrong in and of themselves, but most criminal acts are defined as such by authorities, notably by legislators and the authors of the bills they champion.

It is important to be aware of the various types of criminal activities because one cannot convincingly discuss solutions to the crime problem without reference to specific criminal acts; that is, there are no panaceas or complete solutions to some abstract concept known as "crime." Accordingly, we will discuss the importance of focusing on specific criminal acts later in this chapter, but for now let us briefly discuss the more common varieties of criminal behavior that we face every day. They can be placed in four categories, even though there is some overlap between them: (1) violent crime, (2) property crime, (3) white-collar and organized crime, and (4) public-order crimes.

Violent crime is what most captures our attention and inspires the greatest fear in the minds of most Americans. There are many types of violent crimes, but the types that have received the most attention historically are forcible rape, murder/homicide, assault and battery, and robbery. The common thread running through these types of crimes is that each involves a degree of physical force inflicted on one or more other human beings. This book will pay more attention to crimes of homicide, assault, and battery. The reason for this is that these crimes—and supposed solutions to them—have been researched at great length. Comparatively little research has focused on responses to crimes such as forcible rape. The same holds true for research on other types of crimes, especially those of the white-collar variety.

Property crimes come in many varieties. However, most property crimes fall into the categories of larceny/theft and burglary. Larceny/theft can include such offenses as shoplifting, writing bad checks, credit card theft, auto theft, fraud, and embezzlement. Depending on state law, burglary can come in several varieties. The most common are residential burglaries and commercial burglaries. Some states define theft from (in contrast to theft of) vehicles as a form of burglary. Most of the research on responses to the crime problem has focused heavily on residential and commercial burglaries, car theft, and various forms of larceny. A few studies reviewed throughout subsequent chapters will attest to this.

White-collar crime is ill-defined but generally consists of crimes committed by people during the course of their professional careers. One of the early definitions of white-collar crime was any "crime committed by a person of respectability and high social status in the course of his occupation."[2] More recently, white-collar crime has come to be defined with reference to the specific types of activities it comprises, without reference to precisely who commits it. That is, white-collar crime includes many acts and can be committed not just by the rich, but also by middle-class Americans. It can include tax evasion, credit card fraud, insurance fraud, solicitation of bribes, medical fraud, swindles, influence peddling, securities fraud, overbilling, and so forth.

Finally, public order crimes consist, not surprisingly, of crimes that offend the social order. Often these are called *vice crimes*. They can include prostitution, pornography, gambling, and substance abuse. Even homosexuality and certain paraphilias (also known as fetishes) are considered by some people to offend the social order. The most common types of crimes against the social order that receive attention throughout the criminal justice system include drugs and prostitution. Indeed, the drug problem is so ubiquitous that we will revisit it many times throughout the book. Public order crimes are also important because many recent approaches to the crime problem in the United States advocate targeting low-level crimes, such as street-level drug dealing and prostitution, in an effort to deter more serious crime. This is commonly known as the "broken windows theory," and we will discuss it further in Chapter 4.[3]

The Ever-Expanding Criminal Law

Criminal law is ever-expanding. Not a federal or state legislative session goes by without the addition of more acts deemed criminal to applicable penal codes. It would be impossible to cover all such laws in this book. In the interest of parsimony, then, we will focus primarily on traditional violent and property crimes. This is not to diminish the importance of new criminal laws. It is difficult to dispute that, for instance, terrorism ought to be targeted by the law. The problem is that such novel legal approaches have yet to be subjected to much research.[4] Furthermore, many of them target such a small percentage of people that their overall crime control benefits are probably marginal. We will thus focus on types of crime that are quite prevalent and that take a significant financial toll on our society.

As criminal law continues to expand, the most effective solution to crime is at hand. That solution is decriminalization. In other words, the most effective solution to crime is to reduce the range of activities that are considered criminal. Obviously, doing so is fraught with controversy and quite unrealistic, especially for serious crimes, but it is only fair to point out that while more and more conduct is being defined as criminal, a less criminal law would certainly equate with less crime. Most of us would not want to live in a society with no criminal law, but many people have advocated decriminalization. Decriminalization experiments have been explored as well, such as for medical use of marijuana. We discuss these and similar approaches to the drug problem later in the book.

Incidence of Crime

The incidence of crime can be defined in several ways. First, it is useful to distinguish between the volume of crime, its geographic distribution, and its temporal distribution. The volume is concerned with how much crime takes place. The geographic distribution of crime is concerned with where it takes place. Finally, the temporal distribution of crime is concerned with patterns over time.

The incidence of crime also varies among categories of people. The most common method of understanding the incidence of crime in this way is with reference to: (1) gender, (2) age, (3) race, and (4) social status. That is, the incidence of crime tends to vary between the sexes, between different racial categories, between different age groups, and between different levels of social status (income, marital status, etc.).

Figure 1.1 shows violent victimization trends between 1993 and 2011, the most recent year for which data were available at the time of this writing. Table 1.1 captures the distribution of violent crime by sex, race/ethnicity, age, and marital status. It further classifies crime into the categories of violent crime and *serious* violent crime. Table 1.2 captures the geographic distribution of crime, broken down by region and residential location (urban, suburban, and rural).

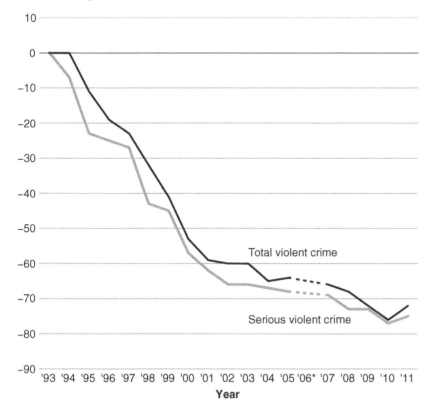

FIGURE 1.1   Percent Change of Violent Victimization Since 1993

Source: Jennifer L. Truman, *Criminal Victimization, 2011* (Washington, DC: Bureau of Justice Statistics, 2012), bjs.gov/content/pub/pdf/cv11.pdf (accessed March 19, 2013).

TABLE 1.1 Rate and Percent Change of Violent Victimization, 2002, 2010, and 2011

Demographic Characteristic of Victim	Violent Crime					Serious Violent Crime[a]				
	Rates[b]			Percent Change[c]		Rates[b]			Percent Change[c]	
	2002	2010	2011	2002–2011	2010–2011	2002	2010	2011	2002–2011	2010–2011
Total	32.1	19.3	22.5	−30%[†]	17%[†]	10.0	6.6	7.2	−28%[†]	9%
Sex										
Male	33.5	20.1	25.4	−24%[†]	27%[†]	10.4	6.4	7.7	−26%[†]	20%
Female	30.7	18.5	19.8	−36[†]	7	9.5	6.8	6.7	−30[†]	−2
Race/Hispanic origin[d]										
White[e]	32.6	18.3	21.5	−34%[†]	18%[†]	8.6	5.8	6.5	−24%[†]	13%
Black[e]	36.1	25.9	26.4	−27[†]	2	17.8	10.4	10.8	−39[†]	4
Hispanic	29.9	16.8	23.8	−20[†]	42[†]	12.3	6.7	7.2	−42[†]	7
American Indian/ Alaska Native[e]	62.9	77.6	45.4	−28	−42[‡]	14.3!	47.3!	12.6!	−12	−73[†]
Asian/Native Hawaiian/other Pacific Islander[e]	11.7	10.3	11.2	−4	9	3.4!	2.3!	2.5!	−25	12
Two or more races[e]	--	52.6	64.6	--	23	--	17.7	26.2	--	48
Age										
12–17	62.7	28.1	37.7	−40%[†]	34%[†]	17.0	11.7	8.8	−48%[†]	−25%
18–24	68.5	33.9	49.0	−28[†]	45[†]	24.7	17.0	16.3	−34[†]	−4
25–34	39.9	29.7	26.5	−34[†]	−11	12.3	7.1	9.5	−22[‡]	34
35–49	26.7	18.2	21.9	−18[†]	21[‡]	7.6	5.6	7.0	−8	24
50–64	14.6	12.7	13.0	−11	3	4.4	3.7	4.3	−4	15
65 or older	3.8	3.0	4.4	17	48	1.8	0.9	1.7	−9	91
Marital status										
Never married	56.3	31.8	35.5	−37%[†]	11%	16.1	11.9	11.7	−27%[†]	−2%
Married	16.0	7.8	11.0	−31[†]	40[†]	5.7	2.2	3.7	−34[†]	70[†]
Widowed	7.1	6.7	3.8	−46[‡]	−43	4.4	3.0!	0.7!	−85[†]	−78[†]
Divorced	44.5	35.2	37.8	−15	7	10.9	11.2	9.2	−15	−18
Separated	76.0	60.2	72.9	−4	21	34.8	18.8	26.4	−24	40

[†]Significant at 95%.

[‡]Significant at 90%.

! Interpret with caution. Estimate based on 10 or fewer sample cases, or coefficient of variation is greater than 50%.

- -Less than 0.5.

[a]Includes rape or sexual assault, robbery, and aggravated assault.

[b]Per 1,000 persons age 12 or older.

[c]Calculated based on unrounded estimates.

[d]The collection of racial and ethnic categories changed in 2003 to allow respondents to choose more than one racial category.

[e]Excludes persons of Hispanic or Latino origin.

Source: Jennifer L. Truman, *Criminal Victimization, 2011* (Washington, DC: Bureau of Justice Statistics, 2012), bjs.gov/content/pub/pdf/cv11.pdf (accessed March 19, 2013).

TABLE 1.2 Rate and Percent Change of Violent Victimization by Household Location, 2002, 2010, and 2011

| Household Location | Violent Crime | | | | | Serious Violence Crime[a] | | | | |
| | Rates[b] | | | Percent Change[c] | | Rates[b] | | | Percent Change[c] | |
	2002	2010	2011	2002–2011	2010–2011	2002	2010	2011	2002–2011	2010–2011
Total	32.1	19.3	22.5	−30%[†]	17%[†]	10.0	6.6	7.2	−28%[†]	9%
Region										
Northeast	28.5	17.2	20.3	−29%[†]	18%	7.1	6.8	6.4	−9%	−6%
Midwest	38.8	22.0	26.3	−32[†]	19[‡]	11.5	7.6	7.8	−32[†]	3
South	27.4	16.6	18.3	−33[†]	10	10.8	5.4	6.5	−40[†]	20
West	35.6	22.4	27.1	−24[†]	21[‡]	9.5	7.5	8.4	−12	12
Location of residence										
Urban	41.0	24.2	27.4	−33%[†]	13%	15.2	9.5	9.7	−36%[†]	3%
Suburban	28.3	16.8	20.2	−29[†]	20[†]	7.8	5.5	5.7	−27[†]	4
Rural	28.6	17.7	20.1	−30[†]	14	7.9	4.7	6.7	−15	42

[†]Significant at 95%.

[‡]Significant at 90%.

[a]Includes rape or sexual assault, robbery, and aggravated assault.

[b]Per 1,000 persons age 12 or older.

[c]Calculated based on unrounded estimates.

Source: Jennifer L. Truman, *Criminal Victimization, 2011* (Washington, DC: Bureau of Justice Statistics, 2012), bjs.gov/content/pub/pdf/cv11.pdf (accessed March 19, 2013).

The incidence of crime varies among individuals. The number of crimes an individual commits within a given time frame is known as *lambda*. The concepts of "career criminals" and "criminal careers" fit in here. Criminologists who favor studying the incidence of crime with reference to individuals commonly invoke terms, such as, *onset, continuity, duration, frequency, escalation, desistance,* and *termination.* Unfortunately, there is little agreement among researchers when it comes to defining lambda. That is, it is practically impossible to know for sure how many crimes are committed by a typical criminal within a specific time frame. Nevertheless, some figures are available. For instance, criminal career researchers have estimated that the annual rate of committing crime for active offenders ranges from 2 to 4 per year for serious assaults and from 5 to 10 per year for robbery and property crimes.[5] Larceny and motor vehicle theft are committed, it appears, at twice the rate of robbery and burglary.

Costs of Crime and Criminals

Crime is obviously a costly societal problem. But it is difficult to come up with accurate estimates of the financial toll it takes on society. The best we can hope for are rough estimates. These rough estimates have been arrived at in two different ways. First, some researchers have sought to assign a monetary value to the number of crimes committed, resulting in estimates of the costs of crime in certain locations and over certain time periods. Second, researchers have estimated the costs of crime committed by individuals.

As to the costs of crime on an aggregate level, there are not as many estimates available as one might expect. But of the studies that are available, it is clear that crime is costly. The RAND Corporation recently took stock of the cost-of-crime literature and determined an average cost for *each incident* of the following offenses:

- Homicide: $8,949,216
- Rape: $217,866
- Robbery: $67,277
- Serious assault: $87,238
- Burglary: $13,096
- Larceny: $2,139
- Motor vehicle theft: $9,079.[6]

Add white-collar crime to these figures, and the amounts become even more shocking. Securities regulators estimate that securities and commodities fraud costs the United States approximately $40 billion per year.[7] Check fraud has been estimated to cost $10 billion per year,[8] and consumers appear to lose roughly $40 billion per year to telemarketing fraud alone![9] Health care fraud costs in excess of $100 billion per year.[10] The list goes on and on. One fact is clear: The aggregate cost of crime in America is almost beyond belief.

If you are not convinced that the costs of crime are beyond belief, consider economist David Anderson's estimates of the "net burden" of crime each year, which includes not just the direct costs of crime but also fear of crime, costs of private security, opportunity costs, and several other factors.[11] "Opportunity costs" refer to the loss of active criminals' and inmates' potential productivity were they not criminal. Ready for the numbers? He estimates that crime costs more than $1 trillion per year, in the United States alone. This translates into $4,118 for each U.S. citizen. Imagine what you could do each year with that kind of money!

Is Fear of Crime Worse Than Crime Itself?

"Fear, in some ways, is a worse problem than crime. While victims suffer the direct consequences of crime when it happens, fear can affect the quality of life of victims and nonvictims over an indefinite period of time."[12] Fear of crime can also lead to withdrawal from the community and a breakdown in social relations among people.[13] It can even suppress investment, discourage new business, and it can contribute to neighborhood deterioration and abandonment.[14] At an individual level, excessive fear can lead to anxiety and depression.[15]

People become fearful of crime for several reasons. They talk about personal victimization experiences.[16] The mass media heighten people's fear through the graphic portrayal of violence.[17] People also watch many reality television shows (e.g., *COPS*), leading them to believe that crime is more prevalent than it really is.[18] Fear of crime can also stem from the location in which a person lives; dangerous areas promote feelings of discomfort and nervousness with respect to the possibility of victimization.[19]

victimization paradox: A high level of fear with a correspondingly low likelihood of victimization.

In general, people fear becoming victims of violent crime much more than their likelihood of being victimized would suggest. Researchers call this the **victimization paradox**. The term refers to high levels of fear and correspondingly low rates of self-reported victimization. Studies have shown, specifically, that women are more fearful of crime than they should be,[20] and so are the elderly.[21] Recent research has shown that fear levels remain high even when the crime rate drops.[22]

APPROACHES, NOT JUST POLICIES

It was tempting to use the term *policy* in the title of this book. Unfortunately, the very mention of policy tends to scare people away. Undergraduates typically dread policy courses because images of dull legalese and laborious reading are quickly conjured up. These images are not wholly misplaced. An in-depth look at actual criminal justice policy can be a tedious endeavor. Consider the U.S. PATRIOT Act of 2001, which was signed into law by former president Bush following the September 11 terrorist attacks on the World Trade Center in New York and the Pentagon. The legislation is nearly 200 pages long, single spaced, and printed in a very small font. Worse still, it was written by lawyers, making it nearly impossible for the layperson to understand. Rest assured, though, that the dreadful heavy-on-law approach is not what this book is about.

Despite the fear and loathing inspired by the word *policy,* we would be remiss not to give some attention to it. After all, legislation is one of the most important responses to the crime problem in America. But there are obviously more ways of dealing with crime. For example, police departments and other criminal justice agencies enact policies in response to crime. Also, certain unofficial approaches (e.g., buying a gun to protect oneself) deserve some consideration. It is these types of approaches to the crime problem with which this book is concerned. The term *approaches* is used to suggest that a wide variety of methods are used to control crime. Let us consider each in more detail.

Laws

Criminal law constitutes the "bread and butter" of crime control. We rely on legal responses to the crime problem more than any other approach. Whether criminal law is enforced uniformly, thoroughly, and consistently is another matter, but all that one has to do is consult the state penal code, and it quickly becomes apparent that we thrive on legal responses to the crime problem.

The legal approach to crime occurs at all levels of government. At the highest level, the U.S. Code prohibits certain actions, especially those that have an interstate dimension. Next, all 50 states have their own criminal codes. These can range from relatively arduous documents to mind-bogglingly complex mountains of paperwork. Finally, cities and counties generally have their own ordinances that are used to proscribe certain types of misconduct.

In this book, we will give attention to the criminal law primarily at the state level. This is because most crime control legislation in the United States is found at the state level. As the need arises, we will focus on crime control legislation arising at other levels of government. Another example is federal sentence enhancements, to which we will turn later.

Official Policies, Written and Unwritten

Another set of approaches to this country's crime problem can be found at the level of the individual public agency. Typically, most criminal justice agencies throughout the United States enact their own policies and procedures that may partly be intended to address the crime problem. Although most such procedures are intended to set forth guidelines for behavior on the job, others are clearly intended to affect crime. In fact, criminal justice agencies can engage in common practices that are more or less unwritten. These, too, can be intended to affect crime.

As an example of a written policy, a police department might enact a policy that describes how its officers are to behave during drug busts. Without such a policy (and sometimes even in spite of one), some officers might be tempted to pocket the goods, which is itself a crime problem. Police departments also have policies that describe how officers are to proceed when serving search and arrest warrants at private residences. If an officer slips up and violates such protocol, the result might be an unlawful entrance into some person's house, itself a form of criminal trespass.

Unwritten policies at the department level are important to crime control as well. It could be, for instance, that the chief of police believes that his or her officers should make aggressive use of investigative detentions in an effort to detect the presence of illegally carried guns. This unwritten approach to crime is not something that could be found "on the books" anywhere, but it is clearly important to crime control.

Let us also consider a softer example of an unwritten policy. Assume that the same police chief argues that community policing is the wave of the future. The chief believes that crime control can be accomplished only with substantial input from citizens and by giving patrol officers more discretion to make their own decisions. This approach to crime cannot be considered part of the legal approach, and it is doubtful that there would be any mention of it in the department's policy manual. It amounts, mostly, to an unwritten response to crime. We will give attention to community policing and numerous other examples of unwritten approaches to crime that are found at the level of the individual police department, court, or corrections agency.

Official policies can also be found outside of the criminal justice system. For example, crime control can be accomplished in our nation's schools. Most of us have heard stories of schools reacting to student shootings by enacting strict policies limiting what students can bring to class. Such is an official policy, and one that is intended to address crime but that takes place somewhat independently of the criminal justice system.

Unofficial Approaches

Unofficial approaches to crime should not be confused with unwritten approaches. Unofficial approaches to crime are those that are undertaken outside of a public agency context. Several examples of unofficial approaches will be discussed in this book; they include those stemming from families, neighborhoods, and individuals. Perhaps the best-known example of an unofficial response to crime is buying a gun to protect oneself. Does it work? Does it really deter crime? We will try to answer this question later in the book.

ON THE IMPORTANCE OF DEFINITIONS

This book is about crime control, about measures that are taken to deal with this country's crime problem. Everyone has his or her opinion about what is best in terms of crime control. Some people favor aggressive law enforcement; others favor softer approaches. There is no certainty as to which approach is the best. But before we can argue for what we believe in, we need to settle on some definitions. And before we can talk about what works and does not work to control crime, it is important to define our terms. We need to define the problem, the possible solutions, and the desired outcome.

For illustration's sake, consider the abortion debate. People have been butting heads for generations over whether women should have the right to terminate their pregnancies. But the abortion debate cannot be settled without attention to definitions.

In fact, the whole debate hinges on one's definition of when human life begins. Does it begin at conception? In the second trimester? The third trimester? Without being able to answer questions such as these, the debate will indefinitely continue to go around in circles. The same can be said for crime control. Without defining our terms, debates over crime and the best solutions to it reduce to mere rhetoric.

Defining the Crime Problem

So far, we have been throwing around the term *crime problem* with wild abandon. The section entitled "The Crime Problem in America" showed that crime is clearly a significant and costly social problem. However, where the rubber meets the road—where crime control is actually supposed to be accomplished—it is essential to define the crime problem. If we cannot define the problem, how do we know what we are targeting?

As has already been indicated, there are no crime control panaceas, and there probably never will be. It is simply unrealistic to believe that there is one uniform solution to crime. If we voluntarily surrendered our civil rights and, say, gave police officers the authority to summarily execute law violators, then perhaps society would be safer. But this is not realistic. Instead, crime control needs to be accomplished on a piecemeal basis, one variety of crime at a time.

How do we define the crime problem? A balance needs to be struck between vagueness and excruciating specificity. Assume that a prosecutor's office has a new strategy that it believes will reduce repeated second-degree burglaries of one particular house on one particular city block. That is probably too specific. For one thing, responses to the crime problem rarely target degrees of offenses. Rather, they tend to target larger geographical areas, even entire states. At the other extreme, a new law that is intended to reduce all index offenses, including homicide, rape, robbery, assault, burglary, larceny, motor vehicle theft, and arson, is probably too vague. Somewhere in the middle is where the appropriate definition of the crime problem lies. See Figure 1.2 for a list of hypothetical crime problems that are sufficiently specific.

Defining the Solution

Crime control also cannot be accomplished without a definition of the possible solutions. In other words, what is to be done to control the crime problem? Again, a balance needs to be struck between ambiguity and exacting precision. To say that community policing

---

1. Purse snatchings at a subway station
2. Homicides in a gang-infested neighborhood
3. Drug sales in a problem neighborhood
4. Fights outside nuisance bars in a given city
5. Rapes at a city park
6. Burglaries in a specific city
7. Auto theft from a particular neighborhood or retail establishment
8. Robbery at banks close to a freeway
9. Drug smuggling in airports
10. Vandalism in a neighborhood

FIGURE 1.2 Hypothetical Crime Problems

> 1. Tough sentences for repeat offenders
> 2. Enhanced supervision of probationers in a county
> 3. Targeting street racing in an industrial area
> 4. Foot patrol in an urban center
> 5. Radar traps on a problem section of a freeway
> 6. Chemical castration for sex offenders
> 7. Outpatient treatment for first-time drug offenders
> 8. Sentence enhancements for crimes committed with guns
> 9. Installing home security systems
> 10. Prosecutor decision not to drop charges in domestic violence prosecutions

FIGURE 1.3 Hypothetical Crime Solutions

(see Chapter 5) is the solution to street-level drug dealing in a given neighborhood is a practically meaningless statement. Community policing is a multifaceted concept that needs definition. If a police department consisting of 1,000 officers decides to put more police officers on foot patrol in the same neighborhood, for example, and decides to call this "community policing," then the solution is more specific. On the other hand, if the same police department decides to decentralize by eliminating one sergeant position, this approach might be too specific—and is probably unlikely to address any pressing problem.

How, then, do we define a solution to the crime problem? Although this might seem to be a difficult question to answer, the answer is actually very simple. If the solution speaks for itself for most laypeople, then it is probably specific enough. As has been indicated, community policing is a somewhat vague concept. It calls out for definition and is probably not familiar to people who have no awareness of changing trends in the criminal justice system. On the other hand, most people can understand the solution to crime when it is stated in terms of the execution of every person who intentionally and with planning takes another person's life. In short, solutions to the crime problem that require clarification and elaboration are rarely specific enough. See Figure 1.3 for a list of hypothetical solutions to crime that are sufficiently specific.

Defining the Desired Outcome

solution (crime control): the means to an end, in this case crime control.

outcome (crime control): that which is likely to be affected by the solution.

The **solution** should not be confused with the **outcome**. Think of the solution as the means and the outcome as the ends. In other words, the outcome is what is likely to be affected by the solution. Because this book is about crime control, most of the outcomes we will consider are crime rates. But what crime rates should be considered outcomes? It depends on the solution. The addition to a police force of a car theft task force is clearly intended to affect the incidence of motor vehicle theft. Likewise, a marijuana "buy-bust" operation would be intended to affect the incidence of marijuana sales in a particular location.

Although it might seem simple to define the desired outcome associated with some response to the crime problem, it is often quite difficult. It is difficult because sometimes crime control programs are developed without much attention to what it is hoped that they will do. Also, some approaches to crime are so complex that it is nearly impossible to settle on a specific definition of success. Consider, again, community policing. We will give careful attention to it in Chapter 5, but for now it serves as a shining example of something with multiple outcomes. It is intended to reduce crime but also to improve police officer morale, make citizens more trusting of the police, change the structure of police departments, improve feelings of neighborhood safety, and reduce fear of crime.

There is nothing fundamentally wrong with a crime control program that has multiple desired outcomes. In fact, if an approach to the crime problem has added benefits besides the reduction of crime, then why not pursue it? The problem with having multiple desired outcomes is that it complicates evaluation. That is, it is difficult to claim that a program is a success when the program is intended to do multiple things. Indeed, such a program can be a success and a failure at the same time! Consider community policing once again. If it fails to reduce crime but improves citizen satisfaction, what conclusion do we draw as to its effectiveness?

In sum, before we can talk about crime control, we need to define our terms. Everyone needs to be on the same page about the type of crime problem under consideration, the supposed solution to it, and the outcomes that solution is likely to produce. Once we agree on these three important criteria—defining the problem, the solution, and the desired outcome—we can begin to consider effectiveness. Unfortunately, though, determining whether a crime control program is effective is not always easy in the social sciences.

EVALUATING SUCCESS: AN IMPOSSIBLE TASK?

By now it should be clear that success cannot be measured without some attention to important definitions. How do we move on to deciding whether an approach to the crime problem is a success or a failure? The short answer is that we conduct an **outcome evaluation** (sometimes called an impact assessment). An outcome evaluation is a method of determining whether some form of social action is a success or a failure. In our case, social action consists of an approach to the crime problem.

outcome evaluation: a method of determining whether some form of social action is a success or a failure.

It is also possible to conduct **process evaluations**. These are a means of determining whether a program or policy is operating as it should be (e.g., that everyone involved is committed and working toward stated goals). We will not focus on process evaluations here. Instead, we will focus on outcome evaluations. Such evaluations are more appropriate for determining whether some approach to the crime problem actually does what it is intended to do.

process evaluation: a method of determining whether a program or policy is operating as it should be.

This book uses the term *evaluation* somewhat loosely. The typical image of an evaluation is a formal study by a university or research organization, usually conducted over some period of time and usually concluding with a large report that is presented to whoever commissioned the study. However, when a researcher conducts, say, a statistical analysis to determine whether the addition of more officers to a police department reduces crime, this is basically an evaluation. Even if the researcher never sets foot in the field but instead researches such an approach from the comfort of his or her "ivory tower," the research can still be considered an evaluation for our purposes. Thus, this book defines evaluation as using social science methodology to determine whether an approach to the crime problem achieves its stated goals.

The Hard and Soft Sciences

Criminal justice and criminology occupy a position in what can be called the **soft sciences**. The soft sciences are the social sciences, those fields that focus on the study of social

soft sciences: the social sciences primarily, fields that focus on the study of social phenomena in their natural settings.

hard sciences:
scientific fields of
study characterized
by research that is
usually conducted
in tightly controlled
laboratory settings
(e.g., chemistry and
biology).

phenomena in their natural settings. The **hard sciences**, by contrast, include the fields of chemistry, physics, biology, and other disciplines in which research is usually conducted in tightly controlled laboratory settings. It is generally rare for the social sciences, which include criminal justice, criminology, sociology, anthropology, political science, economics, and other disciplines, to see research conducted in the laboratory. Perhaps the only exception is the field of psychology; much of its research takes place in the laboratory.

Why is it useful to distinguish between the hard and soft sciences? The answer is that research conducted outside of a laboratory setting is often confounded by events over which the researcher has almost no control. Consider, for example, a researcher's decision to evaluate the DARE (Drug Abuse Resistance Education) program. The DARE program cannot be researched in a laboratory because it takes place in grade schools. If the researcher finds that children who participate in DARE use fewer drugs later in life, how can the researcher know that he or she has ruled out all possible alternative explanations? It is not possible. There are simply too many intervening events that could affect a child's decision to use drugs later in life. It is this problem—research in a social setting—that makes it difficult for researchers to evaluate the successes and failures of approaches to our nation's crime problem.

The Elusive Criminal Justice Experiment

classical experiment:
the gold standard for
scientific research, a
study that includes
(1) a treatment
group and a control
group, (2) a pretest
and a posttest, and
(3) a controlled
intervention.

The ideal technique for conducting research, be it for determining whether a new law reduces crime or whether a new drug cures cancer, is a so-called **classical experiment**. The classical experiment consists of three important elements: (1) a treatment group and a control group, (2) a pretest and a posttest, and (3) a controlled intervention. The treatment group receives the intervention. This can include a new drug or, from our previous example, exposure to an educational program such as DARE. The control group represents "business as usual." It does not get exposed to the intervention. A key component of the classical experiment is that participants are randomly assigned to treatment and control groups. Next, the pretest and posttest are simply measurements before and after the intervention. The "tests" could in fact be tests of knowledge. They could also be measures of the size of a tumor, a person's brain waves, or even one's opinion on an attitude survey. Finally, a controlled intervention is one over which the researchers have total control.

As you have probably realized by now, an experiment of this sort almost never happens in criminal justice and criminology. The fact that social scientists research people in social settings makes such things as random assignment and controlled interventions all but impossible. Suppose we wanted to conduct a classical experiment to determine whether the death penalty deters crime. First, it would be necessary to randomly assign research subjects to treatment and control groups. This means that the researchers—not a jury or a judge—would have to decide who is executed and who is not. Obviously, this is impossible, so it is not even worth considering the other difficulties associated with using a classical experiment to evaluate the death penalty. Such an experiment is just not possible.

The point we are getting at here is that classical experiments are rare in criminal justice and criminology. This inherent limitation of the social sciences thus makes it difficult to determine whether approaches to the crime problem are successes or failures. For every researcher's claim that something works or doesn't work, it is *always* possible to conceive of alternative explanations. That is why the following chapters use phrases such as "appears to reduce crime" or "may reduce crime." It is just not possible, in criminal justice and criminology, to determine successes and failures with absolute certainty. Social phenomena—such as crime—are simply too complex.

You *Can* Prove Anything with Statistics

This book is not a research methods or statistics text, but it is important to have an understanding of the limitations of social science research. It is also important to know that the old adage "You can prove anything with statistics" is more or less true. Many fancy statistical techniques are little more than "smoke and mirrors" that obscure a simple truth: Either something reduces crime or it doesn't. Clearly, it is risky—and possibly offensive—to claim that statistics can be manipulated, but it is rarely the case that only one statistical technique can be applied to a social science research question.

The only real way of knowing how statistics can be used to serve a researcher's interests is to have a fairly in-depth understanding of statistical methodology. It is not assumed that you have this level of knowledge. However, if you want to get a basic grasp of how statistics can be manipulated, carefully examine the literature review in a 1996 study on the relationship between police levels and crime (which we consider more fully in Chapter 3).[23] The authors of that study reviewed 36 previous studies of the relationship, most of which used differing statistical techniques and came up with contradictory conclusions.

Lest you think that the gauntlet is being thrown down to statisticians everywhere, consider two observations on the relative importance of statistical analysis. First, Sherman and his colleagues have been staunch advocates of randomized, controlled experiments for measuring the effectiveness of approaches to the crime problem.[24] The randomized experiment simply compares two groups before and after some intervention. It does not require complex statistical analysis and is arguably the most sophisticated research design that can be conceived of. The point is that one does not need tedious statistics to judge the effectiveness of crime control in America.

Second, James Austin has argued that criminology is irrelevant in part because it has strayed from basic experimental designs. In his words:

> The major weakness in our policy studies is an apparent unwillingness to use experimental designs with the random assignment of subjects conducted in multiple sites by independent researchers. Instead, criminologists have increasingly favored quasi-experimental designs of poorly implemented policies or simulations of proposed policy that rely on untested assumptions, faulty data, and employ questionable mathematical models.[25]

Although Austin's statements might be offensive to many criminologists, his point is at least partially valid: It is not always necessary to resort to complex statistical modeling. Rather, a back-to-basics scientific approach that relies on traditional experimental methods is desirable. Whether or not this is possible, given the nature of the problem we study, experimental methods ought to at least be pursued where feasible. And although experimental designs are not without their faults, their results can be conveyed much more directly and understandably than those of a sophisticated statistical model.

Qualitative and Quantitative Research

There is some degree of tension between **qualitative research** and **quantitative research**. The former refers generally to in-depth research on a specific location or

qualitative research: a largely exploratory method of inquiry characterized by in-depth research on a specific location or group of subjects.

quantitative research: a method of inquiry characterized by the analysis of numerical data designed to represent concepts of interest.

group. The latter refers, for the most part, to less detailed research on a large number of cases (e.g., people, cities, or states). Understood differently, quantitative research usually requires number-crunching; qualitative research is much more descriptive and anecdotal.

Which is better? Some would say that quantitative methods are essential. They claim that it is impossible to understand what works and what does not without some degree of statistical analysis. Others would say that "running the numbers" tells only part of the story. These people claim that in-depth research in specific areas or with a handful of people is more important. In the end, it is impossible to say that quantitative research is better than qualitative research or vice versa. Some people claim that the two methods complement one another and should be used jointly.

This book has a decided quantitative slant. This reflects not only the author's preference but also the majority of research in criminal justice and criminology. But there is some convincing qualitative research in our field that cannot be ignored. From time to time, qualitative research will be given detailed attention. Indeed, it is quite possible for an approach to the crime problem to be a resounding success without being subjected to quantitative analysis.

Macro- and Micro-Level Crime Control

macro-level crime control: consists of approaches to the crime problem that are intended to have a dramatic and desirable effect on crime in an entire neighborhood, city, or state or even across the nation.

It is important to distinguish between **macro-level crime control** and **micro-level crime control**. Macro-level crime control consists of approaches to the crime problem that are intended to have a dramatic and desirable effect on crime in an entire neighborhood, city, or state or even across the nation. Macro-level crime control can also consist of an approach to the crime problem that is intended to affect many people at the same time. Micro-level crime control, by contrast, is more isolated geographically. It is also less concerned with large numbers of research subjects. It can even be concerned with specific individuals.

micro-level crime control: consists of approaches to the crime problem that are more isolated geographically.

Why the distinction between these two types of crime control? Researchers are often hung up on macro-level crime control. That is, they seek to determine whether crime control programs and policies either have an effect on crime in some large geographical area or positively affect a large sample of individuals.[26] This might be because of a desire to find crime control panaceas. But, as has already been indicated, these do not exist. Often overlooked are micro-level attempts to control crime. Accordingly, this book will also give micro-level crime control attention, in an effort to achieve some balance between two often-competing types of research.

A general rule of thumb is as follows: The more resistant to a uniform definition an approach to the crime problem is, the more likely it is that such an approach will be researched at a micro level. Consider two examples. First, hiring more police officers with the intention of increasing the police presence is a simple, understandable crime control strategy. As Chapter 3 will attest, many studies looking at police hiring are macro-level studies. By contrast, approaches to the crime problem that are multifaceted and difficult to define with precision are often researched at the micro level. Community policing is one of the best examples of an approach to the crime problem that defies simple definition. Chapter 5 will provide evidence of this. A closely related problem is the use of micro-level research designs to study macro-level policies and vice versa. For example, researchers have studied the effect of welfare spending on aggregate crime rates, even though the presumed helpful effects of welfare funding are very much geared toward specific individuals. Alternatively, researchers sometimes study individual-level data while trying to draw conclusions about larger city-, county-, or state-level policies. Using macro-level research to draw micro-level conclusions is known as the *ecological fallacy*. Using micro-level research to draw conclusions about macro-level units is known as the *individualistic fallacy*. Both such approaches are mistaken and should be carefully guarded against.

DISPLACEMENT AND DIFFUSION

Some studies suggest that certain methods of crime control lead only to short-term reductions in the problem and can push the problem into neighboring areas. This problem is known as **displacement**. According to a recent study, "[o]ne of the most significant potential negative consequences of crime reduction schemes, whether they are aimed at well-defined geographical locations or specific population groups, is that of crime displacement."[27] The authors of this study base their claim on a long line of research highlighting the unanticipated consequences of crime control efforts in America.[28]

displacement: The spillover or movement of crime (in the case of crime control) into a surrounding area not targeted by the intervention in question.

As has been indicated, the image of displacement that is conjured up in the minds of most criminologists is that of crime being physically pushed into a surrounding area because of some intensive, focused effort to control a problem; but this is only one of six types of displacement, namely, spatial displacement. Other types of displacement include temporal (offenders decide to commit crime at different times of day), tactical (offenders decide to adopt a different modus operandi), target (offenders select a different type of target), crime type (offenders opt for a different kind of criminal activity), and perpetrator, which occurs when offenders who are caught are replaced by new ones.

We focus here on the issue of spatial, or geographic, displacement. Is it really a problem? In two reviews of the issue, researchers concluded that cases of spatial displacement are relatively isolated.[29] These findings have been confirmed by at least one more recent study.[30] In fact, some researchers have found the opposite: that crime reduction schemes can produce a "diffusion of benefit," also known as **diffusion**. This phenomenon is also called a free rider effect and is characterized by a reduction in crime not only in targeted areas, but surrounding areas, as well.[31] Even displacement can have benefits. For example, displacement clearly benefits those who have avoided victimization because of the crime getting pushed into a surrounding area.[32]

diffusion (crime control): a reduction in crime not only in the area targeted by an intervention, but also in surrounding areas. Also referred to as a diffusion of benefit.

Researchers have recently pointed out that identifying displacement or diffusion is plagued by two separate but related problems. First is the difficulty of measuring displacement. That is, how do we know for sure when it has occurred? The second problem is defining a geographic area to which crime is likely to be displaced (or into which diffusion of benefits may be witnessed). Let us consider each of these issues in more depth.

Measuring Displacement and Diffusion

Two recent studies highlight the difficulty of measuring displacement/diffusion. Braga and his colleagues focused on police calls for service and reported crime levels in response to a problem-oriented policing strategy.[33] They found no evidence of displacement when examining calls for service but possible evidence of the displacement of property crime. In a related study, the authors examined only calls-for-service data.[34] They found that calls for service, particularly those for narcotics and public morals offenses, went down in the target area *and* the displacement zone. This, they reported, amounted to a diffusion of benefits associated with the drug enforcement strategy they studied. As these studies attest, displacement can be measured in different ways, often with different results.

Do displacement and diffusion matter? That depends. It depends first on whether you are concerned with a specific area or with the costs that crime can impose over a large space. Many politicians do not care about displacement because they do not need to answer to constituents outside the areas they serve. But many academics and others who are concerned with the bigger picture tend to be very concerned when crime is pushed into surrounding areas. Second, whether displacement and diffusion matter depends largely on definitions and measurement issues.

THE TENTATIVE NATURE OF SCIENTIFIC KNOWLEDGE

All scientific knowledge is tentative. It is neither etched in stone nor timeless. Nearly every valid scientific claim should be stated in terms of the here and now. Additional study, new settings, alternative research designs, different measures, other data, and several related factors make it all but impossible to resolve a scientific question once and for all. The body of scientific knowledge is constantly growing and evolving. In the context of crime control, what appears to work today might not work tomorrow, next year, or in the next millennium. The following sections discuss the various ways in which scientific knowledge is tentative.

The Measures Used

Scientific knowledge can be considered tentative because researchers often use different measures to represent the same phenomenon. Consider the concept of serious crime. One researcher might measure serious crime by focusing on all crimes in the FBI's Crime Index, namely, homicide, rape, robbery, assault, burglary, larceny, motor vehicle theft, and arson. Another researcher might claim that the only truly serious crimes are homicide, rape, robbery, and assault. With these different sets of measures, the two researchers can reach different conclusions about the effectiveness of a particular crime control policy.

Another example of different measures could be used in two community prosecution studies. (Community prosecution is discussed in Chapter 6.) Let's assume that two researchers want to determine whether federal community prosecution funding reduces crime. One researcher might compare crime rates in counties that received funding with crime rates in counties that did not receive funding. Another researcher might look only at counties that received funding and instead focus on how much money each county received, perhaps theorizing that more money equates with less crime. Again, the two researchers could reach different conclusions because they have used different measures. This is one way in which scientific methodology is tentative.

When New Data Become Available

Many researchers in criminal justice and criminology use decennial national census data in their studies. One study based on the 2000 census might reach different conclusions from those of an identical study conducted on 2010 census data. Although it is not always the case that new data change researchers' conclusions, it does happen.

Clearly, the census is not the only data source for criminologists and criminal justice researchers. Countless other data sources exist, and new data sources are emerging from one day to the next. When new data are applied to the same research question, it is not always the case that previous conclusions hold true. This, then, is the second means by which scientific knowledge can be considered tentative.

Alternative Settings: The Generalization Problem

The generalization problem is concerned with the extent to which a researcher's findings can be carried over to another location or series of locations. For instance, if a gardener uproots a tree from the soil where it has flourished and then expects this tree to grow well in a different location, the expectations might prove to be unfounded. Only if the gardener takes careful steps to ensure similar soil and light conditions at the second site can the tree be expected to flourish. This is precisely how social scientific research works: If a researcher declares that some crime control policy is a success in location A (say, California), the same policy might not work in location B (say, Washington). Only if locations A and B mirror each other precisely and only if the policy is exactly the same in both locations can the researcher expect to reach similar conclusions if location B is also studied.

Other Concerns

There are several other reasons why scientific knowledge can be considered tentative. First, researchers often focus on different units of analysis. Units of analysis represent the objects under study. Examples include people, groups, organizations, cities, counties, states, and nations. A study of states might lead a researcher to reach one conclusion, whereas a study of cities in a specific state might lead the same researcher to reach an entirely different conclusion. Indeed, a recent debate over the effect of three-strikes legislation on crime attests to this. One study of states concluded that the legislation has increased the number of homicides,[35] but another study of counties in a single state concluded that three-strikes legislation has reduced several types of criminal activity, including homicide.[36]

New analytical techniques are continually coming to the fore. For example, in 1980, McCleary and Hay published a now-famous study on purse snatchings in the Hyde Park neighborhood of Chicago.[37] They sought to determine whether a program known as Operation Whistlestop had led to a significant reduction in purse snatchings, and their analysis revealed that the intervention had no apparent effect on purse snatchings. However, in a recent study employing a relatively new statistical technique known as a structural times series model, researchers concluded that McCleary and Hay's findings were flawed and that Operation Whistlestop *was* successful.[38]

Researchers often study samples. Samples are subsets of a larger population. For example, 1,000 voters in California is a sample of all voters in California. Alternatively, 100 drug treatment patients could be a subset of a larger group. Samples are generally easier to research because it would be prohibitively costly for the whole population to be examined. The problem is that researchers often use different sample sizes and sampling techniques. The same study conducted on 100 individuals and then on 10,000 individuals could yield contradictory results. Likewise, a random sample of 1,000 people might produce different results from those of a group of 1,000 people who are handpicked by a researcher. Possible differences in sampling and sample sizes should always be on readers' minds when studying the effectiveness of crime control in the United States.

Finally, with respect to time, there are two types of research. In the first type, *cross-sectional research*, a study takes place that is based on data collected at a single point in time. For instance, if one surveys several people today and finds that there is a relationship between fear of crime and prior victimization, this is a cross-sectional design. However, if a researcher followed the same group of people for a longer period of time, then that researcher would be conducting what is known as *longitudinal research*. Why does this matter? First, longitudinal research is more sophisticated and desirable than cross-sectional research. Second, it is not possible to draw conclusions about cause and effect without factoring in the time dimension. Thus, the most convincing research is that which incorporates the time dimensions. As we will see, however, this type of design is relatively uncommon in criminal justice and criminology.

FUNDING AND POLITICAL PRIORITIES

Crime control in the United States is dictated in large part by what is being funded at any given time. As one researcher has observed:

> The selection of which public policies to be evaluated, the research methods to be used, and ultimately the researcher's conclusions are heavily influenced by the amount and source of research funds. Within the United States, the federal government has a virtual monopoly on research. And over the years, a small but highly influential circle of criminologists have exerted a disproportionate influence on what is funded and who gets to do it.[39]

Many of our efforts to control crime—especially those taken by criminal justice agencies—are intimately tied to where the money is. What is being funded is a reflection of political priorities and can be largely connected to who is in the White House, in the governor's mansion, or in the state legislature.

How is this so? It is well known that public agencies in the United States are underfunded. In good times and in bad, there always seems to be a shortage of money for hiring more police officers, building more prisons, providing drug treatment to those who want it, and so forth. This state of affairs causes many criminal justice agencies to seek out additional so-called soft money. Hard money is the money that is given to an agency through the appropriations process, but soft money is sought through funding sources such as units of government (e.g., the Bureau of Justice Assistance in the U.S. Department of Justice) and private foundations.

An example of soft money is that being granted through the Office of Community Oriented Policing Services (the COPS Office) in the U.S. Department of Justice. It provides grants to interested police agencies for the purpose of implementing community policing (see Chapter 3 for further discussion). The COPS Office will not be around forever and, in fact, could disappear in the near future if additional federal funds are not allocated for its continued existence. When the money is no longer there, will police departments be doing as much community policing? Probably not, and at least one recent study appears to support this.[40]

Another example is one that we will consider more fully in Chapter 6. During the years of the Clinton Administration, millions of dollars were allocated for community prosecution programs across the United States. The funds were awarded by the Bureau of Justice Assistance (in the U.S. Justice Department) through a competitive grant process. Those funds have since dried up, and many district attorneys' offices are chasing funds in other areas. The point of this section is that it is important to be aware of the faddish nature of crime control in the United States. When political priorities change and funding reflects different priorities, research becomes complicated.

Criminologists are left asking, "How can we determine whether it works when it is only around for a little while?" In fact, criminologists often do the same thing, that is, follow the most recent funding stream. Federal and state research priorities—and the grants that are given out in support of them—are often directly tied to the criminal justice programs that are being funded at any given time.

Academic Crusaders and Bandwagon Science

As we just saw, funding dictates public policy and guides research. This phenomenon can also be understood as **bandwagon science**. Everyone who has an interest in receiving research funding jumps on the bandwagon and assigns a great deal of priority to researching the current hot topic. There is nothing wrong with this practice; research is costly, and funding should be available to offset the costs. But a potential problem arises when researchers devote all their energies to a specific topic. The problem is that other topics are ignored—topics that are of potentially great importance and lasting influence. In other words, when chasing funding, researchers often ignore other important avenues of criminal justice research that may be just as worthy of their attention.

bandwagon science: focusing research on what is trendy or popular at a given time, perhaps ignoring other worthy problems and avenues of inquiry.

Somewhat related to funding priorities, which are inherently political, is the concept of the **academic crusade**. The conventional view of science is that it is objective and devoid of personal interests, positions, and beliefs. In reality, though, science is regularly used to advance people's political priorities. Interest groups publish what would appear to be objective science, but then an interest group with a different set of priorities will publish objective science that tells a different story. This has occurred with numerous U.S. crime policies, including gun control and the war on drugs, among others. Likewise, there are some academics in the halls of our nation's universities who can be called crusaders, whose mission in life is to convince the world that in the case of crime control, one approach is better than another, even in the face of overwhelming evidence to the contrary.[41]

academic crusade: when research loses objectivity and is used to further a political agenda, often in the face of overwhelming evidence to the contrary.

EVIDENCE-BASED JUSTICE

As should be clear by now, it is not possible to claim with certainty if various approaches to the crime problem "work" or "do not work." The only way to get close to such a claim is to move the discussion deep into the realm of social science methodology. That approach is not what this book is about; instead, the intent is to provide a relatively comprehensive review of the crime control literature. Only minimal reference will be made to the methods that are used in the various studies reviewed throughout the next several chapters.

Determining what types of crime control "work" is difficult. The approach that is taken in this book is to ask the question "On the basis of the available information, what can we safely conclude about the effectiveness of specific approaches to the crime problem?" To this end, after every section that discusses some approach to the crime problem is a section entitled "Does It Work?" These sections summarize the author's impressions of the literature as well as his conclusions about the effectiveness (or the lack thereof) of crime control in America.

There is nothing unique or special about the approach taken in this book. The approach taken is part of a larger evidence-based policy/practice movement that *evidence-based justice:* use of the best available scientific evidence to guide criminal justice policy and practice.

has gained steam throughout the sciences. Focusing on crime control in particular, researchers and policymakers have increasingly become interested in what works and does not work to control crime. This **evidence-based justice** movement seeks to use the most rigorous scientific methodology available to identify and implement crime control techniques that are most likely to make best use of taxpayer monies. This book is just one piece of the evidence-based justice puzzle. It draws on a number of resources aimed at identifying effective solutions to crime. Examples include scientific studies published in academic journals, review treatises, and government resources/publications, including the many resources available on the federal government's recently launched crimesolutions.gov Web site.

Effective Does Not Always Mean Best

Even if an approach to the crime problem appears effective, it might not be the best one. For example, hiring more police officers might reduce crime, but targeting police resources more carefully where they are needed the most could do even more. Drug treatment might reduce drug dependence, but treatment combined with cognitive-behavioral therapies could have an even more pronounced effect. What is important is that while reading this book, do not think that a successful crime control strategy is the best approach. There is a great deal that we can do to effectively control crime, and the odds are that several approaches combined together will do the most to make society safer.

A PREVIEW OF THE BOOK

Crime control in America is inherently complicated. There are innumerable ways in which we go about addressing the crime problem—more ways than can possibly be considered fully in a book of this size. Nevertheless, there are certain approaches to crime that are inherently controversial, that pique our curiosity, and that receive a significant measure of publicity. These are the approaches that are considered throughout the remaining chapters.

That having been said, the approach that this book takes to discussing crime control in America is by focusing on *where crime control originates*. Recall from the earlier discussion that the focus here is on approaches to crime. These approaches can originate at various levels. Formal approaches found in the criminal justice system are one variety. Informal approaches taken at an individual level are common as well. The approaches that are considered throughout the remaining chapters are (1) law enforcement approaches, including police and prosecutor approaches; (2) courts, corrections, and legislative approaches; and (3) approaches beyond the criminal justice system.

Guns and Drugs: The Real Attention Getters

This country's gun and drug problems are such that they cannot be covered thoroughly in any one chapter. For example, gun violence is addressed through everything from policing strategies and sentence enhancements to neighborhood watch programs and self-defense measures. Likewise, drugs can be dealt with via get-tough conservative approaches such as mandatory sentences and less drastic approaches such as education and treatment. Accordingly, it will be necessary to touch on drugs and gun violence on several occasions throughout the remaining chapters rather than having single chapters devoted to each.

Summary

This chapter has covered issues in the identification and evaluation of crime control in America. We began by pointing out that this country has a crime problem. Then we discussed the contours of the crime problem. We learned that there are many types of crimes, that the criminal law continues to expand, and that crime is quite pervasive, costly, and fear-inspiring. The point was also made that this book examines the effectiveness of crime control in America mostly with attention to its effects on index offenses.

After covering the crime problem, this chapter introduced the various approaches taken to deal with it. Approaches to the crime problem include laws, public policies (official and unofficial), and unofficial approaches. The approaches that receive the greatest degree of attention in this book include the first two. Laws and public policies are commonly used to control crime, and people take several unofficial approaches to the crime problem.

To evaluate success, it is necessary to settle on important definitions, including the crime problem; an approach is intended to address, what the solution is, and how it will be evaluated. Once definitions are put forth, it becomes much easier to evaluate the effectiveness of crime control in America. But given that the academic discipline of criminal justice is included within the social sciences, there are many problems that threaten researchers' ability to determine what works and what doesn't to control crime. Several such problems were discussed at great length in this chapter.

This chapter concluded with some attention to the faddish nature of crime control and to the concept of bandwagon science. Both can divert attention from approaches that are in need of additional research but for which there is no funding. The academic crusade—a researcher's decision to push his or her agenda at the expense of good science—was also discussed. There will be "Does It Work?" sections that will appear throughout subsequent chapters. They will serve as summaries of the literature and present the author's opinion regarding the effectiveness of various approaches to the crime problem.

Notes

1. Federal Bureau of Investigation, *Uniform Crime Reports, 2011*, fbi.gov/about-us/cjis/ucr/crime-in-the-u.s/2011/crime-in-the-u.s.-2011/violent-crime/violent-crime (accessed March 19, 2013).

2. Edwin Sutherland, "White-Collar Criminality," *American Sociological Review* 5 (1940): 2–10.

3. James Q. Wilson and George L. Kelling, "Broken Windows: The Police and Neighborhood Safety," *Atlantic Monthly* 249 (1982): 29–38.

4. For what appears to be an isolated exception, see B.L. Smith, K.R. Damphouse, F. Jackson, and A. Sellers, "The Prosecution and Punishment of International Terrorists in Federal Courts, 1980–1998," *Criminology and Public Policy* 1 (2002): 311–38.

5. A. Blumstein, J. Cohen, J.A. Roth, and C.A. Visher, eds., *Criminal Careers and Career Criminals* (Washington, DC: National Academy Press, 1986).

6. Paul Heaton, *Hidden in Plain Sight: What Cost-of-Crime Research Can Tell Us About Investing in Police* (Santa Monica, CA: RAND Corporation, 2010), 5.

7. National White Collar Crime Center, *Securities Fraud* (Richmond, VA: National White Collar Crime Center, 2002).

8. National White Collar Crime Center, *Check Fraud* (Richmond, VA: National White Collar Crime Center, 2002).

9. National White Collar Crime Center, *Telemarketing Fraud* (Richmond, VA: National White Collar Crime Center, 2002).

10. National White Collar Crime Center, *Healthcare Fraud* (Richmond, VA: National White Collar Crime Center, 2002).

11. D.A. Anderson, "The aggregate burden of crime." *Journal of Law and Economics* 42 (1999): 611–42.

12. F.J. Fowler, Jr. and T.W. Mangione, "A Three-Pronged Effort to Reduce Crime and Fear of Crime: The Hartford Experiment," in *Community Crime Prevention: Does It Work?* Ed. D. Rosenbaum (Beverly Hills, CA: Sage, 1986), 87–108.

13. S.W. Greenberg, W.M. Rohe, and J.R. Williams, *Safe and Secure Neighborhoods: Physical Characteristics and Informal Territorial Control in High and Low Crime Neighborhoods* (Washington, DC: National Institute of Justice, 1982); T. Hartnagel, "The Perception and Fear of Crime: Implications for Neighborhood Cohesion, Social Activity, and Community Affect," *Social Forces* 58 (1979): 176–90.

14. J. Garofalo, "The Fear of Crime: Causes and Consequences," *Journal of Criminal Law and Criminology* 72 (1981): 839–57; L. Schuerman and S. Kobrin, "Community Careers in Crime," in *Communities and Crime*, ed. A.J. Reiss, Jr. and M. Tonry (Chicago, IL: University of Chicago Press, 1986), 67–100; W.G. Skogan, *Disorder and Decline: Crime and the Spiral Decay in American Cities* (New York: Free Press,

1990); R.P. Taub, D.G. Taylor, and J.D. Dunham, *Paths of Neighborhood Change: Race and Crime in Urban America* (Chicago: University of Chicago Press, 1984).

15. J.E. Conklin, *The Impact of Crime* (New York: Macmillan, 1975).

16. Paul J. Lavrakas, "Fear of Crime and Behavioral Restrictions in Urban and Suburban Neighborhoods," *Population and Environment* 5 (1982): 242–64.

17. Dennis Rosenbaum and Linda Heath, "The 'Psycho-Logic' of Fear Reduction and Crime-Prevention Programs," in *Social Influence Processes and Prevention*, eds. John Edwards et al. (New York: Plenum, 1990), 221–47.

18. Timothy J. Flanagan and Dennis R. Longmire, *Americans View Crime and Justice: A National Public Opinion Survey* (Thousand Oaks, CA: Sage, 1996); Mary Beth Armstrong and G. Blake Armstrong, "The Color of Crime: Perceptions of Caucasians' and African-Americans' Involvement in Crime," in *Entertaining Crime: Television Reality Programs*, eds. Mark Fishman and Gray Cavender (New York: Aldine de Gruyter, 1998), 19–35.

19. Dan A. Lewis and Greta Salem, *Fear of Crime: Incivility and the Production of a Social Problem* (New Brunswick, NJ: Transaction Books, 1986).

20. V.D. Young, "Fear of Victimization and Victimization Rates among Women: A Paradox?" *Justice Quarterly* 9 (1992): 419–41; M.C. Stafford and O.R. Galle, "Victimization Rates, Exposure to Risk, and Fear of Crime," *Criminology* 22 (1984): 107–85.

21. R.L. Akers, A.J. LaGreca, C. Sellers, and J. Cochran, "Fear of Crime and Victimization among the Elderly in Different Types of Communities," *Criminology* 25 (1987): 487–505.

22. L. Heath, J. Kavanagh, and S.R. Thompson, "Perceived Vulnerability and Fear of Crime: Why Fear Stays High When Crime Rates Drop," *Journal of Offender Rehabilitation* 33 (2001): 1–14.

23. Thomas B. Marvell and Carlisle E. Moody, "Specification Problems, Police Levels and Crime Rates," *Criminology* 34 (1996): 609–46.

24. For a detailed discussion of the merits of experimental research, see Vol. 589 (Sept. 2003) of *The Annals of the American Academy of Political and Social Science*. Sherman edited the issue, and he and several authors argue for expanded use of experimental designs throughout the political and social sciences.

25. J. Austin, "Why Criminology Is Irrelevant," *Criminology and Public Policy* 2 (2003): 557–64.

26. For an example, see Jihong "Solomon" Zhao, Matthew C. Scheider, and Quint Thurman, "Funding Community Policing to Reduce Crime: Have Cops Grants Made a Difference?" *Criminology and Public Policy* 2 (2002): 7–32.

27. K.J. Bowers and S.D. Johnson, "Measuring the Geographical Displacement and Diffusion of Benefit Effects of Crime Prevention Activity," *Journal of Quantitative Criminology* 19 (2003): 275–301.

28. For earlier reviews, see S. Hakim and G. Rengert, *Crime Spillover* (Beverly Hills, CA: Sage, 1981); T.A. Repetto, *Residential Crime* (Cambridge, MA: Ballinger, 1974). See also R. Barr and K. Pease, "Crime Placement, Displacement and Deflection," in *Crime and Justice: A Review of Research*, eds. M. Tonry and N. Morris, vol. 12 (Chicago, IL: University of Chicago Press, 1990), 277–315.

29. R.B.P. Hesseling, "Displacement: A Review of the Empirical Literature," in *Crime Prevention Studies*, ed. R.V. Clarke, vol. 2 (Monsey, NY: Criminal Justice Press, 1995), 197–230; J. Eck, "The Threat of Crime Displacement," *Criminal Justice Abstracts* 25 (1993): 527–46.

30. Michael R. Smith, "Police-Led Crackdowns and Cleanups: An Evaluation of a Crime Control Initiative in Richmond, Virginia," *Crime and Delinquency* 47 (2001): 60–83.

31. See, for example, R.V. Clarke and D. Weisburd, "Diffusion of Crime Control Benefits: Observations on the Reverse of Displacement," in *Crime Prevention Studies*, ed. R.V. Clarke, vol. 3 (Monsey, NY: Willow Tree Press, 1994), 165–83; T.D. Miethe, "Citizen-Based Crime Control Activity and Victimisation Risks: An Examination of Displacement and Free-Rider Effects," *Criminology* 29 (1991): 419–39.

32. G. Barnes, "Defining and Optimising Displacement," in *Crime and Place: Crime Prevention Studies*, eds. J. Eck and D. Weisburd, vol. 4 (Monsey, NY: Criminal Justice Press, 1995), 95–114.

33. A. Braga, D. Weisburd, E. Waring, L. Green-Mazerolle, W. Spelman, and G. Gajewski, "Problem-Oriented Policing in Violent Crime Places: A Randomized Controlled Experiment," *Criminology* 37 (1999): 541–79.

34. D. Weisburd and L. Green, "Policing Drug Hot Spots: The Jersey City Drug Market Analysis Experiment," *Justice Quarterly* 12 (1995): 711–35.

35. T.B. Marvell and C.E. Moody, "The Lethal Effects of Three-Strikes Laws," *Journal of Legal Studies* 30 (2001): 89–106.

36. J.M Shepherd, "Fear of the First Strike: The Full Deterrent Effect of California's Two- and Three-Strikes Legislation," *Journal of Legal Studies* 31 (2002): 159–201; see also T. Kovandzic, J.J. Sloan III and L.M. Vieraitis, "Unintended Consequences of Politically Popular Sentencing Policy: The Homicide Promoting Effects of 'Three Strikes' in U.S. Cities (1980–1999)," *Criminology and Public Policy* 1 (2002): 399–424.

37. R. McCleary and R.A. Hay, *Applied Time Series Analysis for the Social Sciences* (Beverly Hills, CA: Sage, 1980).

38. Patrick T. Brandt and John T. Williams, "A Linear Poisson Autoregressive Model: The Poisson AR(p) Model," *Political Analysis* 9 (2001): 164–84.

39. J. Austin, "Why Criminology Is Irrelevant," *Criminology and Public Policy* 2 (2003): 557–64.

40. John L. Worrall and Jihong Zhao, "The Role of the COPS Office in Community Policing," *Policing: An International Journal of Police Strategies and Management* 26 (2003): 64–87.

41. References have deliberately been left out of this section to avoid any potentially libelous statements.

Crime Control Perspectives

LEARNING OBJECTIVES

- Summarize operational perspectives of criminal justice.
- Summarize political perspectives of criminal justice.
- Explain the goals of crime control.

Crime control perspectives consist of the views people have with respect to how the justice system should operate, the causes of crime, what should be done about crime, and what the proper goals for the criminal justice system should be. We begin by highlighting four operational perspectives. These consist of people's beliefs either about how the justice system should operate or about how it *does* operate. Then we discuss what, for lack of a better term, can be called political perspectives. In this section, we will highlight the leading ideological views with respect to crime control in America. The third major section of this chapter will conclude with a brief introduction to some other perspectives that are neither operational nor necessarily political. Finally, we will conclude with some attention to the goals of criminal justice, including deterrence, retribution, incapacitation, and rehabilitation.

OPERATIONAL PERSPECTIVES

We begin by introducing two conflicting viewpoints about how justice should operate: due process and crime control. Both perspectives are political in the sense that they closely resemble liberal and conservative orientations, but their concern is more with how the justice system should work than with what causes crime, the effects crime has on society, and what should be done about crime. (We cover those issues in the section on political perspectives.) Next, this section introduces the system and nonsystem perspectives. Some people believe that the justice system is a well-oiled machine; others believe that it is a disorganized mess. The funnel model of criminal justice and the criminal justice wedding cake are also introduced, as they are also ways to view the operation of the justice system.

Due Process and Crime Control

Crime control is an exciting topic because of the inherent tension it creates between two competing sets of priorities. On the one hand, there is a serious interest in this country in controlling crime, doing whatever it takes to keep criminals off the streets. On the other hand, because of our democratic system of government, we value people's rights and become angry when these rights are compromised or threatened. Herbert Packer has described these two competing sets of values as the **crime control** and **due process** perspectives (see Figure 2.1 for an overview).[1]

You are probably familiar with the values to which each opposing perspective subscribes because these values are frequently invoked in discussions of criminal justice. Almost without exception, whenever there is disagreement as to how best to approach the crime problem—be it through court decisions or legislative measures—the due process/crime control debate rears its head. A delicate balance has to be achieved between both perspectives.

DUE PROCESS VALUES.   Packer's due process model is first and foremost concerned with people's rights and liberties. It also gives significant weight to human freedom. Due process advocates believe that the government's job is not first and foremost to control crime but rather to maximize human freedom, which includes protecting citizens from undue government influence. Due process values favor minimizing the potential for mistakes, partly because:

> People are notoriously poor observers of disturbing events . . . confessions and admissions by persons in police custody may be induced by physical or psychological coercion

crime control perspective: a belief that the key aim of criminal justice policy is the control of crime, perhaps at the expense of individual liberties and due process protections.

due process perspective: a belief that the key aim of criminal justice policy is the protection of due process and people's rights, even if crime control suffers.

Crime Control Values	Due Process Values
• Follows "assembly line" metaphor	• Follows "obstacle course" metaphor
• Emphasizes quantity over quality	• Emphasizes quality over quantity
• Favors informality	• Prefers formality
• Has faith in the police	• Has faith in the courts
• Makes presumption of guilt	• Makes presumption of innocence
• Seeks to benefit society	• Seeks to benefit suspects
• Is concerned with ends, not means	• Is concerned with means, not ends
• Seeks to maximize police authority	• Seeks to maximize human freedom
• Seeks to control crime at all costs	• Seeks to protect people's rights at all costs
• Puts emphasis on factual guilt	• Puts emphasis on legal guilt

FIGURE 2.1 The Values of Due Process versus Crime Control

Source: J. L. Worrall, *Criminal Procedure: From First Contact to Appeal,* 2004. Boston: Allyn & Bacon, p. 13.

so that the police end up hearing what the suspect thinks they want to hear rather than the truth; witnesses may be animated by a bias or interest that no one would trouble to discover except one specially charged with protecting the interests of the accused (as the police are not).[2]

Due process advocates also believe that all suspects are to be considered innocent until proven guilty, just as we are taught. They place greater emphasis on legal guilt (whether a person is guilty according to the law) than on factual guilt (whether a person actually committed the crime with which she or he is charged).

At the heart of the due process perspective are four sets of ideals: (1) The criminal process looks—or should look—something like an obstacle course; (2) quality is better than quantity; (3) formality is preferred over informality; and (4) a great deal of faith is put in the courts.

That the criminal process should resemble an obstacle course is a metaphorical description. A criminal process that resembles an obstacle course is one that is complex and needs to be navigated by skilled legal professionals. Further, it is one that is somewhat difficult to operate in a predictable fashion. It is the opposite of a process that prides itself on speed and efficiency, values that are of great importance in the crime control perspective. The obstacle course metaphor also stresses that each case needs to pass through several complicated twists and turns before a verdict can be rendered.

Another way to distinguish between due process and crime control is in terms of quantity and quality. The due process view favors quality; that is, a fair and accurate decision at every stage of the criminal process. It stresses that each case be handled on an individual basis, with special attention to the facts and circumstances surrounding each event. In addition, a concern with quality is one that minimizes the potential for error. For example, due process advocates are in favor of having several death penalty appeals because the possibility of executing the wrong person is something to be avoided at all costs.

Due process advocates do not favor informal processes. Because of the potential for human error and bias, they favor a full-blown adversarial criminal process. They also believe that early intervention by judges and other presumptively objective parties (besides, say, the police) is in the best interest of people who find themselves on the wrong side of the law.

Another value that is inherent in the due process perspective is intense faith in the courts as opposed to law enforcement. Due process advocates point out, correctly, that the job of judges is to interpret the U.S. Constitution. This, they argue, helps to provide protection to those who have been charged with crime. Faith in the courts also jibes with the above-mentioned insistence on formality. When guilt and innocence are determined in the courts, an air of fairness and objectivity presides.

CRIME CONTROL VALUES. The crime control model stands in contrast to the due process perspective. It emphasizes the importance of controlling crime, perhaps to the detriment of civil liberties. From a cost--benefit perspective, crime control advocates believe that the benefits to all of controlling crime outweighs the cost of infringing on some individuals' due process protections. Another way to distinguish between the due process and crime control perspectives is to consider the distinction between means and ends; crime control is more concerned with the ends—with wiping out crime or, at a minimum, mitigating its harmful effects. By contrast, due process is concerned with the means, with the methods with which people are treated by criminal justice officials. The end result—either crime or the absence of it—is not of great concern to due process advocates.

The metaphor of an assembly line suggests that the criminal process should be automatic, predictable, and uniform. In other words, every criminal should be treated the same, with minimal variations in terms of charges and sentences. The assembly line metaphor further suggests that the criminal process should be quick and efficient. The goal of the crime control perspective is to move criminals through the justice process as swiftly as possible. A full-blown, adversarial criminal process replete with hearings and other pauses in the interest of the accused are anathema to the crime control view.

As we have seen, the due process model stresses quality over quantity. The crime control model, by contrast, favors quantity over quality. This view is consistent with the assembly line metaphor. The goal is to move as many offenders as possible through the criminal justice system with as little delay as possible. If mistakes are made along the way and someone is wrongfully charged or convicted, so be it. The *overall* goal of ensuring that as many criminals are dealt with as possible takes precedence over any individual's constitutional rights.

Whereas the due process perspective favors the formality of the criminal process, with particular emphasis on the courts, the crime control perspective favors informality. The courts are something to be avoided, and justice should be meted out beyond the walls of a courtroom. Plea bargaining, for instance, is favored because of its swift, behind-the-scenes nature, not to mention that it avoids the need to go to trial. An insistence on informality suggests further that the law enforcement establishment, not the courts, should be more involved in making guilt determinations.

Finally, whereas the due process perspective places a great deal of faith in the courts, the crime control perspective puts a high degree of trust in the police. We are all taught that all suspects are innocent until proven guilty in a court of law. Clearly, courts are charged with making this determination. However, crime control advocates favor "street justice," giving the police vast discretion to decide how people who are suspected of being involved in criminal activity should be dealt with. A fitting description of the crime control perspective is therefore "all criminals are guilty until proven innocent." In other words, all suspects should be considered guilty; if the courts determine otherwise, then so be it.

System and Nonsystem

When people talk about the criminal justice system, they often assume that it is a system. What is a system? There is no one definition, but several have been offered. One is that a system is a group of interacting, interrelated, or interdependent entities. That would seem to characterize the criminal justice system to an extent; police agencies, courts, and correction institutions are certainly working to combat the same problem. But other definitions of *system* stress a condition of harmonious, orderly action. Assuming that we buy into this second definition, we must then ask another question: "Is criminal justice harmonious and orderly?" Many people think not.[3] They think that it is best characterized as a nonsystem. But others believe that the various elements of the U.S. justice system work well together.

A WELL-OILED MACHINE?   The notion that the criminal justice system is a well-oiled machine can be traced to the civics book image of justice. At some point when we were first introduced to the components of the justice system, we were probably taught that all the agencies involved work as a cohesive whole with a common goal: the reduction of crime. As we have (ideally) become more enlightened, though, we have come to learn that certain elements of the justice system do not always work well together. Turf wars between law enforcement agencies can impede the administration of justice. Miscommunication between police departments and prosecutors' office can result in cases being rejected for prosecution. A disconnection between the various agencies that are responsible for the treatment and reintegration of offenders could cause more harm than good. And so on.

Walker has called this the "old idealism," a view that the components of the justice system work well together and rigidly adhere to their organizational missions. This idealized image of criminal justice also suggests that all crimes and criminals are assigned high priority and that everyone who is employed in the justice system selflessly does what he or she is supposed to do. Walker has put it this way:

> This view holds that diligent and hardworking officials enforce the law as it is written in the statutes; a person who commits a crime is duly arrested and prosecuted for that offense; if convicted, he or she receives the prescribed punishment. It is an adversarial system of justice that determines the truth of guilty or innocence through a public contest between prosecution and defense, overseen by an impartial judge.[4]

A DISORGANIZED MESS?   The opposite of the civics book image is a perception that our nation's criminal justice system is a disorganized mess. This is the nonsystem perspective. Those who believe that we have a criminal justice nonsystem claim that everyone who is involved in the control of crime has his or her own priorities and values and therefore does not work well with other agencies. Believers in the nonsystem model also claim that there is much duplication of effort between government agencies and a total lack of communication among those who are responsible for making our nation safer. And to the extent we have a nonsystem, it is also characterized by a disconnection between the various agencies that are involved in the control of crime. It is a classic case of the right hand not knowing what the left hand is doing.

It is probably safe to say that we have (or at least have had) something of a non-system, given the surge in partnerships and cooperative agreements between criminal justice agencies in recent years.[5] For example, federal and local prosecutors have begun to team up to target gun violence. Other such partnerships are discussed later in this book. They have not been pursued out of a desire to socialize but rather out of a desire to work together in pursuit of a common goal: the reduction of crime. Partners in the various collaborations that are evident in the justice system today generally come to the table because they believe that when the flow of information improves, when efforts are not duplicated, and when tools available to each agency in a partnership are used at the same time and in response to the same set of problems, crime can be targeted more effectively.

The Funnel Model of Justice

In 1967, the President's Commission on Law Enforcement and Administration of Justice attempted to model the criminal justice process with a flowchart.[6] That flowchart is reprinted in Figure 2.2. The figure, turned on its side, clearly resembles a funnel. This is what is meant by the funnel model of justice. It shows that the criminal process begins with offenses known to the police, self-reported criminal activity, and the dark figure of criminal victimization. At the other end, after the criminal process has played out, a comparatively small percentage of cases come out of the system. Another noteworthy feature of Figure 2.2 is the large drop-off in cases between the criminal event and a police investigation. It also shows the funnel effect of the criminal justice system.

The funnel model presented in Figure 2.2 is characteristic of a systems perspective of criminal justice. That is, it was developed and organized by people who believe that we have a cohesive, smooth-working justice *system*. The figure further shows that there is a great deal of interconnectedness between the various agencies of the criminal justice system and that they work effectively together toward a common goal. But as we saw in the previous section, it might be that our criminal justice system is in fact a disorganized nonsystem. To the extent that this is true, Figure 2.2 is probably a dramatic oversimplification. One might even argue that a reason for the left-to-right funneling effect is that the various agencies that are involved in the control of crime do not work well together.

The Criminal Justice Wedding Cake

criminal justice wedding cake model: a model of the criminal process emphasizing how cases are processed. Top layer cases are the fewest in number and receive the full gamut of the criminal process while the lowest level cases, which are the greatest in number, receive quick and informal processing.

Some people have argued that the funnel model of the criminal process does not give attention to the priorities that are assigned to various types of crime. In response to this concern, an alternative model of the criminal justice process has been put forth: that of a four-layer wedding cake. The **criminal justice wedding cake model** was first described by Lawrence Friedman and Robert Percival in their book *The Roots of Justice*,[7] but they gave it only three layers. It has since been refined, most notably in Gottfredson and Gottfredson's book *Decision Making in Criminal Justice*.[8] They added a fourth layer to the wedding cake.

The wedding cake (see Figure 2.3) illustrates how offense seriousness relates to how the criminal process plays out. At the top of the cake, the smallest layer, are the so-called celebrated cases. These are cases involving celebrities (e.g., Michael Jackson) or that otherwise receive extensive media coverage (e.g., Scott Peterson). Such cases benefit from a full-blown, drawn-out criminal trial that can take months. The problem is

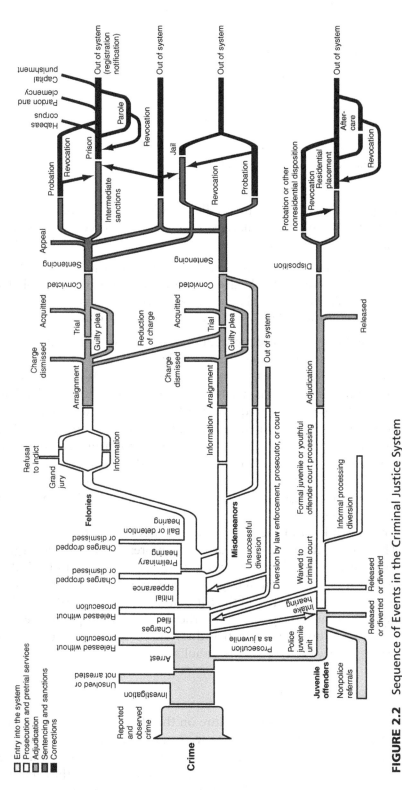

FIGURE 2.2 Sequence of Events in the Criminal Justice System

Source: President's Commission on Law Enforcement and Administration of Justice, *Task Force Report: Science and Technology* (Washington, DC: Government Printing Office, 1967), pp. 58–59.

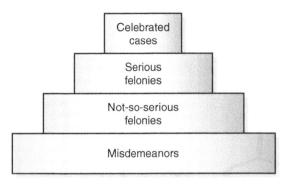

FIGURE 2.3   Criminal Justice Wedding Cake Model

that when a lengthy trial combines with media attention, people come to think that the criminal process works similarly for all types of offenders accused of all types of crime. Walker has made this observation:

> Because of the publicity, celebrated cases have an enormous impact on public perceptions about criminal justice. People mistakenly assume that they are typical of all cases. This fosters the belief that people like Ernesto Miranda (whose cases gave us the *Miranda* warning) are "beating the system" every day through "technicalities."[9]

The second and third layers of the wedding cake consist of felonies. The second-layer felonies consist of serious crimes that usually result in a full-blown trial that is not as involved and drawn-out as trials in celebrated cases. Dismissals are also rare. But down in the third layer, dismissals are more common. Additionally, defendants are allowed to plea-bargain more frequently. If they are convicted, defendants in the third-layer cases often receive probation instead of a prison sentence. What determines whether a case ends up in the second or the third layer? There are generally three factors: the relationship between the victim and the offender, the seriousness of the offense, and the defendant's prior record;[10] serious felonies committed by offenders with lengthy rap sheets against victims who are strangers will almost certainly be placed in the second layer.

Finally, the fourth layer of the criminal justice wedding cake is reserved for misdemeanors. The size of this layer is a metaphorical representation of the large number of misdemeanors relative to felonies. Cases in this layer rarely go to trial. If they do, they are dispensed of quickly, often in large numbers and at the same time. The fourth layer is arguably most representative of the *true* nature of criminal justice in the United States (as compared to the top layer), but it is the layer that most people never see. We get much more worked up over celebrities' dirty laundry than over offenses such as public drunkenness, petty theft, or simple assaults.

POLITICAL PERSPECTIVES

Before we can critically analyze the literature on the effectiveness of crime control in the United States, it is necessary to review various political viewpoints on the subject. One reason for doing so is that throughout the book, some attention will be given to each. Another reason for examining political perspectives is that they tell us a great deal about why certain crime control approaches have come to pass (e.g., conservative policies are often adopted when conservative politicians are elected to influential

Communists --- Socialists --- Marxists --- Liberals --- Middle-of-the-roaders --- Conservatives --- Anarchists

FIGURE 2.4   A Continuum of Political Perspectives

positions). Finally, familiarizing ourselves with such perspectives helps us to think about our own set of beliefs and priorities for addressing important social problems.

An important note about the conflicting viewpoints that we are about to cover is that they are not limited to issues of crime and justice. For example, there are liberal and conservative views on nearly every political issue, not just justice-related ones. Likewise, consensus and conflict perspectives reach well beyond the realm of criminal justice. Our concern here, though, is with the relationship between political values and issues of criminal justice. We want to answer the following questions: (1) What do the perspectives tell us about the causes of crime? (2) What do they tell us about the consequences of crime? and (3) What do they suggest we should do about the crime problem in the United States?

It is also important to note that the perspectives we are about to introduce fall on a continuum of government involvement,[11] a continuum that runs from left to right (see Figure 2.4). At the far left we find conflict thinkers, including (in order of their movement from left to right) communists, socialists, and Marxists. Still other conflict perspectives may fit to varying degrees between each of these,[12] but our concern is going to be with conflict thinking in general, not with the subtle (and sometimes significant) differences between variations of it. Conflict thinkers are generally critical of what they perceive to be an overreaching, overcontrolling, and even oppressive government.

Moving to the right past the conflict perspective we find liberals. Moving farther right still, we find the middle-of-the-roaders. Such people buy into elements of liberal and conservative thinking. As we go even farther to the right we find conservatives, and still farther to the right we find anarchists and other fringe thinkers. We will not move beyond the conservative perspective because very little attention has been given to the anarchist perspective in criminal justice. Anarchists often consist of militia members, survivalists, and others whose views are so far "out there" as to render their beliefs practically useless in terms of informing real-world policies.

Liberals and Conservatives

The due process perspective closely resembles a **liberal perspective**. Liberals often favor the protection of people's rights and liberties to a higher degree than their conservative counterparts do. By contrast, crime control is an important part of the **conservative perspective**. Of course, in reality there can be a great deal of overlap between the two perspectives. Liberals occasionally favor conservative crime control policies, and conservatives can be concerned with protecting the rights of American citizens. But unlike the due process/crime control views, which explain only the administration of justice (or how it *should* be carried out), liberal and conservative viewpoints can be used to explain (1) the causes of crime, (2) the consequences of crime for society, and (3) what should be done about crime. Let us look at each of these in more detail.

CAUSES OF CRIME.   Conservatives believe, simply, that crime is a product of individual choice. That is, people supposedly weigh the costs and benefits associated with committing crime and then act on the basis of the information they have. Crime results,

liberal perspective: with respect to crime control, an emphasis on the protection of people's rights and liberties. Corresponds closely with a due process perspective.

conservative perspective: with respect to crime control, an emphasis on tough punishment and crime control. Corresponds closely with a crime control orientation.

then, when people perceive that the benefits associated with committing a crime outweigh the costs. This rational choice perspective is sometimes called *the classical criminological paradigm,* or *the classical school.* In this sense, it was around well before many of the more "environmental" theories of crime were put forth. But it persists today; some people with conservative leanings tend to favor the rational choice perspective.

If it is assumed that people make rational choices, then deterrence-oriented policies should be adopted. We will consider deterrence as a goal of criminal justice later in this chapter, but for now, note that it is closely tied to the rational choice perspective. One team of authors explains the relationships between the classical schools of criminology, rational choice, and the deterrence theory in this way:

> One of the most widely debated premises underlying attempts to explain crime, among both criminologists and lay persons, is the role of choice. At issue is the degree to which offenders are, or are not, driven by rationality. Both deterrence theory and other explanations falling within the larger rational choice framework assign a greater role to calculating decision-making on the part of the criminal offender than to other approaches. Both are rooted in utilitarian thought, the notion that public policy decisions should maximize pleasure while minimizing pain among the general citizenry.[13]

Liberals believe that crime is a product not of individual choices but of environmental factors. That is, liberals discount the notion of rational decision-making and point to a number of other explanations for crime. These include peer influence, dysfunctional families, blocked opportunities, stigmatization, and a host of other causes of crime. Understood differently, "[m]any theories rooted in the [liberal] paradigm sympathize with offenders, maintaining that social, biological, or psychological pathologies are responsible for their conduct,"[14] according to one source. This liberal take on crime has been termed *positivistic criminology,* or *the positivistic paradigm.*

As should be clear by now, hard-line liberals and conservatives disagree about the causes of crime. But some people buy into both perspectives to varying degrees. A middle-of-the-road take on liberal and conservative explanations for crime might be something like this: People make rational decisions, but their rationality is limited by environmental factors. Another centrist view could be that people are heavily influenced by their environments; anyone who is not mentally defective to some extent gives at least some thought to his or her actions.

CONSEQUENCES OF CRIME FOR SOCIETY. Although conservatives and liberals disagree on the causes of crime, they do agree on the consequences of crime for society. Both believe that crime offends the moral fabric of society and crosses the line between what everyone perceives as acceptable and unacceptable conduct. In other words, both liberals and conservatives believe that there is a general consensus in society about what is wrong and right. This is quite distinct from causes of crime and views on what is the appropriate policy response to the crime problem.

Obviously, there is less than total consensus on what constitutes appropriate and inappropriate behavior. Most people in a civilized society agree that serious crimes such as homicide, robbery, rape, and burglary are not socially acceptable; there is much more disagreement over whether less serious offenses, such as recreational drug use and social gambling, should be targeted by the criminal law. Such disagreement notwithstanding, the fact that there is *any* consensus over what effect crime has on society is what makes liberal and conservative perspectives markedly different from others to which we will turn shortly.

WHAT SHOULD BE DONE ABOUT CRIME?   Conservatives and liberals may agree that certain crimes are unacceptable; they certainly disagree as to what should be done about such crimes. Conservatives generally take a tough-on-crime stance and argue for more criminal justice spending and increased sanctions. They believe that more police should be hired, that justice system officials should be able to do their work unimpeded, and that the more criminals are put behind bars, the safer society will be.

Some conservatives believe that tough sanctions will set criminals on the straight-and-narrow. They believe that time in prison will cause a criminal to reflect on his or her actions, reducing the likelihood that the person will commit more crimes after release. Some conservatives also believe that crime is a problem to be reined and aggressively controlled. They tend not to prioritize prevention, early intervention, and other strategies that are thought to discourage crime before it is committed.

Liberals, by contrast, tend to favor treatment, rehabilitation, job training, and other prevention-oriented methods of addressing crime. This stems from their view that crime is caused by environmental factors. For example, a liberal might look at a drug addict's self-destructive behavior in the context of the environment in which the addict lives. The liberal might then push for a drug treatment program for the addict because without such an intervention that addict might simply return to the same environment on release from prison and fall victim to the same forces that perhaps created the problem in the first place.

These conflicting views on what should be done about crime have led to many lively exchanges over the years. The most tension appears to exist in academic rather than policy circles, however. Why? Probably because, to be elected, liberal politicians often need to take a tough-on-crime stance. Consider the following hypothetical political candidate's agenda for dealing with this country's drug problem and then ask yourself, "Would this person be elected?"

> I feel sincerely that drugs are a social problem, not a crime problem. We need treatment for drug offenders. We also need to reevaluate whether there is a need to incarcerate the large number of nonviolent drug offenders currently residing in our nation's corrections institutions. We could save money be releasing certain prisoners, but drug treatment is sure to be costly, and it certainly won't succeed in the short term. Resources, time, and considerable effort will be necessary, but in the long run society will be safer.

Even after campaigning and winning election, some liberals opt for traditionally conservative crime control policies. Bill Clinton's Violent Crime Control Act of 1994 is a prime example. So there is a blurring of the lines between liberal and conservative thinking with respect to what should be done about crime. Academics, though, do not have to answer to the same constituencies that politicians do; they can militantly adhere to their views on what method of crime control is sure to produce the most desirable results, knowing that their jobs are fairly secure.

Consensus and Conflict

As we have indicated, liberals and conservatives tend to believe that crime offends a more or less cohesive social system. Further, they tend to believe that (1) certain norms and values are the core elements of social life, (2) people are committed to a certain social order, (3) solidarity is evident in the interaction between people of all groups, and (4) everyone willingly submits to a legitimate authority, typically the government. This is known as the **consensus perspective**. The term consensus refers, in general, to

consensus perspective: a set of beliefs that (1) certain norms and values are the core elements of social life, (2) people are committed to a certain social order, (3) solidarity is evident in the interaction between people of all groups, and (4) everyone willingly submits to a legitimate authority, typically the government.

the notion that everyone in a society agrees to be governed. Furthermore, consensus thinkers believe that people agree on which issues are of most concern to social welfare, what effect they have on society, and what should be done about them.

conflict perspective:
a belief that self-
interest, coercion,
division, opposition,
exclusion, hostility,
sectional interests,
political power,
contradictions, and
other such factors
best describe social
interactions.

The opposite of the consensus perspective is the **conflict perspective**. Conflict thinkers believe that self-interest, coercion, division, opposition, exclusion, hostility, sectional interests, political power, contradictions, and other such factors best describe social interactions. As is usually the case with other political perspectives, conflict thinking ranges from fairly extreme to quite mild. The most extreme version of conflict thinking lies in the realms of Marxism, socialism, and communism. These versions of conflict thinking stress the role of tension between classes and oppression of the masses at the behest of the controlling authority. Milder versions of conflict thinking also point to divisions between classes and to the rift between the haves and the have-nots, but they usually stop short of calling for changing the form of government.

The language of capitalism pervades conflict thinking. Specifically, people who adhere to the conflict perspective believe that a free market results in oppression because it necessarily requires two groups of people: the working class and those who control the working class. Conflict thinkers further believe that a small controlling class (i.e., the bourgeoisie) oppresses the working class (i.e., the proletariat) and actively works to keep workers ignorant of the oppression to which they are being subjected (e.g., through control of the popular press). Because capitalism is the market equivalent of democracy, conflict thinkers tend to be very critical of the U.S. system of government. They believe that it results in class divisions, inequality, and, once again, oppression. Let us now examine the differences between consensus and conflict perspectives as they relate to the causes of crime, the consequences of crime, and the methods that are conceived of to deal with it.

CAUSES OF CRIME.   The consensus and conflict perspectives have very different takes on the causes of crime. Recall that consensus thinkers believe that most people in society agree on what behaviors should be considered criminal. They believe that the criminal law reflects society's consensus that certain behaviors are improper. Crime therefore results from people who are not socialized into the mainstream. In other words, criminal behavior results from the fact that some people get socialized into criminal behavior. When people commit crimes, consensus thinkers point to the failures of the agencies of socialization, including families, schools, religious institutions, and the like.

Conflict thinkers believe that crime results from a very different set of circumstances. They believe that capitalism, particularly the tension it creates between the controlling and subject classes, is largely responsible for crime. They believe that crime is a reaction to one's life conditions. Conflict thinkers are also quick to point out that the criminal law reflects not the consensus of society but rather the priorities of the elites. Thus, crime tends to be concentrated in the lower class because the ruling class writes the law to make it look as though crime is the work of the poor. Stated differently, people in the lower class are more likely to be arrested and labeled criminals because the bourgeoisie controls law enforcement agencies.

CONSEQUENCES OF CRIME FOR SOCIETY.   As we pointed out earlier in highlighting the differences between liberal and conservative thinking, consensus thinkers believe that crime offends the conscience of society. To the extent that this occurs, crime creates a tighter bond among people; they unite in opposition to it. Many of us have probably experienced this phenomenon. Perhaps a burglary was committed in our neighbor-hood. If the residents came together in some fashion, perhaps to implement a surveil-lance program, consensus thinkers would be quick to argue that such behavior results from the general agreement among members of society about what is right and wrong. Moving away from crime, many of us have been through traumatic experiences, pos-sibly shared with strangers, in which a unique bond and sense of familiarity quickly developed between the various parties involved. This is also illustrative of consensus thinking.

Conflict thinkers do not believe that crime creates a bond among people. Instead, they believe that crime is divisive insofar as it continues to perpetuate differences between the rich and the poor. More than that, though, crime diverts the lower class's attention away from the exploitation they experience toward members of their own class. They think that crime occurs because of people in their midst rather than because "crime" has been defined by the rich and powerful in a way that benefits them. Conflict thinkers, particularly Marxists, call this *ideology,* a state of false consciousness among the ruled that makes them think that their own interests and those of the ruling class are one and the same. Conflict thinkers further point out that "crime" is a label that exists to serve the interests of the rich, that white-collar criminals often don't receive punish-ment because their crimes are not defined as quite as serious as those of the poor, and that crime creates employment. With respect to the latter issue, conflict thinkers argue that the controlling class has an interest in the presence of crime because of the money its members stand to earn from crime.

WHAT SHOULD BE DONE ABOUT CRIME?   People who believe that society is char-acterized by consensus tend to look for relatively simple solutions to social problems. With respect to crime, most people—liberals and conservatives alike—believe that some penalty should be attached to illegal behavior. Conservatives, of course, favor lengthy prison terms and otherwise getting tough with crime. Some liberals, especially more moderate liberals, also favor stringent sanctions against criminals, but many lib-erals favor rehabilitation, treatment, and other methods of making sure that offenders receive the services they need to reintegrate into society.

Conflict thinkers argue that something much more drastic is necessary to control crime. They do not argue that the justice system should punish criminals or even that the justice system should be involved at all. Instead, they believe the structural condi-tions of society need changing. They point to the widening gap between the rich and the poor and argue that it needs to be closed so that everyone has access to the same products and services. Moderate conflict thinkers favor policies that are intended to ensure a measure of equality between people. With respect to issues of justice, they believe that poor people should receive the same treatment as the more affluent, that justice should be blind, and that people's financial or social status should have little influence on how they are treated.

Extreme conflict thinkers, such as socialists and communists, point to the need for the abandonment of capitalism (because of the inevitable division that it creates between classes) and for forms of government that ensure equality between people. They might advocate socialism, in which the government ensures that everyone has the same access to products and services. Or they might favor communism, a form of socialism that abandons private ownership altogether. Whether socialist or communist systems of government are achievable (or desirable) is certainly open for debate, but if implemented, they would clearly be departures from capitalism and democracy, a development that hard-line conflict thinkers often favor.

OTHER PERSPECTIVES

Still other crime control perspectives can be identified. They are neither operational nor necessarily political, but they represent competing views that people have with respect to questions such as "What are the appropriate sources of information for making justice-related decisions?"; "What is the true priority of criminal justice?"; and "Is there a rift between the academic and real worlds?" We now briefly touch on each.

Faith and Fact

As Walker has observed, there is a great deal of mythology and nonsense surrounding the administration of justice.[15] He even borrowed the term "crime control theology"[16] to explain the misinformation on which people (usually policymakers) rely when deciding how to control crime. As Walker puts it,

> A serious problem with the debate over crime policy is that faith usually triumphs over facts. Both liberals and conservatives begin with certain assumptions that are almost like religious beliefs. Too often, these assumptions are not supported by empirical evidence.[17]

We will see several examples of approaches to the crime problem that do not appear, on the basis of the available research, to be effective, despite strong sentiments to the contrary. For example, many people, even liberals, are in favor of a tough-on-crime position that involves putting more and more offenders away in prison, but the evidence in support of such an approach is virtually absent. At the other extreme, many Americans are supportive of community policing strategies, but there is little available evidence to suggest that these approaches work.

It is clear that many decisions in the arena of crime control (and in other walks of life) are based on myths and half-truths. Entire books have been devoted to this problem.[18] The push in such sources is for decisions to be based on the opposite of faith, namely, fact. But is there such a thing? Is there a source that policymakers can visit that clearly lays out the facts so that crime control can be accomplished effectively and with as little waste as possible? The answer to both the questions is probably not. Several reasons for this were pointed out in Chapter 1. Nevertheless, it is hoped that this book and others like it will take us one step closer to making crime policy decisions with more than just assumptions in mind.

Crime Control and Revenue Generation

We are all taught that the purpose of the criminal justice system is to make us safer, to reduce crime. But what if that is not its purpose at all? What if, instead, the justice system is concerned more with revenue generation than crime control? Certainly, many people's livelihood stems from the existence of crime; nearly everyone who is employed in some aspect of criminal justice earns a living because of the presence of crime. But others have taken this line of thinking to the extreme. For example, Nils Christie's book *Crime Control as Industry* presents the controversial argument that one of the forces that drives criminal justice in the United States is money.

The emergence of private prisons in particular has been sharply criticized by a number of authors. The concern is that allowing the private sector to conduct crime control will cause profit, rather than reducing crime, to become the driving motivation.[19] Such concerns are not limited to the growth in private sector criminal justice activities. Some have even argued that *public* criminal justice agencies are obsessed with profit. One team of authors went so far as to call one aspect of U.S. law enforcement "policing for profit."[20] Their criticism was of the practice of civil asset forfeiture, a practice that we will revisit (with a special eye toward its effects on crime) in a later chapter.[21]

Whether the justice system and the businesspeople who are connected to it are more concerned with money than with crime control is certainly up for debate, and the debate cannot possibly be resolved here. But it is important that the reader keep an eye out for methods of crime control that can be criticized on the grounds that they might elevate revenue generation above crime control. It is well known that resources in public agencies are often in short supply, which could lead some participants to try to improve the bottom line at the expense of other loftier goals.

Politics and Ivory Towers

Academics are often described derisively as ivory tower types who have little connection to the real world. There is a measure of truth to this description because academics do not always communicate their message in such a way that others will listen. This is especially true when it comes to informing policymakers. Because policymakers are often elected politicians, they are bound by a certain set of constraints that do not apply to academics. Academics can also hand down controversial, even radical, recommendations on how to stop crime with little fear of losing their jobs.

Academics often look for root causes of crime, and many academics are convinced (rightly, as much evidence suggests) that crime stems partly from environmental conditions, such as an absence of parental affection, family conflict, inconsistent discipline, blocked opportunities, unemployment, and discrimination. Others are convinced that the root cause of crime is at least partly biological. Either way, the implications that flow from such thinking include family interventions, rehabilitation, the elimination of discrimination, and job creation. Most of these approaches are not politically feasible.

Although politicians might also be concerned with the root causes of crime, they rarely have the luxury of dealing with them. Moreover, politicians might not have the *right* to deal with them (e.g., by intervening in people's family lives). Politicians tend to be more concerned with the real-world tools that are available to deal with crime, how much can be done without stifling opposition, what can be done that is affordable, and, perhaps cynically, what can be done such that one's reelection is certain and credit can be claimed. To the extent that these values prevail, the most politicians can hope to accomplish is to manipulate the risks of crime and the accessibility of criminal targets.

It is always risky to place people into two distinct camps. There are certainly politicians who care deeply about the causes of crime and who try mightily to do what it really takes to control crime. Likewise, there are academics who do a great job of working with policymakers and informing their decisions. For the most part, though, academics and policymakers do not communicate as much as they should. How many politicians read the latest research published by criminologists? Alternatively, how many academics have the ears of powerful politicians in their area? The answer to both questions is, at best, very few. (See Figure 2.5 for a review of the differences between political and ivory tower thinking.)

Political

Common Questions

1. What real-world tools are available to control crime?
2. Can crime control be done with minimal opposition?
3. Can crime control be done with minimal expenditure of funds?
4. Can crime control be done and still guarantee my reelection?
5. Can crime control be done in the short time I'm in office so I can claim credit?

Solutions Pursued

1. Redistribute money.
2. Hire persons who can offer advice.
3. Hire persons who practice surveillance and detection.
4. Build detention facilities.
5. Increase penalties.

Ivory Tower

Common Questions

1. Are there individual predispositions toward crime?
2. What external factors influence crime?
3. What are the root causes of crime?
4. Is society structured in such a fashion to discourage crime?
5. Is the criminal justice system concerned with controlling crime, or does it have other goals in mind?

Solutions Pursued

1. Restructure society.
2. Improvements to social conditions.
3. Improvements to family relationship.
4. Productive interactions between people.
5. Target other environmental conditions linked to crime.

FIGURE 2.5   Differences between Political and Ivory Tower Perspectives

Subsequent chapters will show that the criminal justice system does not do a great deal to effectively control crime. This is especially true for get-tough approaches to the crime problem. One reason for this could be that policymakers are not familiar with what is happening in the halls of academia and with the research that our nation's leading scholars are publishing. If the gap between the ivory tower and political worlds were to be bridged, crime control in America might take on an entirely different face.

GOALS OF CRIME CONTROL

This chapter is about crime control perspectives. So far, we have considered operational and political perspectives, some of which pit one group of thinkers against another. Just as there are differences in how people think the justice system operates (and should operate), there are differences in the goals people believe should have priority. Some believe that our justice system should prize deterrence, that it should actively work to discourage people from committing crime. Others believe that criminals should get their "just deserts" (retribution) or otherwise be locked in prison for a long time (incapacitation). Still others believe that rehabilitation is most important.[22]

Our concern in this book is with the effects of various approaches to the crime problem on the crime problem itself. The language of deterrence will pop up frequently because when the methods of crime control are thought to influence the population of would-be offenders, they are thought to have a deterrent effect. In other words, when crime goes down after, say, a punitive change in the law, then deterrence probably has something to do with the decline. But as we will see, deterrence is fraught with some problems. This could make other goals, such as rehabilitation, more worthy of our attention.

Deterrence

Deterrence, as most of us know, is about discouraging behavior. For our purposes, this means that people should be discouraged from committing crime. How can it be made possible? The general assumption is that tougher sanctions will discourage people from committing crime. But what does it mean to "discourage" people from committing crime? This requires defining specific types of deterrence. As the following subsections will show, there are two different ways of viewing deterrence: The first is concerned with *who* is discouraged from committing crime; the second is concerned with *what* causes people to decide not to violate the law.

GENERAL AND SPECIFIC DETERRENCE. As far as who is discouraged from committing crime, it is necessary to distinguish between general and specific deterrence. **Specific deterrence** occurs, most often, when a person is locked away after being convicted of a crime. As long as such a person stays behind bars, he or she will not be able to commit more crimes in the community. Specific deterrence need not be accompanied by a prison term, however. A first-time offender could be placed on probation, and that sanction alone could lead the offender to steer clear of crime for the duration of his or her lifetime.

General deterrence moves beyond the individual offender. It is concerned with the possibility that some population of people decides not to commit crime because of the threat of sanctions. The population could be incarcerated offenders, career criminals, other would-be criminals, the general public, and so on. Inmates might be discouraged from acting out in prison because of the threat of solitary confinement. Career criminals might decide not to commit another felony for fear of a life prison term. Other would-be offenders might think twice before committing an offense after seeing someone they know being sent to prison for a long time. Members of the public might be deterred from crime because of a change in the law that increases the penalties attached to criminal behavior.

ABSOLUTE AND MARGINAL DETERRENCE. **Absolute deterrence**, according to Daniel Nagin, is the notion that the "collective actions of the criminal justice system exert a substantial deterrent effect."[23] In other words, it is the system as a whole that deters crime. Think of absolute deterrence as meaning that our extensive justice system helps to keep crime at bay. Without it, crime would probably increase.

By contrast, **marginal deterrence** is concerned with incremental changes in various dimensions of the criminal justice system. For example, if hiring more police officers reduces crime (see Chapter 3), then doing so has a marginal deterrent effect. Or, thinking about our current focus, if increasing prison sentence length reduces crime, then, again, it has a marginal deterrent effect. As the reader can probably infer, altered sentence lengths presumably have a *marginal* deterrent effect on crime.

Do not confuse absolute and marginal deterrence with general and specific deterrence. Many of the approaches to crime discussed throughout this book are thought to have a marginal deterrent effect. That is because they can be altered, abandoned, or implemented aggressively. And it is quite possible for marginal deterrence to include both specific and general deterrent effects.

A prime example is the death penalty. The death penalty is a sanction that can be altered (e.g., applied to specific offenses), abandoned (as some states have), or implemented aggressively (some states execute more people than others). At the same time,

---

specific deterrence: *when a sentenced offender is discouraged from committing additional crimes due to his or her capture/incarceration.*

general deterrence: *when others besides the sentenced offender are discouraged from committing additional crime due to sentencing/incarceration practices.*

absolute deterrence: *the belief that the collective actions of the criminal justice system on the whole discourage criminality.*

marginal deterrence: *incremental changes in the deterrability of crime due to changes in various dimensions of the criminal justice system and process.*

the death penalty clearly serves a specific deterrent purpose by putting dangerous offenders to death. Many people also assume that it capably deters would-be criminals from committing serious violations of the law.

THE LIMITATIONS OF DETERRENCE. Of the various types of deterrence, general deterrence is perhaps the most difficult to show, yet it often serves as justification for getting tough on crime and devoting more resources to justice system employment. There are at least three reasons why crime control might not (and might not be able to) have a general deterrent effect on crime. First, deterrence assumes that offenders are knowledgeable, but the literature clearly shows that many serious offenders lack the ability to associate criminal activity with the potential for punishment. As evidence of this, research shows that many serious offenders are high school dropouts and are undereducated.[24] In addition, they often come from backgrounds that are characterized by deprivation and blocked opportunity.[25]

Second, offenders often have substance abuse problems. This diminishes the ability of many offenders to rationally calculate the likely consequences of their actions.[26] Third, and perhaps the most important, the criminal justice system has a poor track record of catching lawbreakers. Research suggests that on the whole, fewer than 50 percent of crimes result in the apprehension of a suspect.[27] According to one author, this means that "[e]ven those offenders who do bother to calculate the odds [of being caught] may convince themselves that they will never be apprehended for their crimes."[28] In short, deterrence will not work if offenders fail to act in a rational manner, calculating the likely costs and benefits associated with criminal activity.

Retribution

retribution: *a goal of criminal justice concerned with punishing criminals on the basis of the severity of their crimes.*

just deserts: *the punishment an offender "deserves." That which one deserves.*

Retribution is concerned, simply, with punishing criminals on the basis of the severity of their crimes. It is not the same as revenge, because revenge implies an action that is undertaken simply to satisfy crime victims. Instead, retribution is more of a societywide view that criminals need to be punished fairly and justly for the crimes they commit. What's more, retribution is an end unto itself. Those who favor it believe that criminals should get their **just deserts** and that little else is necessary. Deterrence and other goals are not of interest to retribution advocates because these goals distract from what is thought to be the core purpose of crime control: proportionate punishment. Retribution has been described in this way:

> To say that someone "deserves" to be rewarded or punished is to refer to his past conduct, and assert that its merit or demerit is reason for according him pleasant or unpleasant treatment. The focus on the past is critical. That a student has written an outstanding paper is grounds for asserting that he deserves an award; but that the award will yield him or others future benefits (however desirable those might be) cannot be grounds for claiming he deserves it. The same holds for punishment: to assert that someone deserves to be punished is to look to his past wrongdoing as reason for having him penalized. This orientation to the past distinguishes dessert from the other purported aims of punishment—deterrence, incapacitation, and rehabilitation—which seek to justify the criminal sanction by its prospective usefulness in preventing crime.[29]

THE LIMITATIONS OF RETRIBUTION. Retribution is limited in at least two ways. Its core concern is with proportional punishment, but there is much evidence that punishments are not decided solely on the basis of the seriousness of the offense. Race, for example, has been shown to influence the severity of a sanction that someone will receive.[30] Another criticism of retribution is that it is myopic; that is, it is only concerned with past behavior and not with the possibility of preventing future crime. This raises an important question: "If we continue to punish with our attention directed backward, then how could we possibly expect the crime problem to change?" The answer is that we need to prioritize different goals of crime control, including deterrence, incapacitation, and rehabilitation.

Incapacitation

As a goal of crime control, **incapacitation** is easy to understand. It amounts to removing criminals from society, usually through incarceration (or sometimes through home confinement, electronic monitoring, or a similar method of restraint). Incapacitation is further concerned with protecting members of society by removing the criminal element. Those who buy into the incapacitation perspective are rarely concerned with loftier goals such as deterrence and rehabilitation. They might not even care whether criminals get their just desserts. Their only preference is for warehousing criminals through some form of restraint.

incapacitation: removing criminals from society, usually through incarceration (or sometimes through home confinement, electronic monitoring, or a similar method of restraint).

THE LIMITATIONS OF INCAPACITATION.   Incapacitation is limited for two reasons. First, it is costly. Simply locking away offenders with little attention to rehabilitation, treatment, deterrence, and other goals takes an enormous amount of resources. Were incapacitation thinkers concerned with, say, deterrence, then if locking offenders away discourages others from crime, there might be cost savings to society through such an approach. But because those who favor incapacitation do not necessarily care about deterrence, little cost savings to society is achieved by locking up criminals. Certainly, it spares the society the costs of an individual offender's criminal activity, but one wonders whether such benefits outweigh the costs of imprisonment.

Like retribution, incapacitation is a fairly short-sighted perspective. It ignores the possibility that people can change or otherwise be reformed. Why lock all criminals away when the behavior of some can be corrected and such offenders can be released back into society without threatening public safety? In a similar vein, the incapacitation perspective ignores a wealth of research that shows that people mature out of criminal lifestyles. Ignoring the fact that people change simply with the passage of time surely imposes significant costs on the justice system.

Rehabilitation

Rehabilitation consists of a planned intervention intended to change behavior. It need not be limited to criminals. For example, athletes participate in rehabilitation when they injure themselves. But our concern is with rehabilitation of criminals. Various methods have been used over the years, including treatment, job training, and cognitive therapy. Because of the breadth of rehabilitation-type programs throughout the United States, an entire chapter of this book is devoted to different varieties of rehabilitation. But as will become apparent, researchers have given much more attention to the effects of deterrence- and incapacitation-oriented approaches to the crime problem.

rehabilitation: a planned intervention intended to change behavior.

THE LIMITATIONS OF REHABILITATION.   There is a key (and perhaps flawed) assumption that underlies rehabilitation: that people can change through some type of planned intervention. It is safe to say, though, that not all criminals can change. Some may be resistant to treatment; others may just be prone to failure. A related limitation of rehabilitation is that it can take time and cost a significant amount of money. This means that people need to be patient and realize that behavior does not change overnight. Americans tend to be somewhat shortsighted with respect to crime control—we want quick fixes—but rehabilitation rarely works in the short term, and it requires significant commitments by those providing it, those receiving it, and those who will live, work, and associate with rehabilitated offenders.

Goals of Crime Control Compared

The differences between the foregoing goals of crime control were well-described in a famous Pennsylvania Supreme Court case (*Commonwealth* v. *Ritter* 13 Pa. D. & C. 285 [1930]). They are presented in the following order: rehabilitation, retribution, incapacitation, and deterrence. In that decision, the court said:

1. As far as the principle of reformation is concerned, however important it may be in the general run of cases, it obviously has little or no application to such a case as the present. Whichever be the penalty here inflicted, the defendant will not again be in contact with society, and since secular law is concerned with one's relation to the community and not primarily with his inward moral development, the spiritual regeneration of a defendant is not, in such a case as this, a dominant factor. In other words, it would not be a practical consideration weighing in favor of life imprisonment that thereby the defendant might be susceptible of moral reformation, whereas the opportunity for this would be denied to him if the death penalty were inflicted.

2. The second theory which has been urged as a basis for the imposition of penalties is that of retribution. This may be regarded as the doctrine of legal revenge, or punishment merely for the sake of punishment. It is to pay back the wrong-doer for his wrong-doing, to make him suffer by way of retaliation even if no benefit result thereby to himself or to others. This theory of punishment looks to the past and not to the future, and rests solely upon the foundation of vindictive justice. It is this idea of punishment that generally prevails, even though those who entertain it may not be fully aware of their so doing. Historically, it may be said that the origin of all legal punishments had its root in the natural impulse of revenge. At first this instinct was gratified by retaliatory measures on the part of the individual who suffered by the crime committed, or, in the case of murder, by his relatives. Later, the state took away the right of retaliation from individuals, and its own assumption of the function of revenge really constituted the beginning of criminal law. The entire course, however, of the refinement and humanizing of society has been in the direction of dispelling from penology any such theory. Indeed, even in classical times moralists and philosophers rejected the idea entirely. Plato puts into the mouth of Protagoras the words: "No one punishes those who have been guilty of injustice solely because they have committed injustice, unless indeed he punishes in a brutal and unreasonable manner. When any one makes use of his reason in inflicting punishment, he punishes, not on account of the fault that is past, for no one can bring it about that what has been done may not have been done, but on account of a fault to come, in order that the person punished may not again commit the fault and that his punishment may restrain from similar acts those persons who witness the punishment."

3. Rejecting, therefore, the theory of retribution as a proper basis upon which to impose the penalty of law, we come to the third principle which has been advocated, namely, the restraint of the wrong-doer in order to make it impossible for him to commit further crime. Here we arrive not only at a justifiable basis for action but at one which is vital to the protection of society. To permit a man of dangerous criminal tendencies to be in a position where he can give indulgence to such propensities would be a folly which no community should suffer itself to commit, any more than it should allow a wild animal to range at will in the city streets. If, therefore, there is danger that a defendant may again commit crime, society should restrain his liberty until such danger be past, and, in cases similar to the present, if reasonably necessary for that purpose, to terminate his life. Admittedly, restraint by imprisonment can never be as wholly effectual as execution, and there are, from time to time, cases where imprisonment may not be sufficient for the protection of society. It is on this ground that it is pertinent to take testimony in regard to the history of a defendant and of the circumstances attending his commission of crime. If his record shows that he is of a dangerous type, or that he habitually commits grave crimes, or that he has a homicidal tendency, or that he is hopelessly depraved, or that he has a savage nature, or that he has committed murder under circumstances of such atrocity and inhuman brutality as to make his continued existence one of likely danger to society, then, in my opinion, the sentence of death is both justifiable and advisable. The community may not be safe with such a man in existence even though he be serving a term of life imprisonment; he may again commit murder within the prison walls, or may escape and again make innocent victims his prey, or may even, by cunning simulation of repentance, obtain a pardon from governmental authorities. . . .

4. This brings us to the final and what must be fairly regarded as one of the most important objectives of punishment, namely, the element of deterrence—the theory which regards the penalty as being not an end in itself but the means of attaining an end, namely, the frightening of others who might be tempted to imitate the criminal. From this angle a penalty is a cautionary measure, aimed at the prevention of further crime in the community. There has been much controversy and an enormous amount of literature on the subject as to whether the death penalty does or does not act as a deterrent. With that controversy we have nothing to do. As before stated, the law of Pennsylvania retains the death penalty as an optional alternative. The real question is not as to whether the death penalty is in general a deterrent, but as to the particular kinds of murder cases in which execution would or would not be most likely to effect deterrence. It becomes a problem of determining the basis upon which to make such classification.[31]

Summary

Four types of crime control perspectives were introduced in this chapter. The first, operational perspective, consisted of people's views about how the justice system operates (or should operate). We looked at crime control and due process, the system and nonsystem perspectives, the funnel model of justice, and the criminal justice wedding cake. Second, we looked at political perspectives. This is where we were introduced to liberal and conservative perspectives as well as consensus and conflict perspectives. Third, we discussed some other crime control perspectives that were neither operational nor necessarily political. They were concerned with whether faith or fact, crime control or revenue generation, or political or ivory tower thinking dominates criminal justice. Finally, this chapter presented several goals of crime control: deterrence, retribution, incapacitation, and rehabilitation. Each represents a perspective insofar as some people tend to favor one goal over another.

Notes

1. Herbert L. Packer, *The Limits of the Criminal Sanction* (Stanford, CA: Stanford University Press, 1968).
2. Ibid., 163.
3. See, e.g., "Criminal Justice Non-System," in R.H. Moore, Jr., T.C. Marks, and R.V. Barrow, eds., *Readings in Criminal Justice* (Indianapolis, IN: Bobbs-Merrill, 1976), 5–13.
4. S. Walker, *Sense and Nonsense about Crime and Drugs,* 5th ed. (Belmont, CA: Wadsworth, 2001), 27.
5. For evidence of this, visit ncjrs.org and perform an abstract search with "collaboration" or "partnership" in the title. Note that the dates of most publications are recent.
6. President's Commission on Law Enforcement and Administration of Justice, *Task Force Report: Science and Technology.* Washington, DC: U.S. Government Printing Office, 1967, 58–9.
7. L.M. Friedman and R.V. Percival, *The Roots of Justice: Crime and Punishment in Alameda County, California, 1870–1910* (Chapel Hill, NC: University of North Carolina Press, 1981).
8. M.R. Gottfredson and D.M. Gottfredson, *Decision Making in Criminal Justice: Toward the Rational Exercise of Discretion,* 2nd ed. (New York: Plenum, 1988).
9. S. Walker, *Sense and Nonsense about Crime and Drugs,* 5th ed. (Belmont, CA: Wadsworth, 2001), 29.
10. Ibid., p. 35; see also C. Spohn and J. Caderblom, "Race Disparities in Sentencing: A Test of the Liberation Hypothesis," *Justice Quarterly* 8 (1991): 306.
11. This is not the only way to represent political beliefs. Circular and multiaxis models are sometimes used. Delving into them would take us too far afield. Interested readers should read W.S. Maddox and S.A. Lilie, *Beyond Liberal and Conservative: Reassessing the Political Spectrum* (Washington, DC: Cato Institute, 1984).
12. Some believe, for example, that fascists should be on the left of a continuum that relates to government power.
13. S.E. Brown, F. Esbensen, and G. Geis, *Criminology: Explaining Crime and Its Context,* 4th ed. (Cincinnati, OH: Anderson, 2001), 177.
14. Ibid., 27.
15. S. Walker, *Sense and Nonsense about Crime and Drugs,* 5th ed. (Belmont, CA: Wadsworth, 2001).
16. See G.C. Thomas and D. Edelman, "An Evaluation of Conservative Crime Control Theology," *Notre Dame Law Review* 63 (1988): 123–60.
17. S. Walker, *Sense and Nonsense about Crime and Drugs,* 5th ed. (Belmont, CA: Wadsworth, 2001), 17.
18. Ibid.; see also V.E. Kappeler, M. Blumberg, and G.W. Potter, *The Mythology of Crime and Criminal Justice,* 2nd ed. (Prospect Heights, IL: Waveland, 1996).
19. See, e.g., D. Shichor, *Punishment for Profit: Private Prisons/Public Concerns* (Thousand Oaks, CA: Sage, 1995).
20. E. Blumenson and E. Nilsen, "Policing for Profit: The Drug War's Hidden Economic Agenda," *University of Chicago Law Review* 65 (1998): 35–114.
21. For additional reading, see J.R. Lilly, "The Corrections-Commercial Complex," *Crime and Delinquency* 39 (1993): 150–66; J. Reiman, *The Rich Get Richer and the Poor Get Prison,* 6th ed. (Boston, MA: Allyn and Bacon, 2001).
22. Some have argued that restoration is a goal of crime control. We touch on restoration in Chapter 11.
23. D. Nagin, "Deterrence and Incapacitation," in *The Handbook of Crime and Punishment,* ed. M. Tonry (New York: Oxford University Press, 1988), 346.
24. Sentencing Project, *Facts about Prisons and Prisoners* (Washington, DC: Sentencing Project, 2001).
25. E. Currie, *Crime and Punishment in America* (New York: Metropolitan Books, 1998); M. Tonry, *Malign Neglect: Race, Crime, and Punishment in America* (New York: Oxford University Press, 1995).
26. Sentencing Project, *Facts about Prisons and Prisoners* (Washington, DC: Sentencing Project, 2001).
27. R.L. Lippke, "Crime Reduction and the Length of Prison Sentences," *Law and Policy* 24 (2002): 17–35.
28. Ibid., 26.
29. A. von Hirsch, *Doing Justice: The Choice of Punishments* (New York: Hill and Wang, 1976), 46.
30. S. Walker, C. Spohn, and M. DeLone, *The Color of Justice: Race, Ethnicity, and Crime in America* (Belmont, CA: Wadsworth, 1996).
31. *Commonwealth* v. *Ritter,* 13 Pa. D. & C. 285 (1930).

Traditional Policing

LEARNING OBJECTIVES

▨ Summarize the relationship between police hiring and crime.

▨ Explain how police resources can be freed up for crime control purposes.

▨ Describe the limitations of reactive and random patrol.

▨ Explain the association between detective work and crime.

▨ Discuss private policing and its relationship to crime.

Traditional policing consists of simple, commonsense, and generally unimaginative policing approaches to the crime problem. Basically, traditional policing amounts to throwing money at crime by hiring more police officers, freeing up resources, and even turning to private policing. Also, traditional policing tends to favor random, preventive patrols, in which police officers drive around in their cars (or patrol on foot) in an effort to either detect crime when it is being committed or deter it. Advocates of traditional policing believe that if officers can be dispatched to the scene of a crime quickly, then the result will be increased apprehension of lawbreakers. Finally, it is sometimes assumed that additional approaches to policing, such as requiring officers to have college degrees, will improve matters. This chapter reviews all of these assumptions—and some others—with a critical eye. First, though, we need to examine the theory that underlies traditional policing.

THE THEORY OF TRADITIONAL POLICING

Traditional policing prizes deterrence theory. Deterrence theory assumes that people can be discouraged from committing crime by the threat of either serious sanctions or apprehension.[1] We will turn to the topic of serious sanctions in Chapter 9, but the threat of apprehension is what is important here. It is often assumed that pouring more money into law enforcement, particularly for the purpose of hiring more police, is an effective crime reduction strategy because of how it presumably influences the decision-making processes of most citizens, including criminals. People who favor more police on the streets argue that the more visible the police presence is, the more likely it is that would-be criminals will be deterred from violating the law.

Obviously, some people cannot be deterred from committing crime. For example, it is doubtful that the presence of additional police officers on the street factors into the decision-making process of a deranged psychopathic killer. Likewise, the abuser in a heated domestic violence incident probably doesn't think twice about the prospects of apprehension. For these types of people, deterrence theory simply does not apply. And if certain people cannot be deterred, then there is no point in throwing large sums of money at the crime problem; deterrence theory falls to pieces. In other words, if deterrence theory does not hold true, if something else is responsible for crime, then most of the approaches that are discussed in this chapter cannot possibly work for all varieties of crime and criminals.

DOES HIRING MORE COPS REDUCE CRIME?

The notion that having more cops equates with less crime is quite appealing. It is difficult for even the most skeptical academic to claim that there is no merit in hiring more police officers. Even so, a debate has raged for decades in response to one simple question: "Does hiring more cops reduce crime?"[2] The debate gained steam in the early 1970s with the now-famous Kansas City Preventive Patrol Experiment. More recently, attention has turned to president Clinton's Violent Crime Control Act of 1994, which resulted in the hiring of some 100,000 police officers in the latter part of the 1990s. In between these times, researchers have debated all aspects of the police hiring controversy. The following sections contain highlights of this literature. First, however, let us consider some reasons that are commonly offered as to why the police *might not* be able to affect crime rates in a significant way.

Reasons Why Hiring More Cops Might Not Reduce Crime

There are several important reasons why simply hiring more police might not affect crime in a significant way. Assume, for example, that 100,000 new police officers were immediately put on the streets throughout the United States. This number is not large in relation to our population, but some people believe that such an addition to the size of our nation's police force could make a difference. Indeed, even former president Clinton thought that such an addition would be beneficial, as 100,000 is roughly the same number of police officers that were hired as a result of the 1994 Violent Crime Control Act (discussed later in this chapter) that was enacted during his administration.

First, an increase of 100,000 in police ranks looks like a dramatic increase on its face, but police officers are not machines that can work around the clock. At a minimum, most police agencies deploy their officers in three shifts. Also, with sick leave, vacation, family emergencies, in-service training, and other such factors, the size of the force can be reduced drastically. Add to that time spent on paperwork, transportation of arrestees, and other duties, and it is likely that fewer than 10,000 of those newly hired officers are patrolling the streets at any given time.

Even assuming that all 100,000 newly hired police officers could be put on the streets at once, there is so much variation from one city to the next that their presence still might not affect crime rates. This can be seen by comparing the police presence and crime rates from one city to the next. Several large cities across the country have approximately the same number of police officers per citizen but very different levels of crime. As Table 3.1 shows, Detroit has 35 police officers per 10,000 residents while Seattle has 22. At first glance, one may be inclined to conclude that Detroit is a safer city, but it is not, at least according to the Uniform Crime Reports. It continues to far outrank Seattle in terms of its violent crime rate.

Several other reasons can be offered for why adding more police will not necessarily reduce crime. First, as the numbers listed in the previous paragraphs suggest, the police presence in America is spread very thin. Even if we could suddenly double the size of our nation's police force, the number of police officers per 10,000 citizens would remain quite small. Next, according to one author, "many actual or potential offenders do not perceive police patrol as a meaningful threat."[3] This means that even with a substantial and visible police presence, some people cannot be deterred from committing crime. Finally, as one critic of hiring more police officers has observed:

> many crimes are inherently not "suppressible" by patrol. . . . Because they usually occur indoors and in the heat of passion, the amount of police patrol out on the street is not going to affect them.[4]

Consider, for instance, the crime of burglary. A burglar who has at least a glimmer of intelligence will try to operate out of view of the police. Most police officers on patrol would not notice that a burglary is taking place or has taken place. Likewise, consider both parties in an abusive relationship. How many domestic violence incidents take place in view of the police? Probably very few. The very term *domestic* suggests that it is something that occurs in a private residence, out of view of authorities. It makes intuitive sense, therefore, that a heightened police presence might not be able to reduce all crime.

Note that these reasons why the police might not be able to reduce certain crimes are speculative; that is, they are not based on research. Also, one should not get the

TABLE 3.1   Fifty Largest Local Police Departments in the United States

Name of Department	Population Served	Full-Time Sworn Personnel		Total Full-Time Employees	
		Number	Per 10,000 Residents	Number	Per 10,000 Residents
New York (NY) Police	8,220,196	35,216	43	51,480	63
Chicago (IL) Police	2,824,434	13,336	47	15,436	55
Los Angeles (CA) Police	3,870,487	9,504	25	12,834	33
Philadelphia (PA) Police	1,435,533	6,778	47	7,610	53
Houston (TX) Police	2,169,544	4,892	23	6,317	29
Washington (DC) Metropolitan Police	588,292	3,913	67	4,493	76
Phoenix (AZ) Police	1,541,698	3,231	21	4,379	28
Dallas (TX) Police	1,239,104	3,122	25	3,739	30
Miami-Dade (FL) Police	1,082,395	3,120	29	4,495	42
Detroit Police (MI) Police	860,971	3,049	35	3,418	40
Baltimore (MD) Police	624,237	2,952	47	3,565	57
Suffolk County (NY) Police	1,308,750	2,644	20	3,234	25
Nassau County (NY) Police	1,030,495	2,600	25	3,922	38
Las Vegas (NV) Metropolitan Police	1,341,156	2,390	18	4,704	35
San Francisco (CA) Police	733,799	2,303	31	2,625	36
Boston (MA) Police	591,855	2,169	37	2,813	48
Memphis (TN) Police	669,264	2,062	31	2,666	40
Milwaukee (WI) Police	572,938	1,960	34	2,436	43
San Diego (CA) Police	1,261,196	1,922	15	2,677	21
Honolulu (HI) Police	905,903	1,911	21	2,406	27
Baltimore County (MD) Police	785,567	1,888	24	2,188	28
Columbus (OH) Police	735,981	1,829	25	2,187	30
San Antonio (CA) Police	1,316,882	1,795	14	2,402	18
Atlanta (GA) Police	497,290	1,701	34	2,177	44
Jacksonville (FL) Sheriff's Office	797,350	1,629	20	2,852	36
Indianapolis (IN) Metropolitan Police	797,268	1,607	20	1,887	24
Cleveland (OH) Police	439,888	1,584	36	1,884	43
Denver (CO) Police	573,387	1,523	27	1,876	33
Prince George's County (MD) Police	647,701	1,522	23	1,823	28
Charlotte-Mecklenburg (NC) Police	733,291	1,481	20	1,927	26
Fairfax County (VA) Police	976,392	1,427	15	1,737	18
New Orleans (LA) Police	220,614	1,425	65	1,693	77
Austin (TX) Police	716,817	1,415	20	2,029	28
Fort Worth (TX) Police	670,693	1,412	21	1,794	27
Kansas City (MO) Police	447,725	1,393	31	2,129	48
San Jose (CA) Police	934,553	1,386	15	1,831	20
St. Louis (MO) Police	348,197	1,348	39	1,863	54
Seattle (WA) Police	585,118	1,277	22	1,767	30

TABLE 3.1   (*Continued*)

Name of Department	Population Served	Full-Time Sworn Personnel		Total Full-Time Employees	
		Number	Per 10,000 Residents	Number	Per 10,000 Residents
Newark (NJ) Police	280,158	1,229	44	1,429	51
Montgomery County (MD) Police	911,528	1,199	13	1,563	17
Louisville (KY) Metro Police	624,030	1,184	19	1,411	23
Metropolitan Nashville (TN) Police	564,169	1,180	21	1,499	27
El Paso (TX) Police	616,029	1,095	18	1,455	24
Cincinnati (OH) Police	332,388	1,062	32	1,309	39
Miami (FL) Police	410,252	1,054	26	1,770	43
Tucson (AZ) Police	523,299	1,052	20	1,456	28
Oklahoma City (OK) Police	542,199	999	18	1,251	23
Tampa (FL) Police	337,220	992	29	1,352	40
Long Beach (CA) Police	473,959	972	21	1,485	31
Albuquerque (NM) Police	513,124	963	19	1,455	28

Source: Brian A. Reaves, *Local Police Departments, 2007* (Washington, DC: Bureau of Justice Statistics, 2010), p. 34, Table 1.

impression that police are unable to reduce crimes that are inherently more visible. To say otherwise is to question the need for a police presence at all. It is necessary to move away from assumptions and anecdotes, focusing instead on what the research shows. The following sections do just that.

Lessons from Kansas City

One of the most important policing studies relevant to police hiring is the now-famous **Kansas City (MO) Preventive Patrol Experiment**.[5] Conducted during 1972 and 1973, the experiment divided the South Patrol District of Kansas City into three groups of patrol beats. *Proactive beats* received two to three times the normal level of patrol. *Reactive beats* received no patrol, only responses to calls for service. *Control beats* kept police patrol levels to normal. Figure 3.1 depicts the various proactive, control, and reactive beats in Kansas City.

Kansas City (MO) Preventive Patrol Experiment: a 1972/1973 experiment structured to understand the relationship between patrol and crime. Generally, the experiment found that the level of patrol had no clear effect on suppressible crimes.

The experiment found that the level of patrol had no effect on crimes that are suppressible by patrol. These included burglaries, auto thefts, larcenies involving auto accessories, robberies, and vandalism. That is, public safety neither improved nor decreased in any of the three beats. What's more, citizens were not even aware of the differences. Specifically, citizens' attitudes toward the police, their feelings of security, and their decisions to report crime did not vary noticeably from one beat to the next. The lessons of Kansas City, therefore, are often touted as evidence that having more police will not reduce crime.[6]

The Kansas City Experiment should not be interpreted as the gospel truth. For example, the authors of the experiment's final report pointed out that their findings might have been misinterpreted, because there was more to the experiment than just a look at whether additional hiring is necessary. Also, some academics have been highly critical of the experiment. Let us briefly consider some of these concerns.

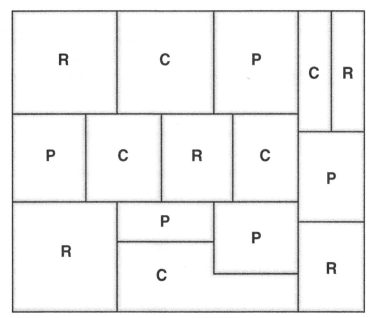

P = Proactive   **C** = Control   **R** = Reactive

FIGURE 3.1   Kansas City Patrol Study Beat Configuration

Source: George L. Kelling, Tony Pate, Doane Dickman, and Charles E. Brown, *The Kansas City Preventive Patrol Experiment: Summary Report* (Washington, DC: Police Foundation, 1974).

MISINTERPRETATIONS.   During the course of the Kansas City Experiment, a number of early findings were published in local newspapers. Among these were claims that hiring additional patrol officers was unnecessary. This claim was then reported on local television channels, causing a fair degree of outrage. However, the authors of the experiment's final report claimed that this and other misinterpretations diminished the importance of the study. They claimed that the experiment should have served as evidence that close attention to what the police do with their time is necessary for effective crime control. In their words:

> Given the distinct possibility that the police may more effectively deal with the problems of crime if they work more closely and systematically with their communities, it may be that an increase rather than a decrease in the number of police is warranted. . . . Police serve a vital function in society, and their presence is of real and symbolic importance to citizens.[7]

CRITICISMS.   In a significant critique of the Kansas City Experiment, one researcher claimed that patrol cars entered reactive beats to respond to calls, which means that they basically created a police presence.[8] How, he claimed, could this have differed from business as usual in the eyes of the citizens of Kansas City? Another pair of researchers concluded that the statistical methods that were used in the Kansas City Experiment were not sophisticated enough to detect differences in crime that could be attributable to the program.[9] In fairness, however, most social science studies can be criticized on similar grounds.

The Post–Kansas City Intellectual Debate

Since publication of the results of the Kansas City Experiment, multiple studies have examined the police–crime relationship.[10] That is, they have sought to determine whether there is a relationship between police presence and crime. Whether a police–crime relationship exists is actually one of the most significantly researched questions in criminal justice, though one of the most overlooked. Why have there been so many different studies? As was mentioned in one of the discussions in Chapter 1, researchers have used different data sources, researched different time periods, relied on different estimation techniques, focused on different units of analysis (e.g., cities versus counties), considered different types of crimes and measures of police presence, and so on. In short, they have sought to improve the generalizability of previous research.

Needless to say, it would be time-consuming and probably redundant to examine every police–crime study in exhaustive detail. Instead, let us briefly consider two important review studies that have concluded that there is virtually no relationship between police presence and crime. Let us also consider some recent studies that have brought the police–crime debate back to the research forefront, showing that, in fact, the police might be able to reduce crime and that having more cops might be desirable.

In 1998, a study was published wherein the author reviewed 22 previous studies of the police–crime relationship.[11] He concluded that 18 of the 22 studies found either no relationship between police and crime or a positive relationship. A positive relationship is not what one would expect because it suggests that as the police presence increases, so does crime. A similar review published in 1996 reviewed 36 previous studies.[12] The authors of that review reported that only 10 of the 36 previous studies found a relationship between police presence and crime, that is, a relationship showing a decrease in crime when the police presence increased. Most recently, a review study "could not support firm conclusions on the deterrent impact of increased police levels on crime rates. . . ."[13] In short, these studies appear to show that there is very little research concluding that it is desirable to hire more police officers.

Methodological problems also abound in this area of research. Marvell and Moody have claimed that previous research in this area is plagued by **simultaneity bias**.[14] More simply, previous researchers have failed to address the possibility that not only might an enhanced police presence affect crime, but crime might also affect police presence. We know, for example, that voters commonly express frustration when public safety is threatened, calling on politicians to give more resources to law enforcement. In a sophisticated analysis that controlled for this possibility, Marvell and Moody found that a heightened police presence does reduce crime to some extent: "Higher police levels reduce most types of crime, particularly at the city level."[15]

These sentiments were echoed by another researcher, who, again using a sophisticated statistical analysis, found that police levels substantially reduced violent crime in a sample of large cities throughout the United States.[16] Another pair of researchers who looked at counties in Florida found that "there was a relationship between police levels and crime rates, such that increased levels of crime caused small increases in police levels, while increased police levels caused sometimes substantial reductions in crime over time."[17] The most recent research suggests there is a "models inverse association between police levels and crime."[18]

Why does all this matter? For one thing, the most recent research seems to fly in the face of traditional assumptions that the police presence is not related to the crime problem. Sophisticated statistical studies also seem to challenge the findings of the Kansas City Experiment. So where does the truth lie? The answer remains somewhat elusive, especially when one examines the relationship between police grant funding and crime.

simultaneity bias:
In the policing crime context, the problem that policing may affect crime and that crime may also affect the number of police. Disentangling the relationship is statistically complicated.

The Violent Crime Control Act of 1994

Violent Crime Control and Law Enforcement Act of 1994: *federal legislation enacted in 1994 that, among other things, created the Office of Community Oriented Policing Services in the U.S. Justice Department.*

Office of Community Oriented Policing Services: *also known by its acronym, the COPS Office, the U.S. Justice Department agency that was primarily responsible (and continues as of this writing) to award community policing-related grants to local law enforcement agencies around the United States. Since 1994, the COPS Office has awarded over $11 billion.*

Former president Clinton signed into law the so-called **Violent Crime Control and Law Enforcement Act of 1994** in September 1994. Title I of the Act, known as the "Public Safety Partnership and Community Policing Act of 1994," permitted the use of $8.8 billion to fund local law enforcement agencies in the fight against crime and to help improve their community policing capabilities. To spend this massive sum of money, the U.S. Department of Justice created a new agency known as the **Office of Community Oriented Policing Services** (a.k.a. the COPS Office). Its job was to administer and supervise the spending.[19]

Since its creation, the COPS office has awarded grants to law enforcement agencies throughout the United States. More than $11 billion has been spent. These grant awards have included funds for the hiring of additional police officers,[20] for innovative community policing programs,[21] and for improving law enforcement technology.[22] COPS funds have also been used to fund regional community policing institutes, research, and training and technical assistance. All in all, the COPS office has provided funding for the hiring of nearly 100,000 new police officers throughout the United States.

All this spending naturally raises the question "Has it affected crime?" That is, $11 billion and more than 100,000 new cops later, are we any better off? Drawing on six years' worth of data and focusing on 6,100 law enforcement agencies serving more than 145 million citizens, the authors of one study sought to determine whether COPS spending reduced crime in America. They concluded: "Our analyses suggest that COPS hiring and innovative grant programs have resulted in significant reductions in local crime rates in cities with populations greater than 10,000 for both violent and nonviolent offenses."[23]

They then took their research a step further and arrived at specific estimates of how many crimes have been prevented as a result of the COPS program. They claimed that "in cities with populations greater than 10,000, an increase in one dollar of hiring grant funding per resident contributed to a corresponding decline of 5.26 violent crimes and 21.63 property crimes per 100,000 residents."[24] Next, they stated that "an increase in one dollar of innovative grant funding per resident has contributed to a decline of 12.93 violent crimes and 45.53 property crimes per 100,000 persons."[25] Their study showed that COPS funding had no effect on crime rates in cities with fewer than 10,000 residents.

Lest you wonder how, for instance, one dollar of hiring money can result in a reduction of 21.63 property crimes per 100,000 residents, remember that the authors stated that one extra dollar *per person* will result in a decline of 21.63 property crimes per 100,000 people. Their results can also be interpreted in this way: One dollar per person will result in a decline of 0.0002163 crimes per person. Regardless of how you interpret their findings, it appears that the COPS funding has had at least some impact on both violent and property crimes throughout the United States. This lends support to some of the recent research suggesting that additional police on the streets can reduce crime. It would appear, then, that the lessons of Kansas City—especially the conclusion that altering patrol levels does not affect crime—do not apply in this day and age. Some even more recent studies continue to support this proposition.[26] But alas, researchers continue to explore the association between grant funding and crime. At least one key study found no association whatsover.[27] There is anything but consensus in this area.

What Happens When the Police Go on Strike?

So far, we have been considering whether the addition of more police officers reduces crime. What about moving to the opposite extreme? Would eliminating the police presence cause an increase in crime? The answer to this second question is important because if crime increases when the police presence disappears, then it is likely that the critics of additional police hiring are wrong.

How is it possible for the police presence to disappear? Historically, there have been occasions when police officers went on strike, thereby practically eliminating the police presence in specific locations. And when the police have gone on strike, crime rates tended to skyrocket.

In one of the more sophisticated studies to date, Makinen and Takala studied crime in Helsinki, Finland, before and during a police strike.[28] They found that there was a significant increase in crime, specifically fights in public and assaults, during the course of the strike. The rates of these crimes increased even though the strike took place during the cold winter months. In another study, examining the Montreal police strike of 1969, researchers found that there were 50 times more bank robberies and 14 times more commercial burglaries during the strike.[29] Several other researchers have reached similar conclusions.[30]

Police strikes almost never happen in modern times. In fact, there are laws nowadays that prohibit the police from going on strike. Some police officers have, however, staged sick-outs, or "blue flues," in which several officers call in sick as a legal alternative to striking. It is therefore unclear whether a strike in this day and age would result in an increase in crime. Indeed, the National Guard could be called in if the police presence were to suddenly become nonexistent.

A Very Thin Blue Line: Is There Really a Police Presence?

As has been discussed already, when we factor in shifts, vacation, sick leave, and the like, the size of the typical police force is reduced substantially. But when we look at precisely what police officers are doing at any given time, a more troubling picture can emerge. It is often said that the police constitute a "thin blue line" between civilization and chaos. Many of us don't know exactly how thin that line can be.

The author once spoke with administrators in a large police department in Southern California. The department serves a population of approximately 300,000 people and employs roughly 300 officers and 600 civilians. When speaking with these administrators, he asked, "How many of your officers are driving around, engaged in routine preventive patrol at any given time?" They answered that approximately six officer were doing so. Needless to say, this answer was a little surprising.

This does not mean that the other 294 officers were off duty or even tied up at the police station. Many of them were out in the field responding to calls, interviewing witnesses, stopping speeders, making arrests, and so forth. The point is that they were still tied up, meaning that only six officers were actively patrolling a city of 300,000 people. Clearly, the thin blue line is more like a thread—or even a hair. This city could be atypical, but it is probably not an isolated example. It is a miracle, then, that the police presence—however minute—can affect crime throughout the United States.

What Are They Doing on the Job?

Some critics of police hiring claim that simply adding more police officers will not reduce crime.[31] Instead, they claim that police officers' efforts need to be directed to specific problems and that the law enforcement enterprise needs to be creative and even businesslike, with a focus on public service. These arguments are convincing and meritorious, and we will consider them more fully in the next two chapters.

However, some research suggests that hiring more police, even with virtually no attention to what they are doing, can reduce crime. Indeed, some of the studies of the Violent Crime Control Act of 1994 that have already been cited support this contention. Zhao and his colleagues, for example, did not consider what COPS-funded officers were doing.[32] Rather, they found that the simple addition of more police officers reduced crime.

Although the COPS grants were funded to increase the amount of community policing throughout the United States, it is not clear to this day how many of the funded agencies actually required that their officers engage in focused community policing activities. This lack of research has been supplemented by at least one study that shows that, regardless of the presence of grant funds, police departments today are—for the most part—going about business as usual,[33] not out of choice but out of necessity.

Does It Work?

Given the police strike literature as well as recent research on the relationship between police presence and crime, it is safe to conclude that hiring additional police officers is not counterproductive. In fact, many sophisticated studies show that as the number of police officers increases, crime rates tend to decline. Moreover, when the number of police officers decreases—and, in the case of strikes, disappears—crime rates tend to move sharply upward.

FREEING UP RESOURCES

As this chapter shows, one of the more common traditional policing strategies is to hire more police. Obviously, though, there are times when police agencies are not in a position to be able to afford additional officers. When times are tight, therefore, police departments might seek to free up their existing resources by engaging in one of these three activities: (1) eliminating two-officer patrols and replacing them with one-officer patrols, (2) implementing so-called 311 systems, and/or (3) focusing carefully on what officers are doing while on patrol and making appropriate adjustments. Two of these approaches are traditional in the sense that they were tried decades ago and have, with some exceptions, fallen into a state of disfavor. In contrast, the 311 system has been implemented relatively recently.

One- versus Two-Officer Patrols

Presumably, a one-officer patrol can cover more ground. Does this approach affect crime? Several published studies[34] suggest the following with respect to one- versus two-officer patrols:

1. Patrol staffing mode has virtually no effect on police effectiveness.
2. Single-officer staffing increases patrol visibility, but the effect on crime is almost nonexistent.
3. Two-officer patrols are, not surprisingly, twice as costly as single-officer patrols.
4. Patrol activity levels are comparable between the two staffing methods.

What about the effect of one- versus two-officer patrols on crime rates, particularly the ability of the police to prevent crime with the added visibility of one-officer patrols? One researcher has noted, "As to the issue of prevention, the limited mathematical data . . . suggest that since visibility is only marginally improved by single-officer patrol, the concurrent deterrent effects should be minimal."[35]

311

Calling the police by dialing 911 is, according to one author, the cornerstone of policing in the United States.[36] Almost anyone can pick up a phone anywhere, dial 911, and most likely receive help in short order. The problem is that people resort to 911 calls too readily. Estimates are that between 40 percent and 80 percent of 911 calls are for non-emergencies.[37] In response to this problem, many jurisdictions across the country have implemented **311 systems** reserved for nonemergency calls. One of the key reasons for 311, relevant in this section, is that it presumably frees up police resources, allowing officers to focus their efforts on more serious problems.

311 system: a nonemergency alternative to the popular 911 system.

Has 311 made a difference? Relatively few researchers have tried to answer this question. Of those who have, their research shows that 311 results in a reduction in 911 calls and can even lead to a reduction in overall 911 and 311 calls.[38] At the same time, though, the research suggests that 311 does not reduce officer response time and does not free up uncommitted blocks of time for patrol officers.[39] These latter findings are particularly relevant in the present context. It appears that 311 does not reduce response time and does not free up resources, making its effect on public safety minimal. Even if response time could be sped up, research that we discuss later in this chapter casts doubt on this method of crime control in America.

Patrol Downtime Studies

Some researchers have studied what police officers do when they are "on the clock." One study shows that patrol time for medium-sized police agencies was about 54 percent.[40] Another found that, of the 24 agencies studied, two-thirds of patrol time was uncommitted.[41] Still another study found that 60 percent of a department's patrol time was uncommitted.[42] The studies on which these findings were based are now somewhat dated, but they have prompted administrators to focus carefully on officers' patrol time. It has been suggested that reducing a police officer's uncommitted time (i.e., his or her **downtime**) from, say, 60 percent to 40 percent would make additional personnel available for other assignments.[43] Unfortunately, this claim has not been subjected to evaluation, so it remains to be seen whether this approach could lead to a noticeable reduction in crime.

downtime: in the patrol context, the time during which a police officer is not actively engaged in controlling or preventing crime. Uncommitted time.

Does It Work?

Available research suggests that switching from two- to one-officer patrols has no effect on crime rates; 311 systems do not look particularly promising in this regard either. Likewise, it does not appear that altering what officers do during downtime while they are on patrol will have a measurable effect on crime. This should not be taken as proof positive that patrol doesn't matter, however. It's just that extant research suggests a minimal relationship between crime rates when downtime is minimized.

THE PROBLEM WITH BEING REACTIVE AND RANDOM

We know, then, that spending more money to add police officers to our nation's police forces does not appear to have a noticeable effect on crime rates. Throwing money at *any* problem, not just crime, is rarely a useful strategy. We know that freeing up resources and eliminating procedural restraints do not appear to be effective either. In this vein, criminological research also shows that traditional, "uncreative" police approaches to the crime problem do not deliver large rewards. First, when the police act in a reactive fashion, that is, when they simply *respond* to calls rather than attempting to stay on top of problems, the crime rate does not appear to fluctuate. Second, when the police attempt to respond rapidly to 911 calls, not much is accomplished in terms of the crime rate. Finally, the practice of engaging in simple random patrol does not appear to influence the crime rate either.

Reactive Policing

reactive policing: The practice of solely responding to calls for service. The oppositive of proactive policing.

Reactive policing, especially waiting to act until *after* a crime has been reported, is not particularly effective. Some people believe that when the police react to a criminal event by arresting someone, others will be deterred from crime. Others believe that when the police act in a reactive manner, it is because they are too busy to do anything else. Either way, researchers have frowned on the reactive approach. As one critic of this practice has noted, "[t]he evidence in support of the reactive arrest hypothesis is remarkably unencouraging."[44]

How have researchers determined that reactive policing does not affect crime rates in a significant way? Two methods have been used. First, researchers have compared the connection between crime rates and arrest rates between several cities. That is, they have sought to determine whether making more arrests has a general deterrent effect on crime. Several sophisticated research studies taking this approach have shown that city-level arrest rates are not clearly associated with the crime problem.[45] That is, there does not appear to be much of a general deterrent effect associated with a heightened arrest rate.

Second, researchers have studied whether increased arrests for certain groups of offenders reduce crime. These researchers have sought to determine whether increasing arrests for specific offenses has a specific deterrent effect. The key to these studies, however, is that the arrests in question are made *after* someone requests police assistance (e.g., by calling 911). As with the previous studies, much of the scientific literature is unsupportive of a *specific* deterrent effect resulting from more arrests of certain individuals. Most of the research in this area has concentrated on reactive arrests for domestic violence.

mandatory arrest: In the policing context, the requirement (usually set by policy) that police officers arrest at least one party after responding to an alleged domestic violence incident.

DOMESTIC VIOLENCE ARRESTS.   There are at least two relevant strains of research concerning domestic violence that are worth mentioning here. Some researchers have found that when states have aggressive anti–domestic violence laws, domestic violence appears to decline.[46] Such studies do not, however, focus on the direct effects of mandatory arrest, which constitutes the second strain of research. Indeed, **mandatory arrests** for domestic violence have been subjected to extensive research. Let us review some of the pertinent findings.

In 1984, Sherman and Berk conducted a study of the Minneapolis Domestic Violence Experiment.[47] The study consisted of random assignment of arrest, separation, and counseling. That is, police officers were required to either arrest the offender, separate the two parties, or counsel both parties but not arrest or separate. Officers were not given the choice of which course of action to take; it was based on random assignment. A six-month follow-up period was used to measure the frequency and severity of domestic violence after the first contact. They found that arrests were the desirable approach. They concluded that arrests should be made in domestic violence situations unless there is clear evidence that an arrest would be counterproductive. Needless to say, their research set off a firestorm of controversy.[48]

Most of the research published following the Minneapolis study is either unsupportive of mandatory arrest for domestic violence or suggests that the arrest–no arrest dilemma is far from black and white. For example, Sherman himself found, in a subsequent study, that arrests had no overall crime reduction effect in repeat domestic violence cases.[49] Another study published in the same year revealed that arrests were no more effective than other police interventions in reducing new incidents of domestic violence.[50] Other researchers have been critical of the popular studies in this area,[51] have suggested that mandatory arrest policies can be easily circumvented,[52] have claimed that victims' desires should not be discounted in domestic violence situations,[53] and have shown that short- versus long-term arrests can affect repeated violence.[54] Still others claim that this area of research is so complex and the research designs so divergent that no meaningful conclusions can be drawn about the costs or benefits of mandatory arrest for domestic violence.[55] But at least one recent study suggests that arrests can reduce future acts of domestic violence.[56]

Rapid Response

Many people believe that if the police could reach crime scenes more quickly (i.e., **rapid response**), they would have a better chance of apprehending criminals. The result, these people assume, would be an eventual decline in crime. The assumption is that criminals will be deterred if, in the back of their minds, they believe the police will respond quickly to calls for service. It is also assumed that the ends of public safety and incapacitation can be served by rapid response. According to one author,

rapid response: In the policing context, prompt response to calls for service. Rapid response assumes that the more quickly the police respond to a call, the more likely it is that they will apprehend the perpetrator.

> [It is assumed] that the shorter the police travel time from assignment to arrival at a crime scene, the more likely it is that police can arrest offenders before they flee. This claim is then extended to rapid response producing three crime prevention effects. One is a reduction in harm from crimes interrupted in progress by police intervention. Another, more general benefit of rapid response time is a greater deterrent effect from the threat of punishment reinforced by response-related arrests. The third hypothesized prevention effect comes from the incapacitation through imprisonment of offenders prosecuted more effectively with evidence from response-related arrests.[57]

Not surprisingly, many researchers have sought to determine whether this assumption is accurate. Rapid response is another traditional policing strategy; there appear to be no recent attempts to restudy it. That is, researchers have all but given up on the effectiveness of rapid response. Let us consider some sample studies.

In what appears to be the first study in this area, Isaacs selected 265 police responses to citizen calls for service by the Los Angeles Police Department.[58] He found, as did researchers in a subsequent study, that the probability of arrest increased when police travel time to the crime scene decreased.[59] However, two studies that were published later failed to find a relationship between response time and the probability of arrest.[60] And most recently, researchers found that response time can be relevant some of the time, particularly if the crime in question is an in-progress burglary.[61]

What are we to make of police response time studies? On the basis of the four studies just cited, the evidence is clearly mixed. Fortunately, a fairly rigorous study was undertaken in Kansas City during the 1970s.[62] The first step in the study was to divide crimes into two types: victim–offender "involvement" crimes, which included such offenses as robbery, assault, and rape, and after-the-fact "discovery" crimes such as burglary and auto theft. This distinction was important because the researchers assumed, rightly, that prompt response to discovery crimes would not matter; the offender would already be gone. Instead, the researchers opted to focus on involvement crimes.

Once the researchers settled on involvement crimes, they then focused on three types of response time. The first was reporting time, the amount of time between the criminal act and the call to 911. The second was dispatch time, the amount of time between the 911 call and when an officer was dispatched. The third was travel time, the amount of time from dispatch to arrival at the crime scene. Despite this sophisticated approach, the researchers found virtually no relationship between reporting time and the probability of arrest. One of the reasons offered for this finding was that people were slow to call police, even for involvement crimes. The researchers also found that cutting travel time would have virtually no effect.

Needless to say, people were somewhat upset at the findings of Kansas City's response time study. In response, the National Institute of Justice commissioned response time studies in four other cities.[63] The results from the four studies provided clear support for the Kansas City findings. That is, the researchers found that response time had virtually no effect on crime. Why was this so? First, people tend to be slow when it comes to reporting crime. Second, most crimes are of the discovery rather than involvement variety. Response time could matter, however, if people called for assistance quickly and there were enough police resources to ensure a prompt response.[64]

Random Patrol

random patrol: The practice of engaging in preventive patrol by unpredictably covering a beat.

Researchers have also been concerned with the extent to which **random patrols** are connected with crime rates. Before the advent of the automobile, police officers patrolled mostly on foot, which limited the geographic area they could cover. Their patrol patterns became fairly predictable with this approach. However, once police agencies acquired automobiles, officers could suddenly cover much more ground. They could also drive around in a fairly random pattern. The reason for being random is so that criminals don't become accustomed to an officer's patrol habits. The hope is that criminals will be deterred from crime by not knowing when a patrol car will happen upon them.

What does the research show about the effectiveness of random patrol? As we have already seen, the Kansas City Preventive Patrol Experiment showed that having more police on patrol did not reduce crime. The experiment found that citizens did not even *notice* the differences in police patrol. Other experiments in the foot patrol context support this finding as well. Specifically, research has shown that adding more police officers to foot patrol for the purpose of walking around and detecting crime did not affect crime rates.[65] Unfortunately, very few other studies have examined the effectiveness of random patrol (either by car or on foot), but the studies that are available paint a discouraging picture about its effectiveness.

Why is the evidence for the effectiveness of random patrol discouraging? It might not be because random patrol is ineffective; rather, it could be that the research designs previously employed in this area are inadequate. Recall from Chapter 1 that true experiments are rare throughout criminal justice. For a true experiment to be applied in the random patrol context, it would be necessary to completely randomize patrol levels. Both the Kansas City Preventive Patrol Experiment and subsequent studies looking at the effect of patrol have been criticized for their failure to assign patrol in a truly random fashion.[66] If a true experiment had been conducted on the relationship between random patrol and crime, the results might have been different.

Even in the absence of an experimental design (or any research for that matter), it should be intuitively obvious, given the nature of policing in the twenty-first century, that random patrols cannot be expected to make a substantial difference. As was indicated earlier in this chapter, many crimes are not suppressible by patrol. They take place behind closed doors and therefore cannot be readily detected. As we also discussed earlier, the police presence in America is spread very thin. Assume that there is a town of 40,000 people that is being actively patrolled by five officers (not an unrealistic assumption). How much crime could those officers realistically prevent by randomly patrolling the city? What if the number of officers were doubled or even tripled? The simple fact is that there are far more people than patrol officers, making it unlikely that random patrol will reduce crime. Random patrol is not unlike playing blackjack in Las Vegas; the odds of reaching 21 are probably about as unlikely as the odds of apprehending a criminal "red-handed."

Does It Work?

It is safe to conclude on the basis of available evidence that being reactive and random is not effective. First, a reactive arrest strategy does not appear to be particularly fruitful. Second, there is little evidence that increasing police response time will reduce crime. Finally, random patrol, while perhaps necessary on one level, does not appear to be linked to the incidence of crime. All in all, these types of traditional police responses to the crime problem have virtually no credible scientific support.

DETECTIVE WORK AND CRIME

Patrol is arguably the most significant priority to most American police agencies. What is the next most important? In terms of the amount of time spent and personnel allocated to it, criminal investigations (i.e., detective work) are next. One researcher showed that, on average, some 60 percent of police personnel are assigned to patrol, and 15 percent are assigned to investigation.[67]

For many aspiring police officers—and even many patrol officers—detective work is something to strive for. It is usually associated with a certain amount of prestige, and a promotion is often necessary to rise to the level of detective. The level of prestige that detectives enjoy is often reinforced in the mass media. Popular television programs portray detectives as intelligent, dedicated, and effective crime-fighters. But what does the research show? Are detectives truly effective? In one of the most comprehensive studies on this subject to date, researchers found, somewhat surprisingly, that detective work is not all that it is made out to be.

The RAND Study

The study just referred to was one done by Peter Greenwood and Joan Petersilia and published by the RAND Corporation.[68] They examined the literature on investigative performance, conducted a survey of all municipal and county law enforcement departments with more than 150 sworn personnel, and visited a number of agencies in person. Their research goals were, among others, to describe investigative practices, assess the contribution of investigations to the achievement of criminal justice goals, and ascertain the effectiveness of certain investigative technologies. Several of their major findings were as follows:

1. Differences in investigative training, staffing, workload, and procedures appear to have no appreciable effect on crime, arrest, or clearance rates.

2. Our data consistently reveal that an investigator's time is largely consumed in reviewing reports, documenting files, and attempting to locate and interview victims on cases that experience shows will not be solved. For cases that are solved (i.e., a suspect is identified), an investigator spends more time in post-clearance processing than he does in identifying the perpetrator.

3. The single most important determinant of whether or not a case will be solved is the information the victim supplies to the immediately responding patrol officer. If information that uniquely identifies the perpetrator is not presented at the time the crime is reported, the perpetrator, by and large, will not be subsequently identified.

4. Latent fingerprints rarely provide the only basis for identifying a suspect.

It would appear that the RAND study is not isolated.[69] In a related study, researchers argued that information from bystanders and victims is key to the success of investigative work.[70] In their words, "[t]he capacity of police to solve most kinds of crime is low. Most Part I offenses known to the police are *not* solved. When crimes are solved and arrests made, it is almost always due to extensive information supplied to police by witnesses and victims as to the identity and whereabouts of the offender."[71] These and other studies do not show that detective work is entirely ineffective, only that not as much crime is solved by detective work as we are led to believe.

Recent Developments

The RAND study was published in 1975. We are now three decades past the release of that study. Is detective work still as ineffective as it was then made out to be? Clearly there are many new investigative techniques and tools. Criminal investigation is increasingly being viewed as a specialized science. Indeed, many criminal investigators in this day and age earned college degrees in fields such as chemistry, physics, and biology. It is safe to conclude that detective work today is not the same as it was 30 years ago. Unfortunately, there is precious little evidence available that can refute the RAND study. The only recent inquiry into the detective function seems to affirm the RAND study findings. In 2010, the National Academy of Sciences published a report on the status of forensic sciences in the United States.[72] It cited a number of problems, including case backlog and evidence errors. For example,

> The fact is that many forensic tests—such as those used to infer the source of toolmarks or bite marks—have never been exposed to stringent scientific scrutiny. . . . Even fingerprint analysis has been called into question.[73]

Does It Work?

Taking steps to improve the effectiveness of detective work is considered a traditional policing strategy because many years have passed since research in this area has been conducted. Police agencies have not stopped hiring and training detectives. Criminal investigation is as sought-after a specialization as it ever was. Nevertheless, the available research suggests that detective work is not as effective as it is made out to be. It is safe to draw at least three conclusions in this regard: (1) Detective work is not as "sexy" as is portrayed in the media; (2) victims and witnesses still play a pivotal role in the apprehension of lawbreakers; and (3) pouring additional resources into the investigations division will probably not have a drastic effect on overall crime rates.

PRIVATE POLICING

The police, as most of us know them, are not the only ones in the business of crime control and prevention. Public police (municipal police departments, sheriff's deputies, state troopers, etc.) work alongside scores of private police and security officials.[74] Indeed, the latter outnumber the former by something like three to one![75]

Recent estimates place the number of people involved in either private policing or security provision at over 2,000,000.[76] David Sklansky has eloquently described the pervasive lack of familiarity with the magnitude of the private security/policing apparatus:

> For most lawyers and scholars, private security is terra incognita—wild, unmapped, and largely unexplored. . . . The neglect is increasingly indefensible. The private security industry already employs significantly more guards, patrol personnel, and detectives than the federal, state, and local governments combined, and the disparity is growing . . . if criminal procedure scholars continue to focus exclusively on the public side of law enforcement, our work is likely to become of steadily more marginal importance.[77]

Private Security Versus Private Policing

Odds are you have seen a security guard in one location or another, perhaps in a Walmart parking lot, in a hotel, at an entrance to a gated community, or at a sporting event. These guards are who we typically think of when thinking about private policing. They represent the proverbial tip of the iceberg, however. In this regard, it is useful to distinguish between **private policing** and **private security**. According to one source, private security refers to the *industry* that provides "for-profit security products and services, which include three broad categories: the provision of guards, equipment, and investigation or consulting services."[78] The homeowner who buys his or her security system does so from the private security industry. "Private policing, by contrast, refers to the acquisition and use of these products and services, as well as the application of specialized knowledge in areas like crime control, investigation, and risk management."[79] In other words, private police are supplied by the private security industry.

The concern here is not with the private security industry per se. If one were to give much attention to it, one would also need—for balance—to discuss the various industries that supply public police agencies with equipment (e.g., firearms, handcuffs, investigative tools, etc.). The interest here is in private policing, with the provision of security, crime prevention, and crime control functions by actual people. Whether it is called "security" or "policing" is not particularly important, but for consistency's sake, I will use the term *private policing* from here on, knowing that private policing owes its livelihood to the private security industry. Private police, then, could be trained personnel supplied by the private security industry. Private police could also refer to ordinary people—trained in the trade or not, and not affiliated with any known security "company"—who are hired to provide security services.

private policing: law enforcement personnel supplied by the private security industry. Private police generally do not enjoy the same authority as sworn police.

private security: industry that provides for-profit security products and services, including guards, equipment, and investigation or consulting services.

Why Private Police?

Three explanations have been offered for the growth in private policing witnessed during the past four decades or so.[80] One is an ideological shift, a preference for a movement toward non-governmental provision of key services. Some people (vast numbers?) are convinced that the private sector can do "better" than the public sector when it comes to the provision of security and criminal justice services. Another explanation for private policing is that it has simply evolved in response to the need to police "mass private property,"[81] notably large shopping malls and other properties that attract large numbers of consumers with little to no public police protection. To that we could add the presence of security guards in gated communities; as the population grows and as those people who can afford it move into gated communities, they often need the services of security personnel. The third explanation is simply an outgrowth of the first two: A belief that public police are incapable of providing the volume and type of policing that people want:

> As we have seen, for over two centuries privately paid entrepreneurs (remember the privateers from Chapter 1?) in both Britain and America have been filling gaps in the police protection offered by public law enforcement. Private police today, moreover, tend at least in broad outline to do the kinds of things that public police departments are faulted for not doing: patrol visibly and intensively, consult frequently with the people they are charged with protecting, and—most basically—view themselves as service providers.[82]

Private Policing Methods

Private policing can also be distinguished from public policing by its methods. Clifford Shearing has identified four such methods.[83] First, private police personnel focus largely on loss control and prevention. Retail security guards, for instance, are in the business of making sure their clients' products are not removed from the store by people who have not paid for them. The term *loss* can also be much broader than lost merchandise. Some private police focus on accident and error prevention. According to one source, "[t]he emphasis on loss also means that private police are disengaged from the moral underpinnings of the criminal law; they focus instead on property and asset protection."[84] "Moral underpinnings" refers to the what's right/what's wrong aspect of the laws public police are charged with enforcing; it is their responsibility to target problems deemed as such by constituents and lawmaking bodies. Private police are not limited by these issues; they do what their clients want (and pay for) without regard to moral issues.

The second main private policing method is prevention: "private police stress preventive means over detection and apprehension to control crime and disorder."[85] Why? Their concern is not so much with punishment of wrongdoers. Rather, it is with preventing the disruption of—most often—legitimate business activities. It is somewhat humorous, in fact, that retailers often place signs reading, "Shoplifters will be prosecuted to the fullest extent of the law," throughout their establishments. For one thing, retailers have limited say over whether someone will be charged with theft (prosecutors make this decision). And their concern with prosecution is typically incidental to their more instant concern of making sure the business doesn't lose money. That is why private police focus heavily on surveillance. If you have spent time in a casino, you know exactly what I am referring to. Casinos go to great pains to "keep an eye on things" and make sure that unscrupulous gamblers do not make off with any ill-gotten gains at the casino's expense.

Private policing is also distinguished from public policing by its focus on "private justice" rather than public justice. As Elizabeth Joh has stated, "[t]hese are functional alternatives to the public police and the criminal justice system."[86] Consider, for example, employee theft from a retail store. What would the store's owner rather do: prosecute the employee and keep him or her on the payroll, or simply fire the employee? The latter choice would be most likely. What about the gambler who counts cards in a blackjack game and gets caught? He or she would sooner be banned from the casino than charged with any criminal violation. "In a private justice system, the resolution of problems is left to the control and discretion of private police and their clients, who may see some incidents as unworthy of the lost time and resources necessary to assist in a public prosecution."[87] Indeed, some businesses are willing to tolerate a certain amount of loss due to the costs that would go along with pursuing formal criminal charges against certain individuals.

The fourth distinguishing feature of private policing is a concern with private rather than public property. Generally, public police do not have the luxury of entering private places without proper cause or an invitation. At the opposite extreme, private police generally couldn't care less about public spaces. Their job is, for the most part, protection of private property. Often they work in quasi-public places, such as privately owned malls that are open to the public, but their loyalties lie to the businesses that employ them, not the shopping public. I do not mean to suggest that public police do not concern themselves with theft and other forms of loss. They clearly do, but that is only part of their mandate. As will become apparent in subsequent chapters, there is much more to policing than crime-fighting (whether by patrolling streets or arresting lawbreakers).

Controversies in Private Policing

Private security is controversial in a number of respects. First, it is important to note that private security is but one part of a larger privatization movement in criminal justice.[88] Private prisons, for instance, have emerged to provide a presumably cost-effective alternative to state-run correctional facilities. Critics charge that privatization turns criminal justice into a for-profit venture, which possibly translates into detrimental cost-cutting measures. Second, some people have charged that private policing is poised to replace public policing, but such a change is quite unlikely.[89] Perhaps the most significant controversy associated with private policing deals with constitutional concerns. In general, because private police are nongovernmental, they are not bound by the same legal requirements as public police.[90]

The U.S. Supreme Court has yet to tackle the issue of private policing head-on. It decided one case involving an amusement park security guard who had been "deputized" by the county sheriff.[91] It ruled that the security guard was a state official and thus was bound by the same legal constraints as public police officers. Beyond that case, the Supreme Court has had little to say. State courts, however, have been much more vocal, and most of them have refused to treat private police as state actors. For example, private police have been exempted from the Fourth Amendment,[92] the *Miranda* rule,[93] and restrictions on entrapment.[94]

Don't construe these favorable-to-private police decisions as granting unbridled power. It is true that some private police do have more power than ordinary citizens. Deputizing private police officers gives them, some of the time, the same authority as public police. Likewise, many private police officers are off-duty public police officers. Yet most private police do not enjoy the same legal powers as public police: "Many private security guards, for instance, possess no greater legal capabilities than do ordinary citizens to forcibly detain persons who are suspected of or have in fact committed a crime.[95] (In many states, ordinary citizens can arrest people for misdemeanors committed in their presence and for felonies that they have probable cause to believe were committed.)[96]

Does It Work?

Despite all the attention to private policing, it remains to be seen whether it is any more or less effective than public policing. In all likelihood, it may fall victim to the same fate as traditional policing in general. This is especially true if private policing is used to engage in traditional functions such as random patrol and rapid response.

COLLEGE DEGREES FOR COPS

Another traditional policing response to the crime problem is to require that police officers attain a certain level of education beyond high school.[97] Relatively few police departments require that their officers have four-year degrees (see Table 3.2), but those that do have such a requirement cite several reasons why college degrees for cops might improve law enforcement's ability to fight crime.

As early as 1973, the National Advisory Commission on Criminal Justice Standards stated:

> Police agencies have lost ground in the race for qualified employees because they have not raised standards. College graduates look elsewhere for employment. Police work has often come to be regarded by the public as a second class occupation, open to anyone with no more than a minimum education, average intelligence, and good health.[98]

The commission found it strange that educational requirements for the police were not increased while other professions were beginning to adopt stringent educational requirements. What is the logic for college degrees for police officers? What is it about a college degree that could improve police performance? In a study published by

TABLE 3.2   Education Requirements for New Officers

Population Served	Total with Requirement	Percent of Departments Requiring a Minimum of—			
		High School Diploma	Some College*	2-Year College Degree	4-Year College Degree
All sizes	98%	82%	6%	9%	1%
1,000,000 or more	100%	62%	38%	0%	0%
500,000–999,999	100	68	16	16	0
250,000–499,999	98	65	9	17	7
100,000–249,999	99	72	16	7	4
50,000–99,999	99	68	14	14	3
25,000–49,999	99	68	15	14	1
10,000–24,999	99	83	7	9	--
2,500–9,999	98	80	5	13	1
Under 2,500	97	87	5	5	1

Note: Detail may not sum to total because of rounding.

--Less than 0.5%.

*Non-degree requirements.

Source: Brian A. Reaves, *Local Police Departments, 2007* (Washington, DC: Bureau of Justice Statistics, 2010), p. 11.

the Police Executive Research Form, researchers identified the following advantages of college education for police officers:

1. It develops a broader base for decisionmaking.
2. College ingrains responsibility and appreciation for people's rights.
3. College creates an ability to flexibly handle difficult situations.
4. College engenders tolerance and empathy.
5. College-educated officers are likely to be less rigid in decision making.
6. College will help officers better communicate with people and respond to the demands of the job.
7. College-educated officers will be more professional.
8. The college experience will make officers less authoritarian in their demeanor.[99]

What does the research show? Strangely, there have been very few studies in this area. In those that have been published, the results are either inconclusive or suggest that college degrees for cops make virtually no difference in terms of their job performance. For example, Sherman and Blumberg studied the impact of higher education on the police use of force. They concluded:

> In short, the present study is far from conclusive about higher education and the use of deadly force. It is even less conclusive about the value of higher education for improving police performance, the many components of which are not necessarily consistent for individual officers.[100]

Several related studies show support for Sherman and Blumberg's findings.[101] Others conclude that the relationship between college education and job performance in policing is practically impossible to understand.[102] At least one study suggests, however, that college education for police officers might reduce their risks of being sued civilly.[103] Beyond that, we cannot conclude with any measure of certainty that higher education for police officers is beneficial. What is more, there is no convincing evidence that college degrees for police result in reduced criminal activity.

Does It Work?

There is no convincing evidence that college-educated police officers are better crime-fighters than officers who are not required to obtain a college degree. Although it is difficult to dispute the argument that college education encourages tolerance and possibly even better problem-solving abilities, an officer's ability to fight crime probably cannot be attributed to his or her level of postsecondary education. This statement should not be cause for abandoning college education requirements for police officers. Instead, the message of this section is that there is currently no convincing relationship between college degree requirements for police and crime rates.

Summary

All in all, most traditional policing approaches do not appear to affect crime rates. A possible exception is hiring more police officers. Recent research on community policing hiring grants—coupled with the police strike literature—suggest that hiring is far from counterproductive. Whether much hiring can continue to take place, however, is unclear. The lack of resources in many public agencies might threaten additional hiring unless additional federal grants are made available.

Apart from hiring, there is little evidence that freeing up police resources by shifting from two- to one-officer patrols, implementing 311, or reducing patrol downtime affects crime. Likewise, being reactive and random does not appear to affect crime.

Finally, hiring additional detectives, turning to private policing, and mandating college degrees for police officers do not appear to affect crime noticeably.

Notes

1. A classic law enforcement study espousing the deterrence theory is Isaac Ehrlich, "The Deterrent Effect of Criminal Law Enforcement," *Journal of Legal Studies* 1 (1972): 259–76.
2. For a summary of the debate, see Thomas B. Marvell and Carlisle E. Moody, "Specification Problems, Police Levels and Crime Rates," *Criminology* 34 (1996): 609–46.
3. Samuel Walker, *Sense and Nonsense about Crime and Drugs: A Policy Guide,* 5th ed. (Belmont, CA: Wadsworth), 81.
4. Ibid.
5. George L. Kelling, Tony Pate, Duane Dieckman, and Charles E. Brown, *The Kansas City Preventive Patrol Experiment: A Summary Report.* Washington, DC: The Police Foundation, 1974.
6. Samuel Walker, *Sense and Nonsense about Crime and Drugs: A Policy Guide,* 5th ed. (Belmont, CA: Wadsworth, 2001), 81.
7. George L. Kelling, Tony Pate, Duane Dieckman, and Charles E. Brown, *The Kansas City Preventive Patrol Experiment: A Summary Report,* in *What Works in Policing,* ed. David H. Bayley (New York: Oxford University Press, 1998), 49.
8. R.C. Larson, "What Happened to Patrol Operations in Kansas City? A Review of the Kansas City Preventive Patrol Experiment," *Journal of Criminal Justice* 3 (1975): 267–97.
9. S.E. Fienbert, L. Kinley, and A.J. Reiss, Jr., "Redesigning the Kansas City Preventive Patrol Experiment," *Evaluation* 3 (1976): 124–31.
10. Illustrative examples include R.W. Bahl, R.G. Gustely, and M.J. Wasylenko, "The Determinants of Local Government Police Expenditure: A Public Employment Approach," *National Tax Journal* 31 (1978): 64–79; D.H. Bayley, *Patterns of Policing: A Comparative International Analysis* (New Brunswick, NJ: Rutgers University Press, 1985); R.A. Carr-Hill and N.H. Stern, "An Economic Model of the Supply and Control of Recorded Offenses in England and Wales," *Journal of Public Economics* 2 (1973): 289–313; C. Cornwell and W.M. Trumbell, "Estimating the Economic Model of Crime with Panel Data," *Review of Economics and Statistics* 72 (1994): 360–66; I. Ehrlich, "Participation in Illegal Activities: A Theoretical and Empirical Investigation," *Journal of Political Economy* 81 (1973): 521–67; J.A. Fox, "Crime Trends and Police Expenditures: An Investigation of the Lag Structure," *Evaluation Quarterly* 3 (1979): 41–58; D.F. Greenberg, R.C. Kessler, and C. Loftin, "The Effect of Police Employment on Crime," *Criminology* 21(1983): 375–94; S. Hakim, "The Attraction of Property Crimes to Suburban Localities: A Revised Economic Model," *Urban Studies* 17 (1980): 265–76; C.R. Huff and J.M. Stahura, "Police Employment and Suburban Crime," *Criminology* 17 (1980): 461–70; K.C. Land and M. Felson, "A General Framework for Building Dynamic Macro Social Indicator Models, Including an Analysis of Changes in Crime Rates and Police Expenditures," *American Journal of Sociology* 82 (1976): 565–604; S. Levitt, "Using Electoral Cycles in Police Hiring to Estimate the Effect of Police on Crime," *American Economic Review* 87 (1997): 270–91; C. Loftin and D. McDowall, "The Police, Crime, and Economic Theory: An Assessment," *American Sociological Review* 47 (1982): 393–401; Thomas B. Marvell and Carlisle E. Moody, "Specification Problems, Police Levels and Crime Rates," *Criminology* 34 (1996): 609–46; T.V. Kovandzic and J.J. Sloan, "Police Levels and Crime Rates Revisited: A County Level Analysis from Florida (1980-1998)," *Journal of Criminal Justice* 30 (2002): 65–76.
11. S. Cameron, "The Economics of Crime Deterrence: A Survey of Theory and Evidence," *Kyklos* 41 (1988): 301–23.
12. Thomas B. Marvell and Carlisle E. Moody, "Specification Problems, Police Levels and Crime Rates," *Criminology* 34 (1996): 609–46.
13. Hyeyoung Lim, Hoon Lee, and Steven J. Cuvelier, "The Impact of Police Levels on Crime Rates: A Systematic Analysis of Methods and Statistics in Existing Studies," *Asia Pacific Journal of Police & Criminal Justice* 8 (2010): 49–82.
14. Ibid.
15. Ibid., 640.
16. S. Levitt, "Using Electoral Cycles in Police Hiring to Estimate the Effect of Police on Crime," *American Economic Review* 87 (1997): 270–91.
17. T.V. Kovandzic and J.J. Sloan, "Police Levels and Crime Rates Revisited: A County Level Analysis from Florida (1980-1998)," *Journal of Criminal Justice* 30 (2002): 73.
18. John L. Worrall and Tomislav V. Kovandzic, "Police Levels and Crime: An Instrumental Variables Approach," *Social Science Research* 39 (2010): 506–15.
19. Jeffrey Roth and Joseph Ryan, "Overview," in *National Evaluation of the COPS Program, Title I of the 1994 Crime Act,* eds. Jeffrey Roth and others (Washington, DC: U.S. Department of Justice), 1–24.
20. The Universal Hiring Program (UHP); the Accelerated Hiring, Education, and Deployment Program (AHEAD); the Funding Accelerated for Smaller Towns Program (FAST); and the Police Hiring Supplement Program (PHS) were used to this end.

21. Some of these grants programs include the Advancing Community Policing Program, Organizational Change Demonstration Centers, and the Distressed Neighborhoods Program.

22. The Making Officer Redeployment Effective (MORE) program was used to this end.

23. Jihong "Solomon" Zhao, Matthew C. Scheider, and Quint Thurman, "Funding Community Policing to Reduce Crime: Have Cops Grants Made a Difference?" *Criminology and Public Policy* 2 (2002): 7–32.

24. Ibid., 7.

25. Ibid., 7.

26. See J. Klick and A. Tabarrok, "Using Terror Alert Levels to Estimate the Effect of Police on Crime," *Journal of Law and Economics* 48 (2005): 267–79; W.N. Evans and E. Owens, "Cops and Crime," *Journal of Public Economics* 91 (2007): 181–201.

27. John L. Worrall and Tomislav V. Kovandzic, "COPS Grants and Crime Revisited," *Criminology* 45 (2007): 159–90.

28. Tuija Makinen and Hannu Takala, "The 1976 Police Strike in Finland," *Scandinavian Studies in Criminology* 7 (1980): 87–106.

29. Gerald Clark, "What Happens When the Police Go on Strike," *New York Times Magazine* Nov. 16, sec. 6(1969): 176–185, 187, 194–195.

30. Johannes Andenaes, *Punishment and Deterrence* (Ann Arbor, MI: University of Michigan Press, 1974); Francis Russell, *A City in Terror: 1919—The Boston Police Strike* (New York: Viking, 1975); A.V. Sellwood, *Police Strike—1919* (London: W.H. Allen, 1978).

31. Samuel Walker, *Sense and Nonsense about Crime and Drugs: A Policy Guide*, 5th ed. (Belmont, CA: Wadsworth, 2001).

32. Jihong "Solomon" Zhao, Matthew C. Scheider, and Quint Thurman, "Funding Community Policing to Reduce Crime: Have Cops Grants Made a Difference?" *Criminology and Public Policy* 2 (2002): 7–32.

33. Edward Maguire, "Structural Change in Large Municipal Police Organizations during the Community Policing Era," *Justice Quarterly* 14 (1997): 701–30.

34. Examples include L.E. Boydstun, M.E. Sherry, and N.P. Moelter, *Patrol Staffing in San Diego: One- or Two-Officer Units* (Washington, DC: Police Foundation, 1977); S.H. Decker and A.E. Wagner, "The Impact of Police Patrol Staffing on Police-Citizen Injuries and Dispositions," *Journal of Criminal Justice* 10 (1982): 375–82; E.H. Kaplan, "Evaluating the Effectiveness of One-Officer versus Two-Officer Patrol Units," *Journal of Criminal Justice* 7 (1977): 325–55; D.A. Kessler, "One- or Two-Officer Cars?: A Perspective from Kansas City," *Journal of Criminal Justice* 13 (1985): 49–64; National Institute of Justice, *Performance Measures for Evaluating One- versus Two-Person Cars* (Washington, DC: National Institute of Justice, 1986).

35. C. Wilson, "*Research on One- and Two-Person Patrols: Distinguishing Fact from Fiction.* Australasian Centre for Policing Research, Report Series No. 94, 1990. Available at acpr.gov.au/pdf/ACPR94.pdf.

36. D.H. Bayley, *What Works in Policing* (New York: Oxford University Press, 1998).

37. L. Mazerolle, D. Rogan, J. Frank, C. Famega, and J.E. Eck, "Managing Citizen Calls to the Police: The Impact of Baltimore's 3-1-1 Call System," *Criminology and Public Policy* 2 (2002): 97–124.

38. Ibid.

39. Ibid.

40. G. Cordner, "While on Routine Patrol: What the Police Do When They're Not Doing Anything," *American Journal of Police* 1 (1982): 94–112.

41. G. Whitaker, "What Is Patrol Work?" *Police Studies* 4 (1982): 13–22.

42. G. Kelling, T. Pate, D. Dieckman, and C. Brown, *The Kansas City Patrol Experiment* (Washington, DC: Police Foundation, 1974).

43. L.K. Gaines, V.E. Kappeler, and J.B. Vaughn, *Policing in America*, 3rd ed. (Cincinnati, OH: Anderson, 1999).

44. Lawrence W. Sherman, "Policing for Crime Prevention," in *Preventing Crime: What Works, What Doesn't, What's Promising*, eds. Lawrence W. Sherman and others (Washington, DC: National Institute of Justice, 1998).

45. David F. Greenberg, Ronald C. Kessler, and Charles H. Logan, "A Panel Model of Crime Rates and Arrest Rates," *American Sociological Review,* 44 (1979): 843–50; David Greenberg and Ronald C. Kessler, "The Effects of Arrests on Crime: A Multivariate Panel Analysis," *Social Forces* 60 (1982): 771–90.

46. For a recent example, see L. Dugan, "Domestic Violence Legislation: Exploring Its Impact on the Likelihood of Domestic Violence, Police Involvement, and Arrest," *Criminology and Public Policy* 2 (2003): 283–312.

47. L. Sherman and R.S. Berk, *The Minneapolis Domestic Violence Experiment* (Washington, DC: The Police Foundation, 1984); the academic version of their report can be found in L. Sherman and R.S. Berk, "The Specific Deterrent Effects of Arrest for Domestic Assault," *American Sociological Review* 49 (1984): 261–72; see also L. Sherman, *Policing Domestic Violence* (New York: Free Press, 1992).

48. At least two academic journals devoted symposia to this topic. See Vol. 36, Issue 5 of the *American Behavioral Scientist* (1993) and Vol. 83, Issue 1 of the *Journal of Criminal Law and Criminology* (1992).

49. L.W. Sherman and D.A. Smith, "Crime, Punishment, and Stake in Conformity: Legal and Informal Control of Domestic Violence," *American Sociological Review* 57 (1992): 680–90.

50. R.A. Berk and others, "The Deterrent Effect of Arrest in Incidents of Domestic Violence: A Bayesian Analysis of Four Field Experiments," *American Sociological Review* 57 (1992): 698–708.

51. See L.G. Mills, "Mandatory Arrest and Prosecution Policies for Domestic Violence: Critical Lit Review and the Case for More Research to Test Victim Empowerment," *Criminal Justice and Behavior* 25 (1998): 306–18.

52. For an example, see T.N. Ho, "Domestic Violence in a Southern City: The Effects of a Mandatory Arrest Policy on Male-versus-Female Aggravated Assault Incidents," *American Journal of Criminal Justice* 25 (2000): 107–18.

53. R.C. Davis, B.E. Smith, and B. Taylor, "Increasing the Proportion of Domestic Violence Arrests That Are Prosecuted: A Natural Experiment in Milwaukee," *Criminology and Public Policy* 2 (2003): 263–82.

54. L.W. Sherman and others, "From Initial Deterrence to Long-Term Escalation: Short Custody Arrest for Poverty Ghetto Domestic Violence," *Criminology* 29 (1991): 821–50.

55. J. Garner, J. Fagan, and C. Maxwell, "Published Findings from the Spouse Abuse Replication Program: A Critical Review," *Journal of Quantitative Criminology* 11 (1995): 3–28.

56. C.D. Maxwell, J.H. Garner, and J.A. Fagan, "The Preventive Effects of Arrest on Intimate Partner Violence: Research, Policy, and Theory," *Criminology and Public Policy* 2 (2002): 51–80.

57. Lawrence W. Sherman, "Policing for Crime Prevention," Chapter 8 in *Preventing Crime: What Works, What Doesn't, What's Promising,* eds. Lawrence W. Sherman and others (Washington, DC: National Institute of Justice, 1998).

58. H. Isaacs, "A Study of Communications, Crimes and Arrests in a Metropolitan Police Department," Task Force Report: Science and Technology, *A Report to the President's Commission on Law Enforcement and Administration of Justice* (Washington, DC: U.S. Government Printing Office, 1967).

59. C. Clawson and S.K. Chang, "The Relationship of Response Delays and Arrest Rates," *Journal of Police Science and Administration* 5 (1977): 53–68.

60. Jan M. Chaiken, "What Is Known about Deterrent Effects of Police Activities," in *Preventing Crime,* ed. James A. Cramer (Beverly Hills, CA: Sage Publications, 1978), 109–35.

61. Abdullah Cihan, Yan Zhang, and Larry Hoover, "Police Response Time to In-Progress Burglary," *Police Quarterly* 15 (2012): 308–27.

62. William Bieck and David A. Kessler, *Response Time Analysis* (Kansas City, MO: Board of Police Commissioners, 1977); see also Tony Pate, Amy Ferrara, Robert A. Bowers, and Jon Lorence, *Police Response Time: Its Determinants and Effects* (Washington, DC: Police Foundation, 1976).

63. William Spelman and Dale K. Brown, *Calling the Police: A Replication of the Citizen Reporting Component of the Kansas City Response Time Analysis* (Washington, DC: Police Foundation, 1981).

64. For a look at the relationship between response time and citizen perceptions of the police, see Stephen Percy, "Response Time and Citizen Evaluation of Police," *Journal of Police Science and Adminstration* 8 (1980): 75–86.

65. Police Foundation, *The Newark Foot Patrol Experiment* (Washington, DC: Police Foundation, 1981); Robert Trojanowicz, "Evaluating a Neighborhood Foot Patrol Program: The Flint, Michigan Project," in *Community Crime Prevention: Does It Work,* ed. Dennis Rosenbaum (Beverly Hills, CA: Sage, 1986), 157–78.

66. David P. Farrington, "Randomized Experiments on Crime and Justice," in *Crime and Justice: An Annual Review of Research,* eds. Michael Tonry and Norval Morris (Chicago, IL: University of Chicago Press, 1982).

67. David H. Bayley, *What Works in Policing* (New York: Oxford University Press, 1998).

68. Peter W. Greenwood and Joan Petersilia, *The Criminal Investigation Process,* Vol. 1: *Summary and Policy Recommendations* (Santa Monica, CA: RAND, 1975).

69. See David H. Bayley, *What Works in Policing* (New York: Oxford University Press, 1998).

70. Wesley G. Skogan and George E. Antunes, "Information, Apprehension, and Deterrence: Exploring the Limits of Police Productivity," *Journal of Criminal Justice* 7 (1979): 217–41.

71. Ibid., 123 in David H. Bayley, *What Works in Policing* (New York: Oxford University Press, 1998).

72. National Academy of Sciences, National Research Council, *Strengthening Forensic Science in the United States: A Path Forward* (Washington, DC: The National Academies Press, 2010).

73. Ibid., 1–6.

74. See, e.g., M.K. Nalla and C.G. Heraux, "Assessing the Goals and Functions of Private Police," *Journal of Criminal Justice* 31 (2003): 237–47.

75. E.E. Joh, "The Paradox of Private Policing," *Journal of Criminal Law and Criminology* 95 (2004): 49–131.

76. W.C. Cunningham and J.J. Strauchs, "Security Industry Trends: 1993 and Beyond," *Security Management* 36 (1992): 27–30, 32, 34–36.

77. D.A. Sklansky, "The Private Police," *UCLA Law Review* 46 (1999): 1165–287, 1166.

78. E.E. Joh, "The Paradox of Private Policing," *Journal of Criminal Law and Criminology* 95 (2004): 67.

79. Ibid.

80. D.A. Sklansky, "The Private Police," *UCLA Law Review* 46 (1999): 1221–2.

81. C.D. Shearing and P.C. Stenning, *Private Policing* (Newbury Park, CA: Sage, 1987).

82. D.A. Sklansky, "The Private Police," *UCLA Law Review* 46 (1999): 1222.

83. C.D. Shearing and P. Stenning, "Modern Private Security: Its Growth and Implications," in *Crime and Justice: A Review of Research,* ed. M. Tonry (Chicago, IL: University of Chicago Press, 1981), 193–246); also see C.D. Shearing and P.C. Stenning, *Private Policing* (Newbury Park, CA: Sage, 1987).

84. E.E. Joh, "The Paradox of Private Policing," *Journal of Criminal Law and Criminology* 95 (2004): 62.

85. Ibid.

86. Ibid.

87. Ibid., 63.

88. See, e.g., D. Shichor and M.J. Gilbert (eds.), *Privatization in Criminal Justice: Past, Present, and Future* (Dayton, OH: Lexis-Nexis Publishing, 2001).

89. D.A. Sklansky, "The Private Police," *UCLA Law Review* 46 (1999): 1166.

90. Ibid., 1230–1.
91. *Griffin v. Maryland*, 378 U.S. 130 (1964).
92. See, e.g., *Wade v. Byles*, 83 F.3d 902 (7th Cir. 1996); *Gallagher v. "Neil Young Freedom Concert,"* 49 F.3d 1442 (10th Cir. 1995); *United States v. Francoeur*, 547 F.2d 891 (5th Cir. 1977); *People v. Taylor*, 271 Cal. Rptr. 785 (Ct. App. 1990); *United States v. Lima*, 424 A.2d 113 (D.C. 1980) (en banc); *People v. Toliver*, 377 N.E.2d 207 (Ill. App. Ct. 1978); *People v. Holloway*, 267 N.W.2d 454 (Mich. Ct. App. 1978); *State v. Buswell*, 460 N.W.2d 614 (Minn. 1990).
93. See, e.g., *United States v. Antonelli*, 434 F.2d 335 (2d Cir. 1970); *City of Grand Rapids v. Impens*, 327 N.W.2d 278 (Mich. 1982).
94. See, e.g., *United States v. Cruz*, 783 F.2d 1470, 1473 (9th Cir. 1986); *State v. Garcia*, 528 So. 2d 76 (Fla. Dist. Ct. App. 1988); *Perez v. State*, 517 So. 2d 106 (Fla. Dist. Ct. App. 1987); *People v. Gorski*, 494 N.E.2d 246 (Ill. App. Ct. 1986); *State v. Farmer*, 510 P.2d 180 (Kan. 1973); *Commonwealth v. Lindenmuth*, 554 A.2d 62 (Pa. Super. Ct. 1989.
95. E.E. Joh, "The Paradox of Private Policing," *Journal of Criminal Law and Criminology* 95 (2004): 64.
96. See, e.g., J. Hall, "Legal and Social Aspects of Arrest Without a Warrant," *Harvard Law Review* 49 (1935): 566.
97. For a recent discussion, see T.J. Hawley, III, "The Collegiate Shield: Was the Movement Purely Academic?" *Police Quarterly* 1 (1998): 35–59.
98. National Advisory Commission on Criminal Justice Standards and Goals, *The Police* (Washington, DC: U.S. Government Printing Office, 1973).
99. D.L. Carter, A.D. Sapp, and D.W. Stephens, *The State of Police Education: Police Direction for the 21st Century* (Washington, DC: Police Executive Research Forum, 1988).
100. L. Sherman and M. Blumberg, "Higher Education and Police Use of Deadly Force," *Journal of Criminal Justice* 9 (1981): 317–31.
101. G. Griffin, *A Study of the Relationship between Level of College Education and Police Patrolmen's Performance* (Saratoga, NY: Twenty One Publishing, 1980); A. Lewis, "Police Halt Push for College Grads," *The Washington Post*, December 17, 1970, D-1; J. Livermore, "Policing," *Minnesota Law Review* 55 (1971): 649–730; more recently, see C.W. Sherwood, "Job Design, Community Policing, and Higher Education: A Tale of Two Cities," *Police Quarterly* 3 (2000): 191–212.
102. T. Eisenberg and R. Reinke, "The Use of Written Examinations in Selecting Police Officers: Coping with the Dilemma," *Police Chief* 40 (1973): 24–8.
103. D. Carter and A. Sapp, "The Effect of Higher Education on Police Liability: Implications for Police Personnel Policy," *American Journal of Police* 8 (1989): 153–66.

Proactive Policing, Directed Patrol, and Other Advancements

LEARNING OBJECTIVES

■ Explain the relationship between proactive arrest strategies and crime.

■ Summarize the effects of directed patrol on crime.

■ Discuss the broken windows approach to law enforcement and whether it is effective.

■ Explain how partnering with other agencies may or may not benefit the police.

■ Summarize the relationship between less-lethal weapons and crime.

■ Know the elements of COMPSTAT and its relationship to crime.

This chapter focuses on proactive policing strategies, directed patrol, and the so-called broken windows law enforcement. Interesting partnerships are also introduced, as is COMPSTAT, which is best understood as a new managerial approach to law enforcement, one that stresses intelligence and accountability. This includes understanding where crime is concentrated and holding law enforcement administrators (e.g., captains and lieutenants) accountable for crime in the areas for which they are responsible. This chapter wraps up by examining technology and less-lethal weapons.

The term *proactive* in the title of this chapter is used in stark contrast to *reactive* policing, which was discussed in the previous chapter. The term *directed* refers to policing with purpose and direction, again contrary to some of the law enforcement strategies that were covered in Chapter 3. The term *creative* is used as a catchall for certain approaches that do not fit neatly into the categories of proactive, directed, traditional policing, or community involvement in policing, the last of which is covered in the next chapter. Examples include partnering, acquiring technology, and considering new managerial approaches.

It is also important to note that the strategies that are discussed in this chapter do not necessarily require the additional expenditure of funds. Indeed, that is one reason they are attractive. It is much easier for cash-strapped police departments to redirect the energies of their officers than to hire more.

PROACTIVE ARRESTS

Do not confuse **proactive arrests** with reactive arrests discussed in Chapter 3. A proactive arrest strategy relies heavily on police-initiated arrests as opposed to arrests made after someone calls for police assistance. When a police department makes arrests primarily *after* someone calls for service, this is known as the *reactive* arrest strategy. As we have already seen, the effectiveness of the reactive approach is not well supported by the scientific literature. In other words, when the police wait around for calls for service, resulting arrests do not appear to affect the crime rate. By contrast, research suggests that proactively arresting certain individuals might have beneficial effects on crime.

proactive arrest:
targeting certain individuals and/or crime types for arrest rather than waiting for a call for service prior to the arrest.

It is also important not to confuse a proactive arrest strategy with arresting people on the basis of the mere possibility that they might commit a crime. When the police arrest someone without probable cause to believe that the person has committed a crime, they violate the Fourth Amendment to the U.S. Constitution. This is not what is meant by a proactive arrest strategy. Rather, proactive arrests follow increased police attention to specific types of criminals and crimes.

The proactive arrest approach also differs from the directed patrol approach discussed later in this chapter. Whereas proactive arrests focus on criminals and crime, directed patrol is more concerned with increasing the law enforcement presence in specific geographical areas. Directed patrol researchers commonly refer to "hot spots" of criminal activity, which reinforces the notion that directed patrol is geographic, not targeted against specific individuals or types of criminal activities.

That having been said, there are two general types of proactive arrests. The first proactive arrest strategy consists of keeping tabs on high-risk repeat offenders in the hope of catching them in the act. The second proactive arrest strategy can involve prioritizing arrests for certain types of offenders, such as drunk drivers and drug dealers. We now look at the relative effectiveness of each approach.

Proactive Arrests for High-Risk Repeat Offenders

Concerning the first proactive arrest approach, one study found that aggressive pre-arrest investigations of certain high-risk offenders made it more likely that those offenders would wind up in prison.[1] In that study, researchers examined the effectiveness of the Repeat Offender Project (ROP), a specialized unit that operated in the Washington, D.C., area during the early 1980s. The Project consisted of assigning 60 police officers to unmarked cars and giving them surveillance and investigative equipment. They were to spend at least half their time targeting individuals who had outstanding warrants and individuals who were thought to be criminally active. According to the authors:

> [ROP] increased the likelihood of arrests of targets, the seriousness of the criminal histories of its arrestees, the probability of prosecution for a felony, the chance of a felony conviction, and the length of the term of those sentenced to incarceration.[2]

Unfortunately, the researchers did not examine the general deterrent effect (if any) that ROP had, making it difficult to conclude that the program reduced crime.[3]

A similar study found that *post*arrest investigations of high-risk offenders, for the purpose of building a stronger criminal case against such individuals, increased the odds that those individuals would be incarcerated.[4] Both of these findings are plausible; if there are certain offenders who have a pattern of criminal conduct, then closely monitoring them and carefully mounting a case against them can be expected to promote a safer community. Whether repeat offender programs reduce overall crime rates, however, is unclear.

Proactive Arrests for Specific Offenses

We now turn to the second type of proactive arrest strategy: prioritizing arrests for certain types of offenses. Clearly, there are many types of crimes that the police might wish to target, but most of the research on this approach to crime has been confined to drug offenders and drunk drivers. It is assumed that when the police aggressively target drug dealers and drunk drivers, they can have a significant effect on crime. It is also assumed that aggressive arrests of drunk drivers cause drunk driving-related crashes to drop off noticeably.

TARGETING DRUG OFFENDERS.   The most researched proactive arrests approach is that of crackdowns on drug offenders. From time to time, this approach is combined with the directed patrol approach discussed in the next section, but we will treat it here as a law enforcement strategy unto itself. Basically, a crackdown occurs when authorities flood a specific area that is known for problems (in this case, drug problems) and seek to remove the criminal element from that area. You might have heard the phrase *weed and seed*. The weeding consists of removing bad elements, particularly criminals. The seed component consists of improving the area (we will discuss this more in later chapters).

The evidence is mixed concerning the effectiveness of drug crackdowns. There are more supportive studies than unsupportive ones, but they do not amount to a significant majority. In fact, researchers have become increasingly critical of drug crackdowns because of their tendency to ignore underlying root causes of crime, to push crime into surrounding areas,[5] and to fix the problem only temporarily.[6] Others have claimed that crackdowns increase the health risks to those who are addicted to drugs and increase fear and uncertainty among members of the community.[7]

Even so, some researchers have concluded that drug crackdowns are necessary and effective. One study showed that violence went down after a crackdown on heroin.[8] Another study on heroin crackdowns was also supportive of the strategy.[9] Yet another study showed that raids of crack houses led to a decline in crime but only for 12 days.[10] A study of an April 1999 crackdown on drugs in seven Virginia neighborhoods showed a 92 percent reduction in reported crime during the crackdown period with no apparent displacement of the problem into surrounding neighborhoods.[11]

But just as many, if not more, studies are unsupportive of crackdowns on the drug problem. For example, one study showed that a police crackdown on the crack market had no effect on violence.[12] Another set of researchers concluded that there were no consistent, desirable changes in the period following an aggressive, anti-drug arrest strategy.[13] Other studies show that buy-bust operations do not affect the illicit drug market[14] and that drug crackdowns in public housing have no measurable effect on crime.[15] It is likely that many crackdowns appear to be ineffective because they do not target the demand side of America's drug problem. As one researcher has observed, the drug market rapidly adapts to its new conditions following proactive arrest strategies.[16]

TARGETING DRUNK DRIVERS. Drunk drivers have also been targeted by proactive law enforcement arrest strategies. But there is a question as to whether the police can actually deter drunk driving, given how few officers per citizen there are. Also, drinking, especially social drinking, is a largely accepted practice in contemporary society. Combine these two facts, and it would seem that the police are fighting an uphill battle when it comes to drunk driving. This is confirmed by the paucity of research that is supportive of proactive arrests for drunk driving.[17]

To the extent that proactive arrests for drunk drivers may have a deterrent effect, it appears to be short-lived. Such was the finding in a famous study concerning the 1967 Road Safety Act in England.[18] The act gave police the authority to conduct a breath test of any driver. Refusal to submit to the breath test was treated the same as a failure. The act appeared to have an initial deterrent effect, but it wore off after three years. This effect, known as "initial deterrence decay,"[19] was also apparent in a 1984 Justice Department study concerning four anti-drinking campaigns in the United States.[20]

An alternative to proactive arrests is the passage of laws aimed at deterring drunk drivers. There is some research suggesting that such laws can have a deterrent effect. For example, two researchers found that drunk driving–related arrests decreased dramatically and continued to decrease in the years following the enactment of strict drunk driving sanctions in California.[21] But an equally convincing study led the author to conclude that "drunken driving deterrence policies appear to have no marginal effect on the demand for alcohol or the level of fatalities."[22]

Still other research shows that it is easy for authorities to avoid aggressive enforcement of anti–drunk driving laws.[23] Local priorities can also influence the enforcement of drunk driving laws, meaning that some areas might not give enforcement of drunk driving a high priority.[24] Some researchers claim that instead of relying on proactive arrests and stiffer legal penalties, the police need more training in how to deal with drunk drivers[25] and that swift and certain sanctions may be beneficial deterrents.[26]

Does It Work?

On the basis of available research, we cannot conclude with any measure of certainty that proactive arrests for repeat offenders reduce overall crime rates. Such programs appear to succeed in apprehending individual repeat offenders, resulting in a specific deterrent effect, but whether a general deterrent results is unclear.

Likewise, proactive arrests for drug offenders and drunk drivers do not appear, across even a majority of studies, to reduce crime. When proactive arrests *do* succeed in reducing crime, their effects appear either to be short-lived or to push crime into surrounding areas.

DIRECTED PATROL

directed patrol: a form of patrol that involves concentrating the police presence in areas where certain crimes are a significant problem.

hot spot: a concentrated area of significant criminal activity, such as a street corner known for drug sales.

Directed patrol is, as the term suggests, patrol with direction. Unlike random patrol, directed patrol involves concentrating the police presence in areas where certain crimes are a significant problem. Two terms that are used in conjunction with directed patrol are *hot spots* and *hot times*. **Hot spots** are concentrated areas of significant criminal activity, such as a street corner that is well-known for its prostitution traffic. Hot times are those times of day when crime is particularly problematic, such as after dark on Friday nights.

Other terms that frequently pop up with reference to directed patrol include *crime peaks,* or those times of day when the frequency of certain crimes increases. Also, directed patrol researchers often refer to *saturation patrols,* which occur when several police officers flood a certain area in an effort to catch criminals and deter would-be offenders. Others refer to directed patrol as *focused patrol.* This term is used to refer to the fact that police *focus* their efforts on certain problems, locations, or times.

Today, police departments are able to identify hot spots and hot times with sophisticated software. Using dispatch data, for example, police departments can plot the concentration of certain offenses, and the times during which they occur, on maps. Figure 4.1 shows a typical crime map. A crime map allows officials to see firsthand where the problems are. Using this information, supervisors allocate personnel to the areas where they are needed most. Directed patrol, therefore, is one way of making the most out of a police department's limited resources.

Classic Studies

The directed patrol approach seems sensible, and many classic studies suggest that this approach is beneficial. Wilson and Boland[27] were among the first researchers to examine the relationship between aggressive policing and crime. They found an inverse relationship between the number of traffic tickets and serious crime. That is, as the number of tickets increased in a certain area, serious crime declined.

Sampson and Cohen extended Wilson and Boland's research.[28] They focused on robbery in 171 U.S. cities and on whether aggressive traffic enforcement reduces robbery. They measured the concept of aggressive traffic enforcement by the number of disorderly conduct and driving-under-the-influence arrests per officer.[29] They found that cities with aggressive traffic enforcement had reduced robbery rates. They concluded that an aggressive traffic enforcement can have both general and specific deterrent effects, by deterring potential robbers and making it more likely that criminals will be caught.

Cordner examined the relationship between aggressive directed patrol on robbery, burglary, auto theft, and theft from vehicles.[30] The strategy that he studied took place

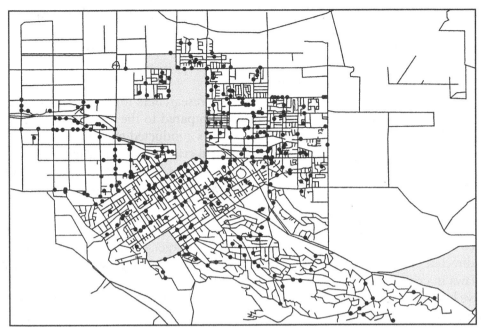

FIGURE 4.1 Crime Map for a Three-Month Period in Redland, California

Source: Center for Criminal Justice Research, California State University, San Bernardino.

in Pontiac, Michigan. There, a special unit of police officers was freed from responding to calls for service and allowed to direct their patrol and investigative efforts toward specific target areas. He found that when police officers engaged extensively in vehicle stops and questioning of suspicious persons, offense rates declined.

In a study of traffic patrol in Indianapolis, researchers analyzed the effect of additional police patrol on offenses such as burglary.[31] Officers patrolled an extra four hours at the end of their shifts, resulting in a heightened police presence. This occurred in eight police beats over a period of six weeks. Through the use of aggressive traffic stops and frequent use of consent searches, crime was reduced. The study even showed crime reductions in surrounding areas.

In a similar study, researchers randomly assigned patrol officers in Dayton, Ohio, into treatment and control groups.[32] In the treatment area, officers were instructed to enforce all traffic laws aggressively. The control area was to continue with business as usual. The researchers found that arrests for offenses involving weapons, drugs, and drunk driving increased in the treatment area but not in the control area. Not all research is supportive of this traffic enforcement–based approach to serious crime, however.[33]

Moving away from traffic enforcement, other researchers have focused on so-called police crackdowns in specific areas. One classic study focused on the high levels of robbery in a New York City precinct. The researcher found that a 40 percent increase in police presence led to a reduction in visible crime.[34] Another study showed that increasing foot patrols on New York City subways reduced robberies.[35] Researchers continue to find that concentrated foot patrols in areas known for an inordinate amount of crime can be effective.[36]

As another example, after the Minneapolis Police Department realized that crime in its city was concentrated in certain areas and at certain times of day, it reorganized its entire police force. The level of patrol was reduced in low-crime areas and at times when the frequency of crime was low. Substantially more patrol was added to high-crime areas and during those times of day when the crime rate was high. A study of this approach revealed that it appeared to be effective.[37] In particular, the research showed that the longer police officers remained at crime hot spots, the greater the amount of time the area was free from criminal activity.

In another analysis of the Minneapolis data, researchers found that with more patrol in high-crime areas, there was less crime compared to the areas with no extra patrol. Similar findings have been reached in studies conducted outside Minneapolis. For example, two separate studies found a decrease in crimes committed outdoors with an increase in patrol targeted specifically at those offenses.[38] Still more studies suggest that targeting crimes at specific times of day can lead to significant reductions.[39]

Lawrence Sherman and the Hot Spots[40]

Research by Sherman[41] and by Sherman, Gartin, and Buerger[42] is among the most cited in the directed patrol literature. These researchers found that aggressive enforcement of the laws in crime hot spots causes crime to decline. Their efforts have spawned an extensive body of hot spots research.[43] Most of the research has concentrated on areas with drug problems and excessive gun violence. Some hot spots interventions, though, do not target just one crime type per se, and they can still be quite effective, as recent research suggests.[44]

DIRECTED PATROL OF DRUG HOT SPOTS. In 1989, the National Institute of Justice initiated the Drug Market Analysis (DMA) program. The DMA program was designed to develop strategies that could be used to address street-level drug crime and effectively target the areas that were plagued by drug activity.[45] More important, the DMA program was intended to help researchers determine what policing strategies prove effective for combating drug problems.

In one DMA study, two researchers reported on the effect of an innovative drug enforcement strategy in Jersey City, New Jersey.[46] Using computer mapping technology, they identified 56 drug hot spots.[47] These hot spots were randomized into experimental and treatment groups. Then police officers engaged in various types of crackdowns on drug activity. These ranged from mini-crackdowns to major, coordinated crackdowns by a large number of officers. The researchers found that crackdowns significantly reduced disorder-related emergency calls for service.

Interestingly, the Jersey City study is one of few criminal justice *experiments,* complete with treatment and control groups as well as random assignment. Accordingly, the findings should be taken seriously. They were based on more than just correlation analysis. But to conclude that directed patrol for drug offenses is effective across the board is a risky proposition. Fortunately, additional research suggests that targeted drug enforcement efforts can reduce crime.[48]

One problem with patrols directed at drug hot spots is that the effects of such patrols can be short-lived. A recent study of police raids for dealing with illegal drug selling at nuisance bars serves as proof positive.[49] The authors concluded that "police intervention suppresses levels of drug dealing during periods of active enforcement, but the effects largely disappear when the intervention is withdrawn."[50] The same study suggests that authorities need to give careful attention to the areas that are targeted for proactive enforcement; some target areas respond to aggressive enforcement better than others.[51]

DIRECTED PATROL OF GUN VIOLENCE HOT SPOTS.   In the early 1990s, the Kansas City Police Department studied the effect of a directed patrol strategy on violent crime. Their directed patrol strategy placed some officers in patrol cars, freed them from the responsibility of responding to calls for service, and instructed them to patrol the neighborhood proactively with a special emphasis on locating and seizing illegally possessed firearms. Findings from the study were impressive: There was a 65 percent increase in gun seizures and a 49 percent decrease in gun-related crime in the target area.[52]

In a study patterned after the Kansas City gun experiment, researchers examined the effects of an initiative implemented by the Indianapolis Police Department.[53] In July 1997, the department implemented directed patrol in two target areas for a total of 90 days. The strategy was summarized as follows:

> The goal was to maximize vehicle stops and thereby create a sense of significantly increased police presence. The theory was that offenders would be deterred by this increased police presence. Additionally, the police anticipated that the large number of vehicle stops would yield seizures of illegal weapons.[54]

What did the research show? Apparently, crime was reduced in one of the target areas but not the other. The researchers concluded that "[t]he impact of directed patrol on gun crime, homicide, aggravated assault with a gun, and armed robbery in the north target beat was similar to that observed in Kansas City."[55] These outcomes did not carry over into the other target area, a result that possibly was attributable to lower directed patrol "dosage levels" in that area. The researchers argued that reductions occurred in the north target beat because there the police maximized stops for suspicious activities and conducted more thorough investigations than were done in the east beat.

Taken together, the results from the Kansas City and Indianapolis studies suggest that directed patrol for the purpose of taking guns out of circulation can have a desirable effect. The Indianapolis study, in particular, suggests that the police can have a specific deterrent effect on gun violence when they target suspicious individuals and activities. The researchers claimed that this "targeted offender approach sends a message of increased surveillance and removes firearms from those individuals most likely to engage in violent crime."[56]

Does It Work?

Directed patrol is now viewed as common sense. Surprisingly, though, it took police departments a long time to realize that this approach is favorable. It was not until the 1970s that the first studies of the directed patrol hypothesis were conducted. But directed patrol did not become commonplace until approximately the 1980s. Now, with crime mapping tools at the disposal of most police departments, almost every police agency in the United States is attempting some manner of directed patrol.

What does the research show? There is remarkable consensus in the literature that directed patrol can reduce certain types of criminal activity. The most convincing evidence comes from studies of directed patrol's effect on gun violence and drug crime. Specifically, research on gun violence from Kansas City and on drug problems in Jersey City suggest that directed patrol is worth pursuing. It is not a panacea, however. There appear to be no studies suggesting that directed patrol has outcomes that are completely intended.

THE BROKEN WINDOWS LAW ENFORCEMENT APPROACH

More than 20 years ago, Wilson and Kelling[57] claimed that if low levels of disorder and deviance are not prioritized by law enforcement, more serious crime will be likely to follow. They also claimed that when signs of disorder are ignored, problems of violence

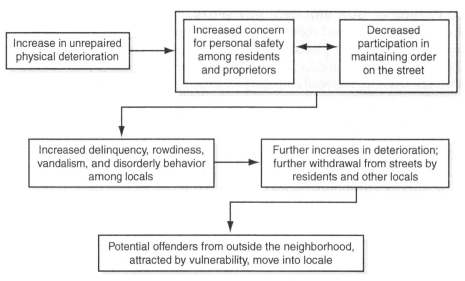

FIGURE 4.2   Broken Windows Theory

Source: Ralph B. Taylor and Adele V. Harrell, *Physical Environment & Crime* (Washington, DC: USDOJ, OJP, 1996).

broken windows theory: an explanation for crime based on the notion that physical decay in a community (such as abandoned buildings) can breed disorder and lead to more serious crime by signaling that laws are not being enforced.

and delinquency will manifest themselves and begin to spiral out of control. Thus, in their view, one way for law enforcement agencies to become effective in reducing serious crime is to begin by targeting minor problems.

Wilson and Kelling's **broken windows theory** of crime seems eminently sensible because it suggests that crime follows a fairly predictable pattern: When minor offenses such as prostitution or low-level drug dealing are ignored, citizens will begin to feel uncomfortable, perceive their neighborhood as unsafe, and curtail their activities. As citizens begin to withdraw in this fashion, the community bonds that presumably existed beforehand begin to break down, providing fertile ground for criminal activity. (See Figure 4.2 for a visual depiction of the broken windows theory.)[58]

Despite its attractiveness, the law enforcement strategy that is supported by Wilson and Kelling's theory has met with mixed reviews by various individuals. Some prominent law enforcement officials have argued that broken windows policing leads to reductions in serious crimes.[59] In his observations of the New York City Police Department, Silverman,[60] an academic, concluded that crime declined in New York in part because of this policing strategy. Numerous other law enforcement commentators favor the broken windows theory and accept it with open arms.

The media, by contrast, have often been sharply critical of the aggressive policing strategies that are supported by the broken windows theory.[61] The broken windows strategy has even been called the "harassment model of policing."[62] In fact, some have argued that the theory is inherently flawed, relying on a misinterpretation of the history of criminal activity in neighborhoods.[63] Despite criticism, however, Wilson and Kelling's ideas continue to be the subject of great attention among law enforcement experts. Many researchers, drawing on their ideas, have refined and extended the broken windows theory[64] even beyond the realm of policing (e.g., to prosecution).

Although few direct tests of the broken windows theory have been published, many researchers have tested some of the ideas that flow from (and led up to) Wilson and Kelling's seminal argument. The literature can be organized into two broad categories: the effects of fear and disorder on crime and the effects of so-called quality-of-life policing strategies on crime and disorder.

Fear, Disorder, and Crime

Skogan was one of the first researchers to examine the relationship between fear, disorder, and crime, phenomena that are considered closely linked by supporters of Wilson and Kelling's broken windows theory.[65] He reported on a survey of 13,000 residents in 40 neighborhoods of six different cities and found that crime and fear were linked to disorder. He concluded that this relationship was even stronger than that between poor socioeconomic conditions and crime. He also concluded that disorder *preceded* crime in the neighborhoods surveyed. His research seemed to provide empirical support for the broken windows theory.

Research subsequent to Skogan's has cast some doubt on his conclusions. For example, one researcher reanalyzed Skogan's data and found that disorder, fear, and crime were not tightly linked.[66] This led two other researchers to conclude that "Skogan's results are extremely sensitive to outliers and therefore do not provide a sound basis for policy."[67] Thus, fear of crime might not be affected when the police target low-level disorder offenses.

Quality-of-Life Policing

Past research also seems to support a policing strategy that is geared toward reducing social and physical disorder but that is less than aggressive in orientation.[68] This strategy assumes that as signs of disorder are reduced, community members will be more inclined to associate with one another, care for their neighborhoods, and work jointly to promote safety and otherwise send a signal that crime is not welcome. Quality-of-life policing has found a wealth of support in the law enforcement community[69] as well as in academia.[70]

The studies addressing quality-of-life policing can be roughly categorized into macro- and micro-level research. Macro-level research in this area looks at the effect of quality-of-life policing on aggregate (e.g., city, county, or state) crime rates. Micro-level studies, by contrast, usually focus on single cities, single neighborhoods, an area consisting of a few blocks, or lower-level units of analysis. Recent research suggests that a micro-level approach is more appropriate for studying broken windows, but macro-level research is nevertheless available and should be reviewed.[71]

MICRO-LEVEL RESEARCH.   One example of a micro-level quality-of-life policing study was published in 1998.[72] The authors of that study examined one community's attempt to deal with disorder crimes, notably joyriding and street drinking, that affected quality of life. The response to the problem was twofold. First, the state alcohol regulation agency assigned undercover agents to the target area, instructing them to make arrests and issue citations for open containers of alcohol. Next, the local police department allocated several patrol cars to the areas where joyriding was prominent. The researchers evaluated this approach in terms of its effect on the serious crimes of robbery and aggravated burglary; they found that the intervention had no effect. Note that they considered serious crime as the outcome because their research proceeded under the broken windows assumption that serious crime can be reduced following aggressive efforts to target low-level quality-of-life crimes. The study appears to cast some doubt on the accuracy of the broken windows theory.

Another recent study of quality-of-life policing also paints a somewhat grim picture of the effectiveness of broken windows policing. Katz and his colleagues studied the effect of the Chandler, Arizona, Police Department's quality-of-life initiative on police calls for service in several categories.[73] These included calls for person crime, property crime, drug crime, suspicious persons, assistance, public morals, physical disorder, nuisance, disorderly conduct, and traffic.[74] They found that quality-of-life policing reduces physical disorder and public morals offenses (e.g., prostitution) but little else. This is not a surprising conclusion, considering that a major component of the Chandler initiative involved policing physical disorder (mainly through code enforcement) and public morals offenses.

Thus, from the evidence of both the Chandler study and the one discussed in the preceding paragraph, localized efforts to do broken windows policing are not resounding successes. But at least one study suggests that when the police cracked down on fare beaters in subways, robberies in the subway system declined.[75] This is consistent with the broken windows theory, suggesting that it might be possible to reduce serious crime by targeting low-level offenses. Yet another recent study—perhaps the most sophisticated to date—revealed that failure to address low-level problems such as litter and unkempt lawns leads to increases in serious crime later.[76]

MACRO-LEVEL RESEARCH. One study found that when the police aggressively target minor problems, the rate of serious crime appears to decline.[77] This conclusion was based on a county-level analysis, looking at crimes and arrests over a period of several years in California. The author found that in counties with more misdemeanor arrests as a percentage of all arrests, serious crime went down. It was not possible to show that aggressive attention to misdemeanors *caused* a reduction in serious crime. It could very well be that counties with low violent crime rates target misdemeanors because of a lack of violent crime.

Does It Work?

Two seasoned researchers recently observed that "the contention that disorder is an essential cause in the pathway to predatory crime is open to question."[78] To assert that broken windows policing might not work would be anathema to many a layperson and law enforcement practitioner, so this much can be said: While the literature is not 100% supportive of broken windows, recent studies paint the strategy in a very favorable light.

PARTNERING

Partnering is today's buzzword in criminal justice. It is happening through all stages of the criminal process, across all levels of government, and between agencies inside and outside the criminal justice system. Police, in particular, are partnering in unprecedented ways with prosecutors, corrections officials, and a host of other stakeholders. As part of this partnering movement, police are also looking "down the road" and trying to prevent additional crimes before they occur, such as through being involved in the reintegration of parolees back into neighborhoods. In short, law enforcement officials are getting tired of the "revolving door" that has all too often characterized criminal justice in the past.

Police–Corrections Partnerships

Police–corrections partnerships are partnerships between police officers and either probation officers or parole officers. A recent government report describes police–corrections partnerships in this way:

> In recent years, police and correctional agencies in many jurisdictions have formed a variety of partnerships in which their staff collaborate to share information or jointly perform services in ways that benefit both agencies. Some of these partnerships are formalized—they are the product of a detailed planning process, have multiagency advisory and oversight boards, and operate pursuant to written procedures. Other partnerships are informal, having evolved because a handful of staff in the two or more agencies involved began talking about better ways to do their jobs. Some partnerships are mainly known only to those directly involved. Others have been widely publicized and have served as prototypes for new programs.[79]

An example of one such partnership was San Bernardino, California's Operation Nightlight Program (patterned after Boston, Massachusetts' Operation Night Light program). It consisted of five two-person teams, each team consisting of one probation officer and one police officer. These teams worked in the field to conduct home visits with juveniles who had been freshly placed on probation. The teams also enforced curfew and truancy violations. They even rewarded well-behaved probationers with trips to sporting events and other activities. The probation and police officers worked together in teams to enforce the conditions of probation. This is but one example of a police–corrections partnership.

Operation Nightlight in San Bernardino was basically an enhanced supervision program. In other words, it ensured that juveniles who were placed on probation received more supervision than they would under normal circumstances.[80] In some jurisdictions around the country, it is not uncommon for probation officers to have caseloads in excess of 100 or even 200. Obviously, this makes supervision of probationers somewhat difficult. Nightlight permitted additional supervision.

Other examples of enhanced supervision programs like Nightlight have been implemented in such locations as Minneapolis, Minnesota (the Minneapolis Anti-Violence Initiative); Clark County, Washington (the Clark County Anti-Gang Unit); New Haven, Connecticut (Project One Voice); Bellevue and Redmond, Washington (Smart Partners Program); and Maricopa County, Arizona (the Neighborhood Probation program).[81] In each of these five locations, police officers pair up with corrections officials, including probation and parole officers, jail personnel, and sometimes other individuals.

Aside from providing enhanced supervision, police–corrections partnerships engage in other activities, such as fugitive apprehension and dealing with serious habitual offenders.[82] Still other teams have been organized for the purposes of sharing information, promoting sex offender registration, reducing prison gang problems, revitalizing neighborhoods, providing services to offenders, and so on.[83]

Although police–corrections partnerships appear promising on their face, there appear to be no published studies examining their effectiveness. The best available evidence suggesting that these partnerships might reduce crime comes from Boston, Massachusetts. Its Operation Night Light program, which began in 1992, saw a substantial reduction in homicides during the heyday of the program. In 1993, there were 93 homicides in Boston, compared to 39 between January 1 and November 30,

1997. And between early 1995 and late 1997, there were *no* homicides among juveniles.[84] These numbers appear to support the program's effectiveness, but there were several other crime control measures in place in Boston during approximately the same period. One of those was Boston's Operation Ceasefire, which we discuss in Chapter 6.

WHAT DOES THE RESEARCH SHOW? To date, few studies have examined the effectiveness of police–corrections partnerships. The only research that is available appears to be an evaluation of Operation Nightlight in San Bernardino, California.[85] Researchers there examined the effect of Nightlight on several types of juvenile arrests in the city of San Bernardino. Using a technique known as time series analysis, they found that the program reduced juvenile arrests for the following felonies: (1) robbery, (2) assault, (3) burglary, (4) theft, and (5) motor vehicle theft. They found that the program had no effect on misdemeanor and status offense (e.g., runaway) arrests, however.

The Nightlight evaluators also explored displacement and diffusion effects associated with the partnership between the San Bernardino Police Department and San Bernardino County Probation. Their catchment areas were, of necessity, whole cities, including Colton, Rialto, and Highland, all of which are contiguous to San Bernardino. They found that Operation Nightlight neither increased nor decreased juvenile arrests in the cities of Colton and Rialto. In Highland, however, there appeared to be some evidence of diffusion, particularly for burglary.

One problem with the Nightlight evaluation was that the authors examined the program's effect on juvenile arrests. Because Nightlight was an enhanced supervision police–corrections partnership, it is possible that arrests would *increase* rather than decrease following enhanced contact between juvenile probationers and authorities. On the other hand, if arrests are considered evidence of criminal activity, then one might expect them to go down following increased collaboration between police and probation officers. In other words, juvenile arrests might not have been the ideal outcome measure for studying the effect of Operation Nightlight because it is unclear whether the program should have caused arrests to increase or decrease.

Multijurisdictional Drug Task Forces

multijurisdictional drug task force: a drug interdiction and eradication team composed of members from law enforcement agencies from multiple jurisdictions and often several other levels of government.

Another example of collaboration and partnering occurs through the use of **multijurisdictional drug task forces.** Such efforts usually team several law enforcement agencies from several jurisdictions, and often several levels of government, together to interdict and eradicate drugs. Such initiatives are extremely popular. For example, during the height of the drug war of the 1980s, 800 task forces were developed and funded by federal grant monies.[86] Task forces have also been found in states such as New Jersey, Kentucky, Indiana, Utah, Idaho, Missouri, Mississippi, Nebraska, and several others. The drugs targeted vary considerably, as do the tactics. Some task forces rely on eradication, while others focus on prevention or an aggressive enforcement through buy-bust operations, and still others work to stem the flow of illicit drugs into the United States.

The question for our purposes is "Do multijurisdictional drug task forces work?" If the focus is on outputs, particularly the amount of drugs seized, the number of arrests made, and the number of charges filed, drug task forces appear to be quite successful. One need only look at the CAMP statistics. Some research also shows that task forces are quite successful in terms of seizing large quantities of drugs and that arrests and prosecutions can increase as a result of such collaboration.[87] Yet not everyone believes that outputs "measure up."[88] When the focus shifts to *outcomes,* that is, whether task forces reduce the drug problem, there is little or no convincing evidence that such an approach works. Instead, most of the available research has been concerned with the implementation of task forces and the relationships among team members.[89] To date, it appears that only one study links drug task forces to reductions in the amount of drugs being dispersed.[90]

Military Partnerships and Militarization

Most of us are familiar with the "war on drugs" or "war on crime" more generally. To some, this connotes nothing more than a serious stance with respect to lawbreaking. To others, the war metaphor means much more. For better or worse, it signals a blurring of the lines between the military and the police. Who cares? The **Posse Comitatus Act**, passed in 1878, generally prohibits the federal military personnel and the National Guard (under federal authority) from engaging in local law enforcement activities. (Note the "federal authority" language; it is quite appropriate and common for state governors to rely on the National Guard for enforcement functions in times of emergency and crisis.) Thus, anything that looks like active collaboration between the military and local police raises some eyebrows.

Posse Comitatus Act: U.S. legislation passed in 1878 that generally prohibits federal military personnel and the National Guard (under federal authority) from engaging in local law enforcement activities.

While there are no apparent signs of the military replacing local police, the two are certainly working together closely. According to Peter Kraska and Victor Kappeler, two researchers who have studied this progression closely: "By the early 1990s, all branches of the military, including most state national guards, were becoming 'socially useful' by involving themselves in both domestic and international drug law enforcement."[91] This pattern, they note, has become more obvious since the end of the Cold War because, in their view, the military has almost been searching for a purpose. Whether this is true today, in light of the war on terror, is not totally clear. On the one hand, the various branches of the military certainly have their hands full in the Middle East. On the other hand, the war on terror begs for collaboration between the police and the military.

Even going back *before* 9/11, however, there were plenty of other signs of police–military partnerships. During the height of the drug war during the 1980s, for instance, the Bush administration created several Department of Defense-sponsored "joint task forces," which included personnel from the military as well as local law enforcement agencies. Their role was to coordinate drug interdiction efforts at the borders and abroad—and interdiction efforts here in the states.[92] "This arrangement required substantial overlap and cooperation between the military and civilian police forces."[93]

THE POLICE–MILITARY CONNECTION.   Perhaps the most concrete example of police–military partnering is that of the **police paramilitary unit (PPU)**, also going by terms like special weapons and tactics (SWAT) teams, tactical units, special operations units, strike teams, and so forth. While these are distinctly law enforcement tools and disconnected from the military in the formal sense, they learn how to operate in much the same way. Indeed, it is not uncommon for PPU members to train with one or more branches of the military. Kraska and Kappeler found that 43 percent of the officers in

police paramilitary unit (PPU): a specially trained and equipped law enforcement unit that trains with one or more branches of the military and uses military tactics and techniques.

the PPUs that they surveyed trained with active military personnel.[94] This, they argue, is changing the face of American policing:

> Initially these units constituted a small portion of police efforts and were limited to large urban police departments. The constructed and publicly understood role of PPUs was confined to rare situations involving hostages, terrorism, or the "maniac sniper." Despite the camouflage of these common assumptions, there have been recent unmistakable signs of intensifying military culture in police departments. Although these units are highly secretive about their operations, obvious expressions of militarism are found throughout contemporary policing in the form of changing uniforms, weaponry, language, training, and tactics.[95]

POLICE PARAMILITARY UNITS. PPUs are obvious to most observers, but most of us don't have occasion to actually see them except in the movies and on television. It is worth pointing out, then, the distinguishing features of these units. Kraska and Kappeler point to several such features[96]:

- Militaristic equipment and technology
- Common use of the Heckler and Koch MP5 submachine gun
- "Tactical, semi-automatic shotguns, M16s, sniper rifles, and automatic shotguns referred to as 'street sweepers'"
- Use of less-than-lethal technology, such as percussion grenades
- Tools for "dynamic entries," such as during the service of high-risk warrants
- Battering rams, hydraulic door-spreaders, and even C4 explosives
- Armored and/or military personnel carriers, and specially-equipped "tactical cruisers"
- Organizational structure that parallels the military and special operations groups (SOGs)
- Wearing black or "urban camouflage," Kevlar helmets, body armor, and so forth
- A focus on "high-risk" work, including warrant service, managing civil riots, responding to terrorism, and dealing with hostage situations and barricaded suspects

Kraska and Kappeler conducted a survey to gauge the extent and use of police paramilitary units. What they found, first, was a growing trend of reliance on PPUs. "In 1982, about 59 percent of the police departments surveyed had a PPU. By 1990, this figure had increased to 78 percent, and by 1995 it reached 89 percent."[97] Their research was limited to cities with more than 50,000 people, but the growth is interesting nonetheless.

They also found increasing "normalization" of PPUs. What this means, in part, is that they are taking on less traditional roles, focusing on problems besides just those of the "high-risk" variety. More than 20 percent of the agencies that responded to Kraska and Kappeler's survey reported using PPUs for proactive patrol work, such as suppressing gang violence, the illicit drug trade, and other problems. One commander of a large city police department reported how his chief bought a "SWAT bus" that could carry upwards of 30 tactical officers in military gear out into town to do patrol work.[98] And in a somewhat ironic twist of events, one department that touted community policing reported this about using PPUs for patrol (and it even used some community policing money to do it!):

> We're into saturation patrols in hot spots. We do a lot of our work with the SWAT unit because we have bigger guns. We send out two, two-to-four-man cars, we look for minor

violations and do jump-outs, either on people on the street or automobiles. After we jump out, the second car provides periphery cover with an *ostentatious display of weaponry.* We're sending a clear message: If the shootings don't stop, we'll shoot someone.[99]

Some would call this creative patrol. Others would say it's antithetical to the ideals of community building and partnering. My intent is not to take sides. It is just interesting to note that while there is all this talk of relationship-building, community justice, citizen interaction, and the like, police departments in *many* cities across America are adopting a very militaristic stance with respect to crime. Consider another interesting observation from frontline personnel on collaboration between the police and the military. This came straight from the mouth of an officer involved in a large city police department's PPU:

> We've had special forces folks who have come right out of the jungles of Central and South America. These guys get into the real shit. All branches of the military service are involved in providing training to law enforcement. U.S. Marshalls act as liaisons between the police and the military to set up the training—our go-between. They have an arrangement with the military through JTF-6 (joint task forces 6) . . . I just received a piece of paper from a four-star general who tells us he's concerned about the type of training we're getting. We've had teams of Navy Seals and Army Rangers come here and teach us everything. We just have to use our judgment and exclude the information like: "at this point we bring in the mortars and blow the place up."[100]

FUSION CENTERS AND INTELLIGENCE-LED POLICING.   Fusion centers are part of the so-called **intelligence-led policing** movement. The term intelligence-led policing originated in the United Kingdom.[101] Specifically, the Kent Constabulary came up with the concept in response to a rise in property crime—a rise that occurred while police resources were being cut. Originally called the *Kent Policing Model*, this approach prioritized calls for service and referred nonemergency calls to other agencies, when appropriate. This freed up resources so that officers could focus on the property crimes that were on the rise. The result was a property crime drop of 24 percent over three years. According to one assessment of this effort,

intelligence-led policing: the collection and analysis of information to produce an intelligence end product designed to inform police decision making at both the tactical and strategic levels. Also called intelligence-driven policing.

> [I]ntelligence-led policing focuses on key criminal activities. Once crime problems are identified and quantified through intelligence assessments, key criminals can be targeted for investigation and prosecution. Because the groups and individuals targeted in Kent were those responsible for significant criminal activity, the ultimate reduction in crime was considerable.[102]

Since it has been imported into the United States, intelligence-led policing has remained largely the same, with some minor twists. For example, it has led to the creation of several **fusion centers** around the United States. These are essentially intelligence-gathering units—often collaborative efforts that serve various agencies. As David Lambert explains,

fusion center: an intelligence-gathering unit, often constituted as a collaborative effort that serves various agencies.

> A fusion center is a "collaborative effort of two or more agencies that provide resources, expertise, and information to the center with the goal of maximizing their ability to detect, prevent, investigate, and respond to criminal and terrorist activity." Fusion centers can identify potential threats through data analysis and enhance investigations through analytical support (e.g., flow charting and geographic analysis).[103]

It remains to be seen whether fusion centers are influential from a crime reduction standpoint. As yet, researchers have not formally examined their effects on crime.

Does It Work?

It is unclear whether partnering between police and corrections agencies reduces crime. Such partnerships are relatively new and are significantly underresearched. Only time and additional research will make it clear whether crime reductions (or arrest reductions) can be expected when police departments and probation agencies pair up to keep tabs on probationers and other such people.

Multijurisdictional collaboration to target the U.S. drug problem seems sensible. Indeed, a few studies show that task forces can remove drugs from circulation and increase arrests that ultimately result in charges. As for their effect on the drug problem, there is no convincing evidence that collaboration of this sort has reduced the movement of drugs, their use, or their sale. Because funding priorities have shifted away from this topic, we might not ever know for sure whether multijurisidictional drug task forces reduce crime.

As for military partnerships and militarization, it is unclear what effect this form of collaboration has on crime. Surely military training is beneficial to police officers who engage in high-risk activities such as crowd control and warrant execution. Other than that, no one has attempted to determine whether militarization is beneficial. Finally, the efficacy of fusion centers has not been formally examined as of this writing.

TECHNOLOGY AND LESS-LETHAL WEAPONS

The technology of law enforcement has changed significantly in the past one hundred or so years. Examples include the invention of the automobile, the spread of radio communications, the birth of forensic investigation, and the advent of computers. These technologies are relatively crude considering what is being developed now—and what is on the horizon.

Safely Ending Pursuits

Numerous technologies have been developed to assist police with interrupting high-speed pursuits. Most readers are probably familiar with spike strips. Recent versions of these make use of hollow spikes that slowly release the air from fleeing suspects' tires so as to bring the vehicle to a safe stop. The spikes can also be retracted remotely so pursuing vehicles can pass by without incident.

Another device that is currently being developed exploits vehicles' onboard computer technology and disrupts fleeing vehicle electronics, kills the ignition, and brings them safely to a stop. According to Jaycor, the company that is developing the product (called the "Titan"):

> For the growing problem of high-speed vehicle pursuit, Titan is refining and miniaturizing the Auto-Arrestor™ system, which uses electromagnetic pulses to disrupt a fleeing automobile's sensitive electronics and safely stop it. The system can be deployed as a permanent or temporary barrier across a road. The electrical energy injected onto the vehicle's frame couples to the ignition system and disables the engine, bringing it to a safe, controlled stop.[104]

There are, of course, options besides technology. For example, most police agencies have some sort of policy governing police pursuits. Their policies bear directly on the incidence of pursuits. A study revealed, for instance, that when Metro-Dade (Florida) adopted a "violent felony only" pursuit policy, the number of pursuits declined markedly.[105] In contrast, Omaha adopted a more lax pursuit policy and witnessed an increase in pursuits of 600 percent in the space of one year.[106] Clearly, then, agencies can manage pursuits with policies—maybe better than with technology.

Crime Detection Devices

We have already seen that the police presence is spread thin in America; officers simply cannot be where all the crime occurs. Fortunately, they have been able to avail themselves of various crime detection technologies. Consider gun detection devices. Shotspotter is one of the companies that manufactures these devices, and several cities throughout the United States have purchased and installed them. These devices use sensitive microphones to identify gunshots, distinguish them from other noises that are not gunfire, and then triangulate the location of the shot so law enforcement officials can respond quickly to the correct location. Research suggests gun detection technology can help police better identify shooting incidents, but not necessarily that such technologies reduce crime.[107]

Less-Lethal Weapons

Less-lethal weapons offer something of a solution to charges of use of excessive force. Less-lethal weapons are designed to disable, capture, or immobilize a suspect rather than kill him or her.

less-lethal weapon: a weapon that is designed to disable, capture, or immobilize, rather than kill.

Efforts to provide law enforcement officers with less-lethal weapons such as stun guns, Tasers, rubber bullets, beanbag projectiles, and pepper spray began in 1987.[108] More exotic types of less-lethal weapons are available nowadays, too. They include snare nets fired from shotguns, disabling sticky foam that can be sprayed from a distance, microwave beams that heat the tissue of people exposed to them until they desist in their illegal or threatening behavior or lose consciousness, and high-tech guns that fire bolts of electromagnetic energy at a target, causing painful sensory overload and violent muscle spasms. The National Institute of Justice says, "The goal is to give line officers effective and safe alternatives to lethal force."[109]

As their name implies, less-lethal weapons are not necessarily *completely* safe. They are simply considered *less* lethal than firearms. On October 21, 2004, for example, 21-year-old Emerson College student Victoria Snelgrove died hours after being hit in the eye with a plastic pepper-spray–filled projectile that police officers fired at a rowdy crowd celebrating the Red Sox victory over the New York Yankees in the final game of the American League Championship Series in 2004. Witnesses said that officers fired the projectile into the crowd after a reveler near Fenway Park threw a bottle at a mounted Boston police officer.[110] The following sections look at three families of less-lethal weapons. There are others besides those we discuss here, but these are perhaps the most widely used.

CONDUCTED ENERGY DEVICES.   The typical **conducted energy device (CED)** (also called electromuscular disruption technology) is the familiar **Taser**. Tasers have one or both of two modes: "probe" and "touch stun." In the probe mode, a cartridge projects and attaches to a suspect's clothing or penetrates the skin with barbs. Between the barbs and pistol-like Taser unit travel two small wires. An electrical charge is then sent down the wires, disabling the suspect. The "touch stun" mode requires touching the suspect with the unit; wires are not used (not unlike a "stun gun"). For obvious reasons, the "probe" mode is safer for the officer.

conducted energy device (CED): a device that uses electrical shock to incapacitate a suspect. Examples are the Taser and the Sticky Shocker. Also called electromuscular disruption technology.

Taser: the most popular conducted energy device in law enforcement use today.

There are some concerns over the use and safety of conducted energy devices. A Police Executive Research Forum (PERF) study called attention to the need for national guidelines governing their use, particularly that of Tasers, and the organization offered over 50 recommendations for proper (and safe) operation of the devices.[111]

The need for such guidelines is critical because despite their supposedly nonlethal nature, conducted energy devices *have* been responsible for some deaths. In fact, Amnesty International, the well-known human rights group, called for a moratorium on Taser use until risks could be properly assessed. According to the Amnesty report, which was published in 2006, the number of Taser-related deaths has passed 150.[112] Amnesty attributes the deaths mainly to Tasers, as though Tasers are the direct and only cause. But the vast majority of the time, suspects who die in these cases are usually high on drugs and/or have heart conditions; the Taser simply "pushes them over the edge."

impact munition:
munitions designed to stun or otherwise temporarily incapacitate a suspect or dangerous individual so that law enforcement officers can subdue and/or arrest the person.

IMPACT MUNITIONS.   **Impact munitions** are nonlethal devices that can be fired at unruly suspects from a distance. According to the National Institute of Justice,

> These devices can be fired at a greater distance from the target, thus reducing the risk to officers and the likelihood they will resort to lethal force. . . . Impact munitions are designed to stun or otherwise temporarily incapacitate a suspect or dangerous individual so that law enforcement officers can subdue and arrest that person with less danger of injury or death for themselves and others.[113]

Impact munitions include foam rubber bullets, wooden dowels, beanbags, and other projectiles that are usually fired from 12-gauge shotguns or 37/40-millimeter gas grenade launchers. For example, Combined Tactical Systems' (CTS) 12-gauge launching cap can fire a large rubber projectile from a distance of 75 to 100 meters. Beanbags can also be fired from these types of devices. The same company's 12-gauge point round is another example of a less-lethal technology. According to CTS, "The point target cartridge round delivers a strong blow to the body with the capability to stun individuals without penetrating the body. The round is designed to be fired at the center mass of an adult subject at distances between 10 and 20 meters."[114] So-called area rounds are 12-gauge shotgun shells full of rubber pellets that deliver strong blows to people without penetrating the skin. "Sponge point grenades" and similar projectiles, fired from grenade launchers, can also do wonders to subdue unruly persons. Even rubber pellet-filled hand grenades have been developed. Finally, flash grenades or "flash-bang stun hand grenades" are available in the law enforcement arsenal. All these devices pose minimal risk of death, though they can certainly cause injury.

Law enforcement officers need to be careful to use impact munitions from proper distances. They are even "less less-lethal" from great distances because they rapidly lose their velocity. When fired from less than thirty or so feet, though, these devices can cause serious injury, including broken bones. Death can even occur if the devices are not used as intended. A National Institute of Justice study of 373 impact munitions incidents found that eight individuals died as a result of injuries sustained from impact munitions.[115] Most of the deaths were caused by broken ribs that pierced the heart or lungs. At least one suspect died as a result of being hit in the neck with a beanbag round.

pepper spray: a so-called lachrymatory (inflammatory) agent that causes irritation to the eyes and skin. Also called oleoresin capsicum, or OC.

PEPPER SPRAY.   **Pepper spray**, or oleoresin capsicum (OC), is a so-called lachrymatory agent, or inflammatory agent that causes irritation to the eyes and skin. Pepper spray causes the eyes to close tightly and tear up, and it may even cause temporary blindness. Also, the mucous membranes of the nose, throat, and sinuses burn, swell, and make breathing difficult. All in all, OC spray is very effective when used to subdue a resistant suspect. Note, however, that pepper spray is not the same as "tear gas."

Pepper spray is aptly called a less-lethal weapon because some people *have* died as a result of it.[116] A study of pepper spray's effectiveness was conducted by researchers at the University of North Carolina.[117] They examined injuries to officers and suspects, and excessive force complaints tied to pepper spray. Concerning officer injuries, the researchers found an overall decline in injuries, but the decline apparently preceded the introduction of pepper spray. The effect varied across police departments. As for suspect injuries, the researchers found fewer of them due to the introduction of pepper spray. Finally, complaints of excessive force declined markedly after pepper spray started being used.

Another study looked at in-custody deaths following the use of pepper spray. Researchers at the University of Texas, Southwestern Medical Center identified 63 such cases and concluded, for the most part, that pepper spray was not the culprit. According to one summary of this research:

> For pepper spray to cause death, it would have to make breathing difficult by closing or narrowing the bronchial tubes. The subject would have to struggle to both inhale and exhale. These effects would be noticeable shortly after the application of pepper spray. Yet, except for the two cases in which the subjects were classified as asthmatics, comments regarding breathing (other than "ceased breathing") were found in only five case reports, none of which referred to a struggle to breathe. In none of these cases did death immediately follow pepper spray application.[118]

The researchers went on to conclude that pepper spray did not cause *or* contribute to death in 61 of the 63 identified cases. The two remaining deaths were of asthmatics whose conditions were exacerbated by pepper spray. Figure 4.3 contains a summary of the causes of death in these 63 cases. "Positional asphyxia" sometimes occurs when suspects are placed, usually with handcuffs behind their backs, in a prone position. The position sometimes makes breathing more difficult.

Category	Number of Cases
Category I: Clear cut	23
IA: Drugs alone	12
IB: Drugs and disease	4
IC: Positional asphyxia	7
Category II: Combined effects	32
IIA: Confrontational situation + drugs	23
IIB: Confrontational situation + disease	5
IIC: Confrontational situation + drugs and disease	4
Category III: Outliers (uncategorizable)	6
Category IV: Asthma	2
Total cases examined in study	**63**

FIGURE 4.3   Causes of Death in Sixty-Three Cases Where Pepper Spray Was Used

Available: www.ncjrs.gov/pdffiles1/nij/195739.pdf

Source: National Institute of Justice, *The Effectiveness and Safety of Pepper Spray, Research for Practice* (Washington, DC: National Institute of Justice, 2003), p. 9.

Does It Work?

By definition, technological advances are relatively new and thus underresearched. We do not exactly know, for example, how effective spike strips are in the pursuit driving context. Likewise, gunshot locators, while surely effective in locating gun shots, do not necessarily get the police there quick enough. Last, less-lethal technologies are certainly advantageous and have assisted police in the apprehension of unruly and dangerous suspects, but their benefits need to be weighed against their costs. This has yet to be done.

COMPSTAT

It's just past seven on the third morning of the new year, and Lawrence, who runs the 10th Precinct in Midtown Manhattan, is standing on a podium in the command control center at police headquarters—the "war room." His face is bright red and a little clammy. His body is wired up tight. He is surrounded by sheaves of statistics, screens filled with computerized maps and charts and N.Y.P.D. bosses who, amazingly, seem to know as much about crime in his precinct as he does. "It's been 30 days since we've seen you, Tom," says Chief of Department Louis Anemone, a dark tone creeping into his voice. "And we're seeing an increase in robberies." "What's the pattern here, Cap?" asks Deputy Commissioner Jack Maple. . . . "What are you doing to take these guys out?"[119]

This is what one reporter observed during an early New York Police Department (NYPD) COMPSTAT meeting, one element of a relatively novel (and quickly growing) mechanism to ensure accountability in police agencies. **COMPSTAT** represents the cutting edge in police accountability. It is not reactive in the sense the internal investigations are; rather, it is a proactive, preemptive attempt to hold high-level supervisors (captains, for example) responsible for problems in the areas for which they are responsible.

During the early years of his tenure as Police Commissioner of New York City, William Bratton called for weekly meetings with representatives from each of the NYPD's eight bureaus. Deputy Commissioner Jack Maple, in conjunction with other high-ranking officials, placed pressure on the bureaus to generate crime statistics, which, surprisingly, were not being kept up to date at the time. Precincts began to measure criminal activity more carefully; then the results were computerized and assembled into a document known as the COMPSTAT Book.[120] The crime figures reported in the COMPSTAT Book would eventually be used to hold precinct commanders responsible for the crime rates in their areas. NYPD leaders then began to hold meetings with precinct commanders, one of which is described in the quote at the beginning of this section.

COMPSTAT is an acronym for "computational statistics" or, in some locations, "compare statistics." It has come to be widely imitated around the country,[121] and several different designations can be identified. One researcher has defined COMPSTAT in this way: "COMPSTAT is a goal-oriented strategic management process that uses computer technology, operational strategy and managerial accountability to structure the manner in which a police department provides crime-control services."[122]

Generally speaking, COMPSTAT emphasizes four important things: (1) accurate and timely intelligence, (2) rapid deployment, (3) effective tactics, and (4) relentless follow-up and assessment.[123] The logic behind the intelligence aspect is that "Information describing how and where crimes are committed, as well as who criminals are, must be available to all levels of policing."[124] Rapid deployment is important because "the most effective plans require that personnel from several units and enforcement functions work together as a team."[125] "Tactics are designed to respond directly to facts discovered during the intelligence gathering process,"[126] and relentless follow-up is necessary to ensure that desired outcomes occur.

New Orleans has had promising results with its version of COMPSTAT (which is called COMSTAT). During 1996, the New Orleans Police Department undertook a major reorganization and philosophical change. All crime-fighting responsibilities were placed under the eight district commanders. New resources were allocated to assist them in accomplishing their mission: reducing crime and violence in one of the most dangerous cities in the country. New Orleans' version of COMPSTAT contained the four elements that were present in New York—intelligence, rapid deployment, effective tactics, and follow-up—but the means by which they were accomplished are particularly interesting. Figure 4.4 depicts the elements of the typical COMPSTAT model.

The last step, relentless accountability, is extremely important and is usually accomplished most effectively in COMPSTAT meetings. According to Jack Maple, former Deputy Commissioner of the NYPD, "the first step to crime reduction itself—the gathering and analyzing of accurate, timely intelligence—has to be quickened by the heat of accountability."[127] New Orleans' COMSTAT program maintains a similar philosophy:

Accountability is paramount in this procedure. Each District Commander is expected to be fully aware of the crimes that take place in his or her area of responsibility and is expected to not only react to these offenses but to take proactive measures to reduce and deter them. In addition, each District Commander must prepare an extensive weekly report on the activity in his or her district.[128]

An important aspect of COMPSTAT consists of crime mapping. Because crime data need to be portrayed clearly and in a timely fashion, computer technology is essential. According to one source, "A powerful software tool, MapInfo 94, became the NYPD's crime radar screen, with attention-grabbing colors and shapes. Red dots indicated drug complaints from the public, blue dots showed drug arrests, green triangles

- Accurate and timely intelligence
  - daily incident reports to unit commanders
  - follow up cases assigned to investigators
  - directed patrols based on offense information
- Rapid deployment
  - uniformed squads deploy to targeted areas
  - plainclothes officers and other tactics used as needed
- Effective tactics
  - thinking outside the box
  - all internal and external resources considered when responding to problems
  - thorough, rapid, and systematic investigation
- Follow-up and assessment
  - critical assessment of police tactics
  - roll call training on crime fighting, evidence gathering, and the like
  - regular COMPSTAT meetings involving district commanders and top executives

FIGURE 4.4 Elements of the Typical COMPSTAT Model

represented shooting incidents, and yellow dots indicated homicides."[129] Computerized images generated by MapInfo 94 brought together all the data in the Compstat books, whereas in the past, crime statistics were not kept or presented in any single source. As another researcher observed, "These visual presentations are a highly effective complement to the COMSTAT report, since they permit precinct commanders and executive staff members to instantly identify and explore trends, patterns, and possible solutions for crime and quality-of-life problems."[130]

The most popular measure of success for precinct commanders is crime—specifically, the lack thereof. However, Garner and Hoover raise questions about the appropriateness of crime as a sole outcome measure.[131] They cite quality-of-life issues as well as citizen complaints as barometers of police performance that agencies that are experimenting with COMPSTAT might wish to consider. The appropriate success measure, they suggest, "communicates what issues are valued most in the department."[132] They also raise concerns about the NYPD version of COMPSTAT, which is rather confrontational. Although NYPD's program was intended to provide greater accountability, increased awareness, improved problem-solving endeavors, and increased managerial control, Garner and Hoover caution that focusing on weekly meetings might be too short-sighted, COMPSTAT might be too aggressive an approach to reducing crime, and it might overemphasize outcomes rather than underlying causes of problems. Indeed, one researcher has observed that "COMPSTAT's approach ignores decades of expert research that has shown that crime levels are determined by vast social forces beyond police control—poverty, racism, [and] demographics."[133]

Does It Work?

Unfortunately, the effect of COMPSTAT on crime has not been extensively researched. Some researchers have attributed drops in crime to COMPSTAT and similar managerial approaches,[134] but to date, no one has conducted an experiment to determine whether COMPSTAT clearly affects crime. Some researchers have, however, employed quasi-experimental designs to examine the effects of COMPSTAT on crime. One evaluation of COMPSTAT in New York found no discernible effects on crime,[135] yet another from Fort Worth, Texas, found that was at least partially responsible for the city's decline in property-related crime.[136]

Summary

The outlook for proactive, directed, and creative policing, while an improvement over traditional approaches, is uncertain. The reason for this is that many such approaches are relatively novel and, as yet, underresearched. The body of directed patrol research is well developed and suggests that law enforcement can reduce crime at drug and gun violence hot spots. The problem with such approaches is that the problem can be displaced (or, alternatively, a diffusion of benefits can be witnessed), and some of the effects do not last for long. Apart from directed patrol, the other approaches that were considered in this chapter deserve much more attention by researchers.

Proactive arrest policies appear capable of generating a specific deterrent effect, but a general deterrent effect seems unlikely. Encouragingly, recent research on the broken windows theory is relatively supportive of policing strategies that target low-level problems with the intent of curbing serious crime. More research is necessary, however, for partnering, in the areas of technology and less-lethal weapons, and for COMPSTAT.

Notes

1. Susan Martin and Lawrence Sherman, "Selective Apprehension: A Police Strategy for Repeat Offenders," *Criminology* 34 (1986): 55–72.
2. Ibid., 170.
3. See also S.E. Martin and L.W. Sherman, "ROP: Catching Career Criminals," in *Police and Policing*, ed. D. Kenney (Westport, CT: Praeger, 1989), 136–149.
4. Allan F. Abrahamse, Patricia A. Ebener, Peter W. Greenwood, Nora Fitzgerald, and Thomas E. Kosin, "An Experimental Evaluation of the Phoenix Repeat Offender Program," *Justice Quarterly*, 8 (1991): 141–68.
5. For some commentary to this effect, see L. Zimmer, "Proactive Policing against Street-Level Drug Trafficking," *American Journal of Police* 9 (1990): 43–74.
6. C. Aitken, D. Moore, and P. Higgs, "The Impact of a Police Crackdown on a Street Drug Scene: Evidence from the Street," *International Journal of Drug Policy* 13 (2002): 189–98.
7. L. Maher and D. Dixon, "The Cost of Crackdowns: Policing Cabramatta's Heroin Market," *Current Issues in Criminal Justice* 13 (2001): 5–22.
8. M. Kleiman, "Crackdowns: The Effects of Intensive Enforcement on Retail Heroin Dealing," in *Street-Level Drug Enforcement: Examining the Issues*, ed. M. Chaiken (Washington, DC: National Institute of Justice, 1988), 3–34.
9. L. Zimmer, "Proactive Policing against Street-Level Drug Trafficking," *American Journal of Police* 11 (1990): 43–74.
10. Lawrence Sherman and Dennis P. Rogan, "Deterrent Effects of Police Raids on Crack Houses: A Randomized, Controlled Experiment," *Justice Quarterly*, Vol. 12 (1995): 755–81.
11. M.R. Smith, "Police-Led Crackdowns and Cleanups: An Evaluation of a Crime Control Initiative in Richmond, Virgnia," *Crime and Delinquency* 47 (2001): 60–83.
12. M. Sviridoff et al., *The Neighborhood Effects of Street-Level Drug Enforcement: Tactical Narcotics Teams in New York* (New York: Vera Institute of Justice, 1992).
13. C.D. Uchida, B. Forst, and S.O Annan, "Modern Policing and the Control of Illegal Drugs: Testing New Strategies in Two American Cities," Research Report. Washington, DC: National Institute of Justice, 1992.
14. Ibid.
15. S. Annan and W. Skogan, *Drug Enforcement in Public Housing: Signs of Success in Denver* (Washington, DC: Police Foundation, 1993).
16. C. Aitken, D. Moore, P. Higgs, et al., "The Impact of a Police Crackdown on a Street Drug Scene: Evidence from the Street," *International Journal of Drug Policy* 13 (2002): 189–98.
17. One of the few exceptions is B.L. Benson, B.D. Mast, and D.W. Rasmussen, "Can Police Deter Drunk Driving?" *Applied Economics* 32 (2000): 357–66.
18. H.L. Ross, "Law, Science, and Accidents: The British Road Safety Act of 1967," *Journal of Legal Studies* 2 (1973): 1–78;

H.L. Ross, *Deterring the Drinking Driver: Legal Policy and Social Control* (Lexington, MA: Lexington Books, 1981).
19. L.W. Sherman, "Police Crackdowns: Initial and Residual Deterrence," in *Crime and Justice: An Annual Review of Research* (Vol. 12), eds. M.W. Tonry and N. Morris (Chicago, IL: University of Chicago Press, 1990), 1–48.
20. Bureau of Justice Statistics, *Jailing Drunk Drivers: Impact on the Criminal Justice System* (Washington, DC: Government Printing Office, 1984).
21. P.T. Kinkade and M.C. Leone, "The Effects of 'Tough' Drunk Driving Laws on Policing: A Case Study," *Crime and Delinquency* 38 (1992): 239–57.
22. J.T. Wilkinson, "Reducing Drunk Driving: Which Policies Are Most Effective?" *Southern Economic Journal* 54 (1987): 322–34.
23. S.D. Mastrofski and R.R. Ritti, "You Can Lead a Horse to Water . . .: A Case Study of a Police Department's Response to Stricter Drunk-Driving Laws," *Justice Quarterly* 9 (1992): 465–91.
24. R.J. Lundman, "City Police and Drunk Driving: Baseline Data," *Justice Quarterly* 15 (1998): 527–46.
25. S.D. Mastrofski and R.R. Ritti, "Police Training and the Effects of Organization on Drunk Driving Enforcement," *Justice Quarterly* 13 (1996): 290–320.
26. J. Yu and W.W. Williford, "Drunk-Driving Recidivism: Predicting Factors from Arrest Context and Case Disposition," *Journal of Studies on Alcohol* 56 (1995): 60–6; J. Yu, "Punishment Celerity and Severity: Testing a Specific Deterrence Model on Drunk Driving Recidivism," *Journal of Criminal Justice* 22 (1994): 355–66.
27. J.Q. Wilson and B. Boland, "The Effect of Police on Crime," *Law and Society Review* 12 (1978): 367–90.
28. R.J. Sampson and J. Cohen, "Deterrent Effects of the Police on Crime: A Replication and Theoretical Extension," *Law and Society Review* 22 (1988): 163–89.
29. At first glance, it would seem that this study fits in the proactive arrests section, but note that Sampson and Cohen studied *aggregate* arrest statistics. This aggregate approach does not mean that any specific city was necessarily engaged in a proactive arrest strategy.
30. G. Cordner, "The Effects of Direct Patrol: A Natural Quasi-Experiment in Pontiac," in *Contemporary Issues in Law Enforcement*, ed. J. Fyfe (Beverly Hills, CA: Sage, 1981), 37–58.
31. A. Weiss and E.F. McGarrell, "The Impact of Increased Traffic Enforcement on Crime" (paper presented at the annual meeting of the American Society of Criminology, Chicago, IL).
32. A. Weiss and S. Freels, "The Effects of Aggressive Policing: The Dayton Traffic Enforcement Experiment," *American Journal of Police* 15 (1996): 45–64.
33. J.H. Jacob and M.J. Rich, "The Effects of Police on Crime: A Second Look," *Law and Society Review* 15 (1981): 109–22.

34. S.J. Press, *Some Effects of an Increase in Police Manpower in the 20th Precinct of New York City* (New York: New York City Rand Institute, 1971).

35. Jan M. Chaiken, M. Lawless, and K. Stevenson, "The Impact of Police Activity on Crime: Robberies on the New York City Subway System," *Urban Analysis* 3 (1975): 173–205; Jan M. Chaiken, "What Is Known about Deterrent Effects of Police Activities," in *Preventing Crime,* ed. James A. Cramer (Beverly Hills, CA: Sage Publications, 1978), 109–35.

36. Jerry H. Ratcliffe, Travis Taniguchi, Elizabeth R. Groff, and Jennifer D. Wood, "The Philadelphia Foot Patrol Experiment: A Randomized Controlled Trial of Police Patrol Effectiveness in Violent Crime Hotspots," *Criminology* 49 (2011): 795–831.

37. Christopher Koper, "Just Enough Police Presence: Reducing Crime and Disorderly Behavior by Optimizing Patrol Time in Crime Hot Spots," *Justice Quarterly* 12 (1995): 649–72.

38. S.J. Press, *Some Effects of an Increase in Police Manpower in the 20th Precinct of New York City* (New York: RAND Institute, 1971); J.S. Dahmann, *Examination of Police Patrol Effectiveness* (McLean, VA: Mitre Corporation, 1975).

39. J.F. Schnelle, R.E. Kirchner, Jr., J.D. Casey, P.H. Uselton, Jr., and M.P McNees, "Patrol Evaluation Research: A Multiple-Baseline Analysis of Saturation Police Patrolling during Day and Night Hours," *Journal of Applied Behavior Analysis* 10 (1977): 33–40.

40. This heading is also the name of Professor Sherman's band, which often plays during the annual American Society of Criminology conference.

41. L. Sherman, "Police Crackdowns: Initial and Residual Deterrence," in *Crime and Justice: A Review of Research* (vol. 12), eds. M. Tonry and N. Morris (Chicago, IL: University of Chicago Press, 1990), 1–48.

42. L. Sherman, P. Gartin, and M. Buerger, "Hot Spots of Predatory Crime: Routine Activities and the Criminology of Place," *Criminology* 27 (1989): 27–55.

43. L. Sherman and D. Rogan, "Effects of Gun Seizures on Gun Violence: Hot Spots Patrol in Kansas City," *Justice Quarterly* 12 (1995): 673–94; D. Weisburd and L. Green, "Policing Drug Hot Spots: The Jersey City Drug Market Analysis Experiment," *Justice Quarterly* 12 (1995): 711–35; A. Braga, D. Weisburd, E. Waring, L. Green-Mazerolle, W. Spelman, and G. Gajewski, "Problem-Oriented Policing in Violent Crime Places: A Randomized Controlled Experiment," *Criminology* 37 (1999): 541–79.

44. Anthony Braga and Brenda J. Bond, "Policing Crime and Disorder Hot Spots: A Randomized Controlled Trial," *Criminology* 46 (2008): 577–607.

45. National Institute of Justice, *Program Plan* (Washington, DC: National Institute of Justice, 1989).

46. D. Weisburd and L. Green, "Policing Drug Hot Spots: The Jersey City Drug Market Analysis Experiment," *Justice Quarterly* 12 (1995): 711–35.

47. For a thorough discussion of the characteristics of the hot spots, see D. Weisburd and L. Green Mazerolle, "Crime and Disoder in Drug Hot Spots: Implications for Theory and Practice in Policing," *Police Quarterly* 3 (2000): 331–49.

48. See, for instance, L.G. Mazerolle, C. Kadleck, and J. Roehl, "Controlling Drug and Disorder Problems: The Role of Place Managers," *Criminology* 36 (1998): 371–404.

49. J. Cohen, W. Gorr, and P. Singh, "Estimating Intervention Effects in Varying Risk Settings: Do Police Raids Reduce Illegal Drug Dealing at Nuisance Bars?" *Criminology* 41 (2003): 257–92.

50. Ibid., 257.

51. Ibid.

52. L.W. Sherman and D.P. Rogan, "The Effects of Gun Seizures on Gun Violence: 'Hot Spots' Patrol in Kansas City," *Justice Quarterly* 12 (1995): 673–93; L.W. Sherman, J.W. Shaw, and D.P. Rogan, *The Kansas City Gun Experiment* (Washington, DC: National Institute of Justice, 1995).

53. E.F. McGarrell, S. Chermak, A. Weiss, and J. Wilson, "Reducing Firearms Violence through Directed Police Patrol," *Criminology and Public Policy* 1 (2001): 119–48.

54. Ibid., 130.

55. Ibid., 142.

56. Ibid., 143.

57. J.Q. Wilson and G. Kelling, "Broken Windows: The Police and Neighborhood Safety," *Atlantic Monthly* March (1982): 29–38.

58. G. Kelling and W. Bratton, "Declining Crime Rates: Insiders' Views of the New York City Story," *Journal of Criminal Law and Criminology* 88 (1988): 1217–31; W. Skogan, *Disorder and Decline* (New York: Free Press, 1990).

59. W. Bratton, "Remark: New Strategies for Combating Crime in New York City," *Fordham Urban Journal* 23 (1996): 781–85; W. Bratton, *Turnaround: How America's Top Cop Reversed the Crime Epidemic* (New York: Random House, 1998).

60. E. Silverman, *NYPD Battles Crime: Innovative Strategies in Policing* (Boston, MA: Northeastern University Press, 1999).

61. D. Kocieniewski and M. Cooper, "Police to Tighten the Scrutiny of All Suspects under Arrest," *New York Times* May 28, 1998, A1; P. O'Hara, "Bratton's Turnaround: Glimpse of the Future or Reinvention of the Past?" *Law Enforcement News* June 24, 1998, 13–4.

62. R. Panzarella, "Bratton Reinvents Harassment Model of Policing," *Law Enforcement News* 24 (1998): 14–5.

63. S. Walker, "Broken Windows and Fractured History: The Use and Misuse of History in Recent Police Patrol Analysis," *Justice Quarterly* 1 (1984): 57–90.

64. G. Kelling and C. Coles, *Fixing Broken Windows* (New York: Free Press, 1996); J. Skolnick and D. Bayley, *The New Blue Line: Police Innovation in Six American Cities* (New York: Free Press, 1986); J. Skolnick and D. Bayley, "Theme and Variation in Community Policing," in *Crime and Justice: A Review of Research* (vol. 10), eds. M. Tonry and N. Morris (Chicago, IL: University of Chicago Press, 1988), 1–38.

65. W. Skogan, *Disorder and Decline* (New York: Free Press, 1990).

66. B. Harcourt, "Reflecting on the Subject: A Critique of the Social Influence Conception of Deterrence, the Broken-Windows Theory, and Order Maintenance Policing New York Style," *Michigan Law Review* 97 (1998): 291–389.

67. J. Eck and E. Maguire, "Have Changes in Policing Reduced Violent Crime?: An Assessment of the Evidence," in *The Crime Drop in America*, eds. A. Blumstein and J. Wallman (Cambridge: Cambridge University Press, 2000) 207–65; see also R. Taylor, "The Incivilities Thesis: Theory, Measurement, and Policy." in *Measuring What Matters: Proceedings from the Policing Research Institute Meetings*, ed. R. Langworthy (Washington, DC: National Institute of Justice, 1999), 65–88.

68. C.M. Katz, V.J. Webb, and D.R. Schaefer, "An Assessment of the Impact of Quality-of-Life Policing on Crime and Disorder," *Justice Quarterly* 18 (2001): 825–76.

69. G. Kelling and W. Bratton, "Declining Crime Rates: Insiders' Views of the New York City Story," *Journal of Criminal Law and Criminology* 88 (1988): 1217–31; W. Bratton, "Remark: New Strategies for Combating Crime in New York City," *Fordham Urban Journal* 23 (1996): 781–85; W. Bratton, *Turnaround: How America's Top Cop Reversed the Crime Epidemic* (New York: Random House, 1998).

70. For example, see D. Roberts, "Forward: Race, Vagueness, and the Social Meaning of Order-Maintenance Policing," *Journal of Criminal Law and Criminology* 89 (1999): 775–836.

71. W. Spelman, "Optimal Targeting of Incivility-Reduction Strategies," *Journal of Quantitative Criminology* 20 (2004): 63–88.

72. K. Novak, J. Hartman, A. Holsinger, and M. Turner, "The Effects of Aggressive Policing of Disorder on Serious Crime," *Policing: An International Journal of Police Strategies and Management* 22 (1999): 171–90.

73. C.M. Katz, V.J. Webb, and D.R. Schaefer, "An Assessment of the Impact of Quality-of-Life Policing on Crime and Disorder," *Justice Quarterly* 18 (2001): 825–76.

74. Ibid., 844.

75. George L. Kelling and Catherine M. Coles, *Fixing Broken Windows: Restoring Order in Our Communities* (New York: Free Press, 1996).

76. B. Brown, D.D. Perkins, and G. Brown, "Crime, New Housing, and Housing Incivilities in a First-Ring Suburb: Multilevel Relationships across Time," *Housing Policy Debate* 15 (2004): 301–45; also see R. Taylor, *Breaking Away from Broken Windows: Baltimore Neighborhoods and the Nationwide Fight against Crime, Grime, Fear, and Decline* (New York: Westview, 2001).

77. John L. Worrall, "Does Targeting Minor Offenses Reduce Serious Crime?: A Provisional, Affirmative Answer Based on an Analysis of County-Level Data," *Police Quarterly* 9 (2006): 47–72.

78. R. Sampson and S.W. Raudenbush, "Disorder in Urban Neighborhoods—Does It Lead to Crime," in *Research in Brief* (Washington, DC: National Institute of Justice, 2001).

79. Dale Parent and Brad Snyder, *Police-Corrections Partnerships* (Washington, DC: National Institute of Justice, 1999), 5.

80. See also Matthew J. Giblin, "Using Police Officers to Enhance the Supervision of Juvenile Probationers: An Evaluation of the Anchorage CAN Program," *Crime and Delinquency* 48 (2002): 116–37.

81. Ibid.

82. Ibid.

83. Ibid.

84. Ibid., 13.

85. Larry K. Gaines and John L. Worrall, *Evaluation Report: San Bernardino County Probation Department's Project Impact/ Nightlight Program* (San Bernardino, CA: California State University, San Bernardino, 2003).

86. See E.F. McGarrell and K. Schlegel, "The Implementation of Federally Funded Multijurisdictional Drug Task Forces: Organizational Structure and Interagency Relationships," *Journal of Criminal Justice* 21 (1993): 231–44.

87. K. Schlegel and E.F. McGarrell, "An Examination of Arrest Practices in Regions Served by Multijurisdictional Drug Task Forces," *Crime and Delinquency* 37 (1991): 408–26.

88. B.W. Smith, D.J. Novak, J. Frank, and L.F. Travis III, "Multijurisdictional Drug Task Forces: An Analysis of Impacts," *Journal of Criminal Justice* 28 (2000): 543–56.

89. See, for example, T.C. Pratt, J. Frank, B.W. Smith, and K.J. Novak, "Conflict and Consensus in Multijurisdictional Drug Task Forces: An Organizational Analysis of Personnel Attitudes," *Police Practice and Research* 1 (2000): 509–25.

90. M.C. Ray, *Assessment of Multijurisdictional Drug Task Forces in Mississippi* (Mississippi Department of Public Safety, 1994).

91. P.B. Kraska and V.E. Kappeler, "Militarizing American Police: The Rise and Normalization of Paramilitary Units," *Social Problems* 44 (1997): 1–18.

92. P.B. Kraska, "Militarizing the Drug War: A Sign of the Times," in *Altered States of Mind: Critical Observations of the Drug War*, ed. P.B. Kraska (New York: Garland), 159–206.

93. P.B. Kraska and V.E. Kappeler, "Militarizing American Police: The Rise and Normalization of Paramilitary Units," *Social Problems* 44 (1997): 1–18, 12.

94. P.B. Kraska and V.E. Kappeler, "Militarizing American Police: The Rise and Normalization of Paramilitary Units," *Social Problems* 44 (1997): 1–18.

95. Ibid.; also see P.B. Kraska, "Enjoying Militarism: Political/ Personal Dilemmas in Studying U.S. Police Paramilitary Units," *Justice Quarterly* 13 (1996): 405–29; P.B. Kraska, "Militarizing Mayberry and Beyond: Making Sense of American Paramilitary Policing," *Justice Quarterly* 14 (1997): 607–29.

96. P.B. Kraska and V.E. Kappeler, "Militarizing American Police: The Rise and Normalization of Paramilitary Units," *Social Problems* 44 (1997): 1–18.

97. Ibid., 6.

98. Ibid.

99. Ibid., 10.

100. Ibid., 12.

101. This section draws from Peterson, *Intelligence-led policing*, 9.

102. Ibid.

103. D. Lambert, "Intelligence-Led Policing in a Fusion Center," *FBI Law Enforcement Bulletin* December (2010), fbi.gov/stats-services/publications/law-enforcement-bulletin/Dec2010/intelligence_feature (accessed January 14, 2011).

104. Accessed on 2/6/2007 from jaycor.com/jaycor_main/web-content//eme_ltlt.html.

105. G.P. Alpert, *Police Pursuit: Policies and Training* (Washington, DC: National Institute of Justice, 1997), 4.

106. Ibid.

107. Peter Scharf, Michael Geerken, and George Bradley, *Draft Technical Report for SECURES Demonstration in Hampton and Newport News, Virginia* (Washington, DC: Department of Justice, 2008).

108. David W. Hayeslip and Alan Preszler, "NIJ Initiative on Less-than-Lethal Weapons," *NIJ Research in Brief* (Washington, DC: National Institute of Justice, 1993).

109. Ibid.

110. Thomas Farragher and David Abel, "Postgame Police Projectile Kills an Emerson Student," *Boston Globe*, October 22, 2004. Web posted at boston.com/sports/baseball/redsox/articles/2004/10/22/postgame_police_projectile_kills_an_emerson_student (accessed July 25, 2005).

111. J.M. Cronin and J.A. Ederheimer, *Conducted Energy Devices: Development of Standards for Consistency and Guidance* (Washington, DC: Police Executive Research Forum, 2006). Available at: policeforum.org/upload/CED-Guidelines_414547688_2152007092436.pdf.

112. Amnesty International. *Amnesty International's Continued Concerns About Taser Use* (Amnesty International, USA, 2006). Available at: web.amnesty.org/library/index/engamr510302006.

113. National Institute of Justice, *Impact Munitions Use: Types, Targets, Effects* (Washington, DC: National Institute of Justice, 2004).

114. National Institute of Justice, *Department of Defense Nonlethal Weapons and Equipment Review: A Research Guide for Civil Law Enforcement and Corrections* (Washington, DC: National Institute of Justice, 2004). Available at: ncjrs.gov/pdffiles1/nij/205293.pdf.

115. National Institute of Justice, *Impact munitions use: Types, Targets, Effects* (Washington, DC: National Institute of Justice, 2004), 3.

116. For some research in this area, see R.J. Kaminski, S.M. Edwards, and J.W. Johnson, "Assessing the incapacitative Effects of Pepper Spray during Resistive Encounters with Police," *Policing: An International Journal of Police Strategies and Management* 22 (1999): 7–29; R.J. Kaminski, S.M. Edwards, and J.W. Johnson, "The Deterrent Effects of Oleoresin Capsicum on Assaults against Police: Testing the Velcro-Effect Hypothesis," *Police Quarterly* 1 (1998): 1–20.

117. National Institute of Justice, *The Effectiveness and Safety of Pepper Spray, Research for Practice* (Washington, DC:

National Institute of Justice, 2003). Available at: ncjrs.gov/pdffiles1/nij/195739.pdf.

118. Ibid., 10.

119. E. Pooley and E. Rivera, "One Good Apple," *Time* 147 (1996): 54.

120. E. Silverman, *NYPD Battles Crime: Innovative Strategies in Policing* (Boston, MA: Northeastern University Press, 1999).

121. D. Weisburd, S. Mastrofski, A.M. McNally, and R. Greenspan, *Compstat and Organizational Change: Findings from a National Survey* (Washington, DC: Police Foundations, 2001); for a review of Compstat-like strategies in six cities, see also M.H. Moore and A.A. Braga, "Measuring and Improving Police Performance: The Lessons of Compstat and its Progeny," *Policing: An International Journal of Police Strategies and Management* 26 (2003): 439–53.

122. W.F. Walsh, "Compstat: An Analysis of an Emerging Police Managerial Paradigm," *Policing: An International Journal of Police Strategies and Management* 24 (2001): 347–62.

123. E. Brady, "Compstat: Mapping, Accountability Equal Less Crime," *USA Today* December 1, 1997, 18A.

124. K. Harries, *Mapping Crime: Principle and Practice* (Washington, DC: National Institute of Justice, 1999), 79.

125. Ibid.

126. Ibid.

127. J. Maple, *The Crime Fighter* (New York: Doubleday, 1999), 93.

128. New Orleans Police Department, *Comstat* (New Orleans, LA: New Orleans Police Department, 1999). Retrieved from acadiacom.net/nopd/constat.htm.

129. E. Silverman, *NYPD Battles Crime: Innovative Strategies in Policing* (Boston, MA: Northeastern University Press, 1999), 104.

130. K. Harries, *Mapping Crime: Principle and Practice* (Washington, DC: National Institute of Justice, 1999), 80.

131. R. Garner and L. Hoover, "The Compstat Craze: Emphasizing Accountability in Policing," (paper presented at the Annual Meeting of the Academy of Criminal Justice Sciences in New Orleans, LA, 2000).

132. Ibid., 11.

133. D. Pederson, "Bullets in the Big Easy," *Newsweek* 128 (1996): 29.

134. E. Silverman, *NYPD Battles Crime: Innovative Strategies in Policing* (Boston, MA: Northeastern University Press, 1999).

135. R. Rosenfeld, R. Fornango, and E. Baumer, "Did Ceasefire, Compstat, and Exile reduce homicide?" *Criminology and Public Policy* 4 (2005): 419–50.

136. Hyunseok Jang, Larry T. Hoover, and Hee-Jong Joo, "An Evaluation of COMPSTAT's Effect on Crime: The Fort Worth Experience," *Police Quarterly* 13 (2010): 387–412.

Community Involvement in Policing

LEARNING OBJECTIVES

- Explain the relationship between community justice, problem-oriented policing, and community policing.
- Summarize the history underlying and reasons behind community policing.
- Provide a definition and examples of community policing.
- Discuss the relevance of structural and attitudinal change in the development of community policing.
- Summarize the research on community policing's effectiveness.
- Explain the concept of third-party policing.

Citizen involvement in policing has become rather popular. First, police officers have increasingly reached out to the community and sought to establish positive relationships and rapport with citizens. Second, citizens have come to police agencies to learn about—and even participate in—various aspects of the policing profession. Finally, community involvement has been a two-way street, with citizens and police collaborating in an effort to address the crime problem. Collectively, these three approaches to citizen involvement have come to be known as **community policing**. This chapter also introduces and discusses the closely related practice of third-party policing.

This chapter treats community policing separately from proactive and other directed policing strategies that were covered in Chapter 4, even though there can be substantial overlap. For example, police could work with citizens to identify problem areas and then proactively arrest people in the problem area. Likewise, the police could learn from concerned citizens that there is a speeding problem in a residential area. They could in turn institute a proactive patrol strategy to address the problem. But there are many policing strategies that involve citizens that are not directly proactive and directed. They are the subject of the next several sections. First, however, let us turn some attention to the broader community justice movement of which community policing is a part, then to problem-oriented policing, community policing's close cousin.

community policing: *an approach to law enforcement premised on the assumption that the police and citizens must work together to control crime.*

COMMUNITY JUSTICE

community justice: *a belief that criminal justice operations should favor innovative, nontraditional approaches to crime that draw heavily on input from and cooperation with the community.*

Community justice is a relatively new and innovative set of ideas about how criminal justice operations ought to be carried out. It favors innovative, nontraditional approaches to crime that draw heavily on input from and cooperation with the community. A recent book points to two fundamental assumptions underlying community justice: "First, it is assumed that within existing jurisdictions, such as states or large cities, there are critically important differences from one community to another, and these differences suggest that criminal justice strategies need to be tailored to fit those differences."[1] In other words, the first assumption underlying community justice is that custom-fit crime control is better than an unimaginative, traditional approach.

"The second assumption is that formal systems of social control, such as the criminal justice system, are not the main mechanisms of public safety. Rather, informal social controls—families, neighbors, social organizations, and friendship relations—form the most important foundation for public safety."[2] This community justice assumption emphasizes that criminal justice agencies (police, courts, corrections) cannot accomplish crime control alone; community participation is essential. Together, these assumptions define the essence of community justice. It is basically an *innovative* and *cooperative* effort to deal with America's crime problem. One of its hallmarks is the collaboration between the justice system and the community.

Community policing is simply a part of this larger community justice movement. Outside of the policing context, community justice has manifested itself in our nation's courts, particularly through the creation of so-called community courts and other problem-solving courts. Drug courts, domestic violence courts, teen courts, reentry courts, and other types of innovative courts all fall under the umbrella of community justice. Corrections agencies are also doing community justice as we have just defined it. Approaches such as restorative justice fit the community justice model, as do partnerships between probation, parole, and private companies, such as treatment facilities. We will discuss courts and corrections approaches to the crime problem in later chapters. This chapter's focus is on the policing component of community justice.

PROBLEM-ORIENTED POLICING

It is useful to think of community justice as a large umbrella under which community policing falls. **Problem-oriented policing**, the focus of this section, is best understood as a specific component of community policing. That is, community policing is the umbrella under which problem-oriented policing falls. Often, problem-oriented policing is viewed as being independent of community policing, and it can proceed without any community involvement whatsoever. See Figure 5.1 for a summary of the relationships between community justice, problem solving, and community policing.

problem-oriented policing: an approach to law enforcement that emphasizes identifying and solving specific problems (e.g., speeding, panhandling, drug sales, etc.).

Problem-oriented policing (also referred to as problem solving) is, as the term suggests, policing that is geared toward identifying and solving problems. Problems can range from serious ones, such as an excessive number of gang shootings in one area of town, to minor ones, such as panhandlers bothering visitors at a local park. Problem solving is about identifying areas, times of days, specific crimes, individuals, and the like that are particularly troublesome and then crafting a creative solution to deal with them.[3]

Problem-oriented policing, which is the brainchild of Herman Goldstein, has much in common with some of the policing strategies that we have already discussed.[4] For example, problem-oriented policing resembles directed patrol because it emphasizes direction and purpose, not just random and reactive patrol. Problem-oriented policing also resembles community policing because it usually relies on input from citizens to help identify problems. Indeed, sometimes the terms *community policing* and *problem solving* are used interchangeably. But much of the time problem solving is viewed as a separate strategy unto itself.

There are at least two ways to distinguish between community policing and problem-oriented policing. First, problem-oriented policing focuses on innovation, independently of contact with citizens. In contrast, for policing to be truly community oriented, it must consist of some degree of citizen involvement. Another, perhaps more controversial, way of distinguishing between the two approaches is that community policing focuses on citizen involvement and satisfaction as an end to itself, whereas problem-oriented policing is concerned with achieving a swift reduction in crime.

Despite problem solving's difference from community policing and community justice, it is still useful to think of the former as a part of both movements. The reason is that problem solving is concerned with the justice system's adaptation and flexibility

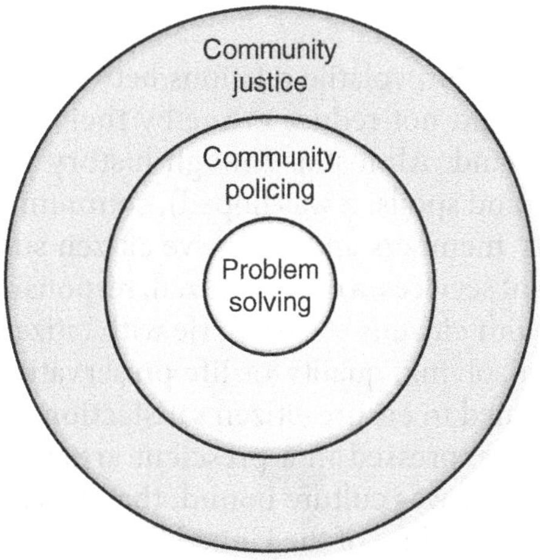

FIGURE 5.1   The Relationships between Community Justice, Community Policing, and Problem Solving

when it comes to the crime problem. This necessitates an understanding of the area, an in-depth understanding of the problem, and some degree of familiarity with the people in the area where a problem exists. It is possible, of course, for problem solving to have no community involvement (direct or indirect), but true problem solving almost always requires some outreach and relationship building with the community.

It is not possible to review a specific literature dealing with problem-oriented policing. Doing so would cause this section to overlap substantially with other sections in this and the previous chapter. Specifically, problem-oriented policing is so connected with either the directed and proactive patrol literature or the community policing literature that it would be redundant to give it much attention unto itself. It is not that case that problem-oriented policing and community policing are one and the same, but much of the research on each approach relies on the same studies.[5]

COMMUNITY POLICING: SOME HISTORY

The central features of community policing can best be understood in a historical context. Accordingly, researchers have divided the development of U.S. policing into three distinct eras: the **political era**, the **reform era**, and the **community era**.[6] During the political era, the authorization for police activities stemmed from political officials. The police provided broad social functions, were decentralized structurally, maintained intimate relationships with citizens, adopted decentralized foot patrol tactics, and worked to ensure the satisfaction of local political machines. U.S. policing was truly politicized near the turn of the twentieth century. Law enforcement positions were frequently granted to individuals who served at the behest of local politicians.[7]

Progressive reformers, discouraged by the decentralized and corrupt method of law enforcement that was in place at the time, advocated extensive reforms. Reformers such as August Vollmer sought to ensure that the police were authorized strictly by legal mandates and that they would focus exclusively on crime control, eschewing service activities that would easily lead to favoritism and loss of objectivity on the part of law enforcement personnel. Consequently, the administrative structure that was adopted during the reform era was centralized, and command was to be structured around military channels. Patrol was to be preventive, stressing rapid response to emergencies and crime control as the top priority of police work. This so-called professional model of policing that was characteristic of the reform era dominated law enforcement management practices until the tumultuous 1960s.

When advances in police research, not to mention volatile relations between the police and the public, revealed that the police could not reduce crime by their own efforts alone, the dawn of the third era was at hand. Almost as though history was repeating itself (with the exception of corruption and spoils, it was hoped), community reformers sought authorization from community members and extensive citizen support, a broad mandate that stressed the provision of services; a decentralized, responsive organizational structure; and intimate relations with citizens. A strong tie with citizens would be achieved through foot patrol, problem solving, quality-of-life preservation, and a host of other tactics, all of which were designed to ensure citizen satisfaction.

The sentiments of the community era were expressed in a prescient article by John Angell.[8] He argued that traditional bureaucracy was culture bound, that bureaucracy is inconsistent with the humanistic democratic values of the United States, that it demanded that employees demonstrate "immature" personality traits, and that it could

political era: an early period of policing characterized by excess corruption and politicization of policing.

reform era: a period of policing characterized by a move toward the professional model of policing. Emphasis on paramilitary organization and preventive patrol.

community era: a recent period of policing characterized by increased involvement by and input from members of the community.

not cope with environmental pressures. The community model would (1) improve community relations, which suffered under the bureaucratic, military model of law enforcement; (2) improve officer morale by allowing them a measure of flexibility in the performance of their duties; and (3) improve interagency coordination.

Reasons for Community Policing

The history of community policing represents a rich and nuanced trail of events and developments. A tendency in the literature has been to assume that community policing has emerged for simple reasons, such as poor police–citizen relations. But there is a great deal more to the origins of the new policing paradigm.

A few writers have called attention to the many reasons for the present community policing era. In a discussion concerning the "drive for change," one researcher has identified three reasons for the changes that are taking place now.[9] The first reason was, not surprisingly, citizen disenchantment with police services. "Minority citizens in inner cities continue[ed] to be frustrated by police who whisk[ed] in and out of their neighborhoods with little sensitivity to community norms and values."[10]

The second reason concerned social science research in the 1970s. Specifically, "research about preventive patrol, rapid response to calls for service, and investigative work—the three mainstays of police tactics—was uniformly discouraging."[11] The third reason for reform suggests that "patrol officers have been frustrated with their traditional role"[12] and that they began to demand improved methods of interacting with citizens. It is sometimes thought that such an approach improves police officer morale.

According to some other authors, community policing can be traced to two interrelated problems.[13] One problem was the isolation of police officers from citizens in patrol cars; the other problem stemmed from fear of victimization and perceptions of a rising crime rate. More specifically, the authors claimed that community policing "rose like a phoenix from the ashes of burned cities" because of

> (1) the isolation of officers in police cars; (2) the narrowing of the police mission to crime fighting; (3) an over-reliance on the scientific approach to management that stressed efficiency and effectiveness; (4) increased reliance on high-tech gadgetry instead of human interaction; (5) insulation of police administration from community input and accountability; (6) a long-standing concern about police violation of human rights; and (7) failed attempts by the police to reach the community, such as PCR, crime prevention, and team policing units.[14]

Still other reasons for the emergence of community policing can be identified. Community policing might be adopted by police organizations for selfish reasons, such as to make rank-and-file officers more content with their jobs.[15] A professional ethic (not to be confused with the professional era) or a desire to emulate progressive police agencies could be responsible for the current and widespread diffusion of community policing. Community policing might be a means of changing the goals of police work (from crime control to service, for example), of shaping public opinion instead of responding to it,[16] or of deflecting attention away from law enforcement officials.[17] Fiscal constraints might have served as a powerful motivator. Political culture and community characteristics could also explain the adoption of community policing.[18] Whatever the reasons for its present popularity, community policing owes its origins to multiple demands and historical contingencies. Figure 5.2 lists 20 possible reasons for community policing—some apparent, others less so.

1. Citizen disenchantment with police services
2. Research on the ineffectiveness of random patrol and quick response times
3. Patrol officers' frustration with traditional, reactive role
4. Isolation of officers from citizens, largely owing to increased use of patrol vehicles
5. Narrow crime-fighting police image
6. Overreliance on bureaucratic and paramilitary structure
7. Overreliance on high-tech gadgetry that diminishes personal interactions
8. Insulation of police administration from community input and accountability
9. Concern about human rights
10. Failure of police, traditionally, to reach out to the community
11. Desire to appear "with it" and professional
12. Desire to emulate other agencies
13. To change the goal of police work from crime control to service
14. To reduce police officers' work load
15. To deflect attention away from police departments to the community
16. A method of saving money
17. Community characteristics
18. Political culture of the surrounding area
19. To improve public image
20. To increase control over the community by adopting multiple strategies

FIGURE 5.2   Possible Reasons for Community Policing

COMMUNITY POLICING: WHAT IS IT?

Community policing is a relatively new approach to law enforcement that is premised on the assumption that the police and citizens must work together to control crime.[19] As one source defines it, community policing is

> a new philosophy of policing, based on the concept that police officers and citizens working together in creative ways can help solve contemporary community problems related to crime, fear of crime, social and physical disorder, and neighborhood decay.[20]

Another source has defined community policing in this way:

> Community policing is a reorientation of policing philosophy and strategy away from the view that police alone can reduce crime, disorder and fear. The strategy is based on the view that police don't help their communities very much by placing primary reliance on random preventive patrolling, rapid response to calls for service irrespective of their urgency, post-incident investigations to identify offenders, and other primarily reactive criminal justice system tactics.[21]

According to the Police Executive Research Forum (PERF), community policing consists of five different perspectives.[22] The first is the *deployment perspective,* which emphasizes the fact that police officers are deployed in a way that moves them closer to citizens. The second perspective is *community revitalization.* This emphasizes the importance of the police and citizens working closely together to improve neighborhoods and make them safer places. Next is the *problem-solving perspective.* Community policing is seen as an approach in which citizens and police work together to identify as well as respond to neighborhood problems. The fourth perspective is that of the *customer.* This emphasizes the importance of the police listening to citizens and serving them. Finally, according to PERF, the fifth community policing perspective is *legitimacy*. This emphasizes bolstering the credibility of the police through police–citizen partnerships.

Cordner has identified four principal dimensions of community policing and some of the common elements within them. The four dimensions of community policing that he identified were the philosophical dimension, the strategic dimension, the tactical dimension, and the organizational dimension.[23]

The philosophical dimension of community policing includes the ideas and beliefs surrounding the new paradigm of policing. Three such ideas underlying community policing include citizen input, an enhanced and broadened police function, and personal service.[24] Community policing can also be identified by its unique strategies, "the key operational concepts that translate philosophy into action."[25] Community policing strategies include, but are not limited to, reoriented operations (e.g., from cruiser patrol to foot patrol), geographical permanency (assigning patrol officers to the same areas for extended periods of time), and an emphasis on crime prevention (e.g., by police officers acting as mentors and role models).

Cordner's third dimension, the tactical dimension, is best understood as a culmination of the first two. "The tactical dimension of community policing ultimately translates ideas, philosophies, and strategies into concrete programs, practices, and behaviors."[26] This dimension stresses constructive interactions between the police and citizens, improved partnerships between law enforcement officials and the public, and problem solving. Finally, the organizational dimension, though not necessarily a fundamental part of community policing, is essential to its development. The structure of police agencies, management, and information services needs to adjust to accommodate community policing through changes such as decentralization, strategic planning, and program evaluation.

COMMUNITY POLICING: IS IT REALLY HAPPENING?

The rhetoric of community policing has become more or less institutionalized in American policing. In Chapter 3, we discussed the Violent Crime Control Act of 1994, the creation of the COPS Office in the U.S. Justice Department, and billions of dollars of grants to local law enforcement agencies to enhance their community policing capabilities. This program and other developments in U.S. policing over the past two decades have put the term *community policing* in nearly every police officer's vocabulary. But is there more to community policing than the term itself? Is community policing really happening, or do police departments just *say* that they're doing community policing? Two strains of research help us to answer these questions: research on changes to police departments and research on whether the rank and file are buying into community policing.

At a glance, this section might seem like a digression from our focus on approaches to the crime problem in America. It is not. If community policing is not really happening, then how can it lead to reductions in crime? With few exceptions, rhetoric does not reduce crime; concrete action is necessary. Therefore, it is critical that we briefly consider research on change and changing perceptions in American policing.

Structural Change

Researchers have questioned whether police departments have actually changed their structure in a way that is consistent with the spirit of community policing. A recent study on trends in police agencies' implementation of community policing from 1995 to 2000 is particularly telling.[27] The authors of that study concluded the following:

"Among organizational changes to support community policing activities, the most rapidly growing were those intended to signal change: revised mission statements and new performance review criteria for community police officers."[28] In other words, police departments are making mostly symbolic changes toward community policing.[29]

The author of another recent study reached the same conclusion: "The police still cling to an institutional definition that stresses crime control and not prevention."[30] He also concluded that "[b]y all available evidence, police organizations (their structures, division of labor, and the like) have not been radically or even significantly altered in the era of community and problem-oriented policing."[31] In short, many police agencies have adopted the basic tenets of community policing but without altering their basic organizational structure in a meaningful way.[32] Additional research appears to confirm the discouraging news that structural change linked to community policing is frustratingly slow.[33]

Attitudinal Change

If American police agencies are slow to change in response to community policing, what about police officers themselves? Here is one author's answer to this important question:

> Police have a remarkable ability to wait out efforts to reform them. Important aspects of police culture mitigate against change. Police resist the intrusion of civilians (who "can't really understand") into their business. They fear that community troublemakers will take over programs and that people will seek to use police for their private purposes or for personal revenge. When police dislike changes proposed from within, they snort that the top brass are "out of touch with the street."[34]

In short, the police are resistant to change. As we have seen, agencies are resistant to structural change. The above passage suggests that police officers themselves will actively take steps to thwart change. In fairness to law enforcement officials, other types of agencies—especially public agencies—also respond slowly to change. Nevertheless, it seems that community policing is being resisted by the police.

Two researchers recently described the efforts to do community policing in two mid-sized U.S. cities.[35] Those cities' police departments attempted four types of community policing: participatory management, community policing training, decentralization of certain police operations, and the creation of special community policing units. The authors then tracked the opinions of the officers in both cities over a six-year period. What they found is that a specialized community policing unit, not full-scale implementation of community policing, is desirable because not all officers will buy in. The researchers also found that despite the presence of different community policing approaches, much law enforcement business proceeded as it always had (e.g., routine patrol).

In a related study, researchers sought to determine whether community policing affects police officers' decisions to use coercion during encounters with suspected criminals.[36] They studied two cities, focusing in particular on whether community policing assignments, community policing training, and community partnerships affected officers' patterns of using coercion. Their analysis showed that neither of these variables had much of an effect on officers' decisions to use coercion, again lending support to previous studies that show how police are resistant to change. And in yet another study concerning alleged resistance to community policing, researchers reached the following conclusion:

> The current transitional period in urban policing in America has left police departments a legacy of fragmented organizational cultures, with a variety of approaches to police work pulling in contradictory directions. . . . Given recent evidence for the effectiveness of

community policing practices, widespread reports of implementation difficulties suggest that this morass may quickly become quicksand, suffocating reform efforts.[37]

THE DEFINITION PROBLEM REARS ITS HEAD

Community policing can be defined in almost innumerable ways. That is, there is an almost limitless choice of alternatives that police departments can pursue to improve police–citizen cooperation.[38] Figure 5.3 offers just a small list of possible approaches. The fact that there are multiple ways to define community policing is both an advantage and a disadvantage. It is advantageous because this suggests that community policing can be custom-tailored to the problems and needs of specific communities. It is disadvantageous because it is nearly impossible to draw generalizations about community policing's effect on crime when it is specifically designed for one location.

Just as there are many possible variations of the community policing theme, there are also many outcomes of potential interest. Researchers have expressed interest in studying the effect of community policing on outcomes such as citizen satisfaction, officer satisfaction, police legitimacy, neighborhood disorder, neighborhood appearance, crime, and fear. Therefore, judging community policing's effectiveness really requires defining which outcome is most important. But because in the end, community policing is intended to affect crime, let us briefly consider what the research tells us about its effect on crime.

Macro- and Micro-Level Research

Recall from Chapter 1 the statement that approaches to the crime problem that are resistant to specific definitions tend to be researched at the micro level. This is the case

1. Departmental sponsorship of a community newsletter
2. Additional officers on foot, bicycle, or horse patrol
3. Use of storefronts
4. Use of a task unit for solving special problems in targeted areas
5. Victim contact program
6. Crime prevention or community policing education of the public
7. Crime prevention or community policing education of officers
8. Fixed assignments of officers to certain neighborhoods
9. Reassignment of some personnel from patrol to crime prevention
10. Taking some officers off 911 response for community contact work
11. Use of a citizen survey to keep police informed of local problems
12. Neighborhood watch
13. Business watch
14. Use of a citizen satisfaction survey
15. Block meetings between police officers and community members
16. Increased hiring of civilians for non–law enforcement work
17. Officers who serve as community liaisons
18. Reassessment of ranks and assignments by the administration
19. Reducing and/or cutting back on middle-management positions
20. Allowing patrol officers to manage selected cases from beginning to end

FIGURE 5.3   Twenty Examples of Community Policing

with community policing. Because it is so easy to conceive of multiple examples of community policing, the literature is almost completely devoid of macro-level research on its effectiveness. The reason for this is that there is no one best definition of community policing. It is inherently a place-specific approach to the crime problem.

Although many common themes—such as citizen participation, decentralization, problem solving, and the like—can be found in community policing programs across the country, this approach to the crime problem is still ill-defined. This means that almost all of the literature directly concerned with community policing's effectiveness (or the lack thereof) has a micro-level orientation. A perusal of the endnotes in the sections throughout the remainder of this chapter will offer evidence of this.

RESEARCH ON COMMUNITY POLICING'S EFFECTIVENESS

The research on community policing's effectiveness can be divided into three categories that correspond to the types of community policing discussed in the first paragraph of this chapter. First, we consider strategies in which the police either physically go out into the community or take steps to improve their public image so that citizens will be more trusting of police and willing to report crime. Second, we will examine strategies in which the police bring people into the world of law enforcement through, most commonly, citizen patrol and citizen police academies. Third, we will look at community policing strategies that rely on mutual exchange of ideas and information between police and citizens. For lack of a better term, this is called *integrated community policing*.

Moving the Police into the Community

The most common approach to community policing has been to move the police out into the community in some fashion. In other words, most of the literature addressing the effectiveness of community policing emphasizes a police-to-citizens approach. Comparatively few studies exist concerning the effectiveness of (1) the citizens-to-police approach and (2) truly collaborative crime control between police and citizens.

It is interesting that most community policing literature focuses on strategies that move the police into the community. It is no accident that this has occurred. Our review of the literature on resistance to community policing suggests that law enforcement agencies wish to maintain a degree of control over their operations. Strategies that move police officers into the community allow departments to maintain control. Alternatives that give citizens strength and authority tend to be met with resistance.

citizen contact patrol: a method of policing typically characterized by door-to-door contacts with residents by police officers.

CITIZEN CONTACT PATROL. One community policing approach that appears promising consists of door-to-door contacts by police officers. This is known as **citizen contact patrol**.[39] This occurs when police officers knock on people's doors, introduce themselves, give out information, and otherwise try to make policing more personal in nature. Police have also used this so-called citizen contact patrol to obtain information about who is carrying guns on the street,[40] to provide citizens with burglary reduction tips,[41] and to offer advice to citizens about how to deal with domestic violence problems.[42]

Researchers have found that such door-to-door visits result in decreased victimization. For example, at least two studies show that door-to-door visits by police led to reductions in victimization.[43] Two other studies found reductions in victimization following door-to-door contacts, but the contacts were supplemented with either storefronts (discussed later in this section)[44] or buy-bust operations.[45] But three additional studies show that door-to-door contacts led to no reductions in victimization.[46] Needless to say, these findings are conflicting. They also make it difficult to draw conclusions about the effect of door-to-door contacts by police on crime.

To sift through some of these conflicting studies, it is useful to consider some of their specific findings. For example, one of the studies showed that door-to-door contacts reduced victimization but largely for vehicular burglaries and minor property crimes.[47] Another researcher concluded that door-to-door contacts worked best in middle-class, predominantly white neighborhoods.[48] Referring to some of the positive outcomes associated with Houston's citizen contact patrol approach, the following observation was made:

> The darker side of these successes came to light in tests of the *generality* of the impact of the programs. Across a number of social indicators—most strongly in terms of race and class—those at the bottom of the local status ladder were severely underrepresented in terms of awareness and contact with the programs, and were unaffected by them. In short, the better-off got better off, and the disparity between area residents grew deeper.[49]

This suggests, on the one hand, that the citizen contact approach to the crime problem has a slim chance of succeeding where it is needed the most. On the other hand, it does not appear that citizens in more disadvantaged areas received the treatment to begin with, so we cannot conclude with certainty that citizen contact patrol is a crime control failure. Nor can we conclude that it is a success.

IMPROVING THE POLICE IMAGE.   Another object of study has addressed whether increased efforts by the police to improve their legitimacy in the minds of citizens reduces crime. One researcher found a strong correlation between citizens' trust of the police and citizens' willingness to obey the law.[50] Similarly, researchers have found that citizens perceive less crime in areas where the trust in the police is high.[51] Another study showed that repeat domestic violence was lowest among arrestees who thought that the police had treated them respectfully.[52] In that study, the researchers concluded: "When police acted in a procedurally fair manner when arresting assault suspects, the rate of subsequent domestic violence was significantly lower than when they did not."[53]

Interestingly, there is a growing literature in place concerning public perceptions of the police.[54] It is closely tied to the movement toward community policing because it is believed that citizens must have confidence in and trust the police if truly collaborative crime control is to be accomplished. Early studies confirm that most citizens view the police positively.[55] Despite some suspicions about state power and authority, law enforcement officers are viewed with relative favor.[56] But such sentiments are not equal across all levels of American society. Many members of minority groups, for example, tend to display contempt for police officers.[57] In contrast, the elderly are more inclined to view the police favorably,[58] as are more affluent individuals.[59] It is unclear what role sex plays in terms of support for the police.[60]

Important for our purposes, some researchers have concluded that when crime is salient in one's life, confidence in the police is undermined.[61] Perceptions of disorder are linked to support (and the lack of support) for the police.[62] There is also evidence to suggest that individuals who "dislike the characteristics of their neighborhoods" are likely to have negative feelings about the police.[63] Together, these findings offer an explanation for police attempts to improve their legitimacy in the eyes of citizens. The logic is that crime control can be accomplished better with a trusting citizenry, one that is inclined to contact—rather than avoid—the police once problems surface. Community policing relies heavily on positive relationships between police and citizens.

ORGANIZING NEIGHBORHOOD WATCH PROGRAMS.   Most people are familiar with **neighborhood watch** programs. All one needs to do is drive through a suburban neighborhood, and one will encounter signs highlighting "Block Watch" and similar programs. These and other neighborhood watch programs are sometimes started by neighborhood residents; at other times, they are started at the urging of local police departments. Most of the research in this area is concerned with the ability of the police to organize neighborhood watch programs for the purpose of reducing criminal activity.

neighborhood watch: also called "neighborhood watch" or sometimes "crime watch," an approach to crime control that relies heavily on citizen volunteers who "scan" a particular area for evidence of wrongdoing and reporting such activity to police. Neighborhood watch programs are sometimes coordinated and organized with a certain degree of local law enforcement involvement.

Unfortunately, the literature devoted to neighborhood watch is almost uniformly unsupportive of this approach to America's crime problem. One study out of Minneapolis sought to determine whether neighborhood watch (with and without police participation) reduced crime. Random assignment was used, which added a level of sophistication to the study, but researchers found no effect on crime.[64] One earlier study showed a link between neighborhood watch and a reduction in burglary for a period of 18 months,[65] but this study appears isolated. For example, researchers in Cincinnati found that neighborhood watches and other community-based organizations had no effect on crime.[66]

Researchers have attributed these findings to the reluctance among citizens to organize neighborhood watch programs in poor, high-crime areas.[67] This reluctance either stems from fear of the police or from distrust between neighbors.[68] To make matters worse, researchers have found that in the areas where neighborhood watch programs flourish (usually middle-class neighborhoods), the programs *increase* rather than decrease fear of crime. This effect was also witnessed in a study of "apartment watch," the equivalent of neighborhood watch for apartments.[69] The scientific literature thus appears to show that police officers who work with citizens to organize neighborhood watch programs in high-crime urban areas could better spend their time on other activities.

HOSTING COMMUNITY MEETINGS.   Sometimes the police host meetings with community members in an effort to identify and deal with specific crime problems and locations. These community meetings are different from neighborhood watch because, unlike neighborhood watch, they are not surveillance-oriented. Instead, they place police officers and community members in the same facility so that they can hash out ideas about crime prevention and control. Community meetings also differ from neighborhood watch in that they are often held in public places, such as a police station, a community center, or city hall. Neighborhood watch is usually organized in neighborhoods.

What does the research show? Not much, because, surprisingly, the effectiveness of community meetings as a crime control mechanism has been subjected to virtually no research. One study of community meetings in Madison, Wisconsin, suggests that community meetings had no effect on crime whatsoever.[70] This was a National Institute of Justice–sponsored evaluation that was carefully conducted. Another study of community meetings, this time in Chicago, suggests that this approach to the crime problem might or might not be effective.[71] That study showed that community meetings led to reductions in certain types of crime and victimization but not others. Before making any claims about the effectiveness of community meetings for crime control, it would be helpful to see additional research.

DISSEMINATING CRIME CONTROL NEWSLETTERS. Police departments have also experimented with disseminating crime control newsletters to community members. These newsletters often contain information on recent developments at the police department, crime statistics in the area, tips for avoiding victimization, and so on. Unfortunately, the research shows that when police officers disseminate these newsletters throughout the community, crime rates remain relatively constant.[72] Other forms of public education, particularly education on domestic violence, appear to be ineffective as well.[73]

One fairly comprehensive study on the use of crime control newsletters focused on Evanston, Indiana; Houston, Texas; and Newark, New Jersey. Although the researchers did not consider the effect of the newsletters on crime, they did reach the following important conclusion:

> There is no evidence that disseminating crime prevention information and crime statistics has any sizable negative effects on the citizenry, at least none as measured by these evaluations. At the same time, there is some evidence that such newsletters may have positive effects in reinforcing citizen coproduction of community safety. In all three cities, those who received the newsletters were overwhelmingly enthusiastic about continuing the dissemination of this type of information.[74]

In other words, although newsletters might not be linked to crime rates per se, their public relations benefits might outweigh their costs.

STOREFRONTS AND SUBSTATIONS. Most of us have happened on a police information booth in a shopping mall or police officers occupying a building in a strip mall. These storefronts and substations are consistent with the spirit of community policing; they bring police officers in closer contact with citizens. The logic is that members of the public might be more likely to talk with police officers in a place that they frequent instead of having to physically go to the police station, which might be inconveniently located. Here is one researcher's description of a storefront in action:

> [Substation] personnel took crime reports and gave and received information, and the police provided a place for people to meet with police. [Substation] officers were freed from routine patrol. . . . The office was to be their base of operations for getting acquainted with neighborhood residents and business people, identifying local problems and helping solve them, seeking ways of delivering better service to the area, and developing programs to draw the police and community closer together.[75]

Somewhat discouragingly, most research suggests that the presence of police offices in storefronts and strip malls does not affect crime.[76]

There is not much convincing evidence that such police substations are necessary to begin with; they tend to pop up in areas where they are needed the least. Placing police officers in strip malls and storefronts might improve public perceptions of the police,[77] but there is no evidence that much else is accomplished. Part of the reason for this might be that substations are largely informational and passive. That is, they are more often concerned with providing information about crime control to the public; comparatively little attention is given to proactive crime control. Some substations are staffed by civilian personnel or volunteers, making it doubtful that they could do much to affect crime rates.

SPECIALIZED PATROLS. Another community policing strategy consists of specialized patrols. The most common is **foot patrol**. This is where officers get out of their cars and patrol their beats on foot in an effort to develop closer relationships with citizens.

foot patrol: an approach to policing that relies primarily on officers patrolling specified beats while on foot.

Naturally, foot patrol works better in some areas than in others. Pedestrian malls and downtown areas obviously lend themselves more readily to foot patrol than suburban and rural areas do. Other specialized patrols include bicycle patrol and horse patrol.

The most researched type of specialized patrol is foot patrol, so we will focus on it. Much research suggests that citizens are more likely to notice police when they patrol on foot,[78] and some research suggests that citizens are more satisfied with police following the implementation of foot patrol.[79] But does this approach reduce crime? One study suggests that foot patrol was associated with a reduction in public order offenses such as vagrancy, disorderly conduct, and vandalism.[80] Another suggested that foot patrol in Flint, Michigan, reduced crime, but the authors of the study did not control for other factors that have been linked to reported crime.[81] In one of the most recent and sophisticated studies on the subject, researchers found that targeted foot patrols in crime hot spots led to significant reductions in violent crime that lasted well after the intervention ended.[82]

OPERATION IDENTIFICATION. Operation Identification is a program whereby property owners can use an engraver to mark their personal possessions in an effort to prevent the items from being stolen or at least to make them easier to recover if they are stolen.[83] Sometimes police will respond to citizen requests by providing them with an engraver. Other times, citizens can check engravers out from the police station. Still other times, the police will sponsor public events at which citizens can learn about crime prevention and have an opportunity to engrave items (such as bicycles) that they bring with them.

Virtually no research is available concerning the effect of Operation Identification and similar identification programs. One of the few published studies examined a burglary prevention program in Portland, Oregon.[84] Officers there began by directly contacting citizens in high-crime areas. The officers then coordinated community meetings at which the program was explained, engraving equipment was distributed, and decals signifying residents' participation in the program were disseminated. Participants were educated about techniques used by burglars and were given several burglary prevention tips.

Clearly, the Portland program did more than supply citizens with engraving equipment, but, again, it is one of few studies in this area. What did the evaluation show? It showed that citizens who participated in the program were more likely to report burglaries, but the program had virtually no effect on property recovery rates. Also, the research was unable to conclude that the program had a dramatic effect on citywide burglary. The rate before the program was 151 burglaries per 1,000 citizens compared to 127 per 1,000 after the program. According to the author of the research report, "These figures indicated that there *may* have been a citywide decline in burglaries."[85] Unfortunately, there was no attempt to include another area to serve as a control group. The only other studies dealing with Operation Identification are government-sponsored evaluations from the 1970s, almost none of which paints Operation Identification in a favorable light.[86]

POLICE-SPONSORED TELEVISION AND WEBSITES. One of the easiest methods for police departments to bring citizens closer is to develop a website. With the proliferation of home computers and the increasing number of people who are connected to the Web, this strategy can both benefit the police and help citizens. The police can benefit, for instance, by giving citizens an opportunity to report on problems in their neighborhood. In fact, some departments allow citizens to complete hot spot reports online and to submit noncriminal complaints electronically. At the same time, citizens can learn about new approaches the department has taken, see pictures of dangerous fugitives, view active warrants, and otherwise develop familiarity with their local police department.

Apart from the obvious community relations gains associated with a website, can this avenue of information dissemination be expected to reduce crime? Unfortunately, it is impossible to know for sure. There are no published studies concerned with the crime control benefits of this technological development. In what appears to be the only article on this subject, the most the author could conclude is that, mostly consistent with what we have already said, websites increase communication, generate leads, increase awareness, and can possibly lead to the apprehension of criminal suspects.[87] Little else is known.

Police departments have also begun to avail themselves of social networking, using Facebook, Twitter, and other programs to reach out to the community, keep citizens posted on recent developments, and assist with criminal investigations. Unfortunately, no research is available as of this writing that considers whether these approaches are effective from a crime control standpoint.

A similar approach to the development of a website is to use television as a medium to get closer to the community. Some police departments, usually in the largest jurisdictions, actually have their own community access channel. Sometimes programs such as "John TV" are broadcast, in which men who are alleged to have solicited prostitutes have their faces and names displayed on television for all to see. Other times, police departments run television shows and TV spots in an effort to improve the ways in which citizens view their local police force. No research is available on the effectiveness of this strategy.

POLICE IN SCHOOLS. Police officers are coming to occupy a significant position in our nation's schools. Police who work in schools are often called **school resource officers**.[88] A national organization known as the National Association of School Resource Officers represents many of these officers from across the United States.[89] Police are also collaborating more with schools, and schools sometimes opt to hire private security personnel to patrol campuses and preserve a safe learning environment.

school resource officer: a police officer stationed primarily in a school (typically a public high school). Most school resource officers (SROs) are specially trained, veteran law enforcement personnel who serve a mix of enforcement, educational, and counseling functions.

The movement of police officers (and related security personnel) into schools can be attributed, in part, to the diffusion of community policing; officers interacting with students might help by improving police–citizen relationships. Here is how one source describes the community policing dimension of police in schools: "Children get to know their community police officers better, develop an understanding of the impact of violence and trauma, and learn adaptive means of dealing with the consequences of exposure to violence and trauma."[90]

On the other hand, police officers are present in schools because of incidents such as the infamous Columbine shooting and the 2012 Sandy Hook Elementary shooting in Newtown, Pennsylvania. In this view, police are there to do little more then preserve school security. This approach might actually weaken relationships between children and police. Regardless of the reasons behind the growing presence of police in schools, a simple question presents itself: Does it reduce crime?

There is much anecdotal evidence suggesting that putting police officers in schools can reduce crime and deviance[91], but there is a dearth of scientific evidence suggesting that this law enforcement approach can make a difference. A researcher in the United Kingdom examined the placement of uniformed police officers on a full-time basis in local elementary schools.[92] Preliminary evaluation findings suggest that the officers were able to reduce truancy and bullying, but the evaluation had not yet been completed as of this writing.

Another study suggests that school–police partnerships are helpful. The study focused on a Truant Recovery Program in the West Contra Costa Unified School District in California.[93] The program was not, however, limited to placing police officers in schools; local police worked with the schools to find and recover truant children. In the study, 178 juveniles were randomly selected for an 18- to 21-month follow-up. Results revealed that the youths who were recovered during truancy sweeps behaved better in schools, but their number of arrests during the follow-up period actually increased.

One of the most recent studies examined a program known as Community Outreach Through Police in Schools. The program, implemented by the Child Development–Community Policing Program at Yale University, is "a short-term, prevention-oriented, school-based group intervention that brings together community police officers and child clinicians as group coleaders to provide weekly sessions for middle school students who are at risk of being exposed to violence in the community."[94] Preliminary evaluation results suggest that the program helps youths to cope with exposure to violence, but the program's effects on crime and deviance among schoolchildren was not examined.

Does It Work?

Police departments around the country have begun to move toward community policing. Part of this approach has entailed moving the police presence out into the community in one way or another. There are many methods of doing this; we have reviewed 10 of the more common (and researched) approaches. With the exception of foot patrol, most of the research is either unsupportive of these approaches or indicates a need for additional study. Few of the approaches appear linked with reductions in crime. They might improve departments' public image and be satisfactory to citizens, but their effects on crime remain to be seen. The exception, again, is foot patrol.

Integrated Community Policing

Thus far, the evidence in favor of community policing is not particularly favorable. This could be because community policing simply does not give enough attention to crime prevention and instead prizes improved police–citizen relations, improved officer morale, and reductions in fear of crime. The lack of favorable evidence might also be due to the fact that this chapter has considered community policing strategies in isolation. That is, we have focused on the independent effects on crime of approaches such as foot patrol, neighborhood watch, and citizen police academies.

What this section is concerned with is an *integrated* approach to community policing. Some of the research that has already been discussed in this chapter dealt with multiple community policing strategies at the same time, but we focused on specific strategies to determine whether—standing alone—they can be expected to reduce crime. To minimize duplication of the previous discussions of community policing approaches, this section turns attention to two important evaluations of community policing programs: in Seattle, Washington, and Hartford, Connecticut. Both were impressive examples of citywide, fully integrated community policing efforts. Both, however, have since been discontinued.

THE SEATTLE APPROACH.   Seattle's Community Crime Prevention Program (CCPP) integrated several of the strategies we have discussed thus far.[95] Mostly in response to a rise in burglaries, officials began by contacting community organizations to alert them of their intentions to target burglary. Focusing on specific locations in the city where burglary was a problem, officials then contacted neighborhood residents. They first sent out mailings alerting residents of their intentions; then a door-to-door contact campaign was started. The intention of the mailings and the contacts was to secure citizen buy-in. The alert reader will note that we have already discussed both of these approaches (newsletters and citizen contact patrol) in isolation.

After contacts had been made, the CCPP program began several primary services. These included organizing a block watch program, beginning an Operation ID program so that residents could mark their property, and conducting home security inspections to inform residents about vulnerabilities to burglary. Again, these approaches were also discussed earlier in this chapter. Seattle's CCPP program was different, however, because it combined all three—along with additional approaches—into a single, uniform, and very deliberate community policing strategy.

On top of the approaches just discussed, officials in Seattle took careful steps to maintain the program so that public interest didn't wane, and advisory services were provided to those who wanted them. In summary, what made the CCPP program somewhat unique is that it targeted a single problem (i.e., burglary). Together with this singular focus, officials used several separate community policing strategies—coupled with citizen contacts and efforts to keep the program alive. Three separate victimization surveys were then conducted. Included in the sample were people who were involved in the CCPP program and people who were not involved in the CCPP program. All three surveys showed modest reductions in burglary, suggesting that an integrated community policing strategy can be effective.[96]

THE HARTFORD APPROACH.   A very different integrated approach was taken in Hartford, Connecticut.[97] There, the police began by assessing the nature of criminal activity in the Asylum Hill area of the city. They paid special attention to the way in which the physical environment contributed to criminal activity (we discuss environmental factors further in Chapter 14). From their analysis of the Asylum Hill area, they decided to target the northern half of the area. They then implemented a three-pronged approach to crime in that area.

First, proposals for changing the physical environment were submitted. This was undertaken in an effort to make the area less conducive to criminal activity. Ultimately, several changes were made to the physical environment, such as restricting traffic flow on certain streets to residential traffic only. Then efforts were taken to organize the community. Before the program, there was one citizen group in the north Asylum Hill area. Over a period of six months, two more organizations were formed. Next, a group of police officers was permanently assigned to the area, and these officers were given a fair degree of autonomy to make their own decisions. This decentralized approach was taken to build lasting relationships and trust between police officers and neighborhood residents.

An evaluation was then conducted after the program had been up and running for some time. Although it did not show the program was a resounding success, it did show that integrative community policing strategies can have some beneficial effects. For example, the evaluators concluded that "[t]here is no doubt that the people in the North Asylum Hill were significantly less fearful and concerned about crime after the program was implemented than one would have expected given the trends in the rest of the city."[98] Examining victimization data, they also concluded that "burglary dropped significantly below its expected levels immediately after the program was implemented, but then rose significantly during the following two years."[99] Although this latter finding was not wholly desirable, at least it showed an initial reduction in one prevalent type of crime.

Does It Work?

Evaluations of integrated community policing efforts are positive. This suggests, on the one hand, that multiple community policing strategies in combination with one another are better than individual strategies in isolation. On the other hand, though, the Seattle and Hartford experiments have long been abandoned, and it is unclear whether they would work today. Unfortunately, the number of rigorous community policing evaluations—especially evaluations of several strategies operating in the same place at the same time—has appeared to taper off.

Bringing the Community to the Police

Thus far, we have examined community policing strategies that are operated largely by the police. The strategies covered are best considered one-way because the police develop and/or coordinate them. Moreover, they are one-way in the sense that the police are the ones who go out into the community to work with citizens in numerous ways. An alternative to these approaches is to bring citizens to the police. Although this is still something that is run and coordinated by the police, it is different insofar as citizens are brought into the law enforcement world. In recent years, this has occurred in two ways: citizen patrol and citizen police academies.

citizen patrol: citizen volunteers who engage in preventive patrol.

CITIZEN PATROL.   There are hundreds, if not thousands, of **citizen patrols** around the United States.[100] Typically, citizen patrols comprise volunteers who engage in preventive patrol. Citizen patrol volunteers are often provided with some type of government vehicle and often patrol the streets during daylight hours. Sometimes, however, citizens volunteer to drive their own vehicles and operate independently of the police. This section considers police-sponsored citizen patrols.

An example of citizen patrol that has received some attention is the Neighborhood Patrol Officers program in Fort Worth, Texas.[101] Started in 1991, the program provided eight hours of training to volunteers covering topics such as rules of conduct, liability issues, and legal considerations. Once training was completed, volunteers were issued an identification badge, a T-shirt, a hat, and a jacket. They also received police radios. Once trained and equipped, the volunteers used their own vehicles to patrol neighborhoods, looking for evidence of serious crimes.

Do citizen patrols work? To date, no formal studies appear to have been completed. One researcher has been especially critical of citizen patrols, arguing that they are evidence of an ever-widening system of control and give legitimacy to traditional, antiquated police strategies (such as routine preventive patrol).[102] One of the few studies that come close to evaluating the effectiveness of citizen patrol reported on a survey of citizens' and police officers' attitudes toward the Guardian Angels, an unsanctioned civilian patrol group that patrols the streets and subways of New York City. Most of the respondents thought that such patrol should be performed by armed, state-sanctioned police.[103] In fact, two other studies suggest that citizen patrol of this sort might exacerbate fear and has no discernible effect on crime.[104]

It is perplexing that citizen patrol has not received more attention from researchers. There is a fascination with uniformed, sworn police officers but apparently not with citizens who perform basic patrol functions. To determine whether citizen patrol works, however, would take a carefully crafted evaluation, ideally with treatment and control groups. Even if such a study were possible, it is doubtful that citizen patrol would prove effective. One need only read the literature on random police patrol that we discussed in Chapter 3. In that chapter, we saw that simple random patrol by police is one of the least effective crime control strategies. There is no reason to suspect that citizen patrol is any more effective.

CITIZEN POLICE ACADEMIES.   Many police departments operate so-called citizen police academies.[105] There are several varieties of citizen police academies, all having a common element: Citizens are given an opportunity to learn about the policing profession and even to experience some of the sensations that uniformed officers experience.[106] This is usually accomplished through a watered-down version of a police academy in which citizens are taught the nature, operations, and complexity of the policing profession.[107] Sometimes citizens even learn to use firearms and otherwise defend themselves from victimization.

It is tempting to ask the question "Do citizen police academies work?" but one must first understand their purpose. It is difficult to fathom any crime reduction benefits associated with citizen police academies; that is not their direct intent. Rather, the academies are more likely to affect citizens' perceptions of the police than to reduce crime. That is what the research suggests. The authors of one recent study found that citizen police academy participants viewed the police more favorably after completing the program.[108] This finding appears to have been replicated in at least two studies.[109]

Other researchers have been critical of citizen patrol academies. One researcher found that the academy participants tend to be mostly community elites and that minorities are drastically underrepresented.[110] The argument has also been raised that citizen patrol academies—like citizen patrol programs—perpetuate a traditional law enforcement strategy and might in fact be antithetical to the spirit of community policing.[111] This argument becomes quite convincing when police departments teach civilians many law enforcement tricks of the trade, such as self-defense techniques.

What can be gleaned from the literature on citizen patrol academies? They appear to improve public perceptions of and attitudes toward the police, but people who participate in the academies might already be more prone to viewing the police favorably before enrolling in the curriculum. As far as the effect of citizen patrol academies on crime, there is no evidence that there is any. We reach this conclusion for two reasons. First, there is a total lack of research on the subject. Second, the practice of giving citizens a window into the law enforcement world is intended to do little more than improve the image of the police.

Does It Work?

Citizen patrol and citizen police academies might have noble purposes. They might also improve police–public relations. Improved relations with the public might be a very desirable outcome for law enforcement organizations. But on the basis of the available literature, there is little evidence suggesting that these approaches should be implemented as crime reduction mechanisms. The random police patrol literature covered in Chapter 3 suggests that citizen patrols cannot reduce crime, and citizen police academies are not really intended to reduce crime at all.

Supporters of citizen patrol and, in particular, of citizen police academies claim that positive relationships between police officers and the public are almost as important as is crime reduction itself. They further claim that citizens who view their police favorably will be more inclined to call on the police when in need. This could lead to an eventual reduction in crime. These arguments are attractive and possibly correct, but because one of the most important purposes of an organized police force is to promote public safety, the police might want to direct their energies more toward methods that are likely to directly further that purpose.

THIRD-PARTY POLICING

third-party policing:
"police efforts to
persuade or coerce
nonoffending persons
to take actions which
are outside the scope
of their routine
activities, and which
are designed to
indirectly minimize
disorder caused by
other persons or to
reduce the possibility
that crime may
occur."

Third-party policing is a recently coined term to describe "police efforts to persuade or coerce nonoffending persons to take actions which are outside the scope of their routine activities, and which are designed to indirectly minimize disorder caused by other persons or to reduce the possibility that crime may occur."[112] Basically, it amounts to formal methods of policing that invoke the use of the **civil law** rather than the criminal law. A criminal law approach to policing has officers arresting people for commission of crimes. A civil law approach, by contrast, has not just the police but other officials relying on civil process, such as nuisance abatement and code enforcement, to reduce crime and disorder.

Michael Buerger and Lorraine Mazerolle, the scholars who first conceived the term *third-party policing*, distinguish it from community policing and problem-oriented policing because of its intended targets: "In community- and problem-oriented policing, the police assume an active quasi-enforcement and managerial role in addition to their more established, hortatory [i.e., encouraging] role as dispensers of expert advice."[113] They go on to argue that community policing and problem solving are simply augmented versions of traditional policing that rely heavily on citizens and guardians (those responsible for places, like landlords) for influence and control over criminals and would-be criminals. Third-party policing is different from this because "it focuses on the places that the guardians control by promoting certain collective responses as a way of controlling individual behavior."[114] In other words, third-party policing is more place-oriented than person-oriented.

Do not confuse third-party policing with environmental criminology, either. Environmental criminology is concerned with the design of "places" such that crime is made more difficult to commit (e.g., access control with a tall security gate). These types of strategies are covered in Chapter 14. Third-party policing is place-oriented, but it is not concerned with "design." Instead, it is about arming guardians with the information and tools they need to take a certain element of law enforcement into their own hands.

There is a possible "dark side" to third-party policing, however. It is not just about encouraging guardians to target problems at the places they are responsible for. It is about *coercing them* to do so. Once again according to Buerger and Mazerolle, "Third-party policing constitutes a return to a compliance model of policing, although the police do not resume inspectorial functions. . . . Rather, these functions are performed by nominal partners of the police, or remain an implied threat behind police negotiations with guardians."

Let's return to our definition of third-party policing. We mentioned "nonoffending" persons. These are the guardians. They are basically persuaded by police to do something about identified problems "or else." Simply put, "third-party policing establishes a control over nonoffending persons and persuades (or coerces) them to engage in activities thought to control crime."[115]

At its core, some would say that third-party policing is about "passing the buck," of turning certain enforcement functions over to those who haven't traditionally done it. Others, though, would argue that this is simply good law enforcement, that it is intended to bring guardians out of the shadows to take control over their properties. The police might, for instance, coerce a slum lord to fix a problem at one of his or her apartment complexes or face possible civil consequences. What do we mean by civil consequences? Let us begin by answering that question, then we will provide some specific examples of this idea of third-party policing.

Beyond the Criminal Law

Police routinely use the criminal law, not to mention local ordinances, curfew statutes, and the like to target crime. Third-party policing is more "outside the box" than this. It primarily invokes civil law provisions. These, according to Buerger and Mazerolle, are "controls imported from the regulatory wing of the civil law [that] include provisions that allow the police to target deviant places, typically crackhouses, blighted homes, and false-front stores (such as 'bodegas' that sell drugs or traffic in black-market food stamps."[116] In truth, the civil law has always been available to the police, but it is with the recent proliferation of problem solving and community policing that officials have turned to more "creative" methods of crime control.

Civil law provisions, like those governing building codes, have been used periodically in law enforcement and, indeed, throughout the public sector to target problems. A dilapidated building that is replete with code violations can be shut down and/or condemned, something officials have done for years. Recently, though, scores of cities have capitalized on civil ordinances, and several have even created their own. San Diego, for example, recently enacted an anti-illegal street racing ordinance that uses civil mechanisms, namely forfeiture, to confiscate racers' cars.

Some Examples of Third-Party Policing

Oakland, California's Beat Health Program is a good example of third-party policing. The program, which is now defunct, operated as follows:

> The Beat Health team will open a "case" (1) after preliminary site visits to a zone that is identified as a potential problem, owing to a high number of narcotic arrests, citizen complaints, or (2) at the request of community groups. Beat Health teams try to establish relationships with place managers (landlords, managers, owners, or tenants of properties) or with others who hold a stake in improving the conditions of the case location. During the intervention, police communicate landlords' rights and tenants' responsibilities, provide ideas for crime prevention measures, and assist civilians in contacting city or community agencies (for legal, ordinance, and rental information). Officers maintain contact with property owners and place managers for [six] months afterward. Beat Health officers also coordinate site visits with the Specialized Multi-Agency Response Team (SMART), composed of a group of city inspectors. Based on initial assessments made by the police, representatives from various agencies such as housing, fire, public works, gas, and electric or vector control are invited to inspect, enforce city codes, and offer solutions to related issues.[117]

The initial contacts were as collegial as possible. The teams attempted to build rapport with the property owners. For those owners who failed to cooperate, however, the more coercive arm of third-party policing was brought to bear on the problem. Interestingly, Mazerolle was one of the evaluators of this program, finding that the most effective means of precipitating change was the identification of sewer and fire violations, which landlords were required to fix.[118] Additionally, the program appeared to have been more successful in commercial rather than residential facilities and third-party policing coupled with traditional enforcement (such as targeting drug offenders) appeared to be the most effective approach.[119]

The Minneapolis Repeat Call Address Policing (RECAP) program began with police officers presenting call histories to the owners and managers of problem properties. Not surprisingly, a number of them knew about the problems; others, though, did not, or deliberately ignored them. Officers then explained that improvements would be mutually beneficial. For example, businesses would attract more customers, and thereby make more profits, if police weren't routinely called to the property and seen arresting people. Owners of rental properties were told that better tenants would be more likely to pay their rent and, of course, add to the bottom line.

The program began with no official mandate from the city and was thus forced to operate only out of the police department. It eventually grew into something larger, however, and it began to partner with other officials, such as those in the city housing inspector's office.[120] The police department's licensing division was also "revived" from a period of dormancy to target problem bar owners:

> When RECAP succeeded in having the licenses of the two most notorious bars revoked (an action unprecedented in recent Minneapolis history), city officials took note of the benefits to be derived from demanding responsible ownership.[121]

The Minneapolis and Oakland stories represent the proverbial tip of the iceberg. Police departments are increasingly wising up to the idea that civil law can work just as well for crime control, in some instances, as criminal law. Beyond the policing realm, other criminal justice officials, particularly prosecutors, are doing the same. Some of the time, prosecutors work closely with the police because they bring to the table the legal knowledge and ability to pursue appropriate actions in court. While third-party policing is catching on, it hasn't been subject to extensive evaluation. A few examples of research were cited, but much more remains to be done in order to identify best practices.

Does It Work?

Third-party policing may look like, as we said, "passing the buck," but in reality it is a creative strategy that police use to get private parties to do their part. It is unrealistic to expect police to do everything. If a landlord is not doing his or her part, then some subtle coercion to get him or her to do so seems eminently sensible. While third-party policing can take on an air of heavy-handedness, most of the time it works through *cooperation* with nonoffending persons. This is why it is covered in this chapter. Whether it is truly effective as crime control, though, remains to be seen. Too few evaluations have been published.

Summary

Community involvement in policing is a ubiquitous phenomenon in this day and age. Countless forms of community policing exist. Police officers are trained in it, books are written on it, and there are even criminal justice classes devoted to it. Taken together with problem-solving policing and the community justice movement, it would appear that we are witnessing a major paradigmatic shift in the way law enforcement is accomplished in the United States. But is this a movement in the right direction? It is difficult to argue that it is not, but the research concerning community involvement in policing is at least a little disheartening.

The message of this chapter is that most community-policing approaches to the crime problem (with the likely exception of foot patrol)— by themselves—do not appear to alter crime rates markedly. Whether police departments move their presence into the community or bring citizens closer to police departments, giving them an eye into the law enforcement world, most research is either unsupportive or uncertain with respect to the effectiveness of each approach. But this does not mean we should throw our arms up in despair. Some studies *do* show that an integrated approach to community policing, one that draws on several strategies simultaneously, can have promising effects. Likewise, third-party policing shows promise, but more research is necessary before we can safely label it "effective."

Notes

1. T.R. Clear and E. Cadora, *Community Justice* (Belmont, CA: Wadsworth, 2003), 1.
2. Ibid., 1–2.
3. V.G. Strecher, *Planning Community Policing* (Prospect Heights, IL: Waveland, 1997).
4. H. Goldstein, *Problem Oriented Policing* (New York: McGraw-Hill, 1990); H. Goldstein, "Improving Policing: A Problem-Oriented Approach," *Crime and Delinquency* 25 (1979): 236–58.
5. See, for instance, L.W. Sherman, J.W. Shaw, and D.P. Rogan, *The Kansas City Gun Experiment: Research in Brief* (Washington, DC: National Institute of Justice, 1995). This publication is often cited as being supportive of both community policing and problem-oriented policing.
6. G.L. Kelling and M.H. Moore, "The Evolving Strategy of Policing," in *Perspectives on Policing* (Vol. 4) (Washington, DC: National Institute of Justice, 1988).
7. J.H. Knott and G.J. Miller, *Reforming Bureaucracy: The Politics of Institutional Choice* (Englewood Cliffs, NJ: Prentice-Hall, 1987).
8. J.E. Angell, "Toward an Alternative to the Classic Police Organizational Arrangements: A Democratic Model," *Criminology* 9 (1971): 185–206.
9. G.L. Kelling, "Police and Communities: The Quiet Revolution," in *Criminal Justice in America: Theory, Practice, and Policy*, eds. B.W. Hancock and P.M. Sharp (Upper Saddle River, NJ: Prentice Hall, 1996), 134–44.
10. Ibid., 138.
11. Ibid.
12. Ibid.
13. R. Trojanowicz, V.E. Kappeler, L.K. Gaines, and B. Bucqueroux, *Community Policing: A Contemporary Perspective*, 2nd ed. (Cincinnati, OH: Anderson, 1988).
14. Ibid., 53.
15. D. Hayeslip and G. Cordner, "The Effects of Community-Oriented Patrol on Police Officer Attitudes," *American Journal of Police—Special Issue on Foot Patrol and Community Policing* 4 (1987): 95–119.
16. P.K. Manning, "Community Policing as a Drama of Control," in *Community Policing: Rhetoric or Reality?* Eds. J.R. Greene and S.D. Mastrofski (New York: Praeger, 1988), 27–45.
17. D. Garland, "The Limits of the Sovereign State: Strategies of Crime Control in Contemporary Society," *British Journal of Criminology* 36 (1996): 445–71.
18. J. Zhao, *Why Police Organizations Change* (Washington, DC: Police Executive Research Forum, 1996).
19. See, for instance, W.G. Skogan and S.M. Hartnett, *Community Policing: Chicago Style* (New York: Oxford University Press, 1997).
20. Robert Trojanowicz and Bonnie Bucqueroux, *Community Policing: A Contemporary Perspective* (Cincinnati, OH: Anderson, 1990).
21. Quotation appearing in William A. Geller and Guy Swanger, *Managing Innovation in Policing: The Untapped Potential of the Middle Manager* (Washington, DC: Police Executive Research Forum, 1995).
22. Police Executive Research Forum, *Themes and Variations in Community Policing* (Washington, DC: Police Executive Research Forum, 1996).
23. G.W. Cordner, "Community Policing: Elements and Effects," in *Critical Issues in Policing: Contemporary Readings*, eds. R.G. Dunham and G.P. Alpert, 3rd ed. (Prospect Heights, IL: Waveland, 1997), 451–68.
24. Ibid.
25. Ibid., 454.
26. Ibid., 458.
27. J.A. Roth, J. Roehl, and C.C. Johnson, "Trends in the Adoption of Community Policing," in *Community Policing (Can It Work?)*, ed. W.G. Skogan (Belmont, CA: Wadsworth, 2003), 3–29.
28. Ibid., 24.
29. See also J. Zhao, Q. Thurman, and N. Lovrich, "Community Oriented Policing Across the U.S.: Facilitators and Impediments to Implementation," *American Journal of Police* 14 (1995): 11–28; J. Zhao, N. Lovrich, and Q. Thurman, "The Status of Community Policing in American Cities," *Policing: An International Journal of Police Strategies and Management* 22 (1999): 152–70.
30. J.R. Greene, "Community Policing and Organization Change," in *Community Policing (Can It Work?)*, ed. W.G. Skogan (Belmont, CA: Wadsworth, 2003), 30–53.
31. Ibid., 49.
32. See, for example, D. Guyot, "Bending Granite: Attempts to Change the Rank Structure of American Police Departments," *Journal of Police Science and Administration* 7 (1979): 253–384.
33. E.R. Maguire, "Structural Change in Large Municipal Police Organizations during the Community-Policing Era," *Justice Quarterly* 14 (1997): 547–76; see also J.A. Roth, ed., *National Evaluation of the COPS Program—Title 1 of the 1994 Crime Act* (Washington, DC: National Institute of Justice, 2000).
34. W.G. Skogan, ed., *Community Policing: (Can It Work?)* (Belmont, CA: Wadsworth, 2003), xxviii.
35. D.P. Rosenbaum and D.L. Wilkinson, "Can Police Adapt?: Tracking the Effects of Organizational Reform over Six Years," in *Community Policing (Can It Work?)*, ed. W.G. Skogan (Belmont, CA: Wadsworth, 2003), 79–108; see also D.P. Rosenbaum, S. Yeh, and D.L. Wilkinson, "Estimating the Effects of Community Policing Reform on Police Officers," *Crime and Delinquency* 40 (1994): 331–53.
36. W. Terrill and S.D. Mastrofski, "Working the Street: Does Community Policing Matter?" in *Community Policing (Can It Work?)*, ed. W.G. Skogan (Belmont, CA: Wadsworth, 2003), 109–35; see also W. Terrill and S.D. Mastrofski, "Situational and Officer Based Determinants of Police Coercion," *Justice Quarterly* 19 (2002): 101–34.
37. R.L. Wood, M. Davis, and A. Rouse, "Diving into Quicksand: Program Implementation and Police

Subcultures," in *Community Policing (Can It Work?)*, ed. W.G. Skogan (Belmont, CA: Wadsworth, 2003), 136–61.

38. Edward R. Maguire and Charles M. Katz, "Community Policing, Loose Coupling, and Sensemaking in American Police Agencies," *Justice Quarterly* 19 (2002): 503–36.

39. M.A. Wycoff, A.M. Pate, W. Skogan, and L.W. Sherman, *Citizen Contact Patrol in Houston: Executive Summary* (Washington, DC: Police Foundation, 1985).

40. L.W. Sherman, J.W. Shaw, and D.P. Rogan, *The Kansas City Gun Experiment* (Washington, DC: National Institute of Justice, 1995).

41. G. Laycock, "Operation Identification, or the Power of Publicity?" *Security Journal* 2 (1991): 67–72.

42. R.C. Davis and B.G. Taylor, "A Proactive Response to Family Violence: The Results of a Randomized Experiment," *Criminology* 35(1997): 307–33.

43. M.A. Wycoff, A.M. Pate, W. Skogan, and L.W. Sherman, *Citizen Contact Patrol in Houston: Executive Summary* (Washington, DC: Police Foundation, 1985); W. Skogan, *Disorder and Decline: Crime and the Spiral Decay in American Neighborhoods* (New York: Free Press, 1990).

44. A.M. Pate and W. Skogan, *Coordinated Community Policing: The Newark Experience. Technical Report.* Washington, DC: Police Foundation, 1985.

45. C.D. Uchida, B. Forst, and S.O. Annan, *Modern Policing and the Control of Illegal Drugs: Testing New Strategies in Two American Cities.* Research Report. Washington, DC: National Institute of Justice, 1992.

46. L.W. Sherman, J.W. Shaw, and D.P. Rogan, *The Kansas City Gun Experiment* (Washington, DC: National Institute of Justice, 1995); C.D. Uchida, B. Forst, and S.O. Annan, *Modern Policing and the Control of Illegal Drugs: Testing New Strategies in Two American Cities.* Research Report. Washington, DC: National Institute of Justice, 1992; R.C. Davis and B.G. Taylor, "A Proactive Response to Family Violence: The Results of a Randomized Experiment," *Criminology* 35 (1997): 307–33.

47. M.A. Wycoff, A.M. Pate, W. Skogan, and L.W. Sherman, *Citizen Contact Patrol in Houston: Executive Summary* (Washington, DC: Police Foundation, 1985).

48. W. Skogan, *Disorder and Decline: Crime and the Spiral Decay in American Neighborhoods* (New York: Free Press, 1990).

49. Ibid., 107.

50. Tom Tyler, *Why People Obey the Law* (New Haven, CT: Yale University Press, 1990).

51. Wesley Skogan and others, *Community Policing in Chicago, Year Three* (Chicago, IL: Illinois Criminal Justice Information Authority, 1996).

52. Raymond Paternoster, Robert Brame, Ronet Bachman, and Lawrence W. Sherman, "Do Fair Procedures Matter?: The Effect of Procedural Justice on Spouse Assault," *Law and Society Review* 31 (1997): 163–204.

53. Ibid., 163.

54. For good reviews of this literature, see M.D. Reisig and R.B. Parks, "Experience, Quality of Life, and Neighborhood Context: A Hierarchical Analysis of Satisfaction with Police," *Justice Quarterly* 17 (2000): 607–30; J.L. Worrall, "Public Perceptions of Police Efficacy and Image: The 'Fuzziness' of Support for the Police," *American Journal of Criminal Justice* 24 (1999): 47–66.

55. D. Black, "Production of Crime Rates," *American Sociological Review* 35 (1970): 733–48.

56. N. Apple and D. O'Brien, "Neighborhood Racial Composition and Residents' Evaluation of Police Performance," *Journal of Police Science and Administration* 11 (1983): 76–84; D. Dean, "Citizen Ratings of the Police: The Difference Police Contact Makes," *Law and Policy Quarterly* 2 (1980): 445–71; E. Erez, "Self-Defined Desert and Citizen's Assessment of the Police," *Journal of Criminal Law and Criminology* 75 (1984): 1276–99.

57. S. Albrecht and M. Green, "Attitudes toward the Police and the Larger Attitude Complex: Implications for Police-Community Relations," *Criminology* 15 (1977): 67–87; T. Jefferson and M.A. Walker, "Ethnic Minorities in the Criminal Justice System," *Criminal Law Review* 28 (1993): 83–95; R.B. Parks, "Linking Objective and Subjective Measures of Performance," *Public Administration Review* 44 (1984): 118–27.

58. I. Hadar and J. Snortum, "The Eye of the Beholder: Differential Perceptions of Police by the Police and the Public," *Criminal Justice and Behavior* 2 (1975): 37–54; D. Walker, R. Richardson, O. Williams, T. Denyer, and S. McGaughey, "Contact and Support: An Empirical Assessment of Public Attitudes toward the Police and the Courts," *North Carolina Law Review* 51 (1972): 43–79.

59. J.L. Worrall, "Public Perceptions of Police Efficacy and Image: The 'Fuzziness' of Support for the Police," *American Journal of Criminal Justice* 24 (1999): 47–66.

60. T. Winfree and C. Griffiths, "Adolescent Attitudes toward the Police," in *Juvenile Delinquency: Little Brother Grows Up*, ed. T. Ferdinand (Beverly Hills, CA: Sage, 1977), 79–99; M.E. Correia, M.D. Reisig, and N.P. Lovrich, "Public Perceptions of State Police: An Analysis of Individual-Level and Contextual Variables," *Journal of Criminal Justice* 24 (1996): 17–28.

61. K.S. Larsen, "Authoritarianism and Attitudes toward the Police," *Psychological Reports* 3 (1968): 349–50.

62. L. Cao, J. Frank, and F. Cullen, "Race, Community Context, and Confidence in the Police," *American Journal of Police* 15 (1996): 3–22; D. Lewis and G. Salem, *Fear of Crime: Incivility and the Production of a Social Problem* (New Brunswick, NJ: Transaction Books, 1986).

63. P. Jesilow, J. Meyer, and N. Namazzi, "Public Attitudes toward the Police," *American Journal of Police* 2 (1995): 67–88.

64. Anthony M. Pate, Marlys McPherson, and Glenn Silloway, *The Minneapolis Community Crime Prevention Experiment: Draft Evaluation Report* (Washington, DC: Police Foundation, 1987).

65. B. Lindsay and D. McGillis, "Citywide Community Crime Prevention: An Assessment of the Seattle Program," in *Community Crime Prevention: Does It Work?* Ed. D. Rosenbaum (Beverly Hills, CA: Sage, 1986), 46–67.

66. B.W. Smith, K.J. Novak, and D.C. Hurley, "Neighborhood Crime Prevention: The Influences of Community-Based Organizations and Neighborhood Watch," *Journal of Crime and Justice* 20 (1997): 69–86; see also D.P Rosenbaum, "The Theory and Research behind Neighborhood Watch: Is It a Sound Fear and Crime Reductions Strategy?" *Crime and Delinquency* 33 (1987): 103–34.

67. Dennis Rosenbaum, Dan A. Lewis, and Jane A. Grant, "Neighborhood-Based Crime Prevention: Assessing the Efficacy of Community Organization in Chicago," in *Community Crime Prevention: Does It Work*? Ed. Dennis Rosenbaum (Beverly Hills, CA: Sage, 1986).

68. See, for example, T. Bennett, *Evaluating Neighborhood Watch* (Basingstoke, UK: Gower, 1990).

69. C. Meredith and C. Paquette, "Crime Prevention in High-Rise Rental Apartments: Findings of a Demonstration Project," *Security Journal* 3 (1992): 161–68.

70. M.A. Wycoff and W.G. Skogan, *Community Policing in Madison: Quality from the Inside Out: An Evaluation of Implementation and Impact.* Technical Report. Washington, DC: Police Foundation, 1993.

71. W. Skogan et al., *Community Policing in Chicago, Year Two* (Chicago, IL: Criminal Justice Information Authority, 1995).

72. Tony Pate, Mary Ann Wycoff, Wesley Skogan, and Lawrence Sherman, *Reducing the Fear of Crime in Newark and Houston* (Washington, DC: Police Foundation, 1986).

73. R.C. Davis and B.G. Taylor, "A Proactive Response to Family Violence: The Results of a Randomized Experiment," *Criminology* 35 (1997): 307–33.

74. P.J. Lavrakas, "Evaluating Police-Community Anticrime Newsletters," in *Community Crime Prevention: Does It Work?* Ed. D. Rosenbaum (Beverly Hills, CA: Sage, 1986), 269–291; see also P.J. Lavrakas, D.P. Rosenbaum, and F. Kaminski, "Transmitting Information about Crime and Crime Prevention to Citizens: The Evanston Newsletter Quasi-Experiment," *Journal of Police Science and Administration* 11 (1983): 463–73.

75. W. Skogan, *Disorder and Decline: Crime and the Spiral Decay in American Neighborhoods* (New York: Free Press, 1990), 96.

76. M.A. Wycoff and W.G. Skogan, *Community Policing in Madison: Quality from the Inside Out: An Evaluation of Implementation and Impact.* Technical Report. Washington, DC: Police Foundation, 1993; C.D. Uchida, B. Forst, and S.O. Annan, *Modern Policing and the Control of Illegal Drugs: Testing New Strategies in Two American Cities. Research Report.* Washington, DC: National Institute of Justice, 1992; A.M. Pate and W. Skogan, *Coordinated Community Policing: The Newark Experience.* Technical Report. Washington, DC: Police Foundation, 1985.

77. See, for example, W.G. Skogan and M.A. Wycoff, "Storefront Police Offices: The Houston Field Test," in *Community Crime Prevention: Does It Work?* Ed. D. Rosenbaum (Beverly Hills, CA: Sage, 1986), 179–99.

78. A.M. Pate, "Community-Oriented Policing in Baltimore," in *Police and Policing: Contemporary Issues*, ed. D.J. Kenney (New York: Praeger, 1989), 112–35; Police Foundation, *The Newark Foot Patrol Experiment* (Washington, DC: Police Foundation, 1981).

79. G. Kelling, *Foot Patrol* (Washington, DC: National Institute of Justice, 1987); but see F. Esbensen, "Foot Patrols: Of What Value?" *American Journal of Police* 6 (1987): 45–65 and A.M. Pate, "Community-Oriented Policing in Baltimore," in *Police and Policing: Contemporary Issues*, ed. D.J. Kenney (New York: Praeger, 1989), 112–35; Police Foundation, *The Newark Foot Patrol Experiment* (Washington, DC: Police Foundation, 1981).

80. F. Esbensen, "Foot Patrols: Of What Value?" *American Journal of Police* 6 (1987): 45–65.

81. R.C. Trojanowicz, "Evaluating a Neighborhood Foot Patrol Program: The Flint, Michigan, Project," in *Community Crime Prevention: Does It Work? Ed. D. Rosenbaum (Beverly Hills, CA: Sage, 1986), 157–78.

82. Jerry H. Ratcliffe, Travis Taniguchi, Elizabeth R. Groff, and Jennifer D. Wood, "Philadelphia Foot Patrol Experiment: A Randomized Controlled Trial of Police Patrol Effectiveness in Violent Crime Hotspots," *Criminology* 49 (2011): 795–832.

83. Do not confuse this version of Operation ID with a responsible tobacco retailing initiative by the same name.

84. A.L. Schneider, "Neighborhood-Based Antiburglary Strategies: An Analysis of Public and Private Benefits from the Portland Program," in *Community Crime Prevention: Does It Work?* Ed. D. Rosenbaum (Beverly Hills, CA: Sage, 1986), 68–86.

85. Ibid., 78.

86. See, for example, U.S. Department of Justice, *Operation Identification Projects: Assessment of Effectiveness: National Evaluation Program.* Phase 1 Summary Report. Washington, DC: U.S. Department of Justice, 1975.

87. M. Alvaro, "Online 'Substations' Enhance Public Safety Efforts," *Police* 24 (2000): 44–7.

88. K.S. Trump, *NASRO School Resource Officer Survey 2002: Final Report on the 2nd Annual National Survey of School-Based Police Officers* (Anthony, FL: National Association of School Resource Officers, 2002).

89. See nasro.org.

90. U.S. Department of Justice, *Community Outreach through Police in Schools* (Washington, DC: Office for Victims of Crime, U.S. Department of Justice, August 2003), 1.

91. See, for example, R.L. Paynter, "Policing the Schools," *Law Enforcement Technology* 26 (1999): 34–6, 38–40; National Crime Prevention Council, "Police Station in a School," *Catalyst* 16 (May 1996): 1–2; M.L. West and J.M. Fries, "Campus-Based Police/Probation Teams: Making Schools Safer," *Corrections Today* 57 (August 1995): 144, 146, 148; W.C. Torok and K.S. Trump, "Gang Intervention: Police and School Collaboration," *FBI Law Enforcement Bulletin* 63(May 1994): 13–6.

92. A.N. Briers, "School-Based Police Officers: What Can the UK Learn from the USA?" *International Journal of Police Science and Management* 5 (2003): 129–42.

93. M.D. White, J.J. Fyfe, S.P. Campbell, and J.S. Goldkamp, "School-Based Partnership: Identifying at-Risk Youth

through a Truant Recovery Program," *Evaluation Review* 25 (2001): 507–32.

94. U.S. Department of Justice, *Community Outreach Through Police in Schools* (Washington, DC: Office for Victims of Crime, U.S. Department of Justice, August 2003), 1.

95. B. Lindsay and D. McGillis, "Citywide Community Crime Prevention: An Assessment of the Seattle Program," in *Community Crime Prevention: Does It Work?* Ed. D. Rosenbaum (Beverly Hills, CA: Sage, 1986), 46–67.

96. Ibid., 65.

97. F.J. Fowler, Jr. and T.W. Mangione, "The Three-Pronged Effort to Reduce Crime and Fear of Crime: The Hartford Experiment," in *Community Crime Prevention: Does It Work?* Ed. D. Rosenbaum (Beverly Hills, CA: Sage, 1986), 87–108.

98. Ibid., 104.

99. Ibid., 105.

100. U.S. Department of Justice, *Citizen Patrol Projects: National Evaluation Program Phase 1 Summary Report* (Washington, DC: U.S. Department of Justice, 1976).

101. J. Hilson, "Fort Worth's Citizens on Patrol Program," *TELEMASP Bulletin* 1(1994).

102. W.J. Einstadter, "Citizen Patrols: Prevention or Control?" *Crime and Social Justice* 21 (1984): 200–12.

103. B.B. Ostrowe and R. DiBiase, "Citizen Involvement as a Crime Deterrent: A Study of Public Attitudes toward an Unsanctioned Civilian Patrol Group," *Journal of Police Science and Administration* 11 (1983): 185–93.

104. D.J. Kenney, "Crime on the Subways: Measuring the Effectiveness of the Guardian Angels," *Justice Quarterly* 3 (1986): 481–96; B. Webb and G. Laycock, *Reducing Crime on the London Underground: An Evaluation of Three Pilot Projects*, Vol. 30, (London: Home Office, 1992).

105. See, for example, V.W. Bumphus, L.K. Gaines, and C.R. Blakely, "Citizen Police Academies: Observing Goals, Objectives, and Recent Trends," *American Journal of Criminal Justice* 24 (1999): 67–79.

106. See, for example, G.A. Aryani, T.D. Garrett, and C.L. Alsabrook, "Citizen Police Academy: Success through Community Partnership," *FBI Law Enforcement Bulletin* 69 (2000): 16–21.

107. E.M. Bonello and J.A. Schafer, "Citizen Police Academies: Do They Just Entertain?" *FBI Law Enforcement Bulletin* 71 (2002): 19–23.

108. M.J. Palmiotto and N.P. Unninthan, "Impact of Citizen Police Academies on Participants: An Exploratory Study," *Journal of Criminal Justice* 30 (2002): 101–6.

109. J.A. Schafer and E.M. Bonello, "Citizen Police Academy: Measuring Outcomes," *Police Quarterly* 4 (2001): 434–48; E.G. Cohn, "Citizen Police Academy: A Recipe for Improving Police-Community Relations, "*Journal of Criminal Justice* 24 (1996): 265–71.

110. W.T. Jordan, "Citizen Police Academies: Community Policing or Community Politics," *American Journal of Police* 25 (2000): 93–118.

111. Ibid.

112. M.E. Buerger and L.G. Mazerolle, "Third-Party Policing: Theoretical Analysis of an Emerging Trend," in *The Police and Society: Touchstone Readings*, ed. V.E. Kappeler, 2nd ed. (Prospect Heights, IL: Waveland, 1999), 402–26.

113. Ibid., 402.

114. Ibid., 403.

115. Ibid., 408.

116. Ibid., 408.

117. Accessed 12/15/2006 from: guide.helpingamericasyouth. gov/programdetail.cfm?id=454.

118. See, e.g., L.G. Mazerolle and J. Roehl, *Controlling Drug and Disorder Problems: Focus on Oakland's Beat Health Program* (Washington, DC: National Institute of Justice, 1999); L.G. Mazerolle, J. Price, and J. Roehl, "Civil Remedies and Drug Control: A Randomized Field Trial in Oakland, California," *Evaluation Review* 24 (2000): 212–41.

119. Ibid.

120. See, e.g., M.E. Buerger, ed., *The Crime Prevention Casebook: Securing High Crime Locations* (Washington, DC: Crime Control Institute, 1992).

121. M.E. Buerger and L.G. Mazerolle, "Third-Party Policing: Theoretical Analysis of an Emerging Trend," in *The Police and Society: Touchstone Readings*, ed. V.E. Kappeler, 2nd ed. (Prospect Heights, IL: Waveland, 1999), 402–26.

Prosecutors and Crime Control

LEARNING OBJECTIVES

▨ Explain the concept of strategic prosecution.

▨ Summarize approaches consistent with the "harder" side of prosecution and their effectiveness.

▨ Summarize approaches consistent with the "softer" side of prosecution and their effectiveness.

▨ Discuss the relationship between plea bargaining and crime control.

In studying the effectiveness of law enforcement in reducing crime, the role of prosecutors is important. Clearly the police are first responders. They are the ones who must confront the crime problem head-on. But the prosecutor's role in crime control is equally important. Without prosecutors, whose job it is to bring formal charges against suspected criminals, it is likely that crime would flourish.

Because prosecutors are often overlooked in our discipline, this chapter begins with a brief review of who prosecutors are. It then discusses the near absence of research devoted to prosecution. After these introductory sections, we turn to two types of prosecution. For lack of a better classification scheme, these will be called the "harder" and "softer" sides of prosecution in America. This chapter concludes with some attention to plea bargaining and its possible effects on crime.

PROSECUTORS

Who Are the Prosecutors?

U.S. attorney: the appointed federal prosecutor.

district attorney: the chief (usually elected) prosecutor at the local (usually county) level.

attorney general: the chief law enforcement official/prosecutor at the state or federal level.

city attorney: the chief legal advisor to citizen government officials and a prosecutor in cases involving city ordinance violations.

There are several types of prosecutors in the United States: U.S. attorneys and their assistants, district attorneys and their deputies, attorneys general, and city attorneys. **U.S. attorneys** are appointed federal prosecutors. **District attorneys** are the elected chief prosecutors. Most often, they are elected to head county offices. Some are elected to head borough offices (e.g., the Borough of Brooklyn, New York). Below the district attorney are several deputy district attorneys who actually litigate most criminal cases in court. There can be hundreds of deputy district attorneys in large, highly populous counties. Most criminal prosecutions of felonies are handled at the county level.

Attorneys general whether state or federal are the chief officials of their jurisdictions. Their role is primarily one of legal advising, rather than prosecution. **City attorneys** are, with some exceptions, the chief legal advisors to city government officials (e.g., the police chief). However, in certain cities around the country, such as Dallas and San Diego, the city attorney is the chief misdemeanor prosecutor. City attorneys are often elected and, like their district attorney counterparts, can supervise a large number of staff. For example, San Diego's city attorney has a staff of over 300 lawyers and nonlegal personnel.

The breakdown of personnel in the typical prosecutor's office is presented in Figure 6.1. It indicates that as of 2007, the most recent year for which data are available as of this writing, there were nearly 80,000 prosecutors (including staff) in the prosecuting offices around the United States. These figures exclude city attorneys, so it is likely that the number of prosecutors exceeds 100,000 when city attorneys who prosecute misdemeanors are taken into account. The point is that although there are not as many prosecutors as police, they still represent a significant percentage of the criminal justice workforce.

The Shift toward Strategic Prosecution

This book uses the term **strategic prosecution** to refer, broadly, to the shift that is taking place in prosecuting attorneys' offices across the nation. Prosecutors are developing creative approaches to the crime problem, some with a get-tough angle and others with a less law enforcement–oriented approach (e.g., community prosecution). Strategic

Job categories[a]	Percent of total full-time equivalent personnel in prosecutors' offices nationwide[b]
Total	100%
Support staff	33%
Assistant prosecutors	32
Investigators	9
Victim advocates	6
Legal services	5
Supervisory/managing Attorneys	7
Chief prosecutor	3
Civil attorneys	2
Other	2
Estimated total full-time equivalent staff	77,927

Note: Table is based on operating budgets, not actual expenditures. Data were missing for 5.5% (128) of offices surveyed. Total budget, total staff, chief prosecutor, and assistant prosecutor values were imputed using data from 2001 and 2007 Census of State Court Prosecutors' Offices, stratified by population served and state. See *Methodology* for details on imputation procedures.

[a]Statistics for job categories were imputed using mean values for valid data from 2007 Census of State Court Prosecutors Offices, stratified by population served.

[b]Full-time equivalent (FTE) is a computed statistic calculated by dividing the total number of hours part-time employees worked by the standard number of hours for a full-time employee (40 hours per week) and then adding the resulting quotient to the number of full-time employees.

FIGURE 6.1   Personnel employed in state prosecutors' offices, 2007

Source: Steven W. Perry and Duren Banks, *Prosecutors in State Courts, 2007—Statistical Tables* (Washington, DC: Bureau of Justice Statistics, 2011).

prosecution represents a marked departure from the traditional role of the prosecutor. Here is one author's description of the traditional prosecutorial role:

> The traditional . . . prosecutor likes to think of himself as the consummate carnivore: a learned lawyer, a compelling oral advocate, a relentless pursuer of the truth who fights crime by putting "bad guys" in jail. His allies in this fight are the . . . investigative agencies. Those agencies identify trends in criminal behavior and "bring" the prosecutor the significant cases.[1]

Strategic prosecution is intended to shift prosecutors' attention from individual criminal cases brought to them by the police to an overall strategy geared toward reducing crime. To illustrate, the same author argues: "Because it is the prosecutor who has the direct connections with . . . investigative agencies, it also falls on the prosecutor to determine whether there are intersections between the case on which the police have focused and cases that other . . . investigative agencies might be working in the same neighborhood."[2] In other words, in strategic prosecution, the prosecutor views himself or herself as one piece in a larger crime control puzzle. Strategic prosecution emphasizes awareness of crime trends, communication, creativity, and cooperation.

THE HARDER SIDE OF PROSECUTION

The harder side of prosecution emphasizes a get-tough approach. Although this is a fairly accurate description, there is little research available that suggests whether a get-tough prosecution approach works. Chapter 3 showed that there is significant research available on the linkage between police levels and crime. Unfortunately, there appears to be no research on the links between either the number of cases prosecuted and crime or prosecution resources and crime. This is baffling to say the least, but it does not mean that there is *no* research on the effectiveness of various prosecution strategies. On the contrary, there is a small amount of research—and some anecdotal evidence—pertaining to get-tough prosecution strategies.

There are probably many more methods that prosecutors have engaged in to aggressively target crime than are presented in this chapter. But there are four such approaches that have received a fair degree of attention in the literature. The first is no-drop prosecution. The second is the juvenile waiver, which generally involves prosecuting certain juveniles as adults. This approach is usually manifested as a policy that requires prosecutors to press charges regardless of the victim's wishes. Third, prosecutors have begun to partner with police departments in an effort to reduce crime. Fourth, local and federal prosecutors have teamed up in an effort to combat crime. Finally, another get-tough prosecution approach is the federal government's Project Safe Neighborhoods initiative.

No-Drop Prosecution Policies

no-drop prosecution: also called evidence-based prosecution, a policy that requires prosecution in domestic violence if the evidence supports it. No-drop prosecution is intended to ignore the victim's preference of whether to prosecute.

A relatively recent example of get-tough prosecution is **no-drop prosecution**. No-drop prosecution is sometimes referred to as evidence-based prosecution and has been primarily applied to domestic violence cases. It emphasizes prosecution irrespective of the victim's wishes. According to one source, it began in San Diego in the late 1980s in response to the high rate of dismissals in domestic violence cases.[3] The problem was that many victims of domestic violence refused to testify in court against their abusers. This meant that prosecutors would decline to pursue criminal charges. No-drop prosecution policies are intended to rectify this problem; prosecutors bring charges (assuming that there is enough evidence) and ignore the desires of the victim.

Not surprisingly, no-drop prosecution policies have been subjected to some criticism. Some people have argued that such policies limit prosecutors' discretion to decide whether charges should be brought against an accused person.[4] Critics have also argued that no-drop prosecution can be harmful to victims. On the one hand, it restricts victim input, which may be both accurate and necessary in some domestic violence cases. On the other hand, an aggressive prosecution strategy can have implications for future violence if the accused person is allowed to return home at some point after being convicted. But at least one author has argued that the benefits of no-drop prosecution outweigh the costs:

> No-drop policies can play an important role in combating domestic violence, because they account for victims' realities, counteract longstanding justifications for inaction, and

transform the statutory promise of justice for battered women into a credible threat of prosecution for their batterers.[5]

So does no-drop prosecution work? Surprisingly, there appears to be only one study that gets close to answering this question. In a National Institute of Justice (NIJ)–funded study, researchers compared 200 domestic violence court cases during the year before the implementation of a no-drop policy and 200 cases that began after the new policy went into effect.[6] The cities of Everett, Washington, and Klamath Falls, Oregon, were the research sites. As was expected, the policy substantially increased guilty pleas and the number of domestic violence cases going to court. The latter increased tenfold.

Although it would seem that no-drop prosecution served its intended purpose in Everett and Klamath Falls, it is not clear whether there was a corresponding decrease in domestic violence incidents. It is unclear, though, whether such a claim *can* ever be made. There are at least two reasons for this. First, according to the NIJ study, no-drop prosecution policies are expensive. This is not surprising, given that they apparently result in more trials. Second, no-drop prosecution might actually deter victims of domestic violence from calling the police because, to the extent that these victims are codependent, a prison sentence could disrupt the home.[7]

Juvenile Waiver

The term **juvenile waiver** refers to trying juveniles as adults, or "waiving" them to adult court. Waivers have been around for some time and have been used on occasion when a juvenile commits a particularly harsh crime and there is a desire to charge him or her in the adult justice system. What has changed recently, though, are the criteria for juvenile waivers. Recent changes have made it easier to try juveniles as adult offenders, a significant departure from the original intent of having a separate juvenile justice system.

In Connecticut, North Carolina, and New York, the jurisdiction of the juvenile court ends after age 15. Offenders who are 16 years of age and older are processed by the adult courts. Ten other states (Georgia, Illinois, Louisiana, Massachusetts, Michigan, Mississippi, New Hampshire, South Carolina, Texas, and Wisconsin) extend the jurisdiction of the juvenile court through a youth's seventeenth birthday. In all other states, the jurisdiction of the juvenile court ends at the eighteenth birthday.[8] These definitions of what constitutes a juvenile have remained relatively constant over time. To get around any restrictions imposed by these age cutoffs, states have enacted legislation that permit the transfer of juveniles to adult courts. Some people would say that this practice is making the age-based distinctions between the juvenile and adult justice systems null and void.

It is not possible to provide an exhaustive list of changes in juvenile waiver criteria, given space constraints. Any effort to do so would also quickly become dated because there are constant changes in this area. Suffice it to say that there is a general trend toward making it easier to try serious—and young—juvenile offenders in adult courts.[9] For example, Colorado legislators enacted a statute that provides for 14- to 17-year olds who have been charged with violent felonies to be tried as adults. California voters recently enacted Proposition 21, an initiative that, among other things, reduced the waiver age from 16 to 14. These changes signal an increasing desire to treat juvenile offenders more harshly than was the case in the past.

Although legislative changes have taken place, it is not clear whether waivers are now being used more commonly and whether they are effective. The vast majority of juvenile cases are still processed in the traditional fashion.[10] One estimate from the mid-1990s showed that 12,000 juveniles were waived to adult court in the space of one year.[11] A more recent trend analysis, though, showed a reduction throughout the latter part of the 1990s in the number of juvenile waivers to adult court.[12] The most dramatic drops were for crimes against persons, which would consist of violent felonies. This trend cannot easily be explained, and unfortunately, data from the year 2000 and later are not yet available. There is also no clear evidence that juvenile waivers affect sentences.[13] We will give some attention to other effects of juvenile waivers and their possible effects on juvenile crime later in this chapter.

Juvenile waivers are a relatively recent phenomenon and therefore have not been subjected to much research. As the reader can probably guess, because they equate with the tough-on-crime approaches that were covered earlier in this book, waivers are probably ineffective. Few researchers appear to have studied the deterrent effect on crime of juvenile waivers. The authors of one study found that Idaho's law, which mandates automatic transfer of some serious juvenile offenders to adult court, had no effect on crime.[14] Similar findings were reported in a study of Georgia's waiver statute.[15]

Other researchers have been critical of juvenile waivers. Some have argued that trying young people as adults and then sentencing them to adult prison is counterproductive because there are few services in such facilities aimed at the needs of juveniles.[16] Others have claimed that juvenile waivers can have unanticipated consequences, such as victimization of youths in adult prison, lengthy pretrial detentions, and net widening.[17] All in all, there is little support for continuing the practice of juvenile waivers, especially from a general deterrence standpoint. Waivers might have a specific deterrent effect, but that appears to be it.

Police–Prosecution Partnerships

police–prosecutor partnership: a crime control strategy that emphasizes collaboration and cooperation between prosecutors and police officers, sometimes even across levels of government.

Police–prosecutor partnerships operate in much the same way as the police–corrections partnerships discussed in Chapter 4. Police–prosecutor partnerships are a relatively new development in criminal justice and, as such, are not commonplace or well researched. Nevertheless, police–prosecutor partnerships are premised on the idea that by working together, criminal justice professionals can more effectively address the problem of crime in our society.

Examples of police–prosecution partnerships have been seen in Maine, Oregon, New Hampshire, and New York City.[18] In 1987 the state of Maine enacted a law that mandated cooperation between investigators and prosecutors to more effectively address the drug problem. The law led to the creation of the Maine Bureau of Intergovernmental Drug Enforcement, an office that became staffed by 50 law enforcement agents and 8 prosecutors.

In Multnomah County, Oregon, the Organized Crime/Narcotics Task Force brought together 12 investigators from several agencies in the area as well as 2 prosecutors. Their job was to work together cooperatively in an effort to reduce the county's illegal narcotics problems. The teams concentrated heavily on the forfeiture of assets obtained from the sale or use of illegal drugs. The teams in New York City focused on gang crime; the teams in New Hampshire focused primarily on misdemeanor violations.

A more recent example of a police–prosecutor team in action was Indianapolis's R.O.A.D. Team, which stands for Rub Out Aggressive Driving. Working together, police and prosecutors in Marion County, Indiana, stepped up their efforts to combat reckless and dangerous driving. Among the tactics that were used in the R.O.A.D. program were strict enforcement of traffic laws and a media campaign that was intended to spread the word that dangerous driving will not be tolerated.[19]

Unfortunately, there is little to no research available at this time that tells us whether these types of partnerships are effective in reducing crime. But this has not stopped prosecutors from teaming up with police officers and vice versa. In fact, partnerships of the type discussed here are gaining momentum around the country. They are bringing a large number of actors together from inside and outside the criminal justice system in a joint effort to control crime. It is doubtful that their efforts will be in vain.

PARTNERING TO REDUCE GUN VIOLENCE. Boston's **Operation Ceasefire** represents a good example of partnering to reduce gun violence. In response to a surge in gun violence, much of which was gang-related, the city called on prosecutors as well as other officials to respond to the problem. Part of Operation Ceasefire's unique approach was meetings that police officers and prosecutors convened with actual and suspected gang members.[20] The prosecutors laid down the law, threatening the gang members with prosecution if gun violence did not cease. Gang members were forced to sign non-violence pacts and forswear possession of guns and ammunition. Whether the gang members actually followed through is unclear, but the researchers who evaluated the program for the National Institute of Justice claimed:

Operation Ceasefire: a popular and successful youth gun violence intervention strategy first introduced in Boston, MA.

> Because Ceasefire was conceived as an intervention aimed at interrupting the overall dynamic of violence in which all Boston gangs and gang members were involved, the operation could not be set up as a controlled experiment, with certain gangs or neighborhoods excluded for purposes of comparison. Some things are clear, however. Youth homicide in the city declined abruptly following the first gang forum in May 1996, and this low level continued through 1998 and 1999.[21]

Federal–State Partnerships

Another approach that local prosecutors have taken is to team up with their federal counterparts: those in the U.S. attorneys' office. One of the key reasons for teaming up with the feds is so that prosecutors can invoke more stringent federal laws to deal harshly with criminals. Local and federal prosecutors have teamed up in response to a variety of crimes, but the most common is teaming up in response to gun violence. The following subsections describe some noteworthy partnerships.

Before getting to the specific examples of local–federal partnerships, readers should be aware that in May 2001, President Bush announced Project Safe Neighborhoods (PSN). The project teams U.S. attorneys with local prosecutors and other law enforcement agencies for the purpose of targeting gun violence. The project will be discussed in more detail later in the chapter. What follow in the next few subsections are examples of federal–local prosecution partnerships that predated PSN. Understand also that while the following partnerships predated PSN, several of them are continuing on and receiving PSN funding.

RICHMOND, VIRGINIA'S PROJECT EXILE. Project Exile was conceived in 1994, shortly after Richmond, Virginia, experienced a significant increase in gun-related homicide. Through a coordinated team effort consisting of contributions from several individuals, the city adopted a three-pronged approach to gun violence.[22] First, federal prosecution was relied on. This was done because federal laws provide stiffer penalties for the use of firearms than Virginia's state law. Next, local, state, and federal law enforcement officials, including both police and prosecutors, worked together in response to the homicide problem. Finally, Project Exile was characterized by extensive community outreach, including a media campaign, both of which were intended to send a message to criminals that gun violence would not be tolerated.

According to official statistics, the homicide rate in Richmond fell from a peak of 160 in 1994 to 69 in 2001, a drop of 57 percent. Project Exile also resulted in a high conviction rate (nearly 75 percent) and the seizure of nearly 1,000 illegal guns. It is difficult to conclude with certainty that Project Exile was responsible for this decline, but it probably did not hurt. According to one study, "While academic studies are needed to evaluate the extent to which these results are due to Project Exile, a positive impact on the Richmond community seems clear."[23] Other researchers agree. According to another study, "Richmond demonstrated significantly greater homicide reductions than comparable cities following the implementation of Project Exile, suggesting the intervention caused the reduction."[24]

TEXAS EXILE. Texas adopted Virginia's Project Exile model in January 2000.[25] It did so for two reasons. First, there was an increase in violent crime in Texas during the late 1990s. Second, nearly 70 percent of violent offenders were reoffending within three years of their release. The project was launched with a $1.6 million grant from the then governor George W. Bush to the state attorney general's office.

Texas Exile consisted of a partnership among several agencies: (1) the Criminal Justice Division of the Governor's Office, (2) the Attorney General of Texas, (3) district and county attorneys, (4) the local U.S. attorney's office, (5) local and state law enforcement agencies, and (6) the Bureau of Alcohol, Tobacco, and Firearms. Besides partnering, one of Texas Exile's key strategies is community outreach. Indeed, the Texas Attorney General's Office dedicated $360,000 to fund a public awareness campaign. The advertising slogan "Gun Crime Means Hard Time" was borrowed from Fort Worth's SafeCities program. Several media were used through which to get the word out, including billboards, radio ads, television commercials, newspapers, bus benches, grocery carts, hats, T-shirts, delivery trucks, posters, and flyers. Figure 6.2 shows a sample advertisement.

Like Richmond's Project Exile, Texas Exile was not subjected to rigorous evaluation, but in the two years after it went into operation, it resulted in nearly 1,500 indictments and 1,000 convictions.[26] In addition, judges sentenced offenders to an average of 72 months in federal prison, there was a massive increase in the prosecution of federal gun cases, and the project had taken some 2,000 illegal guns off the street—all in a two-year period.

Project Safe Neighborhoods

In May 2001, then president Bush announced that $901 million would be set aside over a three-year period to combat gun violence. The resulting program, **Project Safe Neighborhoods** (PSN), which continues to this day, was designed to promote interagency (especially local–federal) coordination to find new and creative ways to deal with gun violence.[27] According to the federal government:

> Project Safe Neighborhoods is a nationwide commitment to reduce gun violence by networking existing local programs that target gun crime and providing these programs with

Since when does a broken tail light lead to federal prison?

Since we found an illegal gun in your trunk.

That's when.

FIGURE 6.2 Advertisement for the Texas Exile Program
Source: www.ProjectSafeNeighborhoods.gov

additional tools necessary to be successful. The goal is to take a hard line against gun criminals through every available means in an effort to make our streets and communities safer. Project Safe Neighborhoods seeks to achieve heightened coordination among federal, state, and local law enforcement, with an emphasis on tactical intelligence gathering, more aggressive prosecutions, and enhanced accountability through performance measures. The offensive will be led by the U.S. Attorney in each of the 94 federal judicial districts across America.[28]

PSN prides itself on a five-pronged approach to gun violence. The five prongs—partnerships, strategic planning, training, outreach, and accountability—and their various constituent elements are presented in Figure 6.3.

The Five Elements of Project Safe Neighborhoods

1. **Partnerships:** Local Gun Crime Task Forces that will include
   - U.S. Attorneys
   - State and Local Prosecutors
   - Special Agents in Charge (ATF, FBI)
   - Chiefs of Police
   - Other community and law enforcement leaders working together
   - Developing district- or statewide strategies to reduce gun violence
   - Preparing gun cases for prosecution in most appropriate jurisdictions
   - Seeking the most appropriate venue for firearm prosecutions

2. **Strategic Plan:** A Proactive Approach
   - Intelligence Gathering
     - Crime mapping
     - Identifying hot spots
     - Tracing
     - Ballistics technology
   - Enforcement Policy
     - Where best to prosecute gun crimes
     - Let states do what states do best
     - Let feds do what feds do best

3. **Training:** Coordinating interagency training and cross-training
   - Training at the National Advocacy Center
   - Regional Gun Crime Training
   - Local Gun Crime Training

4. **Outreach:** Promote aggressive enforcement publicly by showing criminals they will do "Hard Time for Gun Crime"
   - The genius is in the deterrent message to would-be criminals and the supporting prevention message
   - Public Service Announcements
   - Educational Literature
   - Crime Prevention Tool Kits
   - Billboard Advertisements
   - Press Releases and News Articles
   - Other Community Engagement Opportunities

5. **Accountability:** Measuring success based on "outcome" rather than "output." The goal is to reduce the violent crime rate in our communities.

FIGURE 6.3 Project Safe Neighborhoods

Source: U.S. Justice Department, *Project Safe Neighborhoods: America's Network Against Gun Violence* (Washington, DC: U.S. Justice Department, 2004).

Little research is available concerning the effects of PSN. One study published in 2010 found no effects of the program on firearm-related offending.[29] We cannot draw definitive conclusions about the program's effectiveness based on the results of one study, however. More time (and research) will be necessary.

CROSS-DESIGNATION.   It is sometimes the case that state and local prosecutors are chosen to prosecute crimes in federal court. **Cross-designation** permits a local prosecutor to act as a Special Assistant U.S. Attorney (SAUSA). The power to appoint SAUSAs rests with the U.S. Attorney General and is derived from Title 28 of the United States Code, Section 543. Cross-designation typically plays out as follows:

> First, the local chief prosecutor must agree to the cross-designation. This is true because cross-designated prosecutors typically are drawn from the local prosecutor's office, and that office will continue to pay the salary of the SAUSA. Second, the United States Attorney must approve the appointment. Next, a security check is performed. (This can take several months.) Finally, the SAUSA is sworn in before the United States Attorney or the Administrative Officer of the United States Attorney's Office. The SAUSA must be admitted to the appropriate federal district court.[30]

cross-designation: a process by which local prosecutors temporarily act as uncompensated Special Assistant U.S. Attorneys.

This novel approach to the gun violence problem is intended to place local prosecutors in federal courts so that they can avail themselves of the much more punitive federal antigun laws. Cross-designation also tends to take place in the context of local–federal partnerships to reduce gun violence and continues to grow in prevalence as part of the PSN initiative. Whether cross-designation actually reduces gun violence, however, remains to be seen. Researchers have yet to examine the effects of this approach.

Does It Work?

The harder side of prosecution in America has not been extensively researched. In fact, researchers have ignored the effectiveness of *most* prosecution approaches to the crime problem. To date, it appears that only no-drop policies and some federal–state partnerships have been subjected to careful evaluation, and the results are a bit disheartening. No-drop policies might reduce domestic violence but are quite costly. Research on federal–state partnerships—notably Virginia's Project Exile—suggests that other factors besides partnering might have led to a decline in homicides in that city.

THE SOFTER SIDE OF PROSECUTION

Prosecution is not all about dragging suspected offenders into court and "throwing the book at them." There is a softer side of prosecution in America that is as popular (or at least as pervasive) as traditional criminal prosecution. Do not confuse the term *softer* with a soft-on-crime approach, however. Instead, think of the softer side of American prosecution in one of three forms. First, it can manifest itself as a concerted effort to bring victims back into the criminal process. Second, it can be a nontraditional approach to the crime problem that does not always make use of the criminal law. Third, prosecutors sometimes defer criminal charges or sentencing in an effort to minimize the "revolving door" that often puts offenders back on the streets without any meaningful intervention, treatment, or prevention component.

Victim Assistance

Of particular interest to many prosecutors' offices of late has been victim assistance. Historically, victims of crime occupied a secondary position in the criminal process. They were often forgotten by the police and prosecutors. In fact, an early survey conducted in Alameda County, California, (the Oakland area) revealed that only about

12 percent of crime victims were notified that an arrest was made, and approximately 42 percent of victims were never notified of the outcome of their case.[31] In response to victims' concerns, there is a renewed interest in bringing these individuals back into contact with criminal justice professionals. The logic behind this approach to crime control is clear: A satisfied victim is a person who is likely to be cooperative in the future and likely to assist authorities in responding to crime.

The emphasis on pulling victims back into the criminal process has also been manifested outside of police departments and prosecutors' offices. In 1999, the Judiciary Committee of the U.S. Senate sent to the full Senate an amendment to the U.S. Constitution that would protect the rights of crime victims. The proposed amendment was to guarantee restitution to victims of crime, notification of important events, and the right of victims to make statements at sentencing and parole hearings. The proposed amendment never received the required number of votes, but the fact that such a proposal went before the U.S. Senate underscores the importance of victims' rights. Even then president Clinton endorsed the proposal.

It is difficult to dispute the argument that victims should play a role in the criminal process, if only a modest one. How could notifying victims of the progress of their alleged victimizer's case, offering them services, and the like have a detrimental effect on the crime problem? It is practically impossible to conceive of any other answer than "it can't." Nevertheless, there is little research that suggests that our nation's crime problem would improve with increased attention to victims. One reason for this is that victim services are usually provided after the criminal event has already taken place. A possible exception to this rule is domestic violence shelters, which clearly protect victims from further abuse (at least temporarily), but other such programs have failed to show a great deal of promise in terms of their crime prevention attributes.[32]

Of course, one study does not definitively prove that victims' services fail to affect the crime rate. Recent efforts to reach out to victims, such as San Diego County's Victim Assistance Program, are so in-depth and far-reaching that it is hard to believe that they are not beneficial. As of this writing, the San Diego County District Attorney's Office has 29 full-time victim advocates stationed at the courthouses in San Diego County and the headquarters of the San Diego Police Department and the San Diego County Sheriff's Department. Figure 6.4 lists the services provided by the San Diego County District Attorney's Office.

Aside from providing services to crime victims, the victims' rights movement has also resulted in attempts to expand so-called victim's voice laws. Victim's voice laws are laws that give victims the right to make a statement at an offender's sentencing or parole hearing. These statements, known as victim impact statements, either are made orally before the trial judge or parole board or are provided in writing. Written statements are sometimes preferred because an actual appearance may be traumatic for the victim.

One example is California's Proposition 8, which was passed by the state's voters in 1982. It provided that "the victim of any crime, or the next of kin of the victim . . . has the right to attend all sentencing proceedings . . . [and] to reasonably express his or her views concerning the crime, the person responsible, and the need for restitution."[33] Proposition 8 actually requires that the judge take the victim's statement into account when deciding on a sentence.

Opponents of victim's voice laws claim that they bring an element of vengeance into the criminal process. That is, these people claim that criminals receive tougher sentences than they otherwise would because the victim personalizes the criminal act.

Mandatory Services:
- Crisis intervention
- Emergency assistance
- Resource and referral assistance
- Direct follow-up counseling
- Property return assistance
- Orientation to the Criminal Justice System
- Court escort and court support
- Case status and case disposition information
- Notification of family and friends
- Employer notification
- Victim of crime claims assistance

Optional Services:
- Creditor Intervention
- Child care
- Restitution information
- Witness notification
- Funeral and burial arrangements
- Crime prevention information
- Temporary restraining order information
- Transportation assistance
- Court waiting area
- Employer intervention

FIGURE 6.4   County of San Diego District Attorney's Office Victim Services
Source: http://www.sdcda.org/helping/victims/victim-services.html

Given their potential inflammatory effects, it is worth considering what the research shows. Unfortunately, the research does not suggest that victim's voice laws have a deterrent effect on crime. For one thing, many victims of crime do not want to participate in sentencing hearings even if it is their right to do so.[34] Beyond this, there are virtually no published studies on the effect of victim's voice laws on crime. One report shows that such laws have promise, but only in terms of increasing the rate of parole denials. That study, conducted in Pennsylvania, found that parole was denied in 43 percent of cases in which the victim offered a statement compared to only 7 percent of cases in which no such statement was made.[35]

Community Prosecution

Community policing was discussed in Chapter 5. It has revolutionized policing by emphasizing cooperation and collaboration between police and citizens. On the heels of the community policing movement is the rapidly emerging **community prosecution** movement.[36] As of this writing, community prosecution is where community policing was approximately 15 years ago. It is now in full swing in several counties and cities around the United States. It is an exciting crime control development that is reshaping the prosecutor's role in many unmistakable ways.

community prosecution: an approach to crime control and prevention that is intended to improve cooperation and collaboration between prosecutors and individuals outside the criminal justice system, such as community members and business leaders.

Community prosecution is to prosecutors (district attorneys and city attorneys alike) what community policing is to police officers. It is an approach that is intended to improve cooperation and collaboration between prosecutors and individuals outside the criminal justice system, such as community members and business leaders. Here is a more formal definition of community prosecution that was put forth by one of the first authors to write about this emerging law enforcement strategy:

> More than anything else, community prosecution is an organizational response to the grassroots public safety demands of neighborhoods, as expressed in highly concrete terms by the people who live in them. They identify immediate, specific crime problems they want addressed and that the incident-based 911 system is ill suited to handle.[37]

Some prosecutors are quick to say that they have been doing this type of prosecution for many years and that only recently has the term *community prosecution* been attached to the practice. Indeed, many city attorneys, whose jobs often require the prosecution of misdemeanors, claim that community prosecution has been going on for decades. They say that their job has always consisted of dealing with low-level crime problems. Although this is certainly true in some jurisdictions, what makes community prosecution distinctly different from the prosecution of misdemeanors is the two-way relationship between prosecutors and outsiders that was largely absent in the past.

Also, community prosecution—like certain aspects of community policing—is premised on Wilson and Kelling's now-famous broken windows thesis, which claims that low-level offenses should be targeted in an effort to stave off serious crime.[38] Indeed, community prosecution is so connected to the broken windows line of thinking that George Kelling has written about it in a report for the National Institute of Justice. That report, which was authored by Catherine Coles, claims that two trends were occurring in the world of prosecution during the 1990s, both of which ushered in the new community prosecution era:

> First, prosecutors themselves were attempting to develop greater capacities for addressing specific crime problems having a grave impact on public safety and the quality of life. . . . Second, prosecutors met up with the newly developing movement identified widely today as "community justice," which placed pressure on criminal justice agencies to question their "professional" mode of operation, and increase their responsiveness and accountability to citizens.[39]

THE STRUCTURE OF COMMUNITY PROSECUTION. One of the more well-developed community prosecution units is found in the San Diego, California, City Attorney's Office. It is called the Neighborhood Prosecution Unit:

> The neighborhood prosecutors are resources to their respective commands and to the community. They have regular visibility at their respective substations and community centers as well as at weekly meetings. They are at the substations to assist officers, detectives, and command supervisors with prosecution-related issues. . . . The neighborhood prosecutors [also] attend weekly meetings with community members to hear their concerns about quality-of-life crimes, including prostitution, graffiti, drug activity, transient activity, chronic nuisance offenders, and excessive noise.[40]

San Diego's approach is not unique. Other jurisdictions around the country have undertaken a wide array of creative strategies for dealing with crime and public safety. Community prosecutors have targeted everything from repeat offenders and neighborhoods that are plagued by drug dealing to blighted housing and code violations. To this end, prosecutors have used the heavier-handed criminal law approach, civil remedies (such as lawsuits against slumlords), and even techniques that rely on no court involvement whatsoever.

Under President Clinton, community prosecution enjoyed federal funding. The grant program, which was administered by the Bureau of Justice Assistance in the U.S. Justice Department, provided funds for prosecuting attorneys' offices to plan, implement, and enhance community prosecution programs. As of this writing, some agencies are still funded by these grants. But when President George W. Bush was elected, his pet project became Project Safe Neighborhoods (discussed earlier in the chapter), and community prosecution funding all but dried up. Community prosecutors are currently struggling to find funding to keep their programs alive. No federal support for community prosecution is available as of this writing.

NONTRADITIONAL RESTRAINING ORDERS.   Among some of the San Diego city attorney's claimed successes in the area of community prosecution are restraining orders against prostitutes who solicit customers in business districts. San Diego's neighborhood prosecutors have actually helped business owners to file restraining orders against prostitutes out of a concern that prostitutes drive away the businesses' customers. This type of legal assistance is a marked departure from traditionally reactive prosecution strategies.

CODE ENFORCEMENT.   Prosecutors are also relying more and more on code enforcement strategies to target neighborhood quality-of-life issues. For example, each community prosecutor in the Dallas city attorney's office has his or her own code enforcement officer. The theory is that by fixing code violations, neighborhoods will appear cleaner and safer. Consistent with the broken windows theory of crime, it is hoped that improved quality of life will deter serious crime. When code enforcement does not work, Dallas' city attorneys use their civil jurisdiction to file lawsuits against property owners who fail to control criminal activity on their properties or who fail to maintain adequate housing for their lessees.

NUISANCE ABATEMENT.   A nuisance abatement strategy can be seen in Hennepin County, Minnesota. There, assistant district attorneys invoke Minnesota's civil nuisance abatement law to deal with properties that, because of criminal conduct taking place on the premises, adversely affect the neighborhoods in which they are located. First, cease-and-desist notices are sent to property owners. If nothing changes, prosecutors invoke the nuisance abatement law. It requires a showing of two or more "behavioral incidents" (e.g., repeated drug dealing) that signify that a property is a public nuisance. Police and resident testimony can be used to this end. The result is that a property can be effectively shut down and boarded up for a period of one year.

FORFEITURE.   Prosecutors have used civil asset forfeiture (see Chapter 9) as an alternative to criminal prosecution. For example, San Diego's neighborhood prosecutors pushed for a city ordinance that would provide for the forfeiture of cars that are used in illegal street racing incidents. The ordinance passed, and prosecutors can require illegal street racers forfeit their cars. Closely tied to the forfeiture ordinance was a so-called spectator ordinance. The ordinance also made it an arrestable offense to be caught as a spectator at a street racing event.

OTHER CREATIVE APPROACHES. Other recent examples of community prosecution are everywhere. For example, in Austin, Texas, prosecutors operate a reentry initiative that helps offenders who are released from local correctional facilities to transition back into the community. As part of the program, prosecutors leverage resources to provide a better start for released criminals and also warn them of the consequences of reoffending. In Brooklyn, New York, prosecutors practice zone prosecution, which keeps them in one area, trying the cases that arise from the area in which they work. Dallas, Texas, city attorneys organize so-called ACTION (All Coming Together in Our Neighborhood) teams that bring together officials from several public agencies in regular meetings at which creative solutions to the crime problem are developed and implemented. Other prosecutors' offices maintain websites on which interested people can trace the progress of any criminal case within the jurisdiction.

COMMUNITY PROSECUTION RESEARCH. Unfortunately, because community prosecution is relatively new, there are virtually no studies that suggest that it has a substantial effect on the crime problem. Although one report suggests that aggressive prosecution of misdemeanors might reduce serious crime,[41] no other researchers have shown that community prosecution is on the right track. One study has shown that it is sometimes difficult for prosecutors to part with traditional practices,[42] but it is hard to believe that this emerging practice can be harmful. Much anecdotal evidence (cited in the preceding subsections) suggests that many strategies that fall under the rubric of community prosecution can produce desirable results.

Deferred Prosecution

Deferred prosecution amounts to delaying filing of criminal charges against a suspect until he or she fulfills some obligation (or fails to do so). The obligation could be participation in a treatment or diversion program. It could also amount to a probation term. For example, if the suspect successfully completes a period of probation supervision, the prosecutor will forgo criminal charges. This is the approach that has been taken in several jurisdictions around the country. For example, the Kalamazoo County Citizens' Probation Authority, which operated during the late 1970s, allowed suspected offenders an opportunity to complete a pretrial period of probation supervision.[43] If probation was successfully completed, the person's record for the criminal offense was expunged.

Not surprisingly, deferred prosecution raises some concerns. Although it might serve the noble purpose of reducing the stigma of a criminal charge on one's record, some have argued that the practice threatens important constitutional protections.[44] First, the right to counsel might be threatened because deferred prosecution basically amounts to adjudication without trial. Second, deferred prosecution might run counter to the Fifth Amendment's self-incrimination clause. The reason is that it basically coerces the suspect into admitting a degree of guilt, even though a guilty verdict was not obtained, nor was a trial even conducted. Even so, it appears that deferred prosecution has not been limited by our nation's courts.

Surprisingly, deferred prosecution has been subjected to little research. A handful of studies were published in the 1970s,[45] but little has been published since. Therefore, we are unable to determine whether the practice has a measurable effect on program participants or crime rates in general. There are two possible reasons for the lack of research. First, as we have seen, there is surprisingly little research on prosecutors and the effectiveness of their approaches to the crime problem. Second, deferred prosecution looks strikingly similar to diversion. Diversion amounts to steering suspects out of the criminal process and into a treatment or rehabilitation program. The difference between diversion and deferred prosecution is that the former need not involve a prosecution decision.

Deferred Sentencing

Deferred sentencing represents a twist on deferred prosecution. Instead of putting off charges, it puts off sentencing. Furthermore, deferred sentencing requires defendants to plead guilty to a crime, and then, provided that they complete a diversion and/or treatment program, their record will be expunged. A prime example of deferred sentencing in operation, one that has been rigorously evaluated, is Brooklyn, New York's Drug Treatment Alternative to Prison (DTAP) program.[46]

The DTAP program was started by Charles Hynes, Brooklyn's elected district attorney, in response to an alarming increase in drug arrests in Brooklyn during the late 1980s. According to figures from the National Center on Substance and Alcohol Abuse at Columbia University, drug arrests there escalated by some 325 percent between 1981 and 1990.[47] When Hynes assumed his position, 8,182 indictments had been filed against drug felons in Brooklyn in one year. He developed the DTAP program to divert eligible drug offenders into treatment and avoid the traditional revolving-door method of dealing with chronic drug offenders.

Before 1998, the DTAP program was reserved for defendants arrested during buy-bust encounters who had been previously convicted of a nonviolent felony. The program provided for deferred prosecution if eligible defendants agreed to participate in 15 to 24 months of intensive drug treatment and vocational training. Defendants who refused to participate would most likely be convicted and sent to prison. If participants in the DTAP program failed, they would start the process over again—a new prosecution and a new agreement to participate in treatment.

In January 1998, the DTAP program was significantly altered. It changed from a deferred prosecution program to a deferred sentencing program. Now, instead of holding the charges in abeyance, prosecutors obtain guilty pleas from DTAP participants. Sentencing is deferred pending successful completion of the treatment and vocational program, at which point the defendant's guilty plea is withdrawn, and the charges are dismissed. Those who fail in DTAP are brought back to court by the district attorney's special warrant enforcement team, and sentencing takes place.

Because most DTAP participants are second-time predicate felons (i.e., those with previous felony convictions), they face a mandatory prison sentence of between four and a half and nine years in prison under New York State's second felony offender law. Not all DTAP failures are automatically sent to prison; the District Attorney determines, on a case-by-case basis, whether someone should be readmitted to the program. Thus, there is a degree of screening that takes place.

DTAP participants are chosen by the district attorney's office after careful review. Once candidates are chosen, Brooklyn's Treatment Alternatives to Street Crime program screens defendants so that they can be assigned to an appropriate treatment facility. Only the candidates who demonstrate a willingness to participate in a therapeutic community model and who do not have a history of violence or mental disorders may participate in treatment. Once DTAP participants enter treatment, the treatment facilities have the discretion to expel participants for relapses, fights, and other wrongdoing.

The DTAP model has apparently met with some success. The National Center on Addiction and Substance Abuse (CASA) at Columbia University recently concluded an extensive evaluation of the DTAP program. The study, which was funded by the National Institute on Drug Abuse, was designed to compare the benefits of residential treatment for repeat felony drug offenders compared to the traditional approach of prosecution, sentencing, and prison. The evaluation consisted of a sample of 280 DTAP participants and a matched sample of 130 other people who went through the traditional criminal justice process. Another sample of DTAP participants was used to measure changes in employment before and after drug treatment. Finally, data from 1,400 current and former DTAP participants were used to determine treatment retention rates before and after the 1998 changes to a deferred sentencing model.

One of the CASA study's findings was that DTAP participants had rearrest rates that were 26 percent lower two years after they completed the program than those of the matched comparison group. In addition, DTAP participants had reconviction rates that were 36 percent lower two years after completion of treatment than those of the comparison group. DTAP participants were also 67 percent less likely to return to prison after two years, and they were 41 percent less likely to receive a new jail or prison sentence.

The CASA study also found that DTAP participants were less likely to relapse than were offenders who were handled through the traditional criminal process. Moreover, the DTAP program had a high retention rate, more than six times the median stay for most treatment programs. DTAP participants were three and a half times more likely to be employed on exit from the program than before entry.

Finally, the cost savings generated by the DTAP program are impressive. The program's results are achieved at about half the cost of incarceration. CASA researchers reported that it costs $32,975 to put someone through DTAP, whereas the cost is $64,338 to send a person to prison. According to recent figures from the Kings County district attorney's office, the DTAP program, with 708 graduates as of October 1, 2003, has resulted in overall cost savings to New Yorkers of $27,358,640.[48]

DTAP's cost savings estimates also speak to its continuing success. At first glance, the costs associated with treatment might seem unmanageable, but when a drug offender is diverted from prison and successfully completes treatment, significant savings are achieved. Indeed, CASA's evaluation did not factor in cost savings arising from higher employment rates and long-term expenses associated with relapses, rearrests, additional convictions, and lengthy prison terms. Brooklyn's DTAP program is a clear-cut example of community prosecution in action.

Does It Work?

The softer side of prosecution in the United States is relatively new. Community prosecution, for instance, has not been formally evaluated as of this writing. Some of its manifestations, such as code enforcement and nuisance abatement, have led to the closure of problem properties and various neighborhood improvements. Atlanta's Neighborhood Fresh Start, which targets notorious crack houses for closure, appears to have increased property values in targeted neighborhoods.

The case can be made that victim assistance is not really intended to reduce the crime problem, so not much can be said about its effectiveness in the present context. Of the various softer prosecution approaches that have been discussed here, deferred sentencing—coupled with adequate treatment—appears to have a positive effect on drug offenders. Columbia University's evaluation of Brooklyn's DTAP program is one of the most encouraging evaluations of criminal justice policy in recent years.

A PLEA BARGAINING PANDEMIC?

Guilty pleas resulting from plea bargaining are the most common method of securing convictions. The overwhelming majority (90 percent by some estimates) of criminal convictions in the United States result from guilty pleas rather than trials. These guilty pleas are usually the result of some bargaining between the defense attorney and the prosecutor. Both parties stand to gain something from a guilty plea; the prosecutor obtains a conviction, and the defense attorney usually "succeeds" in getting a lesser conviction for his or her client.

Plea bargaining is essential to the administration of justice. If every defendant demanded his or her right to a jury trial and succeeded in such a demand, the criminal justice system would literally collapse. In this vein, arguments against plea bargaining are really like thought exercises; nothing can be done to eliminate plea bargaining because there are just too many criminals and not enough prosecutors.

plea bargaining: an agreement between the prosecutor and the defense attorney such that the defendant pleads guilty in exchange for some concession, such as a reduced charge or sentencing recommendation.

Arguments for and against Plea Bargaining

There are several arguments in support of plea bargaining. These have clearly won out because plea bargaining is a widely accepted practice in the justice system. It is widely accepted because, despite certain drawbacks (discussed below), plea bargaining benefits all members of the courtroom workgroup: the judge, prosecutor, and defense attorney (not to mention the defendant). Prosecutors, judges, and defense attorneys, particularly public defenders, work together on a regular basis, so it is in their interest to work together in an effort to speed up adjudication. Thus, the arguments in support of plea bargaining are really arguments concerning the benefits of reaching plea agreements.

Plea bargaining benefits the prosecution because it provides an increased ability to dispose of a busy caseload. District attorneys are often faced with limited resources and therefore cannot prosecute every case that comes before them. Specifically, the district attorney might opt to pursue charges on cases that have a highly public element and/or are likely to result in guilty convictions. Cases that do not look promising may be prime candidates for a bargain. According to one observer, prosecutors might favor plea bargaining simply because it allows the courtroom workgroup to further its "mutual interest in avoiding conflict, reducing uncertainty, and maintaining group cohesion."[49]

Defense attorneys also benefit from plea bargaining. Public defenders, the most common type of counsel in criminal trials, face resource constraints that are similar to those of prosecutors. Thus, plea bargaining benefits public defenders by allowing quick disposition of cases. It also allows them to focus on cases that they perceive as being more worthy of trial. Bargaining also benefits privately retained counsel because it speeds up the process, which translates into more money for less work. This is not to suggest, however, that defense attorneys are goldbrickers; many jealously guard the interests of their clients.

On one level, plea bargaining benefits the defendant perhaps more than the prosecution or the defense attorney. The obvious reason for this is that the defendant generally receives a lesser sentence (or a lesser charge, which also affects the ultimate punishment) as a result of a plea bargain. On another level, however, as we will see, defendants lose their chance for an acquittal and sometimes important rights, including the right to a trial by jury. But the Supreme Court has said that these costs may be outweighed by the benefits of "avoiding the anxieties and uncertainties of trial."[50]

The court also benefits from plea bargaining. The prompt disposition of cases saves judicial resources. The reason for this should be clear; plea bargaining takes less time than a full-blown trial and does not require the expenses of a jury trial. In fact, to the chagrin of many, even victims may benefit from plea bargaining. A quickly reached plea bargain might give the victim the satisfaction of having the case closed quickly. Victims also might not want to testify or risk the possibility that the prosecution will succeed in obtaining a conviction.[51]

Plea bargaining also poses some problems. One is that in an effort to secure a conviction, the prosecutor will start with the most serious charge and work down from there. That is, prosecutors might "overcharge" as a first step in the bargaining process. This negotiation process is much like that associated with buying a car at a dealership; the dealer usually starts with a ridiculously high price but is willing to negotiate. In the end, however, few buyers end up purchasing a car for its fair market value. The concern with plea bargaining, then, is that defendants will be encouraged to plead guilty to an offense that is more serious than that of which they would be convicted at a trial.

Plea bargaining, according to many commentators, is a method of streamlining the adjudication process; it is prized on efficiency grounds. However, some critics of plea bargaining claim that the practice actually contributes to *inefficiency*. As one researcher observed, "defense attorneys commonly devise strategies whose only utility lies in the threat they pose to the court's and prosecutor's time."[52] Defense attorneys might also lose sight of their responsibility for serving defendants and instead encourage defendants to plead guilty as part of a law confidence game.[53]

Some critics believe not only that plea bargaining is inefficient, but also that it wastes time. These people claim that plea bargaining is not necessary to obtain guilty pleas and that most defendants will plead guilty anyway if they think that there is a high degree of probability that trial would result in a verdict of guilty.[54]

Perhaps one of the best-known criticisms of plea bargaining is that it undermines the integrity of the criminal justice system. Throughout this book, we have covered (and will continue to cover) the complex rules of criminal procedure set forth in the U.S. Constitution and interpreted by the Supreme Court. Critics of plea bargaining claim that the practice circumvents these "rigorous standards of due process and proof imposed during trials."[55]

Another reason that plea bargaining might undermine the criminal process is that it effectively decides the defendant's "guilt" without a trial, an exhaustive investigation, or the presentation of evidence and witness testimony. As was mentioned earlier in this section, the defendant's guilt is in effect decided by the prosecutor. One critic has argued that plea bargaining decisions result from improper considerations:

> One mark of a just legal system is that it minimizes the effect of tactical choices upon the outcome of its processes. In criminal cases, the extent of an offender's punishment ought to turn primarily upon what he did and, perhaps, upon his personal characteristics rather than upon a postcrime, postarrest decision to exercise or not to exercise some procedural option.[56]

Yet another argument against plea bargaining is that it allows criminals to "get away" with their crimes, or at least get lenient sentences. Further, critics claim that reduced sentences might reduce the deterrent effect of harsh punishment. In both cases, plea bargaining might give the impression that defendants can negotiate their way out of being adequately punished for their crimes. At the other extreme, critics of plea bargaining claim that innocent individuals might be coerced to plead guilty. In such situations a plea bargain amounts to an admission of legal guilt when in fact the defendant might not be factually guilty.

Attempts to Limit Plea Bargaining

Concerns over plea bargaining have even led some jurisdictions to abandon the practice. In fact, at one point, the whole state of Alaska banned plea bargaining, which led researchers to conclude that "the efficient operation of Alaska's criminal justice system did not depend upon plea bargaining."[57]

Several other jurisdictions have experimented with restricting the practice of plea bargaining. The experiences of these jurisdictions are perhaps more illustrative than the Alaska experience. (Alaska is not exactly the epicenter of America's crime problem.) Methods of restricting plea bargaining have ranged from outright bans to bans on plea bargains in cases involving certain types of crimes.

One method by which some jurisdictions have restricted plea bargaining is to impose cutoff dates. These cutoff dates prohibit plea bargaining after a case has been in process for a certain amount of time. For example, the Brooklyn district attorney has adopted a cutoff date of 74 days after indictment.[58] Before the deadline, plea bargaining is acceptable. If a case goes all the way to trial within the cutoff period, plea bargaining could conceivably take place all the way through jury deliberations.

Another method of restricting plea bargaining has been to ban pleas. These bans prohibit either some or all types of plea agreements. Alaska is, of course, the most notable example of a total ban. In 1975, Alaska's attorney general banned all forms of plea bargaining in an effort to increase convictions and restore public confidence in the justice system.[59] In a study on the ban, Alaska's Judicial Council found that

> plea bargaining as an institution was clearly curtailed. The routine expectation of a negotiated settlement was removed; for most practitioners justifiable reliance on negotiation to settle criminal cases greatly diminished in importance. There is less face-to-face discussion between adversaries, and when meetings do occur, they are not usually as productive as they used to be.[60]

It is important to understand that Alaska banned plea bargaining but not guilty pleas. Defendants could still plead guilty to the crimes for which they were charged. In fact, the Judicial Council also found that the rate of guilty pleas remained essentially the same in the wake of the ban, suggesting that some degree of behind-the-scenes plea bargaining was perhaps still taking place. Also, in Alaska, the attorney general could hire and fire the district attorneys, which gave the attorney general substantial leverage to ban plea bargaining. In most jurisdictions around the country, district attorneys are elected officials and do not serve at the whim of the state attorney general.

Some jurisdictions have experimented with banning plea bargaining for certain offenses. For example, the Bronx County district attorney enacted a ban on plea bargaining whenever a grand jury returned a felony indictment. This move was seriously criticized, as are most attempts to restrict plea bargaining, but the district attorney stated that the ban "means that society has ceded control to those it has accused of violating its laws; and it means that our system is running us, instead of the other way around."[61] Critics challenged the Bronx County district attorney's ban on postfelony indictment plea bargaining for at least two reasons: It did not eliminate plea bargaining, and the policy encouraged plea bargaining before indictment.[62]

Another approach, which was tried in Philadelphia, was the jury waiver. The jury waiver gives defendants the opportunity to engage in plea negotiations in exchange for giving up their right to a jury trial. Actually, this approach is not plea bargaining in the traditional sense. Instead, the defendant gets his or her day in court, but to receive concessions from the state, the defendant must not demand a jury trial. This process has come to be known as the "slow plea of guilty" insofar as it does not result in the disposition of a case before trial. One researcher described the process in more detail:

> Slow pleas are informal and abbreviated, and consist largely of the defense's presentation of statements concerning the defendant's allegedly favorable personal characteristics. . . . The defense presentation is not concerned with guilt or innocence since it usually is implicitly assumed by all parties involved in the process that the defendant is guilty of at least some wrongdoing.[63]

Still other attempts to restrict or ban plea bargaining have occurred. California attempted to abandon plea bargaining by popular referendum in 1982. The voters passed the referendum, and the resulting statute[64] imposes the following restrictions: no plea bargaining in any case involving (1) a serious felony, (2) a felony in which a firearm was used, or (2) the offense of driving under the influence. Plea bargaining is permissible, however, if the prosecution's evidence is weak, witnesses are unavailable, or a plea agreement does not result in a significantly reduced sentence. Despite the statute, plea bargaining continues almost unabated in California.[65]

El Paso, Texas, also experimented with plea bargaining restrictions. There, two state district judges adopted a policy of prohibiting all plea negotiations in their courts as a method of ensuring equal treatment for similarly situated defendants.[66] Maricopa County, Arizona, adopted a similar approach. Five Maricopa County Superior Court judges adopted a policy that prohibited plea agreements based on stipulated (i.e., agreed-on) sentences. In other words, the judges refused to accept plea agreements that included a negotiated sentence. They believed that sentencing should be a decision left to the trial courts.

Ad Hoc Plea Bargaining

One researcher recently used the term **ad hoc plea bargaining** to refer to some strange concessions that defendants agree to make as part of the prosecutor's decision to secure a guilty plea.[67] He states,

> Ad hoc bargains exist in at least five forms: (1) the court may impose an extraordinary condition of probation following a guilty plea, (2) the defendant may offer or be required to perform some act as a quid pro quo for a dismissal or more lenient sentence, (3) the court may impose an unauthorized form of punishment as a substitute for a statutorily established method of punishment, (4) the State may offer some unauthorized benefit in return for a plea of guilty, or (5) the defendant may be permitted to plead guilty to an unauthorized offense, such as a "hypothetical" or nonexistent charge, a nonapplicable lesser-included offense, or a nonrelated charge.[68]

He also states that ad hoc plea bargaining

> may involve neither a plea nor a sentence. For example, if a defendant charged with public intoxication seeks to avoid a statutorily mandated minimum sentence of ten days in the county jail, the prosecutor might agree to dismiss the charges if the defendant agrees to make a monetary contribution to a local driver's education program.[69]

Even judges can get involved in ad hoc plea bargaining. Colquitt points to one shocking example of this method of bargaining run amok.[70] The case involved a woman who was required to participate in a drug treatment program as a result of several narcotics convictions. The probation officer asked to have the woman removed from the program because she supposedly failed to follow program guidelines. At a hearing to decide on the matter, the woman, "who was wearing a low-cut sweater, bent over several times to remove documents from her purse. Thereafter, the judge dismissed all criminal charges against the woman. When his clerk asked why the charges had been dropped, [the judge] replied, 'she showed me her boobs.'"[71] The judge was subsequently removed from the bench. Some other less extreme examples of ad hoc plea concessions (and some relevant cases) are described in Figure 6.5.

Does It Work?

Plea bargaining is both time-honored and here to stay. Attempts to abolish it are unlikely to succeed, so it is doubtful that any positive effects in terms of crime control will be witnessed. Ad hoc plea bargaining is a relatively recent practice, so its future remains uncertain. Courts have slammed the door on certain types of plea agreements, but others, such as those listed in Figure 6.5, might accomplish a great deal. Researchers would do well to study the effectiveness of creative plea agreements.

---

1. Charitable contributions in lieu of fines or jail terms (e.g., *State* v. *Stellato* 523 A.2d 1345, 1349 [Conn. App. Ct. 1987]; *Ratliff* v. *State* 596 N.E.2d 241, 243 [Ind. Ct. App. 1992])

2. Relinquished property ownership (e.g., *United States* v. *Thao Dinh Lee* 173 F.3d 1258, 1278 [10th Cir. 1999])

3. Agreement not to work in a particular profession or agreement to surrender a professional license (e.g., *United States* v. *Hoffer* 129 F.3d 1196, 1199 [11th Cir. 1997])

4. Voluntary agreement to undergo sterilization (e.g., *State* v. *Pasicznyk* 1997 WL 79501 [Wash. Ct. App. Feb. 25, 1997])

5. Voluntary agreement to undergo surgical castration (e.g., *ACLU* v. *State* 5 S.W.2d 418, 419 [Ark. 1999])

6. Agreement to enter the Army on a four-year enlistment (e.g., *State* v. *Hamrick* 595 N.W. 2d 492, 494 [Iowa 1999])

7. Agreement not to appeal (e.g., *People* v. *Collier* 641 N.Y.S.2d 181 [App. Div. 1996])

8. Shaming punishments (such as bumper stickers for convicted DUI offenders) (e.g., *Ballenger* v. *State* 436 S.E.2d 793, 794 [Ga. Ct. App. 1993])

9. Agreement to seal the records of a case (e.g., *State* v. *Campbell* 21 Media L. Rep. 1895 [Wash. Super. Ct. 1993])

10. Ordering offenders to surrender profits, such as from books written about their crimes (e.g., *Rolling* v. *State ex rel. Butterworth* 741 So.2d 627 [Fla. Dist. Ct. App. 1999])

11. Banishment to another location (e.g., *State* v. *Culp* 226 S.E.2d 841, 842 [N.C. Ct. App. 1976]; *Phillips* v. *State* 512 S.E.2d 32, 33 [Ga. Ct. App. 1999])

12. Pleading guilty to nonexistent crimes (i.e., actions that are not prohibited by law) (e.g., *Bassin* v. *Isreal* 335 N.E.2d 53, 57 [Ill. App. Ct. 1975])

FIGURE 6.5 Examples of Ad Hoc Plea Bargaining Concessions

Source: Adapted from Joseph A. Colquitt, "Ad Hoc Plea Bargaining," *Tulane Law Review* 75(2001): 69. See Colquitt's article for a thorough discussion of various, sometimes stranger, concessions made as a result of ad hoc plea bargaining.

Summary

Prosecutors are arguably the most powerful criminal justice officials. They decide which cases go to court (or are pled out). Without their decisions to take cases forward, the term *revolving-door justice* would be given new meaning. Strangely, though, prosecutors have been all but ignored by criminal justice researchers. Consequently, we know little about the effectiveness of prosecutorial approaches to crime control in the United States.

That having been said, there is some promise in the world of prosecution. Various types of community prosecution have made improvements, mostly on a micro level. Also, deferred sentencing coupled with drug treatment, as in the case of Brooklyn's DTAP program, might be worth pursuing further.

On the flip side, the heavy-handed prosecution approach is either underresearched or ineffective. There are few published evaluations that support no-drop prosecution policies, partnerships between prosecutors and other actors, or the most recent approach to crime in the world of prosecution: Project Safe Neighborhoods. It will be interesting to follow developments in the prosecution literature over the next few years.

Notes

1. Elizabeth Glazer, "Thinking Strategically: How Federal Prosecutors Can Reduce Violent Crime," *Fordham Urban Law Journal* 26 (1999): 573–606.
2. Ibid.
3. R.C. Davis, B.E. Smith, and H.J. Davies, "Effects of No-Drop Prosecution of Domestic Violence upon Conviction Rates," *Justice Research and Policy* 3 (2001): 1–3.
4. K. Robbins, "No-Drop Prosecution of Domestic Violence: Just Good Policy, or Equal Protection Mandate?" *Stanford Law Review* 52 (1999): 205–33.
5. A. Corsilles, "No-Drop Policies in the Prosecution of Domestic Violence Cases: Guarantee to Action or Dangerous Solution?" *Fordham Law Review* 63 (1994): 853–81.
6. For a summary of the research, see R.C. Davis, B.E. Smith, and H.J. Davies, "Effects of No-Drop Prosecution of Domestic Violence upon Conviction Rates," *Justice Research and Policy* 3 (2001): 1–13.
7. Ibid.
8. P. Griffin, P. Torbet, and L. Szymanski, *Trying Juveniles in Adult Court: An Analysis of State Transfer Provisions* (Washington, DC: U.S. Department of Justice, Office of Juvenile Justice and Delinquency Prevention, 1998).
9. P. Torbet and L. Szymanski, *State Legislative Responses to Violent Juvenile Crime: 1996–97 Update* (Washington, DC: U.S. Department of Justice, Office of Juvenile Justice and Delinquency Prevention, 1998).
10. M. Sickmund, A.L. Stahl, T.A. Finnegan, N. Snyder, and J.A. Butts, *Juvenile Court Statistics 1995* (Washington, DC: U.S. Department of Justice, Office of Juvenile Justice and Delinquency Prevention, 1998).
11. J.M. Brown and P.A. Langan, *State Court Sentencing of Convicted Felons* (Washington, DC: U.S. Department of Justice, 1998).
12. C.M. Puzzanchera, *Delinquency Cases Waived to Criminal Court, 1990–1999* (Washington, DC: U.S. Department of Justice, Office of Juvenile Justice and Delinquency Prevention, 2003).
13. J. Fagan, "Separating the Men from the Boys: The Comparative Advantage of Juvenile Versus Criminal Court Sanctions on Recidivism among Adolescent Felony Offenders," in *A Sourcebook: Serious, Violent and Chronic Juvenile Offenders* eds. J.C. Howell, B. Krisberg, J.D. Hawkins, and J.J. Wilson (Thousand Oaks, CA: Sage, 1995), 238–60.
14. E.L. Jensen and L.K. Metsger, "Test of the Deterrent Effect of Legislative Waiver on Violent Juvenile Crime," *Crime and Delinquency* 40 (1994): 96–104.
15. D.A. Risler, T. Sweatman, and L. Nackerud, "Evaluating the Georgia Legislative Waiver's Effectiveness in Deterring Juvenile Crime," *Research on Social Work Practice* 8 (1998):657–67.
16. C.J. Smith, K.S. Craig, K. Block, A. Patrick, and A. Hall, *Maryland Department of Juvenile Justice Partnership to Study Waiver Effects: A Final Report* (Baltimore, MD: University of Baltimore, 2000).
17. D.P. Mears, "Critique of Waiver Research: Critical Next Steps in Assessing the Impacts of Laws for Transferring Juveniles to the Criminal Justice System," *Youth Violence and Juvenile Justice* 1 (2003): 156–172.
18. J. Buchanan, "Police-Prosecutor Teams: Innovations in Several Jurisdictions," *Georgia Trooper* 4 (1990): 35, 37, 39, 41, 43.
19. *R.O.A.D. Team to Target Aggressive Motorists: Marion County Traffic Safety Partnership Launches New Initiative* (Marion County, IN: Marion County Prosecutor's Office, Feb. 28, 2001). Available at indygov.org/pros/traffic/press022801.htm.

20. Boston Police Department, *Operation Cease Fire* (Boston, MA: Boston Police Department, n.d.); see also *A Community-Based Response: One City's Success Story*. Washington, DC: Office of the Attorney General, 1996.

21. Anthony A. Braga, David M. Kennedy, Elin J. Waring, and Anne Morrison Piehl, "Problem-Oriented Policing, Deterrence, and Youth Violence: An Evaluation of Boston's Operation Ceasefire," *Journal of Research in Crime and Delinquency* 38 (2001): 195–225.

22. American Prosecutors Research Institute, *Combating Gun Violence: An In-Depth Look at Richmond's Project Exile* (Alexandria, VA: American Prosecutors Research Institute, 2001). Available at ndaa-apri.org.

23. American Prosecutors Research Institute, *Combating Gun Violence: Promising Practices for America's Prosecutors* (Alexandria, VA: American Prosecutors Research Institute, 2003).

24. R. Rosenfeld, R. Fornango, and E. Baumer, "Did Ceasefire, Compstat, and Exile Reduce Homicide?" *Criminology and Public Policy* 4 (2005): 419–50.

25. Colorado has done the same. Its program, "Colorado Exile," bears several similarities to the Exile programs in Richmond, Virginia, and in Texas.

26. American Prosecutors Research Institute, *Combating Gun Violence: Promising Practices for America's Prosecutors* (Alexandria, VA: American Prosecutors Research Institute, 2003), 33.

27. For further discussion on PSN, see J.A. Calhoun, "Project Safe Neighborhoods: America's Network against Gun Violence Facilitating the Work of Outreach," *USA Bulletin* 50 (2002): 26–8; E. Dalton, "Targeted Crime Reduction Efforts in Ten Communities: Lessons for the Project Safe Neighborhoods Initiative," *USA Bulletin* 50 (2002): 16–25; J. Donovan, "Project Safe Neighborhoods: A Network to Make America's Communities Safer," *USA Bulletin* 50 (2002): 1–5.

28. Retrieved from psn.gov/about/faqs.html.

29. J.C. Barnes, Megan C. Kurlychek, Holly Ventura Miller, J. Mitchell Miller, and Robert J. Kaminski, "Partial Assessment of South Carolina's Project Safe Neighborhoods Strategy: Evidence From a Sample of Supervised Offenders," *Journal of Criminal Justice* 38 (2010): 383–9.

30. American Prosecutors Research Institute, *Cross-Designation and Federal Firearms Laws: What Local Prosecutors Need to Know* (Alexandria, VA: American Prosecutors Research Institute).

31. R. Lynch, "Improving Treatment of Victims: Some Guides for Action," in *Criminal Justice and the Victim*, ed. William McDonald (Beverly Hills, CA: Sage, 1976), 165–76.

32. For example, a survey of 62 victim service programs in North Carolina showed that victim assistance was inadequate. See Robert A. Jerin, Laura J. Moriarty, and Melissa A. Gibson, "Victim Service or Self Service: An Analysis of Prosecution Based Victim-Witness Assistance Programs and Providers," *Criminal Justice Policy Review* 7 (1995): 142–54.

33. See, for example, Candace McCoy, *Politics and Plea Bargaining: Victims' Rights in California* (Philadelphia: University of Pennsylvania Press, 1993).

34. Dean G. Kilpatrick, David Beatty, and Susan Smith Howley, *The Rights of Crime Victims—Does Legal Protection Make a Difference?* (Washington, DC: U.S. Government Printing Office, 1998); see also Edna Erez and Pamela Tontodonato, "The Effect of Victim Participation in Sentencing on Sentence Outcome," *Criminology* 28 (1990): 451–74.

35. William H. Parsonage, Frances Bernat, and Jacquelin Helfgott, "Victim Impact Testimony and Pennsylvania's Parole Decision Making Process: A Pilot Study," *Criminal Justice Policy Review* 6 (1994): 187–206.

36. Community prosecutors are sometimes called *neighborhood prosecutors*. The latter term is used in San Diego, California.

37. Barbara Boland, "What Is Community Prosecution?" *National Institute of Justice Journal* August (1996): 35–40.

38. James Q. Wilson and George L. Kelling, "Broken Windows: The Police and Neighborhood Safety," *Atlantic Monthly* 249 (1982): 29–38.

39. Catherine M. Coles and George L. Kelling, *Prosecution in the Community: A Study of Emergent Strategies: A Cross Site Analysis* (Cambridge, MA: Harvard University, September 1998).

40. *City Attorney's Office—2002 Annual Overview* (San Diego, CA: Office of the City Attorney, Jan. 31, 2003). Available at genesis/sannet/gov/infospc/templates/attorney/news_priorities_main.jsp.

41. John L. Worrall, *Does Broken Windows Law Enforcement Reduce Serious Crime?* (Sacramento, CA: California Institute for County Government, 2002). Available at cicg.org.

42. Gerard Rainville and M. Elaine Nugent, "Community Prosecution Tenets and Practices: The Relative Mix of "Community and Prosecution," *American Journal of Criminal Justice* 26 (2002): 149–64.

43. P.C. Friday, K.R. Malzahn-Bass, and D.K. Harrington, "Referral and Selection Criteria in Deferred Prosecution: The Impact on the Criminal Justice System," *British Journal of Criminology* 21 (1981): 166–72.

44. K.M. Goetsch, "Deferred Prosecution: A Critical Analysis of Michigan Programs," *Detroit College of Law Review* 1978 (1978): 433–56.

45. See, for example, Michigan Office of Criminal Justice, *Model Evaluation Program: An Examination of Deferred Prosecution in Michigan* (Rockville, MD: National Institute of Justice, 1979); San Diego County Probation Department, *San Diego Probation Department Program: Adult Property Crime Deferred Prosecution Project: Evaluation* (Rockville, MD: National Institute of Justice, 1975); Montana Board of Crime Control, *Assessment of Deferred Prosecution in Billings/Yellowstone County* (Rockville, MD: National Institute of Justice, 1978).

46. We will discuss other treatment-oriented components in Chapter 8. Treatment is discussed here in the context of law enforcement only insofar as it heavily involves prosecutors.

47. Center on Addiction and Substance Abuse, *Crossing the Bridge: An Evaluation of the Drug Treatment Alternative-to-Prison (DTAP) Program* (New York: The National Center

on Addiction and Substance Abuse at Columbia University, 2003).

48. Estimates provided by the Office of the District Attorney, Kings County, New York, 2003.

49. Robert A. Weninger, "The Abolition of Plea Bargaining: A Case Study of El Paso County, Texas," *UCLA Law Review* 35 (1987): 265, 267.

50. *Blackledge* v. *Allison*, 431 U.S. 63 (1977), 71.

51. Carolyn E. Demarest, "Plea Bargaining Can Often Protect the Victim," *New York Times* April 15, 1994, A30.

52. Albert Alschuler, "The Prosecutor's Role in Plea Bargaining," *University of Chicago Law Review* 36 (1968): 50–4.

53. A.S. Blumberg, "The Practice of Law as a Confidence Game: Organization and Co-Optation of a Profession," *Law and Society Review* 1 (1967): 15–39.

54. Peter Arenella, "Rethinking the Functions of Criminal Procedure: The Warren and Burger Courts' Competing Ideologies," *Georgetown Law Journal* 72 (1983): 185, 216–9.

55. Alissa Pollitz Worden, "Policymaking by Prosecutors: The Uses of Discretion in Regulating Plea Bargaining," *Judicature* 73 (1990): 335, 336.

56. Albert W. Alschuler, "The Changing Plea Bargaining Debate," *California Law Review* 69 (1981): 652.

57. Michael L. Rubenstein and Teresa J. White, "Alaska's Ban on Plea Bargaining," *Law and Society Review* 13 (1979): 367.

58. Chester Mirsky, "Plea Reform Is No Bargain," *Newsday* March 4, 1994, 70.

59. Teresa White Carns and John A. Kruse, "Alaska's Ban on Plea Bargaining Reevaluated," *Judicature* 75 (1992): 310, 317.

60. Cited in Douglas D. Guidorizzi, "Should We Really 'Ban' Plea Bargaining?: The Core Concerns of Plea Bargaining Critics," *Emory Law Journal* 47 (1998): 753, 775.

61. See statement of Robert T. Johnson, district attorney, Office of the District Attorney of Bronx County, press release, November 24, 1992.

62. Douglas D. Guidorizzi, "Should We Really 'Ban' Plea Bargaining?: The Core Concerns of Plea Bargaining Critics," *Emory Law Journal* 47 (1998): 753, 778.

63. Martin A. Levin, "Urban Politics and the Criminal Courts," *Law and Society Review* 13 (1979): 583–9.

64. California Penal Code 1192.7.

65. *People* v. *Brown*, 223 Cal. Rptr. 66 (Ct. App. 1986), p. 72 & n. 11.

66. See Robert A. Weninger, "The Abolition of Plea Bargaining: A Case Study of El Paso County, Texas," *UCLA Law Review* 35 (1987): 265, 275.

67. Joseph A. Colquitt, "Ad Hoc Plea Bargaining," *Tulane Law Review* 75 (2001): 695.

68. Ibid., 712.

69. Ibid., 711.

70. Ibid, 695.

71. See *Ryan* v. *Comm'n on Judicial Performance*, 754 P.2d 724, 734 (Cal. 1988).

Crime Control through Legislation

LEARNING OBJECTIVES

■ Discuss the history of legislative bans.

■ Summarize legislative approaches to the crime problem, particularly gun violence.

■ Explain the practice of public notification with respect to sex offenders and determine whether it is effective crime control policy.

■ Summarize legislative approaches to the problems of terrorism and white-collar crime.

Thus far we have paid a fair amount of attention to law enforcement approaches to crime. We have seen that the lion's share of crime control by law enforcement consists of actions by police officers. Prosecutors are law enforcement officers as well, but there has been surprisingly little research on the effectiveness of prosecution approaches to America's crime problem. Now we move away from the law enforcement realm and turn to crime control that plays out in legislatures, courts, and corrections institutions.

This chapter begins with a look at legislation aimed specifically at various forms of crime control. It begins with legislative bans, such as bans on guns and certain controlled substances. Then attention shifts to public notification laws, notably those aimed at informing the public of the location of convicted sex offenders. Finally, laws aimed at contemporary problems, notably white-collar crime and terrorism, are considered. In those sections we look at such legislation as the Sarbanes–Oxley Act of 2002 and the anti-terrorism Patriot Act.

Note that this chapter does *not* present an exhaustive review of crime control legislation. Rather, it covers some of the more popular and controversial legislative approaches to crime. It would be impossible, given this limited space, to thoroughly cover state and federal criminal law. Also, as you read through this section of the book, you will note that later chapters touch on legislation to some extent, as well. The three-strikes section of the sentencing chapter (Chapter 9), for example, considers a specific type of law. Three-strikes legislation is best covered there, however, because the concern is with sentencing. The laws considered in this chapter by contrast, are not closely tied to sentencing per se.

LEGISLATIVE BANS

One of the most common approaches to crime control in the United States is for legislators to ban certain devices and substances that are thought to contribute to the crime problem. Untold number of bans have been instituted over the years, and they continue to be popular. Two stand out, however. First, is our nation's experiment with banning certain guns and gun-related products. Also, we have poured a staggering amount of resources into a ban on drugs. Here we turn attention to the research on the effectiveness of these approaches.

Where There's a Demand, There's a Supply

With respect to America's drug problem, it is useful to think in terms of supply and demand in order to understand why we have been unsuccessful in abating the problem. In simple terms, where there is a demand, there will be a supply. This means that so long as the justice system fails to target the demand for drugs that exists, the supply will eventually find its way to consumers. Our nation's response to the drug problem has been decidedly supply-side–oriented, with comparatively few resources devoted to reducing the demand for illicit drugs. In other words, we have waged war on drugs, taking a highly punitive approach to the problem. According to one source:

> The punitiveness is reflected both in budgets and the extent of incarceration. At least three-quarters of the national U.S. drug control budget is spent on apprehending and punishing drug dealers and users, with treatment getting about two-thirds of the remainder. In terms of punishment, the U.S. imprisonment rate for drug offenses alone is much higher than that of most Western European nations for all crimes.[1]

America's tough-on-drugs approach is not concerned purely with interdicting and eradicating illicit substances, however. At the core of the war on drugs is a basic economic assumption that stringently enforced prohibition will raise drug prices to such a high level that the demand for them will disappear, or at least be reduced. But research shows that enforcement does not do a good job of affecting the price of illegal drugs. A number of studies show that drug prices are surprisingly resistant to increased enforcement efforts.[2] It should be clear by now where this section is headed: Bans that do not *directly* address demand are doomed to fail.

Historical Lessons

Critics of America's approach to guns and drugs point to history and its lessons. They argue that past experiences with attempts to ban various products and services have failed miserably. In support of their position, they cite America's experiences with such vices as gambling, prostitution, and alcohol. The crux of their argument is that bans result in one of two problems. First, a ban that is not universally agreed on as constituting effective crime control policy will be circumvented by some, resulting in only partial enforcement. Second, critics of bans argue that criminalization creates a black market where products and services will be provided by profit-seeking criminal syndicates.

GAMBLING AND PROSTITUTION. A series of scandals with nineteenth century lotteries led to prohibition and strict enforcement of gambling activities across the United States—at least until the relatively recent explosion in casino gaming on Indian reservations and in cities such as Las Vegas.[3] The Mafia was also believed to be associated with illegal gambling activities, so it was felt that aggressive enforcement of anti-gambling laws was necessary. Additionally, police corruption was thought to be intimately tied to gambling.[4] But, at the same time gambling was criminalized, there was a widespread perception that it was not the most significant societal ill. According to one study, "gambling cases were handled as low level routine prosecutions, to be disposed of as expeditiously as possible."[5] And another study showed that only 1 in 50 felony gambling convictions resulted in a prison sentence.[6]

The same lessons appear to hold true for prostitution. Presently, all states (with the exception of rural counties in Nevada) have chosen to criminalize prostitution. States' bans on prostitution have resulted in a relatively significant number of arrests. For example, one researcher found that arrests for prostitution in America's sixteen largest cities were on par with the number of arrests for violent crime.[7] But the problem is that few of the arrests appear to result in incarceration.[8] This suggests that judges do not feel prostitution is a particularly serious offense. Indeed, a United States Justice Department survey of crime seriousness appears to confirm this; respondents ranked prostitution 174 out of 204 offenses in terms of its seriousness.

In short, America's attempts to criminalize gambling and prostitution have not produced the desired consequences. Both activities obviously persist—and on a large scale. There also appears to be significant disagreement among Americans as to how serious and damaging both activities really are. Much the same observations can be applied to the war on drugs: Unless there is a fair degree of consensus about the seriousness of the problem, enforcement is bound to be inadequate and partial.

PROHIBITION. America's experiment with the prohibition of alcohol is cited—and quite convincingly—as evidence that continued bans on substances such as drugs are bound to fail. Research suggests that Prohibition resulted in only modest reductions in the consumption of alcohol, despite significant increases in the costs of alcohol resulting from the policy.[9] Research also suggests that Prohibition led to the growth of criminal syndicates that stepped in to fill the void created by criminalization:

> Though organized crime existed in American cities well before Prohibition, the creation of a national market in bootlegged liquor increased its influence, visibility, violence, and wealth. Prohibition also forged connections among gangs in the various cities that had not existed before; much alcohol was imported, and the importers served many cities. This provided the basis for growth of the national Mafia as an organization.[10]

In fairness, some researchers have argued *against* the notion that alcohol Prohibition created a host of problems. They point out, correctly, that the policy did not create criminal penalties for possession of alcohol. Rather, Prohibition criminalized purchase and distribution. They also point to the possibility that enforcement was modest at best. Furthermore, supporters of Prohibition have argued that the policy actually *reduced* problems tied to alcohol. As one author observed, "there can be little doubt that during the few years of Prohibition in Canada, Finland, and the USA, all indicators of alcohol consumption and alcohol problems reached the lowest level achieved in any period for which there are relevant data."[11] And at least one researcher has argued that Prohibition may have been little more than a symbolic attempt to instill temperance and morality in American society.[12] In the end, though, Prohibition was less than a resounding success, and the emergence of criminal syndicates alone may constitute sufficiently convincing evidence that another approach besides use of the criminal law is necessary.

Bans and Their Enforcement

This section is solely concerned with the consequences of banning specific substances and products, notably drugs and guns. We will seek to answer one specific question: What happens when governments criminalize the possession and/or use of guns and drugs? We will not focus on enforcement and sentencing per se. Enforcement was touched on in Chapters 3 through 6. Sentencing will be covered in Chapter 9. Other approaches to problems such as drug use and addiction will be covered later on in the book when we turn attention to treatment, diversion, community-level responses, and other such methods of crime control.

Gun Bans

We are a gun-toting society. Researchers have estimated that there are approximately 200 million guns in circulation in the United States.[13] This translates into roughly one gun for every adult. But it is obviously not the case that every adult owns a gun. Instead, it is estimated that roughly one in two American households has at least one gun.[14] The estimates are slightly lower for handguns, with approximately one quarter of households reporting ownership of a handgun.[15] The estimates vary depending on the group (male/female, white/nonwhite) reporting ownership and the region of the country, among other criteria. But the numbers all tell a similar story: Americans love their guns. Or at least many do.

Of course, a significant percentage of Americans despise guns, for a variety of reasons. Some don't see them as particularly useful for settling disputes. Others see the potential for accidents and mishaps. Still others have been the targets of gun violence—or know someone who has. High-profile shootings like the tragic Sandy Hook Elementary shooting on December 12 also fuel a variety of sentiments, with an underlying thread that guns need to be made less available.

Given the extent to which guns pervade American society, it should be no surprise that guns are associated with a number of problems. Recent estimates suggest that between 30,000 and 40,000 Americans die by gunfire each year.[16] The estimates for handguns are particularly troublesome. When violent crime rates were at their highest in the early 1990s, 930,700 handgun crimes were committed in the space of one year.[17] And in terms of costs, it has been estimated that gun violence costs our society some $100 billion each year.[18] Finally, as Figure 7.1 shows, during 2010, the leading cause of violence-related injury deaths for 15- to 34-year-olds (excluding unintentional motor vehicle traffic accidents) was homicide by firearm.

BAN SPECIFIC GUNS AND GUN POSSESSION.   In response to the costs and consequences of gun violence, the United States has attempted to ban both certain types of guns and the possession of guns at various times and in different places. Two noteworthy types of gun bans are apparent. First, the Gun Control Act of 1968 banned the importation of cheap, small, low-caliber pistols known as "Saturday night specials."[19] But Gary Kleck, a noted gun researcher, argued that such guns are used in only 10 to 27 percent of all crimes committed with handguns.[20]

A similar approach was taken in the 1994 Violent Crime Control Act, which outlawed the manufacture and sale of 19 types of assault weapons.[21] An evaluation of this so-called "assault weapons ban" revealed no discernible effect on violent crime.[22] The law expired in 2004. In the wake of the 2012 Sandy Hook shooting in Newtown, Pennsylvania, several lawmakers sought to resurrect the assault weapons ban, but as of this writing federal efforts have stalled almost completely.

In terms of banning possession, the most oft-cited example of such an approach is Washington, D.C.'s 1976 ban on handgun purchases. The ban was overturned in the U.S. Supreme Court's 2008 *District of Columbia v. Heller* decision.[23] Chicago is another large city that has banned handguns. Its law was implemented in 1982, but was deemed unconstitutional in *McDonald v. City of Chicago*, another Supreme Court case.[24] While little research has focused on the Chicago experience, the Washington, D.C., gun ban has been subjected to a fair amount of research. The suicide effect was stronger than the homicide effect, however. This suggests the law discouraged suicides more than it did homicides.[25]

Drug Bans

America's supply-side approach to drugs has amounted to waging war on the problem. Aggressive steps have been taken at all levels of government to eradicate drugs within our borders and to stop them from coming into the country. The use of criminal law to make it illegal for people to possess, use, and sell drugs is also part of America's drug ban. Many people disagree with this approach, but to flatly ignore the drug problem would be misguided. And legalization may lead to undesirable consequences given the scope of America's drug problem. To this end, let us first discuss the scope of America's drug problem, then we will focus on what the research shows concerning the effectiveness of banning drugs.

THE SCOPE OF AMERICA'S DRUG PROBLEM.   America has a drug problem. We know this for at least three reasons. First, it is estimated that enforcing America's drug laws

10 Leading Causes of Injury Deaths by Age Group Highlighting Violence-Related Injury Deaths, United States – 2010

Age Groups

Rank	<1	1-4	5-9	10-14	15-24	25-34	35-44	45-54	55-64	65+	Total
1	Unintentional Suffocation 905	Unintentional Drowning 436	Unintentional MV Traffic 354	Unintentional MV Traffic 452	Unintentional MV Traffic 7,024	Unintentional Poisoning 6,767	Unintentional Poisoning 7,476	Unintentional Poisoning 9,662	Unintentional Poisoning 4,451	Unintentional Fall 21,649	Unintentional MV Traffic 33,687
2	Homicide Unspecified 154	Unintentional MV Traffic 343	Unintentional Drowning 134	Suicide Suffocation 168	Homicide Firearm 3,889	Unintentional MV Traffic 5,558	Unintentional MV Traffic 4,552	Unintentional MV Traffic 5,154	Unintentional MV Traffic 4,134	Unintentional MV Traffic 6,037	Unintentional Poisoning 33,041
3	Homicide Other Spec., classifiable 82	Homicide Unspecified 163	Unintentional Fire/Burn 89	Unintentional Drowning 117	Unintentional Poisoning 3,183	Homicide Firearm 3,331	Suicide Firearm 2,914	Suicide Firearm 4,092	Suicide Firearm 3,387	Unintentional Unspecified 4,596	Unintentional Fall 26,009
4	Unintentional MV Traffic 76	Unintentional Fire/Burn 151	Homicide Firearm 58	Homicide Firearm 107	Suicide Firearm 2,046	Suicide Firearm 2,594	Suicide Suffocation 1,839	Suicide Poisoning 2,061	Unintentional Fall 2,011	Suicide Firearm 4,276	Suicide Firearm 19,392
5	Undetermined Suffocation 39	Unintentional Suffocation 134	Unintentional Suffocation 31	Suicide Firearm 80	Suicide Suffocation 1,824	Suicide Suffocation 1,910	Homicide Firearm 1,673	Suicide Suffocation 1,965	Suicide Poisoning 1,382	Unintentional Suffocation 3,400	Homicide Firearm 11,078
6	Unintentional Drowning 39	Unintentional Pedestrian, Other 103	Unintentional Other Land Transport 26	Unintentional Suffocation 48	Unintentional Drowning 656	Suicide Poisoning 787	Suicide Poisoning 1,279	Unintentional Fall 1,283	Suicide Suffocation 1,130	Adverse Effects 1,544	Suicide Suffocation 9,493
7	Undetermined Unspecified 35	Homicide Other Spec.. classifiable 84	Unintentional Pedestrian, Other 20	Unintentional Fire/Burn 46	Homicide Cut/Pierce 420	Undetermined Poisoning 580	Undetermined Poisoning 712	Homicide Firearm 1,097	Unintentional Suffocation 613	Unintentional Poisoning 1,402	Suicide Poisoning 6,599
8	Adverse Effects 22	Unintentional Natural/ Environment 52	Adverse Effects 14	Unintentional Other Land Transport 42	Suicide Poisoning 371	Unintentional Drowning 476	Unintentional Fall 493	Undetermined Poisoning 955	Homicide Firearm 533	Unintentional Fire/Burn 1,088	Unintentional Suffocation 6,165
9	Unintentional Fire/Burn 22	Homicide Firearm 43	Unintentional Natural/ Environment 14	Unintentional Poisoning 40	Undetermined Poisoning 282	Homicide Cut/Pierce 438	Unintentional Drowning 409	Unintentional Drowning 578	Undetermined Poisoning 480	Suicide Poisoning 709	Unintentional Unspecified 5,688
10	Unintentional Natural/ Environment 22	Unintentional Struck by or Against 37	Unintentional Poisoning 14	Unintentional Firearm 26	Unintentional Other Land Transport 221	Unintentional Fall 299	Homicide Cut/Pierce 349	Unintentional Suffocation 464	Unintentional Fire/Burn 479	Suicide Suffocation 648	Unintentional Drowning 3,782

Centers for Disease Control and Prevention
National Center for Injury Prevention and Control

Data Source: National Center for Health Statistics (NCHS), National Vital Statistics System.
Produced by: Office of Statistics and Programming, National Center for Injury Prevention and Control, CDC using WISQARS™.

FIGURE 7.1   Causes if Violence-Related Injury Deaths

Source: National Center for Health Statistics, National Vital Statistics Program.

costs the federal government about $4 billion annually.[26] State and local governments spend almost as much, resulting in a drug war whose costs are approaching $11 billion annually.[27] Second, America's drug problem is also evidenced by the amount of money people make from supplying illicit substances to customers. One study estimates that drugs generate approximately $60 billion in annual income to those who supply the product to consumers. This equates to roughly 1 percent of total personal consumption expenditures in the United States.[28]

Third, the extent of the drug problem can be seen through measures of personal drug use. But measuring the scope of America's drug usage is problematic. It is not as simple as tracking sales receipts from retail establishments. Rather, it is necessary to measure drug use indirectly, mostly through the use of surveys. Two key surveys that have been used to measure drug use—especially occasional use—are the **National Survey on Drug Use and Health** (formerly the National Household Survey on Drug Abuse or the NHSDA) and the **Monitoring the Future (MTF)** survey. The former measures self-reported drug use at the household level. The latter measures the same but with a sampling of high school students.

Both the NHSDA and the MTF tell us about the patterns of drug use. They show, for instance, that a majority of the adolescent population experiments with drugs, marijuana being the most common illicit substance of choice.[29] The MTF survey also shows fairly stable trends in marijuana use over several years, as well as other interesting trends in drug use.[30] And the NHSDA shows that nearly 23 million Americans aged 12 or older used illicit drugs at least once in the past month.[31] The National Risk Behavior Survey also tracks trends in illicit drug use. A summary of recent findings appears in Figure 7.2. Regardless of the source, the data show that drugs are a problem in the United States.

Most official surveys fall short when it comes to measuring drug use by addicts. The reasons for this are that dependent users are inherently more transient, less truthful in surveys, and likely not to be found in schools and households. Even so, researchers have estimated that there are almost one million people who are addicted to heroin.[32] It is also estimated that millions of people use cocaine on a regular basis.[33] Furthermore, researchers have concluded that at least two million people qualify as "addicted" to marijuana and report using the drug three times per day.[34] And the drug tests of arrestees, through the recently modified Arrestee Drug Abuse Monitoring (ADAM) program, show that over 60 percent of arrestees in all sites tested positive for at least one of the illicit drugs tested for.[35]

DRUG BAN PROBLEMS.   It can scarcely be disputed that the United States has a drug problem. But has banning drugs worked? While it might help keep the problem at bay, it is also clear that America's approach to illicit drugs has resulted in at least four significant problems.[36] First, prohibition of drugs clearly generates black markets, and people have achieved staggering wealth as a result of their decisions to supply illegal drugs to individuals who want them. For example, one researcher estimated that Rayful Edmond, Jr., the man who was the main cocaine supplier in Washington, D.C., during the late 1980s, made millions of dollars by his early twenties.[37] It is also quite apparent that successful drug traffickers, especially from Mexico, have amassed significant wealth, perhaps in billions of dollars.[38]

Second, it is clear that America's war on drugs has adversely affected inner-city communities. It has resulted in a disproportionate amount of African-Americans going

National Survey on Drug Use and Health: a survey administered by the Substance Abuse and Mental Health Services Administration that measures the prevalence of drug and alcohol use in people 12 years and older.

Monitoring the Future (MTF): an ongoing survey of students that gauges trends in legal and illegal drug use.

Trends in the Prevalence of Marijuana, Cocaine, and Other Illegal Drug Use National YRBS: 1991–2011

The national Youth Risk Behavior Survey (YRBS) monitors priority health risk behaviors that contribute to the leading causes of death, disability, and social problems among youth and adults in the United States. The national YRBS is conducted every two years during the spring semester and provides data representative of 9th through 12th grade students in public and private schools throughout the United States.

YRBSS

Measure	1991	1993	1995	1997	1999	2001	2003	2005	2007	2009	2011	Changes from 1991–2011[1]	Change from 2009–2011[2]
Ever used marijuana one or more times (during their life)	31.3 (28.4–34.4)[3]	32.8 (29.6–36.2)	42.4 (39.4–45.5)	47.1 (44.1–50.1)	47.2 (44.7–49.7)	42.4 (40.5–44.3)	40.2 (37.4–43.1)	38.4 (35.9–41.0)	38.1 (35.5–40.7)	36.8 (34.8–38.8)	39.9 (37.8–42.1)	Increased, 1991–1999 Decreased, 1999–2011	Increased
Tried marijuana for the first time before age 13 years	7.4 (6.3–8.7)	6.9 (5.9–8.2)	7.6 (6.4–8.9)	9.7 (8.4–11.2)	11.3 (9.6–13.2)	10.2 (9.1–11.5)	9.9 (8.6–11.3)	8.7 (7.8–9.6)	8.3 (7.0–9.7)	7.5 (6.7–8.3)	8.1 (7.3–9.0)	Increased, 1991–1999 Decreased, 1999–2011	No change
Used marijuana one or more times (during the 30 days before the survey)	14.7 (12.6–17.0)	17.7 (15.3–20.3)	25.3 (23.5–27.3)	26.2 (24.0–28.5)	26.7 (24.2–29.4)	23.9 (22.3–25.5)	22.4 (20.2–24.6)	20.2 (18.6–22.0)	19.7 (17.8–21.8)	20.8 (19.4–22.3)	23.1 (21.5–24.7)	Increased, 1991–1999 Decreased, 1999–2011	Increased
Used marijuana on school property one or more times (during the 30 days before the survey)	NA[4]	NA	8.8 (7.7–10.0)	7.0 (6.0–8.1)	7.2 (5.9–8.8)	5.4 (4.7–6.2)	5.8 (4.6–7.3)	4.5 (3.9–5.2)	4.5 (3.6–5.5)	4.6 (4.0–5.4)	5.9 (5.1–6.7)	Decreased, 1995–2005 Increased, 2005–2011	Increased
Ever used any form of cocaine one or more times (for example, powder, crack, or freebase, during their life)	5.9 (5.1–6.9)	4.9 (4.1–5.8)	7.0 (5.9–8.3)	8.2 (7.2–9.4)	9.5 (8.2–11.1)	9.4 (8.2–10.7)	8.7 (7.6–9.9)	7.6 (6.7–8.7)	7.2 (6.2–8.2)	6.4 (5.7–7.1)	6.8 (6.2–7.5)	Increased, 1991–1999 Decreased, 1999–2011	No change
Ever used inhalants (sniffed glue, breathed the contents of aerosol spray cans, or inhaled any paints or sprays to get high one or more times during their life)	NA	NA	20.3 (18.3–22.5)	16.0 (14.7–17.3)	14.6 (12.9–16.5)	14.7 (13.1–16.6)	12.1 (10.9–13.4)	12.4 (11.1–13.8)	13.3 (12.1–14.6)	11.7 (10.6–12.8)	11.4 (10.7–12.1)	Decreased, 1995–2003 No change, 2003–2011	No change
Ever used heroin one or more times (also called "smack", "junk", or "China white", during their life)	NA	NA	NA	NA	2.4 (1.9–3.0)	3.1 (2.7–3.6)	3.3 (2.6–4.1)	2.4 (2.0–2.8)	2.3 (1.8–2.8)	2.5 (2.2–2.9)	2.9 (2.5–3.3)	No change, 1999–2011	No change
Ever used methamphetamines one or more times (also called "speed", "crystal", "crank", or "ice", during their life)	NA	NA	NA	NA	9.1 (7.9–10.5)	9.8 (8.3–11.5)	7.6 (6.7–8.7)	6.2 (5.3–7.2)	4.4 (3.7–5.3)	4.1 (3.6–4.6)	3.8 (3.4–4.3)	Decreased, 1999–2011	No change

FIGURE 7.2 Contemporary Drug Use Trends

Source: Centers for Disease Control and Prevention, Youth Risk Behavior Surveillance System, cdc.gov/healthyyouth/yrbs/pdf/us_drug_trend_yrbs.pdf.

	1991	1993	1995	1997	1999	2001	2003	2005	2007	2009	2011	Changes from 1991–2011[1]	Change from 2009–2011[2]
Ever took steroid pills or shots without a doctor's prescription one or more times (during their life)													
	2.7 (2.3–3.2)	2.2 (1.7–2.8)	3.7 (3.1–4.3)	3.1 (2.7–3.6)	3.7 (3.1–4.5)	5.0 (4.4–5.5)	6.1 (4.7–7.8)	4.0 (3.5–4.6)	3.9 (3.4–4.6)	3.3 (2.9–3.8)	3.6 (3.2–4.1)	Increased, 1991–2003 Decreased, 2003–2011	No change
Ever used a needle to inject any illegal drug into their body one or more times (during their life)													
	NA	NA	2.1 (1.6–2.6)	2.1 (1.7–2.7)	1.8 (1.4–2.2)	2.3 (2.0–2.7)	3.2 (2.1–4.7)	2.1 (1.8–2.4)	2.0 (1.5–2.7)	2.1 (1.8–2.5)	2.3 (1.9–2.7)	No change, 1995–2011	No change
Offered, sold or given an illegal drug by someone on school property (during the 12 months before the survey)													
	NA	24.0 (21.4–26.8)	32.1 (29.1–35.3)	31.7 (29.9–33.5)	30.2 (27.8–32.7)	28.5 (26.5–30.6)	28.7 (24.9–32.8)	25.4 (23.3–27.6)	22.3 (20.3–24.4)	22.7 (20.7–24.9)	25.6 (23.6–27.6)	Increased 1993–1995 Decreased 1995–2011	Increased

[1] Based on trend analyses using a logistic regression model controlling for sex, race/ethnicity, and grade.
[2] Based on t-test analyses, p < 0.05.
[3] 95% confidence interval.
[4] Not available.

Where can I get more information? Visit www.cdc.gov/yrbss or call 800–CDC–INFO (800–232–4636).

National Center for HIV/AIDS, Viral Hepatitis, STD, and TB Prevention
Division of Adolescent and School Health

FIGURE 7.2 (Continued)

to prison. For instance, Reuter and MacCoun studied drug selling in Washington, D.C., from 1985 to 1991. They found that 98 percent of people who were arrested for drugs were African-American while that group constituted 65 percent of the population at that time. Other consequences for inner cities include increased violence tied to drug selling.[39] Yet another consequence for inner cities is an apparent reduction in the number of positive adult male role models. Third, much evidence exists suggesting that the criminalization of drugs has had a corrupting influence on law enforcement officials both here and abroad. While many fingers have been pointed at drug enforcement problems in Mexico, there have been a few celebrated incidents of drug-related corruption in the United States.[40] Finally, researchers have pointed out that the war on drugs has resulted in disastrous public health consequences, including increased potency (and resulting unpredictability) of drugs tied to aggressive law enforcement[41] and costs associated with treating addicts and responding to drug-related violence and death.[42]

Does It Work?

Legislative bans have a terrible track record, especially when they do nothing to tap the demand that exists for a particular product or substance. There is some evidence that gun bans may reduce gun violence, but a number of studies suggest otherwise. Surprisingly little research exists concerning the crime control benefits associated with the criminalization of drugs, but given the scope of America's drug problem, it is safe to conclude that criminalization has not achieved its intended purpose. This does not mean, however, that drugs should be legalized. It could be that criminalization is keeping the problem at bay and that legalization would create havoc.

LEGISLATIVE CONTROLS

Another traditional approach to America's crime problem is to restrict and regulate certain behaviors, controlling them through legislation. Nowhere is this more apparent than with gun policy. This section focuses specifically on guns and considers attempts to alter gun designs, regulate drug transactions, and restrict gun ownership by dangerous persons. It also discusses gun buyback programs and the recent debate over whether Americans should be able to carry concealed weapons.

Altering Gun Designs

A relatively recent approach to gun violence, and particularly accidental shootings, is to force gun manufacturers to alter gun designs to promote safety. Examples of alterations include indicators whether the weapon is loaded, trigger locks, and personalized gun technology.[43] Personalized guns prevent the weapon from being fired by anyone other than the owner. With one type of personalized gun, the user wears a magnetic ring that activates the gun once it is held. Another type is a fingerprint recognition system that ensures no one other than the owner can shoot the gun.

The problem with altering gun designs is that it is almost certain not to affect the crime problem. One of the main motivators for design changes is, as indicated, a desire to minimize accidental shootings. While this is a noble goal, it does little to address the huge number of guns currently in circulation.[44] It is also doubtful that altered designs will become ubiquitous because, currently, firearms are exempt from regulation by the Consumer Product Safety Commission (CPSC). The CPSC regulates virtually all consumer products, but not firearms. Legislative change would be necessary before the

CPSC could mandate that all firearm manufacturers integrate safety features into their products.[45]

Regulating Gun Transactions

It is assumed that strict regulations of gun transactions will mitigate the harmful effects of gun violence. Currently, almost anyone can buy a gun, subject to certain restrictions in the Gun Control Act of 1968 (and its 1996 amendments). According to the Act, people who cannot buy guns include minors, adults under indictment or who have been convicted of a felony, people convicted of misdemeanor domestic violence, illegal aliens, people confined because of mental disorders, and a few others. Otherwise, almost any law-abiding American who is of age can walk into a gun dealership in almost any state and expect to return home with a gun—either at the time of purchase or shortly thereafter.

What steps are taken to ensure that persons prohibited from buying guns do not do so? At a minimum, the Gun Control Act of 1968 requires that licensed dealers require buyers to show identification and complete a form attesting that they can legally own a gun. More recently, background checks and "cooling off" periods have been required. (These approaches will be discussed in more detail in the following subsection.) However, these requirements do not necessarily affect private sellers and gun sales in the so-called secondary market. For example, the Gun Control Act does not require nondealers to determine whether gun buyers are eligible.

Fortunately, states can impose their own restrictive requirements on gun sales. Yet, despite such regulations, not all dealers are upstanding. Some turn a blind eye to so-called straw purchases, in which someone who can legally buy a gun buys it for someone else who cannot.[46] Research suggests that the Bureau of Alcohol, Tobacco, Firearms, and Explosives (ATF), the federal agency charged with licensing and inspecting gun retailers, can only inspect a small percentage of the nation's 80,000 licensed dealers each year.[47] Likewise, research also shows that government needs to get better at identifying problem gun dealers before substantial crime control benefits will be reaped.[48] If federal regulations placed significant restrictions on gun sales in the secondary market, perhaps public safety could be improved.

Denying Gun Ownership to Dangerous Persons

As already indicated, the Gun Control Act of 1968 places limitations on who can buy a gun, and some states have imposed their own limitations. One of the most significant attempts to restrict gun ownership among classes of dangerous persons is the Brady Act. The Brady Act, formally called the **Brady Handgun Violence Prevention Act**, went into effect on February 28, 1994, and required that gun dealers in states without background checks conduct (through a chief law enforcement officer) cursory background checks of prospective buyers. Since a background check takes time, the Brady Act also effectively created a waiting period. According to the legislation, this waiting period was not to exceed five days.

While the Brady Act has prohibited many thousands of people from buying guns (see Table 7.1),[49] the Act's effects on public safety are somewhat less clear. One important study, published in the *Journal of the American Medical Association*, compared mortality trends in the 32 states that were required to abide by Brady with the remaining states that were exempt from the legislation.[50] The study found no significant

Brady Handgun Violence Prevention Act: named for James Brady, who was shot by John Hinckley, Jr., in the 1981 assassination attempt on Ronald Reagan; a federal legislation that required background checks on firearms purchasers in the United States.

TABLE 7.1 Estimated Number of Applications and Denials for Firearm Transfers or Permits since the Inception of the Brady Act, 1994–2010

	Number of Applications		
	Received	**Denied**	**Percent Denied**
Total	118,249,000	2,079,000	1.8%
Brady interim period[a]			
1994–1998	12,740,000	312,000	2.4%
Permanent Brady[b]	105,509,000	1,767,000	1.7%
1998[c]	893,000	20,000	2.2
1999	8,621,000	204,000	2.4
2000	7,699,000	153,000	2.0
2001	7,958,000	151,000	1.9
2002	7,806,000	136,000	1.7
2003	7,831,000	126,000	1.6
2004	8,084,000	126,000	1.6
2005	8,278,000	132,000	1.6
2006	8,612,000	135,000	1.6
2007	8,658,000	136,000	1.6
2008	9,900,000	147,000	1.5
2009	10,764,000	150,000	1.4
2010	10,405,000	153,000	1.5

Note: Counts are rounded to the nearest 1,000. Annual numbers may not sum to totals in other tables. For more information on reporting agencies and sample design, see *Methodology*.

[a]From March 1, 1994, to November 29, 1998, background checks on applicants were conducted by state and local agencies, mainly on handgun transfers. See *Presale Handgun Checks, the Brady Interim Period, 1994–98,* NCJ 175034, BJS website, June 1999.

[b]The National Instant Criminal Background Check System (NICS) began operations in 1998. Checks on handgun and long gun transfers are conducted by the FBI and state and local agencies.

[c]November 30 to December 31, 1998, counts are from the NICS operations report for the period and may include multiple transactions for the same application.

Source: Ronald J. Frandsen, Dave Naglich, Gene A. Lauver, and Allina D. Lee, *Background Checks for Firearm Transfers, 2010—Statistical Tables* (Washington, DC: Bureau of Justice Statistics, 2013).

differences in homicides among people over age 25 in Brady states compared to non-Brady states. Juvenile homicides were excluded from the analysis because young people are not permitted to buy guns legally anyway. Another researcher found that Brady even resulted in an *increase* in certain crimes after its implementation![51]

Indeed, the effects of Brady were somewhat short-lived. First, the Supreme Court declared the background check portion of the Act unconstitutional in mid-1997 in the case of *Printz v. United States.*[52] Second, the Act is effectively defunct today because it required that, as of November 30, 1998, its waiting period requirements were replaced with a national instant background check system (hence the switch to the "Permanent Brady" section of Table 7.1). The background system applies not only to handguns, but also to shotguns and rifles. Importantly, though, the instant background check system is not necessarily used in states that were exempt from Brady. But on a positive note, some research suggests that Brady reduced the incidence of suicide among people 55 and older.[53]

Another well-researched approach to gun violence is to deny ownership to persons convicted of certain misdemeanors. As indicated, the Gun Control Act of 1968 prohibits people convicted of misdemeanor domestic violence from buying guns. California has extended this restriction to include *anyone* who has been convicted of a violent misdemeanor. An interesting study was recently published that has sought to determine whether this restrictive law makes a difference. Garen Wintemute and his colleagues compared the criminal histories of a control group of people who succeeded in buying guns before the law went into effect with a treatment group of those who were denied guns after the law was enacted.[54] The researchers found that those in the control group were more likely to be arrested than those in the treatment group, possibly suggesting that the law has improved matters. On the contrary, though, another study suggests that prohibiting gun ownership to those convicted of misdemeanor domestic violence does not affect crime, especially intimate partner homicides.[55] But the same study also suggests that laws that prohibit people with restraining orders from buying guns may actually *reduce* intimate partner homicides.[56]

Buybacks

In something of a twist on gun purchase regulations and restrictions, some states have experimented with **buyback programs**. The city of St. Louis attempted two separate buybacks in the 1990s. The first, in 1991, resulted in 7,500 guns being brought in. The second, in 1994, resulted in 1,200 more guns. The buybacks in St. Louis were evaluated (along with some other buyback programs in other states) and found to have no discernible effect on crime.[57] A number of other jurisdictions around the country continue to utilize buyback programs, but more often than not relatively token amounts are offered in exchange for guns. Phoenix, for example, recently offered $100 grocery cards to people who turned in guns. It is doubtful people will turn in guns valued at hundreds of dollars or more for such a token amount.

> **buyback program:** *a program that offers a token amount of money or some other reward in exchange for turning in a gun to authorities. Buyback programs are intended to remove as many guns as possible from circulation.*

Other problems with buybacks are that they are generally short-lived and voluntary. Also, nothing prohibits someone who participates in the program from going out and buying another gun. And research has shown that people who participate in buyback programs are at a low risk of offending.[58] Buybacks appear to have been at least somewhat successful in other nations, but not in the United States.[59]

The Right-to-Carry Controversy

In yet another twist to the restrict-and-regulate approach to gun violence, some researchers have argued that states should allow people to carry concealed weapons in an effort to deter crime. In essence, their argument is that more guns will equate with less crime. Presently, some 40 states have enacted permissive gun-carrying laws, but several states (California being a prime example) have been resistant to such an approach.[60] These **"right-to-carry" laws** all but guarantee that people who are not barred from purchasing guns can carry guns, often in a concealed manner. Most of the right-to-carry law states have "shall issue" laws, which require permits are issued to applicants who meet the required standards.

> **"right-to-carry" laws:** *state laws that permit certain people to carry concealed weapons.*

Economist John Lott has ignited some controversy by claiming that right-to-carry laws should exist in every state. In his book, *More Guns, Less Crime*, he argues, "Of all the methods studied so far by economists, the carrying of concealed handguns appears to be the most cost-effective method for reducing crime."[61] He and his colleagues have found that the right-to-carry laws have the desirable effect of almost always reducing violent crime.[62] But other research suggests that the effect of right-to-carry laws is modest or slight.[63]

In fact, some researchers have reestimated Lott's data and concluded that the laws do not deter crime. As it now stands, there are almost as many studies that cast doubt on the more guns, less crime argument than support it.[64] Some of these studies even show an *increase* in crime attributable to the laws. In perhaps the most authoritative study written on the subject to date, Kovandzic and Marvell conclude that "we find little evidence that increases in the number of citizens with concealed-handgun permits reduce or increase rates of violent crime."[65]

Does It Work?

With the possible exception of the Brady law, and gun purchase waiting periods in general, restrictions, regulations, and buybacks are failures. Little progress has been made in terms of altering gun designs, and even if gun designs were radically altered, it is doubtful that a reduction in gun violence would result. The reason? There are simply too many *unaltered* guns currently in circulation. This latter problem has led to the creation of gun buyback programs, but these have also produced unsatisfactory results. Next, the regulation of gun transactions and allowing people to carry guns to deter crime have been shown in numerous studies to result in few beneficial effects. Waiting periods may have resulted in decreases in certain crimes (e.g., suicides) and have most definitely kept guns away from many dangerous people. Even so, there is not much convincing research that suggests waiting periods have a general deterrent effect on crime.

PUBLIC NOTIFICATION

Public notification is another legislative approach to the crime problem. This is particularly apparent in the realm of sex offenses, where legislators in some states have seen fit (due to public demand) to require that the whereabouts and pertinent criminal histories of certain convicted offenders be made available to any and all concerned persons, often through the publication of such information on open access websites. So-called Megan's laws are familiar to most, but other laws have been enacted and deserve mention.

Megan's Law

Megan's laws:
named for Megan
Kanka, laws that
require convicted sex
offenders to register
with authorities and
notify the public as
to their whereabouts/
residence/location.

In the summer of 1994, a seven-year-old by the name of Megan Kanka was raped and murdered by a twice-convicted pedophile who had moved into her neighborhood after being released on parole. In response to the crime, the state of New Jersey passed the Sexual Offender Registration Act.[66] Similar laws have since been enacted in other states and have collectively come to be known as "**Megan's laws**."

While Megan's laws differ from state to state, they possess some similarities, thanks in part to the federal government. In 1996, Congress passed its own Megan's law, which requires states to provide communities with information about sex offenders as a condition of receiving federal anticrime funding.[67] And in 2000, Congress required sex offenders to report their status to college administrators in the schools in which they are enrolled.[68]

At both the federal and state levels, Megan's laws generally have one common feature: community notification of sex offenders. What differs from one place to the next is how this notification is given. The so-called active model of notification requires that paroled sex offenders directly notify the community or community members of their states. The passive model requires that sex offenders' information must be available for public scrutiny. The National Sex Offender Public Website provides an example of the passive approach (see Figure 7.3).

LEGAL ISSUES.   Megan's laws are an especially controversial method of crime control because, according to critics, they serve the ends of punishment. Critics point to examples of lynchings and community retaliation against sex offenders who return to the community. Supporters of Megan's laws claim, by contrast, that the laws merely serve an informational purpose; that they are not intended to punish offenders. Even so, the courts have begun to grapple with the constitutionality of Megan's laws.

The most common legal challenge to sex offender registration is based on the Fifth Amendment's double jeopardy provision, which provides that a person who has

FIGURE 7.3   National Sex Offender Public Website

Source: U.S. Justice Department

been convicted or acquitted of a crime cannot be tried or punished for the same offense twice. Double jeopardy occurs when, for the same offense, a person is (1) reprosecuted after acquittal; (2) reprosecuted after conviction; or (3) subjected to separate punishments for the same offense. It is the latter concern that is of most interest to Megan's law critics. To date, however, a double jeopardy challenge has not succeeded.

Critics of Megan's laws have also alleged that the laws constitute cruel and unusual punishment, invade privacy,[69] threaten due process, violate the Fourteenth Amendment's equal protection clause, and run counter to the constitutional protection against ex post facto laws.[70] Despite the many challenges,[71] however, the courts have not sided with sex offenders. An illustrative example is the New Jersey Supreme Court's decision in *Doe v. Poritz*,[72] where it was held that the state's Megan's law did not serve a punitive purpose.[73] The Supreme Court recently reached a similar decision in *Smith v. Doe*.[74]

EFFECTS ON CRIME.   It would appear, given the lack of successful challenges, that Megan's laws are here to stay. But do they work? Do they serve any crime control purpose? These are important questions because, in the end, it is difficult to conceive of any other reason for Megan's laws than the promotion of public safety. Whether the laws are punitive or simply intended to provide information, they exist so that sex offenders will not reoffend once they return to the community.

Some researchers have sought to examine the effects on crime of sex offender registration, but not many. One South Carolina study found that registration had no effect on offender recidivism.[75] A more comprehensive review by the Washington State Institute for Public Policy found the following: "Regarding specific deterrence, the weight of the evidence indicates the laws have no statistically significant effect on recidivism."[76] The review did, however, find that there is a possible *general* deterrent effect associated with sex offender registration, but the conclusions were tentative at best.

In short, we cannot conclude with certainty that Megan's laws have succeeded in their stated purpose. At least one study shows that while many people are supportive of Megan's laws, most are not aware of their local community notification methods.[77] A lack of awareness certainly could threaten the effect of Megan's laws on subsequent sex crimes. Researchers will need to take this problem into account when—and if—they continue to examine the effects of sex offender registration.

More Recent Sex Offender Legislation

Megan Kanka is not the only victim of a heinous sex offense to have a law named after her. Sadly, another victim, Jessica Lunsford, has to be remembered in the same way. She was taken from her bedroom, raped, and murdered by a previously registered sex offender who confessed to the crime. Megan's law fell short because while registration is intended to help police (and concerned citizens) keep tabs on registered sex offenders, John Couey, Lunsford's killer, was staying with his sister and police had lost track of him. So, **Jessica's law** is intended to pick up where Megan's law falls short.

Florida was the first state to enact Jessica's law. The law provides harsh penalties for sex offenders but also a lifetime of GPS electronic monitoring for the offenders. This means that the offenders' whereabouts can be determined at any time, something registration alone cannot ensure. A similar law was enacted in California, as a result of the initiative process, shortly after Florida passed its law.[78]

Jessica's law: named for Jessica Lunsford, laws that provide harsh penalties for sex offenders and require lifetime GPS monitoring of certain offenders.

Closely tied to legislative developments in the area of Megan's law and Jessica's law is the **Adam Walsh Child Protection and Safety Act of 2006**, named for the son of John Walsh, familiar television personality (America's Most Wanted) and founder of the National Center for Missing and Exploited Children. Signed into law in July 2006 by then president George Bush, the law required states to implement, among other things, a three-tiered classification system for sex offenders. The most serious offenders (those in Tier 3) were required to register for life due to the serious nature of their offenses. In other words, the legislation varied the registration requirements based on the seriousness of the underlying offense. Unfortunately, a 2012 study published by the National Institute of Justice found that the tier classification was unrelated to recidivism.[79]

Adam Walsh Child Protection and Safety Act of 2006: named for the son of John Walsh (America's Most Wanted host), federal legislation that requires, among other things, a three-tiered classification system for convicted sex offenders.

Does It Work?

It is difficult to dispute that notifying communities of sex offenders' whereabouts is ideal, and even necessary. The same can be said of monitoring sex offenders' movements. But do Megan's and Jessica's laws reduce crime? That is, do they deter sex offenders? Surprisingly, we cannot say for certain, but the evidence is not encouraging.

The lion's share of studies in this budding area of research suggest sex offender notification and registration do relatively little to reduce crime. They placate the public to some extent, but probably don't do much more beyond that in terms of improving public safety.

OTHER LEGISLATIVE APPROACHES

This section quickly examines legislation aimed at targeting two high-profile contemporary problems: white collar crime and terrorism. To target the former, the Sarbanes–Oxley Act was enacted in an effort to target certain types of so-called white-collar crime. It was followed in 2010 by the Dodd–Frank Wall Street Reform and Consumer Protection Act. Terrorism, on the other hand, has been targeted via the well-known Patriot Act, which was passed in the wake of the 9/11 attacks. It has since been followed by other laws.

White-Collar Crime Laws

Chapter 1 introduced various types of crime, but most of this book has been concerned with violent and property crime, and to a lesser extent public order crimes. We have all but ignored white-collar crime—until now. White-collar crime has recently gained plenty of attention in the light of high-profile corporate and accounting scandals involving companies such as Global Crossing, Enron, Tyco International, and WorldCom (formerly MCI and now part of Verizon). Thousands of employees, investors, retirees, and financial advisors lost their savings, jobs, retirement benefits, and their livelihood as a result of these companies' exploits, especially those of Enron. According to one study, the resulting decline in investor confidence flowing from these scandals "contributed to an *$8 trillion* decline in the U.S. equity markets from 2001 to 2002."[80]

Sarbanes–Oxley Act: named for its original sponsors, Senator Paul Sarbanes (D, Maryland) and Michael Oxley (R, Ohio); federal legislation passed in reaction to high-profile corporate scandals (notably Enron) and requiring new and improved accounting standards for public companies in the United States.

White-collar crime, particularly corporate fraud, has also gained attention of late due to passage of the 2002 **Sarbanes–Oxley Act**, which owes its name to its original sponsors, Senator Paul Sarbanes (D, Maryland) and Michael Oxley (R, Ohio). Formally called the "Public Company Accounting Reform and Investor Protection Act of 2002," the legislation was passed in reaction to the likes of Enron and provides for new and improved accounting standards for public companies in the United States.

One of the Act's most significant accomplishments is the creation of the Public Company Accounting Oversight Board (PCAOB—or "peekaboo"), a private, nonprofit entity whose mission is to oversee the auditors of public companies. Sarbanes–Oxley also contains other important provisions, including the following:

- A requirement that public companies evaluate and disclose the effectiveness of their internal controls as they relate to financial reporting, and that independent auditors for such companies "attest" (i.e., agree, or qualify) to such disclosure
- Certification of financial reports by chief executive officers and chief financial officers
- Auditor independence, including outright bans on certain types of work for audit clients and pre-certification by the company's audit committee of all other non-audit work
- A requirement that companies listed on stock exchanges have fully independent audit committees that oversee the relationship between the company and its auditor
- Ban on most personal loans to any executive officer or director
- Accelerated reporting of insider trading
- Prohibition on insider trades during pension fund blackout periods
- Additional disclosure
- Enhanced criminal and civil penalties for violations of securities law
- Significantly longer maximum jail sentences and larger fines for corporate executives who knowingly and willfully misstate financial statements, although maximum sentences are largely irrelevant because judges generally follow federal sentencing guidelines in setting actual sentences
- Employee protections allowing those corporate fraud whistleblowers who file complaints with OSHA within 90 days to win reinstatement, back pay and benefits, compensatory damages, abatement orders, and reasonable attorney fees and costs[81]

Dodd–Frank Wall Street Reform and Consumer Protection Act: federal legislation signed into law by President Barack Obama following the 2007/2008 financial crisis. It brought a number of financial regulation reforms intended "[t]o promote the financial stability of the United States by improving accountability and transparency in the financial system, to end 'too big to fail,' to protect the American taxpayer by ending bailouts, [and] to protect consumers from abusive financial services practices.

It is difficult to convey the significance of Sarbanes–Oxley. One study described it as "the most sweeping set of changes to U.S. federal securities laws since the New Deal."[82]

On the subject of certification, for example, all period reports to the Securities and Exchange Commission (SEC) must be accompanied by a signed document from the CEO or CFO of the company, called a "Section 906 Certification." Providing false information in such certifications, whether knowingly or willfully, can result in a $5 million fine and up to 20 years in prison. This presumably prevents top executives from claiming ignorance when allegations of corporate fraud surface. Even so, one has to look pretty hard to find any glowing endorsements of Sarbanes–Oxley. Critics argue that the Act fails to hold executives sufficiently accountable and could do better by forfeiting their assets. As it stands now, there are no forfeiture provisions in Sarbanes–Oxley, meaning that corrupt executives can keep their money, toys, houses, and other spoils:

> The privileged position of corporate fraudsters under the law exists in contrast to their weakened and unprotected victims, and typically stands in stark contrast to violators of other criminal statutes. SarbOx's enhanced criminal penalties, while slightly more punitive, are nevertheless inadequate to effectively battle and deter the corporate fraud problem. Meaningful asset forfeiture sanctions are needed to shore up the Act's deterrent impact.[83]

The financial crisis of 2007 and 2008 led to the enactment of more legislation aimed at the problem of white-collar crime. The **Dodd–Frank Wall Street Reform and Consumer Protection Act** was signed into law by President Barack Obama on July 21, 2010. It brought a number of financial regulation reforms intended "[t]o promote the financial stability of the United States by improving accountability and transparency in the financial system, to end 'too big to fail,' to protect the American taxpayer by ending bailouts, [and] to protect consumers from abusive financial services practices . . ."[84] The law is extremely complex and its details are beyond the scope of this book. Even so, it is sufficiently new as of this writing and it is difficult to determine whether it has had a market effect.

Does It Work?

Has Sarbanes–Oxley reduced corporate fraud? Has Dodd–Frank made a difference? On the one hand, perhaps the relative calm of late is indicative of success. On the other hand, for these laws to be effective, they must be enforced with some frequency. As of this writing, though, it appears that only a handful of individuals have been criminally charged under either statute. Some 200 civil cases were filed in the 10 years since Sarbanes–Oxley was enacted[85], but much more time (and of course research!) will be necessary before we can determine whether these and similar laws make a difference.

Anti-Terrorism Laws

On September 14, 2001, in response to the September 11 attacks on the World Trade Center, then president George W. Bush declared a state of emergency, which permitted him to invoke certain presidential powers. These powers include the ability to summon reserve troops, marshal military units, and issue executive orders for the implementation of such things as military tribunals. Congress even took action following September 11. In order to empower the Justice Department, Congress passed the **Patriot Act** on October 26, 2001. President Bush then signed the Act into law on October 27.

Patriot Act: federal anti-terrorism legislation passed after 9/11. Patriot in the Patriot Act is an acronym that stands for "Uniting and Strengthening America by Providing Appropriate Tools Required to Intercept and Obstruct Terrorism."

The word *Patriot* in the Patriot Act is an acronym that stands for "Uniting and Strengthening America by Providing Appropriate Tools Required to Intercept and Obstruct Terrorism." The Act is very long and complex, consisting of 10 parts and over 300 single-spaced pages. Given its staggering size and breadth, the Act is a testament to the fact that Congress *can* move quickly when it needs to.

The Patriot Act made several important changes to past law and practice. First, it centralized federal law enforcement authority in the U.S. Department of Justice. For example, Section 808 of the Act reassigned the authority for investigating several federal crimes of violence from law enforcement agencies, such as the Secret Service and the Bureau of Alcohol, Tobacco, and Firearms, to the Attorney General. The Act also provided for CIA (Central Intelligence Agency) oversight of all domestic intelligence gathering. Prior to the Patriot Act, the CIA's role was primarily concerned with foreign intelligence gathering. The Act also expanded the definition of the terms *terrorism* and *domestic terrorism* to include activities that do the following:

> (A) involve acts dangerous to human life that are a violation of the criminal laws of the United States or of any state; (B) appear to be intended (i) to intimidate or coerce a civilian population; (ii) to influence the policy of a government by mass destruction, assassination, or kidnapping; or (iii) to effect the conduct of a government by mass destruction, assassination, or kidnapping; and (C) occur primarily within the territorial jurisdiction of the United States. (USA Patriot Act 802, 115 Stat. at 376)

There were also several noteworthy changes in criminal procedure attributable to the Patriot Act. Before describing these changes, some background will be informative.

First, the Supreme Court has held that the Fifth and Sixth Amendment rights of due process and access to jury trials apply to all "persons," not just citizens of the United States.[86] In addition, the Supreme Court has held that all undocumented aliens living inside U.S. borders are entitled to the protections enunciated in the Bill of Rights.[87] Specifically, the Court has stated the following:

> The Fifth Amendment, as well as the Fourteenth Amendment, protects every one of these persons from deprivation of life, liberty, or property without due process of law. Even one whose presence in this country is unlawful, involuntary, or transitory is entitled to constitutional protection.[88]

These rights also apply to the exclusion of aliens from within the U.S. borders. That is, proceedings for the deportation of aliens must conform to constitutional requirements, especially due process.[89] In short, legal, illegal, resident, and temporary aliens have historically enjoyed the same constitutional protections as ordinary U.S. citizens. Why does all this matter? In several ways the Patriot Act alters and even abolishes constitutional protections historically available to people under the jurisdiction of the United States, including aliens. Space constraints prevent full coverage of all the relevant changes, but we can consider a couple here. Also see Figure 7.4 for a summary of key Patriot Act provisions, as explained by the U.S. Justice Department.

DETENTIONS. The Patriot Act also has implications for investigative detentions. Section 412 of the Act requires the attorney general to take into custody any alien whom he has "reasonable grounds to believe" is "engaged in any other activity that endangers the national security of the United States."[90] The alien can then be held for seven days. At the end of seven days, the alien must be released, charged criminally, or deported. Importantly, if an alien is detained for purposes related to immigration, rather than suspected criminal activity, he or she can be detained indefinitely. This has been one tool in the war on terrorism; authorities can indefinitely detain illegal immigrants, which obviously raises serious due process concerns.

IMPROVED INTELLIGENCE GATHERING. The Patriot Act has also given enhanced authority to law enforcement in the name of intelligence gathering. For example, the Act modified portions of the Electronic Communications Privacy Act that governs access to stored electronic communications, like e-mail correspondence and voice mail. Wiretap orders, which traditionally were difficult to secure, are now only required to intercept real-time phone communications. As another example of improved intelligence-gathering, Section 206 creates so-called roving wiretap authority. This basically abandons a previous requirement that the government eavesdropper make sure the target is actually using the device being monitored. This means that if a suspected terrorist switches cell phones, the government can continue to listen.

RECENT DEVELOPMENTS. The Patriot Act was set to expire at the end of 2005. In March 2006, President Bush signed into law a "renewal" of the Act. Some changes were put in place. Various civil liberties protections were written into the new version of the Act. Many of these addressed "Section 215" requests, which permit the government to access business and library records. Some examples include the following:

- *Requiring High-Level Approval and Additional Reporting to Congress for Section 215 Requests for Sensitive Information Such as Library or Medical Records*

1. The Patriot Act allows investigators to use the tools that were already available to investigate organized crime and drug trafficking.
   - Allows law enforcement to use surveillance against more crimes of terror.
   - Allows federal agents to follow sophisticated terrorists trained to evade detection.
   - Allows law enforcement to conduct investigations without tipping off terrorists.
   - Allows federal agents to ask a court for an order to obtain business records in national security terrorism cases.
2. The Patriot Act facilitated information sharing and cooperation among government agencies so that they can better "connect the dots."
   - Prosecutors and investigators used information shared pursuant to Section 218 in investigating the defendants in the so-called "Virginia Jihad" case. This prosecution involved members of the Dar al-Arqam Islamic Center, who trained for jihad in Northern Virginia by participating in paintball and paramilitary training, including eight individuals who traveled to terrorist training camps in Pakistan or Afghanistan between 1999 and 2001.
3. The Patriot Act updated the law to reflect new technologies and new threats.
   - Allows law enforcement officials to obtain a search warrant anywhere a terrorist-related activity occurred.
   - Allows victims of computer hacking to request law enforcement assistance in monitoring the "trespassers" on their computers.
4. The Patriot Act increased the penalties for those who commit terrorist crimes.
   - Prohibits the harboring of terrorists.
   - Enhanced the inadequate maximum penalties for various crimes likely to be committed by terrorists: including arson, destruction of energy facilities, material support to terrorists and terrorist organizations, and destruction of national-defense materials.
   - Enhanced a number of conspiracy penalties, including for arson, killings in federal facilities, attacking communications systems, material support to terrorists, sabotage of nuclear facilities, and interference with flight crew members. Under the previous law, many terrorism statutes did not specifically prohibit engaging in conspiracies to commit the underlying offenses. In such cases, the government could only bring prosecutions under the general federal conspiracy provision, which carries a maximum penalty of only five years in prison.
   - Punishes terrorist attacks on mass transit systems.
   - Punishes bioterrorists.
   - Eliminates the statutes of limitations for certain terrorism crimes and lengthens them for other terrorist crimes.

FIGURE 7.4 Counterterrorism Improvements Due to the Patriot Act

Source: U.S. Department of Justice, *Highlights of the USA PATRIOT Act*, justice.gov/archive/ll/highlights.htm.

- *Statement of Facts Showing Relevance to a Terrorism or Foreign Spy Investigation Required for Section 215 Requests*
- *Explicitly Allowing a United States Foreign Intelligence Surveillance Act (FISA) Court Judge to Deny or Modify a Section 215 Request*
- *Requiring Minimization Procedures to Limit Retention and Dissemination of Information Obtained about U.S. Persons from Section 215 Requests*[91]

The Patriot Act has also been amended under the Obama administration. For example, in early 2010, the President signed a one-year extension of several key provisions. The key activities President Obama reauthorized were "court-approved roving wiretaps that permit surveillance on multiple phones, ... seizure of records and property in anti-terrorism operations, . . . [and] surveillance against a so-called long wolf, a non-U.S. citizen engaged in terrorism who may not be part of a recognized terrorist group."[92] This reauthorization is set to expire in 2015. Needless to say, anti-terrorism legislation continues to evolve and what the Patriot Act will look like in a few years is not completely clear.

Does It Work?

The short answer to the question Does it work? is yes. There has yet to be another significant terrorist event in the United States since 9/11. The long answer is more complicated. For example, there is no way to know whether the Patriot Act has been responsible for a few years of freedom from terrorist attacks. Also, for our purposes, can we really expect the Patriot Act to help in the prevention and control of crime as we know it? With the possible exception of the methamphetamine language of the Patriot Act reauthorization, the answer is probably no. Terrorism, while certainly criminal, is not what comes to mind when we talk about crime. Indeed, the FBI did not count the World Trade Center deaths in its homicide counts, reinforcing the point just made:

> The statistics of September 11 are not a part of the traditional Crime in the United States publication because they are different from the day-to-day crimes committed in this country. Additionally, combining these statistics with our regular crime report would create many difficulties in defining and analyzing crime as we know it.[93]

Summary

Enacting laws that criminalize certain types of conduct and substances is, for the most part, an unimaginative, knee-jerk reaction to problems that are far more complex than we sometimes think. Legislative bans are perhaps the most ineffective approach to the crime problem. This is an area where we steadfastly ignore historical lessons and continue to enact criminal laws anyway. Bans also create strange contradictions. For example, more people clearly die each year from tobacco use than from marijuana, but tobacco remains legal when marijuana does not. In a similar vein, gun control, in all its forms, must confront the stark reality that Americans are armed to the teeth. Only when control succeeds in removing the 200 million or so guns in our country will gun violence be reduced.

Laws requiring public notification of the whereabouts of convicted sex offenders are certainly more imaginative than bans, but do they reduce the sex offense problem? Maybe that is not their intent. Even if it is, no one can say for sure as yet, but the research is not too encouraging. Laws targeting white-collar criminals (e.g., Sarbanes–Oxley, Dodd–Frank) and terrorists (e.g., the Patriot Act) suffer from a similar fate, at least for now. We cannot say whether these laws have reduced either problem. Researchers need to get the ball rolling.

Notes

1. R.J. MacCoun and P. Reuter, *Drug War Heresies* (New York: Cambridge University Press, 2001).
2. See, for example, H. DiNardo, "Law Enforcement, the Price of Cocaine, and Cocaine Use," *Mathematical and Computer Modeling* 17 (1993): 53–64; P. Reuter, G. Crawford, and J. Cave, *Sealing the Borders: The Effects of Increased Military Participation in Drug Interdiction* (Santa Monica, CA: RAND, 1988); J. Caulkins and P. Reuter, "What Price Data Tell Us about Drug Markets," *Journal of Drug Issues* 28 (1998): 593–612.
3. J. Ezell, *Fortune's Merry Wheel: The Lottery in America* (Cambridge, MA: Harvard University Press).

4. W. Moore, *The Kefauver Committee and the Politics of Crime, 1950–1952* (Columbia, MO: University of Missouri Press, 1974).

5. P. Reuter and J. Rubinstein, *Illegal Gambling in New York* (Washington, DC: National Institute of Justice, 1982), 133.

6. J. Lasswell and J. McKenna, *Organized Crime in an Inner City Community* (Springfield, VA: National Technical Information Service, 1972); see also R.J. MacCoun and P. Reuter, *Drug War Heresies* (New York: Cambridge University Press, 2001), 132–6.

7. J. Pearl, "The Highest Paying Customers: America's Cities and the Costs of Prostitution Control," *Hastings Law Journal* 38 (1987): 769–90.

8. C.M. Archer, "Hooker Heaven: How Lax Justice Fuels DC's Prostitution Boom," *Washington Post*, January 8, 1995, C1.

9. J.A. Miron and J. Zwiebel, "Alcohol Consumption during Prohibition," *American Economic Review* 81 (1991): 242–7.

10. R.J. MacCoun and P. Reuter, *Drug War Heresies* (New York: Cambridge University Press, 2001), 160.

11. G. Edwards, P. Anderson, T.F. Babor, et al., *Alcohol Police and the Public Good* (Oxford: Oxford University Press, 1994), 131.

12. J. Gusfield, *Symbolic Crusade: Status Politics and the American Temperance Movement* (Urbana, IL: University of Illinois Press, 1963).

13. D. Cook and J. Ludwig, *National Survey on Private Ownership and Use of Firearms: Research in Brief* (Washington, DC: Department of Justice, National Institute of Justice, 1997).

14. J.T. Young, D. Hemenway, R.J. Blendon, and J.M. Benson, "The Polls—Trends: Guns," *Public Opinion Quarterly* 60 (1996): 634–49.

15. Ibid.

16. Centers for Disease Control and Prevention, FastStats, cdc.gov/nchs/fastats/injury.htm.

17. Bureau of Justice Statistics, *Guns and Crime* (Washington, DC: U.S. Government Printing Office, 1994).

18. P.J. Cook and J. Ludwig, *Gun Violence: The Real Costs* (New York: Oxford University Press, 2000).

19. 18 U.S.C. Section 922(b)(1).

20. G. Kleck, *Point Blank: Guns and Violence in America* (New York: Aldine de Gruyter, 1991), 85.

21. 18 U.S.C. Section 922(v).

22. J.A. Roth and C.S. Koper, "Impacts of the 1994 Assault Weapons Ban: 1994–96." Washington, DC: U.S. Government Printing Office, 1999.

23. *District of Columbia v. Heller*, 554 U.S. 570 (2008).

24. *McDonald v. Chicago*, 561 U.S. 3025 (2010).

25. C.L. Britt, G. Kleck, and D.J. Bordua, "A Reassessment of the D.C. Gun Law: Some Cautionary Notes on the Use of Interrupted Time Series Designs for Policy Assessment," *Law and Society Review* 30 (1996): 361–80; D. McDowall, C. Loftin, and B. Wiersema, "Using Quasi-Experiments to Evaluate Firearm Laws: Comment on Britt et al.'s Reassessment of the D.C. Gun Law," *Law and Society Review* 30 (1996): 381–91.

26. drugsense.org/cms/wodclock.

27. Ibid.

28. W. Rhodes, S. Langenbahn, R. Kling, and P. Scheiman, *What America's Users Spend on Illegal Drugs, 1988–1995* (Washington, DC: Office of National Drug Control Policy, 1997).

29. D.B. Kandel, "The Social Demography of Drug Use," *The Milbank Quarterly* 69 (1993): 365–414; J. Shedler and J. Block, "Adolescent Drug Use and Psychological Health: A Longitudinal Inquiry," *American Psychologist* 45 (1990): 612–30.

30. See, e.g., monitoringthefuture.org/data/12data/fig12_1.pdf.

31. U.S. Department of Health and Human Services, *Results from the 2010 National Survey on Drug Use and Health: Summary of National Findings*, oas.samhsa.gov/NSDUH/2k10NSDUH/2k10Results.htm#Ch2.

32. W. Rhodes, M. Layne, P. Johnson, and L. Hozik, *What America's Users Spend on Illicit Drugs, 1988–1998* (Washington, DC: Office of National Drug Control Policy, 2000).

33. W. Rhodes, S. Langenbahn, R. Kling, and P. Scheiman, *What America's Users Spend on Illegal Drugs, 1988–1995* (Washington, DC: Office of National Drug Control Policy, 1997).

34. P.A. Ebener, J.P. Caulkins, S.A. Geschwind, D. McCaffrey, and H.L. Saner, *Improving Data and Analysis to Support National Substance Abuse Policy: Main Report* (Santa Monica, CA: RAND, 1994).

35. Office of National Drug Control Policy, *ADAM II: 2011 Annual Report* (Washington, DC: Executive Office of the President, 2012), 17.

36. This section draws from R.J. MacCoun and P. Reuter, *Drug War Heresies* (New York: Cambridge University Press, 2001), 112–26.

37. E. Walsh, "Edmund Convicted on All Counts in Drug Conspiracy Case," *Washington Post* December 7, 1989, A1.

38. R. Lee and P. Clawson, *The Andean Cocaine Trade* (New York: St. Martin's Press, 1996).

39. This type of violence has been classified as psychopharmacological (violence resulting from the effects of drugs on users), economic-compulsive (violence for the purpose of generating income to buy drugs), and systemic (violence tied to the black market and drug sales). For further discussion, see P. Goldstein, "The Drugs/Violence Nexus: A Tripartite Conceptual Framework," *Journal of Drug Issues* 14 (1985): 493–506.

40. See, for example, L. Gruson, "Corruption Is Brotherly in Philadelphia," *New York Times* November 9, 1986, A4.

41. D.W. Rasmussen and B.L. Benson, *The Economic Anatomy of a Drug War: Criminal Justice in the Commons* (Lanham, MD: Rowman and Littlefield, 1994).

42. H.J. Harwood, D. Fountain, and G. Livermore, *The Economic Costs of Alcohol and Drug Abuse in the United States, 1992* (Rockville, MD: National Institute on Drug Abuse, 1998).

43. J.S. Vernick and S.P. Teret, "A Public Health Approach to Regulating Firearms as Consumer Products," *University of Pennsylvania Law Review* 148 (2000): 1193–2111.

44. Violence Policy Center, "The False Hope of the 'Smart Gun,'" vpc.org, accessed March 12, 2002.

45. As of this writing, Massachusetts is regulating the design of guns sold within its borders.

46. J. Wachtel, "Sources of Crime Guns in Los Angeles, California," *Policing* 21 (1998): 220–39.

47. Bureau of Alcohol, Tobacco and Firearms, *Commerce in Firearms in the United States* (Washington, DC: U.S. Department of the Treasury, 2000); Bureau of Alcohol, Tobacco and Firearms, *ATF Regulatory Actions: Report to the Secretary on Firearms Initiatives* (Washington, DC: U.S. Department of the Treasury, 2000).

48. C.S. Koper, "Federal Legislation and Gun Markets: How Much Have Recent Reforms in the Federal Firearms Licensing System Reduced Criminal Gun Suppliers?" *Criminology and Public Policy* 1 (2002): 151–78.

49. D.A. Manson and D.K. Gilliard, *Presale Handgun Checks, 1996: A National Estimate* (Washington, DC: U.S. Department of Justice, 1997).

50. P.J. Cook and J. Ludwig, *Gun Violence: The Real Costs* (New York: Oxford University Press, 2000).

51. J.R. Lott, *More Guns, Less Crime*, 2nd ed. (Chicago, IL: University of Chicago Press, 2000), 90, 200.

52. *Printz v. United States*, 521 U.S. 898 (1997); the Supreme Court also declared the 1991 Gun Free School Zones Act unconstitutional in 1995 (*United States v. Lopez* 514 U.S. 549 [1995]), but the act was reinstituted in 1996 once its constitutional problems were cleared up.

53. P.J. Cook and J. Ludwig, *Gun Violence: The Real Costs* (New York: Oxford University Press, 2000).

54. G.J. Wintemute, M.A. Wright, C.M. Drake, and J.J. Beaumont, "Subsequent Criminal Activity among Violent Misdemeanants Who Seek to Purchase Handguns," *Journal of the American Medical Association* 265 (2001): 1019–26.

55. E.R. Vigdor and J.A. Mercy, "Disarming Batterers: The Impact of Domestic Violence Firearm Laws," in *Evaluating Gun Policy: Effects on Crime and Violence*, eds. J. Ludwig and P.J. Cook (Washington, DC: Brookings Institution Press, 2003), 157–214.

56. Ibid.

57. See M. Plotkin, ed., *Under Fire: Gun Buy-Backs, Exchanges, and Amnesty Programs* (Washington, DC: Police Executive Research Forum, 1996).

58. C.M. Callahan, P.R. Frederick, and T.D. Koepsell, "Money for Guns: Evaluation of the Seattle Gun Buy-Back Program," *Public Health Reports* 109 (1994): 472–7; M.P. Romero, G.J. Wintemute, and J.S. Vernick, "Characteristics of a Gun Exchange Program, and an Assessment of Potential Benefits," *Injury Prevention* 4 (1998): 206–10.

59. P. Reuter and J. Mouzos, "Australia: A Massive Buyback of Low-Risk Guns," in *Evaluating Gun Policy: Effects on Crime and Violence*, eds. J. Ludwig and P.J. Cook (Washington, DC: Brookings Institution Press, 2003), 121–56.

60. J.A. Dvorak, "Concealed Weapons Laws Taking Hold," *Knight-Ridder Newspapers*, March 1, 2002.

61. J.R. Lott, *More Guns, Less Crime*, 2nd ed. (Chicago, IL: University of Chicago Press, 2000), 20; see also J.R. Lott and D.B. Mustard, "Crime, Deterrence, and Right-to-Carry Concealed Handguns," *Journal of Legal Studies* 16 (1997):1–68.

62. S.G. Bronars and J.R. Lott, Jr., "Criminal Deterrence, Geographic Spillovers, and the Right to Carry Concealed Handguns," *American Economic Review* 88 (1998): 475–79; F. Plassmann and T.N. Tideman, "Does the Right to Carry Concealed Handguns Deter Countable Crimes? Only a County Analysis Can Say," *Journal of Law and Economics* 44 (2001): 771–98; F. Plassmann and J. Whitley, "Confirming More Guns, Less Crime," *Stanford Law Review* 55 (2003): 1315–70.

63. M. Duggan, "More Guns, More Crime," *Journal of Political Economy* 109 (2001): 1086–114; C.E. Moody, "Testing for the Effects of Concealed Weapons Laws: Specification Errors and Robustness," *Journal of Law and Economics* 44 (2001): 799–813; D.E. Olson and M.D. Maltz, "Right-to-Carry Concealed Weapons Laws and Homicide in Large U.S. Counties: The Effect on Weapon Types, Victim Characteristics, and Victim-Offender Relationships," *Journal of Law and Economics* 44 (2001): 747–70; W.A. Bartley and M.A. Cohen, "The Effect of Concealed Weapons Laws: An Extreme Bounds Analysis," *Economic Inquiry* 36 (1998): 258–65; D.A. Black and D.S. Nagin, "Do Right-to-Carry Laws Deter Violent Crime?" *Journal of Legal Studies* 27 (1998): 209–19; H. Dezhbakhsh and P.H. Rubin, "Lives Saved or Lives Lost? The Effects of Concealed-Handgun Laws on Crime," *American Economic Review* 88 (1998): 468–74.

64. I. Ayres and J.J. Donohue III, "Nondiscretionary Concealed Weapons Laws: A Case Study of Statistics, Standards of Proof, and Public Policy," *American Law and Economics Review* 6 (1999): 436–70; I. Ayres and J.J. Donohue III, "Shooting Down the More Guns, Less Crime Hypothesis," *Stanford Law Review* 55 (2003): 1193–314; J. Ludwig, "Concealed-Gun-Carrying Laws and Violent Crime: Evidence from State Panel Data," *International Review of Law and Economics* 18 (1998): 239–54; D. McDowall, C. Loftin, and B. Wiersema, "Easing Concealed Firearms Laws: Effects on Homicide in Three States," *Journal of Criminal Law and Criminology* 86 (1995): 193–206.

65. T.V. Kovandzic and T.B. Marvell, "Right-to-Carry Concealed Handguns and Violent Crime: Crime Control Through Gun Decontrol?" *Criminology and Public Policy* 2 (2003): 363–96.

66. NJ Rev.Stat. Section 2C: 7–8(c) (1995).

67. Megan's Law, Pub. L. No. 104–145, 110 Stat. 1345 (1996).

68. 20 U.S.C. Section 1094(c)(3)(B) (2000).

69. See T.L. Wayt, "Megan's Law: A Violation of the Right to Privacy?" *Temple Political and Civil Rights Law Review* 6 (1996): 139.

70. For further details see J.B. Rudin, "Megan's Law: Can It Stop Sexual Predators—And at What Cost to Constitutional Rights?" *Criminal Justice* 11 (1996): 3–6, 8–10, 63.

71. Some have even argued for a formula-based method of selecting sex offenders for community notification, presumably because such a method would minimize the potential for arbitrary and constitutionally questionable decisions. See N.J. Pallone, J.J. Hennessy, and G.T. Voelbel, "Identifying Pedophiles 'Eligible' for Community Notification Under Megan's Law: A Multivariate Model for Actuarially Anchored Decisions," *Journal of Offender Rehabilitation* 28 (1998): 41–60.

72. *Doe v. Poritz*, 662 A.2d 405 (N.J. 1995).

73. See also E.A. Goodman, "Megan's Law: The New Jersey Supreme Court Navigates Uncharted Waters," *Seton Hall Law Review* 26 (1996): 764–802.

74. *Smith v. Doe*, 123 S.Ct. 1140 (2003); see also *Connecticut Department of Public Safety v. Doe*, 123 S.Ct. 1160 (2003).

75. Elizabeth J. Letourneau, Jill S. Levenson, Dipankar Bandyopadhyay, Debajyoti Sinha, and Kevin S. Armstrong, "Effects of South Carolina's Sex Offender Registration and Notification Policy on Adult Recidivism," *Criminal Justice Policy Review* 21 (2010): 435–58.

76. Washington State Institute for Public Policy, *Does Sex Offender Registration and Notification Reduce Crime? A Systematic Review of the Research Literature* (Olympia, WA: Washington State Institute for Public Policy, 2009), 1.

77. J.L. Proctor, D.M. Badzinski, and M. Johnson, "Impact of Media on Knowledge and Perceptions of Megan's Law," *Criminal Justice Policy Review* 13 (2002): 356–79.

78. J. Peckenpaugh, "Controlling Sex Offender Reentry: Jessica's Law Measures in California," *Journal of Offender Monitoring* 19 (2006): 13–28.

79. Kristen M. Zgoba, Michael Miner, Raymond Knight, Elizabeth Letourneau, Jill Levenson, and David Thornton, *A Multi-State Recidivism Study Using Static-99R and Static-2002 Risk Scores and Tier Guidelines from the Adam Walsh Act* (Washington, DC: National Institute of Justice, 2012).

80. L.H. Nicholson, "The Culture of Under-Enforcement: Buried Treasure, Sarbanes-Oxley, and the Corporate Pirate," *DePaul Business and Commercial Law Review* 5 (2007): 321.

81. en. wikipedia. org/wiki/Sarbanes-Oxley_Act

82. M.H. Hein, C.E. Neimeth, I.N. Rosner, and F.S. Watts, "The Sarbanes-Oxley Act of 2002 Effects Sweeping Changes to the U.S. Federal Securities Laws," *The Journal of Investment Compliance*, Fall (2002): 5–12.

83. L.H. Nicholson, "The Culture of Under-Enforcement: Buried Treasure, Sarbanes-Oxley, and the Corporate Pirate," *DePaul Business and Commercial Law Review* 5 (2007):321–77.

84. Pub. L. 111–203.

85. Kevin Drawbaugh and Dena Aubin, "Analysis: A Decade On, is Sarbanes-Oxley Working?" *Reuters*, July 30, 2012, reuters.com/article/2012/07/30/us-financial-sarbox-idUSBRE86Q1BY20120730.

86. *United States v. Verdugo-Urquidez*, 494 U.S. 259 (1990), 264–266.

87. *Mathews v. Diaz*, 426 U.S. 67 (1976), 77.

88. Ibid.

89. *Shaughnessy v. United States ex rel. Mezei*, 345 U.S. 206 (1953), 212.

90. USA Patriot Act, Pub. L. No. 107-56, 412, 115 Stat. 272, 350 (2001).

91. The full list can be found here: en.wikipedia.org/wiki/ USA_PATRIOT_Act.

92. Associated Press, "Obama Signs Extension of Patriot Act," usatoday30.usatoday.com/news/washington/2010-02-27-Patriot-Act_N.htm.

93. Federal Bureau of Investigation, *Crime in the United States, 2001, Section V: Special Report* (Washington, DC: FBI, 2001).

Crime Control in the Courts and Beyond

LEARNING OBJECTIVES

▨ Explain how the courts can use incapacitative approaches to crime.

▨ Summarize the research concerning the effectiveness of diversion.

▨ Identify the goals of shaming and explain their connection to crime control.

▨ Discuss whether restorative justice is effective crime control policy.

▨ Summarize the purpose and efficacy of anti-gang injunctions.

▨ Explain the concept of a problem-solving court and provide examples of effective problem-solving courts.

Legislatures enact laws, law enforcement officials ensure people abide by those laws, and courts adjudicate those who fail to do so. Courts do much more than simply adjudicate offenders, however. They make decisions that affect suspected offenders' liberty even before trial, such as by setting (or denying) bail. America's courts are also being used in a wide variety of innovative and nontraditional ways. Judges are taking a more active role in sentencing, often personalizing sentences for purposes of embarrassing criminals into discontinuing crime (as is the case with shaming) or crafting individually-based sentences aimed at helping offenders return to the straight and narrow. Injunctions are being used to curb gang violence. Specialized courts are becoming fixtures all over the country and, indeed, steps are being taken to avoid reliance on the courts altogether. Restorative justice replaces the traditional court venue with an informal meeting between parties affected by crime. Diversion programs try to steer offenders out of the justice system to minimize the stigma associated with a criminal conviction. This chapter takes a hard look at each of these court-related approaches to crime.

COURTS AND INCAPACITATION

Courts issue verdicts that affect the liberty of convicted criminals. Sanctions imposed can range from probation all the way through death. But courts also make decisions that affect people's liberty *before* trial. This can be called pretrial incapacitation.

Pretrial Incapacitation

Once a person is arrested, the question as to whether the individual should be temporarily released (either via bail or on his own recognizance) invariably pops up. On the one hand, if the arrestee does not pose a significant risk of flight and has been arrested for a relatively minor offense, pretrial release seems a sensible approach. On the other hand, if the arrestee is likely to fail to appear in later proceedings, he or she should probably be jailed pending additional court proceedings. Many arrestees who are released prior to their trials reoffend (see Table 8.1), which is why it is important to identify effective control mechanisms at this early stage of the criminal process.

The Eighth Amendment states that "[e]xcessive bail shall not be required." This simply means that bail can't be set ridiculously high, not that everyone enjoys a constitutional right to bail. In capital cases, for example, bail has always been denied. Consider what the Supreme Court stated in *Carlson v. Landon*:

> In England, [the Bail] clause has never been thought to accord a right to bail in all cases, but merely to provide that bail shall not be excessive in those cases where it is proper to grant bail. When this clause was carried over into our Bill of Rights, nothing was said that indicated any different concept.[1]

Some critics of judges' decisions to deny bail have argued that because our criminal justice system presumes innocence, everyone should be released; defendants cannot be considered guilty until the state proves guilt beyond a reasonable doubt. However, in *Bell v. Wolfish*, the Supreme Court stated that the presumption of innocence is merely "a doctrine that allocates the burden of proof in criminal trials."[2] And, as we will see, it is quite common for judges to set bail at a fairly high level, making it difficult for some defendants to pay.

TABLE 8.1 Percent of Defendants Released Pretrial Who Committed Pretrial Misconduct for Cases Disposed in Federal District Courts, FY 1995–2010

| Fiscal Year | Number of Released Defendants | Percent of Released Defendants Who Had— | | | | |
| | | At least One Violation | Technical Violations of Bail Conditions | Failed to Appear | Rearrested for— | |
					Felony Offense	Misdemeanor Offense
1995	26,380	16%	12%	3%	2%	2%
1996	26,801	16	13	2	2	2
1997	28,600	17	14	3	2	1
1998	26,246	16	15	2	2	2
1999	30,841	18	17	3	2	2
2000	31,040	18	17	3	2	2
2001	31,320	19	17	3	2	2
2002	32,140	20	18	2	2	2
2003	31,613	20	18	2	2	2
2004	30,952	20	18	2	2	2
2005	27,253	21	19	2	2	2
2006	30,289	22	19	/	/	/
2007	29,325	21	19	/	/	/
2008	32,936	21	19	2	2	2
2009	33,122	19	17	2	2	2
2010	35,564	17	15	1	2	2

Note: Detail may not sum to total because a defendant could have more than one type of violation.

/ Not reported or determined to be unreliable.

Source: Thomas H. Cohen, *Pretrial Detention and Misconduct in Federal District Courts, 1995–2010* (Washington, DC: Bureau of Justice Statistics, 2013), 8.

preventive detention:
The practice of
denying bail to certain
presumably dangerous
defendants.

PREVENTIVE DETENTION. Growing concern over crimes committed by defendants out on pretrial release prompted some reforms.[3] In 1970, for example, the District of Columbia passed the first "preventive detention" statute. The statute authorized denial of bail to "dangerous" persons charged with certain offenses for up to 60 days.[4] Then, Congress passed the Federal Bail Reform Act of 1984,[5] which authorized judges to revoke pretrial release for firearm possession, failure to comply with curfew, or failure to comply with other conditions of release. The act also permitted detention for up to 10 days of an individual who "may flee or pose a danger to any other person or the community."[6] This practice came to be known as **preventive detention.**

The Bail Reform Act of 1984 permits pretrial detention for *more than* 10 days of certain individuals. If it is deemed that no pretrial release condition "will reasonably assure the appearance of the person as required and the safety of any other person and the community," then indefinite detention is acceptable. For a detention of this nature to conform to Fourth and Eighth Amendment restrictions, a hearing must be held to determine whether the case "involves a serious risk that the person will flee; [or] a serious risk that the person will obstruct or attempt to obstruct justice, or threaten, injure, or intimidate a prospective witness or jury."[7]

Does preventive detention reduce crime? For several reasons, the answer appears to be no. First, recall that the main motivation for preventive detention is a concern that defendants who are released back into the community prior to their trial date will commit more crime. Research suggests that, for most offenders, very few are rearrested while on bail.[8] And of those who fail to appear for their scheduled court dates, most appear to have forgotten about their court dates.[9] In other words, very few remain fugitives from justice.

Another reason that preventive detention seems like inadequate crime control policy is that, when available, it may not be used. A study of preventive detention in Washington, D.C., revealed that very few defendants were detained in the days leading up to their trials. Why? Judges were already able to accomplish preventive detention tacitly by setting bail beyond defendants' means.[10] Much the same result appears to have been achieved in light of the 1984 Federal Bail Reform Act. Research shows that relatively few offenders were detained as a result of the statute.[11] Instead, the law just gave legitimacy to a practice that judges had engaged in for years, namely setting bail at a high amount.

Preventive detention is also fraught with problems because, at its core, it relies on predictions of dangerousness. That is, when deciding whether to detain a defendant prior to trial, judges are effectively required to predict the future. Not surprisingly, judges—and everyone else for that matter—are notoriously inaccurate in doing so. In an interesting study, 69 juveniles who were judged "at risk," detained, and then released to the community were compared to a control group of juveniles who were not detained.[12] After 90 days, the at-risk group reoffended at a higher rate, but 60 percent of the at-risk group did not. Stated differently, the majority of at-risk offenders were not rearrested. The authors of the study therefore concluded that "the accuracy of prediction of dangerousness during the pretrial period remains questionable" and "preventive detention appears to be unjustified."[13]

SETTING BAIL AT A HIGH LEVEL. Pretrial release with bail is a common practice. Indeed, 18 U.S.C.A. Section 3142 provides that "upon all arrests in criminal cases, bail shall be admitted, except where the punishment may be death." Most states have adopted similar language in their constitutions. California's constitution, for example, provides that "all persons shall be bailable by sufficient sureties, unless for capital offenses when the proof is evident or the presumption great."[14] But the bail decision is sometimes problematic. This is because, more often than not, judges set bail according to the nature of the offense in question, not according to the accused's ability to pay.[15] A frequent result is that indigent defendants languish in jail cells until their court dates if they cannot afford to pay.

As a general rule, courts should take into account the accused's ability to pay in setting bail—not just the seriousness of the offense. This is because failure to do so may violate the equal protection clause of the Fourteenth Amendment. Also, setting bail without regard to the accused's financial status also leads to irrational bail determinations. But, as a practical matter, it is fair to say that judges often set bail at a deliberately high amount to ensure that the accused is not released to the community prior to trial. The previous section suggested that this occurs to such an extent that preventive detention statutes would appear completely unnecessary.

An interesting question for our purposes is this: Does setting bail at a high amount serve a crime control purpose? This is a difficult question to answer because, in response to many defendants' inability to post bail, professional bail bondsmen have stepped in. These individuals collect a fee from the accused, usually a percentage of bail, then post a bond so the accused can be released. If the accused shows up at trial, the bondsman collects his fee and gets his money back from the court. If the accused fails to show up, then the bondsman loses the amount posted. In order to avoid such an eventuality, bondsmen employ bounty hunters whose job it is to catch the accused and bring him or her before the court.

It is important to note a significant flaw inherent in the bail bondsman system. The problem is that bail bondsmen, not courts, gain a certain degree of power. Regardless of what amount the court sets as bail, bondsmen can then decide who gets released or who stays in jail based on the accused's ability to pay a fee in order to get a bond. Those who can pay the fee effectively buy their freedom, if only temporarily. Those who cannot pay stay in jail. But bail bondsmen certainly make it easier for indigent defendants to gain pretrial release. The only way to know for sure that setting bail at a high amount serves a crime control purpose would probably be to eliminate the bail bond system. Such an eventuality is probably as unlikely as it is undesirable.

Does It Work?

Pretrial incapacitation comes in two varieties: (1) preventive detention and (2) setting bail at a high level. The former has been well-researched, and the evidence available to date suggests that it does not work. One of its biggest problems is that it is difficult to predict future dangerousness. As for setting bail at a high level, the crime control benefits of this approach have not been explored. And even if any such effects exist, they are probably mitigated because of bail bond agents.

DIVERSION

diversion: a term that refers to any number of informal or programmatic methods of steering offenders out of the criminal justice system.

Diversion is a term that refers to any number of informal or programmatic methods of steering offenders out of the criminal justice system. In one sense, diversion has been around since the emergence of community-based corrections. For example, when a judge sentences an offender to probation, the judge may feel that prison would do more harm than good for the offender. The judge has decided, in essence, that the offender should be diverted out of prison into an environment that fosters reintegration.

Another informal method of diversion could be a police officer's decision not to arrest but, instead, to encourage a suspect to do something to get on the straight and narrow. This kind of informal diversion basically amounts to the exercise of discretion, but it still serves as an example of a criminal justice official advocating a different, less enforcement-oriented method of dealing with the crime problem. Our concern in this chapter, though, is with *programmatic* methods of diversion. Programmatic diversion refers to the development of formal programs the sole purpose of which is to divert offenders out of the criminal process.

There was a significant push for diversion programs following the recommendations of the 1967 President's Commission on Law Enforcement and the Administration of Justice.[16] The Law Enforcement Assistance Administration, which resulted from the Commission's efforts, funded several diversion programs. The rationale for the diversion funding was that it would reduce the number of offenders being drawn into the criminal justice system and would prevent the harmful effects of criminal stigmatization that suspects would experience if they went to court and were convicted and put in prison. The goals of diversion, according to one source, are as follows:

> (1) avoidance of negative labeling and stigmatization, (2) reduction of unnecessary social control and coercion, (3) reduction of recidivism, (4) provision of service (assistance), and (5) reduction of justice system cost.[17]

Perhaps a more cynical view of diversion programs is that they amount to a "break" given to certain offenders. For example, some people feel that young and first-time or low-level offenders should be treated with a measure of leniency. Even if offenders are treated with leniency under diversion programs, the leniency they receive is not the same as traditional sanctions like probation, fines, community service, and the like. Instead, diversion programs usually require that offenders complete a specific program as part of their more-lenient-than-normal sentence.

Examples of Programmatic Diversion

Whether programmatic diversion programs are aimed at adults or juveniles, they tend to manifest themselves in one of four forms.[18] First, **pre-charge diversion** refers to the diversion of offenders out of the criminal justice system before they are charged. Second, **deferred prosecution diversion** occurs when an offender has been charged but the actual in-court prosecution is held off until the offender completes treatment or some other program. Then, if the offender completes his or her obligations, the prosecutor will revisit the charges and most likely drop them.[19] These are the most common types of programmatic diversion, and they are what generally come to mind when diversion discussions occur.

Diversion can also occur at the sentencing stage. This is known as **sentencing diversion**. With respect to this third form of diversion, instead of the offender going straight to jail or prison, he or she may be sent to participate in drug treatment, anger management, or some other program. This approach is akin to the hypothetical judge's decision presented earlier and is premised on a belief that prison may do more harm than good for some offenders. Finally, diversion can even occur at the post-incarceration stage (i.e., **post-incarceration diversion**). Importantly, though, most post-incarceration diversion programs are reserved for chronic low-level offenders and are aimed at getting these offenders who keep ending up incarcerated to stop committing crime.[20] These third and fourth types of diversion can be seen as coming a little too late, and they probably defeat some of the goals of diversion altogether. Even so, they at least attempt to get offenders out of the criminal process, even if the intervention comes well after the criminal act.

Diversion Evaluations

It is difficult to summarize diversion research, for three reasons. First, diversion is often used in conjunction with any other number of criminal justice sanctions. Examples of diversion programs are discussed elsewhere in this book, including in the prosecution context and in the treatment and rehabilitation context. Second, very few evaluations are aimed specifically at the effectiveness of diversion in lieu of prison. As one scholar observed, a review of the diversion literature "is largely a commentary on the unknown."[21] Third, many diversion evaluations have been concerned with juveniles, further restricting the volume of research concerned with diversion of

pre-charge diversion: *the diversion of offenders out of the criminal justice system before they are charged.*

deferred prosecution diversion: *when an offender has been charged but the actual in-court prosecution is held off until the offender completes treatment or some other program.*

sentencing diversion: instead of the offender going straight to jail or prison, he or she may be sent to participate in drug treatment, anger management, or some other program.

post-incarceration diversion: programs that are generally reserved for chronic low-level offenders and are aimed at getting these offenders who keep ending up incarcerated to stop committing crime.

adult offenders. But despite these limitations, we can still briefly review some pertinent research and draw conclusions as to whether diversion does or does not reduce recidivism.

Little is known about pre-charge diversion and diversion at the sentencing or incarceration stage,[22] but researchers *have* paid attention to deferred prosecution diversion. For example, one study shows that offenders whose prosecution is put on hold while they complete employment and educational training recidivated at a lower rate than offenders in a matched control group.[23] A subsequent study of deferred prosecution diversion, however, showed no differences between treatment and control groups.[24] One of the more significant efforts to divert offenders out of the criminal justice system was the **Manhattan Court Employment Project**, sponsored by the Vera Institute of Justice. It provided employment to arrested persons who, with the approval of the prosecutor, would have their charges suspended for 90 days. Charges were then dropped if the defendant kept a job. An early evaluation showed the program was a resounding success,[25] but a later evaluation showed it was not.[26] The authors of the later evaluation argued that the clients served by the employment program would not have been prosecuted at all but for the presence of the program.

Manhattan Court Employment Project: a program once sponsored by the Vera Institute of Justice that provided employment to arrested persons who, with the approval of the prosecutor, would have their charges suspended for 90 days. Charges were then dropped if the defendant kept a job.

Does It Work?

Diversion programs seek to steer offenders out of the criminal justice system because of fears that a criminal conviction can have stigmatizing effects. Diversion has been practiced—and continues to be practiced—on an informal level for years. Programmatic diversion has also been practiced. Unfortunately, though, research concerned purely with the effects of diversion is limited. Research that compares offenders who are diverted to offenders who are processed the traditional way is even more difficult to find. There is a clear ethical problem associated with diversion evaluations, in fact. Specifically, randomly assigning offenders to treatment and control conditions results in some offenders receiving the assistance they need, and others not receiving assistance, all in the name of research. Given this limitation and some of the problems with diversion evaluations already discussed, we cannot safely conclude that diverting offenders out of the criminal justice system improves matters.

SHAMING

After Daniel Alvin bilked several people out of money for tickets and a ride to an Atlanta Hawks basketball game, he found himself charged with eight counts of theft. When he stood before Georgia State Court Judge Leon M. Braun, Jr., to receive his sentence, he was given a choice: He could spend six months in jail or he could spend five weekends in jail and walk around the Fulton County Courthouse for a total of 30 hours wearing a sign saying, "I am a convicted thief." He chose the latter option, spent little time incarcerated, and quickly returned to his family. Of course, he had to suffer the embarrassment of passersby honking at him and hurling less-than-complimentary statements in his direction, but Alvin shouldered his burden and was able to escape a lengthy term of incarceration. This is an example of a **shaming** penalty, the topic of this section.

Shame is one of the most important emotions because it can rear its head in almost any social encounter.[27] According to one researcher, "conformity to exterior norms is rewarded by deference and feelings of pride, and nonconformity is punished by lack of deference and feelings of shame. In this analysis, social control involves a biosocial

shaming: the practice of penalizing offenders by appealing to the emotion of shame, such as by requiring offenders to publicly apologize to their victims.

system that functions silently, continuously, and virtually invisibly, occurring within and between members of society."[28] In other words, shame is a behind-the-scenes emotion that can potentially result from any encounter between people. Or, as another researcher has observed, "shame is an emotional cue regarding one's social status. It is a signal that one's position is in jeopardy, that there are real risks associated with loss of status and social exclusion."[29] Given the importance of shame in social encounters, it is no mystery why those in a position to mete out punishment for criminals have picked up on shame—and all its variants—as a powerful form of condemnation.

Shame, while a powerful emotion, is not the same as guilt. We are concerned here not solely with what criminals *themselves* do or do not feel after violating the law. Rather, we are concerned with other people's knowledge of the criminal act and the effect of their knowledge of the crime and their disapproval of the act. There are some offenders who lack a conscience and may feel no remorse whatsoever for committing crime. But shame, particularly the potential for being socially ousted and disdained by others, may have a powerful effect on one's decision whether to obey the law. As one researcher observed, "[a]ssuming that the offender is concerned with social status, the penalty is meant to reaffirm normative standards and deter future transgressions by creating an opportunity for the offender to experience shame."[30] Thus, shame is a two-way street. It always appears in the context of relationships between people.

A Brief History of Shaming

Shaming punishments can be traced to the prebiblical era. In early times, people lived in tight-knit tribes, and banishment from one's community was one of the most shameful forms of punishment known.[31] Also, if you buy into the story of creation, and particularly the biblical account of the Garden of Eden, then you know that Adam and Eve realized they were naked and were ashamed.[32] Shaming penalties later evolved throughout Europe with the development of public torture, torture that would often end in the death of the accused. Similar but less lethal methods of punishment were then transported to America. Offenders often faced time in the pillory or stocks. Serious offenders were branded and mutilated, thus "fixing on [the offenders] an indelible 'mark of infamy' to warn the community of their criminal propensities."[33] As an example of one such punishment, an offender in Williamsburg, Virginia, had his ear nailed to the wooden brace of a pillory. After he served his sentence, authorities tore him away from the pillory without first removing the nail.[34] He became "ear-marked" as a criminal.

As the United States matured and became a more progressive nation, shaming and other brutal forms of punishment fell out of popularity. Punishment moved away from physical to more psychological methods. That is, authorities began to favor institutional forms of punishment that would affect offenders' mental state more than their physical being. At the same time, people were becoming more mobile, which made certain shaming punishments—especially banishment—less attractive; being forcibly removed from one's surroundings no longer carried with it the same permanency and stigmatization. Criminals who were shamed in one community could simply move away and start a new life elsewhere. Throughout the twentieth century, shaming punishments all but disappeared from the United States. But in the 1970s, such penalties—albeit with a less physical component—began to resurface.

One of the first modern shaming cases came out of California. In *People v. McDowell*,[35] a judge required a convicted purse-snatcher to wear taps on his shoes as a condition of probation. It assumed that the taps would alert potential victims to his presence. A decade later, a Florida court ordered a convicted drunk driver, as part of his probation term, to place a bumper sticker on his car that read "Convicted D.U.I.—Restricted License."[36] These two cases signaled the beginning of a growing reliance on shaming punishments. In the following section we will give more attention to examples of shaming penalties; then we will focus on criticisms of shaming, shaming integrated with restorative justice, and the evidence concerning the effect of shaming on criminal activity.

Examples of Shaming Penalties

public exposure penalty: when a criminal's conviction is made visible to several people. Such penalties point the offender out to the public so that the public can respond with disapproval, thereby heightening the offender's sense of shame.

Shaming penalties come in three forms: public exposure, debasement, and apology penalties.[37] **Public exposure penalties** occur when a criminal's conviction is made visible to several people. Such penalties point the offender out to the public so that the public can respond with disapproval, thereby heightening the offender's sense of shame. Public exposure penalties, such as Megan's law, can also serve the dual purpose of letting people know where criminals reside. **Debasement penalties**, though closely related to public exposure penalties, serve the additional goal of lowering the offender's social status. They tend to require offenders to perform humiliating acts. Finally, **apology penalties** are straightforward; they require offenders to express remorse, usually publicly, for committing a particular crime. The following subsections highlight some examples of each of these types of shaming penalties.[38]

debasement penalty: closely related to public exposure penalties, these shaming penalties serve the additional goal of lowering the offender's social status. They tend to require offenders to perform humiliating acts.

PUBLIC EXPOSURE PENALTIES. Public exposure penalties have been applied for drunk driving, child molestation, and battery, among other offenses. For example, on December 10, 1991, Roy Letterlough pled guilty to driving under the influence in New York State. In addition to other sanctions, the judge ordered Letterlough to affix a fluorescent sign to his car that read "Convicted DWI."[39] As for child molesters, a Rhode Island Superior Court judge required an offender to purchase an ad in a local newspaper. The content of the ad was, in relevant part: "I am Stephen Gershausen. I am 29 years old. . . . I was convicted of child molestation. . . . If you are a child molestor, get professional help immediately, or you may find your picture and name in the paper, and your life under control of the state."[40] Likewise, another sex offender was required to post a 4-foot by 8-foot sign reading "Warning, all children. Wayne Burdin is an admitted and convicted child molestor. Parents beware."[41] And, for battery, a defendant was required to remain on his farm and post a sign at the entrance that read: "Warning! A Violent Felon Lives Here. Enter at Your Own Risk!"[42]

apology penalty: the requirement that offenders express remorse, usually publicly, for committing a particular crime.

DEBASEMENT PENALTIES. Debasement penalties are also becoming popular. For example, a Texas judge ordered a defendant in a child custody case to clean the Houston Police Department's mounted patrol unit stables.[43] An offender in a domestic violence case was made to stand before his wife while she was allowed to spit in his face.[44] Slumlords beware: A landlord was sentenced to house arrest in one of his slum dwellings.[45] And a probationer in a halfway house was accused of "acting like a baby" and required to wear diapers outside of his clothes. In the words of the therapist coordinator, "his attitude reflected the actions of a baby, and because of that, as a learning experience for himself, he would wear a diaper. . . . At that counseling session, I told him that that would be his learning experience. If he chose not to accept it, he would have to leave the facility."[46] An appellate court reversed a lower court decision that the probationer violated the conditions of his sentence, but the former court did state, "suffice it to say that a command . . . that an adult male wear diapers in public would certainly be demeaning in the minds of, so called, reasonable men."[47]

APOLOGY PENALTIES. Apology penalties are certainly less embarrassing than public exposure and debasement penalties, but they can nevertheless lead to feelings of shame and related emotions. For example, a student who vandalized 13 schools was required to visit each school and apologize for his actions in front of the student body.[48] In Tennessee, a judge sentenced a man convicted of car theft to three years probation and required that he apologize to a church congregation. For the crime of burglary, an offender was required to print an apology in the newspaper. It read:

> APOLOGY—I, Tom Kirby, wish to apologize to the people of the City of Newport for all of the problems I have caused. I know now what I did was selfish and wrong. I also realized that I have caused a lot of hardships on people that were my friends and also my own family. I want to thank the courts for a second chance to prove that I can be an honest upstanding person. My apologies again for causing any inconveniences to anyone.[49]

REVERSE BURGLARY? Some judges have imposed shaming penalties that do not fit readily into the categories of public exposure, debasement, or apologies. In Tennessee, a judge permitted the victims of burglary to enter the home of the convicted burglar and steal an item.[50] The victims were allowed to keep coming back over a period of time until they found something worth stealing. Not surprisingly, they had to make several trips! Such penalties border on the bizarre and essentially amount to state-sanctioned crime. But they also satisfy the retributive impulses of many Americans.

Criticisms of Shaming

Some people rejoice over shaming penalties. Bringing unfavorable publicity to criminal activity certainly seems warranted. And encouraging criminals to feel bad for their exploits makes perfect sense. At the same time, though, shaming penalties have been attacked on a number of grounds. The most obvious critique is that such penalties violate the Eighth Amendment to the U.S. Constitution. But this criticism may not carry much weight. To understand why this is so, it is worth quickly considering the Supreme Court's definition of cruel and unusual punishment.

To date the U.S. Supreme Court has not decided on the constitutionality of shaming punishments. It has, however, had occasion to decide whether *corporal punishment* (i.e., the infliction of physical pain on a convicted criminal) violates the Eighth Amendment. In *Trop v. Dulles*, the Court stated that the meaning of the Eighth Amendment must be drawn from "the evolving standards of decency that mark the progress of a maturing society."[51] This would seem to suggest that, assuming the United States is a maturing society, corporal punishment would not be allowed, but the Supreme Court has never found that such punishments rise to the level of cruel and unusual punishment.[52] Following the 1994 caning of an American youth in Singapore, one Supreme Court justice said that such forms of punishment would pass Eighth Amendment muster if brought before the Supreme Court.[53] Therefore, it is likely that shaming penalties would not be considered violative of the Eighth Amendment.

If an Eighth Amendment argument is unlikely to succeed, what other criticisms of shaming are available? One is that it amounts to an abuse of judicial discretion. In particular, some feel that when a shaming penalty is imposed as a probation condition, it violates the purpose of probation, which is generally to rehabilitate. In other words, some people feel shaming amounts to punishment and that punitive sanctions should not be imposed as part of a rehabilitative probation scheme.[54] Another criticism is that shaming penalties sometimes bear little resemblance to the initial crime. For example, if a drunk driver were required to carry a sign alerting the public of his or her transgressions, such a penalty would bear little relationship to the crime. The sensible alternative, as we have seen already, is a bumper sticker on the driver's car. But whether a person who demonstrates such irresponsibility behind the wheel should be allowed back on the road is obviously open for debate.

> David Karp identified three more criticisms of shaming penalties. He argues that shaming penalties (1) may be damaging; (2) ignore the context of crime; and (3) run counter to modern criminal procedure.

Braithwaite's Reintegrative Shaming

reintegrative shaming: the practice of merging shaming methods of punishment with the practice of restorative justice.

Given all the arguments against shaming, one wonders why it is even tried. Many of the criticisms are valid, and a strong case can be made that extreme shaming punishments probably do little more than placate victims of crime, but this has not stopped criminologists from advocating less harsh methods of shaming. One prominent example of this push for alternatives is Braithwaite's notion of "**reintegrative shaming**."[55] At the risk of simplifying his version of shaming, what he calls for is basically a merger of some of the shaming methods discussed thus far with the practice of restorative justice. Restorative justice will be taken up later in this chapter, but for now let us briefly discuss it in the shaming context.

Braithwaite argued that the types of shaming already discussed can be counterproductive. In fact, he is one of the critics of shaming who feel that ostracized criminals may band together and form delinquent subcultures or, at best, remain isolated. He further argues that the distance shaming—as we have discussed it so far—can put between offenders and the community may backfire. He doesn't completely dismiss shaming, however. Instead, he argues that shame should be followed by a process of reintegration.

How does reintegration take place? There is no easy answer to this question. Indeed, reintegrative shaming makes several important assumptions that may complicate its ability to be put into practice. For example, where there is a defined lack of community, one is left asking, What is there for the offender to be reintegrated back into? Similarly, when offenders are accused of serious crime, or are repeat criminals, the prospects for reintegrative shaming may be grim. Nevertheless, one common practice of reintegration is to bring offenders before victims and other stakeholders so it can be made clear to offenders that crime is unwelcome. Such confrontation, it is hoped, will lead to feelings of shame on the part of the criminal. We will return to practices such as this in the next main section when we discuss restorative justice, a close cousin to reintegrative shaming.

Shaming and Recidivism

Clearly much attention has been paid to shaming penalties. But do they reduce crime? No one has answered this question—especially with respect to public exposure, debasement, and apology penalties. That is, despite the prevalence of shaming penalties, we do not know whether they make a difference in offenders' lives. However, some attention *has* been paid to reintegrative shaming. Unfortunately, the evidence is not convincing. For example, researchers have found that recidivism rates in highly communitarian societies in which reintegration takes place are no lower than in other nations.[56] Evidence also suggests that while reintegrative shaming may work for some offenders, it certainly doesn't work for all of them.[57] And it is quite possible that shaming can lead to the opposite outcome from what is expected. For example, a team of researchers recently found that offenders brought before a drug court that practiced some principles of reintegrative shaming actually recidivated at a higher level than those not brought before the drug court.[58]

> Despite the lack of evidence in support of shaming, it is still quite possible that shaming works. In fact, a convincing argument can be made that it is more likely to alter behavior because it can be administered quickly compared to other traditional criminal justice sanctions that often follow periods of long delay.

Does It Work?

Shaming penalties satisfy the thirst some Americans exhibit for revenge. The lack of available evidence for the effectiveness of such penalties shows us that that is about all they do. In other words, there is no convincing evidence that bringing unfavorable publicity and attention to criminal activity reduces recidivism. It is *possible* that shaming in conjunction with reintegration may reduce recidivism, but this practice—known as reintegrative shaming—is difficult to put into practice, especially in nations such as ours that do not necessarily have a defined sense of community. To some people, shaming runs counter to constitutional principles and even sends a signal that we are regressing as a society. Shaming may amount to a modern day return to the stocks and the pillory. Such concerns may not be far from the truth given that, to date, no one has presented a convincing case that shaming works.

RESTORATIVE JUSTICE

Restorative justice is difficult to define because the term has been used interchangeably with related approaches such as community justice (see Chapter 5), peacemaking, relational justice, therapeutic jurisprudence, and so forth.[59] But one author has offered a fairly all-encompassing definition, namely that "[r]estorative justice is a process whereby all the parties with a stake in a particular offence [sic] come together to resolve collectively how to deal with the aftermath of the offence [sic] and its implications for the future."[60] Another writer describes restorative justice as "every action that is primarily oriented toward doing justice by repairing the harm that has been caused by a crime."[61] For some people, restorative justice is viewed as a "return to tribal justice and a rejection of retributive Western legal practice. For others, it is a response to the needs of crime victims, who typically are ignored in current practice. For others still, it is an infusion of religious doctrine into secular jurisprudence."[62]

restorative justice: "a process whereby all the parties with a stake in a particular offence [sic] come together to resolve collectively how to deal with the aftermath of the offence [sic] and its implications for the future."

At the core of restorative justice are two concepts: harm and repair (also see Figure 8.1 for a listing of restorative justice concepts). It is thought, first, that crime causes harm. There are several types of harm.[63] One is material harm, particularly the damage to property and lost wages associated with crime. Another is personal or relational harm, which can include physical injury, emotional damage, and even damaged relationships, increased fear, and a reduced sense of community—all of which can occur following a criminal act. It is also useful to distinguish between public and private harm, the latter being harm shouldered by individual victims of crime, and the former being harm to public places and community cohesiveness. The

Restorative Justice—Fundamental Principles

1. Crime is primarily an offense against human relationships, and secondarily a violation of a law (since laws are written to protect safety and fairness in human relationships).

2. Restorative Justice recognizes that crime (violation of persons and relationships) is wrong and should not occur, and also recognizes that after it does there are dangers and opportunities. The danger is that the community, victim(s), and/or offender emerge from the response further alienated, more damaged, disrespected, disempowered, feeling less safe and less cooperative with society. The opportunity is that injustice is recognized, the equity is restored (restitution and grace), and the future is clarified so that participants are safer, more respectful, and more empowered and cooperative with each other and society.

3. Restorative Justice is a process to "make things as right as possible" which includes: attending to needs created by the offense such as safety and repair of injuries to relationships and physical damage resulting from the offense; and attending to needs related to the cause of the offense (addictions, lack of social or employment skills or resources, lack of moral or ethical base, etc.).

4. The primary victim(s) of a crime is/are the one(s) most impacted by the offense. The secondary victims are others impacted by the crime and might include family members, friends, witnesses, criminal justice officials, community, etc.

5. As soon as immediate victim, community, and offender safety concerns are satisfied, Restorative Justice views the situation as a teachable moment for the offender; an opportunity to encourage the offender to learn new ways of acting and being in community.

6. Restorative Justice prefers responding to the crime at the earliest point possible and with the maximum amount of voluntary cooperation and minimum coercion, since healing in relationships and new learning are voluntary and cooperative processes.

7. Restorative Justice prefers that most crimes are handled using a cooperative structure including those impacted by the offense as a community to provide support and accountability. This might include primary and secondary victims and family (or substitutes if they choose not to participate), the offender and family, community representatives, government representatives, faith community representatives, school representatives, etc.

8. Restorative Justice recognizes that not all offenders will choose to be cooperative. Therefore there is a need for outside authority to make decisions for the offender who is not cooperative. The actions of the authorities and the consequences imposed should be tested by whether they are reasonable, restorative, and respectful (for victim(s), offender, and community).

9. Restorative Justice prefers that offenders who pose significant safety risks and are not yet cooperative be placed in settings where the emphasis is on safety, values, ethics, responsibility, accountability, and civility. They should be exposed to the impact of their crime(s) on victims, invited to learn empathy, and offered learning opportunities to become better equipped with skills to be a productive member of society. They should continually be invited (not coerced) to become cooperative with the community and be given the opportunity to demonstrate this in appropriate settings as soon as possible.

10. Restorative Justice requires follow-up and accountability structures utilizing the natural community as much as possible, since keeping agreements is the key to building a trusting community.

11. Restorative Justice recognizes and encourages the role of community institutions, including the religious/faith community, in teaching and establishing the moral and ethical standards which build up the community.

FIGURE 8.1   Restorative Justice Principles

Source: R. Claassen, *Restorative Justice: Fundamental Principles* (Fresno, CA: Center for Peacemaking and Conflict Studies. 1996). Printed by permission. Presented May 1995 at NCPCR; revised May 1996 at UN Alliance of NGOs Working Party on Restorative Justice. © 1996 Ron Claassen.

concern with harm distinguishes restorative justice from other traditional responses to the crime problem such as rehabilitation and retribution. A focus on the harm caused by crime—as opposed to other concerns—is what places restorative justice in a category by itself.

The second key restorative justice concept is, again, repair. That is, those who practice restorative justice are concerned not just with the harm that crime causes, but also with repairing that harm and restoring a sense of community. Such "repair" can include having the perpetrator fix, say, property he or she damaged. It can also include a larger-scale response aimed at improving relationships among people in a given area. As one author puts it, repair "may involve restoring offenders by creating social support, integrative opportunities, and competencies."[64] It may also "involve rebuilding communities by renewing respect for and commitment to the criminal justice system; by fostering new social ties among community members; by enriching the deliberative democratic process; and by focusing attention on community problems so that broader institutional weaknesses, such as in schools or families, can be addressed."[65]

By now you are either intrigued by the possibilities for restorative justice or you are highly skeptical. On the one hand, restorative justice seems eminently sensible. The practice seeks more involvement on the part of crime victims who have historically been left out of the criminal process. It also seeks to reduce the division between criminals and victims that can lead to awkward and tense future relationships, or no relationships at all. On the other hand, though, restorative justice has no chance of succeeding in areas where there is no defined sense of community. Likewise, it is highly unlikely that victims of serious crimes, especially sex crimes, violent assaults, and the like, would be willing to confront the criminal responsible for the harm they suffered. It seems that restorative justice is probably best relegated to tight-knit rural communities and most feasible for first-time offenders who are accused of committing relatively minor offenses.[66] But this has not stopped some researchers from advocating a restorative justice approach for dealing with serious crime, even homicide![67]

We cannot affirm or reject restorative justice without some attention to the available research. In order to give restorative justice a fair shake, we must focus on the scientific literature and determine whether, as a method of crime control, it reduces future criminal activity. First, though, let us briefly highlight two examples of restorative justice in action in order to bring more clarity to the practice.

Examples of Restorative Justice

Given the somewhat loose definitions of restorative justice presented earlier, there are many examples that could be presented here. The National Institute of Justice has organized restorative justice programs into nine categories: (1) victim impact statements; (2) restitution; (3) sentencing circles; (4) community service; (5) family group conferencing; (6) victim–offender mediation; (7) victim impact panels; (8) victim impact class; and (9) community reparative boards.[68] Some of these have been discussed already (e.g., victim impact panels), and some need not receive much attention here because they are either self-explanatory or familiar to you already. For example, most readers should already know what restitution and community service are. Somewhat less clear, however, are sentencing circles and community reparative boards. Accordingly, we will focus on them.[69]

One author recently described a community reparative board in Vermont in the following way:

> Upon conviction of a minor offense—burglary, drunk driving, for example—the judge will sentence the offender to probation with the condition that he or she must appear before the local reparative board. The board meets with the offender and attempts to work out a solution to the problem created by the offense. Victims and other affected parties, such as parents of a youthful offender, are invited to attend. Board meetings vary in length, but average between 35 and 40 minutes. The outcome of the meeting is a negotiated agreement signed by the offender, specifying a set of tasks to be accomplished during a 90-day probationary period. Typically, offenders return to the board for a mid-term review and a final closure meeting before discharge. Offenders who refuse to sign the agreement or fail to comply are returned to the court.[70]

Sentencing circles, another method of implementing restorative justice, have been described in this way:

> A sentencing circle is a community-directed process, conducted in partnership with the criminal justice system, to develop consensus on an appropriate sentencing plan that addresses the concerns of all interested parties. Sentencing circles—sometimes called peacemaking circles—use traditional circle ritual and structure to involve the victim, victim supporters, the offender, offender supporters, judge and court personnel, prosecutor, defense counsel, police, and all interested community members. Within the circle, people can speak from the heart in a shared search for understanding of the event, and together identify the steps necessary to assist in healing all affected parties and prevent future crimes. . . . The sentencing plan may incorporate commitments by the system, community, and family members, as well as by the offender. Sentencing circles are used for adult and juvenile offenders with a variety of offenses and have been used in both rural and urban settings. Specifics of the circle process vary from community to community and are designed locally to fit community needs and culture.[71]

What the Research Shows

Is restorative justice effective? This is a difficult question to answer because what constitutes effectiveness in the restorative justice context may vary depending on researchers' interests. For example, since restorative justice is heavily concerned with the *process* of bringing victims and offenders together, some researchers may be content to conclude that it is effective simply because it accomplishes this goal. One team of researchers has done just this. They claimed that it is more important to focus on the restorative justice process than specifically on crime-related outcomes.[72] It appears that there are several other researchers who feel the same way given the large number of process (as opposed to outcome) evaluations concerned with restorative justice.[73]

Despite the appeal of focusing on process, researchers have still managed to examine the effect of restorative justice on several outcomes. In a recent meta-analysis, three Canadian researchers reviewed 22 unique studies concerned with restorative justice outcomes.[74] They concluded, with respect to victim satisfaction that "participation in a restorative justice program resulted in higher victim satisfaction ratings when compared to a comparison group."[75] This effect was observed for all but 13 of the 35 programs covered in the studies they analyzed. On the contrary, though, offender satisfaction was not increased following participation in a restorative justice program. The authors also concluded that "offenders who participated in restorative justice programs tended to have substantially higher [restitution] compliance rates than offenders exposed to other arrangements."[76]

What about recidivism? The meta-analysis revealed fairly pronounced reductions in recidivism in the programs studied:

> Restorative justice programs, on average, yielded reductions in recidivism compared to non-restorative approaches to criminal behavior. In fact, compared to the comparison/control groups that did not participate in a restorative justice program, offenders in the treatment groups were significantly more successful during follow-up periods.[77]

Unfortunately, it was not clear what *types* of restorative justice programs made up the sample used for the meta-analysis. That is, it cannot be said whether the programs served low-risk or high-risk offenders. Likewise, it was not clear what types of offenses participating offenders were convicted of. In all likelihood, though, it was probably the case that most offenders were accused of minor crimes. Two recently published studies offer some confirmation that restorative justice seems to work best for the least serious types of offenders. One study of two restorative justice programs for *juveniles* showed reductions in recidivism,[78] and another showed reductions in recidivism for offenders *diverted* out of the formal criminal justice process.[79] Clearly the individuals who participated in these programs are among the least crime-prone.

All in all, there are actually very few restorative justice evaluations that are concerned with the programs' effect on recidivism. As one team of researchers recently observed, "we see little attention paid to recidivism as an outcome criterion. Most evaluations of restorative justice programs tend to measure only the number of victim–offender mediation sessions, responses to satisfaction questionnaires, and the number of restitution agreements achieved."[80] All this means that it is not safe as yet to draw any firm conclusions about whether restorative justice reduces crime, much less whether it reduces crime committed by serious offenders.[81] Only a few studies appear to have carefully matched participants in treatment and control groups *and* examined recidivism over time.[82] Both studies were supportive of restorative justice, but the types of programs evaluated were very different.

Does It Work?

The goals of restorative justice—repairing harm, involving victims, and so forth—are certainly worth pursuing. Restorative justice cannot be faulted for trying to improve on traditional and unimaginative responses to criminal activity. But aside from improving people's feelings, and possibly increasing levels of offender restitution, it is not clear whether restorative justice reduces crime. This is so for at least four reasons. First, few evaluations are concerned with recidivism as an outcome. A similar problem was observed in the community policing section of Chapter 5. When attention drifts from recidivism to other concerns, people often lose sight of the fact that many such programs were intended initially to affect crime! Second, it is unclear whether restorative justice works for serious offenders; very little attention has been paid to offense seriousness and to whether the same outcomes will be observed between, say, rapists and status offenders. Third, most of the evidence concerning restorative justice is less than convincing because many of the designs employed by researchers in this area have been weak. Finally, more attention needs to be given to *where* restorative justice works before any blanket recommendations can be made for dispersing it throughout the country.

ANTI-GANG INJUNCTIONS

Gangs pose vexing problems for criminal justice officials. Traditionally, gang crime has been prosecuted through traditional means. For example, in a turf war, a gang member could be charged with murder for shooting a rival gang member. This reactive method of using traditional criminal statutes to combat the problem has obviously not succeeded; gangs still flourish in many areas of the country. This has forced criminal justice officials and lawmakers to resort to alternative strategies. One such strategy is to create new anti-gang laws. These will be discussed shortly. Another approach—a non-legislative one—is the judicial use of anti-gang injunctions.

Anti-gang injunctions (sometimes called "civil gang injunctions"). An injunction is a judicial order requiring a certain form of conduct to cease. In the case of gang injunctions, a court will issue an injunction—often at the request of a prosecutor—that bars gang members from associating with one another. The legal theory behind injunctions of this sort is that gangs, as unincorporated associations, engage in criminal and other activities that constitute a public nuisance. Usually, specific gang members are named in the injunctions and are barred from associating with one other within specific locations. To ensure that the injunction is publicized, law enforcement officials will sometimes contact gang members to make them aware of the order.[83] Violation of the court's order can result in a number of different penalties. According to one study, there were some 32 separate injunctions issued in southern California alone during the 1990s.[84]

Does It Work?

Do gang injunctions work? Surprisingly, this question has not been answered. Gang injunctions have been used in California since the late 1980s, but there appears to be no evidence of the injunctions' effect on the gang problem. Researchers have advocated additional use of injunctions for other types of crime problems, despite the fact that there is little convincing evidence that they actually improve matters.[85]

PROBLEM-SOLVING COURTS

Over the past several years, many nontraditional and experimental courts have sprung up across the United States (see Figure 8.2 for an overview of these developments). They have begun to deal with problems such as drug addiction, domestic violence, child neglect, and neighborhood quality-of-life issues. These so-called **problem-solving courts** (sometimes called special jurisdiction courts,[86] specialized courts, or boutique courts) include drug courts, domestic violence courts, community courts, career criminal courts, traffic courts, family treatment courts, mental health courts, gun courts, homeless courts, DUI courts, parole reentry courts, teen courts, and others. They all target different problems but share a similar mission: to shift the focus from processing cases to achieving meaningful results for defendants by formulating creative, individually tailored sentences—all in an effort to reduce recidivism.

problem-solving court: courts designed to deal with one specific, particularly troublesome offense type, such as drug abuse, domestic violence, or gun violence.

The development of problem-solving courts represents a change in the American judiciary system. Its magnitude cannot be overstated. The Center for Court Innovation (CCI) has developed a list of six principles/practices that make problem-solving courts different from traditional courts.[87] The first is a focus on case outcomes, not so much the process. As one noted community court judge has observed, "outcomes—not just process and precedents—matter. Protecting the rights of an addicted mother is important. So is protecting her children and getting her off drugs."[88]

Another key principle in problem-solving courts is judicial monitoring. Whereas in the past, judges may have handed down a sentence and washed their hands of the case, in problem-solving courts, judges stay involved in the cases from beginning to end. For example, drug court judges closely supervise offenders who are required to participate

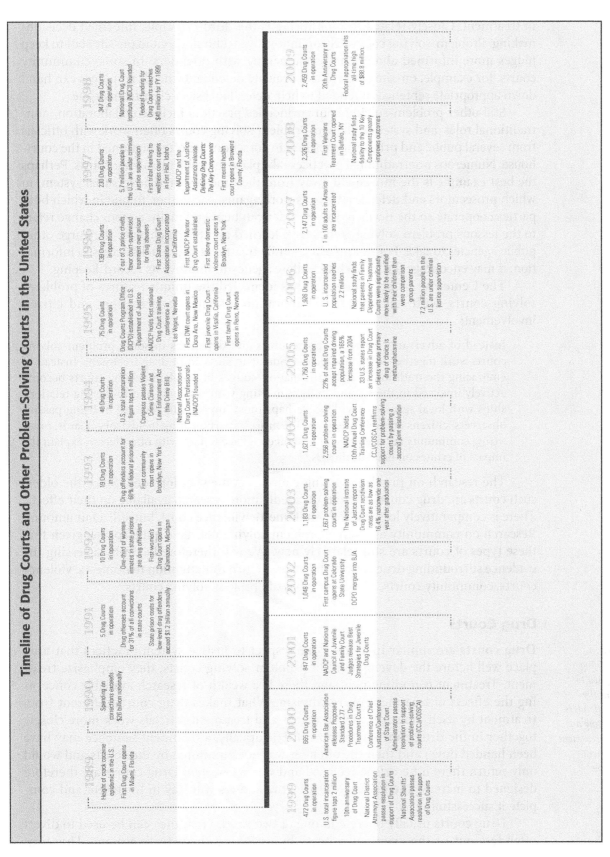

FIGURE 8.2 Timeline of Problem-Solving Courts in the United States

Source: West Huddleston and Douglas B. Marlowe, *Painting the Current Picture: A National Report on Drug Courts and Other Problem-Solving Court Programs in the United States* (Alexandria, VA: National Drug Court Institute, 2011).

in treatment. Closely related to monitoring is the third principle, informed decision-making. Problem-solving courts rely on innovative technologies and on-site staff to keep judges more informed about what is happening with offenders. In some community courts, for example, on-site caseworkers evaluate defendants' needs so judges can hand down appropriate sentences intended to help defendants steer clear from crime.

Still other problem-solving court principles/practices include collaboration, nontraditional roles, and systemic change. Problem-solving courts often work with officials from several public and private agencies, many of whom are often stationed in the courthouse. Numerous nontraditional practices take place in problem-solving courts. Perhaps the best example is the movement away from the time-honored adversarial system, in which prosecutors and defense attorneys work against each other, to one in which both parties cooperate so the needs of the offender can be met. Finally, system change refers to the lessons problem-solving courts have learned and to the changes they urge other public agencies to take. For example, if a family treatment court lacks access to information, it may encourage the local child welfare agency to improve its record-keeping.

The Center for Court Innovation has identified the unique features of problem-solving courts, with reference to collaboration, judicial participation, and citizen involvement:

> Instead of adversarial sparring, prosecutors and defenders in some problem-solving courts work together to encourage defendants to succeed in drug treatment. Instead of embracing the tradition of judicial isolation, judges in problem-solving courts become actively involved in their communities, meeting with residents and brokering relationships with local service providers. Perhaps most importantly, instead of being passive observers, citizens are welcomed into the process, participating in advisory boards, organizing community service projects and meeting face to face with offenders to explain the impact of crimes on neighborhoods.[99]

The research on problem-solving courts is somewhat lopsided. Since the oldest such courts are drug courts, there is decidedly more research available on their effects. There is comparatively less research on domestic violence court, but still a fair amount. Research on community and other problem-solving courts is quite sparse, given that these types of courts are still relatively new. We will therefore begin by assessing the evidence surrounding drug courts, then we will turn our attention to domestic violence courts, community courts, and other types of problem-solving courts.

Drug Courts

drug court: a problem-solving court designed to deal specifically with drug offenders, often providing an avenue for treatment and subsequent rehabilitation.

Drug courts are similar in at least one respect to justice system practices that took place well before the development of problem-solving courts; they emphasize treatment. Treatment is nothing new, and there is a wealth of research available concerning the effects of treatment on recidivism. What makes drug courts different from treatment by itself, however, is that courts and treatment officials work more closely together in the drug court environment. Historically, a treatment sentence may have been handed down and then the offender was not monitored by the courts and would only return there if he or she relapsed and was rearrested. Drug courts are therefore designed to increase the likelihood that drug addicts will stay in treatment and complete it successfully.

Drug courts usually operate in one of two ways. First, they can be used to divert offenders out of the criminal process by assigning them to treatment. This way, assuming offenders complete treatment, they won't carry with them the stigma of a criminal record. Post-adjudication programs, by contrast, either defer sentencing or suspend it in exchange for successful completion of a treatment program. Regardless of which avenue is pursued, the court will then frequently monitor and supervise offenders; frequent hearings and regular contacts with judges are characteristic of drug courts. Since the first drug court was established in Dade County, Florida, in 1989, drug courts have grown rapidly in number. Recent estimates indicate the presence of some 800 drug treatment courts nationwide.[90]

POSSIBLE LIMITATIONS OF DRUG COURTS. Many drug courts are voluntary. That is, offenders are given the choice to participate in drug court or go the traditional route. This has led some critics to argue that they won't reach the offenders most in need— those who are unwilling or uninterested in receiving treatment.[91] Others have criticized drug courts because people often assume, sometimes incorrectly, that drug use is a cause of crime. As one researcher has pointed out, even if drug treatment causes an addict to desist in the short term, if the offender still "runs with the same dangerous crowd, perhaps drinking heavily while complaining about twice-weekly drug testing," his or her likelihood of recidivating can go up.[92] Another possible limitation of drug courts is that they can be limited in scope, concentrating only on offenders' drug use rather than other life circumstances, and the service offenders receive may be too short-lived. Let's now see whether any of these criticisms are valid.

THE EMPIRICAL EVIDENCE. It would be overkill to review all, or even several, of the drug court evaluations currently in print. Fortunately, several detailed reviews of the extensive literature in this area have been published, and they can be summarized here. First, in 1997, the U.S. General Accounting Office (GAO) reviewed 20 drug court evaluations. According to the GAO:

> some studies showed positive effects of the drug court programs during the period offenders participated in them, while others showed no effects, or effects that were mixed, and difficult to interpret. Similarly, some studies showed positive effects for offenders after completing the programs, while others showed no effects, or small and insignificant effects.[93]

In another review of the literature, Belenko pored over the results in 37 separate drug court evaluations.[94] He cautiously concluded that drug courts can favorably affect long-term drug use. He also concluded that "[d]rug courts have achieved considerable local support and have provided intensive, long-term treatment services to offenders with long histories of drug use and criminal justice contacts, previous treatment failures, and high rates of health and social problems."[95] But despite such favorable comments, Belenko also expressed reservations about the current state of the literature. In particular, he was dissatisfied with the scant attention researchers paid to outcomes such as recidivism. He was also discouraged by the small number of studies that followed drug abusers over a long period of time.

The GAO and Belenko drug court reviews were just that: reviews. More recently, a team of researchers conducted a formal meta-analysis of drug court effectiveness. They analyzed the results of 42 separate drug court evaluations and, after doing so, concluded, tentatively that "drug offenders participating in drug court are less likely to reoffend than similar offenders sentenced to traditional correctional options, such as probation."[96] Like the researchers before them, though, they expressed concern over research designs used to evaluate drug courts. First, they were discouraged by the fact that few researchers used pre-post designs with random assignment to treatment and control conditions. Second, many of the designs "made no attempt to statistically control for differences between drug court and comparison participants, and a common comparison group, drug court drop-outs, has a bias favoring the drug court condition."[97] In the most recent meta-analysis published as of this writing, researchers reported that drug court participants recidivate less on the whole than offenders processed in traditional courts.[98] All in all, the news for drug courts is fairly positive.

Even so, our purposes will be well-served if we give two key problems—lack of adequate treatment/control conditions and selection effects—some more attention. Many evaluations of drug courts have compared those who complete treatment to those who were sent to treatment but did not complete. Such people represent a less-than-ideal control group for obvious reasons. Using treatment failures, as opposed to those who go to prison or are sentenced to some other traditional sanction, means, as one researcher has pointed out, that the "successes succeed and failures fail."[99] A relatively small number of drug court evaluations have compared drug treatment participants to those who have not participated in treatment at all.[100] And even fewer relied on random assignment. When random assignment to treatment and control was part of the design, studies present conflicting findings. For example, in one random assignment study researchers found less recidivism among drug court participants,[101] but the authors of a similar study found that drug court participants recidivated at about the same rate as those in the control group.[102]

As already indicated, many drug courts are voluntary. This means, obviously, that some offenders will choose to participate and others will not. It also means that those who *do* participate may differ in some critical way from those who do not. This is known as a selection effect and can have a significant impact on the outcome of any crime policy evaluation. The reason is that those who chose to participate in treatment may also be the ones most likely to discontinue criminal activity. As one team of researchers, whose study was potentially influenced by this problem, concluded, "It is possible that the relationship between participation in drug treatment and reduced recidivism is due to unmeasured variables predicting both."[103] Again, then, the best design to evaluate drug courts—and other criminal justice interventions—is one that randomly assigns subjects to treatment and control conditions.

Domestic Violence Courts

Chapter 3 briefly touched on the effectiveness of arrest in domestic violence incidents. Most of the available literature is unsupportive of the practice. We also saw in Chapter 6 that no-drop policies have been used by prosecutors in an effort to step up convictions in domestic violence cases. The jury is still out with respect to the effectiveness of this approach. The failure of mandatory arrest and the uncertain effects of other methods of intervening in domestic violence situations have led, in part, to the creation of domestic violence courts.[104] Like problem-solving courts more generally, domestic violence courts focus on tailoring interventions to the needs of victims, closely monitoring the offender, and even enlisting community participation. One researcher recently described the advent of domestic violence courts in this way:

> Domestic violence courts seek to coordinate with medical, social service, and treatment providers and establish special procedures and alternative sentencing options to promote

effective outcomes. Success necessitates system-wide collaboration and the ongoing commitment of judges, health care professionals, the police, prosecution, and citizens who witness violent acts.[105]

There are not nearly as many domestic violence courts as drug courts, but recent estimates show that they are nevertheless becoming quite popular in the United States. According to a survey conducted by the National Center for State Courts, there were some 200 domestic violence courts in 1998.[106] More recent estimates suggest that more than 300 courts nationwide are giving specialized attention to domestic violence cases.[107] Not all of these are stand-alone domestic violence courts, however. Some simply reserve time for specialized processing of such cases.[108]

THERAPEUTIC JURISPRUDENCE. At the core of domestic violence courts is the practice of so-called **therapeutic jurisprudence**.[109] Therapeutic jurisprudence amounts to seeing law as a helping profession.[110] It arose from the field of mental health law where, traditionally, there was a focus on the legal rights of mental health patients rather than their treatment needs. It is also concerned with the consequences on social relationships that the law can have. That is to say, therapeutic jurisprudence views law not as an abstract set of rules but as a social process that influences people.

therapeutic jurisprudence: viewing the law as a helping profession rather than a mechanism for punishment. More attention is given to offenders' behavior, emotions, and mental health than traditional legal approaches.

The therapeutic jurisprudence approach has recently been pointed out with respect to the military's "don't ask, don't tell" policy. "Don't ask, don't tell" basically provides that as long as recruits do not talk about their sexual orientation, the military is not permitted to ask about it. This approach to addressing sensitive issues of sexuality may have unanticipated consequences, however. It could lead gay people to feel that their sexual orientation is a taboo topic, and they may be disinclined to talk about it altogether. This possible side effect of justice is what therapeutic jurisprudence is intended to overcome.

Returning to the issue of domestic violence, the therapeutic jurisprudence approach focuses on issues of victim safety and offender accountability. In the past, if an abuser was arrested, he or she (usually he) may have returned home after being released from jail and continued the pattern of abuse. Further abuse was therefore a side effect, or unanticipated consequence, of traditional justice. Domestic violence courts seek to minimize such harmful outcomes that can result from a traditional, unimaginative response to domestic violence. In short, "the therapeutic jurisprudence approach focuses on offender accountability and victim safety, and it requires those who are making decisions to consider the potential benefits and consequences of their decisions on those involved."[111]

A DOMESTIC VIOLENCE COURT IN OPERATION. A recently evaluated drug court can be found in Lexington County, South Carolina. There, all nonfelony domestic violence cases are processed by a specialized criminal domestic violence court. The court is collaborative in the sense that it relies on the services of the sheriff's office investigators, a victim advocate, and a full-time prosecutor. A court administrator handles the administrative tasks, and mental health officials work with the court to diagnose offenders and assign them to proper treatment programs. In addition, the court draws on the services of a legal advocate from a local domestic violence shelter. All parties involved in the court work together to emphasize treatment for offenders and services for victims. Offenders who come before the court often participate in a 26-week group-based cognitive therapy program in exchange for a suspended jail sentence. If they fail treatment, then they serve out their jail term. We will give some attention to the evaluation of this court shortly, but let us consider some additional research concerning domestic violence courts.

THE EVIDENCE. Domestic violence court research is in its infancy. Researchers began by evaluating the implementation of such courts[112] and then by focusing on whether domestic violence courts resulted in added cooperation on the part of victims.[113] More recently, researchers' attention has turned to outcomes such as convictions secured and recidivism.

Courts that give specialized attention to domestic violence appear to gain more convictions than traditional courts.[114] Whether domestic violence courts reduce recidivism remains somewhat unclear, however. To date, there appear to be few studies examining this question. The authors of one such study claimed that recidivism levels did not differ among offenders who received three types of sentencing (a batterer intervention, a batterer intervention and drug treatment, or drug treatment alone) in a domestic violence court setting.[115] The problem with their study, though, was that there was no control group of offenders who were processed in the traditional manner.

In one of the more comprehensive evaluations of domestic violence courts, Gover and her colleagues recently concluded that such courts simultaneously increase arrests and reduce recidivism.[116] Specifically, they found that arrests for domestic violence increased following the implementation of a specialized domestic violence court in Lexington County, South Carolina. In their words, "[t]hese findings lead to the conclusion that the establishment of a centralized court for processing domestic violence cases increased the responsiveness of law enforcement to this crime."[117] They also found that offenders who were processed through the domestic violence court were 50 percent less likely to be rearrested.

A 50 percent reduction seems quite striking, but it is important to point out two features of their evaluation. First, the treatment and control groups were randomly selected, and the latter group consisted of defendants who were processed *prior* to the implementation of the domestic violence court. Second, when examining the court's effect on recidivism, the authors controlled for factors such as race, days in jail prior to trial, employment status, and number of previous charges. Taken together, these two research strategies make the study by Gover and her colleagues more convincing than previous research. In sum, then, there is one relatively sophisticated study concerned with the effects of domestic violence courts on recidivism.

Community Courts

Drug courts and domestic violence courts target their own specific problems. Community courts are more general in terms of the problems they target and the approaches they take to deal with such problems. The Center for Court Innovation answers the question: What is a community court? in this way:

> It can take many forms, but at its core, a community court is about partnership and problem-solving. It's about creating new relationships, both within the justice system and with outside stakeholders such as residents, merchants, churches and schools. And it's about testing new and aggressive approaches to public safety rather than merely responding to crime after it has occurred.[118]

THE MIDTOWN COMMUNITY COURT. One of the earliest community courts, the Midtown Community Court, opened in October of 1993. The court was implemented following a two-year collaborative planning effort between the New York State Unified Court System, the City of New York, and the Fund for the City of New York. The purpose of the court was to provide "accessible justice" for various quality-of-life crimes occurring in and around Times Square. See Figure 8.3 for an overview of how cases flow through the Midtown Community Court.

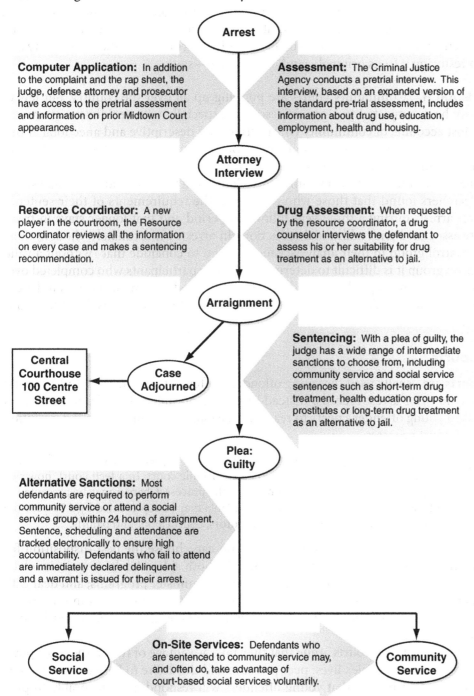

FIGURE 8.3   Midtown Community Court Case Flow Summary

Source: Center for Court Innovation, New York.

The Midtown Community Court developed in response to several concerns.[119] First, traditional courts tended to devote most of their attention to serious crime, not quality-of-life offenses that affect people more directly. Second, community and criminal justice officials were frustrated with the lack of organization in the processing of low-level offenses. Third, community members often felt shut off—and even geographically isolated—from central downtown courts. Fourth, community members, it was felt, should have a stake in the administration of justice because, ultimately, it affected them directly. Finally, there was a desire to have offenders pay back the community and assist in restoring it to its original—and, ideally, safe—state.

THE RESEARCH.   Community courts are popping up all over the country, but few of them have been subjected to rigorous research, especially with recidivism as an outcome. Most accounts of community court activity are descriptive and anecdotal at this point.[120] Either that or they focus on process, perceptions, costs, and benefits, but not necessarily crime.[121] But there are some exceptions.

One study of the Midtown Community Court contained a recidivism analysis.[122] The researchers found that those who completed the requirements of their sentence had fewer arrests during a three-year follow-up period and that longer stays in treatment are associated with additional reductions in arrest. Unfortunately, though, there was no control group in their analysis, causing them to conclude that "without a valid comparison group it is difficult to determine whether participants who completed over 90 days of treatment might have fared as well or accessed treatment services independent of the Court."[123] Three other studies *did* include control groups, but the results were mixed.[124]

Teen Courts

Teen courts are usually used for young offenders (often between ages 10 and 15 years) who have no prior arrest records. Instead of relying on judges for adjudication, teen courts use a young offender's peers to reach a decision. Here is one source's description of the teen court process:

> Teen court defendants may go through an intake process, a preliminary review of charges, a court hearing, and sentencing, as in a regular juvenile court. In a teen court, however, other young people are responsible for much of the process. Charges may be presented to the court by a 15-year-old "prosecutor." Defendants may be represented by a 16-year-old "defense attorney." Other youth may serve as jurors, court clerks, and bailiffs.[125]

Even the judge may be a young person who can choose the best disposition for the case on the basis of the evidence presented by both sides. Adults remain involved in the process, of course (e.g., to oversee the court; administer programs; and deal with budget, planning, and personnel issues). "The key to all teen court programs, however, is the significant role youth play in the deliberation of charges and the imposition of sanctions on young offenders."[126]

Proponents of teen courts argue that they take advantage of two of the most powerful forces in young people's lives: peer pressure and the desire to be accepted by one's peers. They further believe that young offenders will respond more favorably to prosocial youths than to adult authority figures. Teen courts also provide an educational opportunity and an insight into the workings of the judicial system for the young people who serve the roles of judge, attorney, clerk, and so forth.

Notwithstanding the possible benefits associated with teen courts, it is still important to examine the research—and there is a lot of it. Unfortunately, most available studies do not include control groups.[127] Of those studies that have included control groups, the evidence is mixed. Three studies showed no significant differences between teen court participants and youths whose cases were adjudicated in the traditional manner.[128] Only two studies that have been published to date show that teen court participants do better than controls.[129] According to one source, "[r]esearchers are beginning to accumulate a body of findings on the effectiveness of teen courts, but more detailed information is needed for future practice and policy development."[130]

Other Specialized Courts

Many other types of problem-solving courts have begun to appear across the United States. Some have been around for many years; others are being implemented now. There are also mental health courts, whose responsibility is to deal with people who have mental disorders—many of whom do not receive the services and treatment they require through traditional case processing. Courts aimed specifically at the homeless have been developed, and so have reentry courts. Even veterans courts have taken root, as returning war veterans sometimes turn to criminal behavior and need special care and attention to get back on the right path. The list of problem-solving courts is likely to expand, and it will be interesting to trace the research developments in this important area of criminal justice. For now, though, let us briefly examine homeless courts, mental health courts, and reentry courts.

HOMELESS COURTS.   Homeless courts differ perhaps most of all from traditional courts, and even other problem-solving courts. Instead of being used to process new offenses, the courts are often used to resolve outstanding misdemeanor criminal warrants. This approach is taken because, first, several of the homeless are perfectly content remaining homeless and want no part of a justice system intervention. Second, many of the homeless lack the resources to meet the obligations associated with their criminal convictions (e.g., pay a fine) and to show up at court when they are required to do so. This can result in a number of warrants that stack up. Here is how California's Administrative Office of the Courts describes it:

> Resolution of outstanding warrants not only meets a fundamental need of homeless people but also eases court case-processing backlogs and reduces vagrancy. Homeless people tend to be fearful of attending court, yet their outstanding warrants limit their reintegration into society, deterring them from using social services and impeding their access to employment. They are effectively blocked from obtaining driver's licenses, job applications, and rental agreements.[131]

Despite the obvious need for homeless courts, there is virtually no research on whether they work. Only one evaluation appears to have been published as of this writing, and it was concerned largely with the number of cases resolved following the implementation of a homeless court in San Diego.[132] The study's authors found that over 700 cases (for 266 homeless people) were resolved between October 1999 and February 2001. Whether homeless courts help their clients secure gainful employment, receive appropriate social services, or desist from low-level criminal activity is currently unknown.

MENTAL HEALTH COURTS.   Historically, the justice system and mental health agencies have acted independently of one another.[133] Mental health courts are intended to bring these entities together in pursuit of a common goal: providing services to mentally ill offenders. This is a significant development because there are many mentally ill offenders processed by the justice system, many of whom "slip through the cracks."[134] In fact, by some estimates there are more than a quarter-million mentally ill offenders in U.S. prisons and jails,[135] and prisons and jails are not generally equipped to deal with mentally ill offenders. These concerns have led criminal justice officials to seek other options.

The four original mental health courts were located in Broward County, Florida; Anchorage, Alaska; King County, Washington; and San Bernardino, California. Participation in the courts is voluntary and is usually reserved for low-level offenders. In the King County Mental Health Court, a court liaison to the treatment community is present at all hearings and is responsible for linking the defendant with appropriate services. Defendants participate in court-ordered treatment programs and will often have their charges dropped on successful completion of treatment. They are also supervised by probation officers who have small caseloads and have a background in the mental health field.

Mental health courts serve a noble purpose, and it is difficult to argue against enhanced collaboration and coordination between the justice system and social service organizations. Whether such courts actually affect the offenders, though, remains unclear. To date, there are few evaluations of mental health courts, particularly their effects on recidivism. An evaluation of the King County Mental Health Court revealed that those who participated in the program spent less time in detention and were booked on fewer new offenses.[136] Otherwise, most researchers' attention has been drawn to the effects of mental health courts on the utilization of mental health services. For example, researchers who evaluated Broward County, Florida's mental health court found that offenders brought before the court were much more likely to receive mental health treatment than offenders in a comparison group.[137]

REENTRY COURTS.   The Harlem Parole Reentry Court began its operations in June 2001. Its purpose was to "test the feasibility and effectiveness of a collaborative, community-based approach to managing offender reentry, with the ultimate goal of reducing recidivism and prison return rates."[138] The court was developed as part of the U.S. Justice Department's Reentry Court Initiative and was developed through the efforts of the New York State Division of Parole, the Center for Court Innovation, and the New York State Division of Criminal Justice Services. Like homeless courts, most reentry courts—like Harlem's—do not adjudicate new offenses. Instead, they provide oversight and support services to offenders reentering the community. However, when parolees slip up, the courts are there to provide sanctions for inappropriate conduct (and incentives for good behavior).

What makes reentry, mental health, and homeless courts interesting is that the definition of the American criminal court appears to be changing. Many problem-solving courts are moving away from adjudication to monitoring and service provision, tasks that have historically been handled by probation and parole officers and other treatment providers. Does this approach work? In particular, do reentry courts make a difference? Again, only one evaluation has been published (as of this writing) on this subject. Researchers at the Center for Court Innovation in New York published a preliminary evaluation of the Harlem Parole Reentry Court. They compared recidivism rates (reincarcerations and reconvictions) between reentry court participants and a matched sample of traditional parolees. Unfortunately, the evaluation (which again is preliminary) showed few differences between the treatment and control groups. It did, however, show a significant reduction in convictions on non-drug-related offenses within one year of release from prison.

Does It Work?

Drug courts have been around for some time, but other problem-solving courts have not. And since evaluation tends to lag behind implementation, it will be necessary to wait a while for any sort of definitive answer to the question, "Do problem-solving courts work?" For now, though, we can draw some preliminary conclusions. Aside from the fact that there is little available research, we do know that (1) many of the research designs previously employed have their limitations and (2) participation in problem-solving courts is typically voluntary, which can lead to a selection effect. A selection effect occurs when people likely to succeed with treatment (or a related intervention) will select themselves into the problem-solving court environment. To the extent this occurs, problem-solving courts may look more effective than they really are.

Summary

This chapter's focus on crime control in the courts and beyond has led to in-depth discussions of pretrial incapacitation, diversion, shaming, restorative justice, anti-gang injunctions, and problem-solving courts—and the evaluations of each. We found, first, that our ability to predict crime (via preventive detention or setting bail at a high level) is poor. Second, little is known about the efficacy of diversion programs; there are not many stand-alone diversion programs in existence today that fit neatly into the discussion presented in this chapter. Instead, diversion is often part of other approaches to the crime problem, such as job training and drug courts. Therefore, readers will pick up on some of the *indirect* evidence for and against diversion programs by reading other chapters (and sections of the current chapter).

Shaming penalties engender much lively debate, and sometimes a few laughs. But they have been used amply, and research suggests they are becoming more common. Unfortunately, though, there is no evidence that shaming works. Some research suggests that shaming in conjunction with reintegration (á la Braithwaite) can have a favorable effect on offenders, but even that approach has been all but ignored by criminal justice researchers. Much the same conclusion holds for restorative justice, a close cousin to reintegrative shaming—without the shaming part. That is, we don't know whether restoring the community is possible in all places and for all offenders. Anti-gang injunctions, like restorative justice, are contemporary and innovative. But they, too, are underresearched. Finally, problem-solving courts have sprung up with surprising frequency. Much research suggests that drug courts—and possibly domestic violence courts—reduce recidivism, but participation in such courts is often voluntary.

Notes

1. *Carlson v. Landon*, 342 U.S. 524 (1952), 545.
2. *Bell v. Wolfish*, 441 U.S. 520 (1979), 533.
3. See John Goldkamp, "Danger and Detention: A Second Generation of Bail Reform," *Journal of Criminal Law and Criminology* 76 (Spring 1985): 1–74.
4. D.C. Code 1970 Section 23–1322.
5. 18 U.S.C.A. Sections 3141–3150.
6. Ibid., Section 3142(d).
7. Ibid., Section 3142(f).
8. Bureau of Justice Statistics, *Pretrial Release of Felony Defendants, 1992*; Bureau of Justice Statistics, *Felony*

Defendants in Large Urban Counties, 1994. Washington, DC: Government Printing Office, 1998.

9. Bureau of Justice Statistics, *Pretrial Release of Felony Defendants, 1992*, p. 11; Bureau of Justice Statistics, *Felony Defendants in Large Urban Counties, 1994.*

10. *Preventive Detention in the District of Columbia: The First Ten Months* (Washington, DC: Georgetown Institute of Criminal Law and Procedure, 1972); see also Wayne Thomas, *Bail Reform in America* (Berkeley: University of California Press, 1976).

11. Thomas E. Scott, "Pretrial Detention under the Bail Reform Act of 1984: An Empirical Analysis," *American Criminal Law Review* 27.1 (1989): 1–51.

12. Jeffrey Fagan and Martin Guggenheim, "Preventive Detention and the Judicial Prediction of Dangerousness for Juveniles: A Natural Experiment," *Journal of Criminal Law and Criminology* 86.2 (1996): 415–48.

13. Ibid., 445, 448.

14. Cal. Const. Art. I, Section 6.

15. See, for example, M. Paulsen, "Pre-trial Release in the United States." *Columbia Law Review* 66 (1966): 109, 113.

16. T.G. Blomberg, "Widening the Net: An Anomaly in the Evaluation of Diversion Programs," in *Handbook of Criminal Justice Evaluation*, eds. M. Klein and K. Tielman (Beverly Hills, CA: Sage, 1980).

17. T. Palmer, "Juvenile Diversion: When and for Whom?" *California Youth Authority Quarterly* 32 (1979): 14–20.

18. The discussion that follows borrows from J. Nuffield, *Diversion Programs for Adults* (Canada: Public Safety and Emergency Preparedness, 1997). Available at: psepc-sppcc.gc.ca/publications/corrections/199705_e.asp.

19. Strategies such as these were covered in Chapter 5. Deferred sentencing is a more extreme version of deferred prosecution.

20. See, for example, S. Fairhead, *Persistent Petty Offenders* (London: HMSO, 1981).

21. J. Mullen, *The Dilemma of Diversion: Resource Materials on Adult Pre-trial Intervention Programs* (Washington, DC: Law Enforcement Assistance Administration, 1975).

22. What *is* known is most likely covered in other sections of this book. For example, drug courts amount to a form of diversion that occurs at the sentencing stage. Drug courts and other specialized courts are covered later on in this chapter.

23. D.E. Pryor, P.W. Kluess, and J.O. Smith, *Pretrial Diversion Program in Monroe County, NY: An Evaluation of Program Impact and Effectiveness* (New York: Center for Governmental Research, Inc., 1977).

24. J. Austin, *Instead of Justice: Diversion* (Ann Arbor, MI: University Microfilms, 1980).

25. S. Baker-Hillsman and S. Sadd, *The Manhattan Court Employment Project: Final Report* (New York: Vera Institute of Justice, 1972).

26. U.S. Department of Justice, *Diversion of Felony Arrests: An Experiment in Pretrial Intervention* (Washington, DC: Government Printing Office, 1981).

27. T.J. Scheff, "Shame and Conformity: The Deference-Emotion System," *American Sociological Review* 53 (1988): 395–406.

28. Ibid., 405.

29. D.R. Karp, "The Judicial and Judicious Use of Shame Penalties," *Crime and Delinquency* 44 (1998): 277–94.

30. Ibid., 280.

31. H.E. Barnes, *The Story of Punishment: A Record of Man's Inhumanity to Man* (Boston: The Stratford Co., 1930).

32. See the book of Genesis.

33. A. Wooler, "Shame as Punishment; Common in Early America, It's Making a Comeback," *Fulton County Daily Reporter*, October 6, 1997, 5.

34. D.Y. Paschall, Crime and Its Punishment in Colonial Virginia 1607–1776. Unpublished MA thesis, College of William and Mary.

35. *People v. McDowell*, 130 Cal. Rptr. 839, 843 (Ct. App. 1976).

36. *Goldschmitt v. Florida*, 490 So. 2d 123 (Fla. Dist. Ct. App. 1986).

37. D.R. Karp, "The Judicial and Judicious Use of Shame Penalties," *Crime and Delinquency* 44 (1998): 280–3.

38. The following discussion borrows liberally from the examples of shaming penalties discussed in D.R. Karp, "The Judicial and Judicious Use of Shame Penalties," *Crime and Delinquency* 44 (1998): 277–94.

39. *People v. Letterlough*, 86 N.Y. 2d 259 (1995).

40. T.M. Massaro, "Shame, Culture, and American Criminal Law," *Michigan Law Review* 89 (1991): 1880.

41. *State v. Burdin*, 924 S.W. 2d 82 (Tenn. 1996).

42. J. Hoffman, "Crime and Punishment: Shame Gains Popularity," *The New York Times*, January 16, 1997, 1.

43. H. El Nasser, "Paying for Crime with Shame: Judges Say 'Scarlet Letter' Angle Works," *USA Today*, June 25, 1996, 1.

44. D.M. Kahan, "What Do Alternative Sanctions Mean?" *University of Chicago Law Review* 63 (1996): 591–653.

45. Ibid.

46. *Bienz v. State*, 343 So. 2d 913 (Fla. Dist. Ct. App. 1977), 914.

47. Ibid., 915.

48. H. El Nasser, "Paying for Crime With Shame: Judges Say 'Scarlet Letter' Angle Works," *USA Today*, June 25, 1996, 1.

49. N. Tavuchis, *Mea Culpa: A Sociology of Apology and Reconciliation* (Stanford, CA: Stanford University Press, 1991).

50. T. Allen-Mills, "American Criminals Sentenced to Shame," *Sunday Times*, London edition, April 20, 1997, 23.

51. *Trop v. Dulles*, 356 U.S. 86 (1958), 104.

52. See, e.g., *Ingraham v. Wright*, 430 U.S. 651 (1977), 683.

53. "Justice Scaliea Says Caning Likely Constitutional," *San Francisco Chronicle*, May 7, 1994, A1.

54. See, e.g., *People v. Meyer*, 680 N.E.2d 315 (Ill. 1997), 318.

55. J. Braithwaite, *Crime, Shame, and Reintegration* (Cambridge: Cambridge University Press, 1989).

56. E.P. Baumer, R. Wright, K. Kristinsdottir, and H. Gunnlaugsson, "Crime, Shame, and Recidivism: The Case of Iceland," *British Journal of Criminology* 42 (2002): 40–59.

57. L.W. Sherman, H. Strang, and D.J. Woods, *Recidivism Patterns in the Canberra Reintegrative Shaming Experiments (RISE)* (Canberra, Australia: Australian National University Press, 2000).

58. T.D. Miethe, H. Lu, and E. Reese, "Reintegrative Shaming and Recidivism Risks in Drug Court: Explanations for Some Unexpected Findings," *Crime and Delinquency* 46 (2000): 522–41.

59. G. Bazemore and L. Walgrave, "Restorative Juvenile Justice: In Search of Fundamentals and an Outline for Systematic Reform," in *Restorative Juvenile Justice,* eds. G. Bazemore and L. Walgrave, (Monsey, NY: Criminal Justice Press, 1999).

60. Cited in J. Braithwaite, "Restorative Justice: Assessing Optimistic and Pessimistic Accounts," in *Crime and Justice: Review of Research*, ed. M. Tonry, (Chicago: University of Chicago Press, 1999), 5.

61. G. Bazemore and L. Walgrave, "Restorative Juvenile Justice: In Search of Fundamentals and an Outline for Systematic Reform," in *Restorative Juvenile Justice,* eds. G. Bazemore and L. Walgrave (Monsey, NY: Criminal Justice Press, 1999), 48.

62. D.R. Karp, "Harm and Repair: Observing Restorative Justice in Vermont," *Justice Quarterly* 18 (2001): 728.

63. The discussion in this paragraph borrows liberally from D.R. Karp, "Harm and Repair: Observing Restorative Justice in Vermont," *Justice Quarterly* 18 (2001): 729.

64. Ibid., 730.

65. Ibid.

66. For other criticisms of restorative justice see S. Levrant, F.T. Cullen, and B. Fulton, "Reconsidering Restorative Justice: The Corruption of Benevolence Revisited?" *Crime and Delinquency* 45 (1999): 3–27.

67. S. Eschholz, M.D. Reed, and E. Beck, "Offenders' Family Members' Responses to Capital Crimes: The Need for Restorative Justice Initiatives," *Homicide Studies* 7 (2003): 154–81; M.S. Umbreit and B. Vos, "Homicide Survivors Meet the Offender Prior to Execution: Restorative Justice Through Dialogue," *Homicide Studies* 4 (2000): 63–87.

68. National Institute of Justice, *Restorative Justice On-line Notebook* (Washington, DC: National Institute of Justice, U.S. Department of Justice, 2004). Available at: ojp.usdoj. gov/nij/rest-just/.

69. For some attention to other methods of restorative justice and pertinent discussions see S. Eschholz, M.D. Reed, and E. Beck, "Offenders' Family Members' Responses to Capital Crimes: The Need for Restorative Justice Initiatives," *Homicide Studies* 7 (2003): 154–81; E.C. Lemley and G.D. Russell, "Implementing Restorative Justice by Groping Along: A Case Study in Program Evolution," *Justice System Journal* 23 (2002): 157–90; A.W. Dzur and A. Wertheimer, "Forgiveness and Public Deliberation: The Practice of Restorative Justice," *Criminal Justice Ethics* 21 (2002): 3–20; M.S. Umbreit, R.B. Coates, and B. Vos, "The Impact of Restorative Justice Conferencing: A Multi-National Perspective," *British Journal of Community Justice* 1 (2002): 21–48.

70. D.R. Karp, "Harm and Repair: Observing Restorative Justice in Vermont," *Justice Quarterly* 18 (2001): 732.

71. National Institute of Justice, *Restorative Justice On-line Notebook* (Washington, DC: National Institute of Justice, U.S. Department of Justice, 2004). Available at: ojp.usdoj. gov/nij/rest-just/.

72. L. Presser and P. Van-Voorhis, "Values and Evaluation: Assessing Processes and Outcomes of Restorative Justice Programs," *Crime and Delinquency* 48 (2002): 162–88.

73. See, e.g., E.C. Lemley and G.D. Russell, "Implementing Restorative Justice by Groping Along: A Case Study in Program Evolutionary Implementation," *Justice System Journal* 23 (2002): 157–90; A.W. Dzur and A. Wertheimer, "Forgiveness and Public Deliberation: The Practice of Restorative Justice," *Criminal Justice Ethics* 21 (2002): 3–20; G. Maxwell and M. Allison, "Putting Restorative Justice into Practice for Adult Offenders," *Howard Journal of Criminal Justice* 40 (2001): 55–69.

74. J. Latimer, C. Dowden, and D. Muise, *The Effectiveness of Restorative Justice Practices: A Meta-Analysis* (Canada: Department of Justice, Research and Statistics Division, 2001).

75. Ibid., 9.

76. Ibid., 12.

77. Ibid., 14.

78. G. Maxwell and A. Morris, "Restorative Justice and Reconviction," *Contemporary Justice Review* 5 (2002): 133–46.

79. J. Bonta, S. Wallace-Capretta, J. Rooney, and K. McAnoy, "An Outcome Evaluation of a Restorative Justice Alternative to Incarceration," *Contemporary Justice Review* 5 (2002): 319–38.

80. Ibid., 321.

81. M.S. Umbreit, "Restorative Justice: What Works." In *Research to Results: Effective Community Corrections*, ed. P.M. Harris (Lanham, MD: American Correctional Association, 1999).

82. J. Bonta, S. Wallace-Capretta, J. Rooney, and K. McAnoy, "An Outcome Evaluation of a Restorative Justice Alternative to Incarceration," *Contemporary Justice Review* 5 (2002): 319–38; E.F. McGarrell and N.K. Hipple, "Family Group Conferencing and Re-offending among First-Time Juvenile Offenders: The Indianapolis Experiment," *Justice Quarterly* 24 (2007): 222–46.

83. For a description of the process, see B.J. Whitbread and S. Mazza, "Utilizing Civil Injunction to Combat Gangs: Part 2," *Law Enforcement Quarterly* 28 (1999): 34–7.

84. C.L. Maxson, K. Hennigan, and D.C. Sloane, "For the Sake of the Neighborhood? Civil Gang Injunction as a Gang Intervention Tool in Southern California," in *Policing Gangs and Youth Violence*, ed. S.H. Decker (Belmont, CA: Wadsorth, 2003).

85. See, for instance, E.L. Allan, "Policing by Injunction: Problem-Oriented Dimensions of Civil Gang Abatement in the State Of California," (PhD diss., Albany, NY: State University of New York at Albany, 2002).

86. J. Petrila, "An Introduction to Special Jurisdiction Courts," *International Journal of Law and Psychiatry* 26 (2003): 3–12.

87. G. Berman and J. Feinblatt, *Problem-Solving Courts: A Brief Primer* (New York: Center for Court Innovation, 2001).

88. J. Kaye, "Making the Case for Hands-On Courts," *Newsweek*, October 1999, 13.

89. Center for Court Innovation, *Problem-Solving Courts* (New York: Center for Court Innovation, n.d.). Available at: problem-solvingcourts.org/.

90. U.S. General Accounting Office, *Drug Courts: Better DOJ Data Collection and Evaluation Efforts Needed to Measure Impact of Drug Court Programs* (Washington, DC: U.S. General Accounting Office, 2002).

91. M.A.R. Kleiman, "Controlling Drug Use and Crime with Testing, Sanctions, and Treatment," in *Drug Addiction and Drug Policy: The Struggle to Control Dependence*, eds. P. Heymann and W.N. Brownsberger (Cambridge, MA: Harvard University Press, 2001).

92. W.N. Brownsberger, "Limits on the Role of Testing and Sanctions," in *Drug Addiction and Drug Policy: The Struggle to Control Dependence*, eds. P. Heymann and W.N. Brownsberger (Cambridge, MA: Harvard University Press, 2001).

93. U.S. General Accounting Office, *Drug Courts: Overview of Growth, Characteristics, and Results* (Washington, DC: U.S. General Accounting Office, 1997).

94. S. Belenko, "Research on Drug Courts: A Critical Review 2001 Update," *National Drug Court Institute Review* 4 (2001): 1–60.

95. Ibid., 1.

96. D.B. Wilson, M. Ojmarrh, and D.L. MacKenzie, "A Systematic Review of Drug Court Effects on Recidivism," (Paper presented at the annual meeting of the American Society of Criminology, Chicago, 2002), 20.

97. Ibid.

98. Ojmarrh Mitchell, David B. Wilson, Amy Eggers, and Doris L. MacKenzie, "Assessing the Effectiveness of Drug Courts on Recidivism: A Meta-Analytic Review of Traditional and Non-Traditional Drug Courts," *Journal of Criminal Justice* 40 (2012): 60–71; see also Deborah Koetzle Shaffer, "Looking Inside the Black Box of Drug Courts: A Meta-Analytic Review," *Justice Quarterly* 28 (2011): 493–521.

99. J.S. Goldkamp, M.D. White, and J.B. Robinson, "Do Drug Courts Work? Getting Inside the Drug Court Black Box," *Journal of Drug Issues* 31 (2001): 32.

100. Examples include M.W. Finigan, *An Outcome Program Evaluation of the Multnomah County S.T.O.P. Drug Diversion Program* (Portland, OR: NPC Research, Inc., 1998); J.S. Goldkamp and D. Weiland, *Assessing the Impact of Dade County's Felony Drug Court: Research in Brief* (Washington, DC: U.S. Department of Justice, National Institute of Justice, 1993); D.C. Gottfredson, K. Coblentz, and M.A. Harmon, "A Short-Term Outcome Evaluation of the Baltimore City Drug Treatment Court Program," *Perspectives* Winter (1997): 33–8; R.H. Peters and M.R. Murrin, *Evaluation of Treatment-Based Drug Courts in Florida's First Judicial Circuit* (Tampa, FL: Department of Mental Health, Law and Policy, Louis de la Parte Florida Mental Health Institute, University of South Florida, 1998); D.K. Sechrest, D. Shichor, K. Artist, and G. Briceno, *The Riverside County Drug Court: Final Research Report for the Riverside County Probation Department* (San Bernardino, CA: California State University, San Bernardino, 1998); A. Harrell, O. Mitchell, A. Hirst, D. Marlowe, and J. Merrill, "Breaking the Cycle of Drugs and Crime: Findings from the Birmingham BTC Demonstration," *Criminology and Public Policy* 1 (2002): 189–216.

101. D.C. Gottfredson and M.L. Exum, "The Baltimore City Drug Court: One-Year Results from a Randomized Study," *Journal of Research in Crime and Delinquency* 39 (2002):337–56.

102. E.P. Deschenes, S. Turner, and P.W. Greenwood, "Drug Court or Probation? An Experimental Evaluation of Maricopa County's Drug Court," *The Justice System Journal* 18 (1995): 55–73.

103. D. Gottfredson, S.S. Najaka, and B. Kearley, "Effectiveness of Drug Treatment Courts: Evidence from a Randomized Trial," *Criminology and Public Policy* 2 (2003):171–96.

104. K. Little, "Specialized Courts and Domestic Violence," *Issues of Democracy: The Changing Face of U.S. Courts* 8 (2003): 26–31; J. Weber, "Domestic Violence Courts: Components and Considerations," *Journal of the Center for Families, Children, and the Courts* 2 (2000): 23–36.

105. B.J. Ostrom, "Domestic Violence Courts: Editorial Introduction," *Criminology and Public Policy* 3 (2003):105–8.

106. A. Karan, S.L. Keilitz, and S. Denaro, "Domestic Violence Courts: What are They and How Should We Manage Them?" *Juvenile and Family Court Journal* 50 (1999): 75–86.

107. S.L. Keilitz, *Specialization of Domestic Violence Case Management in the Courts: A National Survey* (Washington, DC: National Center for State Courts, 2000).

108. L.S. Levey, M.W. Steketee, and S.L. Keilitz, *Lessons Learned in Implementing an Integrated Domestic Violence Court: The District of Columbia Experience* (Washington, DC: National Center for State Courts, 2001).

109. For an in-depth review of the practice see Volume 4, No.2, of the *Western Criminology Review*.

110. D.P. Stolle, B.J. Winick, and D.B. Wexler, *Practicing Therapeutic Jurisprudence: Law as a Helping Profession* (Durham, NC: Carolina Academic Press, 2000).

111. A.R. Gover, J.M. MacDonald, and G.P. Alpert, "Combating Domestic Violence: Findings from an Evaluation of a Local Domestic Violence Court," *Criminology and Public Policy* 3(2003): 109–32; see also R.B. Fritzler and L.M.J. Simon, "Principles of an Effective Domestic Violence Court," *American Judges Association Court Review* 37 (2000): 1–2.

112. L. Newmark, M. Rempel, K. Diffily, and K.M. Kane, *Specialized Felony Domestic Violence Courts: Lessons on Implementation and Impacts from the Kings County Experience* (Washington, DC: The Urban Institute, 2001).

113. M. Dawson and R. Dinovitzer, "Victim Cooperation and the Prosecution of Domestic Violence in a Specialized Court," *Justice Quarterly* 18 (2001): 593–622.

114. C.C. Hartley and L. Frohmann, *Cook County Target Abuser Call (TAC): An Evaluation of a Specialized Domestic Violence Court, Revised Final Report* (Washington, DC: National Institute of Justice, 2003).

115. N.K. Puffett and C. Gavin, *Predictors of Program Outcome and Recidivism at the Bronx Misdemeanor Domestic Violence Court* (New York: Center for Court Innovation, April 2004).

116. A.R. Gover, J.M. MacDonald, and G.P. Alpert, "Combating Domestic Violence: Findings from an Evaluation of a Local Domestic Violence Court," *Criminology and Public Policy* 3 (2003): 109–32.

117. Ibid., 119.

118. Retrieved from: communityjustice.org.

119. For additional information see M. Sviridoff, *Dispensing Justice Locally: The Implementation and Effects of the Midtown Community Court* (New York: Center for Court Innovation, 1997).

120. See, e.g., D.J. Chase, S. Alexander, and B.J. Miller, "Community Courts and Family Law," *Journal of the Center for Families, Children, and the Courts* 2 (2000): 37–59; J.S. Goldkamp, D. Weiland, and C. Irons-Guynn, *Developing an Evaluation Plan for Community Courts: Assessing the Hartford Community Court Model* (Rockville, MD: National Institute of Justice, 2001).

121. See, e.g., Kelli Henry and Dana Kralstein, *Community Courts: The Research Literature* (New York: Center for Court Innovation, 2011).

122. M. Sviridoff, D.B. Rottman, R. Weidner, F. Cheesman, R. Curtis, R. Hansen, and B.J. Ostrom, *Dispensing Justice Locally: The Impact, Costs and Benefits of the Midtown Community Court* (New York: Center for Court Innovation, 2002).

123. Ibid.

124. For details on these studies, see Kelli Henry and Dana Kralstein, *Community Courts: The Research Literature* (New York: Center for Court Innovation, 2011).

125. J.A. Butts and J. Buck, *Teen Courts: A Focus on Research* (Washington, DC: U.S. Department of Justice, Office of Juvenile Justice and Delinquency Prevention, 2000), 1.

126. Ibid., 2.

127. See K. Butler-Mejia, "Seen but Not Heard: The Role of Voice in Juvenile Justice" (unpublished master's thesis, Fairfax, VA: George Mason University, 1998); P. Harrison, J.R. Maupin, and G.L. Mays, *Teen Court: An Examination of Processes and Outcomes* (paper presented at the annual meeting of the Academy of Criminal Justice Sciences, New Orleans, LA, 2000); A.P. LoGalbo, "Is Teen Court a Fair and Effective Juvenile Crime Diversion Program?" (Unpublished manuscript, Tampa, FL: University of South Florida, 1998); A.P. McNeece, M.K. Falcolner, C. Bryant, and M. Shader, *Hernando County Teen Court: Evaluation of 1996 Continuation Grant Activity* (Tallahassee, FL: Florida State University, Institute for Health and Human Services Research, 1996); K.I. Minor, J.B. Wells, I.R. Soderstrom, R. Bingham, and D. Williamson, "Sentence Completion and Recidivism among Juveniles Referred to Teen Courts," *Crime and Delinquency* 45 (2000): 467–80; R. Rothstein, "Teen Court: A Way to Combat Teenage Crime and Chemical Abuse," *Juvenile Family and Court Journal* 38 (1987): 1–4; SRA Associates, *Teen Court Evaluation of 1994 Activities and Goals: Characteristics, Backgrounds, and Outcomes of Program Referrals* (Santa Rosa, CA: SRA Associates, 1995); M.I. Swink, "Onondaga County Youth Court Recidivism Rates" (unpublished manuscript, Syracuse, NY: Syracuse University, Maxwell School of Citizenship and Public Affairs, 1998); J.B. Wells, K.I. Minor, and J.W. Fox, *An Evaluation of Kentucky's 1997–98 Teen Court Program* (Richmond, KY: Eastern Kentucky University, Center for Criminal Justice Education and Research, 1998).

128. El Dorado County Superior Court, "El Dorado County Teen Court Statistical Overview" (unpublished manuscript, Placerville, CA: El Dorado County Superior Court, 1999); North Carolina Administrative Office of the Courts, *Report on the Teen Court Programs in North Carolina* (Raleigh, NC: North Carolina Administrative Office of the Courts, 1995); C.L. Seyfrit, P. Reichel, and B. Stutts, "Peer Juries as Juvenile Justice Diversion Technique," *Youth and Society* 18 (1987): 302–16.

129. Rod Hissong, "Teen Court—Is It An Effective Alternative to Traditional Sanctions?" *Journal for Juvenile Justice and Detention Services* 6 (Fall 1991): 14–23.

130. J.A. Butts and J. Buck, *Teen Courts: A Focus on Research* (Washington, DC: U.S. Department of Justice, Office of Juvenile Justice and Delinquency Prevention, 2000).

131. California Administrative Office of the Courts, *Homeless Courts* (Sacramento, CA: Administrative Office of the Courts, 2004). Retrieved from courtinfo.ca.gov/programs/collab/homeless.htm.

132. N. Kerry and S. Pennell, *San Diego Homeless Court Program: A Process and Impact Evaluation* (San Diego, CA: San Diego Association of Governments, 2001).

133. For an introduction, see D. Denckla and G. Berman, *Rethinking the Revolving Door: A Look at Mental Illness in the Courts* (New York: Center for Court Innovation, 2001).

134. A. Watson, D. Luchins, P. Hanrahan, M.J. Heyrman, and A. Lurigio, "Mental Health Court: Promises and Limitations," *Journal of the American Academy of Psychiatry and the Law* 28 (2000): 476–82.

135. P.M. Ditton, *Mental Health and Treatment of Inmates and Probationers* (Washington, DC: Bureau of Justice Statistics, 1999).

136. E. Trupin, H. Richards, D.M. Wertheimer, and C. Bruschi, *Mental Health Court Evaluation Report* (Seattle, WA: University of Washington, 2001). Available at cityofseattle.net/courts/pdf/MHReport.pdf. See also E. Trupin and H. Richards, "Seattle's Mental Health Courts: Early Indicators of Effectiveness," *International Journal of Law and Psychiatry* 26 (2003): 33–53.

137. R.A. Boothroyd, N.G. Poythress, A. McGaha, and J. Petrila, "The Broward Mental Health Court: Process, Outcomes, and Service Utilization," *International Journal of Law and Psychiatry* 26 (2003): 55–71.

138. D.J. Farole, *The Harlem Parole Reentry Court Evaluation: Implementation and Preliminary Impacts* (New York: Center for Court Innovation, 2003).

Sentencing

LEARNING OBJECTIVES

▪ Summarize nonprison sentencing options and their effectiveness.

▪ Distinguish between various types of prison sentences.

- Explain the concept of supermax prisons.
- Explain the relationship between sentence length and crime.
- Discuss what is known about the effectiveness of determinate sentencing.
- Discuss what is known about the effectiveness of sentence enhancements.
- Know the relationship beween mandatory sentencing and crime.
- Explain whether capital punishment acts as a general deterrent to crime.
- Summarize the role of castration in the punishment of sex offenders.

This chapter focuses on sentencing approaches to crime. It begins with nonprison sentences, ranging from fines to forfeiture. Then it shifts to more punitive forms of sentencing, including imprisonment, sentence enhancements, mandatory sentencing, supermax prisons, capital punishment, and even castration. Many of the sentencing strategies covered in this chapter have legislative origins. Three-strikes legislation, for example, is an approach to sentencing based on punitive laws that mandate life in prison for third-time felons. Our concern here, though, is more with the sentence than with the law. This stands in contrast to Chapter 7, where our concern was with the laws more than the sentences that can result from them.

NONPRISON SENTENCES

There are several types of penalties that the criminal justice system imposes on people convicted of crime. Two categories of such penalties can be identified: (1) monetary penalties and (2) nonmonetary penalties. Nonmonetary penalties include probation, prison, home confinement, electronic monitoring, and similar sanctions. Probation is covered in the next chapter, as are home confinement and other so-called intermediate sanctions. Prison is covered in this chapter. As for monetary penalties, these include fines, fees, and forfeiture. We begin with these "nonprison" sentences before shifting attention to our country's love affair with the "big house."

Traditional Fines

Fines are the most common punishment used by the criminal justice system today.[1] They are primarily used in cases involving minor offenses. If a fine is imposed, the offender will be ordered to pay a certain amount of money, usually in accordance with the seriousness of the offense. Fines can be imposed in lieu of other punishments or in conjunction with other punishments. A convicted criminal may be forced to pay a certain amount as well as to serve a period of time in prison.

Despite the popularity of fines as a form of punishment, the criminal justice system frequently encounters two problems when attempting to fine criminals. First, in most jurisdictions, the fine to be imposed is defined by law, regardless of the offender's financial position. If a poor offender is convicted of a serious crime, the fine is likely to be high, which means he or she will probably have difficulty paying the required amount.[2] The second problem is an extension of the first. When poor offenders are required to pay large fines, it becomes difficult for the state to collect the money. Many fines go uncollected not only because some offenders cannot pay, but also because many of the collection systems in place across the country are inadequate.[3]

Day Fines

day fine: a monetary form of punishment that takes into account the offender's ability to pay. Day fines often attach a unit value to the seriousness of an offense, which is in then multiplied by a fixed percentage of the offender's income.

In light of the difficulty of collecting fines, some jurisdictions across the United States have experimented with **day fine** systems. Day fines attach a unit value to the seriousness of given offenses. These unit values are then multiplied by a fixed percentage of the offender's income. The result is, ideally, a proportional fine, one that is not unnecessarily burdensome on an offender, but still enough to serve a punishment purpose. Day fines were introduced in Sweden in the 1920s and were quickly adopted by other Scandinavian countries. The concept was also adopted in West Germany in the 1970s and throughout other European nations more recently.

A study of a day fine program in Maricopa County, Arizona, found that day fines were successful in diverting offenders from routine supervision (e.g., probation) and in encouraging greater financial payments.[4] Another study showed that day fines resulted in fewer technical violations and rearrests than did traditional sentencing.[5] However, other research suggests that it is difficult to implement day fine programs and that outcomes may depart from intentions.[6] For example, some offenders may not be able to afford their day fine. Also, it can be difficult to assign dollar values to certain crimes as well as to rank the order of their seriousness. Furthermore, one study finds no difference in recidivism between a day fine system compared to ordinary fines.[7] Despite some gloomy predictions for the success of day fine programs, they have been implemented in a number of areas across the United States, including Des Moines, Iowa; Bridgeport, Connecticut; and Marion, Malheur, Coos, and Josephine counties in Oregon.

Fees

Fees are a relatively new sanction imposed by the criminal justice system. Some jurisdictions require that offenders pay fees for services as another way to hold them accountable for their actions. Fees are not used in lieu of prison or other sanctions. Instead, they are used in conjunction with more traditional methods of punishment, such as probation and prison. Two types of fees are currently being used across the United States: fees for probation and prison fees.

In the presence of inflation and declining support from taxpayers for many criminal justice expenses, it has become necessary for many states to impose probation fees. In fact, some 40 states now impose fees for correctional supervision. In Texas, for example, one half of the cost of probation supervision is paid for by probationers.[8] The logic underlying probation fees is that offenders under community supervision are capable of affording reasonable fees because they are in a position to work for a decent wage.

Critics of fees-for-probation programs cite two arguments.[9] First, critics are concerned that probationers may be incarcerated simply for their inability to pay probation fees. In other words, they imply that it would be unfair to send to prison a probationer who cannot afford the fees he or she is required to pay. Second, critics fear that probation fees will compete with or displace restitution and/or other court-ordered payments.[10] For such programs to be effective, then, it is important that fee collection be systematic and closely monitored to ensure compliance.

With regard to *prison* fees, many states have begun to require inmates to pay for services they receive while serving time. Prisons are anything but cheap to operate, so the logic behind prison fees is that inmates should pay for certain benefits in order to offset costs. Significantly fewer *inmate* fee-for-service programs are in place across the country than probation fee-for-service programs, but they seem to be gaining popularity. Inmates on work release or who work in prison are increasingly being required to pay for such services as postsecondary and college education and medical care.

The Mobile County Metro Jail in Alabama was one of the first to experiment with fees for medical services.[11] The program, which began in 1991, operates as follows: Inmates are first seen by a nurse, who evaluates the inmate's condition and determines if the inmate should see a doctor or a dentist. There is a $10.00 charge to see the nurse and a $10.00 fee to see a doctor or dentist. Free medical services include a medical evaluation on entering the facility, psychiatric services, and emergency services. Inmates pay for all other services. The program in Mobile County has accomplished two goals. First, it has provided substantial revenue to the jail. Second, it has discouraged frivolous claims and unnecessary trips to see a nurse or doctor.

Forfeiture

Forfeiture is another monetary sanction utilized by the criminal justice system. There are two types of forfeiture: civil and criminal. Each will be addressed separately. For now, however, forfeiture needs to be distinguished from seizure. Simply put, the police can seize property (e.g., cash), but forfeiture is a separate action. When something is forfeited, ownership to it (if any) is relinquished. A seizure, on the other hand, implies a temporary action by which ownership is not relinquished.

Criminal forfeiture proceedings are referred to as *in personam*. This means they target people. Criminal forfeiture can only follow a criminal conviction. If criminal forfeiture is sought, the prosecutor must prove beyond a reasonable doubt that the offender is guilty *and* that the property is subject to forfeiture. For example, if, in addition to securing a criminal conviction, the prosecutor can prove beyond a reasonable doubt that the defendant bought his house with the proceeds of the offense for which he is charged, the house can be forfeited. Thus, unlike fines and fees, forfeiture is used to minimize the financial gain associated with certain types of crimes, usually drug offenses.

Civil forfeiture, in contrast to criminal forfeiture, is *in rem*, meaning that it targets property. Civil asset forfeiture does not require a criminal proceeding. It can be pursued altogether independently of a criminal proceeding. Civil forfeiture proceedings can be understood in much the same way as wrongful death lawsuits. Wrongful death lawsuits can be pursued independently (or in lieu) of a trial for homicide. Indeed, all varieties of civil litigation can be pursued independently of criminal proceedings.

Civil asset forfeiture is also controversial because, depending on state law, proceeds can go back to the law enforcement agency that initiated the forfeiture. In some states, local police agencies that are responsible for the seizure of large quantities of cash can receive the cash (to be used for law enforcement purposes) if ownership to it is forfeited. Critics of this practice have argued that civil asset forfeiture creates a conflict of interest between crime control and fiscal management. This has prompted the adoption, at least at the federal level, of a National Code of Professional Conduct for Asset Forfeiture, which appears in Figure 9.1.

The question that concerns us is: "Does asset forfeiture serve a crime control purpose?" Surprisingly, no one has attempted to answer this question. In particular, no one has studied the deterrent effects of an aggressive asset forfeiture policy. The

criminal forfeiture: the relinquishment of ownership of property obtained from criminal activity following a criminal proceeding in which the standard of proof is proof beyond reasonable doubt.

civil forfeiture: the relinquishment of ownership of property obtained from criminal activity following a civil or administrative proceeding in which the standard of proof is the preponderance of evidence.

National Code of Professional Conduct for Asset Forfeiture

1. Law enforcement is the principal objective of forfeiture. Potential revenue must not be allowed to jeopardize the effective investigation and prosecution of criminal offenses, officer safety, the integrity of ongoing investigations, or the due process rights of citizens.

2. The Constitution and Federal Statutes prohibit the improper use of personal characteristics such as race, color, national origin, gender, or religion to target individuals for law enforcement action.

3. No prosecutor's or sworn law enforcement officer's employment or salary shall be made to depend upon the level of seizures or forfeitures he or she achieves.

4. Whenever practicable, and in all cases involving real property, a judicial finding or probable cause shall be secured when property is seized for forfeiture. Seizing agencies shall strictly comply with all applicable legal requirements governing seizure practice and procedures.

5. If no judicial finding of probable cause is secured, the seizure shall be approved in writing by a prosecuting or agency attorney or by a supervisory-level official.

6. Seizing entities shall have a manual detailing the statutory grounds for forfeiture. This manual will include procedures for prompt notice to interest holders, the expeditious release of seized property where appropriate, and the prompt resolution of claims of innocent ownership.

7. Seizing entities retaining forfeited property for official law enforcement use shall ensure that the property is subject to internal controls consistent with those applicable to property acquired through the normal appropriations processes of that entity.

8. Unless otherwise provided by law, forfeiture proceeds shall be maintained in a separate fund or account subject to appropriate accounting controls and annual financial audits of all deposits and expenditures.

9. Seizing agencies shall strive to ensure that seized property is protected and its value preserved.

10. Seizing entities shall avoid any appearance of impropriety in the sale or acquisition of forfeited property.

FIGURE 9.1 National Code of Professional Conduct for Asset Forfeiture

Source: U.S. Justice Department

closest researchers have come is to study the effect of asset forfeiture on law enforcement agencies. And, somewhat controversially, researchers have found that America's law enforcement agencies may be addicted to asset forfeiture.[12] This, according to forfeiture's critics, means that crime control is sometimes not the main concern.

Does It Work?

Fines and forfeiture have been used extensively in our system of criminal justice. Despite their saliency, however, there is almost no research concerning their effect on crime and recidivism. The use of fees is a relatively recent development and, as such, has not been researched adequately. It is doubtful, however, that fees could serve a crime control purpose because their intent is simply to offset the costs of criminal justice sanctions. It is possible (but unknown) that offenders may take their sanctions seriously if they are partly responsible for paying for them.

TYPES OF PRISON SENTENCES

At least four types of sentences can be identified, some of which are closely related to others. **Indeterminate sentencing** gives the judge authority to set the sentence. This form of sentencing empowers the judge to set a maximum sentence, up to what the legislature will allow, and sometimes a minimum sentence, for the offender to serve in prison. Under this system, parole boards usually end up deciding the actual amount of time the offender will spend in prison. This is the most traditional sentencing method, and we will focus on its effects in the next section.

The second type of sentencing is **determinate sentencing**. Determinate sentencing permits the judge to hand down a fixed sentence that cannot later be altered by a parole board. Determinate sentencing has the effect of treating all offenders similarly. It has also had the effect of ensuring that criminals are incarcerated for longer periods of time than may be permissible under indeterminate sentencing. We will give more attention to determinate sentencing shortly.

The third type of sentencing is **mandatory sentencing**. Mandatory sentencing is a form of determinate sentencing, but it differs insofar as it takes discretion away from judges.[13] Three-strikes laws require mandatory sentencing. For example, under California's three-strikes law, if a person who has two "strikeable" felonies on his record commits a third felony of any type, he goes to prison for life. Critics of mandatory sentencing say such laws transfer discretion from judges to prosecutors. We will also consider their effects on crime and recidivism in this chapter.

Finally, **sentence enhancements** are available for certain crimes. While these sentences usually mandate a minimum term of incarceration like mandatory sentencing, it is best to keep them separate for our purposes. It is useful to distinguish between each type of sentencing in the following way: Mandatory sentencing results in a lengthy prison term for any number of criminal acts, but sentence enhancements *increase* one's prison term because of, say, the offender's decision to use a gun during furtherance of the crime.

PRISON STRATEGIES WITHOUT REGARD TO SENTENCE LENGTH

Much of the attention to prisons is concerned with sentence length. That is, will crime be deterred (whether specifically or generally) the longer we put people behind bars? But there are some prison strategies that do not necessarily take sentence length into account. These include selective incapacitation, civil commitment, and the relationship between the number of prisoners and crime rates.

Selective Incapacitation

Criminals are not all created the same. Some are more violent than others, some commit more crimes than others, and so forth. **Selective incapacitation** is an approach to America's crime problem that targets repeat offenders. At its core is a conservative philosophy of specific deterrence. That is, selective incapacitation is intended to keep repeat offenders off the streets so they cannot commit more crimes. Selective incapacitation is not concerned with rehabilitating offenders, or with reintegrating them into the community. Rather, it is all about keeping criminals off the streets.[14]

Selective incapacitation gained popularity as a crime control strategy in the late 1970s and early 1980s. It was strongly endorsed in James Q. Wilson's popular book,

indeterminate sentence: a form of sentencing that empowers a judge to set a maximum sentence, up to what the legislature will allow, and sometimes a minimum sentence, for the offender to serve in prison.

determinate sentence: a form of sentencing that permits the judge to hand down a fixed sentence that cannot later be altered by a parole board.

mandatory sentencing: a sentencing strategy that takes discretion away from judges. The law, not the judge, sets the sentence.

sentence enhancement: a sentencing strategy that increases the length of an offender's sentence due to certain crime-specific circumstances (e.g., hate crimes, crimes committed with guns, etc.).

selective incapacitation: a sentencing strategy that seeks to identify dangerous offenders and imprison them for lengthy periods of time.

Thinking About Crime.[15] He argued that crime could be reduced by one third if each person convicted of a crime received a three-year mandatory sentence. Shortly after Wilson advocated selective incapacitation, The RAND Corporation released a study titled *Selective Incapacitation.*[16] It also offered a great deal of support for selective incapacitation. Its authors claimed that robbery could be reduced by 15 percent with the adoption of selective incapacitation. They further claimed that such a policy would not lead to an increase in prison populations. The RAND study truly put selective incapacitation "on the map," leading to a slew of research on the same subject.

What does selective incapacitation look like? The vague notion that it targets certain repeat offenders for lengthy prison terms does not do the policy justice. At the same time, though, selective incapacitation is difficult to define with precision because it has hardly ever been attempted, especially in this country. It is possible to view policies such as "three strikes" as favoring selective incapacitation, but this book treats such policies as deterrence-oriented given their widespread familiarity to most people, including criminals.

The closest any nation has come to a true policy of selective incapacitation is an Australian approach to dealing with repeat juvenile offenders. Legislation was passed following increased concerns over traffic fatalities resulting from police pursuits of juvenile auto thieves and other offenders. The legislation further provided that some youth could be isolated and incarcerated for a lengthy period of time based on their criminal histories. However, an evaluation of the law revealed that it was a failure.[17]

Returning our attention to the United States, most of the research on selective incapacitation has focused on the difficulties associated with predicting criminal behavior. In this way, the debate over selective incapacitation nearly mirrors the debate over preventive detention; both policies rely on estimates of the number of crimes individuals would commit if they are not incarcerated.[18] Nearly every published study has been harshly critical of the RAND study.[19] They have been critical on two primary grounds: selective incapacitation (1) is unethical and unfair, and (2) results in inaccurate predictions and wrongful incarcerations. Additional criticisms have also been identified.

First, some have argued that selective incapacitation is unethical and discriminatory.[20] Specifically, because the policy relies on estimates of future offending, it is bound to result in false positives from time to time. And when false positives end up in prison, this effectively means that some offenders are not treated equally. Researchers have also argued that most selective incapacitation prediction instruments, such as that advocated in the RAND study, would result in disproportionate numbers of minorities being sentenced to prison.[21] Likewise, one must ask the question: "Is it worth putting innocent individuals (or, at least, not-so-serious offenders) in prison for the purpose of controlling crime?"[22]

By far, most criticism of selective incapacitation has concerned the difficulties associated with predicting future offending. For example, the authors of one study claimed that the differences in arrests between low-rate and high-rate offenders are not sufficiently different to support a policy of selective incapacitation.[23] And, not too long after the RAND study was published, its authors turned around and claimed that the poor predictive accuracy and modest differences in arrest rates of the groups categorized by the selective incapacitation scale do not justify the large differences in sentence lengths for offenders in different risk categories.[24] A recent reanalysis of the RAND selective incapacitation instrument reached precisely the same conclusion.[25]

Selective incapacitation has also been criticized because it assumes that certain offenders never mature out of criminal lifestyles. The criminal career literature presents an entirely different story, however. The decline in crime with age characterizes even the most active criminal offenders.[26] The problem with selective incapacitation, according to this perspective, is that it becomes costly to care for an aging prison population that may not be particularly crime-prone.[27]

Also, simply locking up a serious criminal may not reduce crime because of the replacement effect. For example, if a drug dealer is put in prison pursuant to a selective incapacitation policy, it is quite possible that the dealer will be replaced by another. If the offender is part of an organized crime syndicate, say a burglary or auto-theft ring, then it is all but guaranteed that crimes will continue once the offender is locked up![28]

Despite the volume of research critical of selective incapacitation, it would probably be presumptuous to dismiss this approach outright. One study suggests that the RAND selective incapacitation instrument is quite capable of predicting criminality among low-rate offenders.[29] The author of the study argued that a selective incapacitation–type policy may prove useful for making release decisions, especially when courts mandate the release of certain offenders to ameliorate prison overcrowding.

Civil Commitment

The Fifth Amendment instructs that people cannot be put "twice in jeopardy of life or limb." This constitutionally guaranteed protection against double jeopardy is designed to ensure that a person who has been convicted or acquitted of a crime is not tried or punished for the same offense twice. **Civil commitment** has implications for multiple punishments, however, and, according to some critics, raises double jeopardy concerns. This is because it provides for the incarceration of certain individuals *after* they have served prison time.

civil commitment: the practice of requiring confinement of certain offenders, usually sex offenders and/or the mentally ill, until treatment or a related objective is completed. The decision to confine is not made as part of a criminal proceeding.

Civil commitment comes in several varieties. The most controversial variety is reserved for dangerous sex offenders. After a convicted sex offender serves his time in prison, he can then be "released" and involuntarily committed to a facility. Other varieties of civil commitment exist that do not necessarily target sex offenders. For example, civil commitment has been used for drug addicts.[30] Civil commitment has also been used for individuals with mental disorders[31] and even for juveniles with mental disorders.[32]

The term *civil* in *civil commitment* is intended to convey a message that it is not *criminal* confinement. That is, civil commitment does not need to be preceded by an adversarial criminal trial. And because it is civil in nature, as opposed to criminal, it can be used without violating the Fifth Amendment—or so some courts have said. This is particularly troublesome to critics of civil commitment laws:

> civil commitment statutes, which are based on predictions of future dangerousness and which may facilitate the indefinite incapacitation of even those who can largely control their behavior, threaten to redefine how states punish criminals. Defendants . . . should neither be incapacitated a second time for the same offense, nor institutionalized out of fear that they might in the future again decide to commit a crime.[33]

The Supreme Court considered the constitutionality of civil commitment laws in *Kansas v. Hendricks*.[34] At issue in that case was a statute that allowed additional incarceration of a sex offender who had already served his prison term if the state proved beyond a reasonable doubt that the offender was "likely to engage in predatory acts of violence" because of a mental abnormality or personality disorder. The Supreme Court upheld the Kansas statute by arguing that the law was treatment-oriented and was not intended to serve the goals of retribution or deterrence.[35] More recently, in *Kansas v. Crane*,[36] the Supreme Court held that it must be shown that the person subject to civil commitment has a lack of control, but no clear standard was agreed on. The result, according to one commentator, is that civil commitment will probably remain the same as it has ever been—at least until a more specific Supreme Court decision is reached.[37]

As of 2002, 15 states had enacted statutes focusing on civil commitment of sexually violent criminals.[38] Fourteen of these states have passed legislation that creates inpatient care for those who are committed. This effectively means that these individuals are not free to come and go from care facilities as they see fit. Alternatively, Texas has opted for outpatient treatment and supervision in lieu of confinement. Its law appears somewhat isolated given obvious concerns about the ability of dangerous individuals to leave treatment facilities and return to the community.

The obvious question for our purposes is, "Does civil commitment reduce crime?" No one has answered this question adequately, probably because relatively few individuals are civilly committed. But at least one researcher followed a group of individuals placed in civil commitment for a period of six months.[39] The author of the study concluded that candidates do not tend to be dangerous during the six months following their commitment. Assuming this was not a fluke, it would suggest that civil commitment statutes are not essential for accomplishing crime control in the United States.

More Prisoners, Less Crime?

Chapter 3 critically reviewed the assumption that putting more police on the streets reduces crime. While studies such as the Kansas City Preventive Patrol Experiment are cited as evidence that increasing the police presence does not affect public safety, more recent studies (particularly those of the relationship between community policing grants and crime) suggest that additional law enforcement spending may not be a waste. In addition, the police strike literature showed that eliminating the police presence threatens public safety, so it may not be totally off the mark to think about increasing police spending. Much the same thinking goes into the debate concerning the relationship between prison populations and the crime rate. Indeed, if the prison population and crime were inversely correlated, then the U.S. would be getting safer and safer, according to the data in Figure 9.2.

A common perception among conservatives is that by putting more criminals in prison, public safety will be improved. Some researchers have gone a step further and argued that putting criminals in prison actually saves money! For example, in his well-known study, *Making Confinement Decisions*, Edwin Zedlewski concluded that every dollar spent on imprisoning criminals saves $17 in total social costs.[40] At a glance, these cost savings estimates suggest that liberal use of incapacitation is sensible crime control policy. But, as with many attractive solutions to complex problems, if it looks too good to be true it probably is.

Shortly after Zedlewski published his study, Zimring and Hawkins wrote a scathing critique of it.[41] Their main argument was that Zedlewski misestimated the number of crimes each offender commits in a year. Surprisingly, Zedlewski estimated a total of 187 crimes per year by each offender. Zimring and Hawkins also pointed out that Zedlewski ignored the disagreement in the literature over annual offending rates among criminals. It appears, in fact, that Zedlewski based his cost savings figures on choosing the highest possible estimate of crimes committed per year. Much the same finding emerged in a study by two additional authors, namely that increasing the number of incarcerated offenders will have only marginal effects in terms of crime prevention.[42]

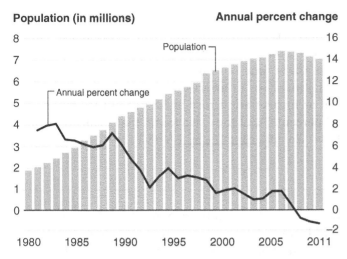

Population (in millions)   **Annual percent change**

FIGURE 9.2 Incarcerated Population, 1980–2011

Source: Lauren E. Glaze and Erika Parks, *Correctional Populations in the United States, 2011* (Washington, DC: Bureau of Justice Statistics, 2011).

It would seem, then, that locking up criminals for the purposes of saving society money and increasing public safety spells guaranteed failure. But it would be risky to draw any conclusions based on two contradictory studies. Fortunately, several other studies examine the relationship between prison populations and crime rates. In fact, it is in this area that most of the academic debate over incarceration has been concentrated. Several researchers have sought to specify the relationship between imprisoning offenders and improving public safety, but, as with the policing research discussed in Chapter 4, there are no clear answers about the efficacy of this approach to crime control in the United States.

One of the most significant problems with researching the relationship between prison populations and crime is known as the *simultaneity effect*. In the prison population/crime context, this simply means that while it seems sensible that the number of incarcerated persons could affect crime, it is also conceivable that crime could affect the number of incarcerated persons. An example of this possibility could be a demand for increased imprisonment among citizens as a result of a sudden surge in, say, drug crime. The fact that the relationship between prison populations and crime can work both ways complicates statistical analysis.

In one of the first studies addressing this problem, Nagin showed that once simultaneity was controlled for, there was virtually no relationship between imprisonment and public safety.[43] But in a very similar study that also controlled for the possibility that crime affects imprisonment rates, a researcher concluded that, indeed, more imprisonment can be expected to reduce crime.[44] He argued that incarcerating one additional prisoner reduces the number of crimes by approximately 15 per year.[45] And in something of a twist in this study, Marvell and Moody applied a sophisticated statistical technique known as a Granger causality test to prison population and crime data.[46] They estimated 16 to 25 index crimes averted per year per additional prisoner, and they found that crime rate changes had virtually no effect on prison populations.[47]

Together, these last two studies suggest that putting more people in prison can reduce crime.[48] But this finding still needs to be reconciled with simple comparisons of the crime rate and the imprisonment rate. It also needs to be reconciled with a recent study that criticized Marvell and Moody's research, concluding that there was a "weak effect of imprisonment on crime between the 1970s and 1990s."[49]

Several researchers have shown that crime rates have remained relatively stable (or even declined) despite substantial increases in imprisonment.[50] For example, one pair of researchers pointed out that as incarceration rose by 78 percent from 1985 to 1992, violent crime increased by 42 percent.[51] But they also found that as incarceration rose by 25 percent from 1981 to 1984, violent crime fell by 9 percent.

SUPERMAX PRISONS

supermax prison: a prison with the most secure level of confinement available. It may be a standalone facility or part of another facility. Supermax prisons are typically reserved for the most violent and disruptive inmates.

This chapter has focused more on sentencing than on types of prisons. This is because the typical prison is fairly consistent from state to state. There are differences in wardens' approaches to running their prisons, and some differences in layout, but for the most part, a prison is a prison. Some are minimum security, others are maximum security, and there is everything in between. What stands out from these traditional prisons, however, is the so-called supermaximum or **supermax prison**. Twenty years ago there was just one of these facilities—in Marion, Illinois. Since then, supermax prisons have appeared on the corrections scene with increased frequency.

Today, the United States has at least 57 supermax prisons that house around 20,000 inmates.[52] One of the most notable is the U.S. Penitentiary Administrative Maximum Facility in Florence, Colorado. Unofficially called ADX Florence, the prison houses such noteworthy offenders as Theodore Kaczynski (the Unabomber), Eric Robert Rudolph (the Olympic Park bomber), and Ramzi Yousef (the 1993 World Trade Center bomber).

What exactly is a supermax prison? Simply speaking, their names describe them aptly; they are prisons with supermaximum security. More specifically, these facilities house dangerous inmates in single cells for 23 hours each day. Inmates are allowed minimal contact with other inmates, and few services are provided to them. A more formal definition is this:

> a highly restrictive, high-custody *housing unit* within a secure facility, or an *entire secure facility*, that isolates inmates from the general prison population and from each other due to grievous crimes, repetitive assaultive or violent institutional behavior, the threat of escape or actual escape from a high-custody facility(s), or inciting or threatening to incite disturbances in a correctional institution.[53]

Not surprisingly, these prisons have been criticized on humanitarian grounds. They have also been criticized, as one author put it, because they allegedly "constitute cruel and unusual punishment, are inhumane, and violate minimum standards of decency."[54] At the same time, though, they are reserved for the "worst of the worst," those who could not remain in traditional prisons.

Our concern is with whether supermax prisons are effective. Relatively little research is available on this subject, but a recently published assessment of supermax prisons offered a somewhat grim assessment:

> On the whole, our examination . . . leads us to be tentatively skeptical about supermax prisons. There is scant evidence that they are effective . . . and some research, including ours, suggests that they may cause many negative effects, preclude investment in other potentially effective strategies, and raise substantial constitutional and humanitarian questions.[55]

Does It Work?

Putting people in prison following criminal convictions is a traditional and often used approach to the crime problem. We spend staggering amounts of money putting people in prison. But the research concerning the relationship between incapacitation and crime is uncertain at best. On the one hand, some studies show decreases in crime when prison populations are increased. On the other hand, simple comparisons of prison population trends and crime rates lead to a different conclusion. Add to this the less-than-convincing research devoted to selective incapacitation and the total lack of research on civil commitment and it becomes clear that the traditional "lock 'em up" approach to crime does not deter crime.

Just because incapacitation does not appear that effective in terms of reducing crime does not mean prisons should be abolished. To suddenly abolish prisons, or even to drastically shorten prison terms, could mean a sudden reduction in any deterrent effects of imprisonment that already exist. It is safe to say that a balance between too much incarceration and not enough is necessary.

As for supermax prisons, one of the negative effects is the possible exacerbation of an inmate's mental illness. The same can be said of health effects; being couped up for 23 hours out of every day certainly is not "healthy." When the authors mentioned precluding investment in other strategies, they were referring to the costs associated with supermax prisons. They are considerably more expensive to build and operate than traditional prisons. The list goes on. Indeed, without any specific attention to the research on supermax prisons, it is safe to draw conclusions about them based on the other research we have discussed thus far; on the whole, prisons do not seem to be resounding successes. Arguably, though, they are necessary evils for a number of different offenders.

DOES SENTENCE LENGTH MATTER?

Many people think that long prison terms are desirable and that they reduce crime. On the one hand, there is a strong desire for retribution and "payback." The thought is that people should be punished for crime and incarcerated for an extended period of time. Other people think that lengthy prison terms serve the ends of crime control. As one researcher has recently observed, "Insofar as they support recent trends in sentencing serious offenders, lawmakers and the general public appear to do so because they believe that longer prison sentences reduce crime or give offenders what they deserve."[56] Whichever view is correct, one fact is certain. Prison sentences per violent crime have tripled in length since 1975.[57]

Thinking about Various Types of Offenders

A uniform policy of increased sentence length for all criminals must confront the reality that there are various types of criminal offenders. Richard Lippke[58] has identified seven categories of offenders:

1. Some serious offenders will be very unlikely to commit further serious crimes because their previous offenses were aberrations, their experiences with the criminal justice system were sufficient to convince them that further offending is unattractive, or they have reached a point in their lives where serious offending has lost its appeal.
2. Some offenders will continue serious offending at low rates, up to the point where the natural workings of age diminish their propensity to offend.
3. Some offenders will continue offending at low rates with little or no drop-off due to aging.
4. Some offenders will continue serious offending at moderate or high rates up to the point where the natural workings of age diminish their propensity to offending.

5. Some offenders will continue serious offending at moderate or high rates and their inclinations to offend will be unaffected by aging.

6. Some offenders will increase their serious offending but, as aging occurs, will gradually decrease it.

7. Some offenders will increase their serious offending and will not decrease it due to aging.[59]

Why is this classification scheme important? First, if the conventional criminological wisdom that criminals mature out of criminal lifestyles is correct, then it behooves lawmakers to focus on those in groups 2, 4, and 6. The reason is that, assuming this thinking is correct, there are very few offenders in groups 3, 5, and 7. Those in group 1 shouldn't be targeted with long sentences because of their short criminal careers. The problem, though, is that the effectiveness of increased prison sentences depends primarily on when those in groups 2, 4, and 6 come into contact with the justice system. As Lippke observes, "The closer they are to middle age when apprehended and convicted, the less significant the incapacitation gains are likely to be."[60]

Can Incarceration Cause Crime?

While conventional thinking suggests that increased incarceration will reduce crime, it is also quite possible that it could *cause* crime. How? Lippke points to six reasons why incarceration may cause crime.[61] First, when criminals are forced to live together in a prison environment, they invariably share information with one another; prison may teach criminals to be better criminals. Second, being in close quarters with one another may cause inmates to act criminally toward one another. Third, it is possible that the violence inmates often experience while incarcerated may be brought back into the community by the released prisoners. Fourth, since the prison experience is unpleasant for most offenders, this may enrage them and thereby contribute toward more crime once they are released. Fifth, prison (not to mention just a criminal conviction) has a stigmatizing effect that can make it difficult for released inmates to make the transition back into society. Sixth, prison can deprive families of the primary breadwinner.[62] These six reasons why prison may cause crime need to be weighed carefully against a policy of lengthy confinement.

Sentence Length and Crime

Surprisingly, there is precious little evidence that links prison sentence length with crime rates. In fact, it appears that only four published studies have examined this topic closely. And, to complicate matters, their findings are contradictory. Two studies show that as the severity of a sentence increases, so do the deterrent effects of punishment.[63] But two other studies are highly critical of these findings.[64] The authors of these latter two studies feel that it is difficult to show a deterrent effect associated with increased sentences.

A significant problem with the studies concerning the correlation between sentence length and crime is that they have been based on surveys! None of them have expressly tested the proposition that altering prison sentences reduces (or increases) crime. Rather, the researchers surveyed the reactions of individuals to hypothetical variations in punishment. For example, in one of the studies, participants were asked to respond to a question asking them what effect an enduring prison term would have on their lives.[65]

Does It Work?

We cannot safely conclude that lengthy prison terms reduce crime. There are four reasons for this. First, the bulk of research in this area is based on hypothetical scenarios posed in survey research. Second, because there are various types of criminal offenders, no uniform policy of lengthy incarceration makes much sense. Third, the possible crime-producing effects of incarceration may be more costly than the expense of housing inmates for a long period of time. Finally, it is not the case that all offenders can be deterred. Some are irrational, morally depraved individuals who act without any thought of the consequences of their actions.

DETERMINATE SENTENCING

Determinate sentencing is a policy of sending offenders to prison for a fixed period of time with no parole.[66] It is basically synonymous with the abolishment of parole.[67] And while it is by no means the most common sentencing method, it stems from a view that parole boards act arbitrarily and are not particularly concerned with the rehabilitation of offenders.[68] Many states passed determinate sentencing laws during the 1970s and 1980s; few, if any, have been enacted in recent years.[69]

There are several varieties of determinate sentencing—each with the common thread that they mandate a specific prison term. Most determinate sentencing laws provide for term reductions for good behavior, but the parole board does not make the decision. Such laws also frequently restrict judges' discretion. For example, some states require that judges choose a sentence within a specified period of, say, 6 to 30 years. Others force judges to choose from a narrower range of years or months.[70] Regardless of their form, determinate sentence laws are highly controversial and have been subjected to intense criticism.[71]

The Hydraulic Displacement of Discretion

Some people feel that a reduction or elimination of discretion in one area of the criminal justice system will simply push that discretion somewhere else, in much the same way a hydraulic pump works. This is known as the **hydraulic displacement of discretion**. Has this effect been witnessed in the context of determinate sentencing laws? At least one researcher tested the possibility and concluded that, contrary to expectations, there was no hydraulic effect associated with determinate sentencing in Minnesota.[72] But an earlier study suggests that a Colorado determinate sentencing law may have enhanced the discretionary power of prosecutors when it took discretion away from parole boards.[73] Accordingly, more research is necessary to determine whether determinate sentencing has displaced discretion.[74]

hydraulic displacement of discretion: the notion that a reduction or elimination of discretion in one area of the criminal justice system will simply push that discretion somewhere else, in much the same way a hydraulic pump works.

Impact on Prison Populations

While our focus here is on crime control, it is worth digressing for a moment to consider the effects of **determinate sentencing laws (DSLs)** on prison populations because that is where most of the research has been concentrated. Specifically, researchers have examined whether DSLs lead to more prison commitments, a greater overall prison population, or both. Six studies show an increase in prison commitments following enactment of DSLs.[75] By contrast, six other studies show either a stable or decreasing number of commitments.[76] The same studies show no consistent effect on overall prison populations, a finding that was replicated in one of the more recent examinations

determinate sentencing law (DSL): a law, typically at the state level, that provides for a determinate sentence, namely a sentence the judge sets that cannot later be altered by a parole board.

of determinate sentencing laws.[77] All in all, there is no clear evidence that DSLs have increased or decreased prison commitments and overall prison populations. Let us now consider their effects on crime.

Impact on Crime

Strangely, it appears that only one published study addresses the possible effects of determinate sentencing laws on crime. In a sophisticated analysis of determinate sentencing laws in 10 states over several years,[78] Marvell and Moody examined the effect of determinate sentencing laws on crime—among other outcomes. They found that the laws have virtually *no* effect on crime rates, even after controlling for several rival explanations. Taken together with their other findings, the authors concluded that DSLs affect neither prison admissions and overcrowding nor crime rates.

Does It Work?

It would be nice if there were more research concerning the effect of determinate sentencing laws on crime. However, considering the Marvell and Moody study alongside several others that show no effect of the laws on prison commitments and populations, it is fairly safe to conclude that determinate sentencing laws have done little to increase public safety. And to the extent that hydraulic displacement of discretion has taken place, criminal justice professionals—especially prosecutors—may have capably bucked the intended changes associated with DSLs.

SENTENCE ENHANCEMENTS

Another tough sentencing approach to the crime problem consists of sentence enhancements for specific offenses and/or offenses committed with specific motivations. Sentence enhancements are usually codified in statutory form and require an added prison term when the offender is eligible. The most commonly referenced (and researched) form of sentence enhancement mandates an additional prison term for crimes committed with guns. A less common—and relatively new—approach to sentence enhancement is to require an additional prison term for hate-motivated offenses. The following subsections consider each of the two in more detail.

Sentence Enhancements for Guns

The most common sentence enhancement approach to the crime problem is one that increases the penalty for a criminal act committed with a gun. So-called firearm sentence enhancement (FSE) laws usually mandate a minimum sentence or an extra prison term for various types of gun violence. FSE laws are not a form of gun control per se; they differ markedly from the policies discussed in Chapter 7 and, indeed, they are viewed as quite acceptable by the pro-gun lobby.[79]

MORE ON DETERRENCE. The most basic assumption underlying FSE laws is that they should reduce gun use through deterrence. In other words, it is assumed that criminals' fear of imprisonment and longer sentences will discourage them from committing crimes with guns. However, one researcher has pointed out that the opposite could occur.[80] Since gun robberies tend to be more lucrative than nongun robberies, then if offenders react to FSE laws by refusing to carry guns, they may have to commit more robberies to sustain the same level of income as would be associated with gun robberies. Likewise, assuming robbers refuse to dispense with their guns, then they may commit more homicides during or following their robberies in an effort to avoid apprehension. Whether these hypothetical outcomes would occur is unclear, but many of the problems associated with deterrence that were introduced earlier apply in the present context.

MORE ON INCAPACITATION.   If we assume that FSE laws cannot do much to deter gun violence, then it is reasonable to assume that they still have an incapacitative effect on crime. Stated differently, the assumption is that crime will be reduced because more dangerous criminals are behind bars because of FSE laws. But is such an outcome likely? Several researchers have answered with a no. First, to have an incapacitative effect on crime, FSE laws must result in apprehension and conviction of criminals. Whether this occurs hinges a great deal on police and prosecutor decision-making.[81] Also, if more offenders are convicted and sentenced to prison, authorities must face the reality that there is already little extra room in America's prisons.[82] In response to these concerns, two studies suggest that FSE laws do not increase prison sentences or admissions,[83] but two additional studies suggest that FSE laws do result in more imprisonment and lengthier terms of incarceration.[84]

STATE-SPECIFIC RESEARCH.   In an early study, Beha examined the effect of Massachussetts' 1975 Bartley–Fox law.[85] It mandated a two-year minimum sentence for crimes committed with a gun. It also increased the penalties for carrying guns without a license. He found little evidence of crime changes in 1975 compared to earlier years. However, subsequent before–after analyses found that homicide, assaults, and armed robbery declined.[86] But then several more researchers analyzed the effect of the Massachussetts law, and its effects became less clear. At least four separate studies conclude that the law reduced different types of crime (e.g., robbery and assault but not homicide, assault only, etc.).[87] All showed some type of reduction, but whether the decline was due to the law or a nationwide decline in gun violence remains unclear.[88]

Another study turned attention toward Arizona's FSE law. McPheters and his colleagues found highly significant reductions in gun robberies but no reductions in non-gun robberies and property crimes.[89] They concluded that Arizona's FSE law made the difference, but they also pointed out that Arizona's robbery rate increased by 75 percent prior to the passage of the FSE law and that the decline may have simply represented a trend back toward normal levels. This latter observation is very important; researchers need to look backward and control for preexisting trends where possible.[90] The downward trend problem is also evidenced in a recent critique of four studies suggesting that FSE laws in Michigan, Florida, and Pennsylvania led to a reduction in crime.[91]

MULTISITE RESEARCH.   Researchers have also examined the effect of FSE laws on several states and/or cities at once. Since some states have FSE laws and others do not, researchers have capitalized on this from a treatment/control standpoint. Treatment states are those with FSE laws; control states have no FSE laws. As an example of this approach, Kleck gathered 1980 data from 170 cities and found that FSE laws have no effect on homicide, assault, or robbery. His study was cross-sectional (meaning that he could not state whether FSE laws *caused*—or did not cause—crime rates to change), however, which makes it somewhat limited.

In what appears to be the most recent study on the subject, two researchers attempted to overcome the deficiencies in past research by examining the effect of FSE laws on various crimes in several states over roughly a 20-year period.[92] Theirs was a sophisticated analysis that attempted to control for numerous rival explanations. In the end, they concluded that there is little evidence that FSE laws reduce crime or gun use. They also found no marked effect on prison admissions or prison populations. They concluded that "[t]his limited impact might be because prosecutors and judges evade the laws' mandates, because the additional penalties add little to those already given for gun crime, because prison capacity limits are reached, because the laws prompt criminals to make greater efforts to evade apprehension for gun crimes, or even because initial increases in prison populations later reduce growth in commitments."[93]

Sentence Enhancements for Hate-Motivated Offenses

A relatively recent approach to sentence enhancements is to require longer prison terms for hate-motivated offenses. There are basically two legislative approaches to hate crimes: (1) stand-alone hate crimes and (2) sentence enhancements for traditional offenses.[94] The latter is what we turn our attention to in the present section.

An example of hate-motivated sentence enhancements in action is a Wisconsin law that came before the Supreme Court in 1993. The law at issue punished an offender's intentional selection of a victim or property based on status characteristics, including race, religion, color, national origin, or ancestry. The case, *Wisconsin v. Mitchell*,[95] dealt with a 19-year-old African-American male who battered a 14-year-old white male. He was sentenced to an additional two-year prison term for selecting his victim on account of his race.[96] The Supreme Court upheld the conviction.

Do sentence enhancements for hate-motivated offenses reduce crime? As of this writing, no one has attempted to answer this question. There are two possible reasons for the oversight. First, the hate crime statutes that are conjured up in our minds have not been around for very long (e.g., the Hate Crime Sentencing Enhancement Act of 1994); perhaps not enough time has yet passed. Second, hate crimes are less common than ordinary crimes, which means it is highly unlikely such laws could have a deterrent effect.[97]

Does It Work?

Hate crime sentence enhancements have not been researched; gun crime sentence enhancements have. So, based on what we know of gun crime sentence enhancements, there is little convincing evidence that they reduce crime. Thinking again in terms of the limitations of deterrence, this finding should not be particularly surprising. Is it likely that most offenders think (or even are aware) of the additional penalties associated with specific types of criminal acts? Probably not.

MANDATORY SENTENCING

So far, this chapter has considered three types of sentences. The first, simply imposing long sentences for specific offenses and offenders, gives enormous discretion to judges. The second, determinate sentencing, restricts the discretion of parole boards but still allows judges to set a prison term. Sentence enhancements, the third method of sentencing, restrict judges' discretion by mandating a prison term for specific aggravating factors associated with crime (e.g., using a gun in a robbery). Mandatory sentencing all but eliminates judicial discretion. It refers, generally, to a sentencing strategy that requires the court to impose either a minimum or specific term of imprisonment.

Some of the research on mandatory sentencing overlaps with the sentence enhancement research. This is particularly true for gun offenses. The line between an enhanced sentence for a crime committed with a gun and a fixed prison term for gun offenses is perilously thin. Accordingly, we will not review the literature on mandatory sentences for gun offenses here. Instead, we will focus briefly on mandatory sentences for drug offenses, drunk driving, and crimes committed by persistent offenders. Then we will give in-depth attention to three-strikes legislation, the most well-known mandatory sentencing policy. Finally, we will discuss the prospects for mandatory death sentences. First, however, let us briefly consider one of the fundamental problems associated with mandatory sentencing.

A Life of Their Own?

It is usually thought that politicians enact crime control policies in response to the public's will. Yet research shows that the public generally favors proportionate, not mandatory, sentencing.[98] And it further appears that there are no valid surveys of public opinion lending support to mandatory sentences.[99] To this end, it is safe to conclude that many mandatory sentences have taken on a life of their own, removed from the will of the public. Politicians continue to tout get-tough measures that ensure lengthy prison terms, even in the face of research that suggests we are not as tough as politicians think we are. Taken together with the many critiques of mandatory sentencing, one wonders why such laws continue to thrive, even in the face of mounting evidence that they are not a resounding success.[100]

Mandatory Sentences for Drug Offenders

Critics of mandatory sentencing point to the large number of nonviolent drug offenders in our nation's prisons (especially our federal prisons) who would not be there but for the presence of mandatory minimum sentencing. In fact, most of the people who are against mandatory sentencing for drug offenders point to the Federal Sentencing Guidelines. Under the Sentencing Reform Act of 1984, Congress created the United States Sentencing Commission and gave it the responsibility for designing a sentencing structure that would avoid "unwarranted sentencing disparity among defendants with similar records who had been found guilty of similar criminal conduct."[101] In November of 1987, the Federal Sentencing Guidelines were enacted. The guidelines were almost immediately attacked by a host of critics. Let us highlight some of their concerns.

One of the most important criticisms of the Federal Sentencing Guidelines centers on the penalties for specific substances. As of this writing, the guidelines demand the same sentence for offenses involving one gram of crack cocaine as for those involving one hundred grams of powder cocaine. This has led some researchers to argue that the discrepancy deliberately[102] or accidentally[103] targets the population of young black men. This concern has been highlighted eloquently by one pair of researchers: "By providing harsher penalties for criminal behavior in which blacks are primarily involved—such as crack offenses—compared to those in which whites are primarily involved—such as powder cocaine offenses—some have argued that the guidelines actually *produce* racially disparate sentencing outcomes."[104]

What does the research show? Are the guidelines really unfair? One study concludes that the defendant's race *does* influence sentencing under the Federal Sentencing Guidelines, even though its framers' intent was to promote fairness and equal treatment.[105] This finding was more or less replicated in two more recent studies.[106] One of the reasons for such discrepancies in sentencing may owe to the fact that the Federal Sentencing Guidelines shift discretion from judges to prosecutors. According to one study, "So long as mandatory minimum sentences, and guidelines anchored by mandatory minimums, are tied to the charges for which the defendant is convicted and prosecutors exercise unfettered discretion in charging decisions, the goals of certainty, uniformity, and the reduction of unwarranted disparity are at risk."[107]

Possible sentencing disparities aside, what are the effects of mandatory minimum sentencing on the drug problem? Surprisingly few answers to this question are available. As indicated earlier, many researchers have studied the effect of mandatory penalties on gun crimes, but the effect of such sentencing on drug crime—owing particularly to the Federal Sentencing Guidelines—has been all but ignored by researchers. The most researchers have done is follow trends in victimization and reported drug use both before and after the enactment of the guidelines. They have concluded that

> federal sentencing policy cannot be expected to have a significant effect on the crimes of most concern to the public when most crime is prosecuted by the states . . ., [and] survey data on the availability of drugs to high school students . . . show that there has been no overall drop since the mandatory minimums were implemented."[108]

Interestingly, one study shows that the criminal justice system reacts to mandatory minimum sentences by seeking to preserve the status quo. Stephen Schulhofer found that although mandatory minimum drug laws increase the probability of incarceration on conviction and the severity of sentences imposed, they also result in fewer overall arrests, indictments, and convictions.[109] The result of such laws, he concluded, is a reduction in the probability of imprisonment *after* the laws go into effect! Findings such as these have led one noted researcher to conclude that "the weight of the evidence clearly shows that enactment of mandatory penalties has either no demonstrable marginal deterrent effects or short-term effects that rapidly waste away."[110]

Mandatory Sentences for Drunk Driving

Between 1975 and 1995, the state of Arizona required mandatory sentences for first-time drunk driving offenders. The law has recently been evaluated and determined to be a failure.[111] The author concluded that drunk driving cannot easily be deterred (the intent of mandatory minimums) because of the irrational nature of drunken driving. In the author's view, drunk drivers do not weigh the costs and benefits associated with driving under the influence. Another earlier study reached the same conclusion. There, authors concluded that Washington State's mandatory two-day jail sentence for drunk drivers failed to affect the incidence of accidents and drunk driving. That study's authors point to a lack of awareness of the law and to variations in enforcement that may have contributed to the failure.[112]

Mandatory Sentences for Persistent Offenders

Some states mandate prison sentences for persistent offenders. Such laws are quite similar to three-strikes laws (the topic of the next section), but still differ in important ways. An example of one such law is Kentucky's Persistent Felony Offender (PFO) statute. Adopted in 1974, the objective of the law is to punish offenders for repeat criminal activity by charging them with a separate count of persistent criminal activity. Then the law mandates that the offender serve 85 percent instead of 50 percent of his or her sentences before being eligible for parole. A study recently sought to determine whether the law was effective as a deterrent to rape.[113] The study tracked 62 rapists over a 15-year period. The authors concluded that the law did not affect recidivism and only serves retributive aims. The authors cited several studies that reached similar conclusions.

Three-Strikes Legislation

Throughout the mid-1990s, many states adopted **three-strikes legislation** in response to the murder of Polly Klass in California by Richard Allen Davis, a repeat offender who was released on parole three months earlier. The state of Washington was the first to pass a three-strikes law. Its Persistent Offender Accountability Act was passed in November 1993. Now, more than half of all states—and the federal criminal justice system—have some version of a three-strikes law.[114] The purpose of three-strikes laws is to remove repeat felons from society for life.[115]

three-strikes legislation: a law that requires a lengthy prison term for an offender convicted of a particular third time felony, usually a serious felony.

THE SUPPORTERS.   Three-strikes advocates argue that such laws protect the public by locking away serious criminals.[116] They also claim that three-strikes laws are capable of deterring would-be offenders.[117] In support of these positions, three-strikes supporters point to a decline in crime that was witnessed during the 1990s. They claim that the passage of three-strikes laws led to this decline,[118] but whether the declines in crime can be attributed to three-strikes laws is not entirely clear.

THE CRITICS.   As already indicated, three-strikes legislation clearly supports specific deterrence; third-strikers cannot commit more crimes because they are in prison. But, according to some critics, a specific deterrent effect is insufficient to justify such a costly crime control policy. They further argue that three-strikes legislation could not possibly have led to any decrease in crime. For example, Zimring, Hawkins, and Kamin raised this point:

> To argue that significant deterrence is taking place in nontargeted populations when no significant reaction can be measured in the targeted groups would break new ground in deterrence theory. Without any visible special decline in the criminality of Three Strikes targets, it does not seem likely that this new law is the moving force behind the general decline in crime.[119]

Similarly, Greenwood and his colleagues argued that specific deterrence is about the most that could be expected as a result of three-strikes legislation.[120] They further argued that only offenders facing their last strike can be deterred because they are the only group threatened with increased penalties under the law.[121] Still others have argued that three-strikes laws are not even intended to serve a deterrent purpose.[122] And, perhaps most important, critics of three-strikes laws claim that society reaps few benefits from the laws because most offenders mature out of criminal lifestyles.[123]

SOME LEGISLATIVE DETAILS.   It is important to note that there are considerable variations in three-strikes laws from one state to the next. Washington's law mandates life in prison for a third conviction on a serious offense. Georgia's law mandates life for a second conviction on a "serious violent felony." California's original three-strikes law required that an offender was "out" if he or she committed *any* felony and had two serious felony convictions on his or her record. The law was changed in 2012, however, to bring it more in line with other states. Figure 9.3 provides a list of the "strikeable" offenses under California law.

TO DETER OR NOT TO DETER. There is a measure of debate in the literature over whether three-strikes is intended to deter crime. On the one hand, three-strikes serves a specific deterrent purpose because it locks dangerous felons away for life. On the other hand, is it reasonable to expect that three-strikes laws deter would-be offenders from committing crime? Stating the question in different terms, is it likely that second-time felons pause and think about the consequences of their actions before committing another crime? Even if they did, is it likely that a life prison sentence would be handed down?

The answers to questions such as these have been subjected to a fair amount of debate in the past few years. Critics of three-strikes laws don't feel that the laws are capable of causing a general deterrent effect, or even that they are supposed to. By contrast, supporters feel that three-strikes laws *can*—and should—have a general deterrent effect. Let us consider each perspective in more detail.

DETERRENCE AND INCAPACITATION. A common problem that arises when studying the effects of crime control legislation is being able to distinguish between deterrence and incapacitation.[124] It is a problem because laws can basically have two effects on crime. One is to deter would-be criminals. The other is to reduce crime by locking up criminals. The problem for researchers, then, is distinguishing between the deterrent and incapacitative effects of crime control legislation.

Researchers are only in the early stages of being able to distinguish between deterrent and incapacitative effects. This is particularly important in the context of three-strikes laws because such laws are intended to affect only a small percentage of criminal offenders. Yet some researchers believe that it is possible for three-strikes laws to deter would-be third-time felons. While, on one level, this seems plausible, can we reasonably expect a large-scale deterrent effect attributable to a law that doesn't affect all criminals? Alternatively, can we reasonably expect a significant reduction in crime because of locking a few serious criminals away for life?

These and several related questions are increasingly becoming important for crime control researchers. To develop a thorough understanding of the effects of legislation on crimes, researchers need to be able to distinguish between deterrent and incapacitative effects. As it now stands, the methods for doing so are rather primitive.[125]

VARIATIONS IN ENFORCEMENT. In Chapter 1, the reader was introduced to various problems with evaluating crime control in the United States. Another problem is relevant here, namely that it is *very* difficult to determine the effects of three-strikes laws without careful attention to how frequently such laws are applied. One researcher found that, at least in California, there is wide variation among counties with respect to how often prosecutors pursue charges under the three-strikes statute.[126] Without considering variations in enforcement, failure to identify a deterrent effect could be attributed to the assumption that states or counties use their strike legislation with the same degree of frequency.

1. Murder or voluntary manslaughter
2. Mayhem
3. Rape
4. Sodomy by force, violence, duress, menace, threat of great bodily injury, or fear of immediate and unlawful bodily injury on the victim or another person
5. Oral copulation by force, violence, duress, menace, threat of great bodily injury, or fear of immediate and unlawful bodily injury on the victim or another person
6. Lewd or lascivious act on a child under the age of 14 years
7. Any felony punishable by death or imprisonment in the state prison for life
8. Any felony in which the defendant personally inflicts great bodily injury on any person, other than an accomplice, or any felony in which the defendant personally uses a firearm
9. Attempted murder
10. Assault with intent to commit rape or robbery
11. Assault with a deadly weapon or instrument on a peace officer
12. Assault by a life prisoner on a noninmate
13. Assault with a deadly weapon by an inmate
14. Arson
15. Exploding a destructive device or any explosive with intent to injure
16. Exploding a destructive device or any explosive causing bodily injury, great bodily injury, or mayhem
17. Exploding a destructive device or any explosive with intent to murder
18. Any burglary of the first degree
19. Robbery or bank robbery
20. Kidnapping
21. Holding of a hostage by a person confined in a state prison
22. Attempt to commit a felony punishable by death or imprisonment in the state prison for life
23. Any felony in which the defendant personally used a dangerous or deadly weapon
24. Selling, furnishing, administering, giving, or offering to sell, furnish, administer, or give to a minor any heroin, cocaine, phencyclidine (PCP), or any methamphetamine-related drug, as described in paragraph (2) of subdivision (d) of Section 11055 of the Health and Safety **Code**, or any of the precursors of methamphetamines, as described in subparagraph (A) of paragraph (1) of subdivision (f) of Section 11055 or subdivision (a) of Section 11100 of the Health and Safety **Code**
25. Any violation of subdivision (a) of Section 289 where the act is accomplished against the victim's will by force, violence, duress, menace, or fear of immediate and unlawful bodily injury on the victim or another person
26. Grand theft involving a firearm
27. Carjacking
28. Any felony offense, which would also constitute a felony violation of Section 186.22
29. Assault with the intent to commit mayhem, rape, sodomy, or oral copulation, in violation of Section 220
30. Throwing acid or flammable substances, in violation of Section 244
31. Assault with a deadly weapon, firearm, machinegun, assault weapon, or semiautomatic firearm or assault on a peace officer or firefighter, in violation of Section 245
32. Assault with a deadly weapon against a public transit employee, custodial officer, or school employee, in violation of Sections 245.2, 245.3, or 245.5
33. Discharge of a firearm at an inhabited dwelling, vehicle, or aircraft, in violation of Section 246
34. Commission of rape or sexual penetration in concert with another person, in violation of Section 264.1
35. Continuous sexual abuse of a child, in violation of Section 288.5
36. Shooting from a vehicle, in violation of subdivision (c) or (d) of Section 12034
37. Intimidation of victims or witnesses, in violation of Section 136.1
38. Criminal threats, in violation of Section 422
39. Any attempt to commit a crime listed in this subdivision other than an assault
40. Any violation of Section 12022.53
41. A violation of subdivision (b) or (c) of Section 11418 and
42. Any conspiracy to commit an offense described in this subdivision.

FIGURE 9.3 Serious Felonies (as "strikes") within the Meaning of *California Penal Code Section 1192.7.(c)*
Source: California Penal Code Section 1192.7(c)

The notion that crime control legislation can be enforced with varying degrees of consistency has set off a debate in the literature. In some three-strikes studies, researchers have simply compared crime rates in states with and without three-strikes laws, with no attention to how often they are enforced.[127]

But as another researcher has argued, simply comparing both types of states "does not provide any information on how often, if at all, states apply their three-strikes laws . . . [and such an approach] will underestimate the legislation's effects in states that do enforce their laws by grouping them with states that never enforce their laws."[128] Accordingly, researchers have recently studied three-strikes laws' effect on crime after controlling for how often the laws are used.[129]

THE RESEARCH. Many researchers have explored the effects of three-strikes legislation on prison populations, court backlogs, and other criminal justice issues.[130] The consensus from these studies is that three-strikes laws have had many detrimental effects on the justice system.[131] But our concern here is with the effect of three-strikes legislation on crime. Some researchers have found that three-strikes legislation deters crime.[132] Others have found that three-strikes laws have failed to reduce crime,[133] and still others have found that the laws actually *increase* crime, particularly homicide.[134] Let us consider some of these studies in more detail.

The Justice Policy Institute and the Sentencing Project were among the first organizations to study the effects of three-strikes legislation on crime.[135] Their research concluded that three-strikes legislation is lousy crime control policy. Unfortunately, a careful look at their research reveals little more than anecdotal evidence about the effect of three-strikes legislation on crime. Similarly, Zimring, Hawkins, and Kamin[136] analyzed the effects of California's three-strikes law on crime, and they concluded that there is none, but they also did little more than compare crime rates prior to and after the law was adopted.

In a related study, researchers found that the three-strikes law is not responsible for California's previously declining crime rates.[137] Their results showed that people in the over-30 age group—those most likely to be subject to three strikes—committed more felonies and were arrested more often following three strikes. But their study only compared crime, arrest, and other data prior to and following the enactment of the three-strikes law. Yet another study concluded that three-strikes legislation does not work, but it amounted to a before–after comparison without any statistical modeling.[138]

Another noteworthy three-strikes law and crime study—one of the first—was published in 1997.[139] The authors examined crime rates in California's 10 largest cities for a period of several months before and after the passage of that state's three-strikes law. They found no deterrent effect that could be attributed to the legislation. In other words, their analysis failed to show an increase or decrease in crime that resulted from three-strikes legislation. A problem with their study was that they were unable to include a control group in the analysis—that is, cities that were not affected by three-strikes legislation.

Employing a state-level analysis and using data from several years, Marvell and Moody found that three-strikes laws actually *increase* the incidence of homicides.[140] They attributed the increase to the possibility that third-strikers have an incentive to kill victims and witnesses in an effort to avoid apprehension (we will revisit the possibility that crime control legislation can *increase* crime in this chapter's section on capital punishment). Marvell and Moody also explored the deterrent and incapacitative effects associated with three-strikes legislation, but found none.

In a replication of Marvell and Moody's research, another team of researchers found that three-strikes laws appear to increase the incidence of homicide.[141] Following an impressive analysis of city-level crime statistics from several states, they concluded that three-strikes laws increased homicides 13 to 14 percent in the short term and 16 to 24 percent in the long term. In addition, they concluded that their findings "lend further support to existing theoretical and empirical research demonstrating the disutility and potentially lethal danger of three-strikes laws."[142]

Shepherd's 2002 analysis of three-strikes legislation in California improved on previous three-strikes research.[143] She found that three-strikes law has resulted in crime reductions throughout the state of California. Her findings were recently confirmed in another California-based study.[144] The authors of that study concluded that three-strikes legislation reduced crime in the short term by deterrence and has also resulted in long-term incapacitation effects on crime. But another study, one of the most recent, suggests that the effect of three-strikes legislation on crime is negligible at best.[145] In the end, we cannot claim with certainty that three-strikes laws have had any marked effect on crime.[146]

Mandatory Death Sentences?

Prior to 1987, Nevada's Capital Murder Statute provided a mandatory death sentence for murders committed by inmates serving life sentences without the possibility of parole. But in June of 1987, the U.S. Supreme Court declared that the statute violated the Fourth and Eighth Amendments to the Constitution.[147] The Court stressed that individuals sentenced to life prison terms enjoy full due process protections, just like any other offenders. The decision was not unanimous, however. The dissent argued that states should be able to summarily execute such murderers, citing deterrence and retribution objectives. As it now stands, capital sentencing hearings must take into account aggravating and mitigating circumstances.

While juries should take aggravating and mitigating factors into consideration when determining whether a death sentence is appropriate, it is not appropriate for judges to do so. Such was the decision in *Ring v. Arizona*.[148] There, the Supreme Court held that allowing a sentencing judge, without a jury, to find aggravating circumstances necessary for imposition of the death penalty violated the Sixth Amendment's jury trial provision.

Does It Work?

Mandatory sentences have been criticized on numerous grounds, but primarily on the grounds that they take discretion away from judges. The result, according to critics, is an irrational sentencing policy—one that can put people in prison for extended periods of time when they could easily be rehabilitated through other means. Add to such critiques the mounting evidence that mandatory sentences neither affect recidivism nor overall crime rates and it becomes quite clear that our nation's mandatory sentencing laws are in some need of reform. While such laws may serve a specific deterrent effect, we are again forced to answer an important question: Does the cost outweigh the benefits? Notwithstanding a handful of studies that show three-strikes legislation may reduce crime, the bulk of research published on mandatory sentencing suggests otherwise.

CAPITAL PUNISHMENT

Capital punishment (known as the death penalty) is perhaps the most attention-getting form of crime control in America. It ignites the fires of debate and invariably occupies much discussion time in many criminal justice classes. Every aspect of the death penalty from its moral dimensions and constitutionality to its potential discriminatory effect and impact on public safety have been written about at great length. Here, however, we are concerned with its effect on crime—in particular, its deterrent effect. Whether the death penalty is moral, constitutional, and/or discriminatory is a topic for another time. Likewise, the costs associated with capital punishment, the lengthy appeals process that fires up the critics, and other concerns are not as important for our purposes as crime control.

Our Stubborn Adherence to Capital Punishment

More than half of the countries in the world have abolished the death penalty, either in law or in practice. Almost every developed nation has done away with it. Countries such as Australia, France, Germany, Italy, Sweden, Switzerland, and the United Kingdom have decided not to carry out executions. Countries that have retained the death penalty include Afghanistan, Botswana, China, Cuba, Egypt, Iran, Iraq, Lebanon, Libya, Nigeria, North Korea, Pakistan, Somalia, the United Arab Emirates, Vietnam, Yemen—and the United States (for the rest of this list see Figure 9.4). Why does the United States adhere so stubbornly to the death penalty? Here is one author's answer:

> The origins of our current against-the-grain death penalty policy can be found in the earlier history of nongovernmental violence that was present in many parts of the United States but particularly rampant in the South. Where nostalgia still exists for vigilante values, citizens are prone to identify with executions as a community process rather than as the activity of a distant and self-interested government.[149]

Afghanistan	Egypt	Lesotho	Somalia
Antigua and Barbuda	Equatorial Guinea	Libya	South Sudan
Bahamas	Ethiopia	Malaysia	Sudan
Bahrain	Gambia	Nigeria	Syria
Bangladesh	Guatemala	North Korea	Taiwan
Barbados	Guinea	Oman	Thailand
Belarus	Guyana	Pakistan	Trinidad and
Belize	India	Palestinian Authority	Tobago
Botswana	Indonesia	Qatar	Uganda
Chad	Iran	Saint Kitts and	United Arab
China	Iraq	Nevis	Emirates
Comoros	Jamaica	Saint Lucia	United States of
Democratic Republic	Japan	Saint Vincent and the	America
of the Congo	Jordan	Grenadines	Vietnam
Cuba	Kuwait	Saudi Arabia	Yemen
Dominica	Lebanon	Singapore	Zimbabwe

FIGURE 9.4   Countries That Retain the Death Penalty for Ordinary Crimes, as of 2001

Source: amnesty.org/en/death-penalty/abolitionist-and-retentionist-countries

But just because the United States is in some unpleasant company with respect to capital punishment does not mean the practice should be abolished without further debate. Let us look at the literature concerning the effectiveness of capital punishment as another method of crime control in the United States.

Does the Death Penalty Deter Crime?

As a specific deterrent, capital punishment clearly works; a person who is dead cannot commit more crimes. What is more interesting, however, is the possible deterrent effect of capital punishment. Whether such an effect exists has been of great interest to many researchers. This is partly due to a famous article by Becker,[150] who argued that crime is a rational behavior committed by individuals who decide whether the "price" of crime is worth it. "Price" includes government-controlled and labor market factors (e.g., threat of punishment and prospects for employment, respectively).

So, what have researchers found with respect to the deterrent effects of capital punishment? The first important study was written by the economist Isaac Ehrlich and was published in 1975.[151] Following a fairly sophisticated statistical analysis, he concluded that one execution would, on average, deter eight murders. Two subsequent but less sophisticated studies lent a measure of support to his findings.[152] An overwhelming number of studies are highly critical of such findings.[153] Their common claim is that the death penalty—either its use or its frequency—does not deter crime. And a 2012 report published by the prestigious National Research Council of the National Academies reviewed more than three decades of death penalty research and reached this damning conclusion:

> . . . the research to date on the effect of capital punishment on homicide is not informative about whether capital punishment decreases, increases, or has no effect on homicide rates. . . . Nothing is known about how potential murderers actually perceive their risk of punishment."[154]

Brutalization?

One of the critiques of Ehrlich's famous study is that he failed to consider the possibility that executions induce additional murders by giving the impression of a lowered respect for human life. Understood differently, it is thought that a publicized execution will lead people to commit additional murders because the former gives the impression that government tolerates killing. Evidence of this so-called **brutalization effect** has been found in four separate studies.[155] We have also seen a measure of support for brutalization in the three-strikes literature discussed earlier.

brutalization effect: the possibility that executions induce additional murders by giving the impression of a lowered respect for human life.

Does It Work?

The lion's share of available evidence suggests that the death penalty does not act as a general deterrent. While a few economists have shown a deterrent effect, their voices are all but drowned out by the host of published studies that suggest otherwise. We cannot claim with certainty, though, that the death penalty serves no deterrent purpose. Certainly at least one criminal at one point in time has thought about the consequences before committing a heinous capital murder. Whether there are enough such individuals to justify the current costs of capital punishment remains to be seen.

CASTRATION

chemical castration: the adminstration to sex offenders of a drug designed to reduce the sex drive (libido).

A relatively recent—and, as such, underresearched—method of dealing with sex crime is **chemical castration** of sex offenders. Supporters of this approach point to the case of Jeffrey Morse, who confessed to police his guilt in the sexual assault of a nine-year-old girl and a similar crime committed some months earlier.[156] Prior to making a plea, Morse discussed with his attorney the possibility of chemical castration in lieu of a lengthy prison term. At his sentencing hearing, four experts testified that castration reduces recidivism in sex offenders, but the state argued against a reduced sentence. The judge denied Morse's request and sentenced him to 26 years in prison, claiming that "the trading of body parts for a lesser sentence" would set a dangerous precedent. Even so, cases like Mr. Morse's have brought the prospect of castration into the criminological limelight.

Methods of Castration

Castration comes in two varieties: surgical and nonsurgical.[157] The surgical method involves removal of a man's testosterone-producing testicles and is irreversible. For this reason, it is rarely used. Chemical castration, by contrast, can be reversed because it relies on drugs. The most common method consists of weekly injections of hormone suppressors that inhibit testosterone production.[158] The most popular such hormone suppressor is a drug known as Depo-Provera, a female hormone compound that suppresses testosterone production. Phenothiazines are another class of drugs that reduce testosterone levels but do not have the side effects associated with Depo-Provera.[159] The obvious problem with drugs, however, is that the effects wear off once they are no longer taken.

European Origins

Chemical castration has been practiced in several European nations, including Belgium, Germany, England, and Denmark. Of these, Germany has been most supportive of the practice, at least historically.[160] Records show some 400 castrations during 1970, but that number has since slowed to about five per year.[161] Denmark was one of the first countries to legally authorize chemical castration, and it has used castration as a method of granting certain offenders early release from prison.[162]

California's Law

Many states have adopted legislation specifically aimed at controlling sex offenders, but only one state appears to have passed a law providing for chemical castration of sex offenders: California. California's chemical castration law was passed by the state's legislature in June 1996. It was subsequently signed into law by then Governor Pete Wilson on September 1, 1996. It took effect on January 1, 1997.[163] The law, which is aimed at protecting victims *under the age of 13*, provides that first-time sex offenders *may* undergo chemical castration at the discretion of the court and that second-time sex offenders *will*, upon parole, undergo chemical castration. Eligible offenses include sodomy and several of its variants, committing a lewd or lascivious act on a child by force or violence, oral copulation or aiding and abetting in forcible oral copulation, and penetration of the genital or anal openings with foreign objects.[164] To date, California's law has withstood constitutional scrutiny.

Effects on Recidivism

Assuming a chemical castration regimen is closely followed, it appears that this approach to dealing with sex offenders succeeds with flying colors. According to one study, "an effective dose of the drug results in an almost total loss of genital functions; the penis is unable to become erect, semen is not produced and orgasm does not occur."[165] In addition, some 20 years of studies in the United States and other countries show that sex offenders who are chemically castrated, usually in conjunction with counseling, have been less likely to reoffend.[166] Of course, chemical castration is not a panacea and it may not work for everyone. Most importantly, careful monitoring to ensure that drugs are faithfully taken (or given) is necessary.

Does It Work?

There is some evidence that castration for certain offenders is an effective crime control policy. But any crime control benefits associated with such an approach must carefully be weighed against possible side effects associated with chemical castration.

Summary

The message of this chapter should be clear: Almost all tough sentencing approaches to the crime problem do not appear to reduce crime. Some penalties, such as three-strikes law and capital punishment, clearly serve a specific deterrent effect. But a wealth of research suggests that they—and other sentences like them—are both costly to implement and almost completely disconnected from crime rates. The same can be said of specific types of prisons, such as those of the supermax variety.

On the upside, fines, fees, and forfeiture may be effective, but there is not enough research to say for sure. Also, evidence suggests that chemical castration of sex offenders, coupled with treatment, may result in reduced recidivism. But the possible undesired side effects associated with castration chemicals may outweigh their benefits. This chapter also reminds us that our discipline is fairly young. While tough sentencing approaches like increased sentence length, determinate sentencing, sentence enhancements, and mandatory sentencing have been researched at some length, other such approaches have not.

Notes

1. S.T. Hillsman, "Fines and Day Fines," in *Crime and Justice: A Review of Research*, eds. M. Tonry and N. Morris, Vol. 12 (Chicago, IL: University of Chicago Press, 1990); S.T. Hillsman, J.L. Sichel, and B. Mahoney, *Fines and Sentencing: A Study of the Use of the Fine as a Criminal Sanction* (New York: Vera Institute of Justice, 1984); S.G. Casale, and S.T. Hillsman, *The Enforcement of Fines as Criminal Sanctions: The English Experience and its Relevance to American Practice* (New York: Vera Institute of Justice, 1986).

2. Sally T. Hillsman, Barry Mahoney, George Cole, and Bernard Auchter, *Fines as Criminal Sanctions* (Washington, DC: National Institute of Justice, 1987).

3. George F. Cole, *Innovations in Collecting and Enforcing Fines* (Washington, DC: National Institute of Justice, 1989).

4. Susan Turner and Judith Greene, "The FARE Probation Experiment: Implementation and Outcomes of Day Fines for Felony Offenders in Maricopa County," *Justice System Journal*, 1 (1999): 1–22.

5. S. Turner and J. Petersilia, "Work Release in Washington: Effects on Recidivism and Corrections Costs," *Prison Journal* 76 (1996): 138–64.

6. Susan Turner and Joan Petersilia, *Day Fines in Four U.S. Jurisdictions* (Washington, DC: National Institute of Justice, 1996).

7. D. Worzella, "The Milwaukee Municipal Court Day-Fine Project," in *Day Fines in American Courts: The Staten Island and Milwaukee Experiments*, eds. D.C. McDonald, J. Green, and C. Worzella (Issues and Practices in Criminal

Justice, National Institute of Justice, Washington, DC, 1992), 61–76.

8. Peter Finn and Dale Parent, *Making the Offender Foot the Bill: A Texas Program* (Washington, DC: National Institute of Justice, 1992).

9. Charles R. King, "Probation Supervision Fees: Shifting the Costs to the Offender," *Federal Probation*, 2 (1989): 43–8.

10. G.R. Wheeler, R.V. Hissong, and T. Macan, "The Effects of Probation Service Fees on Case Management Strategy and Sanctions," *Journal of Criminal Justice* 17 (1989): 15–24.

11. R. Manning, "Inmate Fee for Medical Services Program One Year Later," *American Jails* 3 (July–August 1993): 28–32.

12. J.L. Worrall, "Addicted to the Drug War: The Role of Civil Asset Forfeiture as a Budgetary Necessity in Contemporary Law Enforcement," *Journal of Criminal Justice* 29 (2001): 171–87.

13. For further discussion of the differences, see G.T. Lowenthal, "Mandatory Sentencing Laws: Undermining the Effectiveness of Determinate Sentencing," *California Law Review* 81 (1993): 61–123.

14. Franklin E. Zimring and Gordon Hawkins, *Incapacitation: Penal Confinement and the Restraint of Crime* (New York: Oxford University Press, 1995).

15. James Q. Wilson, *Thinking about Crime* (New York: Basic Books, 1975), 200–2.

16. P.W. Greenwood and A. Abrahamse, *Selective Incapacitation* (Santa Monica, CA: Rand, 1982).

17. R.W. Harding, *Repeat Juvenile Offenders: The Failure of Selective Incapacitation in Western Australia* (Nedlands, Australia: University of Western Australia, 1993).

18. In fact, according to one author, selective incapacitation may be no different from certain traditional practices, such as basing parole decisions on the likelihood that the parolee will reoffend. See M.G. Janus, "Selective Incapacitation: Have We Tried It? Does It Work?" *Journal of Criminal Justice* 13 (1985): 117–29.

19. For helpful reviews, see J. Blackmore and J. Welsh, "Selective Incapacitation: Sentencing According to Risk," *Crime and Delinquency* 29 (1983): 504–28; B. Frost, "Selective Incapacitation: A Sheep in Wolf's Clothing?" *Judicature* 68 (Oct./Nov. 1984): 153–60.

20. A. Hirsch, "Ethics of Selective Incapacitation: Observations on the Contemporary Debate," *Crime and Delinquency* 30 (1984): 175–94.

21. S.H. Decker and B. Salert, "Selective Incapacitation: A Note on its Impact on Minorities," *Journal of Criminal Justice* 15 (1987): 287–99.

22. For a legal scholar's answer to this question, see J. Cohen, "Selective Incapacitation: An Assessment," *University of Illinois Law Review 1984* (1984): 253–90.

23. A. Barnett and A.J. Lofaso, "Selective Incapacitation and the Philadelphia Cohort Data," *Journal of Quantitative Criminology* 1 (1985): 3–36.

24. P.W. Greenwood and S. Turner, *Selective Incapacitation Revisited: Why the High-Rate Offenders Are Hard to Predict* (Santa Monica, CA: Rand, 1987).

25. K. Auerhahn, "Selective Incapacitation and the Problem of Prediction," *Criminology* 37 (1999): 703–34.

26. See M. Gottfredson and T. Hirschi, "True Value of Lambda Would Appear to be Zero: An Essay on Career Criminals, Criminal Careers, Selective Incapacitation, Cohort Studies, and Related Topics," *Criminology* 24 (1986): 213–34.

27. For a recent anti-three strikes argument on these same grounds, see K. Auerhahn, "Selective Incapacitation: Three Strikes and the Problem of Aging Prison Populations: Using Simulation Modeling to See the Future," *Criminology and Public Policy* 1 (2002): 353–88.

28. C.A. Visher, "Career Offenders and Selective Incapacitation," in *Criminology*, ed. J.F. Sheley (Belmont, CA: Wadsworth, 1991), 459–77.

29. K. Auerhahn, "Selective Incapacitation and the Problem of Prediction," *Criminology* 37 (1999): 703–34.

30. T.L. Hafemeister and A.J. Amirshahi, "Civil Commitment for Drug Dependency: The Judicial Response," *Loyola of Los Angeles Law Review* 26 (1992): 39–104.

31. B.J. Bittman and A. Convit, "Competency, Civil Commitment, and the Dangerousness of the Mentally Ill," *Journal of Forensic Sciences* 38 (1993): 1460–6; T. Keville, "Power to Confine: Private Involuntary Civil Commitment as State Action," *New England Journal of Criminal and Civil Commitment* 19 (1993): 61–102.

32. T. Hopcroft, "Civil Commitment of Minors to Mental Institutions in the Commonwealth of Massachusetts," *New England Journal on Criminal and Civil Commitment* 21 (1995): 543–74; D.H. Stone, "Civil Commitment Process for Juveniles: An Empirical Study," *University of Detroit Law Review* 65 (1988): 679–721.

33. P.C. Pfaffenroth, "The Need for Coherence: States' Civil Commitment of Sex Offenders in the Wake of *Kansas v. Crane*," *Stanford Law Review* 55 (2003): 2232–3.

34. *Kansas v. Hendricks* 521 U.S. 346 (1997).

35. For further discussion of the *Hendricks*, see J.K. Cornwell, "Understanding the Role of the Police and Parens Patriae Powers in Involuntary Civil Commitment Before and After *Hendricks*," *Psychology, Public Policy, and Law* 4 (1998): 377–413.

36. *Kansas v. Crane* 534 U.S. 407 (2002).

37. P.C. Pfaffenroth, "The Need for Coherence: States' Civil Commitment of Sex Offenders in the Wake of *Kansas v. Crane*," *Stanford Law Review* 55 (2003): 2229–66.

38. R.K. Bailey, "Civil Commitment of Sexually Violent Predators: A Unique Texas Approach," *Journal of the American Academy of Psychiatry and the Law* 30 (2002): 525–32.

39. R.P. Levin, "Dangerousness of Civil Commitment Candidates: A Six-Month Follow-Up," *Law and Human Behavior* 14 (1990): 551–67.

40. Edwin W. Zedlewski, *Making Confinement Decisions* (Washington, DC: Government Printing Office, 1987).

41. Franklin E. Zimring and Gordon E. Hawkins, "The New Mathematics of Imprisonment," *Crime and Delinquency* 34 (1988): 425–36; see also Franklin E. Zimring and Gordon Hawkins, *Incapacitation: Penal Confinement and*

the Restraint of Crime (New York: Oxford University Press, 1995).

42. J. Cohen and J.A. Canela-Cacho, "Incarceration and Violent Crime," in *Understanding and Preventing Violence: Consequence and Control*, eds. A.J. Reiss, Jr. and J.A. Roth, Vol. 4 (Washington, DC: National Academy of Sciences, 1994).

43. D. Nagin, "Crime Rates, Sanction Levels, and Constraints on Prison Population," *Law and Society Review* 12 (1978): 341–66.

44. S.D. Levitt, "The Effect of Prison Population Size on Crime Rates: Evidence from Prison Overcrowding Litigation," *Quarterly Journal of Economics* 3 (1996): 319–51.

45. Ibid.

46. T.B. Marvell and C.E. Moody, "Prison Population Growth and Crime Reduction," *Journal of Quantitative Criminology* 10 (1994): 109–40.

47. Ibid.

48. See also C.A. Visher, "Incapacitation and Crime Control: Does a 'Lock a 'Lock 'em up' Strategy Reduce Crime?" *Justice Quarterly* 4 (1987): 513–43.

49. R.H. DeFina and T.M. Arvanites, "The Weak Effect of Imprisonment on Crime: 1971–1998," *Social Science Research* 83 (2002): 635–53.

50. For two illustrative examples, see A. Blumstein, "U.S. Criminal Justice Conundrum: Rising Prison Populations and Stable Crime Rates," *Crime and Delinquency* 44 (1998): 127–35.

51. D. Steffensmeier and M.D. Harer, "Bulging Prisons, and Aging U.S. Population, and the Nation's Violent Crime Rate," *Federal Probation* 57 (1993): 3–10.

52. D.P. Mears and J. Watson, "Towards a Fair and Balanced Assessment of Supermax Prisons," *Justice Quarterly* 23 (2006): 232–70.

53. C. Riveland, *Supermax Prisons: Overview and General Considerations* (Washington, DC: National Institute of Corrections, 1999), 6.

54. C. Riveland, "Prison Management Trends, 1972–2025," in *Prisons*, eds. M.H. Tonry and J. Petersilia (Chicago: University of Chicago Press, 1999), 163–203.

55. D.P. Mears and J. Watson, "Towards a Fair and Balanced Assessment of Supermax Prisons," *Justice Quarterly* 23 (2006): 263.

56. R.L. Lippke, "Crime Reduction and the Length of Prison Sentences," *Law and Policy* 24 (2002): 17–35.

57. A.J. Reiss and J.A. Roth, *Understanding and Preventing Violence* (Washington, DC: National Research Council, 1993).

58. Ibid.

59. Ibid., 26–27.

60. Ibid., 27.

61. Ibid., 28.

62. J. Hagan and R. Dinovitzer, "Collateral Consequences of Imprisonment for Children, Communities and Prisoners," in *Prisons*, eds. M. Tonry and J. Petersilia (Chicago: University of Chicago Press, 1999).

63. H.G. Grasmick and G.J. Bryjack, "The Deterrent Effects of Perceived Punishment," *Social Forces* 59 (1980): 471–91; S. Klepper and D. Nagin, "The Deterrent Effect of Perceived Certainty and Severity of Punishment Revisited," *Criminology* 27 (1989): 721–46.

64. R. Paternoster and L. Iovanni, "The deterrent Effect of Perceived Severity: A Reexamination," *Social Forces* 64 (1986): 751–77; R. Paternoster, "The Deterrent Effect of the Perceived Certainty and Severity of Punishment: A Review of the Issues and Evidence," *Justice Quarterly* 4 (1987): 173–217.

65. H.G. Grasmick and G.J. Bryjack, "The Deterrent Effects of Perceived Punishment," *Social Forces* 59 (1980): 480.

66. K.R. Reitz and C.R. Reitz, "The American Bar Association's New Sentencing Standards," *Federal Sentencing Reporter* 6 (1993): 170–1; M. Tonry, *Sentencing Reform Impacts* (Washington, DC: U.S. Department of Justice, 1987), 101.

67. For further discussion, see P.L. Griset, "Determinate Sentencing and Administrative Discretion Over Time Served in Prison: A Case Study of Florida," *Crime and Delinquency* 42 (1996): 127–43.

68. J.D. Casper, "Determinate Sentencing and Prison Overcrowding in Illinois," *Illinois Law Review 1984* (1984): 231–52; D.B. Griswold and M.D. Wiatrowski, "The Emergence of Determinate Sentencing," *Federal Probation* 47 (1983): 28–35.

69. T.B. Marvell and C.E. Moody, "Determinate Sentencing and Abolishing Parole: The Long-Term Impacts on Prisons and Crime," *Criminology* 34 (1996): 107–28.

70. For a discussion of determinate sentencing laws in 10 states, see T.B. Marvell and C.E. Moody, "Determinate Sentencing and Abolishing Parole: The Long-Term Impacts on Prisons and Crime," *Criminology* 34 (1996): 107–28.

71. See, e.g., A. Kassman, "Failure of Determinate Sentencing in Narcotics Convictions: A Look at the California and Federal Judiciary's Paradoxical Implementations of Legislative Sentencing Mandates," *Criminal Justice Journal* 13 (1992): 153–211.

72. T.D. Miethe, "Charging and Plea Bargaining Practices Under Determinate Sentencing: An Investigation of the Hydraulic Displacement of Discretion," *Journal of Criminal Law and Criminology* 78 (1987): 155–76.

73. H.C. Covey and M. Mande, "Determinate Sentencing in Colorado," *Justice Quarterly* 2 (1984): 259–70.

74. See also C. McCoy, "Determinate Sentencing, Plea Bargaining Bans, and Hydraulic Discretion in California," *Justice System Journal* 9 (1984): 256–75.

75. J.D. Casper, D. Brereton, and D. Neal, "The California Determinate Sentencing Law," *Criminal Law Bulletin* 19 (1983): 405–33; J.D. Casper and D. Brereton, "Evaluating Criminal Justice Reforms," *Law and Society Review* 18 (1984): 121–44; D. Howard, *Determinate Sentencing in California* (Lexington, KY: Council of State Governments, 1978); R. Ku, *American Prisons and Jails*, Vol. IV, Supplemental Report—Case Studies in New Legislation Governing Sentencing and Release (Washington, DC:

U.S. Department of Justice, 1980); A.J. Lipson and M.A. Peterson, *California Justice Under Determinate Sentencing: A Review and Agenda for Research* (Santa Monica, CA: Rand, 1980); J.D. Casper, "Determinate Sentencing and Prison Overcrowding in Illinois," *Illinois Law Review* 1984(1984): 231–52.

76. J. Hewitt and T.R. Clear, *The Impact of Sentencing Reform: From Indeterminate to Determinate Sentencing* (Lanham, MD: University Press of America, 1983); R. Ku, *American Prisons and Jails,* Vol. IV, Supplemental Report—Case Studies in New Legislation Governing Sentencing and Release (Washington, DC: U.S. Department of Justice, 1980); S.H. Clark, *Felony Sentencing in North Carolina, 1976–1986: Effects of Presumptive Sentencing Legislation* (Chapel Hill, NC: University of North Carolina, Institute of Government, 1987); D.F. Anspach, P.M. Lehman, and J.D. Kramer, *Maine Rejects Indeterminacy: A Case Study of Flat Sentencing and Parole Abolition* (Portland, ME: University of Southern Maine, 1983); J.H. Kramer, F.A. Hussey, S.P. Lagoy, D. Katkin, and C. McLaughlin, *Assessing the Impact of Determinate Sentencing and Parole Abolition in Maine* (Washington, DC: National Institute of Justice, 1979); J. Sorensen and D. Stemen, "The Effect of State Sentencing Policies on Incarceration Rates," *Crime and Delinquency* 48 (2002): 456–75.

77. T.B. Marvell and C.E. Moody, "Determinate Sentencing and Abolishing Parole: The Long-Term Impacts on Prisons and Crime," *Criminology* 34 (1996) 107–28; see also M.G. Neithercutt, B.G. Carmichael, and K. Mullen, "Perspectives on Determinate Sentencing," *Criminal Justice Policy Review* 4 (1990): 201–13; T.D. Kennedy, "Determinate Sentencing: Real or Symbolic Effects?" *Journal of Crime and Justice* 11 (1988): 1–42; J.R. Hepburn and L. Goodstein, "Organizational Imperatives and Sentencing Reform Implementation: The Impact of Prison Practices and Priorities on the Attainment of the Objective of Determinate Sentencing," *Crime and Delinquency* 32 (1986): 339–65.

78. Marvell and Moody, 1996; their study actually contained data on all states with the non-DSL states serving as a control group.

79. G. Kleck, *Point Blank: Guns and Violence in America* (New York: Aldine de Gruyter, 1991), 337 ff.

80. P.J. Cook, "The Effect of Gun Availability on Violent Crime Patterns," *The Annals of the Academy of Political and Social Science* 455 (1981): 63–79.

81. J.A. Beha, Jr., "And Nobody Can Get You Out: The Impact of a Mandatory Prison Sentence for the Illegal Carrying of a Firearm the Use of Firearms and on the Administration of Criminal Justice in Boston," *Boston University Law Review* 57 (1977): 96–146, 289–333; G. Kleck, *Point Blank: Guns and Violence in America* (New York: Aldine de Gruyter, 1991), 339–42.

82. W.D. Bales and L.G. Dees, "Mandatory Minimum Sentences in Florida: Past Trends and Future Implications," *Crime and Delinquency* 38 (1992): 309–29.

83. C. Loftin, M. Heumann, and D. McDowall, "Mandatory Sentencing and Firearms Violence: Evaluating an Alternative to Gun Control," *Law and Society Review* 17 (1983): 287–318; A. Lizotte and M.S. Zatz, "The Use and Abuse of Sentence Enhancement for Firearms Offenses in California," *Law and Contemporary Problems* 49 (1986): 199–221.

84. J.D. Wright, P.H. Rossi, and K. Daly, *Under the Gun: Weapons, Crime, and Violence in America* (New York: Aldine de Gruyter, 1983), 304–7; L.R. McPheters, R. Mann, and D. Schlagenhauf, "Economic Response to a Crime Deterrence Program: Mandatory Sentencing for Robbery with a Firearm," *Economic Inquiry* 22 (1984): 550–70.

85. J.A. Beha, Jr., "And Nobody Can Get You Out: The Impact of a Mandatory Prison Sentence for the Illegal Carrying of a Firearm on the use of Firearms and on the Administration of Criminal Justice in Boston," *Boston University Law Review* 57 (1977).

86. G.L. Pierce and W.J. Bowers, "The Bartley-Fox Gun Law," *The Annals of the American Academy of Political and Social Science* 455 (1981): 120–37; D. Rossman, P. Floyd, G.L. Pierce, J. McDevitt, and W.J. Bowers, "Massachusetts' Mandatory Minimum Sentence Gun Law: Enforcement, Prosecution, and Defense Impact," *Criminal Law Bulletin* 16 (1980): 150–63.

87. S.J. Deutsch and F.B. Alt, "The Effect of Massachusetts' Gun Control Law on Gun-Related Crimes in the City of Boston," *Evaluation Quarterly* 1 (1977): 543–68; R.A. Berk, D.M. Hoffman, J.E. Maki, D. Roma, and H. Wong, "Estimation Procedures for Pooled Cross-Sectional and Time Series Data," *Evaluation Review* 3 (1979): 385–411; R.A. Hay and R. McCleary, "Box-Tiao Time Series Models for Impact Assessment," *Evaluation Quarterly* 3 (1979): 277–314; S.J. Deutsch, "Intervention Modeling: Analysis of Changes in Crime Rates," in *Methods in Quantitative Criminology*, ed. J.A. Fox (New York: Academic Press, 1981).

88. P.J. Cook, "The Technology of Personal Violence," in *Crime and Justice: A Review of Research,* ed. M. Tonry, Vol. 14 (Chicago, IL: University of Chicago Press, 1991).

89. L.R. McPheters, R. Mann, and D. Schlagenhauf, "Economic Response to a Crime Deterrence Program: Mandatory Sentencing for Robbery with a Firearm," *Economic Inquiry* 22 (1984): 550–70.

90. G. Kleck and E.B. Patterson, "The Impact of Gun Control and Gun Ownership on Violence Rates," *Journal of Quantitative Criminology* 9 (1993): 251.

91. For the critique, see T.B. Marvell and C.E. Moody, "The Impact of Enhanced Prison Terms for Felonies Committed With Guns," *Criminology* 33 (1995): 247–78; for the studies, see C. Loftin and D. McDowall, "One with a Gun Gets You Two: Mandatory Sentencing and Firearms Violence in Detroit," *The Annals of the Academy of Political and Social Science* 455 (1981): 150–81; C. Loftin and D. McDowall, "The Deterrent Effects of the Florida Firearm Law," *Journal of Criminal Law and Criminology* 75 (1984): 250–59; C. Loftin, M. Heumann, and D. McDowall,

"Mandatory Sentencing and Firearms Violence: Evaluating an Alternative to Gun Control," *Law and Society Review* 17 (1983): 287–318; D. McDowall, C. Loftin, and B. Wiersema, "A Comparative Study of the Preventive Effects of Mandatory Sentencing Laws for Handgun Crimes," *The Journal of Criminal Law and Criminology* 83 (1992): 378–94; see also P.H. Blackman, *Firearms and Violence, 1986: An Analysis of the FBI's Uniform Crime Reports and Other Data* (Washington, DC: National Rifle Association, 1988).

92. T.B. Marvell and C.E. Moody, "The Impact of Enhanced Prison Terms for Felonies Committed With Guns," *Criminology* 33 (1995): 247–78.

93. Ibid., 275.

94. B. Levin, "From Slavery to Hate Crime Laws: The Emergence of Race and Status-Based Protection in American Criminal Law," *Journal of Social Issues* 58 (2002): 227–45.

95. *Wisconsin v. Mitchell* 508 U.S. 476 (1993).

96. B. Levin, "Hate Crime: Worse By Definition," *Journal of Contemporary Criminal Justice* 15 (1999): 6–21.

97. For a critique of sentence enhancements for hate-motivated offenses, see M.H. Redish, "Freedom of Thought as Freedom of Expression: Hate Crime Enhancement and First Amendment Theory," *Criminal Justice Ethics* 11 (1992): 29–42.

98. J.V. Roberts, "Public Opinion and Mandatory Sentencing: A Review of International Findings," *Criminal Justice and Behavior* 30 (2003): 483–508.

99. Ibid.

100. For a small sampling of such critiques, see A. Mason, "Mandatory Sentencing: Implications for Judicial Independence," *Judicial Officers Bulletin* 13 (2001): 1, 4–8; R. White, "Ten Arguments Against Mandatory Sentencing," *Youth Studies Australia* 19 (2000): 22–4; W.J. Dickey, *Evaluating Mandatory Minimum Sentences* (Washington, DC: Campaign for an Effective Crime Policy, 1993).

101. 28 U.S.C. 991(b)(1)(B) (Supp. 1993).

102. W.J. Chambliss, "Crime Control and Ethnic Minorities: Legitimizing Racial Oppression by Creating Moral Panics," in *Ethnicity, Race, and Crime: Perspectives Across Time and Space*, ed. D. Hawkins (Albany, NY: State University of New York Press, 1995); M. Tonry, *Malign Neglect* (New York: Oxford University Press, 1995).

103. D.C. McDonald and K.E. Carlson, *Sentencing in the Federal Courts: Does Race Matter? The Transition to Sentencing Guidelines, 1986–1990* (NCJ-145332) (Washington, DC: United States Sentencing Commission, 1993).

104. P. Kautt and C. Spohn, "*Crack*-ing Down on Black Drug Offenders? Testing for Interactions Among Offenders' Race, Drug Type, and Sentencing Strategy in Federal Drug Sentences," *Justice Quarterly* 19 (2002): 1–35.

105. Ibid. 32.

106. C.A. Albonetti, "Sentencing Under the Federal Sentencing Guidelines: Effects of Defendant Characteristics, Guilty Pleas, and Departures on Sentence Outcomes for Drug Offenses, 1991–1992," *Law and Society Review* 31 (1997): 789–822; M.H. Tonry, *Sentencing Matters* (New York: Oxford University Press, 1996).

107. I.H. Nagel and S.J. Schulhofer, "A Tale of Three Cities: An Empirical Study of Charging and Bargaining Practices under the Federal Sentencing Guidelines," *Southern California Law Review* 66 (1992): 561.

108. B.S. Vincent and P.J. Hofer, *The Consequences of Mandatory Minimum Prison Terms: A Summary of Recent Findings* (Washington, DC: Federal Judicial Center, 1994), 11.

109. S.J. Schulhofer, "Rethinking Mandatory Minimums," *Wake Forest Law Review* 28 (1993): 207.

110. M. Tonry, "Mandatory Penalties," in *Crime and Justice: A Review of Research*, ed. M. Tonry, Vol. 16 (Chicago, IL: University of Chicago Press, 1990).

111. H.F. Fradella, "Mandatory Minimum Sentences: Arizona's Ineffective Tool for the Social Control of Driving Under the Influence," *Criminal Justice Policy Review* 11 (2000): 113–35.

112. J.W. Grube and K.A. Kearney, "Mandatory Jail Sentence for Drinking and Driving," *Evaluation Review* 7 (1983): 235–46.

113. J.C. Kunselman and G.F. Vito, "Questioning Mandatory Sentencing Efficiency: A Case Study of Persistent Felony Offender Rapists in Kentucky," *American Journal of Criminal Justice* 27 (2002): 53–68.

114. D. Schichor and D.K. Sechrest, eds., *Three Strikes and You're Out: Vengeance as Social Policy* (Thousand Oaks, CA: Sage, 1996).

115. Bureau of Justice Statistics, *1996 National Survey of State Sentencing Structures* (Washington, DC: Bureau of Justice Statistics, 1998).

116. S. Turner, P.W. Greenwood, E. Chen, and T. Fain, "Symposium: The Impact of Truth-in-Sentencing and Three Strikes Legislation: Prison Populations, State Budgets, and Crime Rates," *Stanford Law and Policy Review* 11 (1999): 75–83.

117. J.M. Shepherd, "Fear of the First Strike: The Full Deterrent Effect of California's Two- and Three-Strikes Legislation," *Journal of Legal Studies* 31 (2002): 159–201.

118. Ibid.

119. F.E. Zimring, G. Hawkins, and S. Kamin, *Punishment and Democracy: Three Strikes and You're Out in California* (New York: Oxford University Press, 2001), 100.

120. P.W. Greenwood, C. Rydell, A.F. Abrahamse, J.P. Caulkins, J. Chiesa, K.E. Model, and S.P. Klien, *Three Strikes and You're Out: Estimated Benefits and Costs of California's New Mandatory Sentencing Law* (Santa Monica, CA: Rand, 1994).

121. Ibid.

122. F.E. Zimring and G. Hawkins, *Incapacitation* (New York: Oxford University Press, 1995).

123. M. Tonry, *Sentencing Matters* (New York: Oxford University Press, 1995).

124. D. Kessler and S.D. Levitt, "Using Sentence Enhancements to Distinguish Between Deterrence and Incapacitation," *Journal of Law and Economics* 42 (1999): 343–63.

125. Ibid.; T.B. Marvell and C.E. Moody, "The Lethal Effects of Three-Strikes Laws," *Journal of Legal Studies* 30 (2001): 89–106.

126. R.C. Cushman, "Effect on a Local Criminal Justice System," in *Three Strikes and You're Out: Vengeance as Public Policy*, ed. D. Shichor and D.K. Sechrest (Thousand Oaks, CA: Sage, 1996).

127. T.B. Marvell and C.E. Moody, "The Lethal Effects of Three-Strikes Laws," *Journal of Legal Studies* 30 (2001): 89–106; T. Kovandzic, J.J. Sloan III, and L.M. Vieraitis, "Unintended Consequences of Politically Popular Sentencing Policy: The Homicide-Promoting Effects of 'Three Strikes' in U.S. Cities (1980–1999)," *Criminology and Public Policy* 1 (2002): 399–424.

128. J.M. Shepherd, "Fear of the First Strike: The Full Deterrent Effect of California's Two- and Three-Strikes Legislation," *Journal of Legal Studies* 31 (2002): 159–201.

129. Ibid.; J.L. Worrall, "The Effect of Three-Strikes Legislation on Serious Crime in California," *Journal of Criminal Justice* (forthcoming).

130. D. Shichor and D.K. Sechrest, eds., *Three Strikes and You're Out: Vengeance as Public Policy* (Thousand Oaks, CA: Sage, 1996).

131. Ibid.

132. J.M. Shepherd, "Fear of the First Strike: The Full Deterrent Effect of California's Two- and Three-Strikes Legislation," *Journal of Legal Studies* 31 (2002): 159–201.

133. L. Stolzenberg and S.J. D'Alessio, "Three Strikes and You're Out: The Impact of California's New Mandatory Sentencing Law on Serious Crime Rates," *Crime and Delinquency* 43 (1997): 457–69.

134. T. Kovandzic, J.J. Sloan III, and L.M. Vieraitis, "Unintended Consequences of Politically Popular Sentencing Policy: The Homicide-Promoting Effects of 'Three Strikes' in U.S. Cities (1980–1999)," *Criminology and Public Policy* 1 (2002): 399–424; T.B. Marvell and C.E. Moody, "The Lethal Effects of Three-Strikes Laws," *Journal of Legal Studies* 30 (2001): 89–106.

135. The Justice Policy Institute study can be found at: cjcj.org/jpi/strikingout.Html. The Sentencing Project Study can be found at: sentencingproject.org/pubs/3strikesnew.Pdf.

136. F.E. Zimring, G. Hawkins, and S. Kamin, *Punishment and Democracy: Three Strikes and You're Out in California* (New York: Oxford University Press, 2001).

137. M. Males and D. Macallair, "Striking Out: The Failure of California's 'Three-Strikes and You're Out Law," *Stanford Law and Policy Review* 11 (1999): 65–72.

138. L.S. Beres and T.D. Griffith, "Did 'Three Strikes' Cause the Recent Drop in California Crime? An Analysis of the California Attorney General's Report," *Loyola of Los Angeles Law Review* 32 (1998): 101–31.

139. L. Stolzenberg and S.J. D'Alessio, "Three Strikes and You're Out: The Impact of California's New Mandatory Sentencing Law on Serious Crime Rates," *Crime and Delinquency* 43 (1997): 457–69.

140. T.B. Marvell and C.E. Moody, "The Lethal Effects of Three-Strikes Laws," *Journal of Legal Studies* 30 (2001): 89–106.

141. T. Kovandzic, J.J. Sloan III, and L.M. Vieraitis, "Unintended Consequences of Politically Popular Sentencing Policy: The Homicide-Promoting Effects of 'Three Strikes' in U.S. Cities (1980–1999)," *Criminology and Public Policy* 1 (2002): 399–424.

142. Ibid. 418.

143. J.M. Shepherd, "Fear of the First Strike: The Full Deterrent Effect of California's Two- and Three-Strikes Legislation," *Journal of Legal Studies* 31 (2002): 159–201.

144. J.R. Ramirez and W.D. Crano, "Deterrence and Incapacitation: An Interrupted Time-Series Analysis of California's Three-Strikes Law," *Journal of Applied Social Psychology* 33 (2003): 110–44.

145. J.L. Worrall, "The Effect of Three-Strikes Legislation on Serious Crime in California," *Journal of Criminal Justice* 32 (2004): 283–96.

146. For the most recent review of this literature available as of this writing, see Mike Males, *Striking Out: California's "Three Strikes and You're Out" Law Has Not Reduced Violent Crime. A 2011 Update*, cjcj.org/files/Striking_Out_Californias_Three_Strikes_And_Youre_Out_Law_Has_Not_Reduced_Violent_Crime.pdf.

147. *Sumner v. Shuman*, 483 U.S. 66 (1987).

148. *Ring v. Arizona*, 122 S.Ct. 2428 (2002).

149. F.E. Zimring, *The Contradictions of Capital Punishment* (New York: Oxford University Press, 2003), x.

150. G.S. Becker, "Crime and Punishment: An Economic Approach," *Journal of Political Economy* 78 (1968): 199–217.

151. I. Ehrlich, "The Deterrent Effect of Capital Punishment: A Question of Life and Death," *American Economic Review* 65 (1975): 397–417.

152. D.O. Cloninger, "Deterrence and the Death Penalty: A Cross-Sectional Analysis," *Journal of Behavioral Economics* 6 (1977): 87–107; J. Yunker, "Is the Death Penalty a Deterrent to Homicide? Some Time Series Evidence," *Journal of Behavioral Economics* 6 (1976): 45–81.

153. The studies include, but are not limited to K.L. Avio, "Capital Punishment in Canada: A Time-Series Analysis of the Deterrent Hypothesis," *Canadian Journal of Economics* 12 (1979): 647–76; A. Barnett, "Crime and Capital Punishment: Some Recent Studies," *Journal of Criminal Justice* 6 (1978): 291–303; B.V. Bechdolt, "Capital Punishment and Homicide and Rape Rates in the United States: Time Series and Cross Sectional Regression Analyses," *Journal of Behavioral Economics* 6 (1977): 33–66; W.J. Bowers and J.L. Pierce, "The Illusion of Deterrence in Isaac Ehrlich's Work on Capital Punishment," *Yale Law Journal* 85 (1975): 187–208; W.J. Bowers, J.L. Pierce, and J.J. McDevitt, *Legal Homicide: Death as Punishment in America 1864–1982* (Chicago: Northwestern University Press, 1984); W.J. Boyes and L.R. McPheters, "Capital Punishment as a Deterrent to Violent Crime," *Journal of Behavioral Economics* 6 (1977): 67–86; S. Brier and S.E. Fienberg, "Recent Econometric Modeling of Crime and Punishment: Support for the Deterrence Hypothesis," *Evaluation Review* 4 (1980): 147–91; B. Forst, "The

Deterrent Effect of Capital Punishment: A Cross-State Analysis of the 1960's," *Minnesota Law Review* 61 (1977): 743–67; S.A. Hoenack and W.C. Weiler, "A Structural Model of Murder Behavior and the Criminal Justice System," *American Economic Review* 70 (1980): 327–41; G. Kleck, "Capital Punishment, Gun Ownership, and Homicide," *American Journal of Sociology* 84 (1979): 882–910; D.L. McKee and M.L. Sesnowitz, "On the Deterrent Effect of Capital Punishment," *Journal of Behavioral Economics* 6 (1977): 217–24; P. Passell, "The Deterrent Effect of the Death Penalty: A Statistical Test," *Stanford Law Review* 28 (1975): 61–80; P. Passell and J.B. Taylor, "The Deterrent Effect of Capital Punishment: Another View," *American Economic Review* 67 (1977): 445–51.

154. D. Nagin and J. Petter, *Deterrence and the Death Penalty* (Committee on Law and Justice at the National Research Council, April 2012). nap.edu/catalog.php?record_id=13363 (accessed December 19, 2012).

155. B.V. Bechdolt, "Capital Punishment and Homicide and Rape Rates in the United States: Time Series and Cross Sectional Regression Analyses," *Journal of Behavioral Economics* 6 (1977): 33–66; W.J. Bowers, J.L. Pierce, J.J. McDevitt, *Legal Homicide: Death as Punishment in America 1864–1982* (Chicago: Northwestern University Press, 1984); D.F. Phillips, "The Deterrent Effect of Capital Punishment: New Evidence on an Old Controversy," *American Journal of Sociology* 86 (1980): 139–48; L. Phillips and S.C. Ray, "Evidence on the Identification and Causality Dispute About the Death Penalty," in *Applied Time-Series Analysis*, eds. O.D. Anderson and M.R. Perryman (Amsterdam: North Holland, 1982).

156. J.M. Bailey and A.S. Greenberg, "Science and the Ethics of Castration: Lessons From the Morse Case," *Northwestern University Law Review* 92 (1998): 1225–46.

157. W.J. Meyer III and C.M. Cole, "Physical and Chemical Castration of Sex Offenders: A Review," *Journal of Offender Rehabilitation* 25 (1997): 1–18.

158. A.G. Carpenter, "Belgium, Germany, England, Denmark, and the United States: The Implementation of Registration and Castration Laws as Protection Against Habitual Sex Offenders," *Dickinson Journal of International Law* 16 (1998): 435–57.

159. Ibid., 441. Chemical castration is also sometimes called "MPA Treatment," for Medroxyprogesterone acetate.

160. N. Heim and C. Hursch, "Castration for Sex Offenders: Treatment or Punishment? A Review and Critique of Recent European Literature," *Archives of Sexual Behavior* 8 (1979): 281–304.

161. A.G. Carpenter, "Belgium, Germany, England, Denmark, and the United States: The Implementation of Registration and Castration Laws as Protection Against Habitual Sex Offenders," *Dickinson Journal of International Law* 16 (1998): 435–57, 443.

162. Ibid.

163. Cal. Penal Code Section 596 (1997).

164. For elaboration, see K.L. Smith, "Making Pedophiles Take Their Medicine: California's Chemical Castration Law," *The Buffalo Public Interest Law Journal* 17 (1998/1999): 123–75.

165. A.G. Carpenter, "Belgium, Germany, England, Denmark, and the United States: The Implementation of Registration and Castration Laws as Protection Against Habitual Sex Offenders," *Dickinson Journal of International Law* 16 (1998): 440.

166. R.I. Lanyon, "Theory and Treatment in Child Molestation," *Journal of Consulting and Clinical Psychology* 54 (1986): 176–182.

Probation, Parole, and Intermediate Sanctions

LEARNING OBJECTIVES

■ Understand the organization and administration of probation and parole in the United States.

■ Summarize the key issues associated with probation and parole, particularly caseloads and recidivism.

■ Distinguish between several types of intermediate sanctions and summarize their effects on crime.

■ Distinguish between intermediate sanctions and hybrid intermediate sanctions.

So far we have focused on many punitive aspects of the criminal justice system. Aggressive law enforcement, tough sentences, and deterrence-based policies all suggest that Americans favors a heavy-handed approach to crime control. But there is much that takes place in the world of crime control that is not so harsh. Such is the focus of this and the next chapter. Here we turn our attention to probation, parole, and intermediate sanctions. Then, sticking with our focus on alternatives to tough sanctions, we will examine the evidence concerning the effectiveness of rehabilitation, treatment, diversion, and other sanctions of a similar variety.

This chapter begins by discussing probation and parole. **Probation** is one of the most frequent sentences handed down by judges and is best understood as an alternative to incarceration. Individuals can be sentenced to probation in the community at a substantially lower cost than sending them to prison.[1] **Parole** is also a form of corrections in the community. Its main difference from probation is that it comes after someone has already served time in prison. Both probation and parole should be viewed as necessary. There are not enough prison cells to handle all offenders.[2] In this way, probation and parole share a great deal in common with plea bargaining. Without them, the criminal justice system would grind to a screeching halt.

Estimates place the number of probationers and parolees in America at close to 5 million (see Table 10.1).[3] This represents roughly 70 percent of all adult criminals under sentence.[4] Add to this estimate the number of juveniles who are placed on probation, and the figure quickly shoots up toward 6 million.[5] More than half of juveniles who receive a juvenile court sanction are placed on probation.[6] In light of these numbers, at least one observer has claimed that the U.S. criminal justice system is mostly a system of community-based sanctioning.[7] Prison and similarly punitive sanctions are the exception rather than the rule.

Probation and parole are reserved for two very different types of offenders. Individuals who are placed on probation (known as probationers) are usually minor offenders who pose minimal risks to public safety. Criminals who are released on parole, while considered less dangerous than those who are kept in prison, are (or were) different from probationers by virtue of having spent time in prison before their parole term begins. We will therefore examine the effectiveness of probation and parole strategies separately.

Probation is clearly a less stringent sanction than prison is. But probation and prison are not the only sentencing options that are available to judges nowadays. Numerous alternatives, collectively known as **intermediate sanctions**, have emerged in recent years. Intermediate sanctions include intensive supervision probation, shock probation, boot camps, electronic monitoring, home confinement, and other approaches. They are "intermediate" in the sense that they lie on a continuum of seriousness between probation and prison. That is, intermediate sanctions are tougher than probation but less harsh than a prison sentence.

This chapter begins with some attention to the organization and administration of probation and parole in the United States. Then it moves into controversial issues associated with probation and parole, including the topic of whether caseloads are linked to public safety. The section on probation and parole also considers the effectiveness of the two strategies. Then we will review the literature on the effectiveness (or the lack thereof) of various intermediate sanctions that are used throughout the United States.

probation: a sentence during which the offender serves his or her time in the community under supervision, subject to specified conditions (e.g., refraining from drug use).

parole: a period of early release for a prison inmate, determined by a parole board, and subject to certain conditions (e.g., retaining a job).

intermediate sanction: a punishment that falls between probation and prison. An example is electronic monitoring.

TABLE 10.1 Persons under Adult Correctional Supervision Over Time

Year	Total Correctional Population[a]	Community Supervision			Incarcerated[c]		
		Total[b]	Probation	Parole	Total	Jail[d]	Prison[e]
2000	6,460,000	4,565,100	3,839,532	725,527	1,937,500	621,149	1,316,333
2001	6,583,500	4,665,900	3,934,713	731,147	1,961,200	631,240	1,330,007
2005	7,050,900	4,946,800	4,162,495	784,354	2,195,500	747,529	1,447,942
2008	7,311,600	5,095,200	4,270,917	828,169	2,307,500	785,533	1,521,971
2009	7,231,400	5,017,300	4,198,155	824,115	2,292,100	767,434	1,524,650
2010	7,079,500	4,887,900	4,055,514	840,676	2,270,100	748,728	1,521,414
2011	6,977,700	4,814,200	3,971,319	853,852	2,239,800	735,601	1,504,150
Average annual percent change, 2000–2010	0.9%	0.7%	0.5%	1.5%	1.6%	1.9%	1.4%
Percent change, 2010–2011[f]	−1.4%	−1.5%	−2.0%	1.6%	−1.3%	−1.8%	−1.1%

Note: The change in the total correctional population was based on the sum of the differences in the probation, parole, local jail, and prison custody populations. Estimates were rounded to the nearest 100 and may not be comparable to previously published BJS reports due to updated information. Total community supervision, probation, parole, and prison custody estimates are for December 31 within the reporting year; jail population estimates are for June 30. See *Methodology*.

[a]Estimates were adjusted to account for some offenders with multiple correctional statuses. For this reason, details do not sum to totals. See *Methodology*.

[b]Includes some offenders held in a prison or jail but who remained under the jurisdiction of a probation or parole agency. The 2008 to 2011 estimates were adjusted to account for offenders with dual community supervision statuses. For this reason, details do not sum to totals. See *Methodology*.

[c]Includes local jail inmates and prisoners held in the custody of state or federal prisons or privately operated facilities.

[d]Totals were estimated based on the Annual Survey of Jails, except the total for 2005, which is a complete enumeration based on the Census of Jail Inmates. See appendix table 4 for standard errors and *Methodology*.

[e]Includes prisoners held in the custody of state and federal prisons or privately operated facilities. The custody prison population is not comparable to the jurisdiction prison population. See text box on page 2 for a discussion about the differences between the two prison populations. See *Prisoners in 2011*, BJS website, NCJ 239808, December 2012, for information on the jurisdiction prison population, which is BJS's official measure of the prison population.

[f]The change in the total correctional population was based on the sum of the differences in the probation, parole, local jail, and prison custody populations. See *Methodology* for more information on the methods used to calculate annual change within each correctional population.

Source: Lauren E. Glaze and Erika Parks, *Correctional Populations in the United States, 2011* (Washington, DC: Bureau of Justice Statistics, 2012).

THE ORGANIZATION AND ADMINISTRATION OF PROBATION AND PAROLE

It is useful to think of probation and parole as both means and ends. They are ends in the sense that they represent a final disposition; probation places someone on supervision in lieu of sending him or her to prison, and parole amounts to a disposition because it results in someone being released from prison. Probation and parole should also be thought of as means to an end. In this sense, they are intended to put someone on the road toward rehabilitation, treatment, reintegration, and other goals. In other words, probation and parole are intended to change offenders so that they don't continue to commit crimes.

Probation

Probation departments play a dual role in the criminal justice system.[8] Probation officers are charged with both protecting public safety and rehabilitating offenders. As protectors of public safety, probation officers act as law enforcement officers, responsible for monitoring probationers' activities and ensuring that probationers comply with court-ordered conditions of probation.[9] In many states, probation officers are sworn peace officers and, as such, possess much the same authority as police officers. Indeed, probation officers are often pulled in two competing directions: the law enforcement direction or the social service direction.

What makes probation different from policing is that it is not always an executive function. Clearly, police officers are charged with enforcement of the criminal law, an executive matter. But the fact that probation officers often serve both law enforcement and social service functions complicates matters. Several states place probation departments under executive control, yet several others place probation under control of the judiciary. In addition, probation is sometimes administered at the local (e.g., county) level and other times at the state level. This makes for a potpourri of probation practices in America. It also complicates research.

Where probation is an executive function, it is usually administered by the state department of corrections. When probation is a judicial function, local courts or the state judiciary control probation officers. Why does this matter? Whether probation is an executive or judicial function can have important implications for its effectiveness. On the one hand, executive branch probation might represent more of a traditional law enforcement role and stress supervision over service. On the other hand, when probation is controlled by the judiciary, probation officers might be more bound by the will of the court and stress services over supervision.

Parole

The decision to grant someone probation is a judicial one. That is, judges decide whether an offender gets probation in lieu of prison or some other sanction. Parole, by contrast, is an administrative act of the executive branch of government. Parole decisions are made by either a parole board or a parole commission. Either entity consists of individuals who are authorized by the executive branch to make such decisions. As is often the case, the parole board or commission represents the interests of the state department of corrections. In addition to deciding who does and does not get paroled, parole boards also determine when revocation and return to prison is necessary.

The organization and administration of parole are generally more consistent than they are for probation. Whereas probation can be administered by the judiciary or the executive branch at either the state or the local level, parole is almost always administered by a state board of corrections. Parole supervision is accomplished through the work of parole officers who work as state employees for the department of corrections. Parole officers, like probation officers, perform both supervisory and service functions. Their job is to ensure that parole conditions are satisfied and that parolees receive necessary services. As is the case with probation officers, though, parole officers are torn between the conflicting goals of enforcing parole terms and assisting in the reintegration into the community of parolees.

Common Probation and Parole Conditions

There are two general types of conditions that are imposed on probationers and parolees. Reform conditions are intended to facilitate the offender's rehabilitation. Drug treatment is an example of a reform condition. Control conditions, by contrast, are intended to ensure adequate monitoring and supervision of the probationer or parolee.

Reform and control conditions help to serve the two common goals of probation and parole in the United States: rehabilitation and the protection of public safety.

Conditions that can be attached to probation and parole are almost too numerous to list. Even so, standard conditions exist across most jurisdictions. Some such conditions include committing no additional crimes, working regularly, supporting dependents, submitting to random drug testing, continuing to reside in the same location, reporting to the probation or parole officer on a consistent basis, allowing the supervising officer to visit at any time, and discontinuing associations with other criminals.

In addition to such standard conditions, probationers and parolees can be required to comply with any number of special conditions. Such conditions are usually tailored to specific offenders on a case-by-case basis. Examples of special conditions include requiring the offender to attend drug treatment, obtain additional education, refrain from going to particular locations, seek counseling, perform community service, pay restitution, remain under house arrest, and many others. Some state-specific special conditions exist also. For example, California requires probationers to sign "Fourth waivers," by which probationers agree to waive their Fourth Amendment rights and be subjected to searches by peace officers at any time. A list of common (discretionary) probation conditions appears in Figure 10.1.

PROBATION AND PAROLE ISSUES

It is difficult to say whether probation and parole reduce crime. Both can be considered crime control policies, but it seems strange to suggest that releasing someone from prison could have the same effect on public safety as locking up a dangerous felon. Because of this, there has been very little research on the link between probation, parole, and public safety. Researchers have instead opted to channel their energies into discussions of several important probation and parole issues. We will consider five such issues: whether (1) probation and parole officers should serve or supervise or do both, (2) caseloads have implications for recidivism and crime rates, (3) probationers and parolees have changed over time such that those who are currently under supervision are more dangerous than their counterparts in the past, (4) probationers and parolees receive the services and treatment they need, and (5) probation and parole impose collateral costs on society that outweigh the benefits associated with keeping offenders out of prison.

To Serve or to Supervise

The romanticized image of probation and parole is one of diligent civil servants carefully monitoring offenders and providing them with the assistance they need to get them back on their feet. This is the image that appears in many introductory criminal justice texts. The same image is conjured up by reading parole and probation department mission statements. But as is the case with other aspects of the criminal justice system, things are not always as they seem. In reality, there is a great deal of tension between the goals of service and supervision, and the latter goal usually wins out. This is so for three reasons. First, more and more people are being put on probation and parole. Second, funding for community corrections has not kept pace with the needs of offenders. Third, caseloads have increased over time, making it difficult for probation and parole officers to put service first.

The number of offenders under supervision in the community is higher today than at any point in history. Between 1980 and today, the number of probationers increased

- support . . . dependents and meet other family responsibilities;
- make restitution to a victim of the offense . . .;
- work conscientiously at suitable employment or pursue conscientiously a course of study or vocational training that will equip him for suitable employment;
- refrain, in the case of an individual, from engaging in a specified occupation, business, or profession bearing a reasonably direct relationship to the conduct constituting the offense, or engage in such a specified occupation, business, or profession only to a stated degree or under stated circumstances;
- refrain from frequenting specified kinds of places or from associating unnecessarily with specified persons;
- refrain from excessive use of alcohol, or any use of a narcotic drug or other controlled substance, . . ., without a prescription by a licensed medical practitioner;
- refrain from possessing a firearm, destructive device, or other dangerous weapon;
- undergo available medical, psychiatric, or psychological treatment, including treatment for drug or alcohol dependency, as specified by the court, and remain in a specified institution if required for that purpose;
- remain in the custody of the Bureau of Prisons during nights, weekends, or other intervals of time, totaling no more than the lesser of one year or the term of imprisonment authorized for the offense, during the first year of the term of probation or supervised release;
- reside at, or participate in the program of, a community corrections facility (including a facility maintained or under contract to the Bureau of Prisons) for all or part of the term of probation;
- work in community service as directed by the court;
- reside in a specified place or area, or refrain from residing in a specified place or area;
- remain within the jurisdiction of the court, unless granted permission to leave by the court or a probation officer;
- report to a probation officer as directed by the court or the probation officer;
- permit a probation officer to visit him at his home or elsewhere as specified by the court;
- answer inquiries by a probation officer and notify the probation officer promptly of any change in address or employment;
- notify the probation officer promptly if arrested or questioned by a law enforcement officer;
- remain at . . . place of residence during nonworking hours and, if the court finds it appropriate, that compliance with this condition be monitored by telephonic or electronic signaling devices, except that a condition under this paragraph may be imposed only as an alternative to incarceration.

FIGURE 10.1 Some Common Probation Conditions

Source: 18 U.S.C. Section 3563.

from just over one million to nearly five million.[10] In fairness, evidence also suggests that the whole adult corrections population (including also those on parole or in prison or jail) has increased during the same period, but the growth rate for probation in particular is fairly dramatic.[11] It is possible that this is the result of a conscious shift in priorities, but it is more likely a by-product of growth in the overall U.S. population. Whatever the reason, one researcher has noted that "2.2 percent of *all* adult residents in the United States are serving criminal justice sentences in the community—about 1 in 27 men, 1 in 160 women."[12]

The community does not always hold probation and parole agencies in high regard. Community corrections as a whole is sometimes viewed as being soft on crime. For example, a 1995 survey showed that 60 percent of people had confidence in the police compared to only 25 percent who had confidence in probation.[13] In another survey, the majority of respondents thought that "community corrections programs are evidence of leniency in the criminal justice system."[14] One of the consequences of this unfavorable image is a lack of funding. Probation and parole agencies receive roughly 15 percent of all corrections funding, despite the fact that they serve some 70 percent of offenders.[15] Furthermore, funding for prisons and jails has risen over time, while funding for probation and parole has remained more or less stagnant.[16]

The result of increasing community corrections populations and less funding is higher caseloads. The 1967 President's Crime Commission recommended ideal caseloads of about 35 per officer. National averages for probation now sit at roughly 175 per probation officer.[17] Parole does not fare much better, with some 75 parolees per parole officer.[18] When attention is turned on urban probation departments in particular, the caseloads in some agencies are no less than shocking. The Los Angeles County Probation Department relies on so-called banked supervision, which consists of no direct supervision or contact for certain low-risk offenders. One probation officer in that agency can be responsible for "supervising" literally thousands of prob ationers. This has prompted the following claim: "Apparently, community supervision has been seen as a kind of elastic resource that could handle whatever numbers of offenders the system required it to."[19] In another noted scholar's words, "it is safe to say that the overall services and monitoring are woefully inadequate to meet the needs of today's community corrections clients."[20]

In short, the combination of more criminals on probation and parole, less funding, and higher caseloads results in little supervision. Little supervision can potentially threaten public safety. One study shows, for instance, that in 1990, just 1 percent of adult probationers and parolees absconded from supervision but that by 1998, 10 percent had done so.[21] A study of community corrections in California shows an even higher percentage: On any day in 1999, some 20 percent of parolees absconded.[22] We will give further attention to the links between caseloads and recidivism shortly. First, though, let us pay some brief attention to the Little Hoover Commission's report on parole in California.

Caseload Concerns

Over the years, probation officers, parole officers, policymakers, and some probation researchers have argued that smaller caseloads would result in more contact between probation officers and probationers. Increasing this contact would in turn decrease the likelihood of recidivism by increasing the level of supervision and access to rehabilitative services.[23] Others simply believe that, as crime control policy, probation and parole are failures regardless of caseload size. Such concerns have prompted three strains of research devoted to (1) probation and recidivism, (2) parole and recidivism, and (3) caseloads and crime.

PROBATION AND RECIDIVISM.   When a person who is placed on probation commits a new crime, this is generally known as a probation failure. But the term *failure* can have different meanings. Researchers who have defined *failure* as reconvictions have found that probation is quite effective.[24] Probation looks more effective still for reincarcerations. That is, relatively few probationers are sent back to prison. If, by contrast, arrests or technical violations are used as measures of probation's effectiveness, the picture is somewhat more disheartening. For example, researchers at the RAND Corporation found that approximately two-thirds of probationers are rearrested during their probation term.[25]

Other studies, however, report that fewer than 50 percent of probationers are rearrested.[26] Indeed, probation researchers have found that when the focus is on the percentage of crime committed by people on probation (instead of arrests, convictions, etc.), probation appears to be surprisingly effective.[27] In their words, "the complete elimination of probation and parole would have a very negligible effect on the burglary and armed robbery rates since more than 90 percent of all burglaries and armed robberies were committed by persons not on probation or parole at the time of their arrest."[28] Perhaps more important than the numbers is the fact that the definition problem (Chapter 1) has once again reared its head; the success and failure of probation and parole hinge to a large extent on how they are defined.

PAROLE AND RECIDIVISM. There is not a wealth of literature concerning parole and recidivism, but what research is available suggests that parole fares comparably to probation. For example, the Bureau of Justice Statistics (BJS) tracked a national sample of parolees who were released from prison in 1983 and found that within three years of their release, 62 percent of them had been rearrested for a felony or serious misdemeanor.[29] Of those, 23 percent were arrested for a violent crime, and 43 percent were sent back to prison. Later studies by the BJS have shown similar results. Nearly half of parolees in 1999 were returned to prison during their parole term.[30] Research also shows that the highest risk period is during the first year after being released on parole, a finding that has been supported in probation research. Recent data are somewhat more encouraging, as Table 10.2 shows. Note that approximately one-third of parolees return to prison. This is still a disturbing amount, of course.[31]

CASELOADS AND CRIME. Studies seeking to link caseload size and recidivism date back more than 30 years. One such study, dubbed the San Francisco Project, was conducted in 1967.[32] Federal probation authorities designated offenders into one of four supervision levels: ideal (caseloads of 40 to 50 offenders per officer), normal (caseloads of 70 to 130), intensive (caseloads of 20 to 25), and minimum (caseloads of several hundred). At the end of two years, the study revealed that there were no significant differences in the number of violations among the probationers placed in the minimum, normal, and ideal caseloads. Each group had violation rates of approximately 23 percent. Somewhat paradoxically, probationers in the intensive caseload group had a violation rate of 38 percent.

In a similar study, Cunniff and Shilton found that the highest absconding rates occurred for those offenders who were supervised by probation officers with caseloads of more than 150.[33] There were no consistent variations, however, between those probationers who were supervised by probation officers with caseloads below 150. The researchers noted that 12 percent of the probationers who were supervised by probation officers whose caseloads ranged from 51 to 100 absconded. In contrast, the absconding rate was actually lower for those who were supervised by probation officers whose caseloads were between 101 and 150 (4 percent). Lower caseloads by themselves would appear to have no direct impact on lowering the absconding rate.

The San Francisco Project and Cunniff and Shilton's research shared a focus on low caseloads and recidivism. They were not evaluations of formal policies per se. Rather, they focused only on how much recidivism occurred in samples of probationers who received more than the traditional level of supervision. Formal efforts to reduce probation caseloads have come to be known as intensive supervision probation (ISP). We will give more attention to ISP in the section on intermediate sanctions.

TABLE 10.2   Type of Parole Exit, 2008–2011

Type of Exit	2008	2009	2010	2011
Total	100%	100%	100%	100%
Completion	49%	51%	52%	52%
Returned to incarceration	36	34	33	32
With new sentence	9	9	9	9
With revocation	25	24	23	21
Other/unknown	1	1	1	2
Absconder	11	9	9	9
Other unsatisfactory exits[a]	2	2	2	2
Transferred to another state	1	1	1	1
Death	1	1	1	1
Other[b]	1	3	1	3
Estimated number[c]	568,000	575,600	562,500	532,500

Note: Detail may not sum to total due to rounding. Distributions are based on parolees for which type of exit was known.

[a]Includes parolees discharged from supervision who did not meet all conditions of supervision, including some who had their parole sentence revoked but were not returned to incarceration because their sentence was immediately reinstated, and other types of unsatisfactory exits; includes some early terminations and expirations of sentence.

[b]Includes parolees discharged from supervision because they were deported or transferred to the jurisdiction of Immigration and Customs Enforcement (ICE), had their sentence terminated by the court through an appeal, were transferred to another state through an interstate compact agreement or discharged to probation supervision, and other types of exits.

[c]Estimates rounded to the nearest hundred. Includes estimates for nonreporting agencies. Estimates are based on most recent data available and may differ from previously published BJS reports. See *Methodology* for a discussion about changes in estimating parole exits from 2000 to 2011.

Source: Laura M. Maruschak and Erika Parks, *Probation and Parole in the United States, 2011* (Washington, DC: Bureau of Justice Statistics, 2012).

An exception to the trend toward studying ISP and recidivism is a recent study that was first published by the California Institute for County Government and later published in an academic journal.[34] The authors of that study used a sophisticated modeling technique to examine the relationship between property crime rates and probation caseloads. After controlling for several factors that have been linked to crime in the past, the authors found that caseloads and crime rates were positively associated with one another; that is, they found that as probation caseloads went up, so did crime. They concluded by arguing that improvements in public safety could result if probation caseloads are reduced.

The astute reader will note the differences in the research designs that were employed to examine links between probation caseloads and crime. The San Francisco Project was a micro-level research design that focused on a sample of probationers. The California Institute for County Government study, by contrast, was macro-level in orientation. It examined the relationship between probation caseloads and crime rates at a county level. What we have, then, are two contradictory findings emerging from two different research designs. Micro-level research shows virtually no link between probation caseloads and crime, but macro-level research suggests a positive association between the two.

Offender Characteristics over Time

So not only are probation and parole underfunded, plagued with high caseloads, and, it would seem, less than effective, but add to these problems a changing offender population, and matters become even worse. Surveys of probation and parole officers reveal, for instance, that they are increasingly becoming concerned with managing offenders because more and more offenders are drug users, sex offenders, and mentally ill.[35] Many also have gang affiliations and no marketable skills with which to get a legitimate job.[36] One author recently reported that nearly three-quarters of parolees are involved in drugs and alcohol.[37] Another 15 percent are mentally ill, and roughly 11 percent are dually diagnosed offenders, that is, those with both mental health and substance abuse problems.[38] However, most probation and parole officers are not equipped to deal with such changes in the client population.

Are Parolees Equipped to Reenter Society?

Presumably, criminals who are put on probation can go about their business and will not suffer many of the harmful and stigmatizing effects that are associated with being placed in prison. Not all probationers are upstanding, of course, and many go back to a life of crime even after being spared a term of incarceration. But matters are far more serious for parolees. Because these individuals will have spent a fair amount of time in prison, we are forced to ask the question "Are they ready to reenter society?" Joan Petersilia's book *When Prisoners Come Home* provides many helpful answers.[39]

As we have already seen, the treatment needs of community corrections clients are not regularly met. With respect to parolees, this is true both inside and outside of prison. As Petersilia observes, "[p]rison work and treatment programs have fallen on hard times. There remains an increasingly large mismatch between the need for programs and program availability."[40]

More frustrating still, even when prisoners are equipped to enter the workforce, the workforce might restrict their participation. For example, employers are increasingly unwilling to hire convicted criminals.[41] And in states such as California, parolees are legally barred from working in professions such as law, real estate, medicine, nursing, education, and others.[42] The implications of a felony conviction for life prospects do not stop with the search for employment:

Convicted felons may lose many essential rights of citizenship, such as the right to vote and to hold public office. . . . Their criminal record may also preclude their receiving government benefits and retaining parental rights, be grounds for divorce, prevent their serving on a jury, and nearly always limits firearm ownership. The restrictions on employment and housing create formidable obstacles to law-abidingness.[43]

On the subject of lost rights, it is amazing to see what **civil disabilities** convicted felons can be saddled with. The Office of the Pardon Attorney in the U.S. Department of Justice recently conducted a complete state-by-state review of rights lost as a result of felony convictions.[44] Figure 10.2 summarizes several of the restrictions that are imposed on convicted felons in California and New York, not just parolees (although parolees are almost always convicted felons). It is safe to say, on the basis of the discussion in this section, that few improvements to public safety are likely to result from any of these restrictions. As Petersilia puts it, "One has to question whether we are jeopardizing public safety by making it so difficult for prison releasees to succeed."[45]

civil disability: a legal right or privilege revoked following a criminal conviction.

Consequences to Society of Prisoner Reentry

There is nothing inherently problematic in returning prisoners to society. Many do indeed complete their parole terms successfully. But parole can still have consequences

California

I. *Rights to Vote, Hold State Office, and Serve on a State Jury; Selected Occupational Disabilities*

A. LOSS OF RIGHTS

The right to vote is suspended while a person is imprisoned or on parole for the conviction of a felony. Cal. Const. art. II, § 4; *Flood* v. *Riggs,* 80 Cal. App. 3d 138, 145 Cal. Rptr. 573 (1st Dist. 1978). Persons who have been convicted of a felony or malfeasance in office, and whose civil rights have not been restored, are disqualified from jury service. Cal. Civ. Proc. Code § 203(a)(5).

Any person convicted of vote-buying, bribery, perjury, forgery, malfeasance in office, or other high crime is disqualified from public office. Cal. Const. art. VII, § 8; Cal. Gov't Code § 1021; Cal. Penal Code § § 67, 68, 74, 88, 98.[1] Earlier similar provisions of California law have been held to extend to federal convictions. *Helena Rubenstein Internat'l* v. *Younger,* 71 Cal. App. 3d 406, 139 Cal. Rptr. 473 (2d Dist. 1980). Additional disqualification statutes include: disqualification from public office for embezzlement of public money or falsification of public account records, Cal. Penal Code § 424; disqualification from holding office as a peace officer upon conviction of felony, Cal. Gov't Code § 1029(a).

A conviction of a crime may result in the denial, suspension, or revocation of a professional or business license if the crime is substantially related to the qualifications, functions, or duties of the business or profession.[2] Cal. Bus. & Prof. Code § 490. Some of these licenses include: law (Cal. Bus. & Prof. Code § 6060(b)); real estate (§ 10177(b)); medicine (§ 2236); nursing (§ 2761(f)); physical therapy (§ 2660(d)). Conviction of certain drug or sex offenses results in suspension and revocation of credentials issued by the State Board of Education or the Commission on Teacher Credentialing, Cal. Educ. Code § 44425, or in the loss of other jobs in the field of education. *E.g.,* Cal. Educ. Code § 44435.

California has a registration requirement for sex offenders, Cal. Penal Code § § 290–290.7, which expressly includes federal offenses. Cal. Penal Code § 290(a)(2). Felony sex offenders and persons convicted of certain violent crimes are required to provide blood and saliva samples for DNA testing. Cal. Penal Code § 290.2.

New York

I. *Rights to Vote, Hold State Office, and Serve on a State Jury; Selected Occupational Disabilities*

A. LOSS OF RIGHTS

A person convicted of a felony under federal law or the law of any state loses the right to vote if he is sentenced to imprisonment and execution of the sentence is not suspended. N.Y. Elec. Law § 5–106. A person convicted of a felony may not serve on a jury. N.Y. Jud. Law § 510(3). A person convicted of a felony (including a federal offense that would constitute a felony under New York law) or a crime that involves a violation of the oath of office, forfeits his office. N.Y. Pub. Off. Law § 30(1)(e). New York does not generally disqualify felons from holding future office, *see* Op. Att'y Gen. 83–60 (1983), although an office holder who forfeits his office is ineligible for the remainder of the term of his office. *See In re Alamo* v. *Strohm,* 74 N.Y.2d 801, 544 N.E.2d 608 (1989). Specific disqualifications, however, are imposed in certain circumstances. *E.g.:* persons convicted of Selective Service violations ineligible for civil office (N.Y. Pub. Off. Law § 3(1)); judges removed from office disqualified from future judicial office (N.Y. Const. art. VI, § 22(h)).

A professional or occupational license may be denied, revoked, or suspended because of a conviction. *E.g.:* trafficking in alcoholic beverages (N.Y. Alco. Bev. Cont. Law § 126(1), (1-a)); attorney (N.Y. Jud. Law § 90(4)).New York has a registration requirement for sex offenders. N.Y. Correct. Law § § 168 to 168-t.

FIGURE 10.2 Civil Disabilities of Convicted Felons

[1]The California Constitution specifically disqualifies persons convicted of vote-buying, and permits laws to be passed disqualifying persons convicted of bribery, perjury, forgery, malfeasance in office, or other "high crimes." Cal. Const. art. VII, § 8. Cal. Gov't Code § 1021 provides that persons are disqualified from any office who are convicted of "designated crimes as specified in the [California] Constitution and laws." Cal. Penal Code § § 67, 68, 74, 88, and 98 define bribery and gratuity offenses.

[2]*See Golde* v. *Fox,* 98 Cal. App. 3d 167, 159 Cal. Rptr. 864 (1st Dist. 1979) (conviction of possession of marijuana for sale is substantially related to business of real estate broker as it shows lack of honesty and integrity); *Windham* v. *Board of Medical Quality Assurance,* 104 Cal. App. 3d 461, 163 Cal. Rptr. 566 (2d Dist. 1980) (federal conviction for income tax evasion is substantially related to the practice of medicine).

Source: M. C. Love and S. Kuzma, *Civil Disabilities of Convicted Felons: A State-by-State Survey, October 1996* (Washington, DC: U.S. Department of Justice, 1997).

for society. Four such collateral consequences have been identified.[46] The first was highlighted in the previous sub-section, namely, that parolees face an uphill battle when it comes to securing gainful employment. Employment prospects aside, parole also affects families and children, neighborhood cohesion, health costs, and levels of domestic violence in the home.[47]

When a person is sent to prison, that can have obvious consequences for families. The breakup of families that can result from a prison term means that for some prisoners, involvement with children in the home is minimized.[48] As one researcher has noted, "[c]hildren of incarcerated and released parents often suffer confusion, sadness, and social stigma; and these feelings often result in school-related difficulties, low self-esteem, aggressive behavior, and general emotional dysfunction."[49] Research also shows that children of imprisoned parents are five times more likely to spend time in prison than are children of parents who are not incarcerated.[50]

When parolees are cycled in and out of prison, this can have detrimental effects on the broader community. In particular, when more and more people are sent to prison, community bonds and informal social control appear to break down. As one researcher describes it, as "family caretakers and role models disappear or decline in influence, and as unemployment and poverty become more persistent, the community, particularly its children, becomes vulnerable to a variety of social ills, including crime, drugs, family disorganization, generalized demoralization and unemployment."[51] In a similar vein, gang loyalties that prisoners develop in prison (often for protection) can be exported into the community on their release, causing additional problems.[52]

Finally, research shows that prisoners and parolees have significantly more health problems than ordinary citizens do. Prisoners received state-sponsored health care while in prison, but when they return to society, they are often unable to cover the costs associated with health care. It has also been estimated that prisoners are infected with HIV at a rate five times higher than the rate of infection in the general population.[53] The prevalence of HIV among prisoners, coupled with the inadequate health care that they receive on release, has led to concerns that released prisoners might be in a position to spread infectious diseases.[54] In sum, not only do parolees themselves affect society when they recidivate, but their release—even when they follow the straight and narrow—can impose significant costs on society.

Improving Probation and Parole

It goes without saying that probation and parole do not live up to their potential. At this time, both mechanisms do more to alleviate prison overcrowding than they do to rehabilitate and reintegrate offenders. Dismal funding levels, high caseloads, and a society that is generally unsupportive of crime control policy that gives the appearance of being soft on crime only make matters worse. These problems have fueled concerns that perhaps *nothing* works. But should we throw up our hands in despair, or can probation and parole themselves be rehabilitated such that society benefits rather than suffers?

Between 1998 and 2000, three separate groups came together to formulate recommendations for the improvement of probation and parole in America. Together, the Reinventing Probation Council, the American Correctional Association, and the Association of State Correctional Administrators identified several promising options to improve a troubled system of community corrections. Drawing on all three organizations' reports, Petersilia identified five of their suggestions:

1. Identify the most dangerous and violent offenders, for whom surveillance through human and technological means is a top priority.
2. Deliver high-quality treatment (particularly for substance abuse) and job training programs to the subgroup of offenders for whom research shows these could be most beneficial.
3. Create the ability to identify and respond quickly to probation and parole violations, particularly those involving drug use.
4. Establish an array of credible intermediate sanction programs to divert true technical violators away from expensive prison cells.
5. Commit to a community-centered approach to offender supervision and management, which means getting officers out of their offices and having them work interactively with victims, law enforcement, offenders, and families.[55]

Reentry Initiatives

In his 2004 State of the Union address, then-President George Bush proposed a four-year, $300 million prisoner reentry initiative to, among other things, expand job training and placement services for parolees. When this much money is offered to criminal justice agencies, they start to salivate at the prospect of receiving some of the funds. Of course, it's not fair to say that agencies implement reentry programs solely for the sake of receiving federal monies. Many are genuinely concerned about the needs of people freshly released from prison. Others, especially the police, realize that without proper services, parolees will be right back on the streets committing crime, which means more work for them.

While most reentry monies have been allocated to departments of corrections and similar entities, many of these agencies have entered into partnerships with police. For example, Boston's Reentry Initiative drew on the services of the Boston Police Department to educate parolees about what they need to know when they reenter society.[56] Marion County, Indiana, held one-time reentry meetings with returning offenders to inform them (1) that the police were aware they were returning to the community and (2) what their likelihood of reoffending was.[57] Fortunately the meetings were also used to point ex-offenders in the direction of support services.[58] A number of similar approaches have been taken all across America.[59] Washington State took this approach:

> [The program] uses community-based storefront locations, staffed by community volunteers and providing office space for police and parole officers. A beat officer is partnered with a parole officer in an effort to better understand the community context facing ex-offenders and facilitating more timely and effective intervention if problems arise.[60]

Another program in Washington State, in the city of Spokane, had police officers working with corrections officers to enforce curfew laws and coupled that effort with the work of volunteer "guardians" who help parolees gain access to services, such as job training.[61] As yet another example, Vermont police officers served on community review boards that reviewed treatment plan options and monitor parolees *before* they enter the community (i.e., when they are in prison) to best steer them in the right direction on release. What is interesting about these developments is the heavy involvement by law enforcement in the parole reentry function. This is another example of partnering for the betterment of the community and crime control:

> While still maintaining separation among agencies and mission, law enforcement agencies are enhancing their role in reentry by receiving and transmitting intelligence about reentering offenders. In addition, law enforcement personnel may meet with offenders before or after prison release to deliver a strong deterrence message. In states including Alabama and Iowa, videotapes have been developed by police, prosecutors, and corrections officials to deliver deterrence messages focused particularly on the sanctions available for felons caught in possession of or using a gun.[62]

Reentry initiatives are fairly new, so there is not much research available. One study looked at the effects of an aftercare program on juvenile boot camp participants' reentry.[63] The program was declared a success. Another study, though, was critical of reentry. Its title, "Good Intentions Meet Hard Realities," is informative.[64] The authors evaluated a program known as "Project Greenlight" and found that participants not only did not perform better than controls, they performed *worse* on measures of recidivism over a one-year period. A recent and quite sophisticated evaluation of an offender rentry program in Minnesota found that increased offender access to community and employment services post-release improved employment, reduced homelessness, improved offenders' networks of social support, and most importantly, reduced reoffending in the treatment group.[65]

Does It Work?

Probation and parole serve two valuable purposes. First, they help to reduce burgeoning prison populations and the associated costs. Second, they are supposed to help criminals either escape the prison experience (as is the case with probationers) or ease back into society following a term of incarceration. Unfortunately, neither policy lives up to the second set of expectations. Community corrections agencies are underfunded and, as research shows, have been relegated to the bottom of the criminal justice priority heap. The result is not enough funding to help people in need and caseloads that are higher than most probation and parole officers can handle. It is safe to say, then, that before probationers and parolees can be rehabilitated, probation and parole need to be rehabilitated first. Some steps have been taken to this end, namely reentry initiatives. And it looks like a properly organized and staffed reentry initiative can make a positive difference in parolees' lives.

INTERMEDIATE SANCTIONS

Intermediate sanctions were defined at the outset of this chapter as more punitive than traditional probation but less punitive than prison. There are two additional features of intermediate sanctions that we must take note of. First, they constitute a relatively new development in the history of criminal justice. Whereas probation and especially parole have been around for a century or so, intermediate sanctions have not been around for nearly as long. Second, though intermediate sanctions are more punitive than, say, probation, they are also intended to be improvements over traditional community corrections. But just because they can be viewed as improvements does not mean that they work particularly well. As the following subsections will attest, improvements to probation supervision and other intermediate sanctions such as electronic monitoring do not have an impressive track record. They have also been criticized on the grounds that they just add layers to an already complex and intrusive criminal justice system. Let us consider this problem of net widening before we turn to the literature on the effectiveness of intermediate sanctions.

The Net Widening Problem

net widening: the phenomenon of intermediate sanctions bring more and more people under some form of social control.

In an effort to improve community corrections, intermediate sanctions of various varieties have come to the fore. This development has come as welcome news to critics of an antiquated system of community corrections. But even when changes are made with the loftiest of intentions, they can have unanticipated consequences. One of these consequences that is particularly troublesome to critics is that intermediate sanctions bring more and more people under some form of social control. This is known as the **net widening** problem. The net is a metaphorical representation of the control that is exercised over the lives of more and more people who find themselves on the wrong side of the law.

The net widening phenomenon was first highlighted by Thomas Blomberg. In a review of juvenile diversion programs, he found that they led to a 32 percent increase in the number of juveniles who were under some form of control.[66] Net widening has been explained by Tonry and Lynch as amounting to political risk aversion; no one, especially politicians, wants to take a risk (such as releasing an offender into the community) that might reflect poorly on them.[67] Thus, it behooves policymakers to give the appearance that "something" is being done to deal with criminals. As one critic of net widening has noted, however, most of the low-risk offenders who are placed in a program because of this risk aversion would succeed without the program.[68] In other words, expanding the criminal justice net probably has no effect on crime.

A Typology of Intermediate Sanctions

There are several methods by which the criminal justice system sanctions and monitors known offenders. Incapacitation and deterrence approaches to the crime problem have already been reviewed. Purely rehabilitative approaches will be the topic of the next chapter. Whether probation and parole serve a deterrent or rehabilitative purpose is unclear, given their somewhat contradictory goals (monitoring and service). That leaves us with intermediate sanctions. According to one author, intermediate sanctions can be placed into two categories.[69] First, *community restraints* require offenders to be restrained in the community. Second, programs that are aimed at providing *structure, discipline, and challenge* include boot camps for adults and juveniles. To these, we can add a third: hybrid varieties of intermediate sanctions. Hybrids combine elements of traditional community corrections with other more (and sometimes less) punitive approaches. We will use this classification scheme throughout the remainder of this chapter.

Community Restraints

The first type of intermediate sanctions, and one of the most researched, is community restraints. Community restraints focus on restricting the mobility of known offenders. One of the earliest forms of this approach is intensive supervision probation, that is, reducing caseloads to provide heightened supervision. Home confinement and electronic monitoring are also methods of community restraints. The former requires offenders to remain in their homes during specific periods. The latter can require offenders to remain at particular locations, but its hallmark consists of tracking the movements of criminals. Given that these two sanctions are usually imposed together nowadays, we will cover them both in a single section.

INTENSIVE SUPERVISION PROBATION. Intensive supervision probation (sometimes called intensive probation supervision or intensive community supervision) basically amounts to reducing caseloads so that probation officers can more effectively monitor and serve probationers. Many probation departments do their own form of intensive supervision, usually reserved for more serious offenders. For example, the San Bernardino County Probation Department has a program known as Success. It is reserved for high-risk probationers, and the probation officers' Success caseloads are approximately 30 per officer. More generally, ISP is any policy of reducing caseloads in an effort to make probation more effective. This approach seems laudable on its face, but the evidence is mixed concerning its effectiveness.

For example, in the mid-1980s, researchers published an evaluation of a Georgia Department of Corrections program that allowed offenders the option of being placed in an ISP in lieu of a prison sentence.[70] To determine program effectiveness, the researchers sampled ISP offenders, regular probationers, and people who had been released from prison. After an 18-month follow-up period, the results revealed that ISP offenders committed fewer and less serious crimes than regular probationers and prison releasees, although they did commit more technical violations than regular probationers did.

Another team of researchers evaluated New Jersey's ISP.[71] One facet of the study was to compare the recidivism rates between two groups: ISP cases and a matched sample of about 100 felony offenders who were sentenced for ISP-eligible crimes (prior to ISP implementation) and who were subsequently released on parole. The results revealed that 12 percent of the ISP offenders were convicted of a new crime compared to 23 percent of the offenders in the matched group. The researchers noted, however, that because the study lacked random assignment, it is difficult to determine whether the results are due to participation in the ISP program.

In 1989, Byrne and Kelly conducted an evaluation of Massachusetts' ISP program.[72] One major focus of the study was to examine and compare recidivism rates between courts with ISPs and courts without ISPs both before and after the implementation of the program. The results revealed there were no overall differences in recidivism rates between the experimental and control courts. The authors of that study did find, however, that as the level of supervision increased, recidivism rates significantly decreased in both courts. These three studies clearly provide a measure of support for ISPs, but more recent studies have cast some doubt on the efficacy of enhanced supervision of probationers.

For example, the RAND Corporation conducted a multisite demonstration project for ISPs in California.[73] Each site identified the offenders who were eligible to participate. Subsequently, RAND randomly assigned each offender into the ISP program or a control group. The study revealed that at the end of the one year follow-up period, about 40 percent of the ISP offenders in each site had technical violations and approximately one-thirds had new arrests. The only significant difference between the experimental and control programs was in Ventura County. The offenders in the ISP program in that county were less likely to be arrested than were the offenders in the control program. But when the average number of arrests per year of street time was used, there was no significant difference between these two groups.

Another RAND study used an experimental design to compare ISP programs in 14 states.[74] The researchers randomly assigned offenders to ISP and control groups, which eliminated many of the problems in previous studies on the subject. They then gathered data on rearrests and technical violations over a period of one year. They found that 37 percent of the ISP clients were rearrested during the follow-up period, compared to 33 percent in the normal supervision group. In addition, the researchers found a significant difference in technical violations between the treatment and control groups. Thirty-eight percent of the control group committed technical violations during one year compared to 65 percent in the treatment group. The researchers' explanation for this perhaps surprising finding was that enhanced supervision gives probation officers more of an opportunity to detect technical violations.

Since the RAND evaluations, several other evaluations of ISP programs have been published. A majority of the research shows, as of this writing, that intensive supervision probation—and even intensive supervision parole—leads to either higher recidivism rates or technical violations (or both).[75] This is not to suggest that all research is unsupportive of ISP, however. For example, one study found that reduced probation caseloads can result in fewer arrests and equal amounts of technical violations between treatment and control groups.[76] Note, though, that the RAND studies are among the most sophisticated to date. They provide fairly convincing evidence that increased supervision is not the panacea that some probation reformers have made it out to be.

Before moving on, it is important to reiterate that this section has been concerned with enhanced supervision alone. Nothing says that a probation department could not only increase supervision of probationers but also provide treatment or otherwise step up service provision such that probationers receive more than just additional contacts. Research shows, for instance, that intensive supervision coupled with drug treatment can lead to a reduction in recidivism.[77] And the RAND researchers found a 10 to 20 percent reduction in recidivism among those ISP clients who actively participated in programs.[78] Additional research is therefore needed before we can conclude with certainty whether enhanced supervision coupled with increased service can reduce crime.

HOME CONFINEMENT AND ELECTRONIC MONITORING. Two explanations are offered for the emergence of **home confinement** and **electronic monitoring** as intermediate sanctions. First, both methods of dealing with offenders are thought to minimize the damaging effects of the prison environment.[79] They also allow offenders to carry on more or less normal lives—of course, with more restrictions than might otherwise have existed. They also enhance offenders' opportunities for rehabilitation and prosocial experiences.[80] Second, home confinement and electronic monitoring have emerged as cost-effective methods of reducing jail and prison overcrowding.[81]

Home confinement and electronic monitoring tend to go hand in hand. This has not always been the case, however. For example, the Federal Home Confinement Program restricted program participants to their residences during specific hours unless they were given permission to leave for employment, education, treatment, or other reasons; there was no electronic monitoring component per se.[82] A preliminary evaluation revealed that there was a low percentage of new criminal conduct among the program's participants.[83] But there are surprisingly few evaluations of pure home confinement programs, that is, home confinement without electronic monitoring.[84] Instead, most of the research in this area is concerned with home confinement coupled with electronic monitoring or, simply, electronic monitoring.

For some reason, though, researchers have steered clear of studying the effect of home confinement and electronic monitoring on recidivism. Instead, most of the existing research is either descriptive or is simply concerned with whether offenders complete their terms of monitoring and confinement.[85] Some researchers have examined the effect of home confinement and electronic monitoring on prison overcrowding and probation violations,[86] but overall there is little research in terms of how both of these

home confinement: a sentence requiring the offender to remain in his or her residence during specified periods.

electronic monitoring: a sentence requiring the convicted offender to wear an electronic device capable of locating authorities as to his or her whereabouts and/or when he/she leaves a specified location. Electronic monitoring usually accompanies home confinement.

intermediate sanctions affect future criminal activity among program participants. As one electronic monitoring researcher has observed,

> To date, we know of no scientific evidence demonstrating that criminal activity is reduced while electronic monitoring is being utilized or after the use of technology with offenders. Currently, the research derived from relatively small samples of offender populations, suggests that when properly utilized, [electronic monitoring] provides another alternative to incarceration, but nothing else.[87]

In one apparent exception to this lack of sophistication in previous research, two academics recently tracked violent male parolees who were supervised via electronic monitoring and compared them to a control group of parolees who were not in the program.[88] They focused in particular on prison recommitments among both groups and concluded that "an [electronic monitoring] component to parole supervision has no significant independent effect on the likelihood of a parolee being recommitted to prison during the follow-up period or on the amount of time before recommitment to prison."[89] They also concluded that electronic monitoring has different effects for various types of offenders. It appeared to delay recommitments to prison of sex offenders. Thus, the researchers concluded that electronic monitoring has no deterrent or rehabilitative effect on parolees' behavior, except for sex offenders.

The notion that electronic monitoring works for some offenders and not others finds a wealth of support in the literature. Indeed, almost all types of criminal justice sanctions work differently for different types of offenders. Research shows, for instance, that younger offenders fail more frequently with electronic monitoring than do older offenders.[90] Women tend to do better than men.[91] The employed also complete electronic monitoring more than the unemployed do.[92] The more extensive a person's criminal record, the more likely it is that he or she will fail.[93] Offenders who have been convicted of minor crimes, such as traffic violations, do better than offenders who have been convicted of serious crime.[94] And so on. Again, these findings are not very different from those for other criminal justice sanctions, suggesting that electronic monitoring in particular is no better (or worse) than traditional methods of dealing with crime. At least one study, though, found marginal improvements in electronically monitored parolees and probationers relative to those who received traditional community services.[95]

Although little research supports electronic monitoring and home confinement, both methods are now being used as more than an intermediate sanction. Electronic monitoring in particular is now used in various jurisdictions for pretrial supervision of criminal defendants.[96] It is also being used for juvenile offenders[97] and as an alternative to incarceration for probation and parole violators.[98] Similarly, home confinement and similar restrictions on people's movement (e.g., curfews) are being resorted to for all manner of criminal offenders, even in the face of mounting evidence that such techniques do not help. Interestingly, the only component of electronic monitoring and home confinement that appears to relate to subsequent criminal activity is the length of confinement. That is, the longer a person is subjected to either sanction, the less likely it is that he or she will be rearrested.[99] This finding flies in the face of the links between prison term length and recidivism touched on in Chapter 9.

GPS MONITORING. Electronic monitoring has traditionally been accomplished with an ankle bracelet worn by the offender. The ankle bracelet, which has a radio transmitter, works together with a field monitoring device (FMD). The FMD is a receiver that is connected to the offender's home telephone. The radio transmitter in the ankle bracelet sends signals to the FMD, which then alerts probation authorities when the probationer is not at home. The problem with this technology is that it tells authorities only where the probationer *is not* rather than where he or she *is*.

In response to some of the limitations of traditional electronic monitoring, some probation departments have implemented GPS (Global Positioning System) monitoring. GPS consists of a group of 21 Department of Defense satellites that circle the earth, constantly transmitting radio signals. If a person wants to know his or her position on the earth, the person can use a GPS receiver. This technology has proven useful in the electronic monitoring arena. Today, both active and passive GPS monitoring takes place. Active monitoring requires the offender to wear a traditional ankle bracelet and carry a portable tracking device (PTD). The offender is required to stay within a certain distance of the PTD at all times. Passive GPS works similarly but does not provide as much detail to authorities about the offender's whereabouts.

Active GPS monitoring has obvious advantages over traditional methods. It can, however, be cost-prohibitive for some agencies. It can also be plagued by some of its own limitations. For example, just because probation officers know where a probationer is at any given time does not mean that the officer knows what the offender is doing. That is to say, the offender could commit a crime without being caught in the act.

Is GPS monitoring effective? Two recent evaluations suggest there is some promise. One study of GPS monitoring in domestic violence cases found participants reoffending less than controls.[100] They also were less inclined to violate "no contact" (orders requiring them to stay away from their victims). Another study looked at the GPS monitoring of sex offenders. The GPS monitored sex offenders fared significantly better than controls. The authors reached this interesting conclusion:

> . . . while one might have hypothesized that the greater the supervision the more likely and quicker the detection of noncompliance and recidivism, it appears that GPS acts as a useful supervision tool, reducing the likelihood and increasing the time until these events.[101]

Structure and Discipline

Although we might hate to admit it, many of us have channel-surfed and happened on a daytime talk show on which parents are seeking advice about how to deal with their wayward sons or daughters. A "solution" that is frequently touted on such shows is to impose a mixture of structure and discipline on the youth's life. This usually entails sending the boy or girl to boot camp, shock incarceration, or a similar program with military organization and rules. In the interest of consistency, we will use the term *boot camp*.

Academics have been unable to resist the pull of boot camps. As a method of dealing with crime—especially crime among juveniles—boot camps have been subjected to incredible amounts of research in the past decade. A search of "boot camps" on the National Criminal Justice Reference Service's website, for example, revealed nearly 200 boot camp publications in a 10-year period. Very few methods of crime control in America have been researched at such great length in such a short period.

ADULT BOOT CAMPS. **Boot camps** began as early as 1983 in Georgia and Oklahoma and then quickly spread throughout America.[102] The earliest boot camps resembled military boot camps. The focus was on structure and discipline. More recently, boot

boot camp: *a short-term correctional camp that follows military structure and discipline. Boot camps are usually reserved for people convicted of minor offenses and are premised on the assumption that criminals need structure and discipline in order to become law-abiding citizens.*

camps have evolved to include some treatment components. Boot camps can be further divided into those catering to adults and to juveniles. Here we focus on the research concerning adult boot camps.

Despite the wealth of attention that has been paid to adult boot camps, no one appears to have conducted an experiment aimed at determining whether they work. The best researchers have done is to compare boot camp releasees with other offenders in the community, controlling for factors that are commonly linked to recidivism (offense seriousness, employment status, etc.). Even so, nowhere else in the criminal justice literature is the research so uniformly unsupportive of an approach. For the most part, the research shows no difference between boot camp participants and similar offenders who do not attend boot camp.[103] This finding is supported in one of the more recent—and most comprehensive—reviews of boot camps:

> In our overall meta-analysis of recidivism, we found no differences between the boot camp and comparison samples. Our analysis predicts that if the comparison sample's recidivism is estimated to be 50 percent, the boot camp sample's recidivism would be estimated to be 49.4 percent, or only 0.6 percent lower. When the individual studies were examined, no significant differences were found between the boot camp samples and the comparisons in the majority of the studies. In only 17 samples out of the total of 44, a significant difference between the experimental and control samples was found; approximately half favored the boot camp while the remaining favored the comparisons. Thus, by whatever criteria are used, there is no evidence that the boot camps reduce recidivism.[104]

Of course, as with most methods of crime control, boot camps cannot be dismissed outright as hopelessly ineffective. Research *does* show that those boot camp participants who stay in the program longer recidivate less than do those who drop out early.[105] It also appears that boot camp participants who attend voluntarily and who receive treatment and services during their term fare better.[106] Finally, the research shows that boot camps can be made more effective when staff are attached to and work closely with program participants.[107] Military structure and discipline alone appear to do little in terms of changing offenders' lives.

JUVENILE BOOT CAMPS. Most research on boot camps has been limited to adults. And as the reader is aware by now, research suggests they do little to prevent or control crime. Much the same holds for juvenile boot camps. Three of four rigorous evaluations (with random assignment to treatment and control conditions) showed more recidivism in the treatment group than in control groups.[108] This does not bode well for juvenile boot camps. The results of one of these evaluations led the California Youth Authority, the organization that oversees many of the state's correctional facilities, to abandon boot camps altogether.

There are several possible explanations for the failure of boot camps. One is that they are too short-lived, making it difficult for the camp practices to be instilled in the youths who go to the camps. Another explanation is that boot camps' use of aggressive and hypermasculine strategies might be counterproductive, actually leading the youths to become more aggressive than they were before program entry. Still another explanation for boot camps' failure could be that they do not target the right problems. Certainly, children can benefit from discipline and structure, but if boot camps do not target other negative influences in a child's life, especially on their return home, then little more than a Band-Aid is applied to a deep-seated and complicated set of problems.

Hybrid Intermediate Sanctions

hybrid intermediate sanction: *the combination of traditional community corrections strategies with other harsh or less punitive sanctions. Examples include shock probation, day reporting centers, and halfway houses.*

As was indicated earlier, **hybrid intermediate sanctions** combine traditional community corrections strategies (e.g., probation and parole) with harsher—or less serious—sanctions. Here we consider five hybrids: (1) shock probation, (2) halfway houses, (3) day reporting centers; (4) foster/group homes for juveniles; and (5) scared straight (for juveniles).

SHOCK PROBATION. **Shock probation** is sometimes called split sentencing. This approach amounts to sentencing a criminal to confinement for a short period followed by a period of supervised release. It is best understood as integrating the community corrections methods discussed at the outset of this chapter with some of the more punitive deterrence-based approaches to crime that we touched on in previous chapters. It is hoped, at least in part, that by sentencing an offender to incarceration followed by supervision, the offender will be deterred from future criminal behavior. At the same time, though, shock probation proceeds under the assumption that incarceration alone is not the best method of dealing with certain offenders. Together, incarceration and supervised release place shock probation in the category of hybrid intermediate sanctions.

shock probation: *sometimes called split sentencing, the practice of sentencing a criminal to confinement for a short period followed by a period of supervised release.*

Does shock probation work? The evidence is not supportive.[109] Studies comparing recidivism levels of shock probationers and traditional probationers show little difference. In fact, some studies show that shock probationers have fared worse. Researchers have found that the time shock probationers spent incarcerated has no bearing on offending.[110] They have also argued that if shock probation is to be used, it should be reserved for first-time offenders because shock probationers with prior records fail at high rates.[111] Still others have argued that shock probation has not been applied fairly, might be racially discriminatory, and can cause administrative problems.[112]

halfway house: *sometimes called community residential centers, prerelease centers, or restitution centers; these are residential facilities intended to ease the transition to regular life for recently-released prison inmates.*

HALFWAY HOUSES. **Halfway houses**, sometimes called community residential centers, prerelease centers, or restitution centers, can also be understood as a form of hybrid intermediate sanctions. They are intended to provide a measure of services to clients, and in this way, they resemble probation and parole, but the literature has cast them in confinement-related terms. Indeed, the term *halfway* is best understood as halfway between prison and returning to the community. Some parolees (or releasees) need a period of readjustment before entering the community. Halfway houses can also be used to house probationers as yet another alternative to incarceration. As with parolees, probationers who the court does not think are fit to reenter the community can be sent to a halfway house for a period of time.

What does the research show? Not surprisingly, the results are mixed. In the 1970s, a team of researchers examined 35 previous studies of halfway houses and their effectiveness.[113] The review showed a series of fairly weak research designs as well as an even division between treatment and control groups in terms of recidivism. A more recent study focused specifically on halfway houses for parolees.[114] Again, the results were mixed. Some halfway houses were linked with lower recidivism rates among clients, but others either had no effect on parolees or made matters worse.

day reporting center: *a facility that allows pretrial releasees, probationers, and parolees to report to a specific facility on a regular basis.*

DAY REPORTING CENTERS. A recent twist on the halfway house strategy is the emergence of **day reporting centers**.[115] Rather than confining them to a facility, day reporting centers allow pretrial releasees, probationers, and parolees to report to a specific facility on a regular basis. People who are required to appear at day reporting centers often receive a number of treatments and services. They might be required to participate in drug testing or treatment. They might also participate in programs that are intended to help them secure employment. Day reporting represents something of an improvement on traditional community corrections programs. This is because they ensure both monitoring *and* treatment. Strangely, though, evaluators have not been drawn to day reporting centers. Consequently, there is little evidence as to their effectiveness. One study showed that longer treatment exposure (i.e., more time engaged in day reporting) is beneficial, but it did not include a control group.[116] One study that did include a control group found virtually no difference between day reporting center clients and traditional probationers.[117] Yet another study showed that when day reporting was added to intensive supervision probation, it made no difference.[118]

FOSTER AND GROUP HOMES. Delinquent youths from broken homes and other family and at-home problems are sometimes placed in foster care or group homes. In **foster care,** as most of us know, the youth moves into a new home where foster parents take over the role of guardianship. **Group homes** are residential facilities, usually homes in ordinary neighborhoods, where several youth live. The homes are staffed 24 hours a day by trained personnel and are often run by companies that own several group homes. Group home operators receive various tax breaks and rent subsidies to offset the costs of taking care of several troubled youths. In fact, the more troubled the youths, the more money the group home operator tends to get. Some people have been especially critical of group home operators because of the amount of money some of them make taking care of troubled children.

group home: small residential facilities intended to serve children or adults in need of special services.

Unfortunately, little is known about the effects of foster care on juvenile delinquency. Researchers have, however, spent a fair amount of time studying group homes. The problem is that they have studied outcomes other than recidivism. For example, researchers have studied staff perceptions and attitudes at group homes,[119] the success rate of youths who are sent to group homes,[120] victimization of resident juveniles,[121] youths who leave group homes,[122] and the differences from one group home to the next.[123] Consequently, we do not know what effect placement in a group home—or a foster home—has on juveniles' future criminality. But group homes and foster parents will continue to provide a valuable and needed service for youths in that middle ground between probation and incarceration.

SCARED STRAIGHT. **Scared straight** refers to a variety of attempts to deter young offenders and at-risk individuals from committing crime.[124] Participants are usually taken to a maximum security prison, where they are told horror stories about prisons and life "on the inside." Video presentations are also used. They can even be bought from Amazon and other online sources. Today, numerous websites are available that serve to allegedly scare kids straight without the need to visit an actual prison.[125] Even stories from youths who are serving adult time can be found on the Internet.

scared straight: any of a variety of attempts to deter young offenders and at-risk individuals from committing crime. Participants are usually taken to a maximum security prison, where they are told horror stories about prisons and life "on the inside."

Scared Straight (originally called the Juvenile Awareness Program) began in the late 1970s when a group of inmates serving life sentences at New Jersey's Rahway State Prison confronted youths with stories of prison life, including rape and murder. An independent news channel in Los Angeles videotaped the confrontation. Three months later, according to the film, 16 of the 17 juveniles who participated became law-abiding. The video won an Academy Award, eight Emmys, and a Peabody Award.

It is used as part of some Scared Straight presentations, even though it was recorded over 25 years ago.

Does Scared Straight work? According to the producers of the original video, it did. But rigorous research that has been published since the video first aired tells a different story.[126] Some researchers have criticized Scared Straight by arguing that it might actually *increase* delinquency.[127] Another researcher has criticized the program by arguing that it presents a distorted image of crime.[128] Still other researchers, who have compared Scared Straight participants with control groups, have also concluded that the program is a failure.[129] In her discussion of Scared Straight, one author reached this conclusion: "Overall, there is no evidence that deterrence programs such as these effectively reduce the future criminal activities of the offender participants."[130]

Does It Work?

With few exceptions, the evidence in favor of intermediate sanctions is either mixed or unsupportive. Admittedly, intermediate sanctions are intended to improve an antiquated system of community corrections in America. But the improvements have yet to materialize. We cannot safely conclude—overall—that community restraints, structure and discipline, or hybrid intermediate sanctions make much of a difference. Petersilia argues that the only way for intermediate sanctions to succeed is for them to include a rehabilitation component, the topic of the next chapter:

> The empirical evidence regarding intermediate sanctions is decisive: Without a rehabilitation component,

reductions in recidivism are elusive. In sum, the ISP evaluations show that programs were seldom used for prison diversion but rather to increase accountability and supervision of serious offenders on probation. In addition, programs did not reduce new crimes, but instead increased the discovery of technical violations and ultimately increased incarceration rates and system costs.[131]

All criticisms aside, there are some favorable findings with respect to certain intermediate sanctions. GPS monitoring, for example, has been carefully evaluated of late and studies suggest it can reduce reoffending in both domestic violence and sex offenders.

Summary

Some people have said that probation and parole are in need of rehabilitation. This is because probation and parole officers are torn between the conflicting goals of service and supervision. Also, caseloads tend to be high for both probation and parole officers, which invariably means that treatment, rehabilitation, and reintegration take a back seat to the supervision function. The evidence also suggests that parolees are not equipped to reenter society following their release from prison, which shows that our traditional system of community corrections is in need of even more reforms. This has prompted critics of probation and parole to argue for improvements, such as the use of intermediate sanctions (see Figure 10.3).

Intermediate sanctions were divided into three categories. Community restraints include intensive supervision probation, home confinement, and electronic monitoring. Structure and discipline programs consist of boot camps for adults and juveniles. Hybrid intermediate sanctions include shock probation, halfway houses, day reporting centers, and others. Each has been developed in response to the limitations and problems associated with probation and parole in America. Most, however, have not made much of a difference. With the possible exception of GPS monitoring of sex offenders and domestic violence offenders, evidence suggests that sanctions without a significant rehabilitation component do little to affect recidivism in community corrections clients.

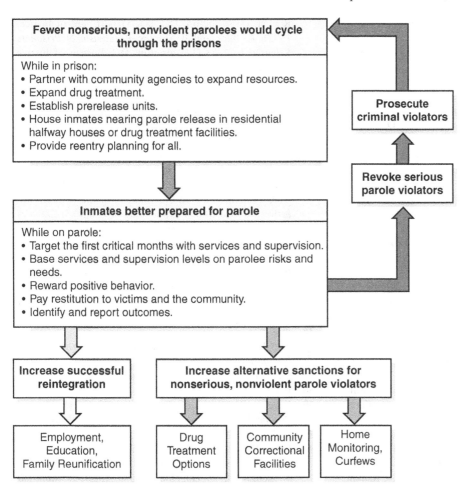

FIGURE 10.3 By Improving the Success of Parolees, the State Could Reduce Crime and Save Money

Source: Little Hoover Commission, *Back to the Community: Safe and Sound Parole Policies: Executive Summary* (Sacramento, CA: Little Hoover Commission, 2003), p. i.

Notes

1. C. Camp and G. Camp, *The Corrections Yearbook 1998* (Middletown, CT: Criminal Justice Institute, 1999).
2. T.R. Clear and H.R. Dammer, *The Offender in the Community* (Belmont, CA: Wadsworth, 2000).
3. A.J. Beck, *Prisoners in 1999* (Washington, DC: Bureau of Justice Statistics, 2000).
4. Ibid.
5. H. Snyder and M. Sickmund, *Juvenile Offenders and Victims: 1999 National Report* (Washington, DC: Office of Juvenile Justice and Delinquency Prevention, 1999).
6. Ibid.
7. J. Petersilia, "Community Corrections," in *Crime: Public Policies for Crime Control,* eds. J.Q. Wilson and J. Petersilia (Oakland, CA: Institute for Contemporary Studies, 2002), 483.
8. Ibid., 484.
9. E.J. Latessa and H.E. Allen, *Corrections in the Community* (Cincinnati, OH: Anderson, 1997).
10. Bureau of Justice Statistics, *At a Glance* (Washington, DC: Bureau of Justice Statistics, 2000), 20.
11. Ibid.
12. J. Petersilia, "Community Corrections," in *Crime: Public Policies for Crime Control*, eds. J.Q. Wilson and J. Petersilia (Oakland, CA: Institute for Contemporary Studies, 2002), 486.
13. D.R. Longmire and B. Sims, *1995 Crime Poll: Texas and the Nation: Executive Summary* (Huntsville, TX: Sam Houston State University, Survey Research Program, Criminal Justice Center, 1995).
14. F. Cullen, B. Fisher, and B. Applegate, "Public Opinion about Punishment and Corrections," in *Crime and Justice: A Review of Research*, ed. M. Tonry (Chicago, IL: University of Chicago Press, 2000), 1–79.
15. Bureau of Justice Statistics, *Justice Expenditure and Employment Extracts* (Washington, DC: U.S. Department of Justice, 1993).

16. P. Langan, "Between Prison and Probation: Intermediate Sanctions," *Science* 264 (1994): 791–4.

17. C. Camp and G. Camp, *The Corrections Yearbook 1998* (Middletown, CT: Criminal Justice Institute, 1999).

18. Ibid.

19. T.R. Clear and A. Braga, "Community Corrections," in *Crime*, eds. J.Q. Wilson and J. Petersilia (San Francisco, CA: Institute for Contemporary Studies, 1995), 423.

20. J. Petersilia, "Community Corrections," in *Crime: Public Policies for Crime Control*, eds. J.Q. Wilson and J. Petersilia (Oakland, CA: Institute for Contemporary Studies, 2002), 488.

21. T. Bonczar and L. Glaze, *Probation and Parole in the United States, 1998* (Washington, DC: Bureau of Justice Statistics, 1999).

22. J. Petersilia, *Challenges of Prisoner Reentry and Parole in California* (Berkeley, CA: California Policy Research Center, 2000).

23. R.M. Carter, J. Robinson, and L. Wilkins, *The San Francisco Project: A Study of Federal Probation and Parole—Final Report* (Berkeley, CA: University of California Press, 1967); R.M. Carter and L.T. Wilkins, "Caseloads: Some Conceptual Models," in *Probation, Parole, and Community Corrections*, eds. R.M. Carter and L.T. Wilkins (New York: Wiley & Sons, 1976), 391–401.

24. E.H. Sutherland, D.R. Cressey, and D.F. Luckenbill, *Principles of Criminology*, 11th ed. (New York: General Hall, 1992), 460.

25. J. Petersilia, "Community Supervision: Trends and Critical Issues," *Crime and Delinquency* 31 (1985): 339–47; J. Petersilia, "Probation and Felony Offenders," *Federal Probation* 49 (1985): 4–9; J. Petersilia, S. Turner, J. Kahan, and J. Peterson, "Executive Summary of Rand's Study, 'Granting Felons Probation: Public Risks and Alternatives,'" *Crime and Delinquency* 31 (1985): 379–92.

26. P.A. Langan and M.A. Cunniff, *Recidivism of Felons on Probation, 1986–1989.* Bureau of Justice Statistics Special Report (Washington, DC: U.S. Department of Justice, 1992); J.T. Whitehead, "The Effectiveness of Felony Probation: Results from an Eastern State," *Justice Quarterly* 8 (1991): 525–43; see also M.R. Geerken and H.D. Hayes, "Probation and Parole: Public Risk and the Future of Incarceration Alternatives," *Criminology* 31 (1993): 549–64, especially p. 555, for an impressive pre-1993 summary of probationer failure rates.

27. M.R. Geerken and H.D. Hayes, "Probation and Parole: Public Risk and the Future of Incarceration Alternatives," *Criminology* 31 (1993): 549–64.

28. Ibid., 557.

29. A. Beck and B. Shipley, *Recidivism of Prisoners Released in 1983* (Washington, DC: Bureau of Justice Statistics, 1989).

30. Bureau of Justice Statistics, *Probation and Parole 1999—Press Release* (Washington, DC: U.S. Department of Justice, 2000).

31. P.A. Langan and M.A. Cuniff, *Recidivism of Felons on Probation, 1986–1989.* Bureau of Justice Statistics Special Report. (Washington, DC: U.S. Department of Justice, 1992); A. Beck and B. Shipley, *Recidivism of Prisoners Released in 1983* (Washington, DC: Bureau of Justice Statistics, 1989).

32. R.M. Carter, J. Robinson, and L. Wilkins, *The San Francisco Project: A Study of Federal Probation and Parole—Final Report* (Berkeley, CA: University of California Press, 1967).

33. M.A. Cunniff and M.K. Shilton, *Variations on Felony Probation: Persons under Supervision in 32 Urban and Suburban Counties* (Washington, DC: U.S. Department of Justice, Bureau of Justice Statistics, 1991).

34. J.L. Worrall, P. Schram, M. Newman, and E. Hayes, *Does Probation Work?: An Analysis of the Relationship between Caseloads and Crime Rates in California Counties* (Sacramento, CA: California Institute for County Government, 2001); J.L. Worrall, P. Schram, M. Newman, and E. Hayes, "An Analysis of the Relationship between Probation Caseloads and Property Crime Rates in California Counties," *Journal of Criminal Justice* 32 (2004): 231–41.

35. J. Petersilia, *When Prisoners Come Home: Parole and Prisoner Reentry* (New York: Oxford University Press, 2003).

36. Ibid.

37. A.J. Beck, *State and Federal Prisoners Returning to the Community: Findings from the Bureau of Justice Statistics* (Washington, DC: Bureau of Justice Statistics, 2000).

38. Ibid.

39. J. Petersilia, *When Prisoners Come Home: Parole and Prisoner Reentry* (New York: Oxford University Press, 2003).

40. Ibid, 102.

41. B. Western, J. Kling, and D. Weiman, "The Labor Market Consequences of Incarceration," *Crime and Delinquency* 47 (2001): 410–28; H.J. Holzer, *What Employers Want: Job Prospects for Less-Educated Workers* (New York: Sage, 1996).

42. J. Petersilia, *When Prisoners Come Home: Parole and Prisoner Reentry* (New York: Oxford University Press, 2003), 113.

43. Ibid., 105.

44. M.C. Love and S. Kuzma, *Civil Disabilities of Convicted Felons: A State-by-State Survey, October 1996* (Washington, DC: U.S. Department of Justice, 1997).

45. J. Petersilia, *When Prisoners Come Home: Parole and Prisoner Reentry* (New York: Oxford University Press, 2003), 105.

46. J. Petersilia, "A Decade of Experimenting with Intermediate Sanctions: What Have We Learned?" *Justice Research and Policy* 11 (1999): 9–24; J. Petersilia, *Challenges of Prisoner Reentry and Parole in California* (Berkeley, CA: California Policy Research Center, 2000).

47. J. Petersilia, "Community Corrections," in *Crime: Public Policies for Crime Control*, eds. J.Q. Wilson and J. Petersilia (Oakland, CA: Institute for Contemporary Studies, 2002), 494.

48. J. Hagan and R. Dinovitzer, "Collateral Consequences of Imprisonment for Children, Communities, and Prisoners," in *Prisons*, eds. M. Tonry and J. Petersilia (Chicago, IL: University of Chicago Press, 1999), 121–62.

49. J. Petersilia, "Community Corrections," in *Crime: Public Policies for Crime Control*, eds. J.Q. Wilson and J. Petersilia (Oakland, CA: Institute for Contemporary Studies, 2002), 494; see also J. Hagan and R. Dinovitzer, "Collateral Consequences of Imprisonment for Children, Communities, and Prisoners," in *Prisons*, eds. M. Tonry and J. Petersilia (Chicago, IL: University of Chicago Press, 1999), 121–62.

50. A. Beck, D. Gilliard, and L. Greenfeld, *Survey of State Prison Inmates, 1991* (Washington, DC: Bureau of Justice Statistics, 1993).

51. E. Anderson, *Streetwise: Race, Class, and Change in an Urban Community* (Chicago: University of Chicago Press, 1990), 4.

52. J. Petersilia, "Community Corrections," in *Crime: Public Policies for Crime Control*, eds. J.Q. Wilson and J. Petersilia (Oakland, CA: Institute for Contemporary Studies, 2002), 495.

53. T.M. Hammett, P. Harmon, and L.M. Maruschak, *1996-1997 Update: HIV/AIDS, STDs, and TB in Correctional Facilities* (Washington, DC: Bureau of Justice Statistics, 1999).

54. D.C. McDonald, "Medical Care in Prisons," in *Prisons*, eds. M. Tonry and J. Petersilia (Chicago: University of Chicago Press, 1999), 427–78.

55. J. Petersilia, "Community Corrections," in *Crime: Public Policies for Crime Control*, eds. J.Q. Wilson and J. Petersilia (Oakland, CA: Institute for Contemporary Studies, 2002), 498.

56. For more on this meeting approach, see E. McGarrell, D. Banks, and N. Hipple, "Community Meeting as a Tool in Inmate Reentry," *Justice Research and Policy* 5 (2003): 5–32.

57. E.F. McGarrell, C.R. Zimmerman, N.K. Hipple, N. Corsaro, and H. Perez, "The Roles of the Police in the Offender Reentry Process, in *Prisoner Reentry and Community Policing: Strategies for Enhancing Public Safety* (Washington, DC: Urban Institute, 2004), 19–53.

58. Ibid.

59. Ibid; also see J.M. Byrne, F.S. Taxman, and D. Young, *Emerging Roles and Responsibilities in the Reentry Partnership Initiative: New Ways of Doing Business* (Washington, DC: National Institute of Justice, 2000).

60. Ibid., 35–6.

61. Ibid., 36; also see F.S. Taxman, J.M. Byren, and D. Young, *Targeting for Reentry: Matching Needs and Services to Maximize Public Safety* (Washington, DC: Bureau of Government Research, 2000).

62. Ibid., 37.

63. M. Kurlychek and C. Kempinen, "Beyond Book Camp: The Impact of Aftercare on Offender Reentry," *Criminology and Public Policy* 5 (2006): 363–88.

64. J.A. Wilson and R.C. Davis, "Good Intentions Meet Hard Realities: An Evaluation of the Project Greenlight Reentry Program," *Criminology and Public Policy* 5 (2006): 303–38.

65. Grant Duwe, "Evaluating the Minnestoa Comprehensive Offender Reentry Plan (MCORP): Results from a Randomized Experiment," *Justice Quarterly* 29 (2012): 347–83.

66. T.G. Blomberg, "Widening the Net: An Anomaly in the Evaluation of Diversion Programs," in *Handbook of Criminal Justice Evaluation*, eds. M.W. Klein and K.S. Teilman (Beverly Hills, CA: Sage, 1980), 572–792.

67. M. Tonry and M. Lynch, "Intermediate Sanctions," in *Crime and Justice: A Review of Research*, ed. M. Tonry, Vol. 20 (Chicago: University of Chicago Press, 1996), 99–144.

68. S. Walker, *Sense and Nonsense about Crime and Drugs: A Policy Guide*, 5th ed. (Belmont, CA: Wadsworth, 2001).

69. D.L. MacKenzie, "Reducing the Criminal Activities of Known Offenders and Delinquents: Crime Prevention in the Courts and Corrections," in *Evidence-Based Crime Prevention*, eds. L.W. Sherman, D.P. Farrington, B.C. Welsh, and D.L. MacKenzie (New York: Routledge, 2002), 330–404.

70. B.S. Erwin, "Turning Up the Heat on Probationers in Georgia," *Federal Probation* 50 (1986): 17–24.

71. F.S. Pearson, *Research on New Jersey's Intensive Supervision Program* (Washington, DC: U.S. Department of Justice, National Institute of Justice, 1987); F. Pearson and A.G. Harper, "Contingent Intermediate Sentences: New Jersey's Intensive Supervision Program, *Crime and Delinquency* 36 (1990): 75–86.

72. J.M. Byrne and L.M. Kelly, *Evaluation of the Implementation and the Impact of the Massachusetts Intensive Probation Supervision Project: A User's Guide to the Machine-Readable Files and Documentation and Codebook* (Washington, DC: U.S. Department of Justice, National Institute of Justice, 1992); J.M. Byrne, A.J. Lurigio, C. Baird, G. Markley, D. Cochran, and G.S. Buck, "The Effectiveness of the New Intensive Supervision Programs," *Research in Corrections* 2(1989): full issue.

73. J. Petersilia and S. Turner, *Intensive Supervision Probation for High-Risk Offenders: Findings from Three California Experiments* (Santa Monica, CA: RAND, 1990); see also J. Petersilia and S. Turner, "An Evaluation of Intensive Probation in California," *Journal of Criminal Law and Criminology* 82 (1991): 610–58.

74. J. Petersilia and S. Turner, *Evaluating Intensive Supervision Probation/Parole: Results of a Nationwide Experiment* (Washington, DC: National Institute of Justice, 1993).

75. See, for example, J. Austin and P. Hardyman, *The Use of Early Parole with Electronic Monitoring to Control Prison Overcrowding: Evaluation of the Oklahoma Department of Corrections Pre-Parole Supervised Release with Electronic Monitoring* (unpublished report to the National Institute of Justice); A. Jolin and B. Stipack, *Clackamas County Community Corrections Intensive Drug Program: Program Evaluation Report* (Portland, OR: Portland State University, Department of Administration of Justice, 1991); E.J. Latessa, *A Preliminary Evaluation of the Cuyahoga County Adult Probation Department's Intensive Supervision Groups* (Cincinnati, OH: University of Cincinnati, 1991); C.J.Z. Mitchell and C. Butter, *Intensive Supervision/Early Release Parole* (Utah Department of Corrections, 1986); National Council on Crime and Delinquency, *Evaluation*

of the Florida Community Control Program (San Francisco, CA: National Council on Crime and Delinquency, 1991).

76. S.K. Jalbert, W. Rhodes, C. Flygare, and M. Kane, "Testing Probation Outcomes in an Evidence-Based Practice Setting: Reduced Caseload Size and Intensive Supervision Effectiveness," *Journal of Offender Rehabilitation* 49 (2010): 233–53; but see the following study by the same authors that found more technical violations in the treatment group: S.K. Jalbert and W. Rhodes, "Reduced Caseloads Improve Probation Outcomes," *Journal of Crime and Justice* 35 (2012): 221–38.

77. M.M. Moon and E.J. Latessa, *The Effectiveness of an Outpatient Drug Treatment Program on Felony Probationers* (paper presented at the annual meeting of the Academy of Criminal Justice Sciences, Kansas City, MO, 1993).

78. J. Petersilia and S. Turner, *Evaluating Intensive Supervision Probation/Parole: Results of a Nationwide Experiment* (Washington, DC: National Institute of Justice, 1993).

79. P.J. Hofer and B.S. Meierhoefer, *Home Confinement: An Evolving Sanction in the Federal Criminal Justice System* (Washington, DC: Federal Judicial Center, 1987).

80. N. Morris and M. Tonry, *Between Prison and Probation: Intermediate Punishment in a Rational Sentencing System* (New York: Oxford University Press, 1990).

81. D.J. Palumbo, M. Clifford, and Z.K. Snyder-Joy, "From Net Widening to Intermediate Sanctions: The Transformation of Alternatives to Incarceration from Benevolence to Malevolence," in *Smart Sentencing: The Emergence of Intermediate Sanctions*, eds. J.M. Byrne, A.J. Lurigio, and J. Petersilia (Newbury Park, CA: Sage, 1992), 229–44.

82. D. Gowen, "Overview of the Federal Home Confinement Program, 1988–1986," *Federal Probation* 64 (2000): 11–8.

83. Ibid.

84. See, for instance, S.J. Rackmill, "Analysis of Home Confinement as a Sanction," *Federal Probation* 58 (1994): 45–52.

85. For an example, see R.R. Gainey, B.K. Payne, and M. O'Toole, "The Relationship between Time in Jail, Time on Electronic Monitoring, and Recidivism: An Event History Analysis of a Jail-Based Program," *Justice Quarterly* 17 (2000): 733–52.

86. K.E. Courtright, B.L. Berg, and R.J. Mutchnick, "The Cost Effectiveness of Using House Arrest with Electronic Monitoring," *Federal Probation* 61 (1997): 19–22; R.J. Lilly, R.A. Ball, G.D. Curry, and R.C. Smith, "The Pride, Inc., Program: An Evaluation of 5 Years of Electronic Monitoring," *Federal Probation* 56 (1992): 42–7; R.J. Lilly, R.A. Ball, G.D. Curry, and J. McMullen, "Electronic Monitoring of the Drunk Driver: A Seven-Year Study of the Home Confinement Alternative," *Crime and Delinquency* 39 (1993): 462–84; D.J. Palumbo, M. Clifford, and Z.K. Snyder-Joy, "From Net Widening to Intermediate Sanctions: The Transformation of Alternatives to Incarceration from Benevolence to Malevolence," in *Smart Sentencing: The Emergence of Intermediate Sanctions*, eds. J.M. Byrne, A.J. Lurigio, and J. Petersilia (Newbury Park, CA: Sage, 1992), 229–94.

87. R. Enos, J.E. Holman, and M.E. Carroll, *Alternative Sentencing: Electronically Monitored Correctional Supervision*, 2nd ed. (Bristol, IN: Wyndam Hall Press, 1999), 74.

88. A.A. Finn and S. Muirhead-Steves, "The Effectiveness of Electronic Monitoring with Violent Male Parolees," *Justice Quarterly* 19 (2002): 293–312.

89. Ibid., 307.

90. S. Roy, "Five Years of Electronic Monitoring of Adults and Juveniles in Lake County, Indiana: A Comparative Study of Factors Related to Failure," *Journal of Crime and Justice* 20 (1997): 141–60.

91. R.R. Gainey, B.K. Payne, and M. O'Toole, "The Relationship between Time in Jail, Time on Electronic Monitoring, and Recidivism: An Event History Analysis of a Jail-Based Program," *Justice Quarterly* 17 (2000): 733–52.

92. K.E. Courtright, B.L. Berg, and R.J. Mutchnick, "Rehabilitation in the New Machine?: Exploring Drug and Alcohol Use and Variables Related to Success Among DUI Offenders Under Electronic Monitoring—Some Preliminary Outcomes," *International Journal of Offender Therapy and Comparative Criminology* 44 (2000): 293–311.

93. J. Bonta, S. Wallace-Capretta, and J. Rooney, "Can Electronic Monitoring Make a Difference?: An Evaluation of Three Canadian Programs," *Crime and Delinquency* 46 (2000): 61–75.

94. R.R. Gainey, B.K. Payne, and M. O'Toole, "The Relationship between Time in Jail, Time on Electronic Monitoring, and Recidivism: An Event History Analysis of a Jail-Based Program," *Justice Quarterly* 17 (2000): 733–52.

95. Martin Killias, Gillieron, Izumi Kissling, and Patrice Villettaz, "Community Services Versus Electronic Monitoring: What Works Better? Results of a Randomized Trial," *British Journal of Criminology* 50 (2010): 1155–70.

96. T.P. Cadigan, "Electronic Monitoring in Federal Pre-Trial Release," *Federal Probation* 55(1991): 31–3; K.W. Cooprider and J. Kerby, "A Practical Application of Electronic Monitoring at the Pretrial Stage," *Federal Probation* 54 (1990): 28–35.

97. M.T. Charles, "The Development of a Juvenile Electronic Monitoring Program," *Federal Probation* 53 (1989): 3–12; J.S. Clarkson and J.J. Weakland, "A Transitional Aftercare Model of Juveniles: Adapting Electronic Monitoring and Home Confinement," *Journal of Offender Monitoring* 4 (1991): 1–15.

98. J.M. Byrne, A.J. Lurigio, and M.A. Baird, "The Effectiveness of the New Intensive Supervision Programs," in *Research in Corrections*, ed. J. Petersilia, Vol. 2, No. 2 (Boulder, CO: National Institute of Corrections, 1989), 1–48; B.S. Erwin, *IPS with Electronic Monitoring Option* (Atlanta, GA: Georgia Department of Corrections, 1989).

99. R.R. Gainey, B.K. Payne, and M. O'Toole, "The Relationship between Time in Jail, Time on Electronic Monitoring, and Recidivism: An Event History Analysis of a Jail-Based Program," *Justice Quarterly* 17 (2000): 733–52.

100. Edna Erez, Peter R. Ibarra, William D. Bales, and Oren M. Gur, *GPS Monitoring Technologies and Domestic*

Violence: An Evaluation Study (Washington, DC: National Institute of Justice, 2012).

101. Stephen V. Gies, Randy Gainey, Marcia I. Cohen, Eoin Healy, Dan Duplantier, Martha Yeide, Alan Bekelman, Amanda Bobnis, and Michael Hopps, *Monitoring High-Risk Sex Offenders with GPS Technology: An Evaluation of the California Supervision Program* (Washington, DC: National Institute of Justice), 5–1.

102. D.L. MacKenzie, "Boot Camp Prisons: Components, Evaluations, and Empirical Issues," *Federal Probation* 54 (1990): 44–52.

103. See, for example, D.L. MacKenzie, R. Brame, D. MacDowall, and C. Souryal, "Boot Camp Prisons and Recidivism in Eight States," *Criminology* 33 (1995): 327–58; D.L. MacKenzie, J.W. Shaw, and V. Gowdy, *An Evaluation of Shock Incarceration in Louisiana* (Washington, DC: National Institute of Justice, 1993); D.L. MacKenzie and J.W. Shaw, "The Impact of Shock Incarceration on Technical Violations and New Criminal Activities," *Justice Quarterly* 10 (1993): 463–87; G.T. Flowers, T.S. Carr, and R.B. Ruback, *Special Alternative Incarceration Evaluation* (Atlanta, GA: Georgia Department of Corrections, 1991).

104. D.L. MacKenzie, D.B. Wilson, and S.B. Kider, "Effects of Correctional Boot Camps on Offending," *Annals of the American Academy of Political and Social Science* 578 (2001): 126–43.

105. D. MacKenzie, R. Brame, D. MacDowall, and C. Souryal, "Boot Camp Prisons and Recidivism in Eight States," *Criminology* 33 (1995): 327–58.

106. Ibid.

107. B.B. Benda, "Survival Analysis of Criminal Recidivism of Boot Camp Graduates Using Elements from General and Development Explanatory Models," *International Journal of Offender Therapy and Comparative Criminology* 47 (2003): 89–100.

108. M. Peters, *Evaluation of the Impact of Boot Camps for Juvenile Offenders: Denver Interim Report* (Washington, DC: U.S. Department of Justice, Office of Juvenile Justice and Delinquency Prevention, 1996); M. Peters, *Evaluation of the Impact of Boot Camps for Juvenile Offenders: Cleveland Interim Report* (Washington, DC: U.S. Department of Justice, Office of Juvenile Justice and Delinquency Prevention, 1996); M. Peters, *Evaluation of the Impact of Boot Camps for Juvenile Offenders: Mobile Interim Report* (Washington, DC: U.S. Department of Justice, Office of Juvenile Justice and Delinquency Prevention, 1996); J. Bottcher, T. Isorena, and M. Belnas, *Lead: A Boot Camp and Intensive Parole Program: An Impact Evaluation: Second Year Findings* (Sacramento, CA: Department of Youth Authority, Research Division, 1996).

109. G.F. Vito, "Developments in Shock Probation: A Review of Research Findings and Policy Implications," *Federal Probation* 48 (1984): 22–7.

110. J. Boudouris and B.W. Turnbull, "Shock Probation in Iowa," *Journal of Offender Counseling Services and Rehabilitation* 9 (1985): 53–67.

111. G.F. Vito and H.E. Allen, "Shock Probation in Ohio: Use of Base Expectancy Rates as an Evaluation Method," *Criminal Justice and Behavior* 7 (1980): 331–40.

112. See, for example, R.J. Michalowski and E.W. Bohlander, "The Application of Shock Probation in Judicial Practice," *International Journal of Offender Therapy and Comparative Criminology* 21 (1977): 41–51; D.M. Petersen and P.C. Friday, "Early Release from Incarceration: Race as a Factor in the Use of Shock Probation," *Journal of Criminal Law and Criminology* 1 (1975): 79–84; W. Ammer, "Shock Probation in Ohio: A New Concept in Corrections after Seven Years in the Courts," *Capital University Law Review* 3 (1974): 33–52.

113. H.E. Allen, R.P. Seiter, E.W. Carlson, H.H. Bowman, J.J. Grandfield, and N.J. Beran, *National Evaluation Program Phase I: Residential Inmate Aftercare, the State of the Art Summary* (Columbus, OH: Ohio State University, Program for the Study of Crime and Delinquency, 1976).

114. E.J. Latessa and H.E. Allen, "Halfway Houses and Parole: A National Assessment," *Journal of Criminal Justice* 10 (1982): 153–63.

115. D.G. Parent, J. Byrne, V. Tsarfaty, L. Valdae, and J. Esselman, *Day Reporting Centers*, Vols. 1 and 2 (Washington, DC: National Institute of Justice, 1995).

116. C. Marin, A.J. Lurigio, and D.E. Olson, "Examination of Rearrests and Reincarcerations among Discharged Day Reporting Center Clients," *Federal Probation* 67 (2003): 24–30; see also R. Sudipto and J.N. Grimes, "Adult Offenders in a Day Reporting Center: A Preliminary Study," *Federal Probation* 66 (2002): 44–50; D. McBride and C. VanderWaal, "Day Reporting Centers as an Alternative for Drug Using Offenders," *Journal of Drug Issues* 27 (1997): 379–97.

117. A. Craddock and L.A. Graham, "Recidivism as a Function of Day Reporting Center Participation," *Journal of Offender Rehabilitation* 34 (2001): 81–97.

118. L.M. Marciniak, "Addition of Day Reporting to Intensive Supervision Probation: A Comparison of Recidivism Rates," *Federal Probation* 64 (2000): 34–9.

119. K.I. Minor, J.B. Wells, and B. Jones, "Staff Perceptions of the Work Environment in Juvenile Group Home Settings: A Study of Social Climate," *Journal of Offender Rehabilitation* 38 (2004): 17–30.

120. B. Haghighi and A. Lopez, "Success/Failure of Group Home Treatment Programs for Juveniles," *Federal Probation* 57 (1993): 53–8.

121. R.J. Mutchnick and M. Fawcett, "Group Home Environments and Victimization of Resident Juveniles," *International Journal of Offender Therapy and Comparative Criminology* 35 (1991): 126–42.

122. A.L. Shostack and R.M. Quane, "Youths Who Leave Group Homes," *Public Welfare* 46 (1988): 29–36.

123. K.M. Kingston, "Comparative Evaluation of Community-Based Group Homes for Delinquents" (unpublished doctoral dissertation. Medford, MA: Tufts University, 1982).

124. J. Hearen and D. Shichor, "Mass Media and Delinquency Prevention: The Case of 'Scared Straight,'" *Deviant Behavior* 5 (1984): 375–86.

125. See, for example, wild-side.com/scared.Html.

126. R.V. Lewis, "Scared Straight—California Style: Evaluation of the San Quentin Squires Program," *Criminal Justice and Behavior* 10 (1983): 209–26.

127. A. Petrosino, C. Turpin-Petrosino, and J.O. Finckenauer, "Well-Meaning Programs Can Have Harmful Effects!: Lessons from Experiments of Programs Such as Scared Straight," *Crime and Delinquency* 46 (2000): 354–79.

128. C. Cavender, "Scared Straight: Ideology and the Media," *Journal of Criminal Justice* 9 (1981): 431–39.

129. J.C. Buckner and M. Chesney-Lind, "Dramatic Cures for Juvenile Crime: An Evaluation of a Prison-Run Delinquency Prevention Program," *Criminal Justice and Behavior* 10 (1983): 227–47; R.V. Lewis, "Scared Straight—California Style: Evaluation of the San Quentin Squire Program," *Criminal Justice and Behavior* 10 (1983): 209–26.

130. D.L. MacKenzie, "Reducing the Criminal Activities of Known Offenders and Delinquents: Crime Prevention in the Courts and Corrections," in *Evidence-Based Crime Prevention*, eds. L.W. Sherman, D.P. Farrington, B.C. Welsh, and D.L. MacKenzie (New York: Routledge, 2002), 341.

131. J. Petersilia, "A Decade of Experimenting with Intermediate Sanctions; What Have We Learned?" *Federal Probation* 62 (1998): 2, 3.

Rehabilitation, Treatment, and Job Training

LEARNING OBJECTIVES

▦ Define and provide examples of rehabilitation for criminal offenders.

▦ Discuss the effectiveness of rehabilitation as crime control policy.

▦ Summarize the research on the effects of drug treatment.

▦ Summarize the research on the effects of sex offender treatment.

▦ Identify various job training interventions and summarize the effectiveness of each approach.

This chapter takes a hard look at rehabilitation, treatment, and job training, approaches to the crime problem that are decidedly less punitive than some of those we have considered earlier in the book. There was a time when each of these attempts to control and prevent crime were considered failures, but as Cullen has observed, "the empirical evidence is fairly convincing—and growing stronger as time passes—that treatment interventions are capable of decreasing recidivism."[1] The public is also changing its views and, for the most part, is highly supportive of treatment. Moreover, many Americans favor the expansion of treatment services, especially in prisons and even more so for juvenile offenders.[2] Although it is true that we remain a fairly conservative lot with respect to crime, there seems to be another side to Americans' thoughts on how to deal with criminals.

A MOVEMENT TOWARD THE LEFT

Before we delve into the scientific evidence concerning treatment, rehabilitation, and job training, it is important to set this chapter's material apart from that covered in earlier chapters. First, think in terms of sentencing goals. Whereas much of the material that was covered in earlier chapters favored the punishment-oriented goals of incapacitation, retribution, and deterrence, the approaches that are covered in this chapter shun such goals. Instead, treatment, rehabilitation, and job training are concerned with "cures" and "fixes," not just attempts to lock offenders up and make them suffer through drawn-out periods of confinement. This chapter therefore signals a movement from the right (the conservative side of the political spectrum) to the left (the liberal side).

One can also distinguish this chapter's content from that presented in earlier chapters by thinking in terms of two broad criminological perspectives, which were introduced in Chapter 2. One view is the so-called classical (classicalist) perspective, which views criminal acts in the context of individual offenders. The other is the so-called positivist perspective, which views crime in an environmental context. To a large extent, the programs and policies that are discussed in this chapter acknowledge the influence of people's surroundings on their behavior. As an example, drug treatment may arm offenders with the wherewithal to "just say no" when confronted with peer pressure to experiment with illicit substances.

Although rehabilitation, treatment, and job training programs acknowledge that the environment can exert harmful consequences on individuals, none of these approaches seeks to alter the environment per se. Instead, we are concerned in this chapter with attempts to alter individual behavior. Attempts to alter the environment itself—be it a community, a school, or even a family—are covered in the last section of this book. As shown in Figure 11.1, this chapter is concerned with methods of targeting individual offenders (and other at-risk people) on the assumption that their life circumstances might be to blame for their criminal acts.

Some Definitions

It is important to clearly define what is meant by each of the terms listed in this chapter's title. Researchers often use one term, namely, rehabilitation, to refer to every step that officials take to treat, train, and otherwise intervene in offenders' lives. By contrast, this chapter's title expressly refers to three separate methods of dealing with crime. The decision to break the material up in this fashion simply reflects the author's belief that a

	Target of Intervention	
	Individuals	**Groups or Communities**
Classical Theory	Deterrence policies Imprisonment Other tough sanctions	"Weeding" programs Order maintenance policing
Positivist Theory	Rehabilitation Treatment Job training	"Seeding" programs Community development Mobilization efforts

FIGURE 11.1   Understanding Crime Control with Reference to Underlying Theories and Targets of Interventions

vast literature can be more easily understood when it is broken into parts. Yet a common thread runs throughout the rehabilitative, treatment, and training-oriented programs that are discussed in the next few pages: "A planned correctional intervention that targets for change internal and/or social criminogenic factors with the goal of reducing recidivism and, where possible, of improving other aspects of an offender's life."[3]

CRIMINALS ARE NOT CREATED EQUAL

People often opine that rehabilitation and treatment programs work for some people and not others. They further claim that both of these methods of dealing with criminals are doomed to fail without willing participants. There is a measure of truth to such statements, but to present a more complete picture, it is worth digressing for a moment to point out that there is an entire field of study devoted to such concerns. In particular, researchers have shown that an offender's level of risk, need, and responsivity to treatment and rehabilitation are important factors.

Risk

Although social scientists have not always been accurate with respect to predicting future criminal activity (see, for instance, the discussion of selective incapacitation in Chapter 7), it is clear that certain individuals are at a higher risk of future criminal activity than others. For example, people with antisocial attitudes, criminal associations, previous convictions and arrests, family problems, substance abuse, and other such afflictions tend to do worse at treatment than do people with "clean" backgrounds.[4] Accordingly, researchers have developed a number of risk assessment instruments, such as the Level of Service Inventory and the Hare Psychopathy Checklist, to predict—with some success—a person's likelihood of reoffending.[5]

   The realization that some offenders are at a higher risk of reoffending and/or treatment failures has also led researchers to conclude that variations in treatment intensity can make all the difference. Andrews and his colleagues found, for instance, that recidivism is reduced when high-risk offenders receive intensive treatment services rather than traditional ones.[6] They also found negligible treatment benefits when intensive treatment was provided to low-risk offenders. In sum, we know that offenders are not all created equal. Some are at higher risk for future crime than others, and treatment intensity generally needs to be varied according to an offender's risk level.[7]

Needs

Criminals (not to mention everyone else) have a variety of different needs. They might need better social skills, an education, substance abuse treatment, housing, and so on. But for treatment and rehabilitation to be effective, programs must target need factors that are most directly linked to criminal activity. These are known as **criminogenic needs**. Another way to understand criminogenic needs is to think of them as the attributes of offenders that are directly linked to criminal behavior.

criminogenic needs: offender attributes that need to be changed in order to reduce the likelihood of offending.

Some of the strongest links to criminal activity are antisocial attitudes, associations with delinquent peers, and skill deficiencies.[8] Offenders might therefore *need* to be relieved of their antisocial attitudes, change their associations, and improve their skills.[9] This chapter will discuss a number of treatment and rehabilitation modalities that are aimed at accommodating offenders' needs. We will also discuss at length job training, which is clearly intended to address offenders' skill deficiencies.

Responsivity

So far in this section, we have seen that risk and need are important factors that can bear on whether treatment or rehabilitation will make a difference in people's lives. Continuing in this vein, research also shows that some people are more *responsive* than others to treatment and rehabilitation. Such "responsivity" has been placed into two categories: general and specific.[10] General **responsivity** is concerned with external factors, such as treatment method (e.g., role-playing versus group discussions) and staff skills.[11] With respect to staff skills, one researcher has observed that "a socially skilled, empathetic and highly verbal staff member may be more likely to actively engage offenders to deal with their problems."[12] Specific responsivity, by contrast, is concerned with people's internal characteristics. Differences in learning styles, intelligence, literacy, anxiety, attention, and the like can have important implications for the effectiveness of a treatment protocol.[13]

responsivity: in the crime control context, the ability of an offender to respond positively to a treatment-related intervention.

REHABILITATION

Rehabilitation amounts to a planned intervention that is intended to change offenders for the better. Researchers have studied four distinct rehabilitation methods at great length. These amount to targeting cognitive skills, anger management, improving victim awareness, and life skills training. These methods fall within the definitions of rehabilitation that were just presented because they target the internal workings of the criminal mind—all in an effort to alter future criminal behavior. Doubtless, there are many other rehabilitative techniques out there, but those that are covered in this section have been subjected to the largest amount of research. Let us see what the evidence shows.

rehabilitation: a planned intervention that is intended to change offenders for the better.

Targeting Cognitive Skills

Cognitive skills are people's mental processes and how they perceive the world around them, solve problems, and make decisions. Cognitive psychologists study people's cognitive skills, identify weaknesses and shortcomings, and then attempt to develop effective treatment regimens. Jean Piaget's work on the moral development of children[14] is one of the pioneering studies in this area. Criminologists have also been attracted to the field of cognitive psychology. For example, Kohlberg's theory of moral development[15] links people's moral development to criminality. Policymakers have also heeded psychologists' calls and have pushed for cognitive therapies aimed specifically at criminals.

There are a host of methods that professionals use to minimize people's dysfunctional attitudes, beliefs, and thought patterns. The field of cognitive psychology has itself split into several subdisciplines. But as one researcher recently pointed out, these diverse methods fall into two relatively distinct categories.[16] The first, which we will call *morals training,* suggests that people can be trained to act in a less morally depraved manner. The second, which we will call *reasoning training,* suggests that people can be trained to make better decisions, weighing the costs and benefits associated with their actions.

MORALS TRAINING. Lawrence Kohlberg, a famous psychologist, argued that people travel through various stages of moral development. He also claimed that during these stages, they make decisions and judgments about what is right and wrong. Kohlberg further argued that criminals might exhibit a different set of morals than law-abiding citizens do.[17] In the 1960s, he and his colleagues found that some criminals were at a lower level in their moral judgment development than were noncriminals, and some recent criminological studies show a link between moral reasoning and criminal behavior.[18]

Unfortunately, there is no agreement as to what constitutes moral behavior. One person might think that personal consumption of marijuana is perfectly acceptable behavior; another might think that using such a substance is amoral and totally unacceptable. Even so, a large majority of people can agree that some actions are morally reprehensible. Sexual assault on a child, for example, is an act that almost all people are unwilling to tolerate. Morals training proceeds under this sense of agreement. It assumes that there is some more or less agreed-upon moral framework that can be pushed on certain people.

Morals training—and virtually all related methods of rehabilitation and treatment—also assumes that people can be changed. That is, it assumes that people's thought processes and attitudes can be permanently altered. Such an assumption is doomed to fail if participants in morals therapy simply go through the motions, with no intentions of changing. Fortunately, the evidence suggests that morals training can exert some positive influence in the lives of criminals. It does not always work and will probably never work for certain offenders, but the evidence is nonetheless encouraging.

A well-known variety of morals therapy is **Moral Reconation Therapy (MRT®).**[19] The term *reconation* stems from *conation,* which means "the aspect of personality characterized by a conscious willing."[20] *Conation* is a popular term in psychology, and the addition of "re" before it suggests an alteration to people's ability to make conscious decisions. MRT "attempts to facilitate a change in the client's process of conscious decision-making. Thus, MRT seeks to increase a client's awareness of decision-making and to enhance appropriate behavior through development of higher moral reasoning."[21]

The MRT treatment curriculum was federally trademarked in the early 1990s, and all of its works and materials are copyrighted. As of this writing, Correctional Counseling, Inc. of Memphis, Tennessee, holds a contract for all sales and distribution of MRT materials in the United States. Therefore, MRT is not free for all interested parties to use. There is a cost associated with it, and the treatment curriculum is marketed by a private company. Even so, MRT therapy has become quite popular. According to one source, MRT therapy has been used on some 400,000 individuals.[22]

Moral Reconation Therapy (MRT): a program that "attempts to facilitate a change in the client's process of conscious decision-making" and "seeks to increase a client's awareness of decision-making and to enhance appropriate behavior through development of higher moral reasoning."

Insofar as MRT materials are available only for a fee, it was deemed impractical to present them here. In addition, MRT therapy differs for specific types of individuals, not all of whom need to be criminals. But one source offers a general description of the MRT process:

> MRT programs utilize workbooks designed for the specific type of client and particular program characteristics. . . . MRT is conducted in open-ended, ongoing groups where participants present a series of homework assignments outlined in the specific MRT workbook utilized. . . . Clients typically make drawings or write very short answers to specific requirements from the workbooks. The essential "treatment" takes place when the participant "shares" his or her work with the group. . . . Depending on the specific program's focus and purpose, MRT groups meet a minimum of once per month to 5 times per week. . . . Facilitators of MRT groups maintain a focus on clients completing and presenting MRT steps or modules in the group and decide on the suitability of a client's work based on objective criteria outlined in MRT training.[23]

MRT has been used frequently with several types of criminal offenders, including those who have been accused of drug use, drunk driving, domestic violence, and sex offenses. Some 70 studies have been published, focusing on everything from cognitive changes and recidivism following MRT treatment to MRT therapy's effects on misconduct and disciplinary infractions on prisoners, parolees, and probationers—both in and out of institutions. It should be pointed out that MRT's developer has published most of the studies, but his research, together with the work published by other independent parties, paints this method of cognitive therapy in a favorable light.

Several studies have looked at MRT therapy's effect on recidivism in drunk drivers.[24] With few exceptions, the studies show lower incarceration levels and fewer non–drunk driving arrests for program participants in comparison to a control group. But after a 30-month follow-up, both the treatment and control groups tend to show similar levels of drunk-driving arrests. Similar outcomes are evident for other types of drug users, especially in a drug court environment (see Chapter 8 for more attention to drug courts).[25]

Four of five studies concerned with recidivism among probationers and parolees showed significantly fewer rearrests and lower reincarceration rates compared to control groups.[26] As for disciplinary infractions in prisons and jails, eight of eight studies show reductions in disciplinary infractions following MRT treatment. The studies were experimental, containing a total of 6,296 MRT participants and over 50,000 controls.[27] Some research also shows promising evidence that MRT positively affects domestic violence offenders[28] and both delinquent and at-risk juveniles,[29] but there are relatively few studies on these types of individuals.[30] MRT's effects on sex offenders also remain unclear.

REASONING TRAINING. Almost all prisons and jails provide some form of rehabilitation or treatment for inmates. Probation and parole officers, despite being saddled with large caseloads, also manage to steer some of their clients toward the services they need. But rehabilitation and treatment alone are not always effective. For example, simply instilling a sense of morals in a person might not change behavior permanently. Likewise, methadone maintenance for a heroin addict might not do much to halt illegal drug use. Research shows, instead, that rehabilitation and treatment work together with some form of reasoning therapy.[31] That is, the most effective methods of rehabilitation do something to improve offenders' ability to make decisions.

Reasoning training assumes that there are some people who do not know how to make proper decisions, and that such people act impulsively without a thought to the possible consequences of their actions. Reasoning training further assumes that people can be trained to make proper decisions. Proper decision making, according to advocates of reasoning training, occurs when people think through the possible consequences of their actions and weigh likely costs and benefits. Reasoning training attempts to improve people's ability to make proper decisions, thus leading to more appropriate future behavior.

There is an irony associated with reasoning training. Although such training falls under the banner of rehabilitation, it basically amounts to training people so that they can be deterred, an inherently conservative strategy. In other words, reasoning training looks much like a tough-on-crime strategy in disguise.

Despite reasoning training's possibly traditional, deterrence-oriented underpinnings, it is arguably necessary. There are many people who do not think about their actions. Such brashness can have many harmful consequences. For example, buying a new car simply because you can make the payment this month doesn't mean that you will be able to make the payment at the same time next year. There is something to be said about engaging in careful decision making. Unfortunately, however, the evidence is mixed with respect to reasoning training.

Reasoning training comes in several guises. The most-researched method of reasoning training is known as **Reasoning and Rehabilitation (R&R)**.[32] The R&R training curriculum was developed by Robert Ross and Elizabeth Fabiano and was first used to treat high-risk probationers in Ontario, Canada. Based on several cognitive theories, the training program relies on audiovisual presentations, reasoning exercises, games, and group discussions in an effort to change clients' decision-making processes. The program comprises thirty-five 90- to 120-minute sessions. Eight specific subject modules are used to teach specific skills. They appear in Figure 11.2. The training begins with problem-solving training and concludes with values enhancement.

Reasoning and Rehabilitation (R&R): a cognitive-behavioral program designed to teach cognitive and others skills that are necessary for prosocial functioning in society.

R&R appears to work rather well for low-risk offenders, but the program's effectiveness is less apparent with high-risk offenders. For example, one pair of researchers found that low-risk R&R participants were reconvicted just over half as often as a control group.[33] But among high-risk offenders, R&R participants had more reconvictions (21 percent) than did the control group (14 percent). Other studies show less recidivism, fewer parole/probation revocations, and fewer readmissions among R&R participants compared to controls,[34] but there remains a lack of consensus with respect to the training's effectiveness. In fact, it appears that the effectiveness (or the lack thereof) of R&R hinges on the outcomes under study. Depending on whether one examines reconvictions, reincarcerations, rearrests, completion rates, revocations, or readmissions, the results differ.[35]

Another example of reasoning training can be found in the Corrective Thinking, or Truthought, Program. In the 1970s, researchers Yochelson and Samenow worked closely with 30 criminals who had been either found not guilty by reason of insanity or deemed incompetent to stand trial. They found that such individuals exhibited distinct thinking patterns and that among these were certain "thinking errors." Building on their research, Rogie Spon built the Truthought training curriculum (called "Charting a New Course"). Much like R&R, it teaches participants to make appropriate decisions and give thought to the consequences of their actions. Truthought further teaches participants to work through various "barriers in thinking." For example, one of the barriers in thinking occurs when criminals perceive themselves as victims (i.e., have a victim stance). The training encourages offenders to take responsibility for their actions.

Module	Description of Module and Cognitive Skill Components
Problem Solving	Offenders are taught to recognize when a problem exists, define a problem verbally, identify feelings associated with problems, separate facts from opinions, assemble necessary information to generate alternative problem solutions, consider all of the consequences, and select the best solution.
Social Skills	Offenders are taught the skills to act pro-socially rather than anti-socially. The skills include: asking for help, expressing a complaint, persuading others, responding to others' feelings, and responding to persuasion, failure, contradictory messages, and complaints. Five steps are used to teach these skills: pre-training, modeling, role-playing, feedback, and transfer of training (using the skills in real life situations).
Negotiation Skills	Offenders are asked to identify their own method of managing interpersonal conflict. They are taught skills to compromise in situations of conflict, specifically by identifying options to problems, identifying consequences to various options, and simulating the information through the use of role plays, practice, and feedback.
Managing Emotions	Offenders are taught the skills to manage their emotions when responding to interpersonal conflict. These skills can prevent them from responding to conflict out of anger or other strong emotional states. Specifically, they focus on recognizing their emotions in these contexts, and using skills such as monitored breathing and self-talk to control their emotions.
Creative Thinking	This module responds to the basic cognitive deficit in an offender's ability to develop alternative views of situations and alternative methods of solving problems or achieving goals. It teaches the offender systematic thinking processes.
Values Enhancement	Offenders are challenged to examine their beliefs and consider their points of view along with the viewpoints of others. No right or wrong values are promulgated in this module. The primary method used to examine values is the use of moral dilemma scenarios, however, values and beliefs are discussed throughout the program as they arise.
Critical Reasoning	In this module, offenders are taught to think carefully, logically, and rationally. This module is designed to increase offenders' intellectual curiosity, objectivity, flexibility, sound judgment, open-mindedness, decisiveness, and respect for other points of view.

FIGURE 11.2   R&R Program Modules and Description of Cognitive Skills Taught

Source: S. Pullen, *Evaluation of the Reasoning & Rehabilitation Cognitive Skills Development Program as Implemented in Juvenile ISP in Colorado* (Denver: Colorado Division of Criminal Justice, 1996).

Truthought was developed in the late 1990s and has not been subjected to much research. However, at least one study suggests that correctional interventions that are based on the Truthought model can be effective.[36] Participants appear to be arrested less often than controls after completion of the program.

Anger Management

Some people exhibit higher anger levels than others. This might be especially true for criminals. Anger management programs have been used to teach offenders to keep their anger in check. Anger management is rarely used as a method of rehabilitation unto itself. Instead, it is usually part of a larger rehabilitation or treatment regimen. Even so, we will focus on whether anger management training itself reduces recidivism and/or leads to other positive outcomes.

Most anger management programs have been used for domestic abusers and drug addicts. With respect to the former, one study shows that subjects who had completed a domestic violence anger management treatment program scored lower on a violent behavior inventory, but recidivism was not examined.[37] In another study of anger management for drug offenders, a team of researchers concluded that those who completed the treatment reoffended at a lower rate than individuals in a control group.[38]

Outside the realm of domestic violence and substance abuse, anger management programs have been used for female prison inmates,[39] young males,[40] violent offenders,[41] parents accused of child abuse,[42] adult prisoners[43] (even murderers![44]), probationers,[45] and other types of offenders. Is it effective when used on such offenders? Most available studies show that anger management either doesn't work or reduces people's levels of anger as measured by various psychological testing instruments.[46] Very few researchers have found that anger management leads to a reduction in recidivism.[47] The studies that do show a reduction in recidivism tend to suffer from weak research designs.[48] Therefore, some people have called for additional research in this area.[49]

Improving Victim Awareness

It is safe to say that many criminals don't give a second thought to the effects of their actions on victims. Victim awareness programs have emerged in response to this lack of concern. The hope is that victim awareness training will lead offenders to appreciate the victim's experience and otherwise understand the impact of their behavior on real people. It is further hoped that victim awareness training will improve offenders' empathy and their understanding of what people go through after being victimized.[50] Victim awareness training has been used as part of a larger restorative justice program (see Chapter 8), but it has also been used by itself to alter offenders' thinking with respect to victims. It has become especially popular for drunk drivers and first-time juvenile offenders.

Unfortunately, not much research has been conducted on victim awareness programs. The only available research has been concerned with so-called victim impact panels (VIPs), which bring victims of drunk driving face to face with drunk drivers. Here is one description of the VIP process:

> A Victim Impact Panel is a group of three or four victims who speak briefly about an impaired driving crash in which they were injured, or in which a loved one was killed or injured, and how it impacted their lives. They do not blame or judge those who listen. They simply tell their stories, describing how their lives and the lives of their families and friends were affected by the crash. . . . The purpose of the panels is to individualize and humanize the consequences of impaired driving, to change attitudes and behaviors, and to deter impaired driving recidivism. Panels also give victims a healing opportunity to share their stories in a meaningful way.[51]

One study of a VIP in California and Oregon showed mixed effects.[52] For example, there was more reckless driving or hit-and-run offenses in the treatment group during the follow-up period but fewer drunk-driving incidents within a year following treatment. Another study shows that VIPs affect offenders' attitudes but not necessarily their empathy toward victims, which is the key target of such interventions.[53] The authors of another more recent study concluded that the panels might reduce drunk-driving recidivism but mostly in the short term.[54] In their words:

> The overall findings suggest that VIPs may reduce DUI recidivism. The results of the five-year follow-up of DUI offenders show that those who participated in the VIP program were much less likely to become DUI recidivists than those who did not attend a VIP session. As would be expected, the results show that there is a diminishment or extinguishment of the VIP effect after the second year. In years three through five, the VIP and comparison group subjects were largely similar with respect to DUI recidivism.[55]

Life Skills Training

life skills: the tools people use to overcome challenges. Examples include drug resistance skills, personal self-management, and general social skills.

Everyone faces difficult decisions and choices throughout their lives. Unfortunately, some people lack the ability to make the appropriate decisions and choices when the time arises. This ability refers, generally, to life skills. **Life skills** consist of the tools people use to overcome life's little challenges. Researchers have identified three specific types of life skills.[56] First, drug resistance skills are usually taught to people at a young age so that they choose clean and sober lifestyles. Drug Abuse Resistance Training (DARE) is a prime example of this approach. It is discussed further in Chapter 13.

The second type of life skills, more relevant in the present context, is personal self-management. Personal self-management is concerned with such things as a person's self-image and understanding of how he or she is influenced by others. It is also concerned with analyzing problem situations, evaluating consequences associated with action, minimizing stress and anxiety, and viewing life challenges in a positive light. The third type of life skills consists of people's general social skills, their ability to interact with others productively and demonstrate assertiveness and confidence (as opposed to passivity and aggression) when surrounded by other people.

One of the most extensive life skills training curriculums is called, not surprisingly, Life Skills Training; it was designed by Gilbert J. Botvin. His program has generally been used with elementary school students and junior high and high school students and has received accolades from the National Institute on Drug Abuse, the U.S. Department of Education, the American Medical Association, and several other organizations. The curriculum has also been evaluated (by Dr. Botvin[57] and independently by others) and appears to reduce criminal activity among juveniles—especially drug use.[58]

It is one thing to teach life skills to noncriminal adolescents. What about criminals? Researchers in San Diego evaluated prison-based life skills training.[59] Inmates were randomly assigned to treatment and control groups. The treatment group received the training; the control group did not. The researchers found that life skills participants, compared to those in the control group, had fewer rearrests and reconvictions after completing the program.[60] But in an equally sophisticated study, another team of researchers was unable to conclude that life skills training worked.[61] They found that life skills training participants were reconvicted *more* than people who received basic cognitive training, but they also found that life skills participants fared better than a "probation only" control group. To explain these seemingly contradictory findings, researchers have concluded that the effects of life skills training vary considerably depending on the population under study.[62]

Does It Work?

The rehabilitation programs that were considered in this section included cognitive skills training, anger management, victim awareness training, and life skills training. There is some overlap between the techniques, and each is an attempt to alter people's thinking patterns. Surprisingly little research has been conducted in this area, and more randomized experiments are needed (and more attention to recidivism, not scores on psychological testing instruments), but the evidence from this section is more encouraging than the research on heavy-handed crime control methods that were discussed in earlier chapters. For example, both morals and reasoning training appear to work with low-level offenders. Anger management might work for some offenders, but victim awareness is difficult to instill. Finally, life skills training might work, but research findings to date have been contradictory. These statements are far from enthusiastically supportive of rehabilitation, but at least they are not as flatly against rehabilitation as researchers are of putting offenders away in prison for long periods of time.

TREATMENT

The term **treatment** used in this section conveys a method of dealing with people who are "addicted" to crime. The best-known (and best-researched) form of addiction in criminal justice is of course drug addiction. It is difficult to dispute that people who are hooked on controlled substances, especially illegal drugs, need treatment to overcome their addiction. Most people also agree that prison alone does little to reduce offenders' dependence on drugs. Accordingly, what we focus on in this section are methods of "curing" people who are addicted to drugs—both in and out of prison.

treatment: as distinguished from rehabilitation, a method of changing for the better people who are "addicted" to particular illegal behaviors, such as illicit drug consumption.

Drug addicts are not the only criminals who have a difficult time desisting from illegal behavior. The literature shows that sex offenders are among the most likely to continue a pattern of illegal behavior. The construct of sexual addiction has even been used to explain sex offender behavior.[63] In response to this, treatment programs for sex offenders sometimes mirror those for drug offenders insofar as they seek to alleviate the offender's dependence on sexually illegal behavior.[64] Accordingly, we begin by reviewing the literature concerned with drug treatment's effectiveness; then we shift our focus to treatment methods for sex offenders.

Treating Drug Addicts

Drug treatment for criminals has, at best, a low priority, given our nation's thirst for locking up criminals with little attention to their individual needs.[65] Even in the face of a host of studies showing that criminal activity and the use of drugs (legal and illegal) go hand in hand,[66] precious little drug treatment takes place in America's correctional institutions. For example, during 1998, there were 95,323 drug offenders under federal supervision, but only about one-third of such offenders participated in drug treatment during that year (see Table 11.1).[67] But a growing body of research is showing that drug treatment is highly effective, especially if it continues over time.[68] And research shows that treatment can work even when offenders want no part of it.[69] As we saw in Chapter 6, for example, forced treatment through deferred sentencing can lead to a significant reduction in recidivism. Here, though, we turn to drug treatment without an express prosecution component.

TABLE 11.1 Inmate Participation in Drug Abuse Treatment Over Time

Program	1990	1991	1992	1993	1994*	1995	1996	1997	1998
Drug Education	5,446	7,644	12,500	12,646	11,592	11,681	12,460	12,960	12,002
Non Residential			644	1,320	1,974	2,136	3,552	4,733	5,038
Residential	441	1,236	1,135	3,650	3,755	4,839	5,445	7,895	10,006
Community Transition			123	480	800	3,176	4,083	5,315	6,951

Program	1999	2000	2001	2002	2003	2004	2005	2006	2007
Drug Education	12,460	15,649	17,216	17,924	20,930	22,105	22,776	23,006	23,596
Non Residential	6,535	7,931	10,827	11,506	12,023	13,014	14,224	13,697	14,392
Residential	10,816	12,541	15,441	16,243	17,578	18,278	18,027	17,442	17,549
Community Transition	7,386	8,450	11,319	13,107	15,006	16,517	16,503	15,466	15,432

Program	2008	2009	2010	2011	Total
Drug Education	23,230	30,775	47,885	41,243	417,693
Non Residential	14,208	14,613	14,507	15,211	182,095
Residential	17,523	18,732	18,868	18,527	255,967
Community Transition	15,466	16,123	16,912	16,873	206,625

*In fiscal year 1994, the drug abuse education policy changed to allow for a waiver if an inmate volunteered for and entered the residential drug abuse treatment program. In addition, data for community transition drug abuse treatment was tabulated by average daily population.

Source: Federal Bureau of Prisons, *Annual Report on Substance Abuse Treatment Programs Fiscal Year 2011* (Washington, DC: Bureau of Prisons, 2011).

IN PRISON. One example of in-prison drug treatment occurs in so-called therapeutic communities, or milieus. The National Institute on Drug Abuse describes therapeutic communities in this way:

> [They] are drug-free residential settings that use a hierarchical model with treatment stages that reflect increased levels of personal and social responsibility. Peer influence, mediated through a variety of group processes, is used to help individuals learn and assimilate social norms and develop more effective social skills.[70]

Some evidence suggests that in-prison therapeutic communities lead to reductions in continued drug use. For example, one team of researchers found that male and female inmates who participated in the therapeutic community model had fewer arrests than did offenders who received either counseling alone or no treatment.[71] Several other studies of the therapeutic community approach to drug treatment show that it works well in comparison to other alternatives.[72] But there are obviously other methods of drug treatment that are provided to prison inmates. Some examples are listed in Figure 11.3.

It is also true that there are many different types of drugs and that treatment effectiveness varies considerably depending on the type of drug targeted. Indeed, there are many other considerations that bear on drug treatment effectiveness—so many that a complete review of the literature in this area would be nothing short of a Herculean task. But it is still possible to identify key findings associated with drug treatment in the criminal justice system.[73]

Type of Treatment	Approach
Detoxification	Where possible, remove drugs from system through detoxification as a first step before effective drug treatment can or should be undertaken.
Self-help groups	Peer support and problem confrontation in a group setting.
Drug testing	Deterrence and maintenance.
Education	Raise awareness of and understanding about a variety of topics, ranging from effects of certain drugs to illogical thinking patterns.
Individual counseling	Psychological counseling in a one-on-one setting, relying on any of a wide range of psychological approaches/modalities (behavioral, psychoanalytic, etc.)
Group counseling	Counseling in a group setting, with a focus on life skills rehearsal, role reversal, and stress management.
Outpatient drug-free	Can include a wide range of approaches, including counseling, education, self-help, 12-step, cognitive behavior therapy.
Milieu therapy	Intensive counseling and separate living conditions—more intensive than individual counseling but less intensive than therapeutic communities.
Family therapy	Therapy for both offender and family.
Inpatient short-term	Medical stabilization and focus on behavioral changes.
Residential programs	Long-term, isolated, comprehensive therapy including social learning, counseling, and education.
Pharmacological maintenance	Medical therapy to address long-term drug use, particularly heroin and alcohol.
Transitional services	Relapse prevention services to help with transition into the community.

FIGURE 11.3 Treatment Approaches in Correctional Settings

Source: D. P. Mears, L. Winterfield, J. Hunsaker, G. E. Moore, and R. M. White, *Drug Treatment in the Criminal Justice System: The Current State of Knowledge* (Washington, DC: Urban Institute, 2003).

First, research shows that drug treatment works when offenders' criminogenic needs are targeted. Such "needs" refer to factors that can be changed (e.g., poor socialization) and that are often linked to criminal activity.[74] Second, treatment is most effective when it is multimodal, that is, designed to target multiple criminogenic needs.[75] Third, as was discussed earlier in this chapter, treatment must proceed on the basis of people's level of responsivity. Fourth, and again based on the discussion at the outset of this chapter, treatment must be designed with knowledge that some offenders show higher risk for failure than others.[76]

Fifth, skill-oriented and cognitive--behavioral treatment methods show more promise than other methods.[77] Sixth, research also shows that drug treatment should be integrated and comprehensive. This means that it should become part of the criminal justice process, not just something that takes place at one stage, such as during incarceration. It also means that treatment should take into account offenders' other needs, such as mental disorders.[78] Seventh, and perhaps most important, researchers advocate a continuum of treatment, not just a one-time program. Continuity of treatment should also come with careful monitoring and case management, according to some researchers.[79]

Eighth, research shows that drug treatment works best when it draws on outside resources such as families and employers. That is, once families, employers, and others pressure offenders to complete drug treatment, the latter tend to fare better.[80] Ninth, the literature suggests that treatment should proceed in appropriate "dosages." In other words, too much treatment can be counterproductive for some offenders. Tenth, drug treatment programs should be carefully implemented (and evaluated) to achieve maximum benefit.[81] Finally, the literature suggests that coerced treatment can work rather well. According to one source, "early criminal justice system intervention can force clients to stay in treatment, resulting in important long-term benefits for offenders and more substantial changes in behavior during treatment."[82]

OUT OF PRISON. Research shows that drug treatment outside the criminal justice system works when it has been preceded by some form of prison-based treatment. In particular, researchers have found that treatment programs that combine therapeutic communities in prison and are later followed by treatment in the community succeed in reducing recidivism.[83] The problem, however, is that it is not known which treatment—in prison or out—leads to the reductions.

In addition, researchers have yet to pay much attention to purely community-based methods of drug treatment, that is, those with no criminal justice component. Most of the research in this area has been tied to treatment with significant justice system involvement. Clearly, there are many treatment programs (e.g., for alcoholics and other drug abusers) that do not involve the justice system, but our concern here is with *criminals,* and little research is available for this population when its members complete treatment on their own outside of prisons and jails.

DRUG TESTING AND TREATMENT. Offenders are often required to submit to drug testing as part of either probation or parole supervision. Urine testing has been one of the more common methods of testing for the presence of drugs. Unfortunately, drug testing falls victim to the same fate as enhanced probation supervision: More supervision does not equal less recidivism. This holds true whether drug testing is implemented as part of probation supervision[84] or during pretrial release periods.[85] As evidence of this, one team of researchers found that three levels of urine testing (no testing, random testing, and frequent testing) had no effect on arrests or convictions.[86] Similar findings were recently reported for juvenile parolees in California, namely, that there were "no improved outcomes from more frequent drug testing."[87] But drug testing in conjunction with other interventions aimed at helping offenders might work.[88]

Treating Sex Offenders

Sex offenders come in all varieties. Examples include exhibitionists, rapists, child molesters, and pedophiles. Sex offenders also vary in terms of the frequency with which they offend. For example, an adult who has sex once with a person under the age of 18 could be convicted of statutory rape, a sex offense. At the other extreme, there are sexual predators who repeatedly commit serious crimes until they are caught. These issues complicate research. Evaluators are often forced to choose between specific offenses and offenders before conducting research. Add to this the fact that sex offenses are among the most underreported, and matters become further complicated. Despite these problems, there is an expanding body of literature concerned with treatment of sex offenders. Like drug treatment, it can be divided into two categories: in prison and out of prison.

IN PRISON. According to one source, "[p]rison-based sex offender treatment programs using cognitive-behavioral treatment are promising methods for reducing sex offense recidivism."[89] For example, one rigorous study showed that a prison-based treatment program for high-risk sex offenders led to a reduction in sex offense reconvictions and reconvictions leading to a return to prison.[90] The program did not appear to affect non-sex offense recidivism, however. Another more recent study *did* look at violent and general recidivism, in addition to sex offense recidivism, and found that in-prison treatment for sex offenders can be effective.[91] In contrast, though, another team of researchers found that a prison-based treatment program for child molesters made little difference.[92]

OUT OF PRISON. Treatment outside the prison context also shows promise. At least three separate studies show reductions in recidivism for treatment of child molesters,[93] exhibitionists,[94] and adult rapists.[95] Interestingly, the three studies show that child molesters and exhibitionists can be treated more easily than rapists. But another recent study suggests that rapists are more amenable to treatment than are child molesters.[96] This latter finding is consistent with a host of studies showing that child molesters are more likely than rapists to reoffend.[97] Recently, a team of researchers evaluated 13 studies that were sufficiently rigorous in scientific terms; they concluded that "non-prison-based sex offender treatment programs were deemed to be effective in curtailing future criminal activity. . . . Prison-based treatment programs were judged to be promising."[98]

THE BIG PICTURE: THREE CHEERS FOR META-ANALYSIS. **Meta-analysis** is a research technique that amounts to synthesizing the literature devoted to a specific topic. In one sense, this book is a meta-analysis because it attempts to summarize a massive amount of literature devoted to crime control in the United States. But true meta-analysis involves pulling several studies together and conducting a statistical analysis to arrive at a single conclusion. In other words, meta-analysis is the use of statistical methods to combine the results of several independent studies. In areas such as drug and sex offender treatment, in which many studies have been conducted, it is useful to turn to meta-analysis for a summary of the literature—and to get an idea of the big picture.

meta analysis: a research technique that amounts to synthesizing the literature devoted to a specific topic.

In one meta-analysis, a researcher analyzed 74 separate sex offender treatment studies.[99] She concluded that individuals who had received treatment reoffended less frequently than controls did. She also found that recidivism levels were lower in studies that were conducted after 1980, which suggests that sex offender treatment methods have perhaps improved over time. But she did find that treatment cannot be short-lived and that offenders need to complete their programs for the best treatment effect. The same researcher recently conducted another analysis of 79 treatment studies encompassing over 11,000 sex offenders.[100] She found that sex offenders who participated in relapse prevention had a rearrest rate of 7.2 percent compared to 17.6 percent in a group of untreated sex offenders. Other meta-analyses show similar results.[101] Other high-profile meta analyses have reached similar conclusions, namely that treatment can be an effective option much of the time.[102]

Does It Work?

All in all, treatment for drug and sex offenders shows promise. Although it is no quick fix and it can cost a fair amount of money, treatment appears to be much more effective than are traditional methods of dealing with crime, such as imprisonment. Treatment coupled with cognitive-behavioral therapies such as those discussed earlier in this chapter appears to be even more effective. Thus, the assumptions that treatment coddles offenders and there is nothing the criminal justice system can do to reduce crime would appear to be wrong. Carefully crafted interventions can make a lasting difference for several types of offenders.

JOB TRAINING

There is an old saying that "the devil makes work for idle hands." For our purposes, this means that unemployed people tend to have more time on their hands than employed people do and thus might be more inclined to commit crime. Although it is certainly not true that all unemployed people commit crime, employment status has long been a factor linked to crime in both micro- and macro-level studies of the causes of crime. To the extent that unemployment is linked to crime, it makes sense to provide job training to people who lack the necessary skills to secure good jobs. In this section, we turn our attention to the effectiveness of job training programs on crime. But first let us give some more attention to the employment–crime connection.

The Employment–Crime Connection

The employment–crime connection has been explored at both the macro and micro levels. Macro-level research has looked at the relationship between unemployment and crime at either the national or the community level. At the national level, researchers have found that when burglary and robbery rates are higher, the unemployment rate is high.[103] Moving to the community level, focusing in particular on states, counties, and cities, researchers have also found a significant relationship between employment and crime.[104] The evidence of a positive connection between employment and crime is even more pronounced when property crimes are separated from violent crimes.[105] More recently, though, crime rates have continued to trend downward while unemployment levels remain unacceptably high, calling into question the employment/crime connection, particularly at the macro level.

At the micro level, researchers have explored whether individual employment status is linked to criminal behavior. For example, studies of the 1945 Philadelphia birth cohort have shown that unemployment is linked to crime.[106] Researchers have also found that among individuals, people tend to commit more property crime during periods of unemployment, but this relationship appears to hold only for people who are predisposed to offend.[107] Others, though, have said that the relationship between unemployment status and crime is spurious and can be explained by other factors such as social control,[108] commitment, and responsibility.[109]

One researcher conducted a review of several analyses of the employment–crime connection and found that the relationship is weak.[110] Some researchers have even found that crime goes up when unemployment *decreases.* For example, auto theft has been shown to increase when the state of the economy improves, most likely because people have more income when economic conditions are good, and some use such income to buy more cars.[111] If there are more cars thieves have a greater opportunity to steal them. Even so, enough research has shown that economic conditions, particularly unemployment levels, are at least *somewhat* connected to the crime rate. This finding has been used to justify a host of programs aimed at improving people's employment status.

Job Training for Convicts

Job training for convicted criminals is very popular. Not as much money is spent on training as, for instance, on custodial costs, but prisons and jails in every state provide programs for inmates that are intended to help them secure jobs on their release. The best known (and best-researched) programs include educational programs, vocational training, corrections industries, and work release. In the following subsections, we will review the available literature concerned with the effect of these approaches on crime and recidivism.

EDUCATION AS JOB TRAINING.   Many criminals are undereducated. As a result, there has been a push to provide Adult Basic Education (ABE) and/or General Education Development (GED) training to convicts. Several researchers have evaluated this approach, but there is little consensus in the literature as to whether ABE/GED training makes a difference.[112] Furthermore, many of the existing evaluations lack scientific merit.[113] And there is concern that education programs may be plagued by the so-called selection effect. That is, those who volunteer for ABE/GED training might already be committed to improving their lives and therefore less likely to reoffend.

Of the available studies that withstand scientific scrutiny, the effects of education training have been found to be modest at best. One researcher found that ABE participants who entered prison with an eighth grade or lower education had a lower rate of rearrests and parole revocations than did people who did not participate in the program, but the difference was barely 6 percent.[114] Similarly, researchers in Texas found that GED completers were rearrested just over 41 percent of the time compared to a rearrest rate of 53.5 percent in a control group.[115] Only one study appears to show a dramatic difference between treatment and controls. Walsh found that in a 42-month follow-up period, 16 percent of GED completers were rearrested compared to a control group with a rearrest rate of 44 percent.[116]

VOCATIONAL TRAINING.   Education clearly gives people a leg up, but education alone is not enough to secure gainful employment most of the time. As a result, another method of job training that is taking place in the criminal justice system is vocational training. **Vocational training** amounts to training a person in a specific job or skill. Images of furniture making and license plate stamping are often conjured up when prison vocational training is discussed, but the reality is that vocational training now comes in several forms. For example, Prison View Golf Course recently opened up at the Louisiana State Penitentiary in Angola, Louisiana. Inmates work to maintain the course and even act as caddies! Elsewhere, inmates learn skills to help them obtain good jobs on their release.

vocational training: training a person in a specific job or skill.

What does the research show? It shows that vocational training carries more promise than does ABE/GED training. For example, Lattimore and her colleagues found that a vocational training program for juvenile inmates led to significantly fewer reconvictions in the treatment group compared to controls.[117] Another team of researchers found that vocational training and apprenticeships for federal prison inmates led to fewer recommitments than were seen among controls.[118] A wealth of other studies also suggest that providing vocational training to known offenders reduces recidivism.[119] In fairness, though, some researchers have actually found that vocational training can make matters worse.[120]

In 1982, Congress enacted the Job Training Partnership Act. It provided money to state governments and was intended to establish programs to provide job training services for economically disadvantaged adults and youths, dislocated workers, and others who face significant employment barriers. The act has undergone significant revisions and was superseded by the Work Investment Act of 1998. But before the revisions went into effect, at least two studies were published concerning the act's effect on ex-offenders, people who clearly face employment barriers. Both studies showed that the act did not achieve its stated purpose when funding was provided to states for the training of ex-offenders.[121] One of the studies even showed that program completers had higher recidivism rates than did controls.[122]

CORRECTIONAL INDUSTRIES.   Correctional industries are closely tied to vocational training. Indeed, inmates often receive vocational training when participating in correctional industries. The term **correctional industry** refers to goods and services that are produced by offenders during incarceration.[123] Incarceration can refer to time in prison or even time in a residential facility of some sort. One author describes correctional industries in this way:

correctional industry: goods and services that are produced by offenders during incarceration.

> Correctional industries produce a wide range of products and services for both government and private sector consumers, including furniture, health technology, automobile parts, institutional and jail products, signs, printing products, textiles and apparel, traffic paint and food products. As well as providing valuable skills and work experience that inmates can use outside of prison, correctional industry experience can provide opportunities for inmates to develop better time management skills, self-discipline and work ethics.[124]

Nearly every state has its own company or government entity that oversees the state's correctional industries. California's Prison Industry Authority, New York's Correctional Industries, and Michigan's State Industries, among others, generally provide work for prison inmates and other incarcerated individuals.[125] Inmates generally receive low pay, and the goods that correctional industries produce often can be sold only to state agencies, not the general public.

Our concern is, of course, with whether correctional industries positively affect inmates and thereby reduce recidivism. Unfortunately, little research is available that examines the effects of correctional industries alone. Instead, most published studies deal with correctional industries along with vocational training and even job assistance. This makes it difficult to separate out the effect of correctional industries on crime. And it could well be that certain inmates voluntarily seek out work while in prison, meaning that such inmates are most likely to change their behavior anyway. But several studies still show modest reductions in recidivism for those who participate in correctional industries.[126]

WORK RELEASE.   Sometimes inmates behave well enough to be released from prison, if only temporarily, to work in the private sector. This is known as **work release**. Obviously this job training method is limited to those inmates who are at the lowest risk of becoming fugitives. Unfortunately, very little research is available concerning the relationship between work release and recidivism. Only one study appears to have been published on the subject.[127] The study produced conflicting findings. On the one hand, work release participants had lower rearrest and reconviction rates than did controls. On the other hand, work release participants were returned to jail or prison at a higher rate than were controls—for new crimes and violations of work release conditions.

work release: the practice of releasing certain jail or prison inmates for specified periods of time so they can participate in the workforce.

Job Training for the General Population

Admittedly, job training for convicts is a bit reactive. It stands to reason, then, that job training for people in the general population who need it could *prevent* crime. People in the general population are clearly in a better position to obtain jobs and job training than ex-offenders are, but not everyone does so. Therefore, it is possible that providing job training to those who most need it will discourage them from committing crimes. It is also probable that job training for young people would have the most pronounced effect on future criminality because it is young people who are at the greatest risk of offending. We know, on the basis of the criminal career literature, that many, if not most, offenders mature out of crime by approximately age 25.

Unfortunately, little research is available that looks at the relationship between criminality and job training for the general population. Instead, most researchers who study this type of job training tend to focus on the type of employment that people secure and the wages they receive following training. In an extensive review of job training programs for people in the general population, including welfare participants, at-risk youths, and other people, Heckman concluded that most programs do not achieve their goals. In his view, only Job Corps, a U.S. Department of Labor program aimed at improving the job prospects for at-risk youths, leads to a significant return on the investment of some $20,000 per participant.

Insofar as employment and crime are linked, it is probably unlikely that job training for the general population will do much to prevent crime. This is especially true for younger people, according to one team of researchers.[128] They concluded, after evaluating a job training program in Baltimore, that "the evidence in this experiment and elsewhere suggests older disadvantaged workers, including those who are known offenders, may be much more responsive (than younger workers) to the opportunity to participate in employment programs."[129] But this statement clearly does not support the extensive use of job training as a crime prevention mechanism.

Housing Dispersal and Mobility Programs

The respected sociologist William Julius Wilson argued in the 1980s that when jobs leave the inner cities and move to the suburbs, this leaves behind an increase in poverty and related social problems.[130] He later argued that to improve the plight of America's inner-city residents, jobs should be brought back to urban centers.[131] Because doing this has proven to be rather difficult,[132] an alternative has been proposed that takes inner-city residents to the suburbs for employment. **Housing dispersal programs** physically move residents to the suburbs; **housing mobility programs** provide transportation to inner-city residents so that they can go to the suburbs to work.

Housing dispersal and mobility programs do not amount to job training per se. They are distinctly different from GED education for inmates, vocational training for at-risk youths, and the like. But they are worth discussing in the present context for two reasons. First, they have been crafted as a method of addressing the employment–crime relationship. It is assumed that employed people, even if they have to go elsewhere for work, will not become criminals. Second, if job training is concerned with enhancing people's prospects for employment, then dispersal and mobility programs are directly related to the subject of this section. But, surprisingly, little research is available concerning their effects on crime.

First, there are a few studies on housing dispersal programs, but only one of them has looked at crime as an outcome.[133] Specifically, Ludwig and his colleagues found that when families move to the suburbs, their children become involved in less criminal

housing dispersal programs: interventions that physically move certain inner-city residents to the suburbs.

housing mobility programs: interventions that provide transportation to inner-city residents so that they can go to the suburbs to work.

activity.[134] The remaining studies show that dispersal programs improve people's levels of employment and life outcome, but that many people are resistant to moving to the suburbs for work, even when they are given an opportunity to do so. These findings have led researchers to focus on housing mobility programs, but to date, there have been no published studies linking them to reductions in crime. Consequently, we cannot draw any conclusions about what effects dispersal and mobility programs have on public safety.

Does It Work?

All in all, there is little or no evidence that job training in the general population prevents crime. This finding also holds for housing dispersal and mobility programs (with the exception of one lone study). As for convicted criminals, there is some evidence that vocational training reduces recidivism. In contrast, there is little evidence that stand-alone education programs, work release, or prison industries without an express job training component lead to reductions in recidivism.

MORE LESSONS FROM META-ANALYSIS

It was advantageous to cover rehabilitation, treatment, and job training separately. This allowed us to decipher a large body of literature and come up with some relatively clear conclusions about what works and what doesn't. At the same time, though, an overall assessment of treatment, rehabilitation, and job training might be worthwhile. In one study, a team of researchers reviewed a total of 302 meta-analyses. Theirs was basically a meta-analysis of meta-analyses dealing with treatment, rehabilitation, and job training for all types of individuals, not just criminals. The researchers concluded that there is no evidence that offenders—and other people—cannot be rehabilitated. Their findings have led to this conclusion by another prominent researcher:

> the meta analysis evidence is reasonably clear about what treatment programs are most successful in reducing recidivism: interventions that are based on social learning or behavioral principles, are structured rather than nondirective, seek to build human capital in offenders, and use more than one treatment modality to address the multiple problems that offenders may be experiencing.[135]

This quote is consistent with the message of this chapter: Rehabilitation, treatment, and job training appear relatively effective. The tough-on-crime view that any attempts to change offenders by any means other than strict punishment is simply misplaced. Americans have a desire to lock up criminals and even a thirst for vengeance against people who violate the law. Although incarceration might temporarily quench this thirst, it leaves some core problems unaddressed. Not only are rehabilitation, treatment, and job training effective, they are, as one researcher has observed, the right things to do:

> I am troubled by what transpires when the correctional system starts to forfeit the rehabilitative ideal and embrace starkly punitive principles. . . . I find it difficult to sustain the view that the absence of a firm commitment to offender treatment fosters more justice and dignity for offenders. . . . [B]y showing concern for the welfare of offenders—with the exchange being that investing in the wayward advances public safety by reducing their risk of recidivating—rehabilitation provides one of the few rationales for not imposing unnecessary pains on those under correctional supervision.[136]

Summary

Rehabilitation, treatment, and job training signal a departure from some of the methods of crime control that were discussed earlier in this book. We found that although many people favor rehabilitation, treatment, and job training, these methods do not work for everyone. Offenders differ in their risk, needs, and responsivity. Effective programs need to take these issues into account. And multifaceted and multidimensional interventions seem most capable of changing offenders for the better.

As for effectiveness, there is much evidence that rehabilitation is effective. In particular, when low-level offenders are targeted for morals and reasoning training, their behavior is favorably altered. Anger management and life skills training also show promise, but victim awareness improvement does not appear to be particularly effective. Rehabilitation is no panacea, but it appears more effective than prison and other harsh sanctions. Treatment shows even more promise, especially when it is coupled with cognitive–behavioral therapies. Finally, there is little evidence that job training of nonincarcerated individuals reduces crime, but prison vocational and work programs appear to be effective for some offenders.

Notes

1. F.T. Cullen, "Rehabilitation and Treatment Programs," in *Crime: Public Policies for Crime Control*, eds. J.Q. Wilson and J. Petersilia (Oakland, CA: ICS Press, 2002), 287.

2. F.T. Cullen, B.S. Fisher, and B.K. Applegate, "Public Opinion about Punishment and Corrections," in *Crime and Justice: A Review of Research*, ed. M. Tonry, Vol. 27, (Chicago: University of Chicago Press, 2000), 1–79; B.K. Applegate, F.T. Cullen, and B.S. Fisher, "Public Support for Correctional Treatment: The Continuing Appeal of the Rehabilitative Ideal," *The Prison Journal* 77 (1997): 237–58; M. Moon, J.L. Sundt, F.T. Cullen, and J.P. Wright, "Is Child Saving Dead?: Public Support for Rehabilitation," *Crime and Delinquency* 46 (1999): 38–60.

3. F.T. Cullen, "Rehabilitation and Treatment Programs," in *Crime: Public Policies for Crime Control*, eds. J.Q. Wilson and J. Petersilia (Oakland, CA: ICS Press, 2002), 255.

4. D.A. Andrews and J. Bonta, *The Psychology of Criminal Conduct* (Cincinnati, OH: Anderson, 1999).

5. J. Bonta, "Risk-Needs Assessment and Treatment Inquiry," in *Choosing Correctional Options That Work: Defining the Demand and Evaluating the Supply*, ed. A.T. Harland (Thousand Oaks, CA: Sage, 1996), 18–32; P. Jones, "Risk Prediction in Criminal Justice," in *Choosing Correctional Options That Work: Defining the Demand and Evaluating the Supply*, ed. A.T. Harland (Thousand Oaks, CA: Sage, 1996), 33–68.

6. D.A. Andrews, J. Bonta, and R.D. Hoge, "Classification for Effective Rehabilitation: Rediscovering Psychology," *Criminal Justice and Behavior* 17 (1990): 19–52; D.A. Andrews, R.D. Zinger, R.D. Bonta, P. Gendreau, and F.T. Cullen, "Does Correctional Treatment Work?: A Psychologically Informed Meta-Analysis," *Criminology* 28 (1990): 369–404.

7. P. VanVoorhis, "An Overview of Offender Classification Systems," in *Correctional Counseling and Rehabilitation*, eds. P. VanVoorhis, M. Braswell, and D. Lester (Cincinnati, OH: Anderson, 1997), 81–110.

8. Ibid.

9. Many other factors are linked to crime but are impossible to change. Examples include age, race, and gender.

10. D.A. Andrews, J. Bonta, and R.D. Hoge, "Classification for Effective Rehabilitation: Rediscovering Psychology," *Criminal Justice and Behavior* 17 (1990): 19–52; D.A. Andrews, R.D. Zinger, R.D. Bonta, P. Gendreau, and F.T. Cullen, "Does Correctional Treatment Work?: A Psychologically Informed Meta-Analysis," *Criminology* 28 (1990): 369–404.

11. S. Kennedy, "Treatment Responsivity: Reducing Recidivism by Enhancing Treatment Effectiveness," *Forum on Corrections Research* (2000): 19–23; S. Kennedy and R. Serin, "Treatment Responsivity: Contributing to Effective Correctional Programming," *The ICCA Journal* April (1997): 46–52; C. Gillis, M. Getkate, D. Robinson, and F. Porporino, "Correctional Work Supervisor Leadership and Credibility: Their Influence on Offender Work Motivation," *Forum on Corrections Research* 7 (1995): 15–7.

12. J. Bonta, "The Responsivity Principle and Offender Rehabilitation," *Forum on Corrections Research* 7 (1995): 34–7.

13. P. VanVoorhis, "An Overview of Offender Classification Systems," in *Correctional Counseling and Rehabilitation*, eds. P. VanVoorhis, M. Braswell, and D. Lester (Cincinnati, OH: Anderson, 1997), 81–110.

14. J. Piaget, *The Moral Judgment of the Child* (London: Kegan Paul, 1932).

15. L. Kohlberg, *Stages in the Development of Moral Thought and Action* (New York: Holt, Rinehart, and Winston, 1969).

16. See D.L. MacKenzie, "Reducing the Criminal Activities of Known Offenders and Delinquents: Crime Prevention

in the Courts and Corrections," in *Evidence-Based Crime Prevention*, eds. L.W. Sherman, D.P. Farrington, B.C. Welsh, and D.L. MacKenzie (New York: Routledge, 2002), 366; see also M.J. Mahoney and W.J. Lyddon, "Recent Developments in Cognitive Approaches to Counseling and Psychotherapy," *The Counseling Psychologist* 16 (1988): 190–234.

17. Some criminologists have argued that this condition is genetically determined. For a review, see H.J. Marens-Willem, "Criminality and Moral Dysfunctions: Neurological, Biochemical, and Genetic Dimensions," *International Journal of Offender Therapy and Comparative Criminology* 46 (2002): 170–82.

18. C. Veneziano and L. Veneziano, "The Relationship between Deterrence and Moral Reasoning," *Criminal Justice Review* 17 (1992): 209–16.

19. G.L. Little and K.D. Robinson, "Moral Reconation Therapy: A Systematic Step-by-Step Treatment System for Treatment Resistant Clients," *Psychological Reports* 62 (1988): 135–51.

20. B.B. Wolman, *Dictionary of Behavioral Science* (New York: Van Nostrand Reinhold, 1973).

21. G.L. Little, "Cognitive-Behavioral Treatment of Offenders," *Addictive Behaviors Treatment Review* 2 (2000): 14.

22. For additional information, see moral-reconation-therapy. com

23. G.L. Little, "Cognitive-Behavioral Treatment of Offenders," *Addictive Behaviors Treatment Review* 2 (2000): 12–21.

24. See, for example, G.L. Little and K.D. Robinson, "Effects of Moral Reconation Therapy upon Moral Reasoning, Life Purpose, and Recidivism among Drug and Alcohol Offenders," *Psychological Reports* 64 (1989): 83–90; G.L. Little and K.D. Robinson, "Treating Drunk Drivers with Moral Reconation Therapy: A One-Year Recidivism Report," *Psychological Reports* 64 (1989): 960–62; G.L. Little and K.D. Robinson, "Relationship of DUI Recidivism to Moral Reasoning, Sensation Seeking, and MacAndrew Alcoholism Scores," *Psychological Reports* 65 (1989): 1171–4; G.L. Little, K.D. Robinson, K.D. Burnette, and E.S. Swan, "Six-Year MRT Recidivism Data on Felons and DWI Offenders: Treated Offenders Show Significantly Lower Reincarceration," *Cognitive-Behavioral Treatment Review* 4 (1995): 1–5.

25. W. Huddleston, "CBTI Payne and Logan County, Oklahoma Drug Court—18 Month Recidivism Study of Graduates and ATTAC Program: 3 Year Recidivism Study of Graduates," *Cognitive Behavioral Treatment Review* 5 (1996): 9; W. Huddleston, "Summary of Drug Court Evaluation: Recidivism Study," *Cognitive Behavioral Treatment Review* 6 (1997): 16–7.

26. The four favorable studies are C.M. Boston, "Changing Offenders Behavior: Evaluating Moral Reconation Therapy in the Better People Program," *Cognitive-Behavioral Treatment Review* 10 (2001): 1–2, 18–9; R. Brame, D.L. MacKenzie, A.R. Waggoner, and K.D. Robinson, "Moral Reconation Therapy and Problem Behavior in the Oklahoma Department of Corrections," *Journal of the Oklahoma Criminal Justice Research Consortium* 3 (1996): 63–84; G. Grandberry, *Moral Reconation Therapy Evaluation Final Report 1998* (Olympia, WA: Washington State Department of Corrections, Planning and Research Section, 1998); and D.L. MacKenzie, R. Brame, A.R. Waggoner, and K.D. Robinson, *Moral Reconation Therapy and Problem Behavior in the Oklahoma Department of Corrections* (Washington, DC: U.S. Department of Justice, 1995). The unfavorable study was W.L. Burnett, "Treating Post-Incarcerated Offenders with Moral Reconation Therapy: A One-Year Recidivism Study," *Cognitive Behavioral Treatment Review* 6 (1997): 2.

27. See A. Black, "Redesigned Programming Pats Off at the Jefferson County, Texas Restitution Center," *Cognitive-Behavioral Treatment Review* 9 (2000): 12–3; R. Brame, D.L. MacKenzie, A.R. Waggoner, and K.D. Robinson, "Moral Reconation Therapy and Problem Behavior in the Oklahoma Department of Corrections," *Journal of the Oklahoma Criminal Justice Research Consortium* 3 (1996): 63–84; G. Grandberry, *Moral Reconation Therapy Evaluation Final Report 1998* (Olympia, WA: Washington State Department of Corrections, Planning and Research Section, 1998); B. Hobler, "First Annual Evaluation Report on the Delaware Life Skills Program: Lower Recidivism and Fewer Rules Violations," *Cognitive Behavioral Treatment Review* 4 (2000): 2–5; C. Lindholm, "Preliminary Outcomes with Moral Reconation Therapy," *Cognitive Behavioral Treatment Review* 7 (1998): 16; D.L. MacKenzie, R. Brame, A.R. Waggoner, and K.D. Robinson, *Moral Reconation Therapy and Problem Behavior in the Oklahoma Department of Corrections* (Washington, DC: U.S. Department of Justice, 1995); H.S. Sandhu, "Drug Offender Treatment at the Bill Johnson Correctional Center in Alva, OK," *Cognitive Behavioral Treatment Review* 7 (1998): 1–7; K. Suitt, "A Study of the Effectiveness of the MRT Program at Jefferson County Restitution Center 2," *Cognitive Behavioral Treatment Review* 10 (2001): 10–1.

28. G.L. Leonardson, "Montana-Based Program Shows Reductions in Domestic Violence Re-arrests after Treatment," *Cognitive Behavioral Treatment Review* 9 (2000): 1–3.

29. A. Wallace, "Results of Moral Reconation Therapy Utilization in the Las Cruces, New Mexico Juvenile Drug Court," *Cognitive Behavioral Treatment Review* 10 (2001): 1–2.

30. For a discussion of the risks associated with implementing MRT in real criminal justice organizations, see T.A. Armstrong, "Effect of Moral Reconation Therapy on the Recidivism of Youthful Offenders: A Randomized Experiment," *Criminal Justice and Behavior* 30 (2003): 668–87.

31. R.R. Ross and E.A. Fabiano, *Time to Think: A Cognitive Model of Delinquency Prevention and Offender Rehabilitation* (Johnson City, TN: Institute of Social Sciences and Arts, 1985).

32. R.R. Ross, E.A. Fabiano, and C.D. Ewles, "Reasoning and Rehabilitation," *International Journal of Offender Therapy and Comparative Criminology* 32 (1988): 29–35.

33. F.J. Porporino and D. Robinson, "An Evaluation of the Reasoning and Rehabilitation Program with Canadian Federal Offenders," in *Thinking Straight*, eds. R.R. Ross and B. Ross (Ottawa: Cognitive Center, 1995), 155–90.

34. G. Johnson and R.M. Hunter, "Evaluation of the Specialized Drug Offender Program," in *Thinking Straight*, eds. R.R. Ross and B. Ross (Ottawa: Cognitive Center, 1995), 215–234; D. Robinson, M. Grossman, and F. Porporino, *Effectiveness of the Cognitive Skills Training Program: From Pilot to National Implementation, B-07* (The Research and Statistics Branch, Ottawa, Correctional Service of Canada, 1991).

35. R.R. Ross, E.A. Fabiano, and C.D. Ewles, "Reasoning and Rehabilitation," *International Journal of Offender Therapy and Comparative Criminology* 32 (1988): 29–35; D. Robinson, *The Impact of Cognitive Skills Training on Post-Release Recidivism among Canadian Federal Offenders.* Research Report, Correctional Research and Development, Ottawa, Correctional Service of Canada, 1995; P. Raynor and M. Vanstone, "Reasoning and Rehabilitation in Britain: The Results of the Straight Thinking on Probation (STOP) Programme," *International Journal of Offender Therapy and Comparative Criminology* 40 (1996): 272–84; C. Knott, "The STOP Programme: Reasoning and Rehabilitation in a British Setting," in *What Works: Reducing Reoffending: Guidelines from Research and Practice*, ed. J. McGuire (New York: John Wiley and Sons Limited, 1995); F.J. Porporino, E.A. Fabiano, and D. Robinson, *Focusing on Successful Reintegration: Cognitive Skills Training for Offenders, R-19* (Research and Statistics Branch, Ottawa, Correctional Service of Canada, 1991).

36. D.J. Hubbard, "Cognitive-Behavioral Treatment: An Analysis of Gender and Other Responsivity Characteristics and Their Effects on Success in Offender Rehabilitation" (PhD dissertation, Cincinnati, OH: University of Cincinnati, 2002).

37. K. Faulkner, C.D. Stoltenberg, R. Cogen, M. Nolder, and E. Shooter, "Cognitive-Behavioral Group Treatment for Male Spouse Abusers," *Journal of Family Violence* 7 (1992): 37–55.

38. H.A. Marquis, G.A. Bourgon, B. Armstrong, and J. Pfaff, "Reducing Recidivism through Institutional Treatment," *Forum on Correctional Research* 8 (1996): 3–5.

39. K.C. Eamon, M.M. Munchua, and J.R. Reddon, "Effectiveness of an Anger Management Program for Women Inmates," *Journal of Offender Rehabilitation* 34 (2001): 45–60.

40. See, for example, S. McCarthy-Tucker, A. Gold, and E. Garcia III, "Effects of Anger Management Training on Aggressive Behavior in Adolescent Boys," *Journal of Offender Rehabilitation* 29 (1999): 129–41; A.G. Escamilla, "Cognitive Approach to Anger Management Treatment for Juvenile Offenders," *Journal of Offender Rehabilitation* 27 (1998): 199–208.

41. G.D. Watt and K. Howells, "Skills Training for Aggression Control: Evaluation of an Anger Management Programme for Violent Offenders," *Legal and Criminological Psychology* 4 (1999): 285–300.

42. R.J. Fetsch, C.J. Schultz, and J.J. Wahler, "Preliminary Evaluation of the Colorado Rethink Parenting and Anger Management Program," *Child Abuse and Neglect* 23 (1999): 353–60.

43. D. Hunter and G.V. Hughes, "Anger Management in the Prison: An Evaluation; Anger Management Program Outcomes," *Corrections Research Forum* 5 (1993): 3–9.

44. S. Napolitano and L.G. Brown, "Strategic Approach to Group Anger Management with Incarcerated Murderers," *Journal of Offender Rehabilitation* 16 (1991): 93–101.

45. P.M. Valliant, L.P. Ennis, and L. Raven-Brooks, "Cognitive-Behavior Therapy Model for Anger Management with Adult Offenders," *Journal of Offender Rehabilitation* 22 (1995): 77–93.

46. For a recent example of the testing approach, see J. Ireland, "Anger Management Therapy with Young Male Offenders: An Evaluation of Treatment Outcome," *Aggressive Behavior* 30 (2004): 174.

47. Those that show a reduction in recidivism include K.C. Eamon, M.M. Munchua, and J.R. Reddon, "Effectiveness of an Anger Management Program for Women Inmates," *Journal of Offender Rehabilitation* 34 (2001): 45–60; and D. Hunter and G.V. Hughes, "Anger Management in the Prison: An Evaluation; Anger Management Program Outcomes," *Corrections Research Forum* 5 (1993): 3–9.

48. More randomized experiments are necessary. See, for example, P.M. Reilly and M.S. Shopshire, "Anger Management Group Treatment for Cocaine Dependence: Preliminary Outcomes," *American Journal of Drug and Alcohol Abuse* 26 (2000): 161.

49. See, for example, R. Serin, *Treating Violent Offenders: A Review of Current Practices* (Ottawa: Correctional Research and Development, 1994); G.V. Hughes, "Anger Management Program Outcomes," *Forum on Corrections Research* 5 (1993): 5–9.

50. D. Shinar and R.P. Compton, "Victim Impact Panels: Their Impact on DWI Recidivism," *Alcohol, Drugs, and Driving* 11 (1995): 73–87.

51. U.S. Department of Transportation, *A How To Guide for Victim Impact Panels.* Available at nhtsa.dot.gov/people/injury/alcohol/VIP/VIP_index.html

52. D. Shinar and R.P. Compton, "Victim Impact Panels: Their Impact on DWI Recidivism," *Alcohol, Drugs and Driving* 11 (1995): 73–87.

53. K. Badovinac, "Effects of Victim Impact Panels on Attitudes and Intentions Regarding Impaired Driving," *Journal of Alcohol and Drug Education* 39 (1994): 113–8.

54. D.G. Rojek, J.E. Coverdill, and S.W. Fors, "Effect of Victim Impact Panels on DUI Rearrest Rates: A 5-Year Follow-Up," *Criminology* 41 (2003): 1319–40.

55. Ibid., 1335–6.

56. The discussion in this and the next paragraph draws heavily from the work of G.J. Botvin, available at lifeskillstraining.com/program.cfm

57. Most of the evaluations of the Life Skills Training program have been conducted by Dr. Botvin, often in collaboration with others. Recent examples of his studies that show favorable outcomes include G.J. Botvin, K.W. Griffin, E. Paul, and A.P. Macaulay, "Preventing Tobacco and Alcohol Use among Elementary School Students through Life Skills Training," *Journal of Child and Adolescent Substance Abuse* 12 (2003): 1–18; and G.J. Botvin, K.W. Griffin, T. Diaz, L.M. Scheier, C. Williams, and J.A. Epstein, "Preventing Illicit Drug Use in Adolescents: Long-term Follow-up Data from a Randomized Controlled Trial of a School Population," *Addictive Behaviors* 25 (2000): 769–74.

58. For an independent evaluation, see R.L. Spoth, C. Redmond, L. Trudeau, and C. Shin, "Longitudinal Substance Initiation Outcomes for a Universal Preventive Intervention Combining Family and School Programs," *Psychology of Addictive Behaviors* 16 (2002): 129–34.

59. R. Melton and S. Pennell, *Staying Out Successfully: An Evaluation of an In-Custody Life Skills Training Program* (San Diego Association of Governments, 1998).

60. For a similar study concerned with female inmates, see P.J. Schram and M. Morash, "Evaluation of a Life Skills Program for Women Inmates in Michigan," *Journal of Offender Rehabilitation* 34 (2002): 47–70.

61. R.R. Ross, E.A. Fabiano, and C.D. Ewles, "Reasoning and Rehabilitation," *International Journal of Offender Therapy and Comparative Criminology* 32 (1988): 29–36.

62. D.K. Cecil, D.A. Drapkin, D.L. MacKenzie, and L.J. Hickman, "Effectiveness of Adult Education and Life-Skills Programs in Reducing Recidivism: A Review and Assessment of the Research," *Journal of Correctional Education* 51 (2000): 207–26.

63. P. Carnes, *Out of the Shadows: Understanding Sexual Addiction* (Minneapolis, MN: CompCare Publications, 1983).

64. T.M. Tays, R.H. Earle, K. Wells, M. Murray, and B. Garrett, "Treating Sex Offenders Using the Sex Addiction Model," *Sexual Addiction and Compulsivity* 6 (1999): 281–8.

65. B.S. Brown, "Program Models," in *Drug Abuse Treatment in Prisons and Jails*, eds. C.G. Leukefeld and F.M. Tims (Rockville, MD: National Institute on Drug Abuse, 1992), 31–7.

66. See, for example, M.R. Chaiken, "Crime Rates and Substance Abuse among Types of Offenders," in *Crime Rates among Drug-Abusing Offenders*, eds. B.D. Johnson and E. Wish (New York: Narcotic and Drug Research, 1986), 12–54; J.A. Inciardi, "Heroin Use and Street Crime," *Crime and Delinquency* 25 (1979): 335–46.

67. Office of National Drug Control Policy, *Drug Treatment in the Criminal Justice System* (Washington, DC: Executive Office of the President, Office of National Drug Control Policy, 2001).

68. D.R. Gerstein and H.J. Harwood, eds., *Treating Drug Problems* (Washington, DC: National Academy Press, 1992).

69. M.D. Anglin and Y.I. Hser, "Treatment of Drug Abuse," in *Drugs and Crime*, eds. M. Tonry and J.Q. Wilson (Chicago, IL: University of Chicago Press, 1990), 393–460; J. Travis, C. Wetherington, T.E. Feucht, and C. Visher, *Drug Involved Offenders in the Criminal Justice System*. Working Paper 96–02. Washington, DC: National Institute of Justice, 1996.

70. National Institute on Drug Abuse, *Research Report Series–Therapeutic Community*. Washington, DC: National Institute on Drug Abuse, 2004. Available at nida.nih.gov/ResearchReports/Therapeutic/Therapeutic2.html#What

71. H.K. Wexler, G.P. Falkin, and D.S. Lipton, "Outcome Evaluation of a Prison Therapeutic Community for Substance Abuse Treatment," *Criminal Justice and Behavior* 17 (1992): 71.

72. See, for example, G. Duwe, "Prison-Based Chemical Dependency Treatment in Minnesota: An Outcome Evaluation," *Journal of Experimental Criminology* 6 (2010): 57–81; S.S. Martin, C.A. Butzon, and J. Inciardi, "Assessment of a Multistage Therapeutic Community for Drug Involved Offenders," *Journal of Psychoactive Drugs* 27 (1995): 109–16; H.K. Wexler, W.F. Graham, R. Koronowski, and L. Lowe, *Evaluation of Amity In-Prison and Post-Release Substance Abuse Treatment Programs* (Washington, DC: National Institute on Drug Abuse, 1995); G. Field, "The Effects of Intensive Treatment on Reducing the Criminal Recidivism of Addicted Offenders," *Federal Probation* 53 (1989): 51–6.

73. The discussion that follows draws heavily from D.P. Mears, L. Winterfield, J. Hunsaker, G.E. Moore, and R.M. White, *Drug Treatment in the Criminal Justice System: The Current State of Knowledge* (Washington, DC: Justice Policy Center, Urban Institute, 2003); F.T. Cullen and P. Gendreau, "Assessing Correctional Rehabilitation: Policy, Practice, and Prospects," in *Criminal Justice 2000: Policies, Processes, and Decisions of the Criminal Justice System*, Vol. 3, (Washington, DC: U.S. Department of Justice, 2000), 109–76; G.G. Gaes, T.J. Flanagan, L.L. Motiuk, and L. Stewart, "Adult Correctional Treatment," in *Prisons*, eds. M.H. Tonry and J. Petersilia (Chicago, IL: University of Chicago Press, 1999), 361–426; National Institute on Drug Abuse, *Principles of Drug Addiction Treatment: A Research-Based Guide* (Bethesda, MD: U.S. Department of Health and Human Services, National Institutes of Health, National Institute on Drug Abuse, 1999).

74. D.A. Andrews, "The Psychology of Criminal Conduct and Effective Treatment," in *What Works: Reducing Offending*, ed. J. McGuire (New York: Wiley, 1995).

75. G.G. Gaes, T.J. Flanagan, L.L. Motiuk, and L. Stewart, "Adult Correctional Treatment," in *Prisons*, eds. M.H. Tonry and J. Petersilia (Chicago, IL: University of Chicago Press, 1999), 364.

76. See, for example, D.A. Andrews and J. Bonta, *The Psychology of Criminal Conduct* (Cincinnati, OH: Anderson Publishing, 1998).

77. F.T. Cullen and P. Gendreau, "Assessing Correctional Rehabilitation: Policy, Practice, and Prospects," in

Criminal Justice 2000: Policies, Processes, and Decisions of the Criminal Justice System, Vol. 3 (Washington, DC: U.S. Department of Justice, 2000), 109–76.

78. M.L. Dennis, *Integrating Research and Clinical Assessment: Measuring Client and Program Needs and Outcomes in a Changing Service Environment*. NIDA Resource Center for Health Services Research Issue Paper. Rockville, MD: National Institute on Drug Abuse, 1998; R.C. Kessler, D.A. McGonagle, S. Zhao, C. Nelson, M. Hughes, S. Eshleman, H. Wittchen, and K. Kendler, "Lifetime and 12-Month Prevalence of DSM-III-R Psychiatric Disorders in the United States," *Archives of General Psychiatry* 51 (1994): 8–19.

79. G. Field, *Continuity of Offender Treatment for Substance Use Disorders from Institution to Community*. Treatment Improvement Protocol (TIP) Series 30. Department of Health and Human Services Publication No. (SMA) 98-3245. Washington, DC: Department of Health and Human Services, 1998.

80. National Institute on Drug Abuse, *Principles of Drug Addiction Treatment: A Research-Based Guide* (Bethesda, MD: U.S. Department of Health and Human Services, National Institute of Health, National Institute on Drug Abuse, 1999).

81. L.L. Harrison and S.S. Martin, *Residential Substance Abuse Treatment (RSAT) for State Prisoners Formula Grant: Compendium of Program Implementation and Accomplishments* (Newark, DE: Center for Drug and Alcohol Studies, 2000).

82. D.P. Mears, L. Winterfield, J. Hunsaker, G.E. Moore, and R.M. White, *Drug Treatment in the Criminal Justice System: The Current State of Knowledge* (Washington, DC: Justice Policy Center, Urban Institute, 2003), 4–9.

83. See, for example, M.L. Prendergast, J. Wellisch, and M.M. Wong, "Residential Treatment for Women Parolees Following Prison-Based Drug Treatment: Treatment Experiences, Needs, and Service Outcomes," *The Prison Journal* 76 (1996): 253–74; H.K. Wexler, W.F. Graham, R. Koronowski, and L. Lowe, *Evaluation of Amity In-Prison and Post-Release Substance Abuse Treatment Programs* (Washington, DC: National Institute on Drug Abuse, 1995); S.S. Martin, C.A. Butzin, and J. Inciardi, "Assessment of a Multistage Therapeutic Community for Drug Involved Offenders," *Journal of Psychoactive Drugs* 27 (1995): 109–16.

84. S. Turner, "Intensive Supervision," *Crime and Delinquency* 38 (1992): 552–6; S. Turner and J. Petersilia, "Focusing on High Risk Parolees: An Experiment to Reduce Commitments to the Texas Department of Corrections," *Journal of Research in Crime and Delinquency* 29 (1992): 34–61.

85. C.L. Britt, M.R. Gottfredson, and J.S. Goldkamp, "Drug Testing and Pre-Trial Misconduct: An Experiment on the Specific Deterrent Effects of Drug Monitoring Defendants on Pretrial Release," *Journal of Research in Crime and Delinquency* 29 (1992): 62–78.

86. E.P. Deschenes, S. Turner, P. Greenwood, and J. Chiesa, *An Experimental Evaluation of Drug Testing and Treatment Interventions for Probationers in Maricopa County, Arizona* (Santa Monica, CA: RAND, 1996).

87. R. Haapanen and L. Britton, "Drug Testing for Youthful Offenders on Parole: An Experimental Evaluation," *Criminology and Public Policy* 1 (2002): 217–44.

88. A. Harrell, O. Mitchell, A. Hirst, D. Marlow, and J. Merrill, "Breaking the Cycle of Drugs and Crime: Findings from the Birmingham BTC Demonstration," *Criminology and Public Policy* 1 (2002): 189–216.

89. D.L. MacKenzie, "Reducing the Criminal Activities of Known Offenders and Delinquents: Crime Prevention in the Courts and Corrections," in *Evidence-Based Crime Prevention*, eds. L.W. Sherman, D.P. Farrington, B.C. Welsh, and D.L. MacKenzie (New York: Routledge, 2002), 371.

90. T. Nicholaichuk, A. Gordon, G. Andre, and D. Gu, *Long-Term Outcome of the Clearwater Sex Offender Treatment* (paper presented at the 14th Annual Conference of the Association for the Treatment of Sexual Abusers, New Orleans, 1995).

91. G. Duwe, "The Impact of Prison-Based Treatment on Sex Offender Recidivism," *Sexual Abuse: A Journal of Research and Treatment* 21 (2009): 279–307.

92. R.K. Hanson, R.A. Steffy, and R. Gauthier, "Long-Term Recidivism of Child Molesters," *Journal of Consulting and Clinical Psychology* 61 (1993): 646–52.

93. W.L. Marshall and H.E. Barbaree, "The Long-Term Evaluation of a Behavioral Treatment Program for Child Molesters," *Behavioral Research and Therapy* 26 (1988): 499–511.

94. W.L. Marshall, A. Eccles, and H.E. Barbaree, "The Treatment of Exhibitionists: A Focus on Sexual Deviance versus Cognitive and Relationship Features," *Behavior Research and Therapy* 29 (1991): 129–35; see also W.L. Marshall, H.E. Barbaree, and A. Eccles, "Early Onset and Deviant Sexuality in Child Molesters," *Journal of Interpersonal Violence* 6 (1991): 323–35.

95. J.K. Marques, D.M. Day, and M. West, "Effects of Cognitive-Behavioral Treatment on Sex Offender Recidivism," *Criminal Justice and Behavior* 21(1994): 28–34.

96. J.K. Marques, D.M. Day, C. Nelson, and M.A. West, "Findings and Recommendations from California's Experimental Treatment Program," in *Sexual Aggression: Issues in Etiology, Assessment and Treatment*, eds. G.C.N. Hall, R. Hirschman, J.R. Graham, and M.S. Zaragoza (Washington, DC: Taylor and Francis, 1993).

97. See, for example, B.M. Maletzky, *Treating the Sexual Offender* (Newbury Park, CA: Sage, 1991).

98. D.M. Polizzi, D.L. MacKenzie, and L.J. Hickman, "What Works in Adult Sex Offender Treatment?: A Review of Prison- and Non-Prison-Based Treatment Programs," *International Journal of Offender Therapy and Comparative Criminology* 43 (1999): 357–74.

99. M.A. Alexander, *Sex Offender Treatment: A Response to Furby et al., 1989 Quasi Meta-Analysis II* (paper presented

at the Annual Meeting of the Association for the Treatment of Sexual Abusers, San Francisco, 1989).

100. M.A. Alexander, "Sex Offender Treatment Efficacy Revisited," *Sexual Abuse: A Journal of Research and Treatment* 11 (1999): 101–16.

101. See, for example, L.S. Grossman, B. Martis, and C.G. Fichtner, "Are Sex Offenders Treatable? A Research Overview," *Psychiatric Services* 50 (1999): 349–61; C.A. Gallagher, D.B. Wilson, P. Hirschfield, M.B. Coggeshall, and D.L. MacKenzie, "A Quantitative Review of the Effects of Sex Offender Treatment on Sexual Re-offending," *Corrections Management Quarterly* 3 (1999): 19–29; G.C.N. Hall, "Sex Offender Recidivism Revisited: A Meta-Analysis of Recent Treatment Studies," *Journal of Consulting and Clinical Psychology* 63 (1995): 802–9.

102. See, e.g., Mark W. Lipsey and David B. Wilson, "The Efficacy of Psychological, Educational, and Behavioral Treatment," *American Psychologist* 48 (1993): 1181–208.

103. P. Cook and G. Zarkin, "Crime and the Business Cycle," *Journal of Legal Studies* 14 (1985): 115–28.

104. T. Chiricos, "Rates of Crime and Unemployment: An Analysis of Aggregate Research Evidence," *Social Problems* 34 (1986): 187–212.

105. Ibid.

106. M. Wolfgang, R. Figlio, and T. Sellin, *Delinquency in a Birth Cohort* (Chicago, IL: University of Chicago Press, 1972).

107. D.P. Farrington, B. Gallagher, L. Morley, R.J. St. Ledger, and D.J. West, "Unemployment, School Leaving and Crime," *British Journal of Criminology* 26 (1986): 335–56.

108. M. Gottfredson and T. Hirschi, *A General Theory of Crime* (Stanford, CA: Stanford University Press, 1990).

109. R.J. Sampson and J.H. Laub, *Crime in the Making: Pathways and Turning Points through Life* (New York: Cambridge University Press, 1993).

110. T. Chiricos, "Rates of Crime and Unemployment: An Analysis of Aggregate Research Evidence," *Social Problems* 34 (1986): 187–212.

111. P. Cook and G. Zarkin, "Crime and the Business Cycle," *Journal of Legal Studies* 14 (1985): 115–28.

112. See D.L. MacKenzie, "Reducing the Criminal Activities of Known Offenders and Delinquents: Crime Prevention in the Courts and Corrections," in *Evidence-Based Crime Prevention*, eds. L.W. Sherman, D.P. Farrington, B.C. Welsh, and D.L. MacKenzie (New York: Routledge, 2002), 358.

113. Ibid.

114. M.D. Harer, "Recidivism among Federal Prisoners Released in 1987," *Journal of Correctional Education* 46 (1995): 98–127.

115. C. Jeffords and S. McNitt, *The Relationship between GED Attainment and Recidivism: An Evaluation Summary* (Austin, TX: Texas Youth Commission, 1993).

116. A. Walsh, "An Evaluation of the Effects of Adult Basic Education on Arrest Rates among Probationers," *Journal of Offender Counseling, Services, and Rehabilitation* 9 (1985): 69–76.

117. P.K. Lattimore, A.D. Witte, and J.R. Baker, "Experimental Assessment of the Effect of Vocational Training on Youthful Property Offenders," *Evaluation Review* 14 (1990): 115–33.

118. W.G. Saylor and G.G. Gaes, *PREP: Training Inmates through Industrial Work Participation and Vocational and Apprenticeship Instruction* (Washington, DC: Federal Bureau of Prisons, 1996).

119. M.D. Harer, "Recidivism among Federal Prisoners Released in 1987," *Journal of Correctional Education* 46 (1995): 98–127; K. Adams, T. Bennett, T.J. Flanagan, J. Marquart, S. Cuvelier, E.J. Fritsch, J. Gerber, D. Longmire, and V. Burton, "A Large-Scale Multidimensional Test of the Effect of Prison Education Programs on Offender Behavior," *The Prison Journal* 74 (1994): 433–39; C. McGee, *The Positive Impact of Corrections Education on Recidivism and Employment* (Illinois Department of Corrections School District 428, 1997); A.M. Piehl, *Learning While Doing Time: Prison Education and Recidivism among Wisconsin Males* (Princeton, NJ: Princeton University Press, 1995); S.V. Anderson, *Evaluation of the Impact of Correctional Education Programs on Recidivism* (Ohio Department of Rehabilitation and Correction, 1995); R.E. Schumacker, D.B. Anderson, and S.L. Anderson, "Vocational and Academic Indicators of Parole Success," *Journal of Correctional Education* 41 (1990): 8–12.

120. H. Bloom, L.L. Orr, G. Cave, S.H. Bell, F. Doolittle, and W. Lin, *The National JTPA Study: Overview of Impacts, Benefits, and Costs of Title IIA* (Cambridge, MA: ABT Associates, 1994); K.R. Van Stelle, J.R. Lidbury, and D.P. Moberg, *Final Evaluation Report, Specialized Training and Employment Project (STEP)* (Madison, WI: University of Wisconsin Medical School, Center for Health Policy and Program Evaluation, 1995); E.A. Downes, K.R. Monaco, and S.O. Schreiber, "Evaluating the Effects of Vocational Education on Inmates: A Research Model and Preliminary Results," *The Yearbook of Correctional Education*, (1995): 249–62; T.P. Ryan, *A Comparison of Recidivism Rates for Operation Outward Reach (OOR) Participants and Control Groups of Non-Participants for the Years 1990 through 1994.* Program Evaluation Report (Washington, DC: Federal Bureau of Prisons, 1997).

121. M.A. Finn and K.G. Willoughby, "Employment Outcomes of Ex-Offender Job Training Partnership Act (JTPA) Trainees," *Evaluation Review* 20 (1996): 67–83; H. Bloom, L.L. Orr, L.L., G. Cave, S.H. Bell, F. Doolittle and W. Lin, *The National JTPA Study: Overview of Impacts, Benefits, and Costs of Title IIA* (Cambridge, MA: ABT Associates, 1994).

122. H. Bloom, L.L. Orr, G. Cave, S.H. Bell, F. Doolittle, and W. Lin, *The National JTPA Study: Overview of Impacts, Benefits, and Costs of Title IIA* (Cambridge, MA: ABT Associates, 1994).

123. T.J. Flanagan, T.P. Thornberry, K. Maguire, and E. McGarrell, *The Effect of Prison Industry Employment on Offender Behavior: Report of the Prison Industry Research Project* (Albany, NY: Hindelang Criminal Justice Research Center, 1988).

124. See D.L. MacKenzie, "Reducing the Criminal Activities of Known Offenders and Delinquents: Crime Prevention in the Courts and Corrections," in *Evidence-Based Crime Prevention*, L.W. Sherman, D.P. Farrington, B.C. Welsh, and D.L. MacKenzie (New York: Routledge, 2002), 364.

125. See nationalcia.org/indlinks2.html for a complete listing.

126. K.E. Maguire, T.J. Flanagan, and T.P. Thornberry, "Prison Labor and Recidivism," *Journal of Quantitative Criminology* 4 (1988): 3–18; W.G. Saylor and G.G. Gaes, *PREP: Training Inmates Through Industrial Work Participation and Vocational and Apprenticeship Instruction* (Washington, DC: Federal Bureau of Prisons, 1996); S.V. Anderson, *Evaluation of the Impact of Participation in Ohio Penal Industries on Recidivism* (Ohio Department of Rehabilitation and Correction, Office of Management Information Systems, 1995).

127. S. Turner and J. Petersilia, "Work Release in Washington: Effects on Recidivism and Corrections Costs," *Prison Journal* 76 (1996): 138–64. See also the N.J. version of the report: S. Turner & J. Petersilia, *Work Release: Recidivism and Corrections Costs in Washington State* (Washington, DC: National Institute of Justice, 1996).

128. I. Piliavin and S. Masters, *The Impact of Employment Programs on Offenders, Addicts, and Problem Youth: Implications from Supported Work* (Madison, WI: University of Wisconsin, Institute for Research and Poverty Discussion, 1981).

129. Ibid., 45.

130. W.J. Wilson, *The Truly Disadvantaged: The Inner City, the Underclass, and Public Policy* (Chicago, IL: University of Chicago Press, 1987).

131. W.J. Wilson, *When Work Disappears: The World of the New Urban Poor* (New York: Alfred A. Knopf, 1996).

132. M.A. Hughes, *Over the Horizon: Jobs in the Suburbs of Major Metropolitan Areas* (Philadelphia, PA: Public/Private Ventures, 1993).

133. J.E. Rosenbaum, "Black Pioneers: Do Their Moves to the Suburbs Increase Economic Opportunity for Mothers and Children?" *Housing Policy Debate* 2 (1992): 1179–213; L.F. Katz, J.R. Kling, and J.B. Liebman, "Moving to Opportunity in Boston: Early Impacts of a Housing Mobility Program" (unpublished manuscript, Washington, DC: National Bureau of Economic Research, 1999); J. Ludwig, G.J. Duncan, and P. Hirschfield, "Urban Poverty and Juvenile Crime: Evidence from a Randomized Housing-Mobility Experiment" (unpublished manuscript, Washington, DC: Georgetown Public Policy Institute, 1999); J. Ludwig, G.J. Duncan, and J.C. Pinkston, "Neighborhood Effects on Economic Self-Sufficiency: Evidence from a Randomized Housing-Mobility Experiment" (unpublished manuscript, Washington, DC: Georgetown Public Policy Institute, 2000).

134. J. Ludwig, G.J. Duncan, and P. Hirschfield, "Urban Poverty and Juvenile Crime: Evidence from a Randomized Housing-Mobility Experiment," *Quarterly Journal of Economics* 116 (2001): 655–79.

135. F.T. Cullen, "Rehabilitation and Treatment Programs," in *Crime: Public Policies for Crime Control*, eds. J.Q. Wilson and J. Petersilia (Oakland, CA: Institute for Contemporary Studies, 2002), 266.

136. Ibid., 289.

Individual, Family, and Household Crime Control

LEARNING OBJECTIVES

■ Discuss the effectiveness of gun use for personal defense.

■ Identify other individual-level methods of crime prevention and control.

■ Summarize varieties of household and family-level crime control.

■ Discuss the effectiveness of household and family-level crime control.

The various methods of crime control that we discussed in Chapters 3 through 11 of this book had significant criminal justice system involvement. We looked at police and prosecution strategies as well as legislative approaches, tough sentencing, probation, and parole—all with significant involvement on the part of criminal justice officials. Even treatment and rehabilitation relied extensively on court involvement and monitoring by police and probation or parole officers. Courts, too, are obviously tied to the justice system. Were this book to have stopped at the last chapter, we would be ignoring the many methods of dealing with crime that do not rely on police officers, prosecutors, and judges. Here we turn our attention to approaches beyond the criminal justice system.

This chapter covers crime control at the individual, family, and household levels. It begins by covering actions that individuals take to control crime; then it shifts focus to crime control that occurs at the level of (though not necessarily by) families and households. For example, some researchers have found an inverse relationship between welfare expenditures and crime, leading them to conclude that more welfare money for families will reduce any need to commit crime to obtain basic necessities. Such crime control is not undertaken by families themselves (government agencies dish out the money), but this type of crime control can still be understood as occurring at the family level.

GOVERNMENT MAY STILL BE INVOLVED

The title of this section of the book is "Approaches beyond the Criminal Justice System." This means that we will move away from our focus on police, courts, corrections, and the various laws and policies that they are charged with enforcing. It does not mean, however, that we will ignore the role of government. Government agencies—especially public assistance entities such as departments of social services—will still play a significant role in many of the approaches discussed here and in the next two chapters.

We begin, though, by considering the effectiveness of actions that individual people take to control crime. Such individual actions rely on virtually no governmental intervention. But family and household crime control, to which we will turn later in this chapter, tend to rely heavily on funding by government organizations. In Chapter 14, we will turn back to some approaches that do not involve government intervention. That chapter will be concerned with crime control by environmental manipulation, including target hardening. An example of target hardening is buying a home security system to deter burglars. One does not need government intervention to buy a home security system.

The reader is advised to keep an eye out for the types of nongovernmental crime controls that were just discussed, as well as others. It should become apparent that there is very little in crime control in America—at least in that which has been researched—that does not rely on a significant amount of government involvement. This raises several important discussion questions: Are we as individuals unable or unwilling to do what it takes to control crime? Is it best that government control crime instead of individuals? Alternatively, is there something else that affects crime that is beyond the control of both government entities and individuals? Keep the first two questions in mind throughout this and the next few chapters. We will return to the third one in Chapter 15.

INDIVIDUAL CRIME CONTROL

There are several methods by which individuals attempt to prevent themselves from becoming victims of crime. (See Table 12.1 for an estimate of the percentage of violent victimizations in which victims took self-protective actions to deter criminals. The table contains the most recent data available as of this writing.) The first and most researched option is to buy a gun and have it available for use in self-defense. Many people believe that having a gun in the house is something of a security blanket and that they can use the gun to defend themselves should an intruder enter. We will not turn this book into a criminal law text by discussing all the legal ramifications of using a firearm in self-defense, but we *will* look at the large body of research that is concerned with whether people can capably defend themselves with guns.

The second type of individual crime control is risk-avoidance behavior. Examples of risk-avoidance behavior include staying inside at night, avoiding certain parts of a neighborhood, and steering clear of dangerous-looking individuals. The third type of individual crime control is risk management. Risk management occurs when individuals cannot stay inside all the time or avoid specific areas or people.[1] An example is not carrying large sums of cash on one's person, thereby minimizing the potential loss

TABLE 12.1   Percent of Violent Victimizations in Which Victims Took Self-Protective Measures

Type of Crime	Number of Victimizations	Percent of All Victimizations		
		All Victimizations	Involving Strangers	Involving Nonstrangers
Total	**2,797,070**	**57.6%**	**55.4%**	**59.8%**
Completed violence	829,360	60.9	53.7	66.1
Attempted/threatened violence	1,967,710	56.3	56.0	56.7
Rape/sexual assault[a]	128,520	63.1	63.9	62.6
Robbery	361,090	65.4	63.5	69.6
Completed/property taken	204,260	54.9	46.2	68.4
With injury	105,540	74.5	77.9	69.7
Without injury	98,720	42.8	27.8	67.5
Attempted to take property	156,830	87.3	89.2	76.5*
With injury	61,070	95.0	100.0	60.1*
Without injury	95,760	83.0	82.9	83.6*
Assault	2,307,460	56.3	53.6	58.8
Aggravated	478,430	57.0	49.5	65.0
With injury	134,410	53.2	50.0	56.1
Threatened with weapon	344,020	58.6	49.3	69.4
Simple	1,829,030	56.1	54.7	57.3
With minor injury	406,940	66.0	65.7	66.2
Without injury	1,422,100	53.8	53.3	54.3

*Estimate is based on 10 or fewer sample cases.

[a]Includes verbal threats of rape and threats of sexual assault.

Source: Michael R. Rand and Jayne E. Robinson, *Criminal Victimization in the United States, 2008* (Washington, DC: Bureau of Justice Statistics, 2011).

associated with robbery victimization. A more extreme example is signing up for a self-defense course to avoid becoming a victim of rape or some other serious crime.

Buying a gun to protect oneself is essentially a form of risk management. It is an action taken to give the impression of self-assuredness and confidence, an impression that, it is hoped, will deter would-be attackers. But because this type of crime control has been subjected to so much research, it is covered in its own section. The section on risk management that comes later in this chapter will focus on less lethal methods of risk management, including victim resistance in violent encounters.

Guns and Personal Defense

People have strong opinions about gun use for personal defense. Mass shootings, such as that which occurred at Sandy Hook Elementary in Newtown, Pennsylvania, in 2012, further fuel the debate over whether people should keep guns in close reach so as to deter would-be mass murderers.[2] Indeed, the NRA recently funded a commission to investigate and come up with recommendations for improving school safety around the country (see nraschoolshield.com). Among the commission's recommendations was training and arming certain school officials to prevent casualties in active shooter situations. Interestingly, though, the commission failed to cite *any* research on the effectiveness of defensive gun use. Here we consider that research.

The first problem with studying the effectiveness of gun use in self-defense is settling on appropriate measures of the phenomenon. Although we can somewhat accurately describe the crime rate with sources such as the Uniform Crime Reports and the National Crime Victimization Survey, there is no direct measure of gun ownership or gun use in the United States. As a result, researchers have had to get creative. It has also proven somewhat difficult for researchers to determine how often people use guns in self-defense.

MEASURING GUN PREVALENCE. The United States has no central registry of guns that are in private hands. Researchers have had to rely on survey measures to assess the extent of gun ownership. One such survey is the General Social Survey. In 1999, the survey revealed that 36 percent of households reported ownership of at least one gun.[3] The most significant problem with the General Social Survey, however, is that it cannot be used to arrive at local-level estimates of gun prevalence. This has forced researchers to rely on any number of proxy measures of gun ownership.

The most reliable measure, according to a recent study, is the number of suicides that are committed with a gun.[4] This measure has outperformed competing measures, including the percentage of homicides that are committed with a gun, membership in the National Rifle Association, and subscriptions to gun-oriented magazines.[5]

Using the number of gun-related suicides to measure gun prevalence reveals substantial regional variation in gun ownership. Such detail cannot be achieved by relying on the General Social Survey. For example, the gun-related suicide numbers show that gun ownership in Louisiana, Alabama, and Mississippi outnumbers ownership in Hawaii and Massachusetts by more than two to one.[6]

HOW OFTEN ARE GUNS USED IN SELF-DEFENSE? Researchers began exploring how often guns are used in self-defense by conducting surveys. For example, a 1994 telephone survey conducted by DataStat revealed that within the preceding 12-month period, more than 500,000 instances of gun use in self-defense against intruders were reported.[7] Survey respondents also claimed that they had successfully fended off attacks nearly 99 percent of the time.[8] Using more recent data, other researchers have found as many as 3.6 million instances of gun use in self-defense each year.[9]

The National Crime Victimization Survey (NCVS) tells a different story. The survey, which is conducted every six months by the Census Bureau, has also been used to arrive at estimates of gun use in self-defense. One such estimate suggests that there were 32,000 instances of defensive gun use in burglary victimizations (80,000 in cases of predatory crime victimization) each year from 1979 to 1987, clearly a much lower number than those arrived at in the DataStat survey.[10] More recently, researchers have used NCVS data to estimate that as many as 108,000 defensive gun uses occur per year, a number that is still far lower than the DataStat estimates.[11] See Table 12.2 for another look at NCVS-based estimates of victim resistance with guns and other techniques.

Which data source should be believed? It appears that researchers have put more faith in NCVS data, for two reasons. First, when both estimates are compared to the annual number of burglaries shown in the NCVS data, it becomes clear that the DataStat survey's estimate of 500,000 uses of guns in self-defense is quite liberal. According to one study, there were roughly 1 million burglaries per year between 1979 and 1987, which would mean that in half of those burglaries, victims used guns in self-defense.[12] This estimate seems quite high.

The second reason why more faith has been put in the NCVS is that its estimates are more consistent with findings from other studies that used neither the NCVS nor DataStat estimates. That is, NCVS estimates perhaps have more external validity than other survey-based measures. For example, a study of 198 Atlanta police reports showed that victims used guns in self-defense in just 1.5 percent of burglaries.[13] It is probably safe to conclude, then, that guns are rarely used in self-defense, especially in the context of burglaries. But this leaves open the question of whether, in those rare instances in which guns are used, people can capably fend off burglars and other criminals.

Before continuing, it is worth mentioning that the NCVS contains its own limitations. First, respondents are never asked about whether they have used a gun in self-defense if they do not first report victimization. For example, a person might fend off a trespasser with a gun, but because criminal trespassing is not measured in the NCVS, this type of gun use would never be reported.[14] Second, if a person *prevents* a crime by using a gun, then the prevented crime would not be reported in the NCVS because it did not technically occur.[15] Third, people might wish to conceal gun use from the government employees who conduct the NCVS survey.[16] Together, these three limitations of the NCVS can result in a downward bias, leading to highly conservative estimates of the extent to which people use firearms to protect themselves from victimization.

AGGREGATE RESEARCH. Researchers have examined the relationship between levels of gun ownership and burglary rates at the state and local level. This type of aggregate research has become popular because of the aforementioned limitations of data sources such as the NCVS and the DataStat survey.[17] It is much easier for researchers to collect city-, county-, or state-level crime data and compare burglary rates to estimates of gun ownership. Assuming that there is a relationship, the one that most of us would expect is a negative one—that is, as gun ownership increases, burglary declines.

John Lott analyzed the relationship between state-level Uniform Crime Reports data and gun ownership for two years (1988 and 1996).[18] He controlled for several other possible explanations of crime (e.g., unemployment) and found that a 1 percent

TABLE 12.2 Percent Distribution of Self-Protective Measures Employed by Victims

Self-Protective Measure	Crimes of Violence	Completed Violence	Attempted/ Threatened Violence	Rape/ Sexual Assault[a]	Robbery Total	Robbery With Injury	Robbery Without Injury	Assault Total	Assault Aggravated	Assault Simple
Total number of self-protective measures	100%	100%	100%	100%	100%	100%	100%	100%	100%	100%
Attacked offender with weapon	1.3	1.8*	1.0*	2.7*	4.2*	4.3*	4.1*	0.6*	1.8*	0.3*
Attacked offender without weapon	7.7	9.5	6.8	2.9*	7.0	10.4*	3.1*	8.1	6.7	8.5
Threatened offender with weapon	0.6*	0.7*	0.6*	0.0*	1.0*	1.8*	0.0*	0.6*	2.4*	0.1*
Threatened offender without weapon	1.0*	0.5*	1.3*	1.9*	1.8*	1.3*	2.2*	0.9*	0.0*	1.1*
Resisted or captured offender	22.3	35.0	16.2	30.9	25.6	31.6	18.9	21.1	18.4	21.9
Scared or warned offender	11.2	11.4	11.0	12.0*	15.2	16.9	13.2*	10.3	10.6	10.2
Persuaded or appeased offender	12.7	9.8	14.1	14.1*	11.3	7.0*	16.2	12.9	9.3	13.9
Ran away or hid	16.2	10.8	18.8	13.6*	14.3	9.4*	19.9	16.7	25.4	14.2
Got help or gave alarm	14.4	9.2	16.9	14.0*	9.3	8.1*	10.7*	15.4	15.0	15.5
Screamed from pain or fear	3.0	7.2	1.0*	6.2*	4.6*	5.9*	3.2*	2.5	2.2*	2.6
Took other measures	9.6	4.1	12.3	1.8*	5.7*	3.1*	8.5*	10.9	8.2	11.7

Note: Detail may not add to total shown because of rounding. Some respondents provided more than one self-protective measure employed.

*Estimate is based on 10 or fewer sample cases.

[a]Includes verbal threats of rape and threats of sexual assault.

Source: Michael R. Rand and Jayne E. Robinson, *Criminal Victimization in the United States, 2008* (Washington, DC: Bureau of Justice Statistics, 2011).

increase in gun ownership led to a 1.6 percent reduction in burglary. His measure of gun ownership was somewhat suspect, however. He relied on voter exit surveys that have been criticized by the authors of subsequent studies.[19]

Another researcher, Mark Duggan, used subscriptions to *Guns & Ammo* magazine as his estimate of gun prevalence.[20] He also improved on Lott's study by including several years of data, not just two. This permitted a more sophisticated statistical model that actually revealed a *positive* relationship between gun ownership and burglary. In other words, he found that burglaries *increased* in areas with high levels of gun ownership.

How could burglary *increase* where people own more guns? One explanation is that guns themselves are the targets of burglars because of their value.[21] As one team of researchers put it, "a gun-rich community provides more lucrative burglary opportunities than one in which guns are more sparse."[22] Whether guns are the targets of burglars probably hinges, though, on the type of burglary being committed and on whether the burglar knows if the dwelling he or she targets is occupied. If a burglar knows that a dwelling is occupied and breaks in anyway (a "hot" burglary), then a gun might not be the target. Guns might become targets during so-called cold burglaries of unoccupied dwellings.

Regardless of what goes on in burglars' heads (we will visit this issue later), before researchers can thoroughly explore the relationship between burglary and gun ownership, they need to differentiate between types of burglaries. Recently, a team of researchers looked specifically at hot burglaries to see whether gun ownership has a deterrent effect. It makes much more sense to look at hot burglaries because if there is any deterrent effect of gun ownership in such instances, it is most certain to take place when victims are at home and can use guns in self-defense. Interestingly, though, the researchers found no deterrent effect. In fact, they found that gun ownership might *increase* burglary, even hot burglaries. In their words:

> We find that gun prevalence has little effect on the fraction of residential burglaries in which someone is at home, and that the hot-burglary victimization rate tends to increase with gun prevalence. These results are robust to alternative specifications and data sets. We conclude that keeping a gun at home is unlikely to provide a positive externality in the form of burglary deterrence.[23]

It appears, then, that guns have little deterrent effect, particularly in the burglary context. But the matter still remains unresolved, for a number of reasons. First, researchers have yet to devote much energy to determining whether other criminals, such as robbers, can be deterred by gun use. An exception appears to be a study looking at the "social costs" of gun ownership. The authors found that gun prevalence and homicide go hand in hand. They concluded: "An increase in gun prevalence causes an intensification of criminal violence—a shift toward greater lethality, and hence greater harm to the community."[24] Second, researchers have criticized the methods that were used by those whose studies we have just summarized.[25] Finally, aggregate research such as that discussed here might mask an occasional success story in which a burglary victim successfully interrupted a criminal's exploits. It also gives no attention to what goes on in the heads of burglars themselves. These latter issues deserve some additional attention.

ANECDOTAL ACCOUNTS. Anecdotal accounts of successful self-defense with a gun flourish[26], but they do not help us here.[27] For one thing, they cannot be validated. And unless we have detailed information about each act of resistance, it is not always possible to separate the effects of gun use from other factors that might deter criminals. For example, a victim's age could influence a criminal's decision to act against him or her more than the mere presence of a gun. Similarly, a criminal might be more willing to attack a victim in private than in public, something that has little to do with the presence or absence of a gun.[28]

ARMED RESISTANCE AND CRIME COMPLETION. Despite the evidence that aggregate gun levels are generally not associated with crime rates some researchers *have* found that armed resistance leads to a reduction in the likelihood that a criminal will complete an attack. Most research in this area has focused on armed resistance in the robbery context, relying on data from the National Crime Victimization Survey, and most of it suggests that armed resistance is associated with a lower probability of robbery completion.[29] In addition, this research shows that armed resistance is generally more effective than is unarmed resistance.[30] The author of one such study concluded that victims who resist by using a gun reported the lowest crime completion rates among eight types of self-protection, some of which are discussed later in this chapter.[31]

ARMED RESISTANCE AND VICTIM INJURY. Just because people might be able to fend off attacks by armed resistance does not mean that they can necessarily do so without injury. This concern has led some researchers to examine the links between armed resistance and victim injury, but the evidence remains somewhat mixed. Three studies, again relying on National Crime Victimization Survey data, have shown that armed resistance is associated with lower levels of victim injury.[32] But another study, using police data, showed that armed resistance was associated with *higher* rates of victim injury.[33] Still another study shows that forceful and nonforceful resistance by female assault victims resulted in an increased likelihood of injury.[34] Whether other, nonlethal forms of resistance lead to victim injury is a topic that we take up later in this chapter, but for now, it remains unclear whether self-defense with a gun increases the likelihood of victim injury (see Table 12.3).

DO CRIMINALS CARE? It is one thing to study gun ownership, aggregate crime rates, anecdotal accounts of deterrence by gun, and the effects of victim resistance. It is quite another to get inside the heads of criminals themselves. A handful of researchers have tried to do so by surveying convicted criminals, notably burglars. This approach of going to the "horse's mouth" has distinct advantages over other methods of research. The most notable advantage is that it allows researchers to determine the extent to which burglars gave thought to the prospect of being shot while they committed the crime.

For example, in 1982, 1,823 state prisoners were surveyed, and 74 percent of the respondents agreed that "one reason burglars avoid houses when people are at home is that they fear being shot."[35] At the same time, though, surveys of convicted criminals reveal that guns are attractive targets in burglaries. Nearly half of the prisoners in the same 1982 survey reported stealing a gun during their lifetimes.[36] As a burglar in one such study claimed, "A gun is money with a trigger."[37]

COMPENSATING RISKS AND OFFSETTING BEHAVIOR. It is not always politically correct to say so, but crime victims sometimes act in ways that increase the probability that they will be injured or attacked. As one researcher has observed, "armed citizens may escalate verbal arguments that otherwise might be defused or ignored or may

TABLE 12.3 Percent of Victimization in Which Protective Measures Were Used by Outcome of Action

Person Using Measure and Type of Crime	Number of Victimizations	Total	Percent of Vctimizations					
			Helped Situation	Hurt Situation	Both Helped and Hurt Situation	Neither Helped Nor Hurt Situation	Don't Know	Not Available
Measure taken by victimdd								
Crimes of violence	2,797,070	100%	66.0	5.7	6.4	10.3	7.2	4.3
Rape/sexual assault[a]	128,520	100%	53.0	8.9*	5.1*	17.3*	5.8*	10.0*
Robbery	361,090	100%	65.1	2.5*	9.9*	12.1	7.1*	3.2*
Assault	2,307,460	100%	66.8	6.1	6.0	9.7	7.3	4.2
Aggravated	478,430	100%	66.0	4.0*	7.4*	10.1	6.1*	6.4*
Simple	1,829,030	100%	67.0	6.6	5.6	9.6	7.6	3.6
Measure taken by others								
Crimes of violence	3,315,580	100%	27.0	7.7	0.7*	34.9	5.9	23.9
Rape/sexual assault[a]	89,450	100%	11.6*	17.8*	0.0*	22.2*	6.0*	42.5
Robbery	366,330	100%	21.7	7.2*	1.0*	48.4	2.9*	18.8
Assault	2,859,790	100%	28.2	7.4	0.6*	33.6	6.2	24.0
Aggravated	595,440	100%	31.5	4.3*	0.9*	32.7	5.9*	24.7
Simple	2,264,350	100%	27.3	8.2	0.6*	33.8	6.3	23.8

Note: Detail may not add to total shown because of rounding. Excludes victimizations in which no self-protective actions were taken. Of those victimizations in which self-protective measures were employed, the victim and/or somebody else may have taken the action. Therefore, the table categories are not mutually exclusive.

*Estimate is based on 10 or fewer sample cases.

[a]Includes verbal threats of rape and threats of sexual assault.

Source: Michael R. Rand and Jayne E. Robinson, *Criminal Victimization in the United States, 2008* (Washington, DC: Bureau of Justice Statistics, 2011).

choose to walk dark streets that would otherwise have been avoided."[38] Such **offsetting behavior** has been documented in a number of other contexts. For example, studies show that improvements in automobile designs have led to riskier driving.[39] Similarly, the introduction of child-resistant packaging for drugs has led to careless storage of such drugs.[40] Returning to the issue of guns, one study shows that one-third of all gun defenders had the option of staying inside their homes and calling the police rather than confronting criminals.[41]

offsetting behavior: when policies intended to reduce risk cause people to act carelessly and put themselves even more at risk.

GUNS AND ACCIDENTAL DEATHS. Several researchers have studied the relationship between gun availability and unintentional firearm deaths,[42] but many such studies are descriptive and do not rely on statistical analysis. One exception is a study in which a team of researchers compared firearm availability to unintentional deaths after controlling for several factors that would affect the latter.[43] The authors found that states with the highest gun ownership had nine times the rate of unintentional firearm deaths of states with the lowest gun ownership:

> There are many potential costs and benefits from having a heavily armed society. . . . The findings suggest that for men and women, African Americans and Whites, and for all age groups, where there are more guns, more people are dying from unintentional gunshot injuries.[44]

One policy that has been implemented in several states in response to unintentional shootings is gun safe storage laws. Several states have passed laws that make gun owners criminally liable if someone is injured when a child gains access to a gun in the home. A team of researchers recently studied the effects of such laws on child mortality due to firearms.[45] They found that among children younger than age 15, unintentional shootings were reduced by 23 percent in states with safe storage laws.

COMPARING THE UNITED STATES TO OTHER NATIONS. So far, the evidence against keeping a gun in the home is mounting. By many estimates, guns are not used very frequently—or effectively—to deter burglars. In addition, a gun in the home can lead to unintended consequences, such as accidental shootings. But some researchers have looked beyond the U.S. borders and compared burglary rates in other nations to those in this country. In general, they have found that residential burglary rates are *higher* in other wealthy nations, such as Canada and the United Kingdom, that do not have nearly as many guns as the United States does. What explanation can be offered for this finding? One possibility is that guns deter criminals; the reason that there are more burglaries in other nations with fewer guns is that burglars do not fear being shot. Another possibility is that something besides the presence of guns explains the differences. For example, burglars in the United States are sentenced to almost twice as much time in prison on average as are burglars in the United Kingdom.[46] Even so, data limitations make it difficult to compare specific crime rates—especially hot burglaries—between nations.[47]

A GUN IN EVERY HOME? In 1982, the city of Kennesaw, Georgia, passed an ordinance requiring every household to keep a gun. A similar law was passed in Nelson, Georgia, in 2013. Some people have said this was forward thinking on the part of government officials who were fed up with trends in burglary. Others have said that the ordinance was little more than symbolic because there was a gun in almost every home before it went into effect. Either way, researchers have jumped on the opportunity to explore whether mandated gun ownership deterred burglary. Unfortunately, given that the level of gun ownership did not change significantly following passage of the ordinance, the results of studies in this area are inconclusive.[48] Indeed, since there was no penalty for failing to comply with the ordinance, it is unlikely that researchers can do much more with Kennesaw to study the deterrent effect (if there is any) of home gun ownership.

Risk-Avoidance Behaviors

risk avoidance behaviors: the actions that people take to avoid being victimized or coming face to face with criminals.

Using a gun in self-defense is about as confrontational as it gets. At the other extreme, **risk-avoidance behaviors** are the actions that people take to avoid being victimized or coming face to face with criminals.[49] Researchers have indeed found that such behaviors are commonplace. Surveys show that between 25 and 45 percent of people have recently refrained from going out at night because of crime.[50] This method of minimizing the potential for victimization appears to be most pronounced in high-crime, inner-city neighborhoods.[51] A litany of other risk-avoidance behaviors exist—so many that people often do not realize that they are engaging in risk-avoidance.

Surprisingly few researchers have explored whether risk-avoidance works. Many studies published in the 1960s and 1970s showed a link between risk-avoidance behaviors, such as not going out at night, and crime. Recently, though, the topic has received scant attention. Perhaps this is because it is obvious that risk avoidance has implications for the possibility of victimization. As Rosenbaum pointed out, "Unless one lives with a violent family member, staying at home behind locked doors and not venturing outside should lower a person's risk of personal victimization because more violent crime occurs outdoors."[52]

CHARACTERISTICS OF VICTIMS. Although there are not many studies concerned directly with the relationship between risk avoidance and victimization, the field of victimology sheds much light on this important type of crime control in America. Specifically, it is helpful to look at the characteristics and behaviors of people and the effects of such factors on the likelihood of victimization. There are two broad classes of such characteristics and behaviors: Those that can be changed and those that cannot be changed. Only the former should be targeted for enhanced crime control.

Victim characteristics that cannot be changed include sex, age, and race. In general, men are more likely than women to become victims of crime. Likewise, younger people are victimized more frequently than the elderly are.[53] Furthermore, ethnic minorities are at a high risk of victimization.[54] See Table 12.4 for a look at murders and nonnegligent manslaughters by victim sex, race, and age.

Obviously, it is not possible to change men into women, young people into the elderly, and minorities into whites. But there are other victim characteristics and behaviors that might lend themselves to change. One is socioeconomic status. The poor are victims of crime, especially violent crime, more often than the rich are, so it could prove useful to assist poorer people such that they can make more money, live in safer neighborhoods, and be at lower risk of victimization. We will consider efforts to improve the socioeconomic status of families—and whole communities—later in this and the next chapter. Marital status also influences victimization risk, so perhaps more marriages are in order for single people.

Improving people's material well-being is easier said than done. And there are single people who don't want any part of marriage. In addition, characteristics such as low socioeconomic status and being unmarried could themselves be caused by other

TABLE 12.4 Murder Victims by Age, Sex, and Race

Age	Total	Sex			Race			
		Male	Female	Unknown	White	Black	Other	Unknown
Murders, total	**13,756**	**10,582**	**3,158**	**16**	**6,655**	**6,587**	**365**	**149**
Percent of total	100.0	76.9	23.1	0.1	48.4	47.9	2.7	1.1
Under 18 years old[1]	1,363	921	442	–	669	640	44	10
18 years old and over[1]	12,393	9,661	2,716	16	5,986	5,947	321	139
Infant (under 1 year old)	201	106	95	–	113	74	9	5
1 to 4 years old	305	163	142	–	164	131	9	1
5 to 8 years old	74	35	39	–	42	27	4	1
9 to 12 years old	70	35	35	–	44	21	5	–
13 to 16 years old	398	317	81	–	189	198	9	2
17 to 19 years old	1,250	1,072	178	–	477	742	22	9
20 to 24 years old	2,432	2,087	344	1	934	1,409	65	24
25 to 29 years old	1,955	1,616	338	1	799	1,101	39	16
30 to 34 years old	1,545	1,221	324	–	654	848	25	18
35 to 39 years old	1,221	963	258	–	581	588	41	12
40 to 44 years old	1,016	741	274	1	552	419	35	10
45 to 49 years old	941	655	286	–	571	340	23	7
50 to 54 years old	708	526	181	1	425	247	27	9
55 to 59 years old	466	314	152	–	293	147	22	4
60 to 64 years old	321	224	97	–	216	90	12	3
65 to 69 years old	231	153	78	–	169	57	4	1
70 to 74 years old	135	86	49	–	105	26	1	3
75 years old and over	294	144	150	–	231	53	10	–
Age unknown	193	124	57	12	96	69	3	24

–Represents zero.

[1]Does not include unknown ages.

Source: U.S. Department of Justice, Federal Bureau of Investigation, *Uniform Crime Reporting Program* (Washington, DC: U.S. Department of Justice, 2012).

factors that are more directly linked to crime. For example, single people also tend to be young, and they are more likely to socialize outside the home, perhaps increasing their potential for becoming victims of crime.

So is there *anything* about crime victims that can be changed and that sheds light on the relationship between risk-avoidance behavior and victimization? Some victimization theories might prove helpful. One such theory, victim precipitation theory, holds that there are two types of victim precipitation: direct and passive. The latter refers to things that people do that unknowingly encourages an attacker (e.g., carrying a shopping bag from an expensive store). The former includes overt actions, such as starting a fight, that increase the potential for victimization. The policy implication for either type of victim precipitation, assuming that the theory is correct, is that people should take steps to minimize their own role in becoming crime victims.

Lifestyle theories have also been put forth to explain why some people are victimized more than others. Some people simply engage in high-risk behaviors, such as drug use, that increase their potential for victimization. Such behavior can have a spiraling effect and put drug users closer to crime geographically (so that they can buy drugs) and otherwise encourage them to hang out in so-called deviant places that are perhaps supportive of the person's lifestyle and habits.[55]

Many other victimization theories have been put forth, and we will not review them extensively here. The point is that risk-avoidance behavior need not simply consist of conscious actions by cautious people who do not want to be victims of crime. People who are at risk of victimization and who either don't know or don't care should be targeted as well. Unfortunately, though, little is done to reach out to such people, and hardly any research on the subject is available.

A SIMPLE EXPLANATION AND A COMPLEX SOLUTION.   Risk avoidance seems like common sense, but for some people it is just not possible. This is probably why little is done to promote risk-avoidance behavior among the people who would benefit most from trying it.

RISK-AVOIDANCE EFFECTIVENESS: FURTHER COMPLICATIONS.   One problem associated with studying the effectiveness of risk avoidance is that when it works, a crime fails to occur, which means that there is no crime to be counted. In other words, successful risk avoidance equates with the absence of crime, and criminal justice researchers do not have good data on crimes that were not successfully completed. In such cases, because there is no crime and no victim, there is no police report or other documentation of the incident. This is partly why the study of victimology came to be; given data limitations, researchers have been forced to look at the characteristics and behaviors of crime victims to develop methods of encouraging such people to avoid becoming crime statistics.

Risk-Management Behaviors

risk management behaviors: the actions that people take when they know that they cannot fully avoid the potential for victimization.

Risk-management behaviors include actions that people take when they know that they cannot fully avoid the potential for victimization. As one source describes it, risk management includes attempts to "make the criminal act more difficult to complete or to minimize the victim's losses (that is, property loss or injury)."[56] Risk management can consist of preventive action that is designed to deter would-be criminals from attacking. For example, if a person hides cash, say, in a money belt, this action is taken to minimize the person's potential for being robbed. But the bulk of the research in this area is concerned with the second form of risk management: resistance. We discussed resistance with a gun earlier on in this chapter. Here, we turn to generally nonlethal mechanisms of resistance and their effectiveness, and we look at vigilantism.

SELF-DEFENSE TRAINING.   Most of us know someone who has taken or is enrolled in a self-defense course. People take such courses for a number of reasons (e.g., to improve their physical fitness and flexibility), but the main reason is so that one can successfully interrupt a criminal attack or otherwise defend oneself during a violent encounter.[57] The question for researchers has been "Does self-defense training work?" But virtually no one has attempted to answer the question. In one of the few published studies on this subject, researchers found that women who enrolled in self-defense courses felt more in control of their bodies and were less fearful of crime.[58] In another study, researchers found that women who enroll in self-defense courses tend to alter their behavior.[59] The problem with both studies is that they do not address the effectiveness of self-defense training, particularly whether it acts as a deterrent to crime or reduces the likelihood of crime completions.

FORCEFUL RESISTANCE. Forceful resistance without a gun can come in two forms.[60] First, forceful physical resistance consists of acts such as hitting, kicking, and biting. Second, forceful verbal resistance includes yelling and threatening the offender. In neither case is the force employed considered deadly. What does the research show about the effectiveness of each approach? Forceful physical resistance tends to reduce the likelihood of crime completion but can increase the likelihood of victim injury, especially in the rape context.[61] More promising are the prospects for forceful verbal resistance. Intended crime victims who display this type of resistance are more likely to see the crime completed than in the case of forceful physical resistance, but there is no clear evidence that forceful verbal resistance leads to an increase in the potential for injury to the victim.

NONFORCEFUL RESISTANCE. Nonforceful resistance also comes in two forms. First, nonforceful physical resistance can include attempts to push the offender away.[62] Second, nonforceful verbal resistance amounts to pleading for the offender to stop and/ or reasoning with the offender. The former method appears to reduce the chances of a crime being completed, but its effect on victim injury remains unclear.[63] Among all the resistance strategies that we have discussed thus far, nonforceful verbal resistance appears to be the least effective. Some studies show, in fact, that it actually contributes to a greater chance of crime completion.[64] However, one recent study, which is arguably one of the most sophisticated to date, suggests that arguing and reasoning with the offender can prove productive:

> Our results unambiguously showed that nonphysical forms of resistance were more effective than either no resistance or physical resistance in reducing a woman's probability of being injured. This was true no matter what the relationship between the victim and her offender, but seemed to be a particularly effective strategy in assaults by strangers. Although overall level of injury was lower in stranger assaults compared with other types, nonphysical resistance by the victim in stranger perpetrated assaults cut her risk of injury by a factor of three.[65]

Most of the research in this area is concerned with rape and, to a lesser extent, robbery. It remains to be seen whether victim resistance strategies work well when other types of crimes are at focus.

VIGILANTISM? THE MINUTEMAN PROJECT AND ILLEGAL IMMIGRATION. Illegal immigration is a hot-button issue today. Border Patrol agents have apprehended their share of undocumented immigrants crossing the U.S.-Mexico border, but there are not enough agents to effectively stem the tide. In response to this concern, citizen groups have stepped up and started to volunteer their time in the name of border protection. One of these efforts, the so-called Minuteman Project,[66] has ascended to national prominence in recent years. It claims to be working in collaboration with the U.S. Border Patrol, but that agency has not officially teamed with or endorsed the Minutemen efforts.

The Minuteman Project (and its sister organization, the Minuteman Civil Defense Corps) consists mostly of civilian volunteers who literally "watch" portions of the

U.S.-Mexico border by foot, car, and helicopter and alert Border Patrol agents to possibly illegal crossings. The Minuteman Project calls itself a "vigilance operation." It does not promote altercations between volunteers and those seeking to cross the border illegally, but instead touts itself as providing a valuable information service to officials whose *legitimate* responsibility is securing the border. The volunteers do, however, work together in armed patrols, and they sometimes detain suspected illegal immigrants until Border Patrol agents arrive.

There is no shortage of critics of the Minuteman Project, many of whom claim the Minutemen are concerned with anything but vigilance. Some critics of the Minutemen went so far as to create Vigilante Watch, another volunteer group whose mission is to "watch the watchers."[67] Even the American Civil Liberties Union (ACLU) has seen some of its members, particularly in Arizona, going out to keep an eye on the Minutemen.[68] The ACLU has also denounced detentions of suspected illegal immigrants by Minutemen volunteers.

Needless to say, there are some heated opinions on both sides of the illegal immigration issue. Should groups like the Minuteman Project be allowed to do what they do? Are the Minutemen vigilantes? What about Vigilante Watch? Should *any* civilian volunteers get involved in active patrolling of our borders and crime prevention? Perhaps the most important question for our purposes is, "Does it work?" By all accounts, the answer seems to be no. Neither government efforts nor those of groups such as the Minutemen have made much of a dent in the illegal immigration problem.

Does It Work?

There is virtually no relationship between levels of gun ownership and crime rates, especially burglary rates. At the individual level, armed resistance with a gun can reduce the likelihood that a crime is completed but might increase the victim's chances of becoming injured. Given the number of accidental shootings and gun-related deaths that take place each year in America, coupled with possible compensating risks and offsetting behavior by armed citizens, one is left wondering whether the costs of our country's stance on firearms outweigh its benefits.

Some readers are bound to take issue with the argument that gun ownership does not deter crime. They might point to high levels of gun ownership in rural areas and to the low crime rates in such areas. Whether gun ownership reduces crime in those areas is unclear. At the very least, there are many other explanations besides gun ownership for why sparsely populated areas see less violence.

As for less lethal methods of individual crime control, much research remains to be done. Risk avoidance seems eminently sensible, but some people cannot take steps to change factors that put them at risk (e.g., being male instead of female). As for risk management, there is little evidence that self-defense training works, but forceful verbal resistance and nonforceful physical resistance appear to do the most to interrupt crime completion and minimize the threat of victim injury.

On one level, using a gun in self-defense is taking the law into one's own hands. This is not what comes to mind most of the time, however, when we talk of vigilantism. Rather, it is the efforts of groups like the Minuteman Project on the U.S.-Mexico border. Has the group made a dent in illegal immigration? As already noted, its founders would certainly say yes, but we still have significant illegal immigration problem in this country.

HOUSEHOLD AND FAMILY CRIME CONTROL

Crime control in households and in families is relatively popular but difficult to evaluate. This is so for at least three reasons.[69] First, consider the example of a program that is designed to educate parents about the wrongs of child abuse. To the extent that such abuse occurs, its effects on children will take a great deal of time to measure. This is because what happens during a child's early years can affect delinquency decades later.

Second, crime control in households and families can be confounded by contextual factors, such as the neighborhood in which a family is located. As one researcher put it, "clinic-based parent training for parents of aggressive elementary school children may work in all neighborhoods in Oregon, but not in many neighborhoods in Chicago."[70] Third, criminal activity in private residences is inherently difficult to measure: "The central problems are low completion rates of personal interviews with victims of family crimes who have been treated, low or inconsistent reporting rates of subsequent crimes to police, and unwillingness to disclose crimes committed in the family during interviews in the home while other family members are present."[71]

The Aim of Crime Control in Households and Families

So far, the aim of crime control in America has been clear. For example, mandatory sentences are intended to deter people from committing additional crimes by threatening would-be criminals with serious sanctions. Buying a gun to keep in the home is clearly intended to promote personal safety. But what is the focus of crime control in households and families? It is twofold. First, such crime control is undertaken with the intent of minimizing abuse in the home, including conventional forms of domestic violence and child abuse. Second, household and family-based crime control is undertaken to discourage children from becoming criminals. This can occur early in children's lives, such as through parent training that is intended to provide new parents with the skills to raise functional and well-behaved children. It can also occur later in a child's life, such as during adolescence when, perhaps, a child suddenly starts to act in an antisocial fashion, causing problems for the family.

How Families Influence Delinquency and Youth Victimization

Some believe that crimes are individual acts, resulting from conscious and rational decisions by people who are seeking instant gratification. To discount the importance of external considerations, especially the role of families in shaping individual behavior, is shortsighted at best. Some families do a great deal to influence delinquency among children as well as victimization of youth (e.g., by child abuse). One researcher has even gone so far as to say that "crime runs in families,"[72] and his is probably not a lone voice.

It has been well documented that criminal and delinquent parents tend to have delinquent and antisocial children.[73] According to one researcher, 63 percent of boys with convicted fathers themselves had criminal convictions, compared to 30 percent among those who did not have convicted fathers.[74] Multiple explanations are offered for such transgenerational delinquency, but one thing is clear: "Having a convicted parent or having a delinquent older sibling was . . . among the best predictors, after poor parental supervision, of juvenile self-reported delinquency."[75] Researchers have also found that children who were born to teenage mothers are at a higher risk of delinquency.[76] The effect becomes more pronounced when the biological father is absent during the child's upbringing.[77] And problems such as parental substance abuse,[78] poor parental supervision,[79] inappropriate discipline,[80] parental rejection of children,[81] abuse and neglect,[82] parental conflict,[83] and a host of other problems can lead to problem behavior in children.

The problem of domestic violence alone can have serious implications for children's behavior later in life. In one recent study, the researchers concluded that domestic violence during the first six months of child rearing is significantly linked to child physical abuse, psychological abuse, and neglect, up to the child's fifth year.[84] Other studies show that repeated child exposure to the trauma of domestic violence can lead to externalized behavior problems later in life.[85] All in all, there is a great deal of consensus that the exposure of children to domestic violence is something to be avoided and prevented. Any form of violence in the home, in fact, can lead to problem behavior during children's adolescent years and beyond. Even in the absence of violence, such situations as parental neglect can produce unfortunate consequences. According to one researcher,

> We know that children who grow up in homes characterized by lack of warmth and support, whose parents lack behavior-management skills, and whose lives are characterized by conflict or maltreatment will more likely be delinquent, whereas a supportive family can protect children even in a very hostile and damaging external environment. . . . Parental monitoring or supervision is the aspect of family management that is most consistently related to delinquency.[86]

So not only can family behavior lead children to act inappropriately as they age, but family types and contexts—apart from parental behavior and neglect—can also influence the probability of children themselves becoming victims in the home. In a recent study by the Office of Juvenile Justice and Delinquency prevention, researchers used NCVS data to explore how families influence youth victimization. They found, for example, that "[y]outh in single-parent families experience significantly higher risks for violence than youth in two-parent families."[87] The researchers also found that length of residence influences the potential for victimization. The relationship may be explained by the bonds that people develop by living in the same area for a period of time, but another explanation is that a short-term residence could itself be explained by a recent disruption in the family. They concluded, in fact, that families might be more important than communities when it comes to predicting victimization of children:

> Although communities can serve as important sources of informal social control and help guard against youth victimization, parents can help reduce their children's risk by recognizing the special difficulties they face due to residential changes and by closely monitoring children's activities when they are away from the home.[88]

Research also shows that children who are born into large families are at a high risk of delinquency.[89] Many explanations of this phenomenon have been offered.[90] One is that as family size increases, the household becomes crowded, leading to angst and frustration in children. Another is that parents cannot effectively supervise all the children in a highly populated home. Still another theory pertains to birth order. Later-born children tend to be more delinquent, according to one researcher.[91] In short, there is much that families do (or fail to do) that leads to delinquency. Some of the factors that are linked to youth delinquency are not necessarily amenable to change, such as family size and divorce; government can do little to keep people married and family sizes small. By contrast, parenting skills, abusive behavior, substance abuse, and other causes of family problems are more tractable. We consider the effectiveness of attempts to change such factors in the next few subsections.

Varieties of Crime Control in Households and Families

Despite the difficulties of evaluating crime control in households and families, there is still much that takes place at this level of analysis. There is also a wealth of available research, much of it from the field of human development that should be reviewed. We will organize such crime control into four categories. First, parent training and education programs will be discussed, with particular emphasis on the effects of such training or education on children's delinquency. Second, the research on family preservation therapy programs will be summarized. Then we will turn our attention to the third and fourth types of crime control in households and families: multisystemic therapy (for families with delinquent juveniles) and family financial assistance, particularly in the form of welfare payments. There are many other types of crime control in households and families, but they tend not to have been adequately researched. Those presented here have been subjected to the most research.

PARENT TRAINING AND EDUCATION.   Just as there are good drivers and bad drivers, there are good parents and bad parents. Some parents, through either a lack of training and education or simply a lack of motivation and interest, act in ways that harm their children. Realizing this, government agencies and other entities have stepped in to fill the void, hoping to make a difference in parents and children's lives before it is too late. An example of one such effort is the federal government's Strengthening Families Program (SFP).[92] Started in 1983, the SFP is a drug abuse prevention program for high-risk, drug-using parents to educate them in appropriate parenting skills. It and other programs have been developed out of fear that dysfunctional family environments lead to problem behavior among children later on in life (see Figure 12.1).

Parent training and education come in many forms. Some of them take place in the home; some take place outside the home. Indeed, parent training and education occur in at least five forms.[93] One method of such training and education consists of home visits by trained professionals, generally during the prenatal period. One such program operating in Elmira, New York, called the Prenatal/Early Infancy Project sought "(1) to improve the outcomes of pregnancy; (2) to improve the quality of care that parents provide to their children (and their children's subsequent health and development); and (3) to improve the women's own personal life-course development (completing their education, finding work, and planning future pregnancies)."[94] This program and others like it have shown a great deal of promise.[95] For example, there appears to be a lower incidence of child abuse in treated families than in untreated families.[96] There also appear to be improvements between treatment and control groups in children's levels of hyperactivity.[97] Perhaps more relevant for our purposes, such programs appear to lead to reductions in arrests and convictions among both mothers and children in treated families.[98]

Parent training and education have also been implemented in conjunction with day care and/or preschool programs for young children. One program, known as the Perry Preschool Project, targeted poor African-American children and their parents. The children participated in a Head Start preschool program in which they were taught thinking and reasoning skills. Steps were also taken to improve their scholastic achievement. Home visits were also conducted at which parent education and other interventions took place. The program appeared to be a resounding success, and its effects appeared to linger for years.[99] Participants were tracked well into their twenties, at which point it was found that they had been arrested at about half the rate of those in the control group. Another such program targeted low-birth-weight infants and their parents. The intervention included home visits and attendance at a special child development center. Researchers who evaluated the program found that the program produced desirable results, but whether the effects lasted long was unclear.[100] Several other

- **Introduction and group building:** This session presents group building exercises and a short lecture on learning theory. Goals include discussing change, focusing on positive thoughts, and encouraging parents to observe their child's good behavior.

- **Developmental expectancies and stress management:** This session discusses physical, mental, social, and emotional development with a focus on appropriate and realistic expectations for children at different ages. A section on stress and anger management teaches parents what to do when they feel overwhelmed.

- **Rewards:** This session covers rewarding children for good behavior, "attends" (describing and emphasizing positive behavior), and providing social rewards. Parents are encouraged to "catch their children being good."

- **Goals and objectives:** This session focuses on setting general goals, defining good behavior, setting behavioral goals and objectives, and making positive statements to children.

- **Differential attention/Charts and spinners:** This session teaches parents the skill of rewarding good behavior and ignoring bad behavior. Charts and spinners are described as a way to encourage good behavior. Charts list and record the child's progress on target behaviors the parent wants to improve (e.g., making the bed, brushing teeth, or cleaning the bedroom). The spinner has rewards for achieving target behaviors the parent and child have chosen together.

- **Communication I:** This session teaches parents about listening and speaking, "I" messages, and roadblocks to communication.

- **Communication II:** This session reinforces concepts covered in the previous session with extensive role-play.

- **Alcohol, drugs, and families:** This session introduces the parent's role in prevention of children's problem behaviors and awareness of at-risk behaviors.

- **Problem solving, giving directions:** This session teaches the basic steps of problem solving and reinforces them with role-play. Making requests, giving clear directions, and delivering effective commands are discussed.

- **Limit setting I:** This session introduces timeouts, overcorrection, positive practice, and the parents' game.

- **Limit setting II:** This session covers the issue of punishment, including how to solve a child's problem behavior by setting appropriate limits.

- **Limit setting III:** This session helps parents continue to solve problems in a variety of situations, including those supplied in the handbook, that may be relevant to their individual needs.

- **Development/Implementation of behavior programs:** This session reviews the process of implementing the abbreviated behavioral program. Parents develop a plan for the first week of a behavior program for their child.

- **Generalization and maintenance:** This session teaches parents to fade rewards (rewarding every other time for several weeks and then rewarding only occasionally if the desired behavior continues), look for naturally occurring rewards, troubleshoot, and maintain behavioral changes in their children.

FIGURE 12.1 Outline of Parent Skills Training Sessions

Source: Family Skills Training for Parents & Children, *Juvenile Justice Bulletin* (Washington DC: United States Department of Justice, OJP, OJJDP, 2000).

researchers have found that parent training and education coupled with treatment in a school, preschool, or other educational venue favorably affect both child behavior and subsequent arrests and other types of delinquency.[101]

Researchers have also studied parent training and education in a clinical setting. Such programs have no at-home component but do tend to include child training in addition to parent training. Unfortunately, the results are not as convincing for this method. Some researchers have found that this method improves child behavior, but little attention has been paid to criminality or to parental behavior.[102] Even when researchers focus squarely on child conduct, a number of studies show that parent training and education in a clinical setting have little desirable effect.[103] Why is this? One explanation is that clinical interventions are short-lived. One such program consisted of only 8 to 10 sessions, compared to training programs with an in-home component that lasted as much as two years.[104] Effectiveness might then depend on the length of the intervention.

School- and community-based parent training and education have been tried as well. The authors of a school-based program in Montreal, Quebec, Canada, describe the parent and child training that occurred in this way:

> The [parent] training procedures included giving parents a reading program, teaching parents to monitor their children's behavior and to give children positive reinforcement for prosocial behavior, training parents to discipline effectively without using abusive punishment, teaching parents family crisis management techniques, and encouraging parents to transfer their new knowledge to new situations. . . . [For the disruptive boys, t]wo types of social skills training were administered by the professionals during lunch time within the context of a small group of four to seven prosocial peers from school, with the ratio being three prosocial peers for each disruptive boy. . . . A prosocial skills training curriculum was implemented in the first year, consisting of nine sessions. . . . In the second year, 10 sessions were given to enhance children's problem solving and self-control in conflict situations.[105]

The results of the evaluation were favorable,[106] as have been evaluations of other school-based child and parent training programs.[107] However, parent training and education (coupled with child education) in a community-based setting do not appear to be as effective. Most evaluations of such programs show little effect on such diverse outcomes as arrests, behavior problems, and self-reported criminal activity.[108] Only one study appears to paint community-based training in a favorable light.[109]

On the whole, parent training and education appear to be effective, but primarily when a home visit dimension is included. Such programs can be effective even without a school-based or clinical component. But there are problems. First, research in this area is plagued by follow-up problems. A handful of researchers have—to their credit—tracked program participants over a long period of time, but to truly ferret out the effects of parent training and education, lengthy follow-up is necessary. This is generally cost-prohibitive. Another problem with the research in this area is that much of it focuses on the behavior, though not necessarily the criminality (or absence of criminality), of program participants. This makes it difficult to conclude whether parent training and education favorably affect crime. At the same time, though, it is doubtful that such training makes matters worse.

FAMILY PRESERVATION THERAPY. More than sixty years ago, John Bowlby theorized that children from broken homes are more likely to grow up delinquent.[110] Much research appears to confirm his theory. For example, studies show that children who experience parental divorce or separation during their first five years of life are at twice the level of risk for a criminal conviction compared to children whose parents stay together.[111] Another study shows that divorce followed by changes in parental figures leads to an even higher rate of child delinquency.[112] Whether it is the broken home or the parental conflict that caused it that leads to youth delinquency is open for debate, but the result is the same: an increase in delinquency. What, then, about divorce predicts delinquency in children? David Farrington answers the question in this way:

> Trauma theories suggest that the loss of a parent has a damaging effect on a child, most commonly because of the effect on attachment to the parent. Life course theories focus on separation as a sequence of stressful experiences and on the effects of multiple stressors such as parental conflict, parental loss, reduced economic circumstances, changes in parent figures, and poor child-rearing methods. Selection theories argue that disrupted families produce delinquent children because of pre-existing differences from other families in risk factors such as parental conflict, criminal or antisocial parents, low family income, or poor child-rearing methods.[113]

family preservation therapy: interventions which seek to improve family relationships and functionality in an effort to prevent and/or control criminal and other inappropriate behavior.

In response to concerns that parental divorce and separation can lead to problem behaviors in children, steps have been taken to keep families intact. Such **family preservation therapy** rarely seeks only to improve relationships between parents, however. Instead, it is usually pursued in response to other problems, such as when a child starts to act inappropriately. Alternatively, family preservation therapy is sometimes pursued when there is evidence of child abuse and/or neglect in a home that is characterized by parental conflict. Only in rare instances is family preservation therapy pursued in an otherwise functional family environment in which parents are divorced or separated (or about to do either) and there is no evidence of child abuse, delinquency, or other problems.

In the late 1980s, there was a significant increase in rates of child maltreatment and the number of children in the American foster care system.[114] In response to these developments, Congress enacted the Omnibus Budget Reconciliation Act of 1993, which authorized $930 million over a five-year period for states to plan and implement family preservation and family support (FPFS) services.[115] This also contributed to the focus of FPFS programs on child safety issues rather than simply family reunification. Because funding was aimed at improving the plight of children from broken homes rather than parental relationships, it led to programs aimed at reducing instances of child abuse and neglect. As a result, researchers were not particularly concerned with children's behavior when they studied family preservation programs. Little is known, then, about their effect on delinquency.[116]

> Family preservation programs thus do not necessarily target the outcomes that are of interest to us here. Even so, it is questionable whether they even do much to improve the predicament of abused and neglected children. Several studies show, for example, that such programs fail to reduce abuse.[117]

Still other researchers have concluded that family preservation therapy does little to affect its intended outcomes.[118] Surely not all such programs are failures, but all in all, the results are not encouraging. Combine this observation with the lack of research on the effect of family preservation therapy on the behavior of children, especially future delinquency, and it appears that the $900-plus million that was spent on such programs in the 1990s could have been better spent elsewhere.

MULTISYSTEMIC THERAPY. Parent training and family preservation therapy have something in common: Both seek to minimize problem behaviors (either in parents or children) before such behaviors can cause serious problems. **Multisystemic therapy (MST)** is different in that it is used well *after* families begin to experience problems with delinquent juveniles. It is a reactive method rather than a preventive method of dealing with crime and delinquency.

MST is an intensive community- and family-based treatment method that targets the many sources of antisocial behavior in delinquent juveniles. It often takes place in more than one place, including home, schools, and community centers. MST also targets everything from interpersonal and cognitive skills to the features of children's environments that contribute to delinquency, including many of the problems (e.g., divorce, parental conflict, peer influence, drug use) that have already been discussed throughout this book. The very term *multisystemic* conveys a focus on multiple factors that are thought to cause delinquency coupled with a systemwide (e.g., drawing on the services of multiple entities besides counselors and family members) approach.

Research on multisystemic therapy is almost uniformly supportive of the practice, giving hope to families with delinquent children. Most relevant for our purposes, several researchers have examined the effects of multisystemic therapy on outcomes such as arrests, criminal convictions, and time incarcerated. For example, two solid studies show reductions in arrests among youths who participated in MST.[119] Another study shows a decline in time spent incarcerated.[120] Still other studies show declines in behavior problems among participating youths.[121] According to one source, "[t]he MST approach to treating serious antisocial behavior in youth provides strong evidence of effectiveness. Ongoing testing of MST . . . offers to provide an even stronger evidentiary base to contribute to policy and legislation for this important subgroup of the offending population."[122]

FINANCIAL ASSISTANCE TO FAMILIES. This section moves away from a focus on parenting, family problems, delinquent children, and the like. Its focus is on financial support for families. Many families lack sufficient resources and therefore might become involved in criminal activity to obtain basic necessities. This concern has led several researchers to examine the connections between welfare spending and serious crime. Most studies link aggregate levels of welfare spending to crime rates, however; there appear to be no studies at the level of individual families that look at whether welfare spending improves people's life conditions.

A common sentiment that many Americans express is that welfare threatens individual responsibility and contributes to an attitude among its recipients that entitlements are due to them, which in turn creates a damaging pattern of dependence on public assistance. As one critic has noted, "[t]he problem with the welfare state is not the level of spending, it is that nearly all of this expenditure actively promotes self-destructive behavior among the poor."[123] Many researchers believe, however, that welfare benefits its recipients and can even *reduce* the crime problem.[124]

One of the first studies examining the links between public assistance and crime was published in 1983. Using a sample of 39 cities, DeFronzo found that Aid to Families with Dependent Children (AFDC) payments, adjusted for cost of living, had significant negative effects on homicide, rape, and burglary rates.[125] Another researcher, who did *not* adjust for cost of living, concluded that AFDC payments were associated with lower urban homicide rates.[126]

Multisystemic Therapy (MST): an intensive community- and family-based treatment method that targets the many sources of antisocial behavior in delinquent juveniles.

Interestingly, one researcher who studied the relationship between welfare participation and crime rates found a positive association between auto theft rates and the percentage of families below the poverty line receiving public assistance.[127] However, a subsequent study criticized his research as failing to include important control variables.[128] The authors of that study argued that had he controlled for the percentage of female-headed households, he might have found a negative, rather than a positive, relationship.

In two subsequent studies, the author controlled for the percentage of female-headed households. Specifically, he found that AFDC payments, adjusted for the cost of living, had a significant inverse effect on the burglary rate.[129] Still other researchers have found a relationship between welfare spending and serious crime.[130] One found that per capita welfare payments and the proportion of state residents receiving welfare benefits were inversely related to state-level property crime rates.[131] Another team of researchers found that the number of poor families on public assistance and welfare payments, the latter being adjusted for cost of living expenses, were inversely related to burglary, larceny, and auto theft.[132]

Still another team of researchers sought to determine how the unemployment rate, inflation, the prison population rate, and "relief" have affected serious crime (i.e., homicides, robberies, and burglaries) over time. They defined *relief* as the "sum of public spending on aid to families with dependent children, categorical public assistance benefits, and other (not elsewhere classified) direct relief."[133] All of their models showed that relief was inversely related to serious crime, but the relationship was significant only for the crime of burglary. They concluded that "relief's demonstrated relation to burglary rates . . . indicate[s] the need for closer scrutiny of this often-neglected aspect of social control."[134] Recently, though, Worrall found that welfare spending does not equate with less crime.[135]

Does It Work?

Household and family crime control comes in many forms, not all of which have been researched. This section has focused only on household and family crime control that has been subjected to the most research. It appears, on the whole, that such crime control can be quite effective. First, a wealth of research suggests that parent training and education can favorably influence child behavior, mostly when it contains an in-home dimension. Most research in this area has focused on child behavior rather than criminality, however. Second, multisystemic therapy for families with delinquent juveniles appears to be effective. Third, increased welfare spending might be associated with a reduction in crime, but it is unclear whether, at the level of individual families, such assistance improves people's life conditions. Finally, family preservation therapy does not appear to do much to help children who are being raised in broken homes.

Summary

There are several methods that people take to protect themselves from victimization. One of the more pronounced methods is gun ownership for personal protection. Many people believe that having a gun in the home will deter criminals and/or could be used effectively in self-defense. This has prompted many a researcher to examine the relationship between gun prevalence and crime. They have found virtually no relationship, especially when the outcome that is at issue is rates of burglary. At the individual level, it appears that armed resistance with a gun can reduce crime completions, but the risks to the victim increase. Also, it is not clear whether costs associated with gun ownership in the United States (e.g., suicides and accidental deaths) are outweighed by the benefits of guns for self-defense.

As for risk avoidance, people can take steps to minimize their potential for becoming crime victims. Avoiding high-crime areas at night, for example, can reduce the likelihood that someone is victimized. However, certain variables that put people at risk of being victimized (e.g., age, race) cannot be changed, so only some forms of risk avoidance can be expected to work. As for risk management, there is no convincing evidence that self-defense training works, but forceful verbal resistance and nonforceful physical resistance

by victims might minimize the potential for victim injury and might decrease the likelihood that the crime is completed. Vigilantism, particularly as manifested in the Minuteman Project, does not look especially effective, either.

Several methods of household and family crime control were also covered in this chapter. We considered these methods because of the many ways in which families can influence the behavior of young people. We found that parent training and education and multisystemic therapy for families with problem children can have a positive influence. Whether financial assistance to families, particularly in the form of welfare payments, affects crime remains unclear. Likewise, there is little evidence suggesting that family preservation therapies keep families together and reduce crime.

Notes

1. It is common to perceive of risk management as a larger umbrella under which risk avoidance falls. The topics are treated separately in this chapter because they seek to accomplish separate objectives.

2. For an overview of the relationship between mass shootings and gun policy, see G. Kleck, "Mass Shootings in Schools: The Worst Possible Case for Gun Control," *American Behavioral Scientist* 52 (2009): 1447–64.

3. T.W. Smith, *1999 National Gun Policy Survey of the National Opinion Research Center: Research Findings* (Chicago: University of Chicago), 52.

4. P.J. Cook and J. Ludwig, "Guns and Burglary," in *Evaluating Gun Policy: Effects on Crime and Violence*, eds. J. Ludwig and P.J. Cook (Washington, DC: Brookings Institution Press, 2003), 74–118.

5. D. Azrael, P.J. Cook, and M. Miller, *State and Local Prevalence of Firearms Ownership: Measurement, Structure, and Trends*, working paper 8570 (Cambridge, MA: National Bureau of Economic Research, 2001).

6. P.J. Cook and J. Ludwig, *Guns in America: Results of a Comprehensive Survey of Gun Ownership and Use* (Washington, DC: Police Foundation, 1996); E.L. Glaeser and S. Glendon, "Who Owns Guns?: Criminals, Victims, and the Culture of Violence," *American Economic Review* 88 (1998): 458–62.

7. R.M. Ikeda, L.L. Dahlberg, J.J. Sacks, J.A. Mercy, and K.E. Powell, "Estimating Intruder-Related Firearm Retrievals in U.S. Households, 1994," *Violence and Victims* 12 (1997): 363–72.

8. Ibid.

9. G. Kleck and M. Gertz, "Armed Resistance to Crime: The Prevalence and Nature of Self-Defense with a Gun," *Journal of Criminal Law and Criminology* 86 (1995): 150–87.

10. P.J. Cook, "The Technology of Personal Violence," in *Crime and Justice: An Annual Review of Research*, ed. M. Tonry (Chicago: University of Chicago Press, 1991), 56.

11. For these and similar estimates, see G. Kleck, "Crime Control through the Private Use of Armed Force," *Social Forces* 35 (1988): 1–21; P.J. Cook, "The Technology of Personal Violence," in *Crime and Justice: An Annual Review of Research*, ed. M. Tonry (Chicago: University of Chicago Press, 1991), 1–71; D. McDowall and B. Wiersema, "The Incidence of Defensive Firearm Use by U.S. Crime Victims, 1987 through 1990," *American Journal of Public Health* 84 (1994): 1982–4; P.J. Cook, J. Ludwig, and D. Hemenway, "The Gun Debate's New Mythical Number: How Many Defensive Uses per Year?" *Journal of Policy Analysis and Management* 16 (1997): 463–9; M.R. Rand, *Circumstances Surrounding Defensive Use of Guns in Crimes Measured by the National Crime Victimization Survey*. Bureau of Justice Statistics Working Paper. (Presented at the 51st Annual Meeting of the American Society of Criminology, Toronto, November 17–20, 1999).

12. P.J. Cook, "The Technology of Personal Violence," in *Crime and Justice: An Annual Review of Research*, ed. M. Tonry (Chicago: University of Chicago Press, 1991), 56.

13. A.L. Kellerman, L. Westphal, L. Fischer, and B. Harvard, "Weapon Involvement in Home Invasion Crimes," *Journal of the American Medical Association* 273 (1995): 1759–62.

14. J. Ludwig, "Gun Self-Defense and Deterrence," in *Crime and Justice: A Review of Research*, ed. M. Tonry (Chicago: University of Chicago Press, 2000), 363–417.

15. D. McDowall, C. Loftin, and S. Presser, *Measuring Civilian Defensive Firearm Use: A Methodological Experiment*. Working Paper. (Albany, NY: University of New York at Albany, 1999).

16. G. Kleck and M. Gertz, "Armed Resistance to Crime: The Prevalence and Nature of Self-Defense with a Gun," *Journal of Criminal Law and Criminology* 86 (1995): 150–87.

17. P.J. Cook and J. Ludwig, "Guns and Burglary," in *Evaluating Gun Policy: Effects on Crime and Violence*, eds. J. Ludwig and P.J. Cook (Washington, DC: Brookings Institution Press, 2003), 74–118.

18. J.R. Lott, *More Guns, Less Crime* (Chicago: University of Chicago Press, 2000), 36.

19. P.J. Cook and J. Ludwig, "Guns and Burglary," in *Evaluating Gun Policy: Effects on Crime and Violence*, eds. J. Ludwig and P.J. Cook (Washington, DC: Brookings Institution Press, 2003), 74–118.

20. M. Duggan, "More Guns, More Crime," *Journal of Political Economy* 109 (2001): 1086–114.

21. P.J. Cook and J. Ludwig, "Guns and Burglary," in *Evaluating Gun Policy: Effects on Crime and Violence*, eds. J. Ludwig and P.J. Cook (Washington, DC: Brookings Institution Press, 2003), 75.

22. P.J. Cook, S. Molliconi, and T.B. Cole, "Regulating Gun Markets," *Journal of Criminal Law and Criminology* 86 (1995): 59–92.

23. P.J. Cook and J. Ludwig, "Guns and Burglary," in *Evaluating Gun Policy: Effects on Crime and Violence*, eds. J. Ludwig and P.J. Cook (Washington, DC: Brookings Institution Press, 2003), 104.

24. P.J. Cook and J. Ludwig, "The Social Costs of Gun Ownership," *Journal of Public Economics* 90 (2006): 379–91.

25. D.B. Kopel, "Comment: Guns and Burglary," in *Evaluating Gun Policy: Effects on Crime and Violence*, eds. J. Ludwig and P.J. Cook (Washington, DC: Brookings Institution Press, 2003), 109–16.

26. See, for example, thearmedcitizen.com.

27. Such accounts can be found on many pro-gun websites, such as thearmedcitizen.com and nra.org.

28. For a detailed list of factors besides guns that might deter criminals, see G. Kleck and M.A. DeLone, "Victim Resistance and Offender Weapon Effects in Robbery," *Journal of Quantitative Criminology* 9 (1993): 55–81.

29. G. Kleck, "Crime Control through Private Use of Armed Force," *Social Problems* 35 (1988): 1–21; E.A. Ziegenhagen and D. Brosnan, "Victim Responses to Robbery and Crime Control Policy," *Criminology* 23 (1985): 675–95.

30. Ibid.

31. G. Kleck, "Crime Control through Private Use of Armed Force," *Social Problems* 35 (1988): 1–21.

32. Ibid.; G. Kleck and M.A. DeLone, "Victim Resistance and Offender Weapon Effects in Robbery," *Journal of Quantitative Criminology* 9 (1993): 55–81; Ziegenhagen and D. Brosnan, "Victim Responses to Robbery and Crime Control Policy," *Criminology* 23 (1985): 675–95.

33. J. McDonald, *Armed Robbery: Offenders and Their Victims* (Springfield, IL: Charles C. Thomas, 1975).

34. R. Bachman and D.C. Carmody, "Fighting Fire with Fire: The Effects of Victim Resistance in Intimate versus Stranger Perpetrated Assaults against Females," *Journal of Family Violence* 9 (1994): 317–30.

35. J.D. Wright and P.H. Rossi, *Armed and Considered Dangerous: A Survey of Felons and Their Firearms*, expanded ed. (New York: Aldine de Gruyter, 1994).

36. Ibid.

37. R.T. Wright and S.H. Decker, *Burglars on the Job* (Boston: Northeastern University Press, 1994).

38. J. Ludwig, "Gun Self-Defense and Deterrence," in *Crime and Justice: A Review of Research*, ed. M. Tonry (Chicago: University of Chicago Press, 2000), 387.

39. S. Peltzman, "The Effects of Automobile Safety Regulation," *Journal of Political Economy* 83 (1975): 677–725; T.L. Traynor, "The Peltzman Hypothesis Revisited: An Isolated Evaluation of Offsetting Driver Behavior," *Journal of Risk and Uncertainty* 7 (1993): 237–47.

40. W.K. Viscusi, "The Lulling Effect: The Impact of Child-Resistant Packaging on Aspirin and Analgesic Ingestions," *American Economic Review* 74 (1984): 324–27.

41. P.J. Cook and J. Ludwig, "Defensive Gun Uses: New Evidence from a National Survey," *Journal of Quantitative Criminology* 14 (1998): 111–31.

42. For examples, see G.L. Carter, "Accidental Firearm Fatalities and Injuries among Recreational Hunters," *Annals of Emergency Medicine* 18 (1989): 406–9; M.D. Dowd, J.F. Knapp, and L.S. Fitzmaurice, "Pediatric Firearm Injuries, Kansas City, 1992: A Population-Based Study," *Pediatrics* 94 (1994): 867–73; J.R. Martin, D.P. Sklar, and P. McFeeley, "Accidental Firearm Fatalities among New Mexico Children," *Annals of Emergency Medicine* 20 (1991): 58–61; P.L. Morrow and P. Hudson, "Accidental Firearm Fatalities in North Carolina, 1976–80," *American Journal of Public Health* 76 (1986): 112–23; N. Sinauer, J.L. Annest, and J.A. Mercy, "Unintentional, Nonfatal Firearm-Related Injuries: A Preventable Public Health Burden," *Journal of the American Medical Association* 275 (1996): 1740–3; A.E. Waller, S.P. Baker, and A. Szocka, "Childhood Injury Deaths: National Analysis and Geographic Variations," *American Journal of Public Health* 79 (1989): 310–5; G.J. Wintemute, S.P. Teret, J.F. Kraus, M.A. Wright, and G. Bradfield, "When Children Shoot Children: 88 Unintended Deaths in California," *Journal of the American Medical Association* 257 (1987): 3107–9.

43. M. Miller, D. Azrael, and D. Hemenway, "Firearm Availability and Unintentional Firearm Deaths," *Accident Analysis and Prevention* 33 (2001): 477–84.

44. Ibid., 483.

45. P. Cummings, D.C. Grossman, F.P. Rivara, and T.D. Koepsell, "State Gun Safe Storage Laws and Child Mortality Due to Firearms," *Journal of the American Medical Association* 278 (1997): 1084–6.

46. P.J. Cook and J. Ludwig, "Guns and Burglary," in *Evaluating Gun Policy: Effects on Crime and Violence*, eds. J. Ludwig and P.J. Cook (Washington, DC: Brookings Institution Press, 2003), 82.

47. Ibid., 79–81.

48. See G. Kleck, *Point Blank* (New York: Aldine de Gruyter, 1991), 136–8; D. McDowall, A.J. Lizotte, and B. Wiersema, "General Deterrence through Civilian Gun Ownership," *Criminology* 29 (1991): 541–59; G. Kleck, "Has the Gun Deterrence Hypothesis Been Discredited?" *Journal of Firearms and Public Policy* 10 (1998): 65.

49. P.J. Lavrakas, J. Normoyle, W.G. Skogan, E.J. Herz, G. Salem, and D.A. Lewis, *Factors Related to Citizen Involvement in Personal, Household, and Neighborhood Anti-Crime Measures: Executive Summary* (Washington, DC: U.S. Department of Justice, 1980).

50. A.D. Biderman, L.A. Johnson, J. McIntyre, and A.W. Weir, *Report on a Pilot Study in the District of Columbia on Victimization and Attitudes towards Law Enforcement* (Washington, DC: U.S. Government Printing Office, 1967); W.G. Skogan and M.G. Maxfield, *Coping with Crime: Individual and Neighborhood Reactions* (Beverly Hills, CA: Sage, 1981).

51. P.J. Lavrakas, S.M. Hartnett, D. Merkle, and D.P. Rosenbaum, *Community Assessment Survey Results in Six Neighborhoods: The Community Responses to Drug Abuse National Demonstration Program Final Process Evaluation Report*, Vol. 3 (Chicago, IL: Center for Research in Law and Justice, University of Illinois at Chicago, 1992).

52. D.P. Rosenbaum, "Community Crime Prevention: A Review and Synthesis of the Literature," *Justice Quarterly* 5 (1988): 333.

53. M. Rand, *Violence-Related Injuries Treated in Hospital Emergency Departments* (Washington, DC: Bureau of Justice Statistics, 1997).

54. U.S. Centers for Disease Control, "Homicide among Young Black Males—United States, 1978–1987," *Morbidity and Mortality Weekly Report* 39 (December 7, 1990): 869–73.

55. R. Stark, "Deviant Places: A Theory of the Ecology of Crime," *Criminology* 25 (1987): 893–911.

56. Ibid., 81.

57. N. Cummings, "Self Defense Training for College Students," *American Journal of College Health* 40 (1992): 183–8; P.A. Follansbee, "Effects of a Self-Defense Program on Women's Psychological Health and Well-Being," *Dissertation Abstracts International* 43 (January, 7-B, 1983): 2388.

58. E.S. Cohen, L.H. Kidder, and J. Harvey, "Crime Prevention vs. Victimization Prevention: The Psychology of Two Different Reactions," *Victimology* 3 (1978): 285–96.

59. D.R. Smith, "A Program Evaluation: The Effects of Women's Self-Defense Training upon Efficacy Expectancies, Behaviors, and Personality Variables," *Dissertation Abstracts International* 44 (June, 12-B, 1984): 3945–6.

60. S.E. Ullman, "Review and Critique of Empirical Studies of Rape Avoidance," *Criminal Justice and Behavior* 24 (1997): 177–204.

61. P.B. Bart and P.B. O'Brien, *Stopping Rape: Successful Survival Strategies* (Elmsford, NY: Pergamon, 1985); R. Block and W.G. Skogan, "Resistance and Nonfatal Outcomes in Stranger-to-Stranger Predatory Crime," *Violence and Victims* 1 (1986): 241–53; G. Kleck and

S. Sayles, "Rape and Resistance," *Social Problems* 37 (1990): 149–62; S.E. Ullman and R.A. Knight, "Fighting Back: Women's Resistance to Rape," *Journal of Interpersonal Violence* 7 (1992): 31–43; R.B. Ruback and D.L. Ivie, "Prior Relationship, Resistance, and Injury in Rapes: An Analysis of Crisis Center Records," *Violence and Victims* 3 (1988): 99–111; J.M. Siegel, S.B Sorenson, J.M. Golding, M.A. Burnam, and J.A. Stein, "Resistance to Sexual Assault: Who Resists and What Happens?" *American Journal of Public Health* 79 (1989): 27–31.

62. Admittedly, trying to push an offender away is somewhat forceful, but the author is relying on a classification scheme that is already relied on in the literature.

63. P.B. Bart and P.B. O'Brien, *Stopping Rape: Successful Survival Strategies* (Elmsford, NY: Pergamon, 1985); R. Block and W.G. Skogan, "Resistance and Nonfatal Outcomes in Stranger-to-Stranger Predatory Crime," *Violence and Victims* 1 (1986): 241–53; W.G. Skogan and R. Block, "Resistance and Injury in Nonfatal Assaultive Violence," *Victimology* 8 (1983): 215–26.

64. P.B. Bart and P.B. O'Brien, *Stopping Rape: Successful Survival Strategies* (Elmsford, NY: Pergamon, 1985); S.E. Ullman and R.A. Knight, "Fighting Back: Women's Resistance to Rape," *Journal of Interpersonal Violence* 7 (1992): 31–43.

65. R. Bachman, L.E. Saltzman, M.P. Thompson, and D.C. Carmody, "Disentangling the Effects of Self-Protective Behaviors on the Risk of Injury in Assaults against Women," *Journal of Quantitative Criminology* 18 (2002): 135–57.

66. Ibid.

67. Their site is vigilantewatch.org.

68. Obtained on 10/30/2006 from aclu.org/immigrants/gen/11742prs20050330.html.

69. L.W. Sherman, "Family-Based Crime Prevention," in *Preventing Crime: What Works, What Doesn't, What's Promising*, eds. L.W. Sherman, D. Gottfredson, D. MacKenzie, J. Eck, P. Reuter, and S. Bushway (Washington, DC: National Institute of Justice, 1997).

70. Ibid.

71. Ibid.

72. D.P. Farrington, "Families and Crime," in *Crime: Public Policies for Crime Control*, eds. J.Q. Wilson and J. Petersilia (Oakland, CA: Institute for Contemporary Studies, 2002), 29–148.

73. J. McCord, "A Comparative Study of Two Generations of Native Americans," in *Theory in Criminology*, ed. R.F. Meier (Beverly Hills, CA: Sage, 1977); L.N. Robins, "Sturdy Childhood Predictors of Adult Outcomes: Replications from Longitudinal Studies," in *Stress and Mental Disorder*, eds. J.E. Barrett, R.M. Rose, and G.L. Klerman (New York: Raven Press, 1979).

74. D.P. Farrington, G. Barnes, and S. Lambert, "The Concentration of Offending in Families," *Legal and Criminological Psychology* 1 (1996): 47–63.

75. D.P. Farrington, "Families and Crime," in *Crime: Public Policies for Crime Control*, eds. J.Q. Wilson and J. Petersilia (Oakland, CA: Institute for Contemporary Studies, 2002), 132.

76. M. Morash and L. Rucker, "An Exploratory Study of the Connection of Mother's Age at Childbearing to Her Children's Delinquency in Four Data Sets," *Crime and Delinquency* 35 (1989): 45–93.

77. A. Conseur, F.P. Rivara, R. Barnoski, and I. Emanuel, "Maternal and Perinatal Risk Factors for Later Delinquency," *Pediatrics* 99 (1997): 785–90.

78. R. Loeber, D.P. Farrington, M. Stouthamer-Loeber, and W. van Kammen, *Antisocial Behavior and Mental Health Problems: Explanatory Factors in Childhood and Adolescence* (Mahwah, NJ: Lawrence Erlbaum, 1998).

79. C.A. Smith and S.B. Stern, "Delinquency and Antisocial Behavior: A Review of Family Processes and Intervention Research," *Social Service Review* 71 (1997): 382–420; D.P. Farrington and R. Loeber, "Transatlantic Replicability of Risk Factors in the Development of Delinquency," in *Historical and Geographical Influences on Psychopathology*, eds. P. Cohen, C. Slomkowski, and L.N. Robins (Mahway, NJ: Lawrence Erlbaum, 1999), 299–329.

80. J. Newson and E. Newson, *The Extent of Parental Physical Punishment in the UK* (London: Approach, 1989).

81. C. Lewis, E. Newson, and J. Newson, "Father Participation through Childhood and Its Relationship with Career Aspirations and Delinquency," in *Fathers: Psychological Perspectives*, eds. N. Beail and J. McGuire (London: Junction, 1982), 174–93.

82. C.S. Widom, "The Cycle of Violence," *Science* 244 (1989): 160–66; J. McCord, "A Forty Year Perspective on Effects of Child Abuse and Neglect," *Child Abuse and Neglect* 7 (1983): 265–70.

83. M. Wadsworth, *Roots of Delinquency* (London: Martin Robertson, 1979); L. Pagani, R.E. Tremblay, F. Vitaro, M. Kerr, and P. McDuff, "The Impact of Family Transition on the Development of Delinquency in Adolescent Boys: A Nine-Year Longitudinal Study," *Journal of Child Psychology and Psychiatry* 39 (1998): 489–99.

84. W.M. McGuigan and C.C. Pratt, "The Predictive Impact of Domestic Violence on Three Types of Child Maltreatment," *Child Abuse and Neglect* 25 (2001): 869–83.

85. B.E. Carlson, "Children Exposed to Intimate Partner Violence: Research Findings and Implications for Intervention," *Trauma, Violence, and Abuse* 1 (2000): 231–342.

86. C.A. Smith and S.B. Stern, "Delinquency and Antisocial Behavior: A Review of Family Processes and Intervention Research," *Social Service Review* 71 (1997): 382–420.

87. J.L. Lauritsen, *How Families and Communities Influence Youth Victimization* (Washington, DC: U.S. Department of Justice, Office of Juvenile Justice and Delinquency Prevention, 2003), 4.

88. Ibid., 10.

89. D.G. Fischer, "Family Size and Delinquency," *Perceptual and Motor Skills* 58 (1984): 527–34; L. Ellis, "The Victimful-Victimless Crime Distinction, and Seven Universal Demographic Correlates of Victimful Criminal Behavior," *Personality and Individual Differences* 3 (1988): 525–48.

90. For a review, see D.P. Farrington, "Families and Crime," in *Crime: Public Policies for Crime Control*, eds. J.Q. Wilson and J. Petersilia (Oakland, CA: Institute for Contemporary Studies, 2002), 136.

91. Ibid.

92. K.L. Kumpfer and C.M. Tait, *Family Skills Training for Parents and Children* (Washington, DC: U.S. Department of Justice, Office of Juvenile Justice and Delinquency Prevention, 2000).

93. The following discussion draws from D.P. Farrington and B.C. Welsh, "Family-Based Crime Prevention," in *Evidence-Based Crime Prevention*, eds. L.W. Sherman, D.P. Farrington, B.C. Welsh, and D.L. MacKenzie (New York: Routledge, 2002), 22–55.

94. D.L. Olds, C.R. Henderson, C. Phelps, H. Kitzman, and C. Hanks, "Effects of Prenatal and Infancy Nurse Home Visitation on Government Spending," *Medical Care* 31 (1993): 155–74.

95. See, for example, R.P. Barth, S. Hacking, and J.R. Ash, "Preventing Child Abuse: An Experimental Evaluation of the Child Parent Enrichment Project," *Journal of Primary Prevention* 8 (1988): 201–17; H. Kitzman, D.L. Olds, C.R. Henderson, C. Hanks, R. Cole, R. Tatelbaum, K.M. McConnochie, K. Sidora, D.W. Luckey, D. Shaver, K. Engelhardt, D. James, and K. Barnard, "Effect of Prenatal and Infancy Home Visitation by Nurses on Pregnancy Outcomes, Childhood Injuries, and Repeated Childbearing: A Randomized Controlled Trial," *Journal of the American Medical Association* 278 (1997): 644–52.

96. C.P. Larson, "Efficacy of Prenatal and Postpartum Home Visits on Child Health and Development," *Pediatrics* 66 (1980): 191–7.

97. J.M. Strayhorn and C.S. Weidman, "Follow-up One Year after Parent-Child Interaction Training: Effects on Behavior of Preschool Children," *Journal of the American Academy of Child and Adolescent Psychiatry* 30 (1991): 138–43.

98. D.L. Olds, J. Eckenrode, C.R. Henderson, H. Kitzman, J. Powers, R. Cole, K. Sidora, P. Morris, L.M. Pettitt, and D. Luckey, "Long-Term Effects of Home Visitation on Maternal Life Course and Child Abuse and Neglect: Fifteen-Year Follow-up of a Randomized Trial," *Journal of the American Medical Association* 278 (1997): 637–43; D.L. Olds, C.R. Henderson, R. Chamberlin, and R. Tatelbaum, "Preventing Child Abuse and Neglect: A Randomized Trial of Nurse Home Visitation," *Pediatrics* 78 (1986): 65–78; D.L. Olds, C.R. Henderson, R. Cole, J. Eckenrode, H. Kitzman, K. Luckey, L. Pettitt, K. Sidora, P. Morris, and J. Powers, "Long-Term Effects of Nurse Home Visitation on Children's Criminal and Antisocial Behavior: 15-Year Follow-up of a Randomized Controlled Trial," *Journal of the American Medical Association* 280 (1998): 1238–44.

99. L.J. Schweinhart, H.V. Barnes, and D.P. Weikart, *Significant Benefits: The High/Scope Perry Preschool Study through Age 27* (Ypsilanti, MI: High/Scope Press, 1993).

100. Infant Health and Development Program, "Enhancing the Outcomes of Low-Birth-Weight, Premature Infants:

A Multi-site, Randomized Trial," *Journal of the American Medical Association* 263 (1990): 3035–42; C.M. McCarton, J. Brooks-Gunn, I.F. Wallace, C.R. Bauer, F.C. Bennett, J.C. Bernbaum, R.S. Broyles, P.H. Casey, M.C. McCormick, D.T. Scott, J. Tyson, J. Tonascia, and C.L. Meinert, "Results at Age 8 Years of Early Intervention for Low-Birth-Weight Premature Infants: The Infant Health and Development Program," *Journal of the American Medical Association* 277 (1997): 126–32.

101. See, for example, T.M. Field, S.M. Widmayer, S. Stringer, and E. Ignatoff, "Teenage, Lower-Class Black Mothers and Their Preterm Infants: An Intervention and Developmental Follow-Up," *Child Development* 51 (1980): 426–36; D.L. Johnson and J.N. Breckenridge, "The Houston Parent-Child Development Center and the Primary Prevention of Behavior Problems in Young Children," *American Journal of Community Psychology* 10 (1982): 305–16; D.L. Johnson and T. Walker, "Primary Prevention of Behavior Problems in Mexican-American-Children," *American Journal of Community Psychology* 15 (1987): 375–85; J.R. Lally, P.L. Mangione, and A.S. Honig, "The Syracuse University Family Development Research Program: Long-Range Impact of an Early Intervention with Low Income Children and Their Families," in *Parent Education as Early Childhood Intervention: Emerging Directions in Theory, Research and Practice*, ed. D.R. Powell (Norwood, NJ: Ablex, 1988), 79–104. W.L. Stone, R.D. Bendell, and T.M. Field, "The Impact of Socioeconomic Status on Teenage Mothers and Children Who Received Early Intervention," *Journal of Applied Developmental Psychology* 9 (1988): 391–408; C. Webster-Stratton, M. Kolpacoff, and T. Hollinsworth, "Self-Administered Videotape Therapy for Families with Conduct-Problem Children: Comparison with Two Cost-Effective Treatments and a Control Group," *Journal of Consulting and Clinical Psychology* 56 (1988): 558–66.

102. C. Webster-Stratton, M. Kolpacoff, and T. Hollinsworth, "Self-Administered Videotape Therapy for Families with Conduct-Problem Children: Comparison with Two Cost-Effective Treatments and a Control Group," *Journal of Consulting and Clinical Psychology* 56 (1988): 558–66; A.E. Kazdin, T.C. Siegel, and D. Bass, "Cognitive Problem-Solving Skills Training and Parent Management Training in the Treatment of Antisocial Behavior in Children," *Journal of Consulting and Clinical Psychology* 60 (1992): 733–47; S. Spaccarelli, S. Cotler, and D. Penman, "Problem-Solving Skills Training as a Supplement to Behavioral Parent-Training," *Cognitive Therapy and Research* 16 (1992): 1–18; C. Webster-Stratton and M. Hammond, "Treating Children with Early-Onset Conduct Problems: A Comparison of Child and Parent Training Interventions," *Journal of Consulting and Clinical Psychology* 65 (1997): 93–109.

103. J. Szapocznik, A. Rio, E. Murray, R. Cohen, M. Scopetta, A. Rivas-Vazquez, O. Hervis, V. Posada, and W. Kurtines, "Structural Family versus Psychodynamic Child Therapy for Problematic Hispanic Boys," *Journal of Consulting and Clinical Psychology* 57 (1989): 571–78; T.J. Dishion,

G.R. Patterson, and K.A. Kavanagh, "An Experimental Test of the Coercion Model: Linking Theory, Measurement, and Intervention," in *Preventing Antisocial Behavior: Interventions from Birth through Adolescence*, eds. J. McCord and R.E. Tremblay (New York: Guilford, 1992), 253–82; T.J. Dishion and D.W. Andrews, "Preventing Escalation in Problem Behaviors with High-Risk Young Adolescents: Immediate and 1-Year Outcomes," *Journal of Consulting and Clinical Psychology* 63 (1995): 538–48.

104. See, for example, P. Long, R. Forehand, M. Wierson, and A. Morgan, "Does Parent Training with Young Noncompliant Children Have Long-Term Effects?" *Behavior Research Therapy* 32 (1994): 101–7.

105. R.E. Tremblay, L. Pagani-Kurtz, L.C. Masse, F. Vitaro, and R.O. Pihl, "A Bimodal Preventive Intervention for Disruptive Kindergarten Boys: Its Impact through Mid-Adolescence," *Journal of Consulting and Clinical Psychology* 63 (1995): 560–68.

106. Ibid.

107. I. Kolvin, R.F. Garside, A.R. Nicol, A. MacMillan, F. Wolstenholme, and I.M. Leitch, *Help Starts Here: The Maladjusted Child in the Ordinary School* (London: Tavistock, 1981); J.D. Hawkins, R.F. Catalano, D.M. Morrison, J. O'Donnell, R.D. Abbott, and L.E. Day, "The Seattle Social Development Project: Effects of the First Four Years on Protective Factors and Problem Behaviors," in *Preventing Antisocial Behavior: Interventions from Birth through Adolescence*, eds. J. McCord and R.E. Tremblay (New York: Guilford, 1992), 128–61; J.D. Hawkins, R.F. Catalano, R. Kosterman, R. Abbott, and K.G. Hill, "Preventing Adolescent Health-Risk Behaviors by Strengthening Protection during Childhood," *Archives of Pediatrics and Adolescent Medicine* 153 (1999): 226–34; D.J. Pepler, G. King, W. Craig, B. Byrd, and L. Bream, "The Development and Evaluation of a Multisystem Social Skills Group Training Program for Aggressive Children," *Child and Youth Care Forum* 24 (1995): 297–313; J.B. Reid, J.M. Eddy, R.A. Fetrow, and M. Stoolmiller, "Description and Immediate Impacts of a Preventive Intervention for Conduct Problems," *American Journal of Community Psychology* 27 (1999): 483–517.

108. L. Bank, J.H. Marlowe, J.B. Reid, G.R. Patterson, and M.R. Weinrott, "A Comparative Evaluation of Parent-Training Interventions for Families of Chronic Delinquents," *Journal of Abnormal Child Psychology* 19 (1991): 15–33; E. Mullin, K. Quigley, and B. Glanville, "A Controlled Evaluation of the Impact of a Parent Training Programme on Child Behaviour and Mothers' General Well-Being," *Counseling Psychology Quarterly* 7 (1994): 167–79; A.V. Harrell, S.E. Cavanagh, and S. Sridharan, "Evaluation of the Children At Risk Program: Results 1 Year after the End of the Program." *Research in Brief* (Washington, DC: National Institute of Justice, 1999).

109. P. Chamberlain and J.B. Reid, "Comparison of Two Community Alternatives to Incarceration for Chronic Juvenile Offenders," *Journal of Consulting and Clinical Psychology* 66 (1998): 624–33.

110. J. Bowlby, *Maternal Care and Mental Health* (Geneva: World Health Organization, 1951).

111. I. Kolvin, F.J.W. Miller, M. Fleeting, and P.A. Kolvin, "Social and Parenting Factors Affecting Criminal-Offence Rates: Findings from the Newcastle Thousand Family Study (1947–1980)," *British Journal of Psychiatry* 152 (1988): 80–90.

112. B.R. Mednick, R.L. Baker, L.E. Carothers, "Patterns of Family Instability and Crime: The Association of Timing of the Family's Disruption with Subsequent Adolescent and Young Adult Criminality," *Journal of Youth and Adolescence* 19 (1990): 201–20.

113. D.P. Farrington, "Families and Crime." in *Crime: Public Policies for Crime Control*, eds. J.Q. Wilson and J. Petersilia (Oakland, CA: Institute for Contemporary Studies, 2002), 142.

114. M. Chaffin, B.L. Bonner, and R.F. Hill, "Family Preservation and Family Support Programs: Child Maltreatment Outcomes across Client Risk Levels and Program Types," *Child Abuse and Neglect* 25 (2001): 1269–89.

115. N. Ashan, "The Family Preservation and Support Services Program," *The Future of Children* 6 (1996): 157–60.

116. One exception to this observation can be found in H.C. Coleman and J.M. Jenson, "Longitudinal Investigation of Delinquency among Abused and Behavior Problem Youth Following Participation in a Family Preservation Program," *Journal of Offender Rehabilitation* 31 (2000): 143–62, but the researchers found virtually no effect of family preservation on child behavior patterns.

117. B.J. Blythe, M.P. Salley, and S. Jayaratne, "A Review of Intensive Family Preservation Services Research," *Social Work Research* 18 (1994): 213–24; D.S. Gomby, P.L. Culross, and R.E. Behrman, "Home Visiting: Recent Program Evaluations—Analysis and Recommendations," *The Future of Children* 9 (1999): 4–26.

118. P. Schene, "Overview of Evaluative Research on Family Preservation," *Protecting Children* 10 (1994): 7–10.

119. S.W. Henggeler, G.B. Melton, and L.A Smith, "Family Preservation Using Multisystemic Therapy: An Effective Alternative to Incarcerating Serious Juvenile Offenders," *Journal of Consulting and Clinical Psychology* 60 (1992): 953–61; S.W. Henggeler, G.B. Melton, L.A. Smith, S.K. Schoenwald, and J.H. Hanley, "Family Preservation Using Multisystemic Treatment: Long-Term Follow-Up to a Clinical Trial with Serious Juvenile Offenders," *Journal of Child and Family Studies* 2 (1993): 283–93.

120. S.K Schoenwald, D.M. Ward, S.W. Henggeler, S.G. Pickrel, and H. Patel, "Multisystemic Therapy Treatment of Substance Abusing or Dependent Adolescent Offenders: Costs of Reducing Incarceration, Inpatient, and Residential Placement," *Journal of Child and Family Studies* 5 (1996): 431–44.

121. S.W. Henggeler, G.B. Melton, M.J. Brondino, and D.G. Schere, "Multisystemic Therapy with Violent and Chronic Juvenile Offenders and Their Families: The Role of Treatment Fidelity in Successful Dissemination," *Journal of Consulting and Clinical Psychology* 65 (1997): 821–33.

122. D.P. Farrington and B.C. Welsh, "Family-Based Crime Prevention," in *Evidence-Based Crime Prevention*, eds. L.W. Sherman, D.P. Farrington, B.C. Welsh, and D.L. MacKenzie (New York: Routledge, 2002), 45–8.

123. R. Rector, "Requiem for the War on Poverty: Rethinking Welfare after the L.A. Riots," *Policy Review* 61 (1992): 40–6.

124. F.F. Piven and R.A. Cloward, *Regulating the Poor: The Functions of Public Welfare* (New York: Vintage, 1971).

125. J. DeFronzo, "Economic Assistance to Impoverished Americans: Relationship to the Incidence of Crime," *Criminology* 21 (1983): 119–36.

126. S.F. Messner, "Geographic Mobility, Governmental Assistance to the Poor, and Rates of Urban Crime," *Journal of Crime and Justice* 9 (1986): 1–18.

127. R. Rosenfeld, "Urban Crime Rates: Effects on Inequality, Welfare Dependency, Region, and Race," in *The Social Ecology of Crime*, eds. J.M. Byrne and R.J. Sampson (New York: Springer-Verlag, 1986), 116–30.

128. L. Hannon and J. DeFronzo, "Welfare and Property Crime," *Justice Quarterly* 15 (1998): 273–87.

129. J. DeFronzo, "AFDC, A City's Racial and Ethnic Composition, and Burglary," *Social Service Review* 70 (1996): 464–76.

130. J. DeFronzo, "Welfare and Homicide," *Journal of Research in Crime and Delinquency* 34 (1997): 395–406; L. Hannon, "AFDC and Homicide," *Journal of Sociology and Social Welfare* 24 (1997): 125–36; J. DeFronzo and L. Hannon, "Welfare Assistance Levels and Homicide," *Homicide Studies* 2 (1998): 31–45.

131. J. Zhang, "The Effect of Welfare Programs on Criminal Behavior: A Theoretical and Empirical Analysis," *Economic Inquiry* 35 (1997): 120–37.

132. L. Hannon and J. DeFronzo, "Welfare and Property Crime," *Justice Quarterly* 15 (1998): 273–87; L. Hannon and J. DeFronzo, "The Truly Disadvantaged, Public Assistance, and Crime," *Social Problems* 45 (1998): 383–92.

133. J.A. Devine, J.F. Sheley, and M.D. Smith, "Macroeconomic and Social Control Policy Influences on Crime Rate Changes, 1948–1985," *American Sociological Review* 53 (1988): 407–20.

134. Ibid., 417; for other such studies, see D.S. Grant and R. Martinez, "Crime and the Restructuring of the U.S. Economy: A Reconsideration of the Class Linkages," *Social Forces* 75 (1997): 769–99; M.B. Chamlin, J.K. Cochran, and C.T. Lowenkamp, "A Longitudinal Analysis of the Welfare-Homicide Relationship: Testing Two (Nonreductionist) Macro-Level Theories," *Homicide Studies* 6 (2002): 39–60.

135. J.L. Worrall, "Reconsidering the Relationship between Welfare Expenditures and Serious Crime: A Panel Data Analysis with Implications for Social Support Theory," *Justice Quarterly* 22 (2005): 364–91.

Crime Control in the Community and in Schools

LEARNING OBJECTIVES

▨ Explain the social ecology of crime.

▨ Summarize the effectiveness of financial assistance to communities.

▨ Discuss other methods of community-based crime control and their effectiveness.

▨ Explain the role of schools in crime prevention/control.

▨ Identify the most effective school-based crime prevention/control initiatives.

As the last chapter revealed, much crime control takes place with little justice system involvement. Individualized efforts such as buying a gun to protect oneself or managing risks do not rely on any intervention by police officers, court officials, or corrections officers. Likewise, family- and household-based crime control need not contain a criminal justice system component, although such methods of crime control can clearly be expected to influence outcomes such as crime and delinquency. In this spirit, we continue now with additional approaches to the crime problem those that take place in the community and in schools. Some of the efforts that are discussed in this chapter rely on *some* justice system involvement (e.g., police officers lecturing to school students about the perils of drug use), but this is not a requirement.

Crime control in the community and schools comes in nearly countless forms. Many innovative and highly effective school-based efforts might not find their way into the pages of this book because they simply have not been subjected to much research. The same is true for community-based initiatives. American communities take untold numbers of approaches—formal and informal—that either have not come to the attention of researchers or are only now beginning to gain publicity. The various methods of crime control in this chapter, like those covered in previous chapters, are those that have been researched at some length. As before, it will become apparent that some of the approaches that are covered in the next few pages should be replicated throughout the country and others should be abandoned in favor of more effective interventions.

COMMUNITY CRIME CONTROL

There are two general ways to view community crime control. The first is crime control that comes through financial assistance to communities. This requires that some outside entity, usually some arm of the government, intervene in an effort to improve the physical and/or economic conditions of a specific area. Enterprise zones and community development block grants serve as examples and will be discussed at some length later in this section.

The second way to view community crime control is to focus on what community members themselves do to control crime. Such approaches do not necessarily rely on outside input or assistance, although they certainly can. Examples of such approaches include block watch programs, anti-gang initiatives, and youth mentoring. Of course, there are still other methods of community crime control, such as after-school programs that do not fit neatly into either of these two categories. To this end, the remainder of this section breaks community crime control into two sections: financial assistance to communities and other methods of community crime control. First, though, let us define the term *community* and briefly touch on the social ecology of crime.

What Is Community?

There is no clear definition of the term *community*, except to say that it is not a city, metropolitan area, county, or state. A city boundary, for example, is somewhat artificial and politically defined. This is especially true in highly urban areas where one city runs right into the next with few noticeable changes. The same holds true, for the most part, with counties and states. Oftentimes, one can cross a county or state boundary and not notice any difference in terms of physical layout, population demographics, and so forth.

Communities, then, are lower units of analysis. They include neighborhoods and other more or less homogeneous areas within larger aggregates. As one researcher has observed, communities possess more "ecological integrity," in that they usually follow natural boundaries and are more socially homogenous.[1] But because it can be difficult to gather data at the community level, researchers often rely on census tracts because there can be several of them within a specific city or metropolitan area.[2] For our purposes, it is important to be aware that the term *community* refers to any number of distinct social collectives that are less populous than cities, counties, and higher-order aggregates.

The Social Ecology of Crime

By now, most readers are aware that multiple theories exist to explain crime. Some such theories (e.g., low self-control) seek to explain the criminal behavior of individuals. Others seek to explain patterns of criminal activity in the aggregate, such as at the community, city, county, state, or nationwide level. Several of the theories that have been put forth to explain aggregate crime rates have been lumped into the so-called social ecological model of crime.

The term *social* in *social ecological* refers to human interaction. The term *ecological* refers to the relationships between human groups and their physical and social environments. The social ecology of crime can then be understood as explanations of crime that result from human interaction in the context of specific environmental characteristics.

One of the first examples of the social ecological model of crime is Shaw and McKay's classic book *Juvenile Delinquency and Urban Areas*.[3] They argued that environmental characteristics such as low economic status, ethnic heterogeneity, and community mobility work together to explain variations in crime and delinquency among juveniles. They later expanded on their initial work and showed that high rates of crime in the Chicago area persisted over time, despite the characteristics of individuals in the city.[4] This led them to effectively abandon individually based explanations of crime and focus instead on community characteristics that are thought to explain crime patterns. Recently, a host of researchers have expanded on Shaw and McKay's research, attempting to explain variations in community-level crime rates.[5] Several such explanations are discussed in the following subsections.

POVERTY.   It is well known that crime tends to affect poor people more than those who are well-off. But depending on the measures of crime and poverty that are employed, the location of the research, and other factors, the relationships can be complex and confusing. For example, researchers have shown a direct relationship between poverty and violence.[6] Yet other researchers have shown that the relationship is weak or absent.[7] These contradictory findings could be explained by something else, such as population mobility. One team of researchers found that population mobility and poverty did not by themselves explain rates of violent crime but that together they did a good job of explaining neighborhood violence.[8]

MOBILITY AND CHANGE.   Population mobility is basically turnover of people. It occurs when some people—sometimes many people—move out of a community and others move in. Shaw and McKay found that turnover reduced stability and lessened informal social control (e.g., neighbors who know each other keeping an eye out for wrongdoing), thereby leading to increases in crime. Not as many researchers have looked at the effect of population mobility on crime in comparison to the effects of poverty on crime, but what studies are available paint a fairly clear picture: Population mobility appears to increase crime. At least three studies that are directly concerned with the effect of population mobility on crime have found a positive relationship between both variables.[9] That is, they have found that low community stability is associated with crime.

RACIAL COMPOSITION. Shaw and McKay found that delinquency was concentrated in heterogeneous urban neighborhoods. For example, they found that areas with more than 70 percent black or foreign-born residents experience twice as much crime as did more homogeneous areas.[10] This finding has led a host of researchers to examine the effects of racial composition on crime. The consensus in the literature nowadays is that the percentage of blacks in a neighborhood is positively—and often strongly—related to the incidence of violent crime.[11] This does not mean, however, that an increase in black residents in a given neighborhood *causes* more crime. Other factors such as family composition, poverty, and mobility could be working together with racial composition to explain neighborhood crime rates.[12]

POPULATION DENSITY. Population density refers to how crowded neighborhoods are. Crowding could explain crime in at least two ways. First, it stands to reason that more crime will occur where there are more people. This is a reason why urban crime rates tend to be much higher than rural crime rates. Second, crowding could cause people to become frustrated by cramped living conditions and act criminally. Either way, a few researchers have examined the linkages between population density and crime rates. As one pointed out, "the most dangerous city blocks are relatively large in population and area with high concentrations of primary individuals and apartment housing."[13] Other researchers found that increases in high-density housing and renter-occupied dwellings were associated with increases in crime.[14] Still other researchers have found that population density is linked to crime, even after controlling for factors such as poverty and racial composition.[15] As can be seen in the bottom panel of Table 13.1, crime is concentrated more in urban areas than in suburban areas.

MORE ON FAMILIES. In Chapter 12, we examined the role of families in both instigating criminal activity and preventing it. Family structure fits into the social ecological model of crime as well. In particular, researchers have focused on family disruption, often relying on measures such as the percentage of single-mother households, female-headed households, or the divorce rate to explain community-level crime rates. In other words, this view holds that young people commit crime not because of their individual family situations but because of some broader community consequence of low parental supervision. As the noted sociologist Robert Sampson has put it,

> This conceptualization focuses on the community-wide effects of family structure and does not require that it is the children of divorced or separated parents that are engaging in crime. For instance, youth in stable family areas, regardless of their own family

TABLE 13.1 Rate and Percent Change of Violent Victimization by Household Location

| Household Location | Violent Crime | | | | | Serious Violence Crime[a] | | | | |
| | Rates[b] | | | Percent Change[c] | | Rates[b] | | | Percent Change[c] | |
	2002	2010	2011	2002–2011	2010–2011	2002	2010	2011	2002–2011	2010–2011
Total	32.1	19.3	22.5	–30%[†]	17%[†]	10.0	6.6	7.2	–28%[†]	9%
Region										
Northeast	28.5	17.2	20.3	–29%[†]	18%	7.1	6.8	6.4	–9%	–6%
Midwest	38.8	22.0	26.3	–32[†]	19[‡]	11.5	7.6	7.8	–32[†]	3
South	27.4	16.6	18.3	–33[†]	10	10.8	5.4	6.5	–40[†]	20
West	35.6	22.4	27.1	–24[†]	21[‡]	9.5	7.5	8.4	–12	12
Location of residence										
Urban	41.0	24.2	27.4	–33%[†]	13%	15.2	9.5	9.7	–36%[†]	3%
Suburban	28.3	16.8	20.2	–29[†]	20[†]	7.8	5.5	5.7	–27[†]	4
Rural	28.6	17.7	20.1	–30[†]	14	7.9	4.7	6.7	–15	42

[†]Significant at 95%.

[‡]Significant at 90%.

[a]Includes rape or sexual assault, robbery, and aggravated assault.

[b]Per 1,000 persons age 12 or older.

[c]Calculated based on unrounded estimates.

Source: Jennifer L. Truman, *Criminal Victimization, 2011* (Washington, DC: Bureau of Justice Statistics, 2012).

situation, have more controls placed on their leisure-time activities, particularly with peer groups. . . . Neighborhood family structure may thus influence whether neighborhood youth are provided the opportunity to form a peer-control system free of supervision by adults.[16]

Indeed, many researchers have found that family structure can explain community-level crime rates. One study showed that rates of victimization were two or three times as high in neighborhoods with a high degree of family disruption than in those with a low degree of disruption.[17] The same study showed that the percentage of female-headed households explained more crime than racial composition did. Similar findings have been reported in subsequent studies, namely, that family composition is often highly associated with crime.[18]

SOCIAL DISORGANIZATION AND COLLECTIVE EFFICACY. Thus far, it appears that poverty, mobility, racial composition, density, and family composition exert independent effects on crime (See Figure 13.1). But what is it about all of these factors together that explains crime? Social disorganization theory has been put forth in response to this question. The theory holds that some communities are "disorganized" because of the inability of people in them to supervise and control potentially delinquent persons.[19] Communities may also be disorganized because they lack the informal social controls that come through friendships and other acquaintances.[20] As one researcher put it, "[t]he social disorganization approach views local communities and neighborhoods as a complex system of friendship, kinship, and acquaintanceship networks, and

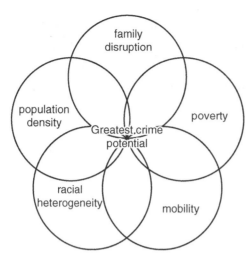

FIGURE 13.1 Ecological Model of Crime

collective efficacy:
"...shared
expectations and
mutual engagement by
residents in local social
control."

formal and informal associational ties rooted in family life and ongoing socialization processes."[21]

An offshoot of the social disorganization theory is the notion of **collective efficacy**. Robert Sampson, who coined the term, has argued that social networks alone cannot explain trends in crime. Instead, he feels that the willingness of community members to come together and confront neighborhood problems, especially crime, is more important. When there is sufficient trust among neighborhood residents and a desire among residents to work for the common good, the residents are said to be in an area characterized by high levels of collective efficacy. In Sampson's words, "[j]ust as individuals vary in their capacity for efficacious action, so too do neighborhoods vary in their capacity to achieve common goals. . . . Collective efficacy is thus a task-specific construct that refers to shared expectations and mutual engagement by residents in local social control."[22] Several researchers have examined the effect of collective efficacy on crime, and most have found that where it is present, crime rates tend to be markedly lower.[23]

CONCENTRATED DISADVANTAGE. So far, we have examined the independent effects of variables such as poverty and racial composition on crime rates. But there is evidence that some of these variables operate together in such a way as to explain even more variations in the crime rate. In particular, the combination of variables such as poverty, family disruption, and racial composition seems to have a severe effect on crime. Various combinations of these variables have been termed **concentrated disadvantage**.[24] Researchers are increasingly relying on concentrated disadvantage to explain community-level crime rates.

concentrated
disadvantage: the
combination of
various community-
level variables
(e.g., single-parent
households, racial
composition) into
a single measure
or index of social
conditions most
linked to crime and
related problems.

COMMUNITIES AND CRIME: A TWO-WAY RELATIONSHIP? By now, the linkages between poverty, mobility, racial composition, population density, family composition, and crime are fairly clear. Up to this point, though, we have conceived of the relationship as being one-way. That is, we have looked only at what effect poverty and other variables have on crime, not at the effect that crime may have on neighborhood characteristics. As one researcher has pointed out, "crime itself can lead to simultaneous demographic 'collapse' and a weakening of the informal control structures and mobilization capacity of communities, which in turn fuels further crime."[25] In fact, several studies have shown the detrimental effect crime can have on communities. It generates fear and withdrawal[26] and even influences people's decisions to move to different neighborhoods.[27]

Financial Assistance to Communities

Clearly, there is a link between community conditions and crime. The relative importance of, say, poverty in comparison to family composition is not totally clear, nor are researchers confident that community conditions cause crime rather than the other way around. What is clear, though, is that undesirable community characteristics, especially high poverty and urban blight, seem to go hand in hand with crime. This has prompted a host of initiatives that were devised to clean up high-crime urban neighborhoods and infuse such areas with a renewed sense of community.

ENTERPRISE ZONES. **Enterprise zones** are economically depressed areas where incentives are provided to employers such that job development is encouraged.[28] Companies that are located in enterprise zones are eligible for substantial tax credits, provided that they hire qualified individuals—often poor people who are in need of employment (the intent of the programs is not to encourage people to leave otherwise decent jobs in surrounding areas). For example, companies can benefit from hiring tax credits, sales tax credits, and business expense deductions above and beyond what an ordinary company would receive. Companies that are located in enterprise zones can also get lower interest rates on loans, be given preference for state contracts, and receive a host of other benefits—all in the name of creating jobs in impoverished areas.

enterprise zone: an economically depressed areas where incentives are provided to employers such that job development is encouraged.

Most states have enterprise zones, the development of which is overseen by some government agency. Colorado's Office of Economic Development and International Trade oversees that state's efforts. In New Jersey, it is the Urban Enterprise Zone Authority that supervises zone development, and the equivalent agency in Ohio is the Ohio Department of Development. Most states now have several enterprise zones. According to one source, the median population for enterprise zones is 4,500 and approximately 1.8 square miles in size.[29]

The logic behind enterprise zones is sensible enough. It is relatively clear that rates of poverty and unemployment go hand in hand with crime. Added employment, then, might lead to a reduction in crime. Enterprise zones can also provide for company growth and possibly wage increases, making a previously impoverished area more desirable to live in. But what does the research show? Unfortunately, there do not appear to be any studies that looked at the effect of enterprise zones on crime. Instead, most research in this area has been concerned with outcomes such as employment levels and job creation. However, it appears that enterprise zones don't do much for job creation and community improvement. Three recent and sophisticated studies show that for the most part, enterprise zones have done little to stimulate employment in their targeted areas.[30] In fairness, some studies have shown improvements in enterprise zones, but their research designs were somewhat less sophisticated.[31]

COMMUNITY DEVELOPMENT BLOCK GRANTS.   In 1974, the Community Development Block Grant program was created. It remains today and is overseen by the U.S. Department of Housing and Urban Development. The program provide so-called formula grants to state and local governments through several channels. Such channels include (1) "entitlement communities," which provide grants to cities and counties to develop housing and expand economic opportunities for low- and moderate-income families; (2) state-administered block grants, by which states receive federal monies, set priorities, and then award grants to local communities to improve economic development; (3) loan guarantees; and (4) disaster recovery assistance, among other channels.[32]

Many criminal justice agencies have applied for and received community development block grants. For example, the Dallas City Attorney's Office has received funding for its community prosecution efforts. Unfortunately, though, little research is available on the Community Development Block Grant program, and virtually none looking at its effect on crime. Part of the reason for this is that the program is highly decentralized and the funding goes to a host of different agencies and projects, each of which can have different goals in mind for the spending. This makes an overall examination of the program's effect difficult to conduct. Also, it is difficult for researchers to separate out the effect of grants on public safety, given the range of other factors that can affect crime and other such outcomes. Only one evaluation of the overall effect of the Community Development Block Grant program has been conducted.[33] The results of the evaluation were favorable, but again crime was not an outcome of interest to the evaluators.

Other Methods of Community Crime Control

There is much community crime control in America that does not rely directly on federal or state funding for its support. This is not to say that such initiatives do not require funding; most do. Their key component is not economic revitalization, though, which tends to require a wealth of time and resources. The other methods of community crime control to which we will now turn our attention include the mobilization of residents to discourage crime, anti-gang initiatives, youth mentoring programs, after-school programs, and publicity campaigns. This may seem like a hodgepodge list of community crime control, but, as before, these are the approaches that have come to the attention of researchers. And remember that community crime control differs from justice system–initiated crime control. Chapter 5, for example, discussed community policing, a strategy that relies heavily on community involvement. But community policing is mainly a police-initiated strategy. The strategies discussed here may—and often do—emerge following some community effort to control crime.

MORE ON COMMUNITIES.   Before we turn to the remaining community crime control strategies, it is worth reiterating the importance of the social ecological model of crime. All of the strategies and initiatives discussed below assume that there is something lacking in the community that needs repair and regeneration. What is lacking can include not just a defined sense of community and a willingness among residents to come together in opposition to crime, but also fear and hesitancy to act as people would in a safer environment. Kelling and Coles, in their important book *Fixing Broken Windows*, describe such a process in this way:

> [D]isorderly behavior unregulated and unchecked signals to citizens that the area is unsafe. Responding prudently, and fearful, citizens will stay off the streets, avoid certain areas, and curtail their normal activities and associations. As citizens withdraw physically, they also withdraw from roles of mutual support with fellow citizens on the streets, thereby relinquishing the social controls they formerly helped to maintain within the community, as social atomization sets in. Ultimately the result for such a neighborhood . . . is increasing vulnerability to an influx of more disorderly behavior and serious crime.[34]

MOBILIZING RESIDENTS.   Community mobilization comes in many forms. It can come "from the creation of formal community development organizations," or "the mobilization of resources from outside the community to help solve local problems like crime and unemployment."[35] Another author has described it as "the transfer of economic and political resources to empower local communities, to give youth a stake in conformity, and to relieve the frustration of blocked aspirations and relieve deprivation that induces delinquency."[36] Stated more simply, community mobilization occurs when people come together and work together, in our case, to address a specific crime problem.

No one knows for sure on how many occasions people have come together collaboratively to reduce crime. Surely the number is large. But in a recent review of community anti-crime mobilization efforts, a team of researchers was only able to identify four such initiatives that have been subjected to research.[37] The programs they reviewed were: (1) Mobilization for Youth, a New York program that provided individual and family services, job training, and education; (2) the Hartford Experiment, a community effort with recreation programs, a targeted policing component, and environmental modifications; (3) the Violent Juvenile Offender Research and Development Program, which provided crisis intervention, mediation, and family support, among other services, for families with delinquent children; and (4) the Neighborhood Anti-Crime Self-Help Program, a combination of neighborhood watch, crime prevention education, youth employment programs, and recreation activities.

The study involving New York's Mobilization for Youth program did not include crime, or any similar measure, as an outcome; the remaining three programs did. Unfortunately, though, evaluation results were not encouraging. The Hartford Experiment was associated with reductions in robbery and burglary, but only in the short term.[38] The researchers attributed this finding to the fact that the police presence was not as pronounced during the third and fourth years of the experiment. Evaluations of the remaining two programs showed only modest, if any, reductions in crime.[39] In addition, none of the programs appeared to have a pronounced effect on the level of community mobilization, quality of life, fear of crime, and other important outcomes. Most of the remaining evidence in favor of community mobilization is little more than anecdotal.[40]

ANTI-GANG INITIATIVES.   The U.S. gang problem is not to be taken lightly. This is especially true in high-crime urban areas. By some estimates, there are nearly a million active gang members in the United States, perhaps more.[41] Even rural areas are not immune from gang activity. In response to this problem, communities have adopted two broad categories of anti-gang initiatives.[42] The first is prevention, which amounts to discouraging prospective gang members from joining gangs. Such programs tend to target high-risk youth in crime-prone areas, a population that tends to have a disproportionate amount of gang involvement. But prevention does not work all the time, and invariably, some youths join gangs. This leads to the second type of anti-gang initiative: gang intervention. Gang interventions target active gang members and seek to redirect members' energies toward more productive pursuits.

What does the evidence show with respect to prevention? One popular prevention program, known as Gang Resistance Education and Training (GREAT), has been subjected to much research, but because it takes place in schools, we will cover it in the next major section of this chapter. Researchers have identified at least three other gang membership prevention programs.[43] The first and oldest such program was the New York Boys Club. Started in 1927, the program provided recreational, health, and vocational services to at-risk youths. But an evaluation at the end of the program showed that it had no noticeable effect on delinquency and truancy among participating youths.[44]

Another program, called the House of Umoja (Swahili for "unity within the family"), was instituted in Philadelphia in the 1970s. It provided both residential and nonresidential services for youths between the ages of 13 and 19. Services included education, job training, employment assistance, counseling, and various activities that were intended to promote constructive behavior. One researcher claimed that the program reduced gang homicides, but the evaluation failed to control for alternative explanations.[45] Yet another program, Chicago's BUILD program, targeted eighth graders and provided gang prevention education and after-school services. An evaluation of it revealed no significant differences in gang membership between treatment and control groups.[46] Needless to say, the evidence in favor of gang membership prevention—outside a school setting—is not particularly encouraging.

If prevention is ineffective, then what about anti-gang interventions? Does intervening in the lives of active gang members reduce gang violence and involvement? The evidence here is somewhat more encouraging. The bulk of evaluations of anti-gang intervention show that such programs meet their intended goals. For example, a Los Angeles program called the Latino Hills Project, which had project staff working with gang members to provide employment assistance, tutoring, recreation, and counseling, showed a reduction in gang member arrests, but the effects were short-lived.[47] A program in Chicago intervened in crisis situations (e.g., a shooting) to reduce inter-gang violence. An evaluation did not show a decline in gang violence, but it did show an escalation that was not as serious as that in comparison areas.[48]

One of the best-known anti-gang interventions was the Boston Gun Project, also called Operation Ceasefire.[49] Implemented in 1996, the program came on the heels of a dramatic upsurge in firearm-related deaths among young people in Boston. The program consisted of contacts between gang members and criminal justice officials as well as aggressive enforcement of firearms laws. An evaluation of the program showed a 69 percent reduction in youth homicide.[50] The evaluation also showed a decline in gun assaults and overall gang violence.[51] To be sure that Boston wasn't witnessing the same declines that other cities might have been, the researchers examined crime trends elsewhere in the United States. They concluded that "Only Boston experienced a significant reduction in the monthly count of youth homicides coinciding with the implementation of the Operation Ceasefire program."[52]

Another Ceasefire program was implemented in Chicago in 1999. Though it was distinct from the Boston approach, it still contained several similar elements. And it, like the Boston approach, was focused on gang violence and relied heavily on street-level interventions, including from ex-gang members. An in-depth evaluation of the program heralded it a success[53], but other evaluations of Ceasefire-like programs have not given such interventions the most glowing reviews.[54]

More recently, Pittsburgh's One Vision One Life program used a similar approach to that implemented in Boston, Chicago, and elsewhere. Relying heavily on street-level work and intelligence gathering, the program attempted to prevent potentially violent disputes with a six prong strategy: ". . . mediation and intervention in conflicts, provision of alternatives for persons most at risk for violence, strong community coalitions, a unified message of no shooting, a rapid response to all shootings, and programs for youths at risk for violence."[55] Unfortunately, an evaluation found the program had virtually no effect on homicides in the areas in which it was implemented.[56]

Despite these less than favorable evaluations, at least some interventions into gang members lives show promise. As one pair of researchers recently put it, "it is our conclusion that gang intervention programs focused on reducing cohesion among juvenile gangs and individual juvenile gang members, but not increasing gang cohesion, is a promising community crime prevention modality."[57] In closing, note that although some of the programs that we discussed in this section (e.g., Operation Ceasefire) relied on some justice system involvement, not all did. This suggests that community members can come together some of the time, marshal their resources, and fight crime effectively.

YOUTH MENTORING. Closely tied to anti-gang initiatives is the practice of youth mentoring. Indeed, one of the explanations for why youths join gangs is because of the sense of family that gang memberships can bring. Further, they might seek such family connections because they come from broken homes or suffer from a lack of parental involvement and affection. Youth mentoring is premised on the same ideas. It assumes that some youths do not have positive role models in their lives and that with proper intervention by concerned volunteers such youths can be motivated to steer clear of crime and take up any number of constructive activities in place of delinquency. Although the mentoring strategy closely mirrors anti-gang interventions, it is different in at least one sense. Mentoring programs tend to target children at a younger age, say, at age 8 to 10 years, rather than during their adolescent years.[58]

One example of a mentoring program took place in Berkeley, California. Called Companionship Therapy, the program consisted of tutoring, mentoring, conversations, and weekly meetings and activities with youth aged between 10 and 11 years. A program in Hawaii, called the Buddy Program, adopted a similar approach. The first Buddy Program assigned 42 children, ages 11 to 17 years, to one of three treatment groups or a control group. The mentors in the treatment groups received $10 to spend on each youth per month. How the money was spent differed among the treatment groups, however. Two groups spent the money on the mentored youths, while the third gave the youths money contingent on positive behavior. Still other examples of youth mentoring programs can be identified, but most have a common element: close and regular contacts between at-risk youths and volunteers.

Big Brothers and Big Sisters of America (BBBSA): a popular youth mentoring program in which volunteers interact regularly with youths in one-to-one settings.

The **Big Brothers and Big Sisters of America (BBBSA)** is familiar to most of us. It has been providing adult support, mentorship, and friendship to youth for nearly 100 years. Volunteers interact regularly with youths in one-to-one settings. An orientation is required for all volunteers, and each volunteer goes through an extensive screening process. Youth participants in the program are also assessed so that they can be matched properly with volunteers. Matches are carefully sought, and supervision takes place throughout the duration of the partnership.

What does the research show? Much of it suggests that mentoring programs can have a positive effect on youth participants. For example, an evaluation of the Buddy Program showed a decline in truancy and problem behaviors among youths in the treatment group.[59] The treatment group that had the most favorable results was the one that provided money to youth following constructive behavior. A later evaluation of the Buddy Program simply compared mentored youths with nonmentored youths. It showed declines in truancy among youths with delinquent histories but, interestingly, not among those who did *not* have delinquent histories.[60]

Evaluations of the BBBSA program routinely show reductions in drug use, abusive behavior, and improved relationships between participants, their families, and peers. Evaluations also show improvements in academic performance and attitudes following BBBSA mentorship.[61] Other evaluations of youth mentoring programs show favorable outcomes,[62] but it appears that most researchers in this area have not been concerned with crime as an outcome. Only two studies appear to have included criminal activity as one outcome, and their results suggest that mentoring can reduce crime, particularly among youths with criminal histories.[63]

AFTER-SCHOOL PROGRAMS. Evidence shows that violent juvenile crime peaks between 3:00 p.m. and 4:00 p.m., or at roughly the same time that school gets out.[64] This is in stark contrast to adult violent crime, which tends to increase hourly starting at 6:00 a.m., peak at around 11:00 p.m., and then decline hourly until the early morning hours (see Figure 13.2 for evidence of this).[65] In addition, in comparing school days to nonschool days, it is clear that the 3:00 p.m. crime peak occurs only on school days, although children who are delinquent in the hours directly after school tend to be delinquent at other times as well.[66] On nonschool days, juvenile violent crime patterns mirror those of adults.[67] One implication that flows from this finding is that longer school days—and more school—might prevent juvenile crime. But such a turn of events is unlikely, so an alternative is to keep children occupied once the school day is over.

What is it about the period after school is out that seems to breed crime? The director of the Office of Juvenile Justice and Delinquency Prevention has described the phenomenon in this way:

> The real problem area is not the school itself but the world our children return to after the dismissal bell rings. In today's society, fewer and fewer children have a parent waiting

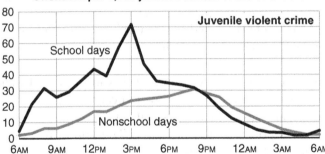

Offenders per 1,000 juvenile violent crime offenders

Note: Violent crimes include murder, violent sexual assault, robbery, aggravated assault, and simple assault. Data are from law enforcement agencies in 35 states and the District of Columbia.

FIGURE 13.2 Peak Times for Juvenile Offending

Source: Office of Juvenile Justice and Delinquency Prevention, ojjdp.gov/ojstatbb/offenders/qa03301.asp

for them at home when school lets out. As a result, youth often supervise themselves and younger siblings after school with varying degrees of oversight by parents and guardians. Most juveniles are responsibly engaged in an array of positive activities, such as sports, clubs, or homework, or they "hang out" harmlessly with friends. However, for youth who have few activities available, whose friends are prone to negative behavior, or who experience other risk factors, the unsupervised hours between school and dinnertime offer ample opportunity to go astray.[68]

Concerns such as this have led to the development of numerous after-school programs aimed at minimizing youthful idleness after school. For school-based programs alone, federal funding grew from $40 million in 1997 to nearly $800 million in 2001.[69] Those numbers say nothing of similar programs that do not include school involvement. As evidence of public concern with—and desire for—after-school programs, California voters recently passed an initiative championed by Governor Arnold Schwarzenegger, approving $550 million in spending for such programs. Funding for the program is uncertain, given the state's fiscal crisis (as of this writing), but the vote nevertheless demonstrated intense public interest in what children do in the hours immediately after school.

Do after-school programs reduce crime? Surprisingly few evaluations are available on this subject, but from those that are available, the evidence is encouraging. Several do not include crime or delinquency as an outcome,[70] but a handful do. For example, one study of a Boys Club program in Louisville, Kentucky, that provided recreational facilities to children of ages 5 to 17 and also had them participate in various group activities, showed that the program led to a reduction in delinquency.[71] A program in Canada, this one focusing on skill development in children, appeared to lead to a decline in arrests among participating juveniles.[72] And still another Boys and Girls Club evaluation showed reduced drug activity, arrests, and other outcomes.[73] It would be nice, though, to see more research on this subject. Certain questions remain unanswered. As one researcher has observed,

> The danger of violent conflicts being generated by club activities is just as open a question as the potential benefits of the programs. Careful research is needed to assess the

net frequency of such conflicts with and without recreation, since shootouts can start off the basketball courts as well as on them. The potential prevention benefits from such programs may well exceed the benefits of prison, perhaps at much lower cost. But we will never know unless we invest in careful evaluation research.[74]

PUBLICITY CAMPAIGNS.   In an important study, Cohen and Felson presented their routine activities theory of crime.[75] They argued that for crime to occur, there must be a motivated offender, the absence of capable guardians, and suitable targets. In Chapter 3, we looked at the relationship between police levels and crime. The police, in Cohen and Felson's view, can be considered capable guardians, despite the fact that they might not be totally effective in reducing crime. We will look at criminal opportunities in the next chapter. What is important here is the motivated offender component of routine activities theory. In particular, it is important to consider offenders' perceptions as to whether there are sufficient criminal opportunities.[76]

What could influence an offender's decision to commit a crime or refrain from doing so? One answer is publicity, especially the publicity of anticrime campaigns. Assuming that offenders make rational decisions, weighing the costs and benefits associated with criminal activity, then publicity might work as follows:

> [offenders] may hear about a police operation through criminal networks, by seeing increased police patrols in an area, or by seeing posters or signs that publicize a scheme. Such knowledge, whether real or perceived, will undoubtedly affect an offender's view concerning the risks or reward involved in committing a crime within a general area or at a specific address.[77]

The notion that offenders can be deterred from crime as a result of publicity has led many a policymaker to clearly announce the latest crime control initiative. And, in contrast to much of what we have seen so far in this chapter, it appears that publicity, properly executed, can have a substantial deterrent effect on crime. For example, one researcher argued that posted signs alerting people that closed-circuit cameras are in operation deter crime.[78] Another study showed that posted signs alerting drivers that speed cameras were in use, even if they really weren't, caused drivers to slow down measurably.[79]

In a recent study of various crime prevention programs in the United Kingdom, a team of researchers found that publicity (including radio interviews, newspaper articles, television appearances, leaflets, posters, stickers, community meetings, alerts to known offenders, and other methods) was associated with significant reductions in burglary.[80] The authors even found that before the implementation of burglary prevention schemes, there were reductions that came purely from publicity (an anticipatory effect) rather than being caused by publicity and enforcement working together. They concluded as follows:

> The . . . results suggest that it may be advisable for scheme organizers to invest in publicity as a relatively straightforward and cost-effective method of enhancing the impact of crime prevention measures. Moreover, that it may also be prudent to implement publicity campaigns as interventions in their own right.[81]

Publicity is important in the anti-drug context, too. The Midwestern Prevention Project relied heavily on the dissemination of an antidrug message through a coordinated system of school, community, parental, and particularly media involvement. Evaluations of the program found it led to reductions in cigarette and alcohol use in treatment groups, but not enough evidence was available to determine whether the program favorably affected illicit drug use.[82]

Does It Work?

Community crime control comes in many forms and can rely on some, little, or no justice system involvement. Regardless of its form, community crime control is closely tied to the social ecological model of crime, which holds, generally, that community features such as poverty, unemployment, and broken homes can contribute to crime, delinquency, and other types of antisocial behaviors.

Two broad categories of community crime control were identified in this section, the first focusing on financial assistance to communities and the second on other types of interventions. There is no convincing evidence that enterprise zones and community development block grants affect crime rates. Nor does it appear that community mobilization or gang membership prevention programs affect people's behavior. Not enough research has been conducted on youth mentoring programs. On the positive lighter side, though, gang member interventions, some after-school recreational programs, and publicity campaigns show a great deal of promise.

SCHOOL-BASED CRIME CONTROL

We have already seen that crime in the hours immediately after school is problematic. After-school programs have emerged to fill the void left by parents and other guardians who cannot always be present to supervise children in the late afternoon hours. In general, schools are safe places, and crime in schools is relatively uncommon. But crime in schools is not entirely absent. As a result, schools have adopted a number of techniques to make students safer while they are being educated. Schools also do a great deal to shape children's behavior. Such interventions can be expected to affect behavior off school grounds. Accordingly, the following subsections discuss the role of school officials in controlling crime both in and out of educational institutions.[83]

Crime in Schools

In the 1960s and 1970s, surveys of public school teachers showed that the most serious classroom problems were tardiness, talking in class, and gum chewing.[84] The priority assigned to such "problems" has since waned. Nowadays teachers and students alike complain about drugs, gangs, violence, and other types of serious crimes.[85] Add to these notorious incidents such as the Sandy Hook Elementary school shooting, and people's concerns over crime in school become even more pronounced. The popular press has gone so far as to say that violence in our nation's schools could be interfering with education.[86] The Centers for Disease Control and Prevention *Youth Risk Behavior Surveillance* study reveals the following with respect to student victimization (this is for 2011, the most recent year for which data are available as of this writing):

- 12% reported being in a physical fight on school property in the 12 months before the survey.
- 5.9% reported that they did not go to school on one or more days in the 30 days before the survey because they felt unsafe at school or on their way to or from school.
- 5.4% reported carrying a weapon (gun, knife, or club) on school property on one or more days in the 30 days before the survey.

- 7.4% reported being threatened or injured with a weapon on school property one or more times in the 12 months before the survey.
- 20% reported being bullied on school property and 16% reported being bullied electronically during the 12 months before the survey.[87]

The Role of Schools in Crime Control

School officials can take a pronounced role in controlling crime. One method of doing so is controlling crime on school grounds. This can take place through target hardening, violence prevention, and student-based problem solving.[88] Target hardening includes the use of metal detectors, surveillance cameras, locks, and other technologies that either make the commission of crime difficult or heighten its costs. Violence prevention programs tend to target at-risk youths by pulling them aside for counseling and skill development. An example of such an approach is the Second Step treatment program. It seeks to improve students' empathy and reduce impulsive behavior and anger levels. Student-based problem solving brings teachers and police officers together with students, usually for a few hours a week during school, to identify and solve school problems.

Another type of school-based crime control focuses on crimes that juveniles commit not just in school but outside it. Examples include programs such as Drug Abuse Resistance Education (DARE). The program takes place in schools, but it intends to do more than target school drug use. Teachers who are involved in the DARE program, usually police officers, hope to encourage youths not to experiment with drugs ever—not just in school. The same can be said about GREAT. A school-based program, GREAT hopes to discourage youths from joining gangs.

A number of other interventions that are intended to alter youth behavior, thinking strategies, and the like can also be identified. To sort through the wide array of school-based crime control methods, we will break the discussion down into two categories. First, we will focus on interventions that target the school environment. Most such interventions are intended to make schools a safer place. Second, we will focus on programs that target individual students, programs that hope to alter youth behavior both inside and outside of school.

The Role of the Government in School-Based Crime Control

The federal government has spent a great deal of money on crime control in America's schools. Some of the funded programs, including DARE, the Learn and Serve America Program, the Drug-Free Schools Program, and GREAT, will be discussed briefly below. Other prominent federally funded school crime control programs include the High Risk Youth Demonstration Program, the Youth Violence Prevention Program, Community Schools, the Youth Services and Supervision Program, and the Juvenile Mentoring Program (JUMP). Unfortunately, federal funding for crime control in schools has not kept pace with the growing costs of education—and a growing student body nationwide. State and local governments, foundations, and other entities fund school programs as well, but such funding is not as common.

Targeting the School Environment

As is usually the case with other social institutions, including prisons, colleges, and government agencies, some schools are run better than others. The logic here is that a school that is run better can reduce everything from learning deficiencies to criminal activity. As one researcher has observed, "[s]chools in which the administration and faculty communicate and work together to plan for change and solve problems have higher teacher morale and less disorder. . . . Schools in which students notice clear school rules and reward structures and unambiguous sanctions also experience less disorder."[89]

Presumably, altering the school environment can have several beneficial effects. But what exactly is the school environment? The term *environment* is used loosely to refer to such activities as making crime more difficult to commit, making and enforcing clear rules, altering classroom designs and instruction techniques, and otherwise improving schools so that antisocial behavior is minimized and learning is improved.

To simplify this complex area of crime control in the United States we will organize school environment interventions into five categories: (1) building administrative capacity, (2) normative education, (3) managing classrooms and education, (4) separate classrooms for high-risk youths, and (5) gun and drug-free school programs.[90]

BUILDING ADMINISTRATIVE CAPACITY.   Successful businesses have highly competent CEOs. Successful schools tend to have good administrators. That is, they have **administrative capacity**. When a school is run poorly, a host of problems can result. The concern that some schools need improvement on the administrative side has led to various attempts to build administrative capacity in school. Basically, this approach amounts to improving the way in which schools are managed by principals, their equivalents, and their staff. Two prominent initiatives have been taken toward this end. One, which began with funding from the Office of Juvenile Justice and Delinquency Prevention, was called Program Development Education (PDE).[91] The other is Comer's School Development Program (SDP).[92]

administrative capacity: the capability of a administrator to successfully run and operate a school.

The PDE program has operated mostly in secondary schools. An example of it in operation is the Baltimore Junior High School PDE project. The program was put in place to help schools define problems and develop and achieve various goals. Each school's principal first selected a school improvement team, consisting of teachers, a guidance counselor, administrators, a social worker, a school psychologist, and a parent liaison. The team worked for a year to develop a plan to improve classroom management and instructional techniques. The plan also provided for regular reports to parents concerning students' classroom behavior, a parent volunteer program, a community support program, extracurricular activities, revisions to the school's discipline program, and a career exploration intervention. The SDPs follow a similar pattern but tend to operate in grade schools rather than secondary schools.

What effect does building administrative capacity have on crime? Interestingly, it appears to have a pronounced—and desirable—effect. Several studies show reductions in outcomes such as drop-out rates, truancy, antisocial behavior, aggression, and crime.[93] Of nearly 10 studies published on this topic, only one[94] suggested that building administrative capacity can make matters worse. Given the weight of the evidence in favor of this approach to crime control in America, one researcher has concluded: "Taken as a set, these school-wide management strategies are effective for reducing crime . . . substance abuse . . . and antisocial/aggressive behavior."[95]

NORMATIVE EDUCATION. Attempts to build administrative capacity focus on administration, not so much on students. An alternative approach to targeting the school environment includes setting norms, guidelines, and expectations for behavior in students.[96] This is known as **normative education**. Many programs that fall within this area focus on drug use, bullying, dating, and general crime prevention. They differ from programs such as DARE (discussed in a later subsection) because unlike DARE and its progeny, they simply tell youths how they are expected to act, rather than directly arm them with the social tools to, say, resist drugs. In other words, normative education basically amounts to teaching schoolchildren how to behave in an acceptable and law-abiding manner.

normative education: an alternative approach to targeting the school environment includes setting norms, guidelines, and expectations for behavior in students.

An example of normative education in operation is the Safe Dates Program. Safe Dates is a dating violence prevention program. It combines school activities, such as role-playing and classroom instruction, with community activities, including the provision of special services for youth in abusive relationships. Another example of normative education is the Start Taking Alcohol Seriously (STARS) program. It combines classroom instruction, often by trained nurses, with "key facts" postcards that educate parents about how they can discourage alcohol use by their children and family take-home lessons. Take-home lessons can include alcohol avoidance contracts that both parents and children sign.

Normative education sounds sensible enough, but does it reduce crime? Again, the results of several evaluations are encouraging. Several evaluations of a variety of normative education programs all show desirable outcomes.[97] Such programs appear to reduce not only crime but alcohol and drug use, antisocial behavior, and aggression.[98] Not a single evaluation appears to show increases in any of these outcomes; they show only decreases. The author of an extensive review of normative education program evaluations has claimed that "[p]rograms aimed at establishing norms or expectations for behavior have been demonstrated in several studies of reasonable methodological rigor to reduce alcohol and marijuana use . . . delinquency . . . and anti-social or other aggressive behaviors."[99]

MANAGING CLASSROOMS AND EDUCATION. A traditional classroom approach to instruction, if there is such a thing, can promote effective learning. But a growing body of evidence is showing that students learn better when the teacher/student ratio is lowered, different learning styles are accommodated, classroom activities are augmented with out-of-class activities, and so forth.[100] An example of this movement toward alternative classroom and education strategies is the well-known "Child Development Project."[101] It consists of five components, including cooperative learning, diversity education, developmental discipline (rewarding positive behavior and allowing students to participate in classroom management), community building, and home schooling. Another example is the Effective Classroom Management[102] approach of teaching sixth graders communication skills, problem-solving techniques, and self-esteem enhancement techniques.

The range of methods for improving classroom instruction is vast, in terms of not only the ages of students served, but also the goals, philosophies, and theories underlying each approach. It would be impossible in such a short space to do justice to the diversity of interventions that have been tried over the years. Doing so would require a book-length review of everything that has been learned in the field of education over the past several decades. Fortunately, the range of studies with crime and delinquency as outcomes shortens the list. A recent review identified nearly 20 studies of classroom interventions.[103] Several of the high-quality evaluations that are listed in the review show reductions in crime, drug and alcohol use, drop-out rates, truancy, antisocial behavior, and aggression,[104] but an equally large number of studies show little or no effect.[105] One reason for the contradictory findings is that the diversity of classroom interventions makes it difficult to draw any blanket conclusions. Even so, attempts to improve classroom instruction do not appear to make students any worse off than they would be in a traditional classroom environment.

SEPARATE CLASSROOMS FOR AT-RISK YOUTHS. Placing disruptive, problem students in the same classroom with everyone else can hamper effective instruction for the good students. This has led to programs that separate high-risk youths by either placing them in different classrooms in the same school or placing them in different schools (alternative schools, adult schools, etc.). Such programs have also been used to ease the transition from middle school to high school. An example of the latter approach is the School Transitional Environment Project (STEP).[106] The program amounted to a school within a school and provided students with guidance, counseling, and specialized instruction aimed at improving their chances of success in high school. Another program targeting at-risk youths provided them with enhanced social studies and English education coupled with law-related education, each with a significant student participation component. Relatively few researchers have examined the effectiveness of these approaches, but evidence shows that separate "schools within a school" can reduce delinquency and drug use,[107] conduct problems,[108] and truancy.[109] Little is known about the effect of alternative schools on the outcomes in which we are interested.[110]

Targeting Students

Each of the strategies that we discussed in the preceding section was aimed at changing the school environment, usually with the motivation of indirectly affecting students in a positive way. The interventions and strategies to which we now turn are focused not on school environments per se but much more directly on students themselves. Each of the approaches that we are about to discuss could work—and quite possibly work well—in even the most poorly run school. We examine instructional interventions, including DARE and GREAT, behavior modification programs, and job training in schools. Through it all, our concern is with the effects of these interventions on crime and problem behaviors in young people.

INSTRUCTIONAL INTERVENTIONS. In an important study, Botvin identified four different methods of instruction to discourage drug use and crime in juveniles.[111] The first is *information dissemination,* which consists of teaching students about drugs, crime, and their effects. *Fear arousal,* the second method, points out the risks of criminal behavior, especially illegal drug use. An example is Partnership for a Drug Free America's "this is your brain on drugs" campaign. The third instructional method is *moral appeal.* This involves appealing to students' understanding of right and wrong and teaching them about the evils of crime. Finally, *affective education* focuses on self-esteem building and relationship development. Botvin also claimed that none of these methods is particularly effective in altering behavior. In place of these approaches, researchers have begun to advocate instructional efforts that improve students' resistance skills, that is, their ability to say no to drug use and other deviant activities.[112]

Gottfredson and her colleagues have identified two primary methods of teaching students resistance skills. One combines traditional instructional methods (e.g., lectures) with what they call cognitive-behavioral or behavioral modeling.[113] In their words, "[t]hese programs . . . rely on cognitive-behavioral and behavioral methods, such as modeling behaviors, providing opportunity for practice of behaviors, giving specific and frequent feedback about new behaviors, providing cues for prompt behavior, and using techniques to generalize the new behavior to different settings."[114] In other words, this first approach is basically interactive education. The second method of teaching students resistance skills simply relies on traditional lecture-based instruction, with little to no interaction between students and instructors.

An example of the first method is the Children of Divorce Intervention Program.[115] School officials and parents referred children to the program, and the children would participate in 15 group sessions with trained group leaders. The goals of the program were to provide a supportive group environment, help students to express divorce-related feelings, enhance self-esteem, teach coping skills, and the like. Another example was the Programs to Advance Teen Health (PATH) program.[116] It was designed to sensitize students to the pressures of using tobacco. It also taught students methods of responding to the pressures. Students practice refusing offers of tobacco while trying to maintain friendships and support other friends who refused offers of tobacco. The program's traditional instructional component consisted of a series of seven video presentations.

Again, these examples represent the tip of the iceberg; many similar instructional programs have operated, and continue to operate, throughout the United States. They target everything from tobacco, alcohol, and illegal drug use to violence, anger, and other varieties of unacceptable behavior. But do they work? Much evidence suggests that they do.[117] Such interventions appear to reduce drug use, drop-out rates, truancy, antisocial behavior, and a number of other conduct problems.[118] And they appear to work well across a wide age span that covers elementary, junior high, and high school students.

But what about traditional instructional methods that don't rely on a significant degree of interaction between students and instructors? Some show promise,[119] but others show little or no effect. Two popular examples of instructional methods that rely more on lecture and traditional teaching methods than on an interactive style are DARE and GREAT. Because each has received much attention, we will cover them separately in the next two subsections.

Drug Abuse Resistance Education (DARE): an anti-drug education program delivered primarily to fifth and sixth graders. The primary curriculum is delivered by uniformed police officers in a classroom visitation context.

DRUG ABUSE RESISTANCE EDUCATION. The **Drug Abuse Resistance Education (DARE)** program began in 1983 as a joint venture between the Los Angeles Police Department and the Los Angeles Unified School District. It is now the most common and best-known drug use prevention program in America. A majority of school districts in all 50 states appear to participate in DARE.[120] The program's primary component is police officer visitations to classrooms. The core curriculum consists of 17 lessons that are presented to students in grade 5 or 6. Students learn about social pressures to use drugs, strategies to overcome such pressures, and consequences of drug use. In addition, they are taught about alternatives to drugs, responsible decision making, self-esteem issues, and other topics. A summary of the DARE curriculum for elementary school[122] is as follows:

Responsibility

Decision Making

Drug Information

Risk & Consequences

Peer Pressure

Stress

Confident Communication

Nonverbal Communication

Listening

Bullying

Helping Others

Getting Help

Given the extent to which DARE has survived the test of time and is ubiquitous in America's schools, one would think that it would be easy to locate demonstrated evidence of its effectiveness. Surprisingly, though, there is little—very little. Almost all published evaluations of DARE show that the program has little to no effect on drug use.[121] Some show short-term effects, but the effects of the program over time do not support its continued use.[123] Meta-analyses of DARE (studies that summarize the results of several other studies) also show that DARE fails to reduce drug use.[124] Even students tend to give DARE mixed reviews.[125] One team of researchers called DARE "very popular but not very effective,"[126] and another researcher has suggested that it is "warm and fuzzy" crime control.[127] Therein might lie the explanation for DARE's persistence; the popularity it enjoys among school officials and law enforcement officers and the favorable publicity that police receive from it perhaps combine to keep DARE in American schools for some time to come.

GANG RESISTANCE EDUCATION. Modeled after DARE, the **Gang Resistance Education and Training (GREAT)** program relies on uniformed police officers who introduce students to conflict resolution skills, cultural sensitivity, and the downside of joining a gang. The program began in 1992 as a joint venture between the Phoenix Police Department and the Bureau of Alcohol, Tobacco, and Firearms. It has since expanded such that GREAT programs currently operate in many schools in all 50 states in the United States.[128] The objectives of the GREAT program are to reduce gang activity and teach students about the consequences that can follow once someone joins a gang. The curriculum consists of eight lessons, and the program serves middle-school students on a weekly basis. The eight lessons in the GREAT program are as follows:

Gang Resistance Education and Training (GREAT): a DARE-like program that relies primarily on uniformed police officers who introduce students to conflict resolution skills, cultural sensitivity, and the downside of joining a gang.

1. Acquaint students with the program and the officer(s) doing the instruction.
2. Students learn about crimes and crime victims, including the consequences of crime for communities.

3. Students learn cultural sensitivity and the harmful effects of prejudicial attitudes and behavior.
4. Students learn conflict resolution skills.
5. Students learn how to satisfy their needs without joining a gang.
6. Students learn about how drugs affect schools and communities.
7. Students are taught about their responsibilities.
8. Students learn about goal setting.[129]

Very little research is available concerning the effect of GREAT. Two evaluations have shown small but desirable effects on the attitudes and behaviors of students who participate in the program,[130] but another evaluation conducted two years after students were exposed to the program showed no effect.[131] Research also shows that students, teachers, and parents are satisfied with the GREAT curriculum.[132] The most sophisticated evaluation of GREAT that has been reported to date was conducted by researchers at the University of Nebraska–Omaha.[133] They found, after following program participants for several years, that GREAT improved prosocial attitudes. It did not, however, affect participants' decisions to join gangs or not. In addition, the research was based on student surveys rather than official data (such as arrest histories), making it difficult to gauge the program's effect on criminal behavior. Overall, though, GREAT appears to show more promise than DARE.

BEHAVIOR MODIFICATION.   DARE, GREAT, and other instructional interventions tend to contain a significant curricular component. That is, they tend to follow a more or less ordered lesson/lecture plan. A different method of targeting individual students is one that does *not* contain a curricular component but instead seeks to modify inappropriate behavior through a system of punishments and rewards. These types of interventions have been implemented—and researched—at three levels of analysis: classrooms, groups, and individuals.[134] Regardless of the level of analysis, though, what they all have in common is the goal of changing the behavior of individual students.

An example of the first approach was a program called Vandalism and Violence Prevention. Through it, teachers used various strategies to reduce vandalism and other forms of disruptive behavior in schools. Although the instruction was carried out in a classroom setting (as opposed to in one-on-one meetings), it was intended to modify the behavior of individual students. Another program was the Good Behavior Game, which put students together in small groups within classrooms. Teams were rewarded for achieving certain behavioral standards. An individual-based approach, in comparison to the group or classroom approach, might reward good behavior by giving individual students something special.

Behavior modification appears to be quite effective, especially when it is used to target at-risk individuals such as disruptive students. Such interventions, though diverse in their focus and methods, appear to reduce truancy and other types of inappropriate—though noncriminal—behaviors.[135] Unfortunately, not many studies in this area have used crime as an outcome. The evidence of those that have, however, suggests that behavior modification can have important crime prevention benefits.[136]

OTHER METHODS OF CRIME CONTROL IN SCHOOLS.   The most the previous sections did was present a cursory review of the research on crime control in schools. Many different strategies have been undertaken to alter school environments, teach students, and modify behavior—all in the hope of reducing crime and other problem behaviors. But there are many other types of interventions that cannot be reviewed here owing to space limitations. For example, one intervention that was absent from the previous discussion is the Student Assistance Program, which is funded by federal Drug-Free Schools and Communities money. It does not appear to have been evaluated, however.[137]

Mentoring and tutoring programs have also been implemented in an effort to keep students in school and deter them from crime, as have work study and job training programs. But because we discussed some such approaches earlier (e.g., mentoring in the section on community crime control), we will not revisit them here. Still other examples of crime control in schools include recreational and other after-school programs that are connected to schools. Those that we touched on earlier in this chapter tend to operate independently of schools. Other methods of supervising young people in the hours after school, including through community service, have been tried, again in the hope of reducing crime. Most such interventions have not been evaluated with great frequency, so it is difficult to draw any firm conclusions about their effects on crime.[138]

Does It Work?

Crime in schools is a problem. Therefore, schools have done much to alter the behavior of students so as to minimize crime and other unconstructive activities. With the possible exception of improving classroom instruction, most interventions that target the school environment appear to be effective. With respect to individual students, interventions that teach students resistance skills and other noncurricular interventions that are intended to change problem behavior appear to be effective. DARE, however, appears to be a failure, and the effects of GREAT remain somewhat uncertain. Several other methods of intervening in students' lives exist, but most have not been sufficiently evaluated.

Summary

Community crime control assumes that communities can be improved in such a manner as to prevent crime. Such improvements can presumably come from financial assistance, efforts to mobilize citizens, anti-gang initiatives, after-school programs, youth mentoring, and other strategies. Of these, only anti-gang interventions (particularly those that target active gang members), after-school recreation programs, and publicity campaigns appear to be associated with reductions in crime. With respect to after-school programs, however, more research is necessary before we will know for sure whether they reduce crime.

Although it might be difficult for communities on the whole to control crime, it appears that interventions taking place in America's schools are quite effective. Interestingly, though, the most publicized of these efforts (i.e., DARE) tends to be the least effective. Several lesser-known approaches that seek to alter the school environment, including how schools are managed, appear to be effective. Likewise, several interventions that target at-risk students, and even students who are not necessarily at risk, have shown demonstrable effects on crime. To be successful, though, such programs should either equip students with appropriate crime resistance skills or seek to modify their behavior through a system of rewards and punishment.

Notes

1. R.J. Sampson, "The Community," in *Crime: Public Policies for Crime Control,* eds. J.Q. Wilson and J. Petersilia (Oakland, CA: Institute for Contemporary Studies, 2002), 601.

2. R.J. Sampson, "What 'Community' Supplies," in *Urban Problems and Community Development,* eds. R.F. Ferguson and W.T. Dickens (Washington, DC: Brookings Institution Press, 1999), 241–92.

3. C. Shaw and H. McKay, *Juvenile Delinquency and Urban Areas* (Chicago: University of Chicago Press, 1942).

4. C. Shaw and H. McKay, *Juvenile Delinquency and Urban Areas*, revised ed. (Chicago: University of Chicago Press, 1969).

5. See, for example, R. Bursik, "Social Disorganization and Theories of Crime and Delinquency: Problems and Prospects," *Criminology* 26 (1988): 519–52; R.J. Sampson and W.B. Groves, "Community Structure and Crime: Testing Social Disorganization Theory," *American Journal of Sociology* 94 (1989): 774–802; L.M. Vieraitis, "Income Inequality, Poverty, and Violent Crime: A Review of the Empirical Evidence," *Social Pathology* 6 (2000): 24–45.

6. R. Block, "Community, Environment, and Violent Crime," *Criminology* 17 (1979): 46–57; G.D. Curry and I. Spergel, "Gang Homicide, Delinquency, and Community," *Criminology* 26 (1988): 381–406.

7. S. Messner and K. Tardiff, "Economic Inequality and Levels of Homicide: An Analysis of Urban Neighborhoods," *Criminology* 24 (1986): 297–318; R.J. Sampson, "Neighborhood and Crime: The Structural Determinants of Personal Victimization," *Journal of Research in Crime and Delinquency* 22 (1985): 7–40, R.J. Sampson, "Neighborhood Family Structure and the Risk of Criminal Victimization," in *The Social Ecology of Crime*, eds. J. Byrne and R. Sampson (New York: Springer-Verlag, 1986).

8. D.R. Smith and G.R. Jarjoura, "Social Structure and Criminal Victimization," *Journal of Research in Crime and Delinquency* 25 (1988): 27–52.

9. R. Block, "Community, Environment, and Violent Crime," *Criminology* 17 (1979): 46–57; R.J. Sampson, "Neighborhood and Crime: The Structural Determinants of Personal Victimization," *Journal of Research in Crime and Delinquency* 22 (1985); R. Taylor and J. Covington, "Neighborhood Changes in Ecology and Violence," *Criminology* 26 (1988): 553–90.

10. C. Shaw and H. McKay, *Juvenile Delinquency and Urban Areas*, revised ed. (Chicago: University of Chicago Press, 1969), 155.

11. R. Block, "Community, Environment, and Violent Crime," *Criminology* 17 (1979): 46–57; S. Messner and K. Tardiff, "Economic Inequality and Levels of Homicide: An Analysis of Urban Neighborhoods," *Criminology* 24 (1986): 297–318; R.J. Sampson, "Neighborhood and Crime: The Structural Determinants of Personal Victimization," *Journal of Research in Crime and Delinquency* 22 (1985): 7–40; D. Roncek, "Dangerous Places: Crime and Residential Environment," *Social Forces* 60 (1981): 74–96; D.R. Smith and G.R. Jarjoura, "Social Structure and Criminal Victimization," *Journal of Research in Crime and Delinquency* 25 (1988): 27–52.

12. R.J. Sampson, "Neighborhood and Crime: The Structural Determinants of Personal Victimization," *Journal of Research in Crime and Delinquency* 22 (1985): 7–40; see also J.F. Short, *Poverty, Ethnicity, and Crime* (Philadelphia, PA: Westview Press, 1997).

13. D. Roncek, "Dangerous Places: Crime and Residential Environment," *Social Forces* 60 (1981): 74–96.

14. L. Schuerman and S. Kobrin, "Community Careers in Crime," in *Communities and Crime*, eds. A.J. Reiss and M. Tonry (Chicago: University of Chicago Press, 1986), 67–100.

15. R.J. Sampson and J.L. Lauritsen, "Violent Victimization and Offending: Individual-, Situational-, and Community-level Risk Factors," in *Understanding and Preventing Violence: Social Influences,* eds. A.J. Reiss Jr. and J. Roth (Washington, DC: National Academy Press, 1994), 1–114.

16. R.J. Sampson, "The Community," in *Crime: Public Policies for Crime Control,* eds. J.Q. Wilson and J. Petersilia (Oakland, CA: Institute for Contemporary Studies, 2002), 229.

17. R.J. Sampson, "Neighborhood and Crime: The Structural Determinants of Personal Victimization," *Journal of Research in Crime and Delinquency* 22 (1985): 7–40; R.J. Sampson, "Neighborhood Family Structure and the Risk of Criminal Victimization," in *The Social Ecology of Crime*, eds. J. Byrne and R. Sampson (New York: Springer-Verlag, 1986), 25–46.

18. S. Messner and K. Tardiff, "Economic Inequality and Levels of Homicide: An Analysis of Urban Neighborhoods," *Criminology* 24 (1986): 297–318; D.R. Smith and G.R. Jarjoura, "Social Structure and Criminal Victimization," *Journal of Research in Crime and Delinquency* 25 (1988): 27–52.

19. R.J. Sampson and W.B. Groves, "Community Structure and Crime: Testing Social Disorganization Theory," *American Journal of Sociology* 94 (1989): 774–802.

20. R. Bursik, "Social Disorganization and Theories of Crime and Delinquency: Problems and Prospects," *Criminology* 26 (1988): 519–52.

21. R.J. Sampson, "The Community," in *Crime: Public Policies for Crime Control,* eds. J.Q. Wilson and J. Petersilia (Oakland, CA: Institute for Contemporary Studies, 2002), 230–1.

22. R.J. Sampson, "The Community," in *Crime: Public Policies for Crime Control,* eds. J.Q. Wilson and J. Petersilia (Oakland, CA: Institute for Contemporary Studies, 2002), 232; see also Sampson, J. Robert, Stephen Raudenbush, and Felton Earls, "Neighborhoods and Violent Crime: A Multilevel Study of Collective Efficacy," *Science* 277 (1997): 918–24.

23. For examples, see R. Taylor, S. Gottfredson, and S. Brower, "Block Crime and Fear: Defensible Space, Local Social Ties, and Territorial Functioning," *Journal of Research in Crime and Delinquency* 21 (1984): 303–31; O. Simcha-Fagan and J. Schwartz, "Neighborhood and Delinquency: An Assessment of Contextual Effects," *Criminology* 24 (1986): 667–704; R.J. Sampson and W.B. Groves, "Community Structure and Crime: Testing Social Disorganization Theory," *American Journal of Sociology* 94 (1989): 774–802; D. Elliott, W.J. Wilson, D. Huizinga, R.J. Sampson, A. Elliott, and B. Rankin, "The Effects of Neighborhood Disadvantage on Adolescent Development," *Journal of Research in Crime and Delinquency* 33 (1996): 389–426;

B. Warner and P. Wilcox Rountree, "Local Social Ties in a Community and Crime Model: Questioning the Systemic Nature of Informal Control," *Social Problems* 44 (1997): 520–36; P. Wilcox Rountree and B.D. Warner, "Social Ties and Crime: Is the Relationship Gendered?" *Criminology* 37 (1999): 789–812; P. Bellair, "Informal Surveillance and Street Crime: A Complex Process," *Criminology* 38 (2000): 137–70; R.J. Sampson, S. Raudenbush, and F. Earls, "Neighborhoods and Violent Crime: A Multilevel Study of Collective Efficacy," *Science* 277 (1997): 918–24.

24. R.J. Sampson and W.J. Wilson, "Toward a Theory of Race, Crime, and Urban Inequality," in *Crime and Inequality,* eds. J. Hagan and R. Peterson (Stanford, CA: Stanford University Press, 1995), 37–56.

25. R.J. Sampson, "The Community," in *Crime: Public Policies for Crime Control,* eds. J.Q. Wilson and J. Petersilia (Oakland, CA: Institute for Contemporary Studies, 2002), 238.

26. W. Skogan, *Disorder and Decline* (New York: Free Press, 1991); R.J. Sampson and S. Raudenbush, "Systematic Social Observation of Public Spaces: A New Look at Disorder in Urban Neighborhoods, "*American Journal of Sociology* 105 (1999): 603–51.

27. R. Bursik, "Delinquency Rates as Sources of Ecological Change," in *The Social Ecology of Crime,* eds. J. Byrne and R. Sampson (New York: Springer-Verlag, 1986); W. Skogan, *Disorder and Decline* (New York: Free Press, 1991), 25–46.

28. See, for example, R.A. Erickson and S.W. Friedman, "Comparative Dimensions of State Enterprise Zone Policies," in *Enterprise Zones: New Dimensions in Economic Development,* ed. R.E. Green (Newbury Park, CA: Sage Focus Edition, 1991), 155–76.

29. Ibid.

30. D. Bondonio and J. Engberg, "States' Enterprise Zone Policies and Local Employment: What Lessons can be Learned?" *Regional Science and Urban Economics* 30 (2000): 519–49; J. Engberg and R. Greenbaum, "State Enterprise Zones and Local Housing Markets," *Journal of Housing Research* 10 (1999): 163–87; R. Greenbaum and J. Engberg, "An Evaluation of State Enterprise Zone Policies: Measuring the Impact on Urban Housing Market Outcomes," *Policy Studies Review* 17 (2000): 29–46.

31. Examples include U.S. Department of Housing and Urban Development, *Expanding Housing Choices for HUD-Assisted Families* (Washington, DC: U.S. Department of Housing and Urban Development, Office of Policy Development and Research, 1996); Office of the Auditor General, California, *A Review of the Economic Activity in the State's Enterprise Zones and Employment and Economic Incentive Areas* (Sacramento, CA: CAO, 1988).

32. hud.gov/offices/cpd/communitydevelopment/programs/index.cfm.

33. Urban Institute, *Federal Funds, Local Choices: An Evaluation of the Community Development Block Grant Program* (Washington, DC: Urban Institute, Center for Public Finance and Housing).

34. G.L. Kelling and C.M. Coles, *Fixing Broken Windows: Restoring Order and Reducing Crime in our Communities* (New York: Free Press, 1996), 20.

35. L.W. Sherman, "Communities and Crime Prevention," in *Preventing Crime: What Works, What Doesn't, What's Promising,* eds. L.W. Sherman, D.C. Gottfredson, D.L. MacKenzie, J.E. Eck, P. Reuter, and S.D. Bushway (Washington, DC: U.S. Department of Justice National Institute of Justice, 1997), 9.

36. T. Hope, "Community Crime Prevention," in *Crime and Justice: Review of Research,* eds. M. Tonry and D.P. Farrington (Chicago, IL: University of Chicago Press, 1995), 35.

37. See B.C. Welsh and A. Hoshi, "Communities and Crime Prevention," in *Evidence-Based Crime Prevention,* eds. L.W. Sherman, D.P. Farrington, B.C. Welsh, and D.L. MacKenzie (New York: Routledge, 2002), 165–97.

38. F.J. Fowler and T.W. Mangione, "A Three-Pronged Effort to Reduce Crime and Fear of Crime: The Hartford Experiment," in *Community Crime Prevention: Does it Work?* Ed. D.P. Rosenbaum (Beverly Hills, CA: Sage, 1986), 87–108.

39. J. Fagan, "Neighborhood Education, Mobilization, and Organization for Juvenile Crime Prevention," *Annals of the American Academy of Political and Social Science* 494 (1987): 54–70; S.F. Bennett and P.J. Lavrakas, "Community-Based Crime Prevention: An Assessment of the Eisenhower Foundation's Neighborhood Program," *Crime and Delinquency* 35 (1989): 345–64.

40. For examples, see R. Stewart-Brown, "Community Mobilization: The Foundation for Community Policing," *FBI Law Enforcement Bulletin* 70 (2001): 9–17; T.M. Green and S. Sakamoto-Cheung, "Model for Community Mobilization: Putting the 'Community' in Community Policing," *Police Chief* 65 (1998): 86–9; J.M. Scheb and W. Lyons, "Communities: Mobilizing against Crime, Making Partnerships Work," *Judicature* 82 (1998): 66–9.

41. Office of Juvenile Justice and Delinquency Prevention, *1997 National Youth Gang Survey: Summary* (Washington, DC: Office of Juvenile Justice and Delinquency Prevention, U.S. Department of Justice, 1999).

42. B.C. Welsh and A. Hoshi, "Communities and Crime Prevention," in *Evidence-Based Crime Prevention,* eds. L.W. Sherman, D.P. Farrington, B.C. Welsh, and D.L. MacKenzie (New York: Routledge, 2002), 165–97; J.C. Howell, "Promising Programs for Youth Gang Violent Prevention and Intervention," in *Serious and Violent Juvenile Offenders: Risk Factors and Successful Interventions,* eds. R. Loeber and D.P. Farrington (Thousand Oaks, CA: Sage, 1998), 284–312.

43. See B.C. Welsh and A. Hoshi, "Communities and Crime Prevention," in *Evidence-Based Crime Prevention* eds. L.W. Sherman, D.P. Farrington, B.C. Welsh, and D.L. MacKenzie (New York: Routledge, 2002), 173.

44. F.M. Thrasher, "The Boys' Club and Juvenile Delinquency," *American Journal of Sociology* 41 (1936): 66–80.

45. R. Woodson, *A Summons to Life: Mediating Structures and the Prevention of Youth Crime* (Cambridge, MA: Ballinger, 1981).

46. D.W. Thompson and L.A. Jason, "Street Gangs and Preventive Interventions," *Criminal Justice and Behavior* 15 (1988): 323–33.

47. M. Klein, *From Association to Guilt: The Group Guidance Project in Juvenile Gang Intervention* (Los Angeles, CA: University of Southern California, 1968); M. Klein, *Street Gangs and Street Workers* (Englewood Cliffs, NJ: Prentice-Hall, 1971).

48. I.A. Spergel, "The Violent Gang Problem in Chicago: A Local Community Approach," *Social Services Review* 60 (1986): 94–129.

49. D.M. Kennedy, A.M. Piehl, and A.A. Braga, "Youth Violence in Boston: Gun Markets, Serious Youth Offenders, and a Use-Reduction Strategy," *Law and Contemporary Problems* 59 (1996): 147–96.

50. A.A. Braga, D.M. Kennedy, and A.M. Piehl, *Problem-Oriented Policing and Youth Violence: An Evaluation of the Boston Gun Project*. Final report submitted to the National Institute of Justice (Cambridge, MA: John F. Kennedy School of Government, Harvard University, 1999).

51. D.M. Kennedy, A.M. Piehl, and A.A. Braga, "Youth Violence in Boston: Gun Markets, Serious Youth Offenders, and a Use-Reduction Strategy," *Law and Contemporary Problems* 59 (1996): 147–96.

52. A.A. Braga, D.M. Kennedy, and A.M. Piehl, *Problem-Oriented Policing and Youth Violence: An Evaluation of the Boston Gun Project*. Final report submitted to the National Institute of Justice (Cambridge, MA: John F. Kennedy School of Government, Harvard University, 1999), 42.

53. W.G. Skogan, S.M. Hartnett, N. Bump, and J. Dubois, *Evaluation of CeaseFire-Chicago* (Washington, DC: National Institute of Justice, 2009).

54. D.J. Boyle, J.L. Lanterman, J.E. Pascarella, and C. Cheng, *Impact of Newark's Operation CeaseFire* (Neward, NJ: Violence Institute of New Jersey, University of Medicine and Dentistry of New Jersey, 2010); D.W. Webster, J.S. Vernick, and J. Mendel, *Interim Evaluation of Baltimore's Safe Streets Programs* (Baltimore, MD: Johns Hopkins Bloomberg School of Public Health, 2009).

55. Jeremy M. Wilson, Steven Chermak, and Edmund F. McGarrell, *Community-Based Violence Prevention: An Assessment of Pittsburgh's One Vision One Life Program* (Washington, DC: National Institute of Justice, 2010), xvii.

56. J.M. Wilson and S. Chermak, "Community-Driven Violence Reduction Programs: Examining Pittsburgh's One Vision One Life," *Criminology and Public Policy* 10 (2011): 993–1027.

57. B.C. Welsh and A. Hoshi, "Communities and Crime Prevention," in *Evidence-Based Crime Prevention* eds. L.W. Sherman, D.P. Farrington, B.C. Welsh, and D.L. MacKenzie (New York: Routledge, 2002), 180.

58. L. Sherman, "Communities and Crime Prevention," in *Preventing Crime: What Works, What Doesn't, What's Promising*, eds. L.W. Sherman, D.C. Gottfredson, D.L. MacKenzie, J.E. Eck, P. Reuter, and S.D. Bushway (Washington, DC: U.S. Department of Justice, National Institute of Justice, 1997), 20.

59. W.S.O. Fo and C.R. O'Donnell, "The Buddy System: Relationship and Contingency Conditioning in a Community Intervention Program for Youth with Nonprofessionals as Behavior Change Agents," *Journal of Consulting and Clinical Psychology* 42 (1974): 163–9.

60. W.S.O. Fo and C.R. O'Donnell, "The Buddy System: Effect of Community Intervention on Delinquent Offenses," *Behavior Therapy* 6 (1975): 522–4.

61. D.C. McGill, S.F. Mihalic, and J.K. Grotpeter, *Blueprints for Violence Prevention, Book Two: Big Brothers and Big Sisters of America* (Boulder, CO: Center for the Study and Prevention of Violence, 1998).

62. C. Dicken, R. Bryson, and N. Kass, "Companionship Therapy: A Replication in Experimental Community Psychology," *Journal of Consulting and Clinical Psychology* 45 (1977): 637–46; J.P. Tierney and J.B. Grossman, *Making a Difference: An Impact Study of Big Brothers/Big Sisters* (Philadelphia, PA: Public/Private Ventures, 1995).

63. W.S.O. Fo and C.R. O'Donnell, "The Buddy System: Effect of Community Intervention on Delinquent Offenses," *Behavior Therapy* 6 (1975): 522–4; A. Hahn "Extending the Time of Learning," in *America's Disconnected Youth Toward a Preventive Strategy*, ed. D.J. Besharov (Washington, DC: Child Welfare League of America Press, 1999): 233–65.

64. H.N. Snyder and M. Sickmund, *Violence after School* (Washington, DC: Office of Juvenile Justice and Delinquency Prevention, U.S. Department of Justice, 1999).

65. Ibid.

66. D.C. Gottfredson, G.D. Gottfredson, and S.A. Weisman, "The Timing of Delinquent Behavior and Its Implications for After-School Programs," *Criminology and Public Policy* 1 (2001): 61–86.

67. Ibid.

68. Ibid.

69. J.B. Grossman, K. Walker, and R. Raley, *Challenges and Opportunities in After-School Programs: Lessons for Policymakers and Funders* (Philadelphia, PA: Public/Private Ventures, 2001).

70. See, for example, K.E. Walker and A.J.A. Arbreton, *After-School Pursuits: An Examination of Outcomes in the San Francisco Beacon Initiative* (Philadelphia, PA: Public/Private Ventures, 2004).

71. R.J. Brown and D.W. Dodson, "The Effectiveness of a Boy's Club in Reducing Delinquency," *Annals of the American Academy of Political and Social Science* 322 (1959): 47–52.

72. M.B. Jones and D.R. Offord, "Reduction of Anti-Social Behavior in Poor Children by Nonschool Skill Development," *Journal of Child Psychology and Psychiatry* 30 (1989): 737–50.

73. S.P. Schinke, M.A. Orlandi, and K.C. Cole, "Boys and Girls Clubs in Public Housing Developments: Prevention

Services for Youth at Risk," *Journal of Community Psychology*, OSAP Special Issue(1992): 118–28.

74. L. Sherman, "Communities and Crime Prevention," in *Preventing Crime: What Works, What Doesn't, What's Promising,* eds. L.W. Sherman, D.C. Gottfredson, D.L. MacKenzie, J.E. Eck, P. Reuter, and S.D. Bushway (Washington, DC: U.S. Department of Justice, National Institute of Justice, 1997).

75. L.E. Cohen and M. Felson, "Social Change and Crime Rate Trends: A Routine Activity Approach," *American Sociological Review* 44 (1979): 588–608.

76. See, for example, M.J. Smith, R.V. Clarke, and K. Pease, "Anticipatory Benefit in Crime Prevention," in *Crime Prevention Studies*, ed. N. Tilley, 13(2002): 71–88; R.V. Clarke and R. Homel, "A Revised Classification of Situational Crime Prevention Techniques," in *Crime Prevention at the Crossroads,* ed. S.P. Lab (Cincinnati, OH: Anderson, 1997).

77. S.D. Johnson and K.J. Bowers, "Opportunity Is in the Eye of the Beholder: The Role of Publicity in Crime Prevention," *Criminology and Public Policy* 2 (2003): 497–524.

78. R.H. Schneider and T. Kitchen, *Planning for Crime Prevention: A Transatlantic Perspective* (London: Routledge, 2002).

79. C. Corbett and F. Simon, *The Effects of Speed Cameras: How Drivers Respond.* Road Safety Research Report 11 (London: DETR, 1999).

80. S.D. Johnson and K.J. Bowers, "Opportunity Is in the Eye of the Beholder: The Role of Publicity in Crime Prevention," *Criminology and Public Policy* 2 (2003): 497–524.

81. Ibid., 518.

82. M.A. Pentz, D.P. MacKinnon, B.R. Flay, W.B. Hansen, C.A. Johnson, and J.H. Dwyer, "Primary Prevention of Chronic Disease in Adolescence: Effects of the Midwestern Prevention Project on Tobacco Use," *American Journal of Epidemiology* 130 (1989): 713–24; C.Chou, S. Montgomery, M.A. Pentz, L.A. Rohrbach, C.A. Johnson, B.R. Flay, and D.P. MacKinnon, "Effects of a Community-Based Prevention Program on Decreasing Drug Use in High-Risk Adolescents," *American Journal of Public Health* 88 (1998): 944–8.

83. Much of the discussion in this section could not have taken place but for the thorough review of the literature put together by D.C. Gottfredson, D.B. Wilson, and S.S. Najaka, "School-Based Crime Prevention," in *Evidence-Based Crime Prevention,* eds. L.W. Sherman, D.P. Farrington, B.C. Welsh, and D.L. MacKenzie (New York: Routledge, 2002), 56–164.

84. National Institute of education, *Violent Schools—Safe Schools: The Safe School Study Report to Congress* (Washington, DC: U.S. Department of Education, 1978).

85. National School Safety Center, "School Crime: Annual Statistical Snapshot," *School Safety* (Winter 1989).

86. J. Hall, "The Knife in the Book Bag," *Time*, May 22, 1993; T. Toch, T. Guest, and M. Guttman, "Violence in Schools: When Killers Come Home," *U.S. News and World Report*, November 8, 1993.

87. cdc.gov/violenceprevention/pdf/schoolviolence_factsheet-a.pdf.

88. D.J. Kenney and S. Watson, *Crime in the Schools: Reducing Conflict with Student Problem-Solving* (Washington, DC: National Institute of Justice, Research in Brief, July 1999).

89. D.C. Gottfredson, D.B. Wilson, and S.S. Najaka, "School-Based Crime Prevention," in *Evidence-Based Crime Prevention,* eds. L.W. Sherman, D.P. Farrington, B.C. Welsh, and D.L. MacKenzie (New York: Routledge, 2002), 71.

90. With the exception of gun- and drug-free school programs, this categorization scheme closely mirrors that outlined by D.C. Gottfredson, D.B. Wilson, and S.S. Najaka, "School-Based Crime Prevention," in *Evidence-Based Crime Prevention,* eds. L.W. Sherman, D.P. Farrington, B.C. Welsh, and D.L. MacKenzie (New York: Routledge, 2002).

91. G.D. Gottfredson, "A Theory-Ridden Approach to Program Evaluation: A Method for Stimulating Researcher-Implementer Collaboration," *American Psychologist* 39 (1984):1101–12; G.D. Gottfredson, D.E. Rickert, D.C. Gottfredson, and N. Advani, "Standards for Program Development Evaluation Plans," *Psychological Documents* 14 (1984): 32 (ms. no. 2668).

92. J.P. Comer, "The Yale-New Haven Primary Prevention Project: A Follow-Up Study," *Journal of the American Academy of Child Psychiatry* 24(1985): 54–160; J.P. Comer, N.M. Haynes, and M. Hamilton-Lee, "School Power: A Model for Improving Black Student Achievement," *The Urban League Review* (1987/88): 111–2, 187–200.

93. See, for example, D.J. Kenney and T.S. Watson, "Reducing Fear in the Schools: Managing Conflict through Student Problem Solving," *Education and Urban Society* 28 (1996): 436–55; D.C. Gottfredson, "An Evaluation of an Organization Development Approach to Reducing School Disorder," *Evaluation Review* 11 (1987): 739–63; D.C. Gottfredson, "An Empirical Test of School-Based Environmental and Individual Interventions to Reduce the Risk of Delinquent Behavior," *Criminology* 24 (1986): 705–31; T.D. Cook, H.D. Hunt, and R.F. Murphy, *Comer's School Development Program in Chicago: A Theory-Based Evaluation* (Chicago, IL: Institute for Police Research, Northwestern University, 1998); J.P. Comer, N.M. Haynes, and M. Hamilton-Lee, "School Power: A Model for Improving Black Student Achievement," in *Black Education: A Quest for Equity and Excellence,* eds. W.D. Smith and E.W. Chunn (New Brunswick, NJ: Transaction Publishers, 1989).

94. D.C. Gottfredson, G.D. Gottfredson, and LG. Hybl, "Managing Adolescent Behavior: A Multiyear, Multischool Study," *American Educational Research Journal* 30 (1993): 179–215.

95. D.C. Gottfredson, D.B. Wilson, and S.S. Najaka, "School-Based Crime Prevention," in *Evidence-Based Crime Prevention,* eds. L.W. Sherman, D.P. Farrington, B.C. Welsh, and D.L. MacKenzie(New York: Routledge, 2002), 77.

96. Ibid.

97. For Safe Dates, see V.A. Foshee, K.E. Bauman, X.B. Arriaga, R.W. Helms, G.G. Koch, and G.F. Linder, "An Evaluation of Safe Dates, An Adolescent Dating Violence Prevention Program," *American Journal of Public Health* 88 (1998): 45–50; and V.A. Foshee, G.F. Linder, K.E. Bauman, S.A. Langwick, X.B. Arriaga, J.L. Heath, P.M. Mc Mahon, and S. Bangdiwala, "The Safe Dates Project: Theoretical Basis, Evaluation Design, and Selected Baseline Findings," *American Journal of Preventive Medicine* 12 (1996): 39–47; for drug and alcohol prevention see B.U. Wilhelmsen, J.C. Laberg, and K. Klepp, "Evaluation of Two Student and Teacher Involved Alcohol Prevention Programmes," *Addiction* 89 (1994): 146–52; C.A. Johnson, M.A Pentz, M.D. Weber, J.H. Dwyer, N. Baer, D.P. MacKinnon, W.B. Hansen, and B.R. Flay, "Relative Effectiveness of Comprehensive Community Programming for Drug Abuse Prevention with High-Risk and Low-Risk Adolescents," *Journal of Consulting and Clinical Psychology* 58 (1990): 447–56; D.P. MacKinnon, C.A. Johnson, M.A. Pentz, J.H. Dwyer, W.B. Hansen, B.R. Flay, and E.Y. Wang, "Mediating Mechanisms in a School-Based Drug Prevention Program: First-Year Effects of the Midwestern Prevention Project," *Health Psychology* 10 (1991): 164–72; M.A. Pentz, E.A. Trebow, W.B. Hansen, D.P. MacKinnon, J.H. Dwyer, C.A. Johnson, B.R. Flay, S. Daniels, and C. Cormack, "Effects of Program Implementation on Adolescent Drug Use Behavior: The Midwestern Prevention Project (MPP)," *Evaluation Review* 14 (1990): 264–89; for bullying prevention, see D. Olweus and F.D. Alsaker, "Assessing Change in a Cohort-Longitudinal Study with Hierarchical Data," in *Problems and Methods in Longitudinal Research: Stability and Change*, eds. D. Magnusson, L.R. Bergman, G. Rudinger, and B. Torestad (Cambridge: Cambridge University Press, 1991), 107–32; D. Olweus, "Bully/Victim Problems among Schoolchildren: Basic Facts and Effects of a School Based Intervention Program," in *The Development and Treatment of Childhood Aggression*, eds. D.J. Pepler and K.H. Rubin (Hillsdale, NJ: Lawrence Erlbaum, 1991), 411–48.

98. For details on which outcomes are affected by which programs, see D.C. Gottfredson, D.B. Wilson, and S.S. Najaka, "School-Based Crime Prevention," in *Evidence-Based Crime Prevention,* eds. L.W. Sherman, D.P. Farrington, B.C. Welsh, and D.L. MacKenzie (New York: Routledge, 2002), 80–1.

99. Ibid., 83.

100. D.D. Brewer, J.D. Hawkins, R.F. Catalano, and H.J. Neckerman, "Preventing Serious, Violent, and Chronic Juvenile Offending: A Review of Evaluations of Selected Strategies in Childhood, Adolescence, and the Community," in *A Sourcebook: Serious, Violent, and Chronic Juvenile Offenders,* eds. J.C. Howell, B. Krisberg, J.D. Hawkins, and J.J. Wilson (Thousand Oaks, CA: Sage, 1995), 61–141.

101. V. Battistich, E. Schaps, M. Watson, and D. Solomon, "Prevention Effects of the Child Development Project: Early Findings from an Ongoing Multisite Demonstration Trial," *Journal of Adolescent Research* 11 (1996): 12–35.

102. E. Schaps, J.M. Moskowitz, J.W. Condon, and J. Malvin, "A Process and Outcome Evaluation of an Affective Teacher Training Primary Prevention Program," *Journal of Alcohol and Drug Education* 29 (1984): 35–64.

103. D.C. Gottfredson, D.B. Wilson, and S.S. Najaka, "School-Based Crime Prevention," in *Evidence-Based Crime Prevention,* eds. L.W. Sherman, D.P. Farrington, B.C. Welsh, and D.L. MacKenzie (New York: Routledge, 2002).

104. See, for example, J.M. Moskowitz, E. Schaps, G.A. Schaeffer, and J.H. Malvin, "Evaluation of a Substance Abuse Prevention Program for Junior High School Students," *The International Journal of the Addictions* 19 (1984): 419–30; J.H. Malvin, J.M. Moskowitz, G.A. Schaeffer, and E. Schaps, "Teacher Training in Affective Education for the Primary Prevention of Adolescent Drug Abuse," *American Journal of Drug and Alcohol Abuse* 10 (1984): 223–35; G. Johnson and R. Hunter, *Law-Related Education as a Delinquency Prevention Strategy: A Three-Year Evaluation of the Impact of LRE on Students* (Boulder, CO: Center for Action Research, 1985); J.D. Hawkins, H.J. Doueck, and D.M. Lishner, "Changing Teaching Practices in Mainstream Classrooms to Improve Bonding and Behavior of Low Achievers," *American Educational Research Journal* 25 (1988): 31–50; S.N. Sorsdahl and R.P. Sanche, "The Effects of Classroom Meetings on Self-Concept and Behavior," *Elementary School Guidance and Counseling* 20 (1985): 49–56.

105. See, for example, J.M. Moskowitz, E. Schaps, and J.H. Malvin, "Process and Outcome Evaluation in Primary Prevention: The Magic Circle Program," *Evaluation Review* 6 (1982): 775–88.

106. O. Reyes and L.A. Jason, "An Evaluation of a High School Drop-Out Prevention Program," *Journal of Community Psychology* 19 (1991): 221–30.

107. D.C. Gottfredson, "Changing School Structures to Benefit High-Risk Youths," in *Understanding Troubled and Troubling Youth: Multidisciplinary Perspectives,* ed. P.E. Leone (Newbury Park, CA: Sage, 1990), 246–71.

108. A. Hausman, G. Pierce, and L. Briggs, "Evaluation of Comprehensive Violence Prevention Education: Effects on Student Behavior," *Journal of Adolescent Health* 19 (1996): 104–10.

109. R.D. Felner, M. Ginter, and J. Primavera, "Primary Prevention during School Transitions: Social Support and Environmental Structure," *American Journal of Community Psychology* 10 (1982): 277–90.

110. D.C. Gottfredson, D.B. Wilson, and S.S. Najaka, "School-Based Crime Prevention," in *Evidence-Based Crime Prevention,* eds. L.W. Sherman, D.P. Farrington, B.C. Welsh, and D.L. MacKenzie (New York: Routledge, 2002), 93–4.

111. G.J. Botvin, "Substance Abuse Prevention: Theory, Practice, and Effectiveness," in *Drugs and Crime,* eds. M. Tonry and J.Q. Wilson (Chicago, IL: University of Chicago Press, 1990), 461–519.

112. Ibid. See also D.C. Gottfredson, D.B. Wilson, and S.S. Najaka, "School-Based Crime Prevention," in

Evidence-Based Crime Prevention, eds. L.W. Sherman, D.P. Farrington, B.C. Welsh, and D.L. MacKenzie (New York: Routledge, 2002), 56–164.

113. D.C. Gottfredson, D.B. Wilson, and S.S. Najaka, "School-Based Crime Prevention," in *Evidence-Based Crime Prevention,* eds. L.W. Sherman, D.P. Farrington, B.C. Welsh, and D.L. MacKenzie (New York: Routledge, 2002), 97.

114. Ibid.

115. J.L. Pedro-Carroll and L.J. Alpert-Gillis, "Preventive Interventions for Children of Divorce: A Developmental Model for 5 and 6 Year Old Children," *Journal of Primary Prevention* 18 (1997): 5–23.

116. H.H. Severson, R. Glasgow, R. Wirt, P. Brozovsky, L. Zoref, C. Black, A. Biglan, D. Ary, and W. Weissman, "Preventing the Use of Smokeless Tocacco and Cigarettes by Teens: Results of a Classroom Intervention," *Health Education Research* 6 (1991): 109–20.

117. For examples, see J. Arbuthnot and D.A. Gordon, "Behavioral and Cognitive Effects of a Moral Reasoning Development Intervention for High-Risk Behavior-Disordered Adolescents," *Journal of Consulting and Clinical Psychology* 54 (1986): 208–16; J. Arbuthnot, "Sociomoral Reasoning in Behavior-Disordered Adolescents: Cognitive and Behavioral Change," in *Preventing Antisocial Behavior: Interventions from Birth through Adolescence,* eds. J. McCord and R.E. Tremblay (New York: Guilford Press, 1992), 283–310; R.E. Tremblay, J. McCord, H. Boileau, P. Charlebois, C. Gagnon, M. LeBlanc, and S. Larivee, "Can Disruptive Boys Be Helped to Become Competent?," *Psychiatry* 54 (1991): 148–61; R.E. Tremblay, L. Pagani-Kurtz, F. Vitaro, L.C. Masse, and R.O. Pihl, "A Bimodal Preventive Intervention for Disruptive Kindergarten Boys: Its Impact Through Mid-Adolescence," *Journal of Consulting and Clinical Psychology* 63 (1995): 560–68; J. McCord, R.E. Tremblay, F. Vitaro, and L. Desmarais-Gervais, "Boys' Disruptive Behaviour, School Adjustment, and Delinquency: The Montreal Prevention Experiment," *International Journal of Behavioral Development* 17 (1994): 739–52.

118. D.C. Gottfredson, D.B. Wilson, and S.S. Najaka, "School-Based Crime Prevention," in *Evidence-Based Crime Prevention,* eds. L.W. Sherman, D.P. Farrington, B.C. Welsh, and D.L. MacKenzie (New York: Routledge, 2002), 114.

119. R. Cook, H. Lawrence, C. Morse, and J. Roehl, "An Evaluation of the Alternatives Approach to Drug Abuse Prevention," *The International Journal of the Addictions* 19 (1984): 767–87; R.L. Spoth, C. Redmond, and C. Shin, *Randomized Trial of Brief Family Interventions for General Populations: Adolescent Substance Use Outcomes Four Years Following Baseline* (Ames, IA: Iowa State University, Institute for Social and Behavioral Research, 1999); L. LoSciuto and M.A. Ausetts, "Evaluation of a Drug Abuse Prevention Program: A Field Experiment," *Addictive Behaviors* 13 (1988): 337–51; C.L. Perry, M. Grant, G. Ernberg, R.U. Florenzano, M.C. Langdon, A.D. Myeni, R. Waahlberg, S. Berg, K. Anderson, K.J. Fisher,

D. Blaze-Temple, D. Cross, B. Saunders, D.R. Jacobs, Jr., and T. Schmid, "WHO Collaborative Study on Alcohol Education and Young People: Outcomes of a Four-Country Pilot Study," *The International Journal of the Addictions* 24 (1989):1145–71.

120. Law Enforcement News, *Truth or DARE: Washington Cities Shelve Anti-Drug Curriculum* (New York: John Jay College of Criminal Justice, 1996).

121. For a short list, see S.T. Ennett, D.P. Rosenbaum, R.L. Flewelling, G.S. Bieler, C.L. Ringwalt, and S.L. Bailey, "Long-Term Evaluation of Drug Abuse Resistance Education," *Addictive Behaviors* 19 (1994): 113–25; M.A. Harmon, "Reducing the Risk of Drug Involvement among Early Adolescents: An Evaluation of Drug Abuse Resistance Education (DARE)," *Evaluation Review* 17 (1993): 221–39; C. Ringwalt, S.T. Ennett, and K.D. Holt, "An Outcome Evaluation of Project DARE (Drug Abuse Resistance Education)," *Health Education Research* 6 (1991): 327–37; D.P. Rosenbaum, F.L. Flewelling, S.L. Bailey, C.L. Ringwalt, and D.L. Wilkinson, "Cops in the Classroom: A Longitudinal Evaluation of Drug Abuse Resistance Education (DARE)," *Journal of Research in Crime and Delinquency* 31 (1994): 3–31.

122. dare.org/d-a-r-e-s-keepin-it-real-elementary-curriculum-design/ (accessed October 28, 2013)

123. R.L. Dukes, J.B. Ullman, and J.A. Stein, "Three-Year Follow-Up of Drug Abuse Resistance Education," *Evaluation Review* 20 (1996): 49–66.

124. S.T. Ennett, N.S. Tobler, C.L. Ringwalt, and R.L. Flewelling, "How Effective Is Drug Abuse Resistance Education? A Meta-Analysis of Project DARE Outcome Evaluations," *American Journal of Public Health* 84 (1994):1394–1401.

125. S. Kernus, "Students Give DARE Mixed Reviews," *Juvenile Justice Digest* 24 (1996): 2–5.

126. R.R. Clayton, C.G. Leukefeld, N.G. Harrington, and A. Cattarello, "DARE (Drug Abuse Resistance Education): Very Popular but Not Very Effective," in *Intervening with Drug-Involved Youth,* eds. C.B. McCoy, L.R. Metsch, and J.A. Inciardi (Thousand Oaks, CA: Sage, 1996), 101–9.

127. R. Abshire, "DARE: 'Warm and Fuzzy' or Solid Success?" *Law Enforcement Technology* 23 (1996): 28–9, 32–3, 52.

128. F. Esbensen, D.W. Osgood, T.J. Taylor, D. Peterson, and A. Freng, "How Great Is G.R.E.A.T.? Results from a Longitudinal Quasi-Experimental Design," *Criminology and Public Policy* 1 (2001): 87–118.

129. Ibid., 88.

130. F. Esbensen and D.W. Osgood, *Research in Brief: National Evaluation of G.R.E.A.T.* (Washington, DC: U.S. Department of Justice, 1997); F. Esbensen and D.W. Osgood, "Gang Resistance Education and Training (G.R.E.A.T.): Results from the National Evaluation," *Journal of Research in Crime and Delinquency* 36 (1999): 194–225; D.J. Palumbo and J.L. Ferguson, "Evaluating Gang Resistance Education and Training (GREAT): Is the Impact the Same as That of Drug Abuse Resistance Education (DARE)?" *Evaluation Review* 19 (1995): 591–619.

131. F. Esbensen, "The National Evaluation of the Gang Resistance Education and Training (G.R.E.A.T.) Program," in *The Modern Gang Reader*, eds. J. Miller, C.L. Maxson, and M.W. Klein, 2nd ed. (Los Angeles, CA: Roxbury, 2001).

132. F. Esbensen, D.W. Osgood, T.J. Taylor, D. Peterson, and A. Freng, "How Great Is G.R.E.A.T.?: Results from a Longitudinal Quasi-Experimental Design," *Criminology and Public Policy* 1 (2001): 87–118.

133. Ibid.

134. See D.C. Gottfredson, D.B. Wilson, and S.S. Najaka, "School-Based Crime Prevention," in *Evidence-Based Crime Prevention*, eds. L.W. Sherman, D.P. Farrington, B.C. Welsh, and D.L. MacKenzie (New York: Routledge, 2002), 124–5.

135. B.D. Brooks, "Contingency Management as a Means of Reducing School Truancy," *Education* 95 (1975): 206–11; B.H. Bry, "Reducing the Incidence of Adolescent Problems through Preventive Intervention: One- and Five-Year Follow-Up," *American Journal of Community Psychology* 10 (1982): 265–76; E.R. Gerler, Jr., "A Longitudinal Study of Multimodal Approaches to Small Group Psychological Education," *The School Counselor* 27 (1980): 184–91.

136. D.C. Gottfredson, "Changing School Structures to Benefit High-Risk Youths," in *Understanding Troubled and Troubling Youth*, ed. P.E. Leone (Newbury Park, CA: Sage, 1990).

137. W.B. Hansen and P.M. O'Malley, "Drug Use," in *Handbook of Adolescent Health Risk Behavior*, eds. R.J. DiClemente, W.B. Hansen, and L.E. Ponton (New York: Plenum Press, 1996), 161–92.

138. For a review of these and other interventions and for a discussion of the lack of research in this area, see D.C. Gottfredson, D.B. Wilson, and S.S. Najaka, "School-Based Crime Prevention," in *Evidence-Based Crime Prevention*, eds. L.W. Sherman, D.P. Farrington, B.C. Welsh, and D.L. MacKenzie (New York: Routledge, 2002), 56–164.

14

Reducing Criminal Opportunities through Environmental Manipulation

LEARNING OBJECTIVES

▨ Explain the theories underlying environmental criminology.

▨ Summarize the methods by which environmental manipulation occurs.

▨ Discuss the effectiveness of environmental manipulation in residential areas.

▨ Discuss the effectiveness of environmental manipulation in and around businesses.

▨ Discuss the effectiveness of environmental manipulation in parking garages, open spaces, and other public areas.

Nearly every method of crime control that we have already discussed in this book has taken an offender-specific focus. The assumption has been that people can be changed in some way. The change could be as simple as discouraging someone from committing crime because of the threat of serious sanctions. Such is the case with deterrence-based policies. We have also reviewed a large body of literature concerned with programs and interventions that are intended to change people's thinking processes.

Regardless of whether the approaches we discussed involved a criminal justice component, each approach has sought to do something with criminals. In this chapter, we turn such thinking on its head. We do so by assuming that little can be done to change offenders. If this assumption is correct, then the only way to control crime is to make it harder to commit.

To make crime more difficult to commit, it stands to reason that some features of the physical environment need to be changed. Think, for example, of a typical maximum security prison. With high walls, guard towers, razor wire, and other physical features, prisons are designed to make it difficult for inmates to escape. Prisons do this well; rare are the occasions when inmates escape from such facilities. Although we are not concerned here with keeping prisoners confined, we *are* concerned with the design of places. For example, it might prove interesting to determine whether enhanced lighting discourages criminals from preying on commercial properties during the late night hours. Or we might want to measure the effect of home security systems on the burglary rate. Each of these strategies is intended to make it difficult for offenders to complete crimes.

SOME PERSPECTIVE

environmental criminology: *a focus on crime with particular attention to the built environment. Environmental criminology is concerned with reducing the frequency of criminal events through careful examination and manipulation of physical spaces.*

There is nothing particularly new or exciting about the material that is presented in this chapter. It is basically a review of the state of knowledge in the field of **environmental criminology**. Environmental criminology is a fairly recent offshoot of traditional criminology. The latter, as we have already seen, is concerned with why offenders commit crime. The former assumes that there is little that can be done to control criminals. Further, there is not much of a concern in environmental criminology with *why* people commit crime. The focus is instead on what can be done about crime.

In many ways, this chapter is consistent with the title of this book. A focus on crime control assumes that crime already exists. In the same spirit, environmental criminology assumes that crime already exists and that we should make it tougher to commit. It does little to search out and fix the root causes of crime. Instead, it applies some fairly superficial fixes to deep-seated and complex problems.

situational crime prevention: *the reduction of opportunity for people to commit crime.*

Environmental criminology is not totally reactive to the crime problem, however. One of its variants, **situational crime prevention**, assumes that situations can breed crime and can be targeted to discourage future criminal activity. Clarke has described this particular approach in the following way:

> Situational crime prevention can be characterized as comprising measures (1) directed at highly specific forms of crime (2) that involve the management, design, or manipulation of the immediate environment in as systematic and permanent a way as possible (3) so as to reduce the opportunities for crime and increase the risks as perceived by a wide range offenders.[1]

So situational crime prevention contains a significant environmental component. It seeks to alter the environment so that crime is difficult to commit. But that is not the whole story. There is something of a theoretical basis to situational crime prevention and other methods of crime prevention by environmental design. That basis is a rational offender perspective, a view that criminals weigh the costs and benefits of their actions before they act. This view holds that criminals make conscious decisions to commit crime only after careful thought. In this way, situational crime prevention prizes deterrence.

Environmental crime prevention is clearly undertaken to discourage people from breaking the law. For example, a sign informing people that they are being videotaped in a public area might discourage criminals from acting. Other than the rational offender perspective, though, there is very little concern in environmental crime prevention for theories that explain the behaviors of individuals. In sum, although environmental criminologists and situational crime prevention advocates might be somewhat concerned with what goes on in criminals' heads, that is not their only concern. As one author has put it:

> Individual behavior is a product of an interaction between the person and the setting. Most criminological theory pays attention only to the first, asking why certain people might be more criminally inclined or less so. This neglects the second, the important features of each setting that help to translate criminal inclinations into action.[2]

Another term that is used to describe the strategies discussed in this chapter is **Crime Prevention Through Environmental Design (CPTED)**. Some might argue that CPTED, situational crime prevention, and environmental criminology are different from one another, but to the extent that there are differences between each, they are very subtle. When all is said and done, each assumes that crime is not evenly distributed across time and especially space. The implication for policy, then, is that times and spaces that have a disproportionate amount of crime should be targeted for a fix. Indeed, the fix may be implemented well before crime is ever committed (see Figure 14.1).

Crime Prevention Through Environmental Design (CPTED): similar to environmental criminology and situational crime prevention, any of a number of efforts designed to reduce opportunities for criminal offending through manipulation of the physical environment.

A QUICK RETURN TO THEORY

Why are we returning to theory again when it appears that environmental criminology is not concerned with why criminals offend? Just because advocates of the strategies that are covered in this chapter might not be concerned with individual offenders' motivations does not mean that they discount theory entirely—quite the contrary. Environmental criminologists rely on several theories. With one exception, the theories explain why crime is concentrated in certain places and at certain times, not why people step outside the bounds of the law. We now review four such families of theoretical perspectives.

Rational Offenders

The **rational offender perspective** consists of the view that criminals weigh the costs and benefits of violating the law. According to one source, they "commit crimes that require the least effort, provide the highest benefits, and pose the lowest risks."[3] Risks are perceived as low if it is easy for the offender to access the area where the crime is committed, he or she can get out quickly, and the chances of being seen are absent or minimal. Environmental features weigh heavily because when there are barriers or design features (such as lights) that would call attention to suspicious individuals, then people can be discouraged from committing crimes.

rational offender perspective: the view that criminals weigh the costs and benefits of violating the law.

Target Hardening	Access Control	Deflecting Offenders
Strong doors (magnetic locking, foam-core steel) Locks (deadbolt) Window screens Reinforced glass (marine glazing) Alarms	Doors and gates locked Interior areas fenced off Visitor check-in booths Guard houses Number of entrances and exits reduced Pass-card system in use Key access to laundry rooms and elevators Indoor and outdoor spaces divided into smaller, easily identifiable areas Resident IDs checked Buzzer and intercom systems [Metal] detectors Assigned parking places Parking stickers	Traffic patterns changed Streets and alleys closed "No Parking" or "No Standing" zones created
Closing Crack Houses and Repairing "Broken Windows"	**Cameras and Other Formal Surveillance**	**Surveillance by Employees**
Garbage-strewn lots cleaned up Abandoned cars towed Abandoned houses boarded up 24-hour graffiti removal	Closed-circuit television Portable camera systems Police call boxes Trained resident patrols Police substations On-site security offices Kobans (mini-stations)	Housing authority staff Bus drivers Crossing guards Mail handlers Utility company workers Social services staff
Improving Natural Surveillance	**Removing Inducements to Crime**	**Signage and Bans on Use**
Improved street and interior lighting Non-see-through fencing and barriers removed Trees and hedges pruned Alcoves and other interior blind spots removed Vulnerable areas redesigned or relocated	Vacant apartments rented Overnight street parking banned	"Drug-Free Zones" Posted guest and visitor policies "No Trespassing" signs

FIGURE 14.1 Summary of CPTED Strategies and Tactics

Source: J. D. Feins and J. C. Epstein, *Solving Crime Problems in Residential Neighborhoods: Comprehensive Changes in Design, Materials, and Use* (Washington, DC: United States Department of Justice, National Institute of Justice, 1997).

routine activities theory: *a theory of crime claiming that crime results when three factors are present: motivated offenders, suitable targets, and an absence of guardians.*

The rational offender perspective can be attributed significantly to Cohen and Felson's **routine activities theory.**[4] They argued that when offenders are motivated to commit crime, crime will be easier to commit when targets are easy to access and the chances of being caught are minimal. To these three elements—motivated offenders, suitable targets, and an absence of guardians—researchers have added others. For example, researchers have argued that motivated offenders have **handlers**, or people who discourage them from committing crime (e.g., family members and other acquaintances).[5] **Place managers** also act to influence motivated offenders. These are people who discourage crime by controlling places.[6] Another modification of routine activities theory is the view that although offenders make rational decisions, they do so subject to important environmental constraints.[7]

handler: one who discourages another from committing crime.

place manager: one who discourages crime by controlling a particular place.

Crime Pattern Theory

The rational offender perspective assumes that criminals decide to commit crime. It is not unlike traditional (and other more recent) criminological theories because of its offender-specific focus. Another theoretical perspective that does not rely so much on what individual offenders think is **crime pattern theory**. This view examines the behavior of known criminals, focusing on the places they visit. As one author has put it, "[w]hereas the routine activities perspective concentrates on evaluations of potential victims, guardians, and place managers at an offense site, the [crime pattern theory] view focuses on the chances that the potential offender will even be likely to consider the site in the first place."[8]

crime pattern theory: the study of crime by examination of the places criminals frequent.

Crime pattern theorists look at offenders' **behavior space**. Behavior space consists of the locations that offenders frequent during the courses of their daily lives. These theorists also look at offenders **awareness space**. This consists of the areas with which offenders are familiar. Crime pattern theorists then look at the interplay between the two phenomena.[9] Places where offenders rarely go and with which they are not familiar will likely not be targeted for crime. But familiar places where offenders often go become suitable targets. For example, a home repair person might identify a worthy target for burglary during the course of his or her job. In short, crime pattern theory combines elements of the rational offender perspective with special attention to the environment, particularly the places that offenders frequent.

behavior space: the locations that offenders frequent during the courses of their daily lives.

awareness space: the areas with which offenders are familiar.

Territorial Functioning and Defensible Space

Humans, like many other living organisms, are territorial. This understanding has been transplanted into the field of environmental criminology because it sheds some light on why people commit crime. But unlike the rational offender perspective and crime pattern theory, the territorial functioning/defensible space perspective is concerned with such issues as the attachment people have to the areas immediately surrounding them. This is called **territorial cognition**. According to one source, these cognitions are manifested in the thoughts that are theorized to go through offenders' heads: "How responsible I feel for what happens there; how concerned I am about its appearance and upkeep; how much privacy I expect to have there; what kinds of persons I expect to encounter and how I may respond to them."[10]

territorial cognition: the attachment people have to the areas immediately surrounding them.

Closely tied to territorial functioning is the notion of **defensible space**. Developed by Oscar Newman, defensible space theory proposes "a model which inhibits crime by creating a physical expression of a social fabric which defends itself."[11] Understood differently, defensible space theory is concerned not just with how the physical characteristics of communities can influence offenders but also with how such characteristics can influence law-abiding residents:

defensible space: a concern not just with how the physical characteristics of communities can influence offenders but also with how such characteristics can influence law-abiding residents.

> For residents, the appearance and design of the area can engender a more caring attitude, draw the residents into contact with one another, lead to further improvements and use of the area, and build a stake in the control and elimination of crime. For potential offenders, an area's appearance can suggest that residents use and care for their surroundings, pay attention to what occurs, and will intervene if an offense is seen.[12]

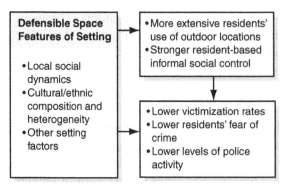

FIGURE 14.2 Defensible Space Theory

Source: R. B. Taylor and A. J. Harrell, *Physical Environment and Crime* (Washington, DC: United States Department of Justice, National Institute of Justice, 1966).

Newman identified four elements of defensible space: territoriality, natural surveillance, image, and milieu. Territoriality refers to people's connection to their surroundings and their desire to exercise some control of the area. Natural surveillance is concerned with environmental design, particularly the design of a place such that legitimate users can observe the activities of acquaintances and strangers. Image is about designing an area to give the appearance that crime is not welcome. Finally, milieu is concerned with the placement of a home or other structure characterized by a low crime rate. Newman compared two different public housing projects and found that crime was higher on the property that provided easy access to strangers. Crime was also higher in the project with more people because it was difficult, given the amount of foot traffic, for legitimate users to distinguish strangers from familiar faces. See Figure 14.2 for an overview of defensible space theory.

The Return of the Broken Windows Theory

We covered the broken windows approach to law enforcement in Chapter 4. The theory underlying the broken windows approach is that low-level crimes and disruptive behavior should be targeted in an effort to stave off the threat of more serious crime. The broken windows theory is actually part of a larger family of theories known collectively as the **incivilities thesis**. Incivilities are defined as "low-level breaches of community standards that signal erosion of conventionally accepted norms and values."[13] Individual perceptions of incivilities operate to enhance people's fear of crime[14] and may also send a signal that a particular area is out of control, possibly increasing the incidence of crime.[15]

incivilities thesis: the view that minor breaches of community standards can create and/or lead to various problems, including crime. The broken windows theory is one example of the incivilities thesis.

Wilson was one of the first to identify possible linkages between incivilities and enhanced levels of fear.[16] He argued that when incivilities are present, people become more fearful and tend to alter their behavior, possibly staying indoors or avoiding areas that they perceive as threatening. Shortly after Wilson called attention to incivilities, a team of researchers argued that it is not so much incivilities themselves that inspire fear but rather a more general sense of "urban unease."[17] The common thread running throughout these two versions of the incivilities thesis was a focus on individual psychological processes quite apart from community structure and higher-order concepts.

Later, Hunter argued that fear of crime was influenced by the prevalence of crime *and* incivilities.[18] He further argued that incivilities and crime influenced each other simultaneously and that both problems were affected directly by neighborhood disorder. On the heels of Hunter's contribution came Wilson and Kelling's famous broken windows theory, another variant—as we have already indicated—of the incivilities thesis.[19] They argued that signs of incivility lead to people's withdrawal from public places. Such withdrawal, they argued, emboldens offenders, which causes people to become fearful and withdraw even more, thereby providing fertile ground for more serious types of crimes.

In a book that was published four years after the broken windows theory was put forth, two researchers asserted that incivilities and crime operate interactively to affect levels of fear.[20] For example, they claimed that when crime is high and incivilities are especially problematic, people's fear will skyrocket. By contrast, when crime is high but incivilities are less prevalent, people will be less fearful. Their study was especially important because it assumed that incivilities and crime have unique origins, in contrast to the broken windows view that one problem leads directly to the other.

Skogan has provided some of the most detailed treatment of how incivilities affect fear.[21] Rather than focusing specifically on individual perceptions of fear, however, he sought to explain neighborhood-level change. Specifically, he argued that disorder (his term for incivilities) "plays an important role in sparking urban decline."[22] Incivilities, he claimed, have detrimental effects on informal social control and community morale and can even threaten the housing market, making people want to leave the area for more peaceful pastures. Skogan's version of the incivilities thesis is perhaps the most developed of all its competitors.

What does the incivilities thesis have to do with the reduction of criminal opportunities? Assuming that incivilities are linked to crime, as Wilson and Kelling argued, then improving the design of spaces to minimize the potential for incivilities can lead to a reduction in crime. If, according to one researcher, "[t]he window isn't fixed or the graffiti isn't erased, and residents become more fearful and withdraw from efforts to control events on the street block, local rowdies act bolder and vandalize further, and the process spirals onward."[23] This thinking combines elements of the rational offender perspective with some of the other theoretical approaches that have already been discussed.

HOW ENVIRONMENTAL MANIPULATION OCCURS

There are almost as many ways to structure environments to prevent crime as there are to design other environmental features. For example, home designs are limited only by architects' imaginations and the laws of physics. Landscapers have almost limitless choices for laying out yards, gardens, and planting beds. The same holds for environmental crime prevention: Methods of reducing criminal opportunities are almost limitless. Fortunately, it is possible to develop a categorization scheme to sort though the complexity.

One such scheme was put forth by Kushmuk and Whittemore in the early 1980s.[24] Although their research was concerned largely with CPTED, it also applies to other attempts to reduce criminal opportunities through environmental design. The researchers identified four methods to reduce criminal opportunities: (1) access control, (2) surveillance, (3) activity support, and (4) motivation reinforcement. Let us consider each in more detail.

Access Control

Access control refers, not surprisingly, to methods of controlling access. It seeks to limit access only to legitimate users. Most of us are familiar with access control; our cars have keys that are designed so that only we can enter the car without having to break, say,

access control: one or more methods of limiting access to place, such as legitimate users.

a window; apartment and condominium complexes often have locked doors that only residents can open; ATMs will provide cash only with the proper PIN code; and so forth.

Another way to view access control is **target hardening**. This includes efforts to make it more difficult for criminals to target specific locations. Features such as high fences, bulletproof glass, security alarms, motion sensors, and locked gates are all intended to make it less easy for criminals to act. Even the design of residential communities can have access control in mind; limiting the number of exits, for example, might make a neighborhood less appealing to a burglar.

target hardening:
any of a number of
efforts to make it
more difficult for
criminals to target
specific locations.

Surveillance

surveillance (in
environmental
criminology): any
method of ensuring
that offenders will
be seen.

Surveillance includes any method of ensuring that offenders will be seen. The method of surveillance that is conjured up in most of our minds is the use of security cameras. But other, more subtle methods of surveillance exist as well. For example, a home builder might put windows on all sides of a house so that while people are inside, they can view the entire perimeter of the home. Homes might also be designed so that doors face the street. This provides an opportunity for easy access to the house, but it also allows passersby to see what is happening at the house. Even plentiful street lighting can make it easier to spot people who should not be there.

The design of sidewalks, public parks, retail establishments, government buildings, and a host of other facilities can be undertaken with an eye toward surveillance. Ironically, even allowing access to many people can have crime prevention benefits. A public place with much foot traffic might not be attractive to criminals because when there are more people, there are more eyes, which heighten the amount of informal surveillance. Whether formal or informal, surveillance activities are all concerned with deterring criminals, with making them think twice about violating the law because of the chances that they might be caught.

Activity Support

activity support:
"functions that
assist and enhance
interaction between
citizens and other
legitimate users in
the community."

A less obvious method of environmental design is **activity support**. This includes "functions that assist and enhance interaction between citizens and other legitimate users in the community."[25] This could include the building of a community center or a clubhouse in a gated community. Such facilities often host activities and otherwise function to bring people together. Consistent interaction causes residents to become familiar faces to one another and improves communal bonds. Locating playgrounds where children's parents can observe them at play can serve a similar function of bringing people together. Much research shows that where community bonds are strong, crime rates tend to be lower.

Motivation Reinforcement

motivation
reinforcement: any
of a number of
strategies concerned
with encouraging
residents and users
of an area to have
positive attitudes
about their living
and working
environment.

Closely tied to the notion of activity support is **motivation reinforcement**. This is concerned with encouraging residents and users of an area to have positive attitudes about their living and working environment. This can work together with the previous concepts, particularly surveillance, to make crime a less attractive option to those who might otherwise commit it. Motivation reinforcement can also be a by-product of activity support. When people come together regularly, they form bonds, which can enhance a feeling of territoriality, a concern that a location does not become overrun by crime and serves to exclude people who should not be there.

THE EFFECTIVENESS OF ENVIRONMENTAL MANIPULATION

Now that we have an understanding of the theories behind environmental criminology and the various techniques that are used to reduce criminal opportunities, it is time to look at what the research shows. Many studies have been concerned with the effectiveness of this approach to crime control, and they tend to fit in four broad categories. One looks at the effectiveness of reducing criminal opportunities in residential areas. The second turns attention to business. The third focuses on transportation. The fourth is concerned with public areas, including parking garages and open spaces.

Residential Areas

Much research has focused on environmental design in high-traffic residential areas, especially housing projects. But traditional residential locations have come to the attention of researchers as well. Residential design has focused both on the areas around residences and on the areas inside them. Common strategies include attempts to restrict pedestrian access, target hardening, property marking, closed-circuit television (CCTV), and other multifaceted interventions that are intended to reduce criminal opportunities.[26]

RESIDENCES. One of the most common methods of discouraging crime at places, particularly residences, is target hardening. Target hardening of residences has most often been accomplished with the use of improved locks and doors as well as home security systems.[27] Surprisingly, though, there is not a great deal of research available on the effectiveness of this approach. One study of a target-hardening strategy in an English public housing complex found that burglary declined by as much as 90 percent in treatment relative to control areas.[28] In another study of target-hardening in the United Kingdom, a researcher found that burglary declined by 52 percent in the treatment area.[29] The author of this second study also examined displacement effects and concluded that target hardening did not lead to a significant increase in burglary in the areas surrounding the target residences.

Another residential approach to crime prevention through environmental design is property marking. We briefly touched on this approach (called Operation Identification) in Chapter 5. Operation Identification has operated somewhat extensively in the United States and has relied significantly on police involvement. Here we look at property identification techniques that do not necessarily involve a significant policing component. What does the research show? Again, there is not much research (as was pointed out in Chapter 5) on this subject from programs in the United States. There is, however, some evidence from other nations.

One study from residences in Canada showed an increase in burglary following a property identification campaign—hardly a desired result.[30] That study contained no control group, however. Another study from the United Kingdom showed the opposite: a significant reduction in burglary following property marking.[31] What can we conclude from these contradictory findings? All we can say is that it remains to be seen whether property identification strategies make crime more difficult to commit or deter offenders.

AREAS SURROUNDING RESIDENCES. Target hardening of residences might make crime more difficult to commit, but it does not appear that property marking works too well. What about environmental manipulations in the areas surrounding residences?

Much more research has been conducted in this area. The two most common methods of targeting the areas surrounding residences have been attempts to restrict pedestrian access and movement and the use of closed-circuit cameras, also called closed-circuit television (CCTV).

There are many methods by which pedestrian access can be restricted, diverted, or altered.[32] One such approach, again in a public housing complex, involved four strategies: reducing the number of foot traffic routes through the project, the creation of smaller areas within the larger project, improved lighting, and physical alterations to the building to make it more aesthetically pleasing. An evaluation of the initiative reported a 54 percent reduction in crime, but there was no control group.[33]

Another approach that has been used to restrict pedestrian access came once again from the United Kingdom. In another public housing project, it was thought that elevated walkways connecting various parts of the facility were responsible for increases in robbery. Partial reductions in crime were reported following the intervention, but because there was no control group, it is difficult to determine whether the removal of the pathways effectively reduced crime.[34] An entry phone was also added at about the same time, so any resultant declines in crime might have been due to its addition.

One of the more significant attempts to restrict pedestrian access to residents hails from Chicago. In yet another public housing project, several manipulations took places. They included police inspections of buildings in the project, new enclosures around ground-floor entrances, the addition of guard stations with metal detectors, the use of resident identification cards for entrance to the building, and security patrols by residents and other entities. The result of the manipulations was, according to one team of researchers, a significant reduction in several types of crimes.[35] However, the evaluation was based on residents' perceptions of crime rather than official crime statistics. In addition, there was once again no control group, so it is difficult to say whether the reductions that residents reported were due to the manipulations to the housing project or other changes.

CCTV basically amounts to the use of security cameras to monitor places and discourage crime. Technically, security cameras do not make crime harder to commit, but their use still constitutes an environmental manipulation, making it important to discuss their effectiveness here. The use of security cameras can be both cheap and expensive. Expensive uses can be found where several live cameras monitor the activities of people in public (and sometimes private) places. Expensive systems often have guards or other observers watching a series of television monitors for evidence of impropriety. At the other extreme, fake cameras are sometimes installed in an effort to give the appearance that people's activities are being monitored. Whether CCTV can be expected to reduce crime is unclear, as was pointed out in a recent review of research:

> It is argued that CCTV (especially if well publicized) may prevent crime because potential offenders are deterred by their increased subjective probability of detection. Also, CCTV may increase the true probability of detection, may increase pedestrian usage of places and hence further increase the subjective probability, may encourage potential victims to take security precautions, and may direct police and security personnel to intervene to prevent crime. . . . [However,] CCTV could also cause crime to increase. For example, it could give potential victims a false sense of security and make them more vulnerable because they relax their vigilance or stop taking precautions, such as walking in groups at night and not wearing expensive jewelry. It may encourage increased reporting of crimes to the police and increased recording of crimes by the police. CCTV may also cause crime to be displaced to other locations, times, or victims.[36]

One available study showed a decline in burglary following the use of CCTV, but it was yet again plagued by the lack of a control group.[37] Another researcher evaluated a police-led CCTV intervention consisting of 63 cameras placed in a town center, parking garages, and arterial streets in Doncaster, England. Two years after the start of the program, crime in the treatment area declined by 21.3 percent, but crime in the control area increased by 11.9 percent. The author concluded that displacement did not occur and that the use of the cameras effectively reduced crime.[38] But two other studies show little to no benefits associated with camera surveillance, either in subways[39] or parking garages.[40] And a study of CCTV in Philadelphia offered a fairly lukewarm assessment concerning the efficacy of this approach.[41] Needless to say, the jury is still out.

COMPREHENSIVE APPROACHES. Target-hardening, CCTV, and the like tend to reflect a singular approach to crime control. Even extensive efforts to restrict pedestrian access by altering the physical appearance of buildings and hiring guards do not represent a wide-ranging approach to environmental manipulation. Multifaceted, comprehensive interventions that combine many of the manipulations already discussed, as well as others not discussed, are the focus of this short section. Two such interventions have been subjected to a fair amount of research. One seeks to reduce repeat victimization at residences, most often apartment buildings. The other seeks to reduce drug dealing at rental properties. Let us consider the effectiveness of each approach.

With respect to repeat victimization at apartments, several comprehensive approaches have been taken. One in Canada included apartment watch (much like neighborhood watch), target hardening, property marking, improvements to lighting, and several other interventions. Reported burglaries dropped substantially in the period after the intervention, but evidence suggests that they might have been on the decline already.[42]

A comprehensive approach in the United Kingdom combined many of the manipulations that we have already discussed with two other unique interventions. At the public housing complex where the intervention took place, residents bought gas for heating and cooking from a coin-operated machine. The machine often held large amounts of cash, making it an attractive target for burglars. The meters were removed for this reason. In addition, a "cocoon neighborhood watch" was implemented, during which several residents would watch a residence that had been subjected to numerous burglaries. An evaluation of the project suggested that it had a dramatic effect on burglary.[43]

Another interesting comprehensive environmental design approach implemented a graduated response to crime. Residents who reported their first burglary victimization received a "bronze" response, during which police would dispense crime prevention advice. First-time victims would also benefit from the cocoon neighborhood watch that was just discussed. Residents who reported their second burglary victimization would receive additional police patrol, and warning stickers were affixed to their dwellings. If a residence was burglarized three times, video surveillance and even more intense patrolling were used. An evaluation of the project showed a significant reduction in burglaries.[44] Further, there was little evidence in the evaluation that burglaries were displaced to surrounding areas; on the contrary, it appeared that burglaries actually went down outside the target area.

Environmental manipulations for the purpose of curbing drug dealing at rental properties have also been evaluated at some length. What makes these approaches different from the other approaches that have been discussed so far in this chapter is their unique approach to environmental manipulation. In particular, they have relied on nuisance abatement laws either to close down problem properties or to produce changes in ownership. Nuisance abatement methods are premised on research that shows that drug dealing tends to be concentrated in smaller rental units where landlords do not always have the resources to drive out the criminal element.[45] When properties are abandoned by their owners, they can become even more attractive to drug dealers.[46]

Policymakers have thus used the civil law to compel property owners to take steps to control crime at the places they own. When they do not, properties can be closed down and/or forfeited, making possible a change in ownership (or even to have the property demolished). A number of evaluations suggest that this approach is highly effective at curbing illegal drug dealing at rental properties.[47] Although this approach to the crime problem can rely significantly on law enforcement involvement (especially that of prosecutors), it still fits nicely in this chapter because it amounts to a manipulation of the physical environment. But instead of targeting properties for changes directly, nuisance abatement initiatives do so indirectly, by compelling property owners to change their ways. The result, it is hoped, is physical improvements to rental properties, including added surveillance and monitoring of people who frequent them.

Life Behind the Wall: Gated Communities

Safety and crime in gated communities are topics of great interest to residents, but the academic community has practically ignored such issues, even in spite of a surge in the number of gated communities and community associations over the past 35 years. Of the research that is available, it is somewhat evenly divided across two gated community types: (1) fee-based gated communities and (2) gated communities without fees.

As researchers have pointed out, "The assessments in fee-based communities ostensibly provide extra services that those residents have willingly accepted to pay as a condition of entrance into their living space."[48] Accordingly, residents should *expect* more in the way of service, and perhaps security, from fee-based neighborhoods and the associations that run them, but researchers have yet to determine with any measure of certainty whether such expectations are grounded in reality.

People who move into gated communities do so for a number of reasons. Often the neighborhoods have strong homeowners' associations that pride themselves on maintaining standards and protecting property values. Families are often drawn to the communities, as well, perhaps because of socializing functions. Recreational opportunities, such as tennis, golf, and boating even serve as draws. Above all else, though, the promise of feeling safe and secure ranks right at the top.[49] Guards, cameras, high walls, gates, and security patrols add to these perceptions.

People who live in gated communities, whether fee-based or otherwise, do report stronger feelings of safety and security than those living in non-gated communities,[50] but there can be a downside to security. As one team of researchers noted, "The security features of the area provide inhabitants with a measure of safety, but it may soothe the households into a state of blitheness."[51] Living inside walls could also promote a "siege mentality," leading people to be fearful of others who do not appear to belong, including strangers, contractors, and delivery personnel.

Perceptions of safety and security draw people to gated communities, but living in a gated community does not immunize one from crime. Actual safety, as measured by crime, does not appear to be significantly different in affluent gated versus non-gated communities.[52] This is a controversial claim to make, but it has a sound basis in the scientific literature.[53] As one study put it, "Idealized community concepts may just be something that was invented from the home owner's imperfect recollections of his or her childhood living environment."[54] Thus, actual crime may be linked to other factors, such as median income, that have little to do with whether a community is gated.

The last chapter reported that community efforts to mobilize in the name of crime control have not proven particularly effective—based on what the scientific literature tells us. This does *not* mean, however, that communities should avoid efforts to improve relationships between neighbors and strengthen ties among residents. Improvements in this regard are essential. Why? People who associate with one another regularly, who *know* one another, will come to the assistance of each other when the need arises, rally in response to crime, engage in collective surveillance, and thereby discourage would-be criminals from coming into the neighborhood.

Improvement of bonds between residents is especially critical in gated communities. One would think that a gated and secure community itself is sufficient to strengthen ties between people and encourage friendship and familiarity. But there are two features of gated communities that inhibit such relationships. First, there is an obvious *physical* barrier between such neighborhoods and "outsiders." Walls, security gates, guard booths, and the like discourage those who don't belong from entering. They also insulate the residents of gated communities from those who live "outside the walls," even though people on the outside may not be that much different in terms of demographic factors.

Next, there is an impression that once a person makes it past that physical barrier and becomes a permanent resident in a gated community, everyone will get along, friendships will be built, neighbors will know each other, and people will associate more often than if they lived in communities on the "outside." This is an inaccurate assessment. Recent research reveals, for example, that gated communities exacerbate social barriers.[55] The authors of one study found that "gated residents' rights and responsibilities are, by and large, confined to legalities, rather than extending to a commitment to enhance social networks either within the development or the adjacent wider community."[56] In other words, there is not enough of a sense of community in gated communities.

The term *community* may in fact be a euphemism, and even intentionally so: "Sense of community to a gated resident may be only of a secondary or tertiary concern, while separation, control, or predictability may be of higher importance."[57] Another researcher said this in reference to the growth in and broadening appeal of gated communities:

> This retreat to secured enclaves with walls, gates, and guards materially and symbolically contradicts American ethos and values, threatens public access to open space, and creates yet another barrier to social interaction, building of social networks, as well as increased tolerance of diverse cultural/racial/social groups.[58]

It remains to be seen whether this author's impressions are correct, but here is a less controversial observation that many residents of gated communities can probably sympathize with:

> By choosing higher levels of protection, residents also forgo typical levels of neighborhood social interaction. Social control is no longer exercised by direct face-to-face contact, but instead by authority figures, usually a private security force employed by the association.[59]

Several factors are associated with residents' satisfaction in gated communities. One of them, for example, is age. Older people tend to be more satisfied.[60] This information is not particularly useful, though, because the community's age composition cannot be easily altered. Another factor associated with gated community residents' satisfaction is their knowledge about crime or, rather, their *lack* of knowledge.

A recent study revealed that residents who do not know about crime in their neighborhoods, even if it exists, tend to be more satisfied:

> A person's knowledge of crime, or the awareness that crime is present, and how it affects the feeling of an individual has toward his or her neighborhood surroundings were shown in our analysis to be significant dynamics in fee-based communities[61]

In simple terms, the authors found that people who were ignorant of crime were more content—this *despite* the reality of crime. That is, the study did not find as much high satisfaction in communities where crime was absent as it did in communities where people were unaware of it. This suggests that, perhaps, "ignorance is bliss."

Does It Work?

Many evaluations of environmental manipulations are not particularly sophisticated because they failed to include a control group. Even so, with the possible exception of property marking, the lion's share of the evidence suggests that when residences are targeted for physical changes, crime—especially burglary—tends to go down. This is an important finding because many environmental manipulations need not be that costly. Added surveillance by neighbors, for example, does not cost anything. And changes to the physical environment do not require that policymakers delve deeply into social problems, such as broken families and poverty, that are inherently difficult to fix. A problem is that environmental manipulations of residences could go "too far" and have unintended effects, as may be the case with gated communities.

Businesses

Residential areas face their share of crime, but businesses are especially vulnerable because they often have more that is worth stealing.[62] This is true of many types of businesses, especially retail establishments, banks, and bars and taverns. Crime at businesses can take place both during and after normal operating hours. This means that environmental manipulations need to be undertaken with the idea in mind that some crimes, especially burglaries and other thefts, can take place at any time. What makes matters even worse is that businesses are sometimes victimized by the very people that work in them. Thus, for crime control to succeed, it needs to target both the traditional criminal element and employees who step outside the limits of the law. The interventions that are discussed in the next three subsections take these issues into account.

STORES.   Convenience stores have come to the attention of environmental criminologists. Some such stores are robbed at a rather high rate, giving rise to a number of changes and interventions that are intended to reduce crime. One such intervention consists of using two clerks instead of one during operating hours. The thinking behind this approach is that criminals will be deterred when faced with having to rob two people instead of one. Does this method work? There are no clear answers to this question. Some studies show an association between the number of clerks and crime,[63] but others do not.[64]

The city of Gainesville, Florida, went so far as to enact an ordinance *mandating* that two clerks at a time work in convenience stores. An evaluation of the ordinance showed long-term reductions in robberies, but whether the changes were due to the ordinance is unclear.[65] Other environmental manipulations in convenience stores include the use of security cameras (sometimes with monitors that patrons can see), silent alarms, and the like, but there have been surprisingly few studies of their effectiveness. The studies that are available tend to present contradictory findings,[66] making it difficult to conclude that environmental manipulations in convenience stores effectively reduce robbery.

Convenience stores also face burglaries after hours. Sometimes criminals attempt to disarm security alarms. Other times, they crash vehicles through the front windows of such stores and make off with as much merchandise as possible before authorities arrive. Store owners often react by installing sophisticated security systems and by barricading their properties to minimize the potential for damage. Unfortunately, it is not clear whether these methods work. The only sophisticated research in this area comes out of the United Kingdom and is concerned largely with repeat burglaries of convenience stores. Evidence suggests that comprehensive efforts to monitor premises and manipulate properties to make them less attractive to criminals are effective.[67] Unfortunately, the available research is not clear as to which specific interventions affect after-hour burglaries more than others. It is at least safe to say that such efforts do not make matters worse.

Shoplifting is also a problem for convenience stores, not to mention all other retail establishments. Most of us are familiar with the security measures that stores take. In addition to CCTV, many retailers—especially apparel retailers—rely on so-called **electronic article surveillance (EAS)**. These are the tags that are placed on merchandise that clerks remove at the time of purchase. When the tags are not removed, they set off an alarm when the person who has the articles in his or her possession tries to leave the store. A similar, though less common, approach consists of using ink tags to mark items that are improperly removed from the premises. The ink permanently stains the item, effectively making it worthless. These two methods of crime control have been subjected to a fair amount of research. The evaluations are almost uniformly supportive of these strategies; EAS and ink tags have led to some significant reductions in shoplifting.[68] CCTV also appears to effectively curb shoplifting activity.[69]

electronic article surveillance (EAS): theft-prevention devices that are placed on merchandise. Clerks remove them at the time of purchase.

As if shoplifting, burglaries, and robberies are not problems enough for retailers, employees sometimes steal. Unfortunately, little research is available on the extent of the problem—or on what can be done to prevent it. Only one researcher appears to have tested whether measures taken by employers reduce employee theft.[70] That researcher examined whether increases in the frequency of inventorying, particularly of items that were prone to employee theft, reduced employer losses. Such "shrinkage" in store inventory was all but eliminated following the change in inventorying practices. Even items that were not targeted for inventorying were stolen at a lower rate. This change was attributed to the diffusion of benefits phenomenon (see Chapter 4). Additional methods of deterring employee theft are available. For example, employers often use security cameras and other surveillance techniques to monitor employees' as well as customers' activities. Such methods have not been of much interest to researchers, however.

BANKS. The movie *L.A. Story,* starring Steve Martin, highlighted the problem of crime at banks, particularly the automated teller machines (ATMs) outside them.

In the movie, there was a line of customers and a line of robbers at one ATM. As a customer withdrew cash, the next robber in line would step up and introduce himself by saying something like, "Hi, I'm John. I'll be your robber tonight." Though a slight departure from reality, that part of the movie was based somewhat on real-world events. Movies and television shows are also replete with less comedic depictions of bank robberies. Whatever the approach, they all remind us that banks are attractive targets to people who are looking to make a quick buck. At the same time, though, most banks are incredibly secure, especially from burglars. But robbers are often more brazen, leading to changes in the physical appearance of banks to deter criminals.

Despite the attractiveness of banks as targets for criminal activity, little research is available on what security measures are most effective. CCTV clearly "captures" robbers on video, but people who are committed to stealing money often foil the camera by disguising themselves. (Of course, the same strategy is used in convenience and other retail store robberies.) Other measures that banks use include stationing security guards inside and/or outside the bank, providing protective screens and/or bulletproof glass for tellers to work behind, installing time-lock safes that employees cannot withdraw money from, and so forth. Several such measures have been evaluated and appear to be associated with reductions in bank robberies,[71] but many of the research designs in this area are weak. Many do not contain control groups, and the studies do not always make clear whether declines in robbery were due to the interventions or to some other occurrence not measured by researchers.

BARS AND TAVERNS. Alcohol and crime often go hand in hand. For this reason, it is no surprise that bars and taverns face a large amount of criminal activity, especially fights and other forms of assault and battery. Not all bars are created equal, of course. Some seem to be hot spots for crime, while others remain relatively crime-free. Such variances can stem from the area where the bar or tavern is located. They can also be explained by everything from managerial practices to security measures. These latter issues have come to the attention of a few researchers. One study of bars in Australia, for example, showed that training for bouncers, crowd control, and improved relationships with the police reduced assaults.[72] Changes in management practices, especially in the form of a code of practice for bar owners, appear to work also.[73] Finally, when servers are trained not to serve alcohol to visibly intoxicated people, assaults can be reduced.[74]

Does It Work?

Businesses are not immune from crime. On the contrary, they can be attractive targets. In response to this, numerous environmental manipulations have been undertaken over the years to make it more difficult to commit crime at retail stores, banks, and drinking establishments. Whether such manipulations work, though, is not entirely clear. There is some convincing evidence that businesses can curb shoplifting by marking their merchandise. There is also evidence that additional inventorying by employers can reduce employee theft. As for measures that banks and other money-handling establishments take, it remains relatively unclear what works. Finally, bars and taverns might be able to reduce assaults on the premises by improved managerial practices. Whether environmental manipulations work for other types of businesses remains somewhat unclear; the research in this important area of crime control is in its infancy.

Transportation

So far, we have seen that residential areas and businesses have come to the attention of environmental criminologists. The same holds for public transportation. Crime on subways, buses, and other transit systems affects many cities throughout the United States. Larger cities, such as New York, retain specific law enforcement officials to patrol mass transit. Add air travel to mass transit and the problem gets even more attention. There is admittedly less crime aboard airlines relative to buses and subways, but events such as the September 11, 2001, terrorist attacks have brought attention to the need for additional security aboard America's many airlines. The following subsections briefly touch on environmental manipulations in public transit, in airports, and aboard airplanes.

PUBLIC TRANSIT.   Several types of crimes take place in buses and subways, including vandalism, robberies and assaults of passengers, attacks on drivers, fare evasion, and other less serious actions. Of course, not all subway and bus systems are besieged by crime. Some, such as the Washington, D.C., Metro System, are relatively safe compared to other systems around the nation.[75] Others, however, can amount to a Mecca for criminal activity. Before it was redesigned, the New York Port Authority Bus Terminal was called "Hell" by a team of researchers who evaluated the changes that were implemented.[76] Many changes have been put in place recently out of concerns that transit systems are terrorist targets, but it is safe to say that crime has not disappeared. A large number of studies concerned with crime on public transit systems suggest that crime is still very much a problem worthy of attention by policymakers and researchers.

Several interventions have been made to improve the physical appearance of mass transit. One was an intensive graffiti cleanup effort on the New York subway. Those who planned the initiative thought that it would make passengers feel safer and deprive vandals of the gratification received by witnessing their work. The initiative was successful in removing graffiti, but it is not clear whether riders' attitudes changed. Also, an evaluation showed a decrease in the number of vandalism arrests, which might indicate either a reduction in crime or a reduction in law enforcement interest in arresting vandals.[77] A study out of Australia, however, showed that a graffiti cleanup, coupled with additional law enforcement, led to a 42 percent reduction in reported crimes against persons.[78] Because this study was concerned with reported crime rather than arrests, it is probably safe to say that graffiti cleanup and added law enforcement can make mass transit safer.

More comprehensive transit cleanup efforts have shown even more promise. One effort (mentioned above) to clean up the New York Port Authority Bus Terminal consisted of not only graffiti cleanup and added law enforcement, but also closure of certain spaces and improved shopping. Unlike the efforts just described, this one took on a distinctly environmental tone, and the concern was with doing something about places in the bus terminal that were plagued by a fair degree of crime. The comprehensive approach was associated with significant reductions in robberies and assaults in the station.[79] A similar approach added CCTV and a publicity campaign aimed at informing people, especially young people, of the initiative. An evaluation showed a decline in vandalism on the buses that received CCTV.[80] Indeed, even buses that did not have cameras aboard faced less vandalism. The researcher attributed this finding to a diffusion of benefits.

Besides trying to reduce vandalism on public transit, officials have also sought to reduce robberies of bus drivers. Nowadays it is commonplace for most buses to have so-called exact fare systems, which require cash-paying passengers to drop change into a secure box. These boxes were put in place to reduce robberies of bus drivers, who had previously been required to carry a fair amount of cash to make change when necessary. Evaluations of the exact fare systems show dramatic—as much as 90 percent—reductions in robberies of bus drivers after their implementation.[81] Another study showed that protective screens around bus drivers led to a 90 percent reduction in robbery.[82] It appears, then, that much can be done—and done effectively—to reduce robberies of bus drivers.[83]

Another crime problem on public transit has been fare evasion. This occurs when people jump toll gates and board subways without paying. It can also occur when people board buses without paying (assuming that the act goes unnoticed by the driver). In an effort to reduce fare evasion, especially on subway systems, several changes to the physical outlay of terminals have been implemented. An example of one such approach was redesign of ticket machines to make them difficult to foil. Another consists of redesigning toll gates so that fare jumping becomes physically impossible. Even personnel changes (e.g., adding more attendants during rush hour and/or relying on volunteers to serve as public transit monitors) have been used. The hope is that more vigilant employees will catch fare evaders before it is too late. Evaluations of these strategies show that they are quite effective.[84]

AIRPORTS. In this day and age, airports are about the last place where someone would want to commit serious crime. But even before September 11, 2001, considerable attention was paid to crime at airports and aboard airplanes. Interventions that were put into effect before then include the addition of air marshals, improvements to doors in airplanes, passenger baggage screening, and extradition treaties between nations to facilitate the prosecution of hijackers. Of course, metal detectors were also put in place in our nation's airports well before 9/11. Unfortunately, though, there have been few evaluations of the effectiveness of these interventions. Certainly, several of them failed miserably on that dark day in the fall of 2001. Even so, it is probably safe to conclude that improvements to airport and airplane security have not made matters worse.

Of the evaluations that *are* available, one researcher found that the air marshal program led to a reduction in hijackings.[85] Two other studies show that implementation of baggage screening has been associated with reductions in hijackings.[86] It remains to be seen whether metal detectors are as effective as their proponents claim them to be. This is especially true in light of several publicized oversights by the screeners who monitor luggage as it passes through magnetometers. Interestingly, there appear to be no published studies on this subject. Instead, researchers have been more concerned with metal detectors in the nation's schools and, as we saw earlier in this chapter, certain public housing projects. This is yet another area that is in need of additional study.

Does It Work?

It is clear that efforts to clean up mass transit and make transit employees safer are associated with reductions in crime. Physical improvements to subway terminals that are designed to discourage fare evasion have also proven to be quite effective at increasing revenues for mass transit systems. As for airports, though, there is little research on which to draw any conclusions. Passenger screening and air marshals appear to have produced declines in airline hijackings over the years, but there are few evaluations in this area. Airports are certainly more secure today than they were before 9/11. But security does not always go hand in hand with safety.

Other Places

Residences, businesses, and mass transit have received the lion's share of environmental criminologists' attention. But there are several other places that have been redesigned in order to make it more difficult for crimes to be completed. Examples include parking garages, open spaces, pay phones, and parking meters.

PARKING GARAGES. Car theft and burglary can be a problem at parking garages, especially when there is little monitoring of the vehicles that are temporarily stored there. The addition of guards, security attendants, and CCTV (in various combinations) has been used in an effort to curtail the problem. Research shows that although guards and security attendants might capably deter criminals,[87] there is no convincing evidence that CCTV makes a difference.[88] One aspect of parking garage improvements that remains to be evaluated by researchers is access and exit control. It stands to reason that access and exit control should discourage car theft, but whether such changes discourage criminals from breaking into cars while they are parked is unclear. Also, it is unclear whether improvements to parking facilities are associated with reductions in other types of crime, such as assaults and robberies. Add to these concerns the cost of employing attendants and/or security guards, and the result could be a dramatic increase in parking costs.

OPEN SPACES. When people are asked what problems they are most concerned with in their neighborhoods, residents of high-crime neighborhoods often complain about a lack of lighting.[89] Findings such as these have prompted many a campaign to improve lighting throughout neighborhoods that face a disproportionate amount of crime. They have also prompted many an evaluation. Several studies of lighting's effectiveness are quickly becoming dated,[90] but a handful of recent studies tend to paint this crime control strategy in a favorable light (no pun intended), indicating that added lighting can reduce crime in public areas.

In one study from London, researchers compared reported crimes before a lighting campaign went into effect with statistics from afterward.[91] There was no control area, and the study revealed that there were declines in crime at night but also during the day. On the one hand, the daytime decrease could be construed as evidence that lighting makes no difference; crime went down regardless of time of day. On the other hand, this counterintuitive finding could be explained by diffusion. A critic of the London study raised this exact point and claimed that lighting *can* reduce crime.[92]

Fortunately, two recent studies of the relationship between street lighting and crime were sophisticated. One study, again from London, compared crime rates in two similar housing projects after one received lighting improvements; the other served as a control. Before- and after-victimization surveys of residents showed a 41 percent decline in victimization in the treatment area compared to 15 percent in the control area. Further, the researchers found no evidence of displacement.[93] Another study of public housing in the United Kingdom, again with a control group, showed similar reductions.[94] In addition, the study showed evidence of diffusion, a reduction in crime in the areas surrounding the target housing project. Add to these studies a series of other studies showing beneficial effects of added lighting, and it becomes quite clear that crime rates go down when darkened areas are brightened up.[95]

An important caveat with respect to lighting and crime is that most evaluations in this area have focused on *public* spaces, as the title of this subsection's heading suggests.

It is unclear whether lighting is advantageous for residential use. (How many offenders does it take to unscrew a light bulb?) There is also something to be said about dark areas. Although they might provide effective cover for criminals, it is difficult for criminals to identify targets in areas that are not illuminated!

Another method of controlling crime in open spaces—by environmental design—is to close streets and restrict traffic. The reasoning behind this approach is that when criminals have easy access to their targets, they will commit more crimes. The notion of restricting access is commensurate with environmental criminologists' belief that crime is a given and that steps should be taken to make it more difficult to complete. Street closures can also trap criminals. As one author put it:

> Closing streets makes escaping more difficult. In the case of prostitution cruising and drive-by shootings, the offenders are likely to follow a circular driving pattern in their search for targets. By making circular driving patterns harder and increasing the chances that offenders will find themselves at the end of a dead-end street, criminal behavior may be thwarted.[96]

Are street closures effective? The evidence is somewhat inconclusive. For example, one study showed that street closures in Miami Shores, Florida, had no significant effect on robberies and assaults.[97] The study compared Miami Shores to two control areas, so its design was fairly sophisticated. But a study of street closures in Dayton, Ohio, showed declines of 26 and 50 percent for overall crime and violent crime, respectively. Thus, two similar approaches produced conflicting results.

When stepped-up enforcement is added to the mix, however, the results are more encouraging. Two British evaluations of street closures that were coupled with an added police presence showed significant reductions in crime.[98] Similar results were reported in an evaluation of the Los Angeles Police Department's Operation Cul-De-Sac. Put into effect in 1990, the initiative saw the placement of traffic barricades on 14 streets in a South Central L.A. neighborhood that had significant drug activity and a number of shootings. An evaluation compared the target area with surrounding neighborhoods and revealed a 65 percent decline in crime in the treatment area.[99] Even more important, during the two years when the barriers were in place, there was only one killing in the target area (see Figure 14.3).[100] Sadly, though, once the barricades were removed, homicides rose 800 percent in comparison to the rate in the surrounding areas.[101]

Additional methods of crime control in open spaces include CCTV. We have already discussed this approach in the context of residential areas, businesses, and mass transit, so we will not go into detail again. Suffice it to say that several evaluations of CCTV in public areas show reductions in crime after cameras were installed, but some of the studies did not contain comparison groups and failed to state whether reported crime reductions were significant (as opposed to chance occurrences).[102]

PARKING METERS AND PUBLIC PHONES.   Parking meters and public telephones have been targets for criminals over the years. When they are not constructed of sturdy material or can be foiled with ease by criminals, cities and phone companies lose out on substantial revenues. Accordingly, steps have been taken to harden targets and make it easier both to detect fraud and to apprehend criminals. For example, improvements to the design of pay phones coupled with electronic monitoring of phone booths (to identify and apprehend criminals) have been associated with reductions in vandalism and theft.[103] Another phone study showed that hardened coin boxes and rapid repair of broken phones led to a reduction in vandalism.[104] Efforts to prevent telephone toll fraud have also been effective.[105]

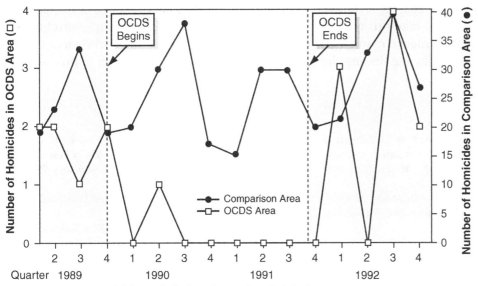

FIGURE 14.3 Homicides Fell during Operation Cul de Sac

Source: J. Lasley, *"Designing Out" Gang Homicides and Street Assaults* (Washington DC: United States Department of Justice, National Institute of Justice, 1998).

As for parking meters, unscrupulous parkers have used slugs (coins and similar objects designed to make a machine think that U.S. currency has been inserted) to foil parking meters. This has prompted cities to install slug-proof parking meters. An evaluation of slug-proof parking meters in New York City revealed an increase in revenue.[106] Warning stickers alone, however, were not effective.[107] In contrast to some of the strategies that we have discussed however, target hardening—even without added law enforcement activity—can serve as an effective deterrent to criminal activity.

Does It Work?

Fraud at pay phones and parking meters can be minimized with relative ease. Warning stickers are not enough, though. Steps must be taken to harden targets and make it tougher for criminals to cheat the phone or meter's technology. As for parking facilities, paid guards and/or security officers appear to make a difference. Finally, various methods of crime control by environmental design in open spaces appear effective. These include lighting campaigns, street closures with added enforcement, and possibly CCTV. The effects of the latter appear somewhat unclear, however.

Summary

We began this chapter by situating its material within the broader field of environmental criminology. We then pointed out that environmental criminologists are not usually concerned with the goings on in criminals' heads. Instead, their explanation for crime is that it is largely opportunistic—that people commit crime when it is easy to do so. Various theoretical perspectives behind this thinking, including the rational offender perspective and crime pattern theory, were then introduced. We also covered four broad methods by which environmental manipulation occurs: access control, surveillance, activity support, and motivation reinforcement.

The last major section of this chapter reviewed the effectiveness of various steps taken to reduce criminal opportunities by environmental manipulations. There is no point in reviewing the findings in detail here (the summary sections above did that). It is safe to say, though, that crime control through environmental designs is one of the more effective strategies that we have touched on in this book.

Notes

1. R.V. Clarke, "Situational Crime Prevention: Its Theoretical Basis and Practical Scope," in *Crime and Justice: A Review of Research*, eds. M. Tonry and N. Morris (Chicago: University of Chicago Press, 1983), 225.

2. M. Felson and R.V. Clarke, *Opportunity Makes the Thief: Practical Theory for Crime Prevention*, vol. 8 (London: Home Office, 1998), 1.

3. R.B. Taylor, "Physical Environment, Crime, Fear, and Resident-Based Control," in *Crime: Public Policies for Crime Control*, eds. J.Q. Wilson and J. Petersilia (Oakland, CA: Institute for Contemporary Studies, 2002), 416–7.

4. L.E. Cohen and M. Felson, "Social Change and Crime Rate Trends: A Routine Activity Approach," *American Sociological Review* 44 (1979): 588–608.

5. M. Felson, "Those Who Discourage Crime," in *Crime and Place*, eds. J.E. Eck and D. Weisburd, Crime Prevention Studies, vol. 4 (Monsey, NY: Criminal Justice Press, 1995), 53–66.

6. R.B. Taylor, "Social Order and Disorder of Streetblocks and Neighborhoods: Ecology, Microecology, and the Systemic Model of Social Disorganization," *Journal of Research in Crime and Delinquency* 33 (1997): 113–55.

7. H. Simon, *Sciences of the Artificial*, 3rd ed. (Cambridge, MA: MIT Press, 1996).

8. R.B. Taylor, "Physical Environment, Crime, Fear, and Resident-Based Control," in *Crime: Public Policies for Crime Control*, eds. J.Q. Wilson and J. Petersilia (Oakland, CA: Institute for Contemporary Studies, 2002), 419.

9. P. Brantingham and P. Brantingham, "Notes on the Geometry of Crime," in *Environmental Criminology*, eds. P. Brantingham and P. Brantingham (Beverly Hills, CA: Sage, 1981), 588–605.

10. R.B. Taylor, "Physical Environment, Crime, Fear, and Resident-Based Control," in *Crime: Public Policies for Crime Control*, eds. J.Q. Wilson and J. Petersilia (Oakland, CA: Institute for Contemporary Studies, 2002), 420.

11. O. Newman, *Defensible Space* (New York: Macmillan, 1972).

12. S.P. Lab, *Crime Prevention: Approaches, Practices, and Evaluations*, 4th ed. (Cincinnati, OH: Anderson, 2000), 27.

13. R.L. LaGrange, K.F. Ferraro, and M. Supancic, "Perceived Risk and Fear of Crime: Role of Social and Physical Incivilities," *Journal of Research in Crime and Delinquency* 29 (1992): 311–34.

14. D.D. Perkins, A. Wandersman, R.C. Rich, and R.B. Taylor, "The Physical Environment of Street Crime: Defensible Space, Territoriality, and Incivilities," *Journal of Environmental Psychology* 13 (1993): 29–49; R. Taylor and M. Hale, "Testing Alternative Models of Fear of Crime," *Journal of Criminal Law and Criminology* 77 (1986): 151–89.

15. J.Q. Wilson and G. Kelling, "Broken Windows," *Atlantic Monthly* 211 (1982): 29–38.

16. J.Q. Wilson, *Thinking about Crime* (New York: Basic Books, 1975).

17. J. Garofalo and J. Laub, "The Fear of Crime: Broadening Our Perspective," *Victimology* 3 (1978): 242–53.

18. A. Hunter, "Community Change: A Stochastic Analysis of Chicago's Local Communities, 1930–1960," *American Journal of Sociology* 79 (1974): 923–47.

19. J.Q. Wilson and G. Kelling, "Broken Windows," *Atlantic Monthly* 211 (1982): 29–38.

20. D.A. Lewis and G. Salem, *Fear of Crime* (New Brunswick, NJ: Transaction Books, 1986).

21. W. Skogan, *Disorder and Decline: Crime and the Spiral Decay in American Cities* (New York: Free Press, 1990).

22. Ibid., 2.

23. R.B. Taylor, "Physical Environment, Crime, Fear, and Resident-Based Control," in *Crime: Public Policies for Crime Control*, eds. J.Q. Wilson and J. Petersilia (Oakland, CA: Institute for Contemporary Studies, 2002), 422.

24. J. Kushmuk and S.L. Whittemore, *A Reevaluation of the Crime Prevention through Environmental Design Program in Portland, Oregon* (Washington, DC: National Institute of Justice, 1981).

25. Ibid.

26. This classification scheme and much of the discussion that follows draws from J.E. Eck, "Preventing Crime at Places," in *Evidence-Based Crime Prevention*, eds. L.W. Sherman, D.P. Farrington, B.C. Welsh, and D.L. MacKenzie (New York: Routledge, 2002), 241–94.

27. D.J. Evans, "Levels of Possession of Security Measures against Residential Burglary," *Security Journal* 14 (2001): 29–41.

28. N. Tilley and J. Webb, *Burglary Reduction: Findings from Safer City Schemes*, vol. 51 (London: Home Office, 1994).

29. P. Allatt, "Residential Security: Containment and Displacement of Burglary," *Howard Journal of Criminal Justice* 23 (1984): 99–116.

30. T. Gabor, "The Crime Displacement Hypothesis: An Empirical Evaluation," *Crime and Delinquency* 26 (1981): 390–404.

31. G. Laycock, *Property Marking: A Deterrent to Domestic Burglary?* Vol. 3 (London: Home Office, 1985); G. Laycock,

"Operation Identification, or the Power of Publicity," *Security Journal* 2 (1991): 67–72.

32. K.J. Bowers, S.D. Johnson, and A.F.G. Hirschfield, "Closing Off Opportunities for Crime: An Evaluation of Alley-Gating," *European Journal of Criminal Policy and Research* 10 (2004): 285–308.

33. O. Newman, *Community of Interest* (Garden City, NY: Anchor Press, 1980); O. Newman, *Creating Defensible Space* (Washington, DC: U.S. Department of Housing and Urban Development, 1996).

34. B. Poyner, "Lessons from Lisson Green: An Evaluation of Walkway Demolition on a British Housing Estate," in *Crime Prevention Studies*, ed. R.V. Clarke, vol. 3 (Monsey, NY: Criminal Justice Press, 1994), 127–51.

35. S.J. Popkin, V.E. Gwiasda, D.P. Rosenbaum, A.A. Anderson, L.M. Olson, A.J. Lurigio, and N. Taluc, *An Evaluation of the Chicago Housing Authority's Anti-Drug Initiative: A Model of Comprehensive Crime Prevention in Public Housing* (Cambridge, MA: Abt Associates, 1995).

36. B.C. Welsh and D.P. Farrington, *Effects of Closed Circuit Television Surveillance on Crime: Protocol for a Systematic Review.* Available at http://www.aic.gov.au/campbellcj/reviews/2003-11-CCTV.pdf.

37. M.R. Chatterton and S.J. Frenz, "Closed-Circuit Television: Its Role in Reducing Burglaries and the Fear of Crime in Sheltered Accommodation for the Elderly," *Security Journal* 5 (1994): 133–9.

38. D. Skinns, "Crime Reduction, Diffusion and Displacement: Evaluating the Effectiveness of CCTV," in *Surveillance, Closed Circuit Television, and Social Control*, eds. C. Norris and G. Armstrong (Aldershot, England: Ashgate, 1998), 175–88.

39. R. Grandmaison and P. Tremblay, "Evaluation des effets de la tele-surveillances sur la criminalite commise dans 13 stations du Metro de Montreal," *Criminologie* 30 (1997): 93–110.

40. B. Poyner, "Situational Crime Prevention in Two Parking Facilities," *Security Journal* 2 (1991): 96–101.

41. See, e.g., J.H. Ratcliffe, *Video Surveillance of Public Places* (Washington, DC: Center for Problem-Oriented Policing, 2006).

42. C. Meredith and C. Paquette, "Crime Prevention in High-Rise Rental Apartments: Findings of a Demonstration Project," *Security Journal* 3 (1992): 161–9.

43. D.H. Forrester, M.R. Chatterton, and K. Pease, *The Kirkholt Burglary Prevention Demonstration Project, Rochdale*, vol. 13 (London: Home Office, 1988).

44. S. Chenery, J. Holt, and K. Pease, *Biting Back II: Reducing Repeat Victimization in Huddersfield* vol. 82 (London: Home Office, 1997).

45. J.E. Eck, "A General Model of the Geography of Illicit Retail Marketplaces," in *Crime and Place*, eds. J.E. Eck and D. Weisburd, vol. 4 (Monsey, NY: Criminal Justice Press, 1995).

46. W. Spelman, "Abandoned Buildings: Magnets for Crime?" *Journal of Criminal Justice* 21 (1993): 481–95.

47. L. Green, "Cleaning Up Drug Hotspots in Oakland, California: The Displacement and Diffusion Effects," *Justice Quarterly* 12 (1995): 737–54; L. Green, *Policing Places with Drug Problems* (Thousand Oaks, CA: Sage, 1996); J.E. Eck and J. Wartell, "Improving the Management of Rental Properties with Drug Problems: A Randomized Experiment," in *Civil Remedies and Crime Prevention*, eds. L. Mazerolle and J. Roehl, vol. 9 (Monsey, NY: Criminal Justice Press, 1998), 161–86; L. Mazerolle, J. Roehl, and C. Kadleck, "Controlling Social Disorder Using Civil Remedies: Results for a Randomized Field Experiment in Oakland, California," in *Civil Remedies and Crime Prevention*, eds. L. Mazerolle and J. Roehl, vol. 9 (Monsey, NY: Criminal Justice Press, 1998), 141–60.

48. D.W. Chapman and J.R. Lombard, "Determinants of Neighborhood Satisfaction in Fee-Based Gated and Nongated Communities," *Urban Affairs Review* 41 (2006): 771.

49. E.J. Blakely and M.G. Snyder, *Fortress America: Gated Communities in the United States* (Washington, DC: Brookings Institution Press, 1997); E. McKenzie, "Private Gated Communities in the American Urban Fabric: Emerging Trends in Their Production, Practices, and Regulation" in *Gated Communities: Building Social Division or Safer Communities?* (Glasgow: University of Glasgow, 2003).

50. T.W. Sanchez, R.E. Lang, and D.M. Dhavale, "Security Versus Status? A First Look at the Census's Gated Community Data," *Journal of Planning Education and Research* 24 (2005): 281–91.

51. D.W. Chapman and J.R. Lombard, "Determinants of Neighborhood Satisfaction in Fee-Based Gated and Nongated Communities," *Urban Affairs Review* 41 (2006): 775.

52. See, e.g., G. Wilson-Doenges, "An Exploration of Sense of Community and Fear of Crime in Gated Communities," *Environment and Behavior* 32 (2000): 597–611.

53. Wilson-Doenges 2000; E.J. Blakely and M.G. Snyder, *Fortress America: Gated Communities in the United States* (Washington, DC: Brookings Institution Press, 1997).

54. Ibid., 776.

55. S. Blandy and D. Lister, "Gated Communities: (Ne)gating Community Development?" *Housing Studies* 20 (2005): 287–301.

56. Ibid., 287.

57. D.W. Chapman and J.R. Lombard, "Determinants of Neighborhood Satisfaction in Fee-Based Gated and Nongated Communities," *Urban Affairs Review* 41 (2006): 776.

58. S.M. Low, "The Edge and the Center: Gated Communities and the Discourse of Urban Fear," *American Anthropologist* 103 (2001): 45–58.

59. T.W. Sanchez, R.E. Lang, and D.M. Dhavale, "Security Versus Status? A First Look at the Census's Gated Community Data," *Journal of Planning Education and Research* 24 (2005): 284.

60. D.W. Chapman and J.R. Lombard, "Determinants of Neighborhood Satisfaction in Fee-Based Gated and Nongated Communities," *Urban Affairs Review* 41 (2006): 769–99.

61. Ibid., 792.

62. B. Fisher and Johanna W. Looye, "Crime and Small Business in the Midwest: An Examination of Overlooked Issues in the United States," *Security Journal* 13 (2000): 45–72.

63. R.D. Hunter and C.R. Jeffrey, "Preventing Convenience Store Robbery through Environmental Design," in *Situational Crime Prevention: Successful Case Studies,* ed. R.V. Clarke (Albany, NY: Harrow and Heston, 1992), 194–204; National Association of Convenience Stores, *Convenience Store Security Report and Recommendations* (Alexandria, VA: National Association of Convenience Stores, 1991).

64. N.G. LaVigne, "Crimes of Convenience: An Analysis of Criminal Decision-Making and Convenience Store Crime in Austin, Texas" (unpublished M.A. thesis, Austin Texas: University of Texas at Austin, 1991).

65. W. Clifton, Jr., *Convenience Store Robberies in Gainesville, Florida: An Intervention Strategy by the Gainesville Police Department* (Gainesville, FL: Gainesville Police Department, 1987); J.V. Wilson, *Gainesville Convenience Store Ordinance: Findings of Fact. Conclusions and Recommendations* (Washington, DC: Crime Control Research Corporation, 1990).

66. See, for example, W.J. Crow and J.L. Bull, *Robbery Deterrence: An Applied Behavioral Science Demonstration—Final Report* (La Jolla, CA: Western Behavior Sciences Institute, 1975).

67. G. Taylor, "Using Repeat Victimization to Counter Commercial Burglary: The Leicester Experience," *Security Journal* 12 (1999): 41–52.

68. For examples, see R.L. DiLonardo, "Defining and Measuring the Economic Benefit of Electronic Article Surveillance," *Security Journal* 7 (1996): 3–9; J. Bamfield, "Electronic Article Surveillance: Management Learning in Curbing Theft," in *Crime at Work: Studies in Security and Crime Prevention,* ed. M. Gill (Leicester: Perpetuity Press, 1994), 3–9; D.P. Farrington, S. Bowen, A. Buckle, T. Burns-Howell, J. Burrows, and M. Speed, "An Experiment on the Prevention of Shoplifting," in *Crime Prevention Studies,* ed. R.V. Clarke, vol. 1 (Monsey, NY: Criminal Justice Press, 1993), 93–120; R.L. DiLonardo and R.V. Clarke, "Reducing the Rewards of Shoplifting: An Evaluation of Ink Tags," *Security Journal* 7 (1996): 11–4.

69. A. Beck and A. Willis, "Context-Specific Measures of CCTV Effectiveness in the Retail Sector," in *Surveillance of Public Space: CCTV, Street Lighting and Crime Prevention,* eds. K. Painter and N. Tilley, vol. 10 (Monsey, NY: Criminal Justice Press, 1999).

70. B. Masuda, "Displacement vs. Diffusion of Benefits and the Reduction of Inventory Losses in a Retail Environment," *Security Journal* 3 (1992): 131–6.

71. For examples, see R.V. Clarke and G. McGrath, "Cash Reduction and Robbery Prevention in Australian Betting Shops," *Security Journal* 1 (1990): 160–3; R.V. Clarke, S. Field, and G. McGrath, "Target Hardening of Banks in Australia and Displacement of Robberies," *Security Journal* 2 (1991): 84–90; P. Ekblom, *Preventing Robberies at Sub-Post Offices: An Evaluation of a Security Initiative,* vol. 9 (London: Home Office, 1987); C. Grandjean, "Bank Robberies and Physical Security in Switzerland: A Case Study of the Escalation and Displacement Phenomena," *Security Journal* 1 (1990): 155–9; T.H. Hannan, "Bank Robberies and Bank Security Precautions," *Journal of Legal Studies* 11 (1982): 83–92; R.T. Guerette and R.V. Clarke, "Product Life Cycles and Crime: Automated Teller Machines and Robbery," *Security Journal* 16 (2003): 7–18.

72. R. Homel, M. Hauritz, R. Wortley, G. McIlwain, and R. Carvolth, "Preventing Alcohol-Related Crime through Community Action: The Surfers' Paradise Safety Action Project," *Crime Prevention Studies* 7 (1997): 35–90.

73. M. Felson, R. Berends, B. Richardson, and A. Veno, "Reducing Pub Hopping and Related Crime," in *Policing for Prevention: Reducing Crime, Public Intoxication and Injury,* ed. R. Homel, vol. 7, (Monsey, NY: Criminal Justice Press, 1997), 115–32.

74. S.L. Putnam, I.R. Rockett, and M.K. Campbell, "Methodological Issues in Community-Based Alcohol-Related Injury Prevention Projects: Attribution of Program Effects," in *Experience with Community Action Projects: New Research in the Prevention of Alcohol and Other Drug Problems,* eds. T.K. Greenfield and R. Zimmerman, vol. 14 (Rockville, MD: Center for Substance Abuse Prevention, 1993), 32–42.

75. See, for example, N.G. LaVigne, "Safe Transport: Security by Design on the Washington Metro," in *Preventing Mass Transit Crime,* ed. R.V. Clarke, vol. 6 (Monsey, NY: Criminal Justice Press, 1996), 163–98.

76. M. Felson, M.E. Belanger, G.M. Bichler, C.D. Bruzinski, G.S. Campbell, C.L. Fried, K.C. Grofik, I.S. Mazur, A.B. O'Regan, P.J. Sweeney, A.L. Ullman, and L.M. Williams, "Redesigning Hell: Preventing Crime and Disorder at the Port Authority Bus Terminal," in *Preventing Mass Transit Crime,* ed. R.V. Clarke, vol. 6 (Monsey, NY: Criminal Justice Press, 1996), 5–92.

77. M. Sloan-Howitt and G.L. Kelling, "Subway Graffiti in New York City: "Getting Up" vs. "Meaning It and Cleaning It," *Security Journal* 1 (1990): 131–6.

78. K. Carr and G. Spring, "Public Transport Safety: A Community Right and a Communal Responsibility," in *Crime Prevention Studies,* ed. R.V. Clarke, vol. 1 (Monsey, NY: Criminal Justice Press, 1993), 147–55.

79. M. Felson, M.E. Belanger, G.M. Bichler, C.D. Bruzinski, G.S. Campbell, C.L. Fried, K.C. Grofik, I.S. Mazur, A.B. O'Regan, P.J. Sweeney, A.L. Ullman, and L.M. Williams, "Redesigning Hell: Preventing Crime and Disorder at the Port Authority Bus Terminal," in *Preventing Mass Transit*

Crime, ed. R.V. Clarke, vol. 6 (Monsey, NY: Criminal Justice Press, 1996), 5–92.

80. B. Poyner, "Video Cameras and Bus Vandalism," *Journal of Security Administration* 11 (1988): 44–51.

81. J.M. Chaiken, M.W. Lawless, and K.A. Stevenson, *Impact of Police on Crime: Robberies on the New York City Subway System* (R-1424-NYC) (New York: The New York City Rand Institute, 1974); R.V. Clarke, ed., *Situational Crime Prevention: Successful Case Studies* (Albany, NY: Harrow and Heston, 1992), 216.

82. B. Poyner and C. Warne, *Violence to Staff: A Basis for Assessment and Prevention* (London: Tavistock, 1986).

83. See also N. Westmarland and J. Anderson, "Safe at the Wheel?: Security Issues for Female Taxi Drivers," *Security Journal* 14 (2001): 24–90.

84. For examples, see R.V. Clarke, "Fare Evasion and Automatic Ticket Collection in the London Underground," in *Crime Prevention Studies*, ed. R.V. Clarke, vol. 1 (Monsey, NY: Criminal Justice Press, 1993), 135–46; R.V. Clarke, R. Cody, and M. Natarajan, "Subway Slugs: Tracking Displacement on the London Underground," *British Journal of Criminology* 34 (1994): 122–38; S. DesChamps, P. Brantingham, and P. Brantingham, "The British Columbia Transit Fare Evasion Audit: A Description of a Situational Prevention Process," *Security Journal* 2 (1991): 211–8; H. van Andel, "Crime Prevention That Works: The Case of Public Transport in the Netherlands," *British Journal of Criminology* 29 (1989): 47–56; R.R. Weidner, "Target Hardening at a New York City Subway Station: Decreased Fare Evasion—At What Price?" in *Preventing Mass Transit Crime*, ed. R.V. Clarke, vol. 6 (Monsey, NY: Criminal Justice Press, 1996), 117–32.

85. W.M. Landes, "An Economic Study of U.S. Aircraft Hijacking, 1961–1976," *Journal of Law and Economics* 21 (1978): 1–32.

86. P.W. Eastreal and P.R. Wilson, *Preventing Crime on Transport* (Canberra: Australian Institute of Criminology, 1991); P. Wilkinson, *Terrorism and the Liberal State* (New York: John Wiley and Sons, 1977).

87. See, for example, P. Barclay, J. Buchley, P.J. Brantingham, P. Brantingham, and T. Whinn-Yates, "Preventing Auto Theft in Suburban Vancouver Commuter Lots: Effects of a Bike Patrol," in *Preventing Mass Transit Crime*, ed. R.V. Clarke, vol. 6 (Monsey, NY: Criminal Justice Press, 1996) 133–61; G. Laycock and C. Austin, "Crime Prevention in Parking Facilities," *Security Journal* 3 (1992): 154–160; B. Poyner, "Situational Crime Prevention in Two Parking Facilities," *Security Journal* 2 (1991): 96–101; B. Poyner, "Lessons from Lisson Green: An Evaluation of Walkway Demolition on a British Housing Estate," in *Crime Prevention Studies*, ed. R.V. Clarke, vol. 3 (Monsey, NY: Criminal Justice Press, 1994) 127–50.

88. For evidence of the conflicting findings, see N. Tilley, *Understanding Car Parks, Crime, and CCTV: Evaluation Lessons from Safer Cities*, vol. 42 (London: Home Office, 1993).

89. See, for example, J.L. Worrall, J. Ross, and M. Macon, *Community Prosecution Needs Assessment Survey Summary* (San Bernardino, CA: Center for Criminal Justice Research, California State University, San Bernardino, 2004).

90. J.M. Tien, V.F. O'Donnell, A. Barnett, and P.B. Mirchandani, *Phase I Report: Street Lighting Projects* (Washington, DC: U.S. Government Printing Office, 1979).

91. S. Atkins, S. Husain, and A. Storey, *The Influence of Street Lighting on Crime and Fear of Crime*, vol. 28 (London: Home Office, 1991).

92. K. Pease, "A Review of Street Lighting Evaluations: Crime Reduction Effects," in *Surveillance of Public Space: CCTV, Street Lighting, and Crime Prevention*, eds. K. Painter and N. Tilley, vol. 10 (Monsey, NY: Criminal Justice Press, 1999), 47–76.

93. K. Painter and D.P. Farrington, "The Crime Reducing Effect of Improved Street Lighting: The Dudley Project," in *Situational Crime Prevention: Successful Case Studies*, ed. R.V. Clarke, 2nd ed. (Guilderland, NY: Harrow and Heston, 1997).

94. K. Painter and D.P. Farrington, "Improved Street Lighting: Crime Reducing Effects and Cost-Benefit Analysis," *Security Journal* 12 (1999): 17–32; K. Painter and D.P. Farrington, "Street Lighting and Crime: Diffusion of Benefits in the Stoke-on-Trent Project," in *Surveillance of Public Space: CCTV, Street Lighting, and Crime Prevention*, eds. K. Painter and N. Tilley, vol. 10 (Monsey, NY: Criminal Justice Press, 1999), 77–122; B.C. Welsh and D.P. Farrington, "Value for Money? A Review of the Costs and Benefits of Situational Crime Prevention," *British Journal of Criminology* 39 (1999): 345–68.

95. For additional studies, see J. Ditton and G. Nair, "Throwing Light on Crime: A Case Study of the Relationship between Street Lighting and Crime Prevention," *Security Journal* 5 (1994): 125–32; K. Painter, "The Impact of Street Lighting on Crime, Fear, and Pedestrian Use," *Security Journal* 5 (1994): 116–24.

96. J.E. Eck, "Preventing Crime at Places," in *Evidence-Based Crime Prevention*, eds. L.W. Sherman, D.P. Farrington, B.C. Welsh, and D.L. MacKenzie (New York: Routledge, 2002), 27.

97. R. Atlas and W.G. LeBlanc, "The Impact on Crime of Street Closures and Barricades: A Florida Case Study," *Security Journal* 5 (1994): 140–5.

98. R. Matthews, "Developing More Effective Strategies for Curbing Prostitution," in *Situational Crime Prevention: Successful Case Studies*, ed. R.V. Clarke (Albany, NY: Harrow and Heston, 1992), 74–82; R. Matthews, *KerbCrawling, Prostitution, and Multi-Agency Policing*, vol. 43 (London: Home Office, 1993).

99. J.R. Lasley, *Using Traffic Barriers to "Design Out" Crime: A Program Evaluation of LAPD's Operation Cul-De-Sac*. Report to the National Institute of Justice. Fullerton, CA: California State University, Fullerton, 1996.

100. Ibid.

101. Ibid.

102. B. Brown, *CCTV in Town Centres: Three Case Studies,* vol. 68 (London: Home Office, 1995); J. Ditton and E. Short, "Yes, It Works, No, It Doesn't: Comparing the Effects of Open-Street CCTV in Two Adjacent Scottish Town Centres," in *Surveillance of Public Space: CCTV, Street Lighting, and Crime Prevention,* eds. K. Painter and N. Tilley, vol. 10 (Monsey, NY: Criminal Justice Press, 1999), 201–23; R. Armitage, G. Smyth, and K. Pease, "Burnley CCTV Evaluation," in *Surveillance of Public Space: CCTV, Street Lighting, and Crime Prevention,* eds. K. Painter and N. Tilley, vol. 10 (Monsey, NY: Criminal Justice Press, 1999), 225–50; L.G. Mazerolle, D.C. Hurley, and M. Chamlin, *Surveillance Cameras in Cincinnati: An Analysis of the Impacts across Three Study Sites* (Cincinnati, OH: Division of Criminal Justice, University of Cincinnati, 1999).

103. M. Barker and C. Bridgeman, *Preventing Vandalism: What Works?* Vol. 56 (London: Home Office, 1994).

104. G. Bichler and R.V. Clarke, "Eliminating Pay Phone Toll Fraud at the Port Authority Bus Terminal in Manhattan," in *Preventing Mass Transit Crime,* ed. R.V. Clarke, vol. 6 (Monsey, NY: Criminal Justice Press, 1996).

105. N.G. LaVigne, "Rational Choice and Inmate Disputes over Phone Use on Rikers Island," in *Crime Prevention Studies,* ed. R.V. Clarke, vol. 3 (Monsey, NY: Criminal Justice Press, 1994); J.F. Decker, "Curbside Deterrence: An Analysis of the Effect of a Slug Rejection Device, Coin View Window, and Warning Labels on Slug Usage in New York City," *Criminology* 10 (1972): 127–42.

106. J.F. Decker, "Curbside Deterrence: An Analysis of the Effect of a Slug Rejection Device, Coin View Window, and Warning Labels on Slug Usage in New York City," *Criminology* 10 (1972): 127–42.

107. Ibid.

15

Putting It All Together and Explaining Crime Trends

LEARNING OBJECTIVES

▦ Summarize crime control successes, failures, and uncertainties.

▦ Identify the three important themes that ran throughout this book.

▦ Discuss explanations for aggregate crime trends.

This book has taken a piece-by-piece approach with respect to the effectiveness of crime control in the United States. We have looked at specific methods of crime control and their effects on various types of crimes. We have also reviewed a large number of evaluations written by a diverse collection of authors from all across the planet. We have *not* thus far attempted to put everything together and come up with explanations of large-scale, aggregate shifts in crime. We have also ignored the dramatic decline in crime that was witnessed during the 1990s and the explanations that have been offered for it. In this chapter, we part ways with the approach taken until now and turn our attention to the explanations researchers have put forth to explain overall crime trends. First, though, let us quickly review Chapters 3–14 and identify three important themes that emerged from the material presented therein.

A QUICK REVIEW

It is not the intent of this section to reiterate all the material presented in earlier chapters. "Does It Work?" sections and summaries did this. Here, we will simply provide a list of what appears to be effective, what does *not* appear to be effective, and what has yet to be researched adequately. The conclusions that are reached in this section are the author's and do not necessarily reflect any degree of consensus in the research community. In fact, some readers are bound to take exception to some of the statements in this section.

Any attempt to summarize what works and what doesn't is likely to be met with some criticism and skepticism. It should be. Social problems such as crime are difficult to deal with. Researching crime control is even more difficult. What's more, the crime problem continues to change, and new studies are published on an almost daily basis. The statements listed in the following subsections should not be construed as the gospel truth; they are tentative and subject to change, and they surely will over time.

The lists were drawn up on the basis of a review of the literature. The types of crime controls that are designated "effective" have been shown in a number of studies to reduce some crime, be it aggregate crime rates or recidivism in small groups of criminals. Had a requirement been imposed that all studies cited in this book employ classical experimental designs, the lists in the next three subsections would be drastically shorter. Readers will note that the lists presented here closely parallel those that are presented in other crime policy books.[1]

Effective Crime Control

Several methods of crime control appear, on the basis of the available evidence, to have at least a slight effect on crime. They might not affect all types of crimes in all places. Also, some may affect individual behavior while others are intended to affect aggregate crime rates. Some work through deterrence; others are rehabilitative. Remember once again that our concern in this book is with effects on *crime*, not other outcomes. All in all, it is an eclectic collection. The approaches include:

1. Hiring more police (with careful attention to allocation, etc.) (Chapter 3)
2. Directed patrol of drug and gun violence hot spots (Chapter 4)
3. Broken windows policing (Chapter 4)
4. Deferred sentencing, especially of drug offenders (Chapter 6)

5. Drug courts—but voluntariness problem persists (Chapter 8)
6. Chemical castration of certain sex offenders, coupled with counseling (Chapter 9)
7. Morals and reasoning training for low-level offenders (Chapter 11)
8. Treatment (with a cognitive-behavioral component) for drug and sex offenders (Chapter 11)
9. Some correctional industries and prison vocational training (Chapter 11)
10. Parent training and education (Chapter 12)
11. Multisystemic therapy for families (Chapter 12)
12. Certain anti-gang interventions (Chapter 13)
13. Big Brother and Big Sisters (Chapter 13)
14. Certain publicity campaigns (Chapter 13)
15. Building school administrative capacity (Chapter 13)
16. Normative education in schools (Chapter 13)
17. Certain school interventions to teach students resistance skills, but not DARE and GREAT (Chapter 13)
18. Student behavior modification programs (Chapter 13)
19. Targeting residences for environmental improvements/modifications (Chapter 14)
20. Electronic article surveillance in retail establishments (Chapter 14)
21. Increased inventorying to deter employee theft (Chapter 14)
22. Improving the physical appearance of mass transit facilities (Chapter 14)
23. Security measures to improve mass transit operators' security (Chapter 14)
24. Anti–fare evasion initiatives (Chapter 14)
25. Target hardening of pay phones and parking meters (Chapter 14)
26. Guards/security officers stationed in parking garages (Chapter 14)
27. Additional street lighting (Chapter 14)

Failures

The following methods of crime control appear, on the basis of the available evidence, to have virtually no effect on crime:

1. One-officer in lieu of two-officer patrols (Chapter 3)
2. 311 (Chapter 3)
3. Reactive policing (Chapter 3)
4. Random patrol (Chapter 3)
5. Rapid police response to 911 calls (Chapter 3)
6. More detectives (Chapter 3)
7. College degrees for cops (Chapter 3)
8. Proactive arrests of specific offenders, including drug offenders (Chapter 3)
9. Moving the police into the community to engage in a specific strategy such as citizen contact or to organize neighborhood watch programs (Chapter 5)
10. Bringing the community to the police (Chapter 5)
11. Victim assistance (Chapter 6)
12. Attempts to abolish plea bargaining (Chapter 6)
13. Preventive detention (Chapter 7)
14. Most methods of restricting and regulating guns, with the possible exception of the Brady Bill (Chapter 7)
15. Gun buybacks (Chapter 7)

16. Sentence enhancements for gun crime (Chapter 9)
17. Mandatory sentencing in all its forms, including three-strikes laws (Chapter 9)
18. Capital punishment for adults and juveniles (Chapter 9)
19. Intensive supervision probation and parole (Chapter 10)
20. Home confinement and electronic monitoring (Chapter 10)
21. Boot camps for adults and youth (Chapter 10)
22. Scared Straight (Chapter 10)
23. Family preservation therapy (Chapter 12)
24. Gang membership prevention (Chapter 13)
25. DARE (Chapter 13)

Uncertainties

The following methods of crime control have not been researched sufficiently, so it is difficult to conclude whether they work or don't work:

1. Private policing (Chapter 3)
2. Police–corrections partnerships (Chapter 4)
3. Multijurisdictional drug task forces (Chapter 4)
4. Military partnerships and militarization (Chapter 4)
5. Technology and less-lethal weapons (Chapter 4)
6. Compstat (Chapter 4)
7. Fusion centers (Chapter 4)
8. Third-party policing (Chapter 5)
9. Integrated/multifaceted community policing initiatives (Chapter 5)
10. No-drop prosecution policies (Chapter 6)
11. Juvenile waivers (Chapter 6)
12. Police–prosecutor partnerships (Chapter 6)
13. Federal–state prosecution partnerships (Chapter 6)
14. Project Safe Neighborhoods (Chapter 6)
15. Community prosecution (Chapter 6)
16. Deferred prosecution (Chapter 6)
17. Setting bail at a high level (Chapter 7)
18. Incapacitation methods, including selective incapacitation and involuntary civil commitment (Chapter 7)
19. Gun bans and the criminalization of drugs (Chapter 7)
20. Patriot Act (Chapter 7)
21. Sarbanes-Oxley Act of 2002 (Chapter 7)
22. Sex offender registration (Chapter 7)
23. Jessica's Law (Chapter 7)
24. Anti-gang injunctions (Chapter 8)
25. Stand-alone diversion programs (Chapter 8)
26. Shaming (Chapter 8)
27. Restorative justice (Chapter 8)
28. Problem-solving courts, with the possible exception of drug courts (Chapter 8)
29. Fines, fees, and forfeiture (Chapter 9)
30. Long prison sentences (Chapter 9)
31. Supermax prisons (Chapter 9)
32. Determinate sentencing (Chapter 9)

33. Sentence enhancements for hate crimes (Chapter 9)
34. Traditional probation and parole (Chapter 10)
35. Hybrid intermediate sanctions (Chapter 10)
36. Anger management (Chapter 11)
37. Improved victim awareness (Chapter 11)
38. Life skills training (Chapter 11)
39. Prison education programs (Chapter 11)
40. Prison work release (Chapter 11)
41. Job training for the general population (Chapter 11)
42. Housing dispersal and mobility programs (Chapter 11)
43. Reentry initiatives (Chapter 11)
44. Self-defense with a gun and guns as deterrents to individual victimization (Chapter 12)
45. Risk avoidance and risk management (Chapter 12)
46. Increase welfare spending (Chapter 12)
47. Minuteman Project (Chapter 12)
48. Financial assistance to communities (Chapter 13)
49. Community mobilization (Chapter 13)
50. Youth mentorship (Chapter 13)
51. After-school programs (Chapter 13)
52. Improving classroom instruction (Chapter 13)
53. Separate classrooms for at-risk youths (Chapter 13)
54. Other school-based interventions aimed at specific students (Chapter 13)
55. GREAT (Chapter 13)
56. Closed-circuit television in residential/public areas (Chapter 14)
57. Two clerks instead of one in convenience stores (Chapter 14)
58. Security systems and barricades in retail establishments (Chapter 14)
59. Bank security measures (Chapter 14)
60. Bar and tavern security measures (Chapter 14)
61. Airport security (Chapter 14)
62. Street closures (Chapter 14)
63. Gated communities (Chapter 14)

THREE IMPORTANT THEMES

Three important themes have emerged throughout this book. From time to time, they were stated outright. Other times, it was necessary to read between the lines to get a grasp of them. The first theme is that the solution to crime appears to lie beyond the justice system. The second theme is that early intervention is necessary if we are to effectively combat crime. The third theme is that criminal justice is a relatively young discipline. Consequently, much research remains to be done. A quick glance at the "Uncertainties" list presented in the preceding section serves as proof of this statement. Let us briefly elaborate on each of these themes.

Beyond the Justice System

The most effective methods of controlling crime discussed in this book did not rely extensively on justice system involvement. This is not to say that the justice system is ineffective, however. Surely, it keeps the problem at bay. For example, there is much that happens in the world of law enforcement that makes a dent in the crime problem, but this book (and the research on which it draws) has shown that several of the most effective methods of crime control have little to do with police, courts, and corrections.

This observation is not new. For example, the authors of a 1997 report to Congress identified "underlying structural conditions" as being intimately tied to the crime problem.[2] The author of another book on policy responses to America's crime problem made this observation: "The truth about crime policy seems to be that most criminal justice-related policies will not make any significant reduction in crime."[3] Still other criminologists have argued that fewer resources should be spent on criminal justice policy and prison building.[4]

Early Intervention Is Key to Success

In the spirit of moving beyond the justice system, the evidence also shows that early intervention, especially in the lives of juveniles, is key to success. This was a common theme pointed out throughout this book. Programs and initiatives that target at-risk individuals *before* crime is committed enjoy a fair degree of success. Even more success seems apparent when early intervention is targeted at young people. Bad habits die hard, and when good habits are instilled early on, much stands to be gained. This is true not just of the crime problem, but also of a host of other social issues and problems. For example, young people learn (or fail to learn) fiscal management, languages, social etiquette, responsibility, respect for others, and so on at an early age.

The justice system is somewhat ill suited to do much early intervention because it basically reacts to crime. The police arrest suspects *after* the commission of a crime. Prosecutors charge *after* suspects have been identified. Trials are held *after* crimes are committed. Sanctions are handed down *after* trial. Sure, the police and other criminal justice agencies do a fair amount of early intervention (e.g., DARE), but such strategies are rarely given high priority. At best, police officers, prosecutors, judges, and corrections workers are not adequately trained to intervene in people's lives before crimes are committed. At worst, prioritizing early intervention surely threatens jobs; an absence of crime means no employment for police and other people who fight crime.

More Research Is Needed

Compared to other disciplines in the social sciences, criminal justice is relatively young. Criminal justice programs popped up across the United States during the 1970s, whereas disciplines such as psychology and sociology had been around for many years before that.[5] Some people have even argued that "criminal justice is an academic discipline in practice but not yet in theory."[6] Whether criminal justice is truly its own discipline is not exactly germane to the points this book is trying to get across, but the very idea that criminal justice has yet to define itself underscores the fact that it has not been around for long. The consequence? Much research remains to be done.

The need for more research does not just stem from the novelty of criminal justice—and, importantly, criminal justice evaluation. The amount of research that is currently available also relates to the funding (especially the lack thereof) that is available for such research. Much crime control in the United States is undertaken in a knee-jerk fashion and is premised on policies that are enacted by politicians who have little idea about the underlying causes of crime. Some of the costliest justice initiatives of the past several decades, such as the Clinton Administration's community policing funding (see Chapter 3), have had almost no research component.

To be sure, there is a movement toward prioritizing research. Books on evidence-based crime prevention are being published in increasing numbers.[7] Communities of scholars are beginning to put their heads together and identify effective social policies. The most recent example is the federal government's crimesolutions.gov project. Unfortunately, funding for research has not kept pace with these developments. Indeed, resources available for evaluation are becoming harder to come by. More funding is necessary so that the body of knowledge about effective crime control continues to grow.

It is disheartening that so little is known about so many methods of crime control. This chapter has identified some 60 types of crime control that have yet to be adequately researched—and the list is far from exhaustive. Untold billions of dollars are being spent on interventions that might or might not work and that might or might not be based on sound ideas and theories. This theme is arguably more important than turning our attention outside the justice system and prioritizing early intervention; much research shows that these methods work, but much more research is necessary before we can know for sure.

EXPLAINING CRIME TRENDS

At the outset of this chapter, it was pointed out that we have yet to address large-scale shifts in crime. That is, we have yet to examine explanations for nationwide crime trends, especially the crime drop that occurred throughout the 1990s—and carried through 2010 (there was a significant uptick in 2011 and 2012).[8] On the contrary, most of the approaches that we have discussed thus far in this book have sought to target crime on a fairly small scale, by focusing either on specific offenders or on specific locations. Rehabilitation programs, for instance, are intended to change the behavior of individual offenders. Rehabilitation cannot be expected to lead to drastic reductions in the overall crime rate unless a huge number of offenders participate in rehabilitation. Similarly, requiring a young person to participate in boot camp cannot realistically be expected to lead to noticeable reductions in crime. The same is true for nearly every other method of crime control that has been presented so far. Together, though, they may be responsible for shifts in the U.S. crime rate.

Unfortunately, it is all but impossible to identify a combination of crime control policies that, when operating together, reduce crime significantly. Researchers have enough trouble trying to determine whether a single intervention, such as aggressive policing, reduces crime in a target area, after controlling for other possible explanations. When they try to determine what effect several interventions have on crime at the same time and in the same place, their research task is made more complicated. This problem besieged research on Boston's well-known Operation Ceasefire (see Chapter 6). The program appeared to be a resounding success, but researchers could not tell exactly which of its components was responsible for the dramatic reductions in homicide. Instead of undertaking the difficult task of identifying which combination of piecemeal, localized approaches reduces crime most effectively, some researchers have instead offered explanations for trends in the overall crime problem in the United States.

To understand why researchers have been concerned with the nation's crime rate, it is necessary to develop an appreciation for what happened with crime during the decade of the 1990s. We have already pointed out that it went down. But to say only that

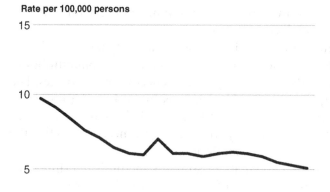

FIGURE 15.1 Homicide Victimization, 1993–2011

Note: Homicide is injuries inflicted by another person with the intent to injure or kill resulting in death, by any means. Excludes homicides due to legal intervention and operations of war. Justifiable homicide is not identified in WISQARS. See appendix table 4 for rates.

[a]Homicide estimates that occurred as a result of the events of September 11, 2001, are included in the total number of homicides.

[b]Preliminary estimates retrieved from Hoyert, D.L. & Xu, J.Q. (2012). Deaths: Preliminary data for 2011. *National Vital Statistics Reports, 61(6)*.

Source: J. Truman, L. Langton, and M. Planty, *Criminal Victimization, 2012* (Washington, DC: Bureau of Justice Statistics, 2013).

it went down is a colossal understatement. Homicide rates dropped 43 percent from a peak in 1991 to 2001, reaching the lowest rate in 35 years![9] Homicide is the most accurately measured and serious crime, making it a useful indicator to track shifts in crime (see Figure 15.1). But homicide is not the whole story. In terms of percentage changes, every type of serious crime declined during the 1990s. What's more, both the Uniform Crime Reports (UCR) and the National Crime Victimization Survey (NCVS) offered evidence of this. The UCR showed 33.6 and 28.8 percent reductions in violent and property crime, respectively.[10] NCVS estimates of the same offenses were 50.1 percent for violent crime and 52.8 percent for property crime.[11] These trends continued mostly downward through 2010, as shown in Figure 15.2.

What is even more striking about these numbers is that they were universal. That is, they affected all geographic areas and demographic groups, something that cannot necessarily be said about some of the methods of crime control that we have discussed throughout this book. The 1990s crime drop also caught nearly everyone by surprise. Researchers were actually forecasting *increases* in crime during the 1990s. An example is James Alan Fox's 1996 prediction that "the next crime wave will get so bad that it will make 1995 look like the good old days."[12] At about the same time, noted criminologist James Q. Wilson offered this grim prediction: "Just beyond the horizon there lurks a cloud that the winds will soon bring over us. The population will start getting younger again. . . . Get ready."[13] Another author wrote, "It is not inconceivable that the demographic surge of the next 10 years will bring with it young male criminals who make the . . . Bloods and Crips look tame by comparison."[14] Even then-President Clinton claimed

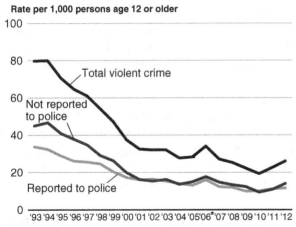

Rate per 1,000 persons age 12 or older

FIGURE 15.2   Violent Victimization, 1993–2012

Note: See appendix table 1 for estimates and standard errors.

*Due to methodological changes in the 2006 NCVS, use caution when comparing 2006 criminal victimization estimates to other years. See *Criminal Victimization, 2007*, NCJ 224390, BJS web, December 2008, for more information.

Source: J. Truman, L. Langton, and M. Planty, *Criminal Victimization, 2012* (Washington, DC: Bureau of Justice Statistics, 2013).

that "[w]e've got about six years to turn this juvenile crime thing around, or our country is going to be living with chaos."[15]

These doom-and-gloom predictions did not come true. Crime went down—and dramatically. Why? Several explanations have been offered. And the same explanations continue today as researchers seek to explain the continued downward trend in serious crime.

Some of the explanations involve the application of methods that have already been discussed in this book (e.g., more concealed weapons permits for interested Americans). Others have not been discussed. Some are commonsense in nature, though not necessarily accurate. And still others are wildly controversial and have engendered much lively discussion and debate. Altogether, it appears that 13 explanations have been offered. For ease of exposition, the following sections divide explanations into three categories. Some explanations are liberal, some are conservative, and some cannot easily be called liberal or conservative. Whether these explanations work independently or together is left to the reader to decide. And the debate over whether the following explanations are plausible or absurd will not be resolved here. The remaining sections simply present these explanations in overview fashion.[16]

Liberal Explanations

Liberal explanations for crime focus on the role of the environment (see Chapter 2). In general, people who subscribe to a liberal political perspective believe that crime is not entirely an individual act consisting of conscious decisions by rational people. Instead, a person's surroundings, upbringing, and other external factors are thought to better explain one's tendency toward delinquency than do individual cost–benefit decisions. This view stands in contrast to the conservative argument that crime occurs when people decide that the benefits of stepping outside the limits of the criminal law outweigh the costs.

Five key liberal explanations for downward crime trends have been identified. They include economic conditions, demographic shifts, citizen attitudes, family conditions, and gun control. How each might have reduced crime and how each has at its core a degree of liberal theorizing are the subjects of the next five subsections.

ECONOMIC CONDITIONS.   A fitting point of departure is one of the most commonly cited reasons for the crime decline of the 1990s: the strong state of the U.S. economy. The decade of the 1990s was indeed a period of strong economic growth. Real GDP per capita grew by nearly 30 percent from 1991 to 2001. The unemployment rate fell from 6.8 percent in 1991 to 4.8 percent in 2001. According to one researcher, "If macroeconomic performance is an important determinant of crime rates, then the economy could explain falling crime."[17]

Several researchers have claimed that these economic conditions had a significant effect on crime during the 1990s. A report from the California Department of Justice reached this conclusion:

> Economic institutions completed a period of downsizing and plant relocations during the 1980s. This was followed by a recent period during which workers experienced revitalized individual and collective effectiveness in addressing perceived economic injustices. This, along with historical distance from the events that caused broad and deep distrust and disregard for many economic institutions, contributed partly to the recent decline in property crime.[18]

Some researchers have even claimed that reductions in *violent* crime during the 1990s can be tied to the strong state of the economy:

> As of 1993 the [economic] expansion reached into the bottom of the earnings distribution and began to raise the wages that were available to low-skilled young men. . . . We see the increase of wages beginning around 1993, which is precisely when we see the decline in youth homicide. All the evidence together suggests that the expanding economy, particularly the improved wage opportunities for young men, may have played an important role in the recent decline in violence.[19]

But others believe the state of the economy probably had little to do with crime trends during the 1990s. To be sure, many researchers have shown that crime rates and economic variables are closely intertwined. When job opportunities are plentiful, this appears to be associated with a reduction in crime, especially property crime. The reduction is only a modest one, though. In a review of several studies published over the past few decades, Steven Levitt noted that most researchers have found, roughly, that a one percentage point increase in the unemployment rate is associated with a one percentage point increase in the property crime rate. According to Levitt, "Based on these estimates, the observed 2 percentage point decline in the U.S. unemployment rate between 1991 and 2001 can explain an estimated 2 percent decline in property crime (out of an observed drop of almost 30 percent)."[20] Note that this observation is for property crime. Levitt and a number of other economists have shown little to no relationship between economic conditions and violent crime.[21]

A problem with the economic conditions/crime relationship has been observed in recent years. As of this writing, crime continues—for the most part—to be trending downward, but this has all been happening even in the face of a serious economic recession that began around 2008. Indeed, there is much more to explaining crime trends than examining the state of the economy.

DEMOGRAPHIC SHIFTS.   Some of the ominous predictions of an increase in crime during the 1990s and beyond cited in their reasoning the number of young people in the population. This is another common explanation for shifts in America's crime problem (even today) and it is part of an argument that demographic shifts, beyond just the number of young people, affect crime rates. But most criminologists agree that demographics probably have little to do with crime. One reason for this is that, contrary to some popular beliefs, the percentage of young people in the population declined during the 1980s and early 1990s when crime was on the rise.[22] As one team of researchers recently observed,

> The crime surge of the late 1980s and early 1990s occurred while the size of the most crime-prone age group (18–24-year-olds) was declining. Likewise, predictions of a coming storm of increasingly violent youth predators, based in large part on demographic forecasts, never came to fruition. The analysis of recent crime trends in America serves as a reminder that demographics are only part of the story.[23]

So the percentage of young people in the population might have little to do with crime. But the aging of the baby boom generation might. It is well known that the elderly commit little crime and are victimized relatively rarely. According to one author, people over the age of 65 experience less than one tenth the amount of victimization that teenagers do.[24] As Levitt observed, "Given that the share of the elderly population increased during the 1990s, a purely demographically driven decline in crime might be expected."[25] Thus, as more people approach old age, less crime is bound to occur.

The growth of the elderly population would seem to suggest that demographic shifts during the 1990s *did* have the effect of sending crime rates downward. Indeed, one researcher found that overall changes in the age distribution in the United States might have reduced crime by a few percentage points.[26] But when he later reflected on his findings, he concluded that "demographic shifts may account for a little more than one-sixth of the observed decline in property crime in the 1990s, but are not an important factor in the drop in violent crime."[27] All in all, then, the age composition of the U.S. population, be it heavy on the old or light on the young, does not appear to influence crime markedly.

Researchers have also considered the effects of immigration trends on crime. One study found city violent crime rates decreased as the concentration of immigrants increased.[28] Several explanations have been offered for this phenomenon. For example, "in many cases, compared with native groups, immigrants seem better able to withstand crime-facilitating conditions than native groups."[29]

CITIZEN ATTITUDES.   Attitudes do not directly affect crime, but their manifestations might. What this means is that over the years, people across the United States have become frustrated with crime. Frustration with crime might have become especially pronounced during the late 1980s, when crime was at its peak before the 1990s decline. Frustration with crime has prompted many people to form various community associations that are intent on fighting off crime. This, as we have seen in the policing chapters, can occur when residents work with the police to improve neighborhoods. It can also occur with little police involvement; citizens can participate in block watch and other types of surveillance programs. Attitudes therefore might have affected crime in the 1990s, but only indirectly, as attitudes influence people to do something about crime.

Have citizen attitudes made a difference? Better yet, have the various efforts that people have taken in response to their frustration with crime helped matters? Several researchers have claimed that community anticrime associations have made significant contributions to the decline in crime throughout the 1990s.[30] Another researcher came to this conclusion: "Neighborhood organizations working in conjunction with community police have aided the recent reduction in the crime rate."[31] Whether organized community responses to crime have really made a difference, however, remains somewhat unclear. Many of the evaluations of community policing, which were reported in Chapter 5, for example, suggested that some community efforts to control crime just do not work. But the discussion in Chapter 13 suggested there are some things that residents can do to effectively reduce crime.

FAMILY CONDITIONS. In Chapter 12, we saw evidence that family conditions can affect crime. Divorces, broken homes, and the like can have a detrimental effect on children, possibly placing them on a path toward delinquency. Not surprisingly, some people have claimed that reductions in crime during the 1990s can be traced to family conditions. But this is not because families became more cohesive during that period. In fact, some evidence suggests that during that time, the number of marriages was actually decreasing.[32] In addition, people are getting married at an older age, and the divorce rate shows no signs of declining.

How could fewer marriages, getting married at an older age, and more divorce lead to a *reduction* in crime? Does this not stand in stark contrast to the discussion in Chapter 12? It may, but not necessarily for the crime of homicide. As we have already seen, homicides declined markedly during the 1990s. There are certainly several reasons for the decline, but one that some researchers offer is a decline in domesticity, that is, a decline in marriages, an increase in the number of people getting married later in life, and an increase in divorce (especially between 1960 and 1980).[33] The logic is straightforward: Many homicides occur between intimate partners, so when there are fewer intimate partners, there is bound to be less homicide.

In addition to the decline in domesticity, women's participation in the workforce has been increasing over time, allowing women to become more financially independent. Furthermore, legal advocacy for women and the surge in domestic violence services have made it easier for women to escape relationships that involve violence and turmoil. According to one author, "[t]he decline has been partly due to fewer young people having spouses, and partly due to women being more financially independent and having more options for leaving bad relationships."[34] One researcher estimated that 9 percent of the homicide reduction from 1993 to 1996 was accounted for by the decrease in domestic murders, the latter of which could be linked to the developments discussed throughout this section.[35]

Changes in family conditions might have reduced homicides, but one is left wondering what effect the other consequences of the apparent decline in domesticity could have on crime. Later marriages often result in children being born later, so it is doubtful that this trend affects crime. But an increase in divorce probably does not help matters. And there is certainly nothing wrong with not getting married, but when children are raised by single parents, their chances of becoming delinquent rise dramatically. As we saw in Chapter 12, "[y]outh in single-parent families experience significantly higher risks for violence than youth in two-parent families."[36]

GUN CONTROL. Gun control is a policy response, whereas economic conditions, demographic shifts, citizen attitudes, and changes in family composition are less intentional. Even so, gun control represents another liberal explanation for the crime decline of the 1990s. It is another environmental explanation in the sense that guns contribute to crime and, as such, should be targeted for control. The old adage "Guns don't kill people, people do" is antithetical to liberal thinking. Liberals prefer something along the lines of "Guns kill, not people." Their view is that enhanced gun control will reduce crime, both by making guns difficult for criminals to obtain and by encouraging responsible gun ownership so that the number of accidental shootings will be reduced. Conservatives tend to be vehemently opposed to gun control in most of its forms (see Chapter 7 for some additional discussion).

Guns, as the reader knows by now, are ubiquitous in America; some 200 million (or more) guns are in private hands.[37] And nearly two-thirds of all homicides in the United States result from guns.[38] One researcher even found that higher rates of handgun ownership might be causally related to violent crime.[39] For these reasons, a number of gun control initiatives have been implemented, at both the state and national levels, over the past few decades. But what about gun control that was put into effect during the 1990s? The Brady Handgun Violence Prevention Act, discussed in Chapter 7, would seem to have reduced gun violence because it placed limits on who could purchase guns. But researchers have since found almost no reduction in violent crime that can be attributed to the Brady law.[40] And because most criminals do not buy their guns from licensed dealers, such legislation is bound to have little effect.[41]

What about other methods of gun control? There is no need to revisit all of them here, as we have already discussed most of them earlier in the book. We can, however, once again emphasize that gun control does little to affect crime, mostly because of the black market in illegal weapons.[42] And many researchers are in agreement that gun buyback programs, handgun bans, assault weapons bans, and other methods of either regulating or restricting gun ownership have not made a significant dent in the problem of gun violence in the United States. In a relatively thorough review of most methods of gun control implemented over the past several years, Levitt claimed that "[t]here is . . . little or no evidence that changes in gun control laws in the 1990s can account for falling crime."[43]

It is difficult to dispute that some gun control works for some people, and liberals will certainly take exception to some of the research cited here and in earlier chapters, but one cannot dispute the fact that America has a gun problem that has not gone away, despite many efforts to control it. As evidence of this, Garen Wintemute, an expert in gun violence and policy responses to it, has made this observation:

> Screening buyers, [the] Brady [bill] and its state-level analogs, waiting periods, and background checks work. They reduce rates of criminal activity involving guns and violence among people who are screened out and denied purchase of a gun—about 25 to 30 percent of those screened. [However, these laws] appear not to have had a substantial, if any, effect on [overall] crime rates. The resolution of that apparent paradox is that under current criteria so few people are denied the purchase of a firearm under Brady and its state-level analogs relative to the number of people who purchase guns every year that an impact on that select group is too small at the population level to be noticed.[44]

Conservative Explanations

Generally speaking, conservatives do not believe that crime drops are fortuitous or can be attributed to factors that no one saw coming. They believe, instead, that conscious efforts to aggressively fight crime make all the difference. They further believe that criminals violate the law because they perceive benefits from doing so; increase the costs of crime, and people will be deterred from crime. Finally, conservatives believe that crimes are inherently individual acts, acts that result from decisions by rational people.

Each of the methods discussed in the next five subsections reflects a strong degree of conservative thinking. More and better policing, sending more criminals to prison, more concealed weapons for law-abiding citizens, increased use of capital punishment, and other criminal justice policy responses stem from a belief that crime should be fought with zeal and that the best way to control crime is to directly target individuals' decision-making processes; make the costs of crime too high to bear, and people will presumably be deterred from violating the law.

MORE AND BETTER POLICING.   It is probably risky to assert that more policing leads to crime reductions, but the author has done just that. In Chapter 3, we saw that there is much convincing evidence that having more police on the streets equates with crime reduction. And looking past all the scientific evidence, it makes perfect sense on an intuitive level that more police will apprehend criminals and reduce crime. To insist otherwise is to argue that for every new police officer who is added to the streets, a new criminal will work against him or her. Sure, there is a replacement effect associated with certain types of criminals (e.g., drug dealers), but it seems eminently sensible that more cops on the streets will make people safer. For the eternal skeptics out there (this book's author is one, believe me), the discussion of a police strike presented in Chapter 3 certainly shows that taking away the police presence can only make matters worse.

Of course, although the evidence that having more cops on the streets means less crime is not 100 percent convincing, there is some strong evidence that how police are used makes a big difference. In this vein, many commentators have argued that the crime reductions in the 1990s were the result of many innovative policing strategies that were implemented during that period. Several such strategies can be discerned, and they were presented in Chapters 4 and 5. They include community policing, broken windows policing, proactive policing, collaborative partnerships, and the like. But whether these efforts directly affected crime is also less than crystal clear. One reason for this is that crime declined in cities that instituted such strategies *and* in cities that did not. Even if innovative policing strategies, especially more aggressive broken windows–oriented approaches, have reduced crime, an unanticipated consequence could result:

> Critics . . . have warned that irrespective of any correlation between aggressive policing and lower crime rates, the strategy may be generating community hostility toward the police that in the long run will undermine their crime-fighting capacity.[45]

Conservatives disagree with such reasoning, however. They cite studies such as those reported in Chapter 3, as well as some others that have not been cited in this book that show adding police officers to the streets equates with less crime.[46] They also cite statistics that the American police force grew by some 14 percent during the 1990s, at the same time that crime was trending downward significantly.[47] One researcher recently estimated that the increase in police during the 1990s explains somewhere between one-tenth and one-fifth of the overall decline in crime that was observed during that decade.[48] The same researcher has argued that adding more police officers to the streets is a cost-beneficial practice:

> Annual expenditures on police are approximately $60 billion, so the cost of the 14 percent increase in police is $8.4 billion a year. . . . If the increase in police reduced crime by

5–6 percent, then the corresponding benefit of crime reduction is $20–25 billion, well above the estimated cost. Thus, . . . the investment in police appears to have been attractive from a cost-benefit perspective.[49]

MORE PRISONERS. Although policing may have made a dent in crime during the 1990s, the same cannot so easily be said for imprisonment. But conservatives once again believe that adding more criminals to the nation's prison population can reduce crime. It is easy to understand their logic, because we have managed to stuff a huge number of criminals into America's correctional institutions over the past several years, the greatest increase having taken place at the same time crime went down dramatically. Almost half of the growth in the prison population that occurred between 1950 and 2000 took place during the 1990s. Researchers have attributed the increase to changes in U.S. drug laws, the incarceration of drug offenders, increased parole revocations resulting in reincarceration, and longer sentences for those who are convicted of crime.[50]

It is easy to understand why prison could, at least in theory, reduce crime. That is because it might serve the dual purposes of incapacitation and deterrence. On the one hand, crime rates might go down because would-be criminals are deterred from the threat of incarceration. On the other hand, crime rates might go down because criminals are locked up and cannot commit more crimes. This incapacitation effect says nothing about the crime and violence that takes place in prisons, but a criminal who is locked up in prison obviously cannot victimize ordinary citizens.

Whether a deterrent effect of imprisonment exists is difficult to prove. It assumes, for example, that people make rational decisions and can be deterred by the threat of sanctions. Additionally, an incapacitation effect might be difficult to detect because, relative to the total population of criminals, there are not many criminals locked up in prison. But these concerns have not stopped researchers from trying to demonstrate that additional imprisonment will reduce crime. Levitt has argued, for example, that "the increase in incarceration over the 1990s can account for a reduction in crime of approximately 12 percent for [violent crime] . . . and 8 percent for property crime, or about one-third of the observed decline in crime."[51] Other researchers have reached similar conclusions, claiming that roughly one-quarter of the crime drop during the 1990s was due to having more criminals off the streets.[52] According to one of these researchers, though, continuing to lock up criminals might not yield benefits for very long:

> We've gone about as far as we can go with prison expansion. In the early 1970s, each additional [prison] bed we built reduced the number of violent crimes on the street by anywhere between 3 and 3.5. That number stayed fairly constant throughout the 1970s. Since 1980 or so it has been dropping, and especially since 1990 it has been dropping like a rock. That means that each additional prison bed is going to reduce violent crime by about 1.1—about a third as much as it did in the early 1970s.[53]

OTHER CRIMINAL JUSTICE POLICIES. As this book has shown, there are many criminal justice policies besides hiring more police and locking up criminals. These include prosecution strategies, drug treatment, and rehabilitation, among many others. Whether they have reduced crime nationwide remains unclear and probably unlikely. The main reason for this conclusion is that the most dominant policy response to the crime problem over the past several decades has been the increased use of imprisonment and/or law enforcement expansion (more police and more prosecutors). Comparatively little has been spent on alternative methods of controlling crime. This phenomenon creates an unfortunate cyclical process: Less money spent on, say, rehabilitation means that fewer researchers will look into its effectiveness; and when there is not a wealth of evidence to convince even the most ardent conservative that rehabilitation works, the traditional approaches of building prisons and hiring police and prosecutors will continue to dominate.

MORE CONCEALED WEAPONS PERMITS.   As we saw in Chapter 7, some researchers have argued that reductions in crime can be expected when more people are given permits to carry concealed weapons. Economists John Lott and David Mustard claimed, in fact, that enormous reductions in violent crime have occurred in states that have made it easy for citizens to carry guns (so-called shall issue states). Recently, though, a slew of studies have been published claiming that Lott and Mustard's conclusions were flawed.

MORE CAPITAL PUNISHMENT.   In the 1980s, 117 prisoners were put to death in U.S. prisons. That number shot up to 478 during the 1990s. It is not surprising, then, that some people have argued that the crime decline of the 1990s can be attributed in part to the increased use of capital punishment. As we saw in Chapter 9, several researchers have tried to show a reduction in crime due to the death penalty.[54] But it is doubtful that additional death sentences, especially those carried out during the 1990s, have made society safer. One reason for this is that the death penalty is still rarely used. Add to this the lengthy delay between sentencing and execution, and it is highly unlikely that criminals can be effectively deterred by such a sanction. Also, if we rely on some of the most liberal estimates of the deterrent benefit of capital punishment (again, see Chapter 9), only about a 1.5 percent decrease in the nationwide homicide rate would have been observed during the 1990s—less than one twenty-fifth of the observed declines.[55] Finally, although it is conceivable that additional executions might deter people from committing murder, people know that one cannot get sentenced to death for less serious offenses, many of which also saw dramatic declines during the 1990s.

Other Explanations

A few other explanations for the crime drop of the 1990s can be identified. They are neither fully conservative nor fully liberal. One is that a cultural renewal took place during the 1990s. Another is the waning of the crack epidemic, another change that cannot be explained solely on the basis of conservative or liberal theories or policies. Finally, some researchers have offered the controversial explanation that the decline in crime during the 1990s stems from the legalization of abortion!

CULTURAL SHIFTS.   Could crime rates have gone down during the 1990s because Americans have become more civilized? At least some commentators seem to think so. One of them noted that together with such changes as increased SAT scores, fewer teen pregnancies, and an increase in charitable giving, the reduction in crime signaled a cultural renewal. As evidence of this, one researcher argued that increased youth access to violent entertainment during the 1990s did not result in an increase in crime.[56] For example, assault rates in California plummeted after violent video games such as *Mortal Kombat* (1992), *Doom* (1993), and *Quake* (1996) surfaced. The 1990s also witnessed an increase in gangsta-rap music, R-rated movies, and Internet use. Yet none of these changes equated with an increase in crime. The explanation, then, could lie in some fundamental cultural shifts that could have taken place during the period. According to one source:

> The recent crime rate decrease has been cited as an indicator of a future increase in national civility. Determining if the crime rate and level of national civility are related causally or are both the result of a third factor is difficult and as yet unresolved. However, this conjecture is interesting as it suggests an impending change in national mood and conscience.[57]

WANING OF THE CRACK EPIDEMIC.   Whether a cultural shift is taking (or has taken) place in the United States is not exactly clear. The waning of the crack epidemic of the 1990s, however, is real (see Figure 16.2). During the mid-1980s, the crack market began to grow. Once it expanded significantly, several researchers began to tie patterns of violence to the presence of the drug.[58]

But what explains the waning of the crack epidemic? Why did it taper off during the 1990s? Not many researchers have tried to answer these questions, but there are nevertheless some possible explanations. One is that young people came to learn of the harmful consequences of experimenting with a drug as addictive as crack.[59] Another is that stepped-up policing efforts, some of which are described in this chapter and elsewhere, made the difference.[60] Yet another explanation is that drugs such as crack follow a natural course and begin to fall out of favor as new substances become available:

> The popularity of a particular drug—such as crack cocaine—tends to start within a limited subpopulation. Sometimes use of a drug catches on and the rate of use increases dramatically until it is widespread. At some point the drug may go out of favor, leading to a slow but steady ebb in its use.[61]

LEGALIZATION OF ABORTION.   The U.S. Supreme Court's 1973 decision in *Roe* v. *Wade* legalized abortion in the United States. More recently, some researchers have tied this controversial decision to declines in crime. Two reasons have been offered for the presumed link. One is that unwanted children are at a greater risk for crime. Several researchers have found that adverse home environments negatively affect children.[62] This leads to the second reason why abortions and crime might be intertwined, namely, that the legalization of abortion leads to a decrease in the number of unwanted children. Researchers have found, in fact, that the legalization of abortion was associated with roughly a 5 percent drop in birthrates in the United States.[63]

In the first published study linking abortion and crime, two economists found that between 1985 and 1997, homicide rates fell 25.9 percent in states with high abortion rates.[64] By comparison, during the same period, there was a 4.1 percent *increase* in homicides in states with low abortion rates. But the authors of the study did more than compare abortion and crime rates. They used a sophisticated statistical modeling strategy to rule out several other possible explanations, such as changes in economic conditions and various crime control initiatives, for the reduction in crime during the 1990s. They published a study a few years later that confirmed their initial findings, and other researchers have concluded that abortion and crime could be linked.[65] Other researchers are not convinced, however.[66] Some believe that some other factor was at work during the 1990s, and they express serious concerns that Donohue and Levitt were effectively calling for more abortions if we want crime to decline.

Summary

Crime control in America takes place in a number of institutional settings. One such setting is the criminal justice system; another is families; yet another is schools; and so on. In each of these institutional settings, some methods of crime control are effective, and others are not. It appears, on the basis of the discussion in this chapter and the presentation throughout the rest of the book, that a combination of justice system efforts and individual, family, school, and community efforts help to make America safer. Others, though, are a colossal waste of money, though they continue to flourish.

Three important themes emerged in this book. One is that the solution to crime does not lie wholly within the criminal justice system. Much effective crime control does not have to rely on the police, courts, or corrections. Next, the research that is reviewed in this book confirms that many of the most effective programs and initiatives targeted people *before* they become criminal. Early intervention is therefore key. Finally, criminal justice is still in its infancy; much additional research is necessary before we can develop a thorough understanding of what works and what does not work to control crime.

Chapters 3 through 14 looked at crime control on a piece-by-piece basis. Possibly lost in the discussion were explanations for the dramatic decline in crime *nationwide* that took place during the 1990s and on up through 2010. Thirteen different explanations for the decline—some liberal, others conservative, and still others in between—were reviewed in the second half of this chapter. Whether economic conditions, criminal justice system efforts, demographic and cultural shifts, increases in abortion, or some other factor made the difference is not clear as yet. Researchers will continue working tirelessly to explain past and current crime trends as well as to forecast what the future holds in store.

Notes

1. See, for example, J.Q. Wilson and J. Petersilia, eds., *Crime: Public Policies for Crime Control* (Oakland, CA: Institute for Contemporary Studies, 2002); L.W. Sherman, D.P. Farrington, B.C. Welsh, and D.L. MacKenzie, eds., *Evidence-Based Crime Prevention* (New York: Routledge, 2002).

2. L.W. Sherman, D. Gottfredson, D. MacKenzie, J. Eck, P. Reuter, and S. Bushway, *Preventing Crime: What Works, What Doesn't, What's Promising* (Washington, DC: U.S. Department of Justice, National Institute of Justice, 1997).

3. S. Walker, *Sense and Nonsense about Crime and Drugs*, 5th ed. (Belmont, CA: Wadsworth, 2001), 290.

4. J.F. Short, *Poverty, Ethnicity, and Crime* (Philadelphia, PA: Westview Press, 1997).

5. J. Sorenson, A.G. Widmayer, and F.R. Scarpitti, "Examining the Criminal Justice and Criminological Paradigms: An Analysis of ACJS and ASC Members," *Journal of Criminal Justice Education* 5 (1994): 149–66.

6. O. Marenin and J. Worrall, "Criminal Justice: Portrait of a Discipline in Process," *Journal of Criminal Justice* 26 (1998): 465–80.

7. L.W. Sherman, D.P. Farrington, B.C. Welsh, and D.L. MacKenzie, eds., *Evidence-Based Crime Prevention* (New York: Routledge, 2002); also see H.D. Barlow, *Crime and Public Policy: Putting Theory to Work* (Philadelphia, PA: Westview Press, 1995).

8. J. Truman, L. Langton, and M. Planty, *Criminal Victimization, 2012* (Washington, DC: Bureau of Justice Statistics, 2013).

9. S.D. Levitt, "Understanding Why Crime Fell in the 1990s: Four Factors That Explain the Decline and Six That Do Not," *Journal of Economic Perspectives* 18 (2004): 163–90.

10. Ibid.

11. Ibid.

12. J. Fox, *Trends in Juvenile Violence: A Report to the United States Attorney General on Current and Future Rates of Juvenile Offending* (Washington, DC: Bureau of Justice Statistics, 1996).

13. J.Q. Wilson, "Crime and Public Policy," in *Crime*, eds. J.Q. Wilson and J. Petersilia (San Francisco: ICS Press, 1995), 507.

14. J. DiIulio, "Help Wanted: Economists, Crime, and Public Policy," *Journal of Economic Perspectives* 10 (1996): 3–24.

15. Allpolitics, "Clinton Unveils Flurry of Plans to Fight Crime." Available at http://images.cnn.com/ALLPOLITICS/1997/02/19/clinton.crime/

16. Several recent sources on this subject are available. They include S.D. Levitt, "Understanding Why Crime Fell in the 1990s: Four Factors That Explain the Decline and Six That Do Not," *Journal of Economic Perspectives* 18 (2004): 163–90; J. Travis and M. Waul, *Reflections on the Crime Decline: Lessons for the Future?* (Washington, DC: Urban Institute, Justice Policy Center, 2002); L.A. Marowitz, *Why Did the*

Crime Rate Decrease through 1999? (And Why Might It Decrease or Increase in 2000 and Beyond?) (Sacramento, CA: California Department of Justice, 2000); A. Blumstein and J. Wallman, *The Crime Drop in America* (New York: Cambridge University Press, 2000).

17. S.D. Levitt, "Understanding Why Crime Fell in the 1990s: Four Factors That Explain the Decline and Six That Do Not," *Journal of Economic Perspectives* 18 (2004): 163–90.

18. L.A. Marowitz, *Why Did the Crime Rate Decrease through 1999? (And Why Might It Decrease or Increase in 2000 and Beyond?)* (Sacramento, CA: California Department of Justice, 2000), p. 17.

19. Cited in J. Travis and M. Waul, *Reflections on the Crime Decline: Lessons for the Future?* (Washington, DC: Urban Institute, Justice Policy Center, 2002), 15.

20. S.D. Levitt, "Understanding Why Crime Fell in the 1990s: Four Factors That Explain the Decline and Six That Do Not," *Journal of Economic Perspectives* 18 (2004): 163–90.

21. See, for example, W. Friedman, "Volunteerism and the Decline of Violent Crime," *The Journal of Criminal Law and Criminology* 88 (1998): 1453–74.

22. J. Travis and M. Waul, *Reflections on the Crime Decline: Lessons for the Future?* (Washington, DC: Urban Institute, Justice Policy Center, 2002).

23. Ibid., 13.

24. C. Perkins, *Age Patterns of Victims of Serious Violent Crime* (Washington, DC: U.S. Department of Justice, Bureau of Justice Statistics, 1997).

25. S.D. Levitt, "Understanding Why Crime Fell in the 1990s: Four Factors That Explain the Decline and Six That Do Not," *Journal of Economic Perspectives* 18 (2004): 163–90.

26. S. Levitt, "The Exaggerated Role of Changing Age Structure in Explaining Aggregate Crime Changes," *Criminology* 37 (1999): 537–99.

27. S.D. Levitt, "Understanding Why Crime Fell in the 1990s: Four Factors That Explain the Decline and Six That Do Not," *Journal of Economic Perspectives* 18 (2004): 163–90.

28. J.I. Stowell, S.F. Messner, K.F. McGeever, and L.E. Raffalovich, "Immigration and the Recent Violent Crime Drop in the United States: A Pooled, Cross-Sectional Time-Series Analysis of Metropolitan Areas," *Criminology* 47 (2009): 889–928.

29. R. Martinez, Jr. and M.T. Lee, "On Immigration and Crime." In *Criminal Justice 2000: The Changing Nature of Crime, Volume I*, eds. G. LaFree and R.J. Bursik (Washington, DC: National Institute of Justice, 2000), 486.

30. Stephen Machin and Costas Meghir "Crime and Economic Incentives," *Journal of Human Resources* 39 (4) (2004): 958–79.

31. L.A. Marowitz, *Why Did the Crime Rate Decrease Through 1999? (And Why Might It Decrease or Increase in 2000 and Beyond?)* (Sacramento, CA: California Department of Justice, 2000), 15.

32. A. Blumstein and R. Rosenfeld, "Explaining Recent Trends in U.S. Homicide Rates," *Journal of Criminal Law and Criminology* 88 (1998): 1175–216.

33. Ibid.

34. L.A. Marowitz, *Why Did the Crime Rate Decrease Through 1999? (And Why Might It Decrease or Increase in 2000 and Beyond?)* (Sacramento, CA: California Department of Justice, 2000), 19.

35. G. Witkin, "The Crime Bust," *U.S. News and World Report*, May 25, 1998, 28.

36. J.L. Lauritsen, *How Families and Communities Influence Youth Victimization* (Washington, DC: U.S. Department of Justice, Office of Juvenile Justice and Delinquency Prevention, 2003), 4.

37. P. Cook and J. Ludwig, *Guns in America: Results of a Comprehensive Survey of Gun Ownership and Use* (Washington, DC: Police Foundation, 1996).

38. S.D. Levitt, "Understanding Why Crime Fell in the 1990s: Four Factors That Explain the Decline and Six That Do Not," *Journal of Economic Perspectives* 18 (2004): 163–90.

39. M. Duggan, "More Guns, More Crime," *Journal of Political Economy* 109 (2001): 1086–114.

40. J. Ludwig and P. Cook, "Homicide and Suicide Rates Associated with Implementation of the Brady Handgun Violence Prevention Act," *Journal of the American Medical Association* 284 (2000): 585–91.

41. J. Wright and P. Rossi, *Armed and Considered Dangerous: A Survey of Felons and Their Firearms* (New York: Aldine de Gruyter, 1994).

42. P. Cook, S. Molliconi, and T. Cole, "Regulating Gun Markets," *Journal of Criminal Law and Criminology* 16 (1995): 59–92.

43. S.D. Levitt, "Understanding Why Crime Fell in the 1990s: Four Factors That Explain the Decline and Six That Do Not," *Journal of Economic Perspectives* 18 (2004): 163–190.

44. Cited in J. Travis and M. Waul, *Reflections on the Crime Decline: Lessons for the Future?* (Washington, DC: Urban Institute, Justice Policy Center, 2002), 16.

45. J. Travis and M. Waul, *Reflections on the Crime Decline: Lessons for the Future?* (Washington, DC: Urban Institute, Justice Policy Center, 2002), 19.

46. T. Marvell and C. Moody, "Specification Problems, Police Levels, and Crime Rates," *Criminology* 34 (1996): 609–46; H. Corman and H.N. Mocan, "A Time-Series Analysis of Crime, Deterrence, and Drug Abuse in New York City," *American Economic Review* 90 (2000): 584–604; S. Levitt, "Using Electoral Cycles in Police Hiring to Estimate the Effect of Police on Crime," *American Economic Review* 87 (1997): 270–90.

47. S.D. Levitt, "Understanding Why Crime Fell in the 1990s: Four Factors That Explain the Decline and Six That Do Not," *Journal of Economic Perspectives* 18 (2004): 163–90.

48. Ibid.

49. Ibid., 177.

50. I. Kuziemko and S. Levitt, "An Empirical Analysis of Imprisoning Drug Offenders," *Journal of Public Economics* 88 (2004): 2043–66.

51. S.D. Levitt, "Understanding Why Crime Fell in the 1990s: Four Factors That Explain the Decline and Six That Do Not," *Journal of Economic Perspectives* 18 (2004): 163–90.

52. J. Travis and M. Waul, *Reflections on the Crime Decline: Lessons for the Future?* (Washington, DC: Urban Institute, Justice Policy Center, 2002). Also see J. Conklin, *Why Crime Rates Fell* (Boston: Allyn and Bacon, 2003).

53. Cited in J. Travis and M. Waul, *Reflections on the Crime Decline: Lessons for the Future?* (Washington, DC: Urban Institute, Justice Policy Center, 2002), 18.

54. Two examples that are not cited there include H. Dezhbakhsh, P. Rubin, and J. Shepherd, *Does Capital Punishment Have a Deterrent Effect?: New Evidence from Post-Moratorium Panel Data* Mimeo (Atlanta, GA: Emory University, 2002); N. Mocan and R.K. Gittings, "Getting Off Death Row: Commuted Sentences and the Deterrent Effect of Capital Punishment," *Journal of Law and Economics* 46 (2003): 453–78.

55. S.D. Levitt, "Understanding Why Crime Fell in the 1990s: Four Factors That Explain the Decline and Six That Do Not," *Journal of Economic Perspectives* 18 (2004): 163–90.

56. M. Males, "Punishing Teens to Protect Them; Curfews and Other Efforts to Control Youth Behavior May be Undermining Social Order," *Los Angeles Times*, May 25, 1998, M1.

57. L.A. Marowitz, *Why Did the Crime Rate Decrease Through 1999? (And Why Might It Decrease or Increase in 2000 and Beyond?)* (Sacramento, CA: California Department of Justice, 2000), 18.

58. A. Blumstein and R. Rosenfeld, "Explaining Recent Trends in U.S. Homicide Rates," *Journal of Criminal Law and Criminology* 88 (1998): 1175–216; P. Cook and J. Laub, "The Unprecedented Epidemic in Youth Violence," in *Crime and Justice: An Annual Review of Research*, ed. M. Tonry (Chicago: University of Chicago Press, 1998), 34–51; P. Goldstein, H. Brownstein, P. Ryan and P. Bellucci, "Crack and Homicide in New York City: A Case Study in the Epidemiology of Violence," in *Crack in America: Demon Drugs and Social Justice*, eds. C. Reinarman and H. Levine (Berkeley, CA: University of California Press, 1997), 113–30; D. Cork, "Examining Space-Time Interaction in City-Level Homicide Data: Crack Markets and the Diffusion of Guns

among Youth," *Journal of Quantitative Criminology* 15 (1999): 379–406; J. Grogger and M. Willis, "The Emergence of Crack Cocaine and the Rise in Urban Crime Rates," *Review of Economics and Statistics* 82 (2000): 519–29.

59. J. Travis and M. Waul, *Reflections on the Crime Decline: Lessons for the Future?* (Washington, DC: Urban Institute, Justice Policy Center, 2002), 14.

60. Ibid.

61. B.L. Golub and B.D. Johnson, *Cracks' Decline: Some Surprises across U.S. Cities* (Washington, DC: U.S. Department of Justice, National Institute of Justice, 1997).

62. R. Loeber and M. Stouthamer-Loeber, "Family Factors as Correlates and Predictors of Juvenile Conduct Problems and Delinquency," in *Crime and Justice: An Annual Review of Research*, eds. M. Tonry and N. Morris (Chicago: University of Chicago Press, 1986); R. Sampson and J. Laub, *Crime in the Making: Pathways and Turning Points through Life* (Cambridge, MA: Harvard University Press, 1993).

63. P. Levine, D. Staiger, T. Kane, and D. Zimmerman, "*Roe v. Wade* and American Fertility," *American Journal of Public Health* 89 (1999): 199–203.

64. J. Donohue and S. Levitt, "Legalized Abortion and Crime," *Quarterly Journal of Economics* 116 (2001): 379–420.

65. J. Donohue and S. Levitt, "Further Evidence That Legalized Abortion Lowered Crime: A Reply to Joyce," *Journal of Human Resources* 39 (2003): 29–49; A. Sen, *Does Increased Abortion Lead to Lower Crime?: Evaluating the Relationship between Crime, Abortion, and Fertility* (Waterloo, Ontario: University of Waterloo, 2002); C. Pop-Eleches, *The Impact of an Abortion Ban on Socio-Economic Outcomes of Children: Evidence from Romania* (New York: Columbia University, 2002).

66. T. Joyce, "Did Legalized Abortion Lower Crime?" Working Paper No. W8319. Cambridge, MA: National Bureau of Economic Research, 2001; J.R. Lott and J. Whitley, "Abortion and Crime: Unwanted Children and Out-of-Wedlock Births," Working Paper no. 254 (New Haven, CT: Yale Law School, 2001).

APPENDIX

An Ultra-Brief Introduction to Criminal Justice in the United States

The purpose of this appendix is to briefly introduce readers to the criminal justice system in the United States. It is intended for those with little or no understanding of who and what make up the criminal justice system and how it operates. Those of you who have already been introduced to the criminal justice system, perhaps through an introductory text and/or course, need not read any further. Of course, if it has been a while since you were introduced to the criminal justice system, then this appendix can serve as a refresher.

Most introductory books and courses on the criminal justice system begin by defining what the criminal justice system is. Rather than trying to define what the criminal justice system is here, this book defines it in Chapter 2 (see the section entitled "Operational Perspectives". There, the argument is presented that what the criminal justice system is depends a great deal on one's personal beliefs. It would also be redundant to present definitions of the criminal justice system twice over.

Other topics that pop up early in introductory criminal justice courses and texts are (1) definitions of crime, (2) sources of crime statistics, (3) victimization, (4) causes of crime, and some others. To avoid duplication, this appendix will not discuss definitions of crime, causes of crime, or victimization. Those topics are covered in sufficient detail—for our purposes—in Chapters 1, 2, and 12, respectively. First, the section on Types of Crimes in Chapter 1 provides some definitions of crime. Second, the section in Chapter 2 on political perspectives sheds light on some of the explanations people offer for crime. (For more detail readers should consult an introductory criminology text.) Third, victimization is briefly discussed in Chapter 12.

SOURCES OF CRIME STATISTICS

Because this book is concerned largely with what works and doesn't work to control crime, it is first necessary to briefly discuss sources of crime statistics. In general, there are two sources on which researchers have relied over the years. The first is the FBI's Uniform Crime Reports (UCR) (see fbi.gov/ucr/ucr.htm#cius). It consists of crimes reported to the police. Local law enforcement agencies report their data to the FBI, which then compiles the statistics. Local law enforcement agencies in some states also report their crime statistics to state-level agencies, and the numbers that they report are often the same numbers reported to the FBI.

An important feature of the UCR is its distinction between Part I and Part II offenses. Part I offenses include homicide, forcible rape, robbery, aggravated assault, burglary, larceny-theft (usually over a certain amount), motor vehicle theft, and arson. Together, these eight offenses make up the crime index. The crime index is what is often reported when the press, criminal justice agencies, politicians, and other people discuss crime trends in America. Part II offenses include all other less serious offenses that are reported to the FBI. Our concern in this book is largely with the crime index, either in whole or in part.

Crimes that are reported to the police do not represent all crimes. For various reasons, some crimes are never reported. Also, because crimes are reported to the FBI from several states, there are bound to be some inconsistencies because of the various definitions of crime in different states. In response to this and similar limitations of the UCR, victimization surveys have emerged. The most noteworthy is the National Crime Victimization Survey (NCVS), conducted by the U.S. Bureau of the Census in cooperation with the Bureau of Justice Statistics in the U.S. Justice Department. It provides detailed data on criminal victimizations (as opposed to crimes reported) and, as such, comes closer to the "dark figure" of crime.

Both the UCR and the NCVS are limited because they do not provide estimates of the total number of crimes. As was mentioned, the UCR is compiled on the basis of crimes reported to the police. The NCVS contains data only on victimizations. What about crimes that are neither reported to police nor reflected in victimization surveys? Self-report surveys have been used to address the weaknesses of the UCR and NCVS, but they are relatively uncommon. We are forced, for the most part, to resort to the UCR and NCVS. So note that when this book discusses the effect of some approach on crime, it is most likely referring to estimates resulting from either of these two data collection strategies.

THE ACTORS

There are several actors (i.e., people) involved in the criminal justice system. Many introductory books list them in the same order in which the criminal process plays out. This necessitates some degree of understanding of the criminal process. Because we haven't yet covered the criminal process, another method of familiarizing ourselves with the actors in the criminal justice system is to think in terms of the organization of our system of government. The U.S. government of course consists of three branches: the executive, the legislative, and the judicial. Most criminal justice actors occupy part of the executive branch, but other important actors can be found in the legislative and judicial branches.

Indeed, looking at the criminal justice system in terms of executive, legislative, and judicial functions does more than simplify matters. It reminds us that the legislative branch in particular does a great deal to shape the makeup and operations of the criminal justice system. Legislatures pass laws and allocate funding, so their role in crime control in America is critical. In other words, thinking in terms of executive, legislative, and judicial crime functions also reminds us that criminal justice is not just about cops, prosecutors, courts, and prisons.

Before continuing, it is worth mentioning that there are countless other people who are involved in some way with the criminal justice system but who are not employed by the government per se. Private service providers, such as substance abuse counselors, do not occupy a position in either branch of government. The same holds for private security guards and a host of other people who might be involved in the control and prevention of crime. Indeed, there are many *government* employees who participate in crime control but who are not considered part of the criminal justice system. Public school teachers, for example, often teach students about the importance of steering clear of a criminal lifestyle, but teachers are not considered criminal justice actors.

Because it would be impossible to list the titles and affiliations of all people—inside and outside of government—who are involved in the control of crime, our focus in this section is on identifying the key players who are involved in the administration of justice in the United States. For those who are interested in what takes place *outside* the criminal justice system, Chapters 12 and 13 introduce readers to some of the strategies—and people—who are involved in individual-, family-, school-, and community-based crime control.

Executive Branch

The executive branch of government is charged with execution of the laws. The two types of criminal justice actors who are responsible for this execution of the law are law enforcement officers and prosecutors. Law enforcement officers enforce the law by investigating crime and apprehending criminal suspects. Prosecutors take things further by selecting certain cases for formal criminal charges. Assuming that criminal charges are filed, prosecutors, as representatives of the executive branch, are responsible for presenting the state's case against the offenders.

Law enforcement officers can be found at the federal, state, and local levels. At the highest level are various federal law enforcement agencies, including the Federal Bureau of Investigation, the U.S. Customs Service, and the Bureau of Alcohol, Tobacco, and Firearms. These agencies are charged with enforcing federal laws. Likewise, state law enforcement agencies are typically responsible for enforcing state laws. Finally, local law enforcement agencies include municipal police departments, sheriff's departments, and other specialized agencies (e.g., university police).

Prosecutors are also found at different levels of government. At the federal level are appointed U.S. attorneys and their assistants. These prosecutors, found in each of 94 federal districts, are responsible for bringing appropriate charges against criminals who violate federal laws. District attorneys represent the government at the local level, usually in county or borough offices. They are the people who come to mind most often when we think of prosecutors. They are responsible for prosecuting the bulk of crime. City attorneys, though, sometimes are responsible for prosecutions, but generally for misdemeanors and usually in large cities.

Legislative Branch

The legislative branch is responsible for making laws. Legislators are criminal justice actors, then, because their job is to (among other things) define what behaviors are considered criminal. The U.S. Congress handles this task for the federal government. State legislatures handle this task at the state level. But because most criminal justice activity (arrests, prosecutions, and convictions) takes place at the local level, state legislatures are of profound importance in criminal justice. As has been shown throughout this book, there are many examples of laws made by legislatures that are intended to affect crime.

Of course, legislators do much more than make law. They control the purse strings. The U.S. Congress allocates funds for federal (and many local level) criminal justice system efforts. State legislatures also allocate funds for criminal justice expenditures. Funding levels vary over time, and political priorities shift. The result is a fluid criminal justice system. It expands and contracts over time. It also prioritizes certain types of crimes (and certain types of offenders) at one point in time but not necessarily in another. Legislatures also allocate funding for research, an important practice that informs much of the discussion presented in this book.

Judicial Branch

The judicial branch is where one finds the courts. As with law enforcement officers and legislators, courts are found at the federal, state, and local level. Federal district courts are where people who violate federal laws are prosecuted. Violations of state laws are generally prosecuted at the local level, most often in county superior courts. Thus, courts and everyone employed by them (judges, court reporters, bailiffs, etc.) can be considered criminal justice actors. Courts can be thought of as bridging the gap between executive and legislative functions; they put criminal defendants who were brought to them by law enforcement officials on trial for violations of the law defined by legislatures.

Within each state (and at the federal level), there are various levels of courts. Trial courts are what we discussed in the previous paragraph. But appellate courts (at both levels) and supreme courts (again at both levels) review decisions by the lower courts. For example, if a trial court finds a defendant guilty, then the defendant may appeal. If an appeal is granted, it will be reviewed by an appellate court. When there is conflict between trial and appellate courts and/or when important legal and constitutional issues are raised, appeals will often arrive at a state supreme court or at the U.S. Supreme Court. Decisions issued by state supreme courts, and especially the U.S. Supreme Court, often have important implications for criminal justice.

THE PROCESS

There is no easy or concise way to describe the criminal process. The 1967 President's Crime Commission attempted to do this.[1] They described the criminal process with the flowchart (shown on page XX in Chapter 2), but their flowchart is not perfect. This is because there are countless variations—at the federal and state levels—in how criminal cases are handled. Further, depending on the seriousness of a case, the criminal process can assume different forms.

Almost all introductory criminal justice texts present an overview of the criminal process, as this book does now, but because of the variation from one jurisdiction to the next, you should take steps to familiarize yourself with the criminal process in the area where you reside. That having been said, let us now turn to a "typical" overview of the criminal process.

Pretrial

A typical criminal case begins with a complaint. This complaint might come in the form of a 911 call from a citizen, a report to the police that one has been victimized, or the actions of a law enforcement officer who observes a crime in progress. If a citizen reports the crime, the police will usually follow up on the complaint by performing an investigation. If a police officer observes a crime, not as much investigation is necessary. In the former instance, the police must take steps to confirm the observations of the citizen. A police officer's observations, by contrast, do not require as much investigative scrutiny. In fact, when an officer observes a crime in progress, he or she will probably arrest the suspect on the spot. This arrest will then be subjected to judicial scrutiny in a hearing at which a judge will decide whether there was probable cause to arrest the suspect.

Once the police have identified a suspect in a crime reported by a citizen, they will approach a judge and seek either an arrest warrant or search warrant. In either case, the police must be able to show probable cause that the evidence they seek will be found in the place to be searched and/or that the suspect was the one who committed the crime. If this burden is met, an arrest or search warrant, or both, will be issued, and the police

---

[1]President's Commission on Law Enforcement and Administration of Justice, *Task Force Report: Science and Technology* (Washington, DC: Government Printing Office, 1967), 58–9.

will go to arrest the suspect named in the arrest warrant or search the premises named in the search warrant. The probable cause burden that is required for search and arrest warrants is not to be taken lightly and has spawned a great deal of debate in the courts.

The role of the police during the pretrial process cannot be overemphasized. In the period between first contact between an officer and a suspect up to the point at which the suspect is arrested and detained the police role is complex and multifaceted. The U.S. Constitution, particularly the Fourth Amendment, places significant restrictions on what the police can and cannot do when they investigate crime and handle suspects. That is why courses on criminal procedure are found in many criminal justice curricula; they devote extensive attention to the role of the police in the criminal process and to the constitutional guidelines the police are required to abide by.

If, as has been indicated, a police officer arrests a suspect for a crime committed in his or her presence, no warrant is necessary. But it is also true that warrants are not always required for arresting suspects or searching their residences based on a citizen complaint. Many contingencies arise in which the police are permitted to arrest or search without a warrant. Suspects who evade authorities, seek to destroy evidence, or are likely to inflict harm on others create circumstances in which the police must act quickly. Indeed, in many other walks of law enforcement life, the police may be forced to make split-second decisions to arrest or search without the protection of a warrant.

Once a suspect has been arrested—be it pursuant to an arrest warrant, a warrant to search, or other method—he or she will be searched. This is done for the protection of the police and to discover contraband that might be in the suspect's possession. Then the suspect will be transported to the police station and booked. Booking is the process in which the suspect is fingerprinted, processed, photographed, and probably placed in a holding cell. The suspect might also be required to submit to testing (such as a breathalyzer) and possibly be required to participate in a lineup.

After booking, the police will present their case to the prosecutor (usually by filing a report of some sort and/or contacting the prosecutor). If the prosecutor believes that the evidence is persuasive enough, he or she will bring charges against the suspect, subject to certain restrictions specified in the U.S. Constitution and clarified by the Supreme Court. The suspect will now be considered the defendant. If the charges are minor, the police might release the suspect, rather than detaining him or her, in which case the suspect will be required to appear at court at some later date.

Suspects who have been booked, placed in detention, and charged with a crime then face a number of different court hearings, depending on the seriousness of the crime. Misdemeanors, because of their not-so-serious nature, tend to be fast-tracked. A misdemeanor defendant might appear at only one court hearing at which the judge will decide guilt or innocence. Felony defendants, by contrast, face a longer road. If, as we have seen already, the suspect is arrested without a warrant, he or she will be granted a hearing at which the judge will decide whether the arresting officer had appropriate justification to make the arrest. This hearing may be merged with other hearings.

The next step in the criminal process is arraignment. At the arraignment, the suspect comes before a judge and is, at a minimum, informed of the charges against him. The defendant will also be notified of his right to counsel, of his right to remain silent, and other important rights. He will also be allowed to make a plea. Common pleas are guilty, not guilty, and nolo contendere; the last is akin to a plea of "no contest." A public defender might be assigned at this stage, particularly if the defendant is unable to afford his own representation. Probable cause might also be determined at this stage if

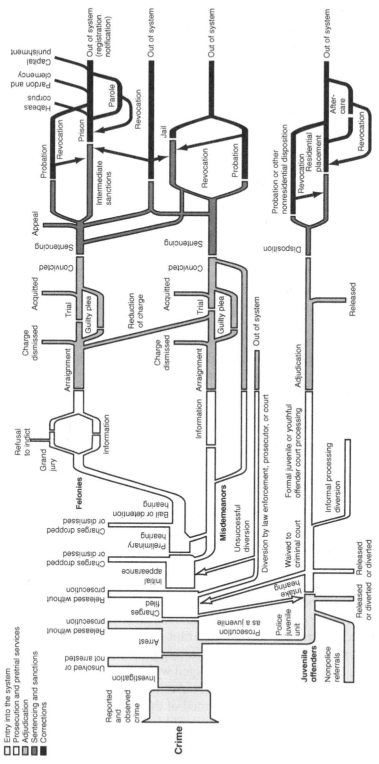

FIGURE 1 Sequence of Events in the Criminal Justice System

Source: President's Commission on Law Enforcement and Administration of Justice, *Task Force Report: Science and Technology* (Washington, DC: Government Printing Office, 1967), 58–9.

a separate hearing is not required. Finally, trial might take place at the arraignment, but only for misdemeanors, and a bail determination could be made as well.

If the bail determination is not fused with the arraignment, a separate hearing might be warranted. In deciding whether bail should be granted, the judge will take such factors into account as the seriousness of the crime as well as the defendant's prior record, likelihood of flight, and level of dangerousness. The defendant's financial status might also be taken into account in deciding whether bail should be granted. Either way, bail (if it is granted) is generally set at an amount that ensures the defendant's appearance at trial. If a defendant cannot afford bail, a bail bond agent may supply a bond for a fee. Bail can also be denied; the Eighth Amendment to the U.S. Constitution does not guarantee the right to bail, only that it cannot be excessive.

It is important to note that the prosecutor's method of filing charges varies from one state to the next. Some states require that the prosecutor proceed by *information*, a document that describes the charges the prosecutor is filing. Other states require that the prosecutor proceed by a grand jury indictment. That is, the grand jury decides whether charges should be filed, usually with the advice and assistance of the prosecutor. Some states require or allow both methods of filing charges, depending on the nature of the case.

In jurisdictions where the prosecutor proceeds by information, she or he is usually required to show that the charging decision is appropriate. This is accomplished in a so-called preliminary hearing. At the preliminary hearing, the prosecutor makes out what is known as a prima facie case of the defendant's guilt. A preliminary hearing can also be required in grand jury jurisdictions. In such a jurisdiction, the prosecutor might be required to present her or his case at a preliminary hearing before seeking a grand jury indictment.

Adjudication

Once the pretrial process has concluded and the charges stand, a trial might or might not take place. If the defendant pleads guilty at arraignment, then a trial is not necessary. In such an instance, special steps must be taken to ensure that the defendant's guilty plea is valid. The defendant might also agree to a plea agreement by which, in exchange for leniency from the prosecutor and/or the court, he or she pleads guilty to the crime for which he or she is charged. Plea bargaining of this nature can occur at any stage of the criminal process, however. That is, a suspect can reach a plea agreement with the prosecutor as early as the pretrial stage and, in fact, well into jury deliberations. In either case, the plea bargain, if there is one, must be accepted by the court. The judge makes this determination.

If the defendant pleads not guilty, the case is set for trial. Trials are usually scheduled for some date well after arraignment. This allows both sides—the prosecution and the defense—to prepare their respective cases. A balance needs to be achieved between providing enough time for both sides to present effective arguments and protecting the defendant's Sixth Amendment right to a speedy trial. During this preparation process, discovery takes place. Discovery is the process by which both sides to a criminal case—the prosecutor and the defense attorney—learn what evidence the other side will present. Work product and strategy are off limits, but the identities of witnesses who will testify, the physical evidence in possession of both parties, and other items are all fair game in the discovery process.

At trial, the prosecutor bears the burden of proving that the defendant is guilty beyond a reasonable doubt. Once the prosecution presents its case, the defense steps in and presents its case. In doing so, it seeks to cast doubt on the prosecutor's evidence. Criminal trials bounce back and forth in this fashion until both sides "rest." Once the prosecution and defense have finished presenting their cases, a verdict must be reached. Depending on the seriousness of the offense, the verdict is decided by either a judge or jury. Judges decide the defendant's fate in what are known as bench trials, but only for offenses that are likely to result in less than six months' imprisonment. Juries decide the verdict when the offense at issue is more serious. Special steps must be taken in either instance to ensure the impartiality of either the judge or the jury.

Beyond Conviction

The criminal process does not necessarily end once the verdict has been read. Sentencing usually takes place at a separate hearing. The guilty party might be sentenced to death (for a capital crime), committed to prison, fined, placed on probation, or subjected to a host of other possible sanctions. Probation is the most common sanction, but imprisonment (and, of course, death) are much more serious. When a person is sentenced to death or otherwise committed to prison, it might seem as though the criminal process has just begun. The appeals process can drag out for years after the criminal trial and sentencing.

Appeals come in two varieties: automatic and discretionary. Most convicted criminals are entitled to at least one automatic appeal (also known as an appeal of right). Automatic appeals must be heard by an appellate court. With discretionary appeals, however, it is up to the appellate court to decide whether the appeal will be heard. Excessive discretionary appeals are what supporters of the death penalty and other serious sanctions lament.

Appeals are not the only method of challenging guilty verdicts. Habeas corpus—a method of what is commonly called "collateral attack"—is a right guaranteed in the U.S. Constitution that provides that every convicted criminal can petition a court to decide on the constitutionality of his or her confinement. All that is granted, however, is the right to file a petition, a request to be heard. The decision whether to grant a prisoner's habeas petition is up to the reviewing court. A prisoner who has exhausted all available appellate mechanisms and is denied habeas review will languish in prison until his or her term is up.

A Note Concerning Sanctions

The description in the preceding three subsections was of the criminal process, with little attention to what takes place after conviction—and after appeals and habeas corpus petitions (assuming that both are unsuccessful). It was pointed out that convicted criminals are often placed on probation or sentenced to prison. These are traditional sanctions and perhaps the most common ones that are available to the courts. But there are many others, including diversion, intermediate sanctions, treatment, rehabilitation, and others. Such sanctions—and their relative effectiveness—are an important part of this book.

Sanctions are intended to discourage people from committing crime. A prison sentence, for example, puts a criminal behind bars so that he or she cannot continue to violate the law. Prison sentences and other such sanctions may also send a message to would-be criminals that crime is not acceptable behavior (see the section on deferrence in Chapter 2 for a discussion of this). There is much more to controlling crime than sanctions, however. Legal approaches to the crime problem, policy changes, and countless informal approaches are taken in this country, as well. They are also discussed at great length throughout this book.

NAME INDEX

SUBJECT INDEX

A

ABE. *See* Adult Basic Education (ABE)

Abortion, legalization of, 399

Absolute deterrence, 41

Academic crusade, 21

Academics, 35, 39, 259

Access control, 363–364

ACLU. *See* American Civil Liberties Union (ACLU)

ACTION (All Coming Together in Our Neighborhood) teams, 140

Activity support, 364

ADAM. *See* Arrestee Drug Abuse Monitoring (ADAM)

Adam Walsh Child Protection and Safety Act of 2006, 167

Ad hoc plea bargaining, 146–147

Administrative capacity, 343

Adult Basic Education (ABE), 287

Adult boot camps, 260–261

AFDC. *See* Aid to Families with Dependent Children (AFDC)

After-school programs, 338–340

Aid to Families with Dependent Children (AFDC), 319–320

Airports, 374

Alcohol, 372

American Civil Liberties Union (ACLU), 312

Anger management, 278–279

Anti-gang initiatives, 335–337

Anti-gang injunctions, 191–192

Anti-terrorism laws, 169–172

Apology penalties, 184, 185

Armed resistance, 305

Arrestee Drug Abuse Monitoring (ADAM), 157

Asset forfeiture, 139, 211–212

At-risk youths, 345

Attitudes, 393–394

Attorneys general, 126

Awareness space, 361

B

Bail, 177, 178, 179–180

Bail Reform Act of 1984, 178

Bandwagon science, 21

Banks, 371–372

Bans, legislative, 152–160

Bars and taverns, 372

BBBSA. *See* Big Brothers and Big Sisters of America (BBBSA)

Beat Health Program, 119

Behavior modification, 348

Behavior space, 361

Bell v. Wolfish, 177

Big Brothers and Big Sisters of America (BBBSA), 338

Boot camps, 260–261

Border Patrol agents, 312

Boston Gun Project, 336–337

Brady Handgun Violence Prevention Act, 161–163

Broken windows theory, 79–82, 362–363

Brooklyn (NY) Drug Treatment Alternative to Prison (DTAP). *See* Drug Treatment Alternative to Prison (DTAP) program

Brutalization effect, 233

Buddy Program, 337–338

BUILD program, 336

Bureau of Alcohol, Tobacco, Firearms, and Explosives (ATF), 161

Businesses, 370–372

Buyback programs, 163

C

California's chemical castration law, 234

Capital punishment, 41–42, 232–233, 398. *See also* Death penalty

CASA. *See* National Center on Addiction and Substance Abuse (CASA)

Caseload concerns, 248–250

Castration, 234–235

CCI. *See* Center for Court Innovation (CCI)

CCPP. *See* Community Crime Prevention Program (CCPP)

CCTV. *See* Closed-circuit television (CCTV)

CED. *See* Conducted energy device (CED)

Center for Court Innovation (CCI), 192, 194, 198, 202

Chemical castration, 234–235

Child abuse, 312–313, 318

Children of Divorce Intervention Program, 346

Citizen attitudes, 393–394

Citizen contact patrol, 108–109

Citizen patrols, 116–117

Citizen police academies, 117

City attorneys, 126

Civil asset forfeiture, 139, 211–212

Civil commitment, 215–216

Civil disabilities, 251, 252

Civil gang injunctions. *See* Anti-gang injunctions

Civil law, 118

Classical experiment, 14–15

Classroom approach, 344–345

Closed-circuit television (CCTV), 366–367, 371, 372, 375, 376

Code enforcement, 82, 139

Cognitive skills, 274–275

Collective efficacy, 332